Criminal Justice

D0165142

Visit the *Criminal Justice, third edition* Companion Website at **www.pearsoned.co.uk/davies_crim** to find regular updates in the field of criminal justice.

We work with leading authors to develop the strongest educational materials in law, bringing cutting-edge thinking and best learning practice to a global market.

Under a range of well-known imprints, including Longman, we craft high quality print and electronic publications which help readers to understand and apply their content, whether studying or at work.

To find out more about the complete range of our publishing, please visit us on the World Wide Web at: **www.pearsoned.co.uk**

DAVIES, CROALL AND TYRER

Criminal Justice

An Introduction to the
Criminal Justice System
in England and Wales

Third Edition

PEARSON

Longman

Harlow, England • London • New York • Boston • San Francisco • Toronto
Sydney • Tokyo • Singapore • Hong Kong • Seoul • Taipei • New Delhi
Cape Town • Madrid • Mexico City • Amsterdam • Munich • Paris • Milan

Pearson Education Limited

Edinburgh Gate
Harlow
Essex CM20 2JE
England

and Associated Companies throughout the world

Visit us on the World Wide Web at:
www.pearsoned.co.uk

First published 1995
Second edition 1998
Third edition published 2005

© Malcolm Davies, Hazel Croall and Jane Tyrer 1995, 2005

The rights of Malcolm Davies, Hazel Croall and Jane Tyrer to be identified
as authors of this work have been asserted by them in accordance with the
Copyright, Designs and Patents Act 1988.

All rights reserved. No part of this publication may be reproduced, stored in
a retrieval system, or transmitted in any form or by any means, electronic,
mechanical, photocopying, recording or otherwise, without either the prior
written permission of the publisher or a licence permitting resricted copying
in the United Kingdom issued by the Copyright Licensing Agency Ltd,
90 Tottenham Court Road, London W1T 4LP.

ISBN 0 582 47320 9

British Library Cataloguing-in-Publication Data
A catalogue record for this book is available from the British Library

Library of Congress Cataloging-in-Publication Data
Davis, Malcolm, 1946-
   Criminal Justice : an introduction to the criminal justice system in
England and Wales / Davis, Croall, and Tyrer. – 3rd ed.
      p. cm
   Includes bibliographical references and index.
   ISBN 0-582-47320-9
   1. Criminal justice, Administrations of – England. 2. Criminal procedure –
England. 3. Law enforcement – England. 4. Corrections – England. I.I Croall,
Hazel, 1947- II. Tyrer, Jane, 1951- III. Title.
   KD7876.D38 2005
   364.942–dc22   2004061628

10 9 8 7 6 5 4 3 2 1
08 07 06 05

Typeset in 9.5/12.5pt ITC Century Book by 3
Printed in Great Britain by Henry Ling Ltd., at the Dorset Press, Dorchester,
Dorset

The publisher's policy is to use paper manufactured from sustainable forests.

We would like to dedicate this book to Michael Molyneux for his inspiration as a teacher to generations of students and colleagues in the Law School at Thames Valley University

The publisher's policy is to use paper manufactured from sustainable forests.

Brief contents

Full contents

PART A
Introduction to criminal justice   1

CHAPTER 1
What is criminal justice?   3

CHAPTER 2
What is crime?   35

PART B
Criminal justice process: law enforcement   113

CHAPTER 5
Crime prevention and reduction   115

CHAPTER 6
The police   140

PART C
Criminal justice process: criminal courts

CHAPTER 9
Criminal courts, judiciary and pre-trial procedure

CHAPTER 10
The trial and establishing guilt

PART D
Criminal justice process: penal system — 289

CHAPTER 13
Prisons   364

CHAPTER 14
Probation service and community penalties   398

Supporting resources

Visit **www.pearsoned.co.uk/davies_crim** to find valuable online resources

Companion Website for students
- Regular updates to keep you up-to-date in this field of law

For more information please contact your local Pearson Education sales representative or visit **www.pearsoned.co.uk/davies_crim**

List of figures

List of tables

Preface

Since the publication of the second edition there have been so many changes in the way criminal justice agencies do business that it seemed possible at one stage that we would not be in a position to encompass within one textbook the scope and scale of the changes. Furthermore, the pace and persistence of legislative reforms has at times overwhelmed the academic and media pundits' ability to report and make sense of them. How these changes will settle down is not, at the time of publication in 2005, clear.

A number of reviews and reports preceded the reform – the most wide-ranging was Lord Justice Auld's detailed and comprehensive review of the criminal courts, judiciary and criminal procedure which led to the reforms in the Criminal Justice Act 2003.

The New Labour Government came to office under Prime Minister Tony Blair in 1997 and was re-elected in 2001. Its modernising agenda for reform has varied in scope. There have been nominal changes of titles – for example, stipendiary magistrates became district judges, and the probation order was renamed as a community rehabilitation order and subsequently became incorporated into a single generic community order. New agencies became established, such as the Public Defender Service and the Sentencing Guidelines Council. Others were abolished. At the time of publication it seems most probable that the historic role of the Lord Chancellor will be reformed if not abolished. Already gone are the petty sessional divisions; and the establishment of the National Offender Management Service (NOMS) is likely to result in the loss of the separate identities of the probation and prison services.

To the many changes and continuing challenges that the criminal justice system was facing within the United Kingdom, such as crime rates, fear of crime and race relations, we have had to incorporate the implications of the globalisation of criminal activities as represented in its most dramatic and brutal form by the terrorist events in the United States of America on 11 September 2001. Furthermore, globalisation means that international fraudsters, not limited by national boundaries and bureaucracies, can use new technology more creatively than law enforcement agencies. Greater geographic mobility allows people to move from jurisdiction to jurisdiction to avoid prosecution, and organised gangs ship people, weapons and drugs to wherever there is bountiful market.

The twenty-first century already begins to see some trends that will distinguish it from the twentieth century. A new criminal justice paradigm will need to incorporate a global dimension in response to global crime problems but also in England and Wales where the loss of sovereignty over legal and crime issues seems increasingly likely as the European Union moves ever closer to establishing a federal constitution.

Furthermore, the twenty-first century has already manifested a re-awakening in the light of terrorist attacks on western countries, a concern with issues of public safety in a way that the seventeenth century writer on law and order, Thomas Hobbes, would have recognised. The late twentieth century concern with the human rights of the defendant and criminal have been supplemented in the twenty-first century by a public safety agenda.

Despite all this, police officers in the United Kingdom still do not carry weapons unless they are part of a specialist unit such as airport security or VIP protection. More unarmed community support officers are appearing on the streets to deal with anti-social behaviour that was previously ignored by the official system as too trivial.

To make sense of these events and reforms we have made changes to the substantive content of the chapters as well as to the organisation of the third edition of the book.

Regarding the substantive changes to the content of the chapters we have incorporated the many recent legislative and policy developments introduced since 1997. In addition, in the third edition we have encompassed the initiatives and impact of the following:

- The Human Rights Act 1998
- The continuing pervasive influence of EU policy making
- Lord Justice Auld's report on the criminal trial and procedure
- John Halliday's report on sentencing
- Crime prevention
- New police community support officers
- The enhanced concern with the role of victims
- Cross-border crimes, globalisation and terrorism
- The Macpherson report on the Stephen Lawrence murder
- The increasing influence of changes in information technology with regard to crime investigation and the organisation and administration of criminal justice agencies
- New agencies: Youth Justice Board, Public Defender Service, National Offender Management Service, Sentencing Advisory Panel, Sentencing Guidelines Council
- New sentences: Drug Treatment and Testing Order, Parenting Order, Anti-social Behaviour Order, Referral Orders.
- Renamed community sentences: e.g. the Probation Order became the Community Rehabilitation Order and then became one aspect of a generic community order.
- The Criminal Justice Act 2003

Regarding the logic of the textbook and its organisation, we have added more chapters in the third edition and have divided them into the following parts:

- **Part A: Introduction to criminal justice**: What is criminal justice? What is crime? Victims, crime prevention, and governmental, administrative and political context of criminal justice in England and Wales.

- **Part B: Criminal justice process – law enforcement**: police, prosecution, diversion, mentally ill offenders, youth justice.

- **Part C: Criminal justice process – criminal courts**: pre-trial criminal procedure, the trial and establishing guilt.

- **Part D: Criminal justice process – penal system**: sentencing, punishment, penal paradigms, prisons, probation service and community penalties.

There are new and enhanced sections on:

- Europe
- probation
- human rights
- youth justice (a new additional chapter)
- victims (a new additional chapter)
- crime prevention (a new additional chapter).

New exercises and student activities, as well as updated references, have been added in the third edition of *Criminal Justice*, and a list of useful websites added.

Finally we have added a new website that provides an opportunity for information on up to the minute changes and developments in law and practice.

Malcolm Davies, Thames Valley University, Ealing, London
Hazel Croall, Glasgow Caledonian University
Jane Tyrer, Buckinghamshire Chilterns University College

December 2004

Author's acknowledgements

The authors would like to thank the anonymous reviewers of the second edition whose thoughtful insights and constructive suggestions influenced the shape and content of the third edition.

Publisher's acknowledgements

We are grateful to the following for permission to reproduce copyright material:

Tables 1.1, 1.2, 2.2, 9.1, 9.2, 9.3, 9.4, 9.5, 9.6, 9.7, 10.1, 10.2, 10.3, 11.1, 12.2, 13.2, 13.3, 13.4, 14.1 and Figures 2.1, 2.2, 3.1, 3.2, 6.3, 7.1, 7.2, 7.3, 8.1, 8.2, 8.3, 12.1, 12.2, 12.3, 14.1, 14.2 from HMSO; Figure 1.2 extract from article 'Tribal Elders Punish Aborigine Car Thieves', *The Daily Telegraph*, 18 June 1994: © Telegraph Group Limited, London, 1994; letter on page 14 from Michael Zander in *The Times*, 12 August 1994; Figure 4.1 reproduced by permission of The Conservative Party; letter on page 93 from Andrew Rawnsley in *The Observer*, 10 November 2002: Copyright Guardian Newspapers Limited 2002; Figure 5.2 from *Crime Prevention and Community Safety: Politics, policies and practices*, Longman, (Crawford, 1998); extract on page 138 by J. Q. Wilson and G. L. Kelling 'Broken Windows: The police and neighbourhood safety' in *The Atlantic Monthly*, March 1982; Figure 6.2 adapted from *Handbook of Policing*, Willan Publishing (Mawby and Wright, 2003); Figure 6.4 from *The Times*, 21 February 1998. © Times Newspapers Limited, 1998. Photo © Photonews Service; Figure 10.2 from *The Times*, 1 March 1995. © Times Newspapers Limited, 1995; Figure 11.1 *Magistrates' Association Sentencing Guidelines*, reproduced with permission of the Magistrates' Association, www.magistrates-association.org.uk; Extract 1 on page 329 'Kiosk theft justifies jail' from *The Times*, 10 May 1993. © Times Newspapers Limited, 1993; Figure 13.1 'The Panopticon' from *The Works of Jeremy Bentham*, (Bowering, 1843), reproduced by permission of The British Library.

In some instances we have been unable to trace the owners of copyright material, and we would appreciate any information that would enable us to do so.

Table of cases

Chronology of key dates in the development of criminal justice in England and Wales

The following gives a list of significant dates referred to in the text. Added comments indicate key developments in the criminal justice system in England and Wales.

1717 Transportation Act

1779 Penitentiary Act

1784 Transportation Act

1816 Millbank penitentiary opened in London

1823 Gaol Act

1824 Vagrancy Act

1829 Metropolitan Police Improvement Act. The Metropolitan Police Force was established

1833 Factory Act

1842 Pentonville prison opened

1853 Penal Servitude Act. Ends short terms of transportation and Parkhurst Prison opens with a regime designed for young offenders

1854 Reformatory School Act

1856 County and Borough Police Act

1861 Offences Against the Person Act

1867 End of transportation

1877 Prison Act. The Prison Commission was established with responsibility for all prisons in the country: the first chairman was Sir Edmund Du Cane

1878 Criminal Investigation Department (CID) of the Metropolitan Police was established

1879 Prosecution of Offences Act

1895 Gladstone Committee Report on prisons

1883 Trial of Lunatics Act allowed juries to bring in a guilty but insane verdict

1898 Prison Act

1898 Criminal Evidence Act

1901 Borstal experiment introduced

1907 Probation of Offenders Act

1908   Prevention of Crime Act. Borstal system and preventive detention introduced

1908   Children Act. Restrictions on the imprisonment of children

1913   Mental Deficiency Act. Mentally deficient persons were diverted out of the prison system

1919   Police Act followed the Police Strike and the formation of the Police Federation

1925   Criminal Justice Act

1933   Children and Young Persons Act. Reformatories and industrial schools were replaced by approved schools

1936   Open prison was established near Wakefield

Prison Officers' Association was founded

End to arrows on uniforms and treadmills

1936   Public Order Act

1948   Criminal Justice Act. Abolished penal servitude, prison with hard labour and whipping. Introduced corrective training, preventive detention and detention centres

1949   Royal Commission on Capital Punishment

1957   Homicide Act

1961   Criminal Justice Act. Minimum age of imprisonment was raised from 15 to 17. Greater use was encouraged of borstal training instead of prison for offenders under 21

1962   Royal Commission on the Police

1963   Prison Commission abolished and replaced by the Prison Department

1964   Criminal Procedure (Insanity) Act

1964   Police Act

1965   Murder (Abolition of Death Penalty) Act

1966   Mountbatten Report. Following the escape of the Russian spy George Blake from Wormwood Scrubs prison, Earl Mountbatten conducted an inquiry into prison security

1967   Criminal Justice Act. Introduction of the suspended sentence and discretionary parole. Courts were empowered to suspend any sentence of imprisonment not exceeding 2 years. Parole allowed an inmate to apply for parole after serving one-third of their sentence. Abolition of preventive detention and corrective training and corporal punishment in prisons. Introduction of majority jury verdicts

1968   Firearms Act

1968   Criminal Appeal Act

1969   Children and Young Persons Act. Introduced care and supervision orders and replaced approved schools and remand homes with community homes

1971   Misuse of Drugs Act

1971   Courts Act. Abolished Assizes and Quarter Sessions and established the Crown Court

1972　Road Traffic Act. Introduced the breathalyser

1972　Criminal Justice Act. Introduced community service orders

1974　Juries Act

1974　Rehabilitation of Offenders Act

1976　Bail Act

1977　Criminal Law Act. Allowed the court to suspend a sentence of imprisonment in part

1979　Report of the May Committee on the Prison Services. A policy of positive custody was advocated

1980　Magistrates' Courts Act

1981　Scarman Report on riots in Brixton

1981　Contempt of Court Act

1981　Royal Commission on Criminal Procedure

1982　Criminal Justice Act. Reduction of the parole eligibility criteria from 12 to 6 months. Statutory criteria for sentencing young offenders to a custodial sentence. Borstal training replaced by youth custody

1983　Mental Health Act

1984　Police and Criminal Evidence Act. Introduced the PACE Codes to cover police stop and search, questioning of suspects and detention in police custody

1985　Prosecution of Offences Act. Established the Crown Prosecution Service

1986　Public Order Act

1986　Drug Trafficking Offences Act made laundering of cash derived from the sale of drugs illegal and allowed confiscation of money made through drug dealing

1988　Criminal Justice Act. Extension of statutory criteria for custodial sentences for young offenders

1988　Legal Aid Act

1988　Road Traffic Act

1990　White Paper, *Crime, Justice and Protecting the Public*

1990　Criminal Justice (International Cooperation) Act introduced a new power for police and customs officers to seize cash discovered on import or export which is reasonably suspected of being derived from or intended for use in drug trafficking and enabled the UK to request and provide assistance to all countries

1991　Criminal Justice Act. Introduced the combination order, unit fine and a sentencing framework

1991　Report on the Prison Disturbances of April 1990 (chairman, Lord Justice Woolf). It recommended wide-ranging changes to the nature of prison regimes and the need for greater coordination throughout the criminal justice system

1991   Criminal Procedure (Insanity and Unfitness to Plead) Act

1993   Royal Commission on Criminal Justice (chairman, Lord Runciman)

1993   Bail (Amendment) Act

1993   Criminal Justice Act repealed the unit fine

1994   Sexual Offences Act

1994   Criminal Justice and Public Order Act. Secure training order, revised bail law, right to silence redefined, new offences relating to collective trespass, raves and squatters; new offence of male rape and reduction in the age of homosexual consent to 18

1994   Police and Magistrates' Courts Act. New process of funding and monitoring police performance and changed the organisation and funding of magistrates' courts. Home Secretary was given the power to set the objectives for the Police Service which have to be included in the local policing plan

1995   Criminal Appeal Act established the Criminal Cases Review Commission to review and investigate possible miscarriages of justice in England, Wales and Northern Ireland. It became operational on 31 March 1997 and it took over the powers formerly exercised by the Home Secretary to refer a conviction or sentence on indictment to the Court of Appeal

1995   Learmont report on prison security

1996   Criminal Procedure and Investigations Act introduced new rules on the disclosure of evidence and the timing of the plea. Restored committal proceedings to replace the unimplemented transfer proceedings and introduced plea before venue

1997   Firearms (Amendment) Act outlawed ownership of handguns above .22 calibre

1997   Protection from Harassment Act

1997   Sex Offenders Act established the Sex Offender Register

1997   Crime (Sentences) Act introduced mandatory life sentence for adults convicted of a second serious offence such as rape or robbery with the use of a firearm, and minimum custodial sentences of 7 years for those reconvicted of trafficking in Class A drugs

1997   White Paper, *No More Excuses*, proposed a range of proposals to improve the effectiveness of the youth court in preventing offending by children and young people. This is now the principal aim of the youth justice system

1998   White Paper, *Modernising Justice*

1998   Consultation Paper, *Joining Forces to Protect the Public*

1998   Crime and Disorder Act introduced Drug Treatment and Testing Orders and the Sentencing Advisory Panel

1999   Access to Justice Act. Legal Service Commission established to oversee reformed legal aid scheme. Introduces Criminal Defence Service (CDS). The purpose of the Criminal Defence Service (CDS) is to secure the provision of advice, assistance and representation, according to the interests of justice, to people suspected of a criminal offence or facing criminal proceedings

1999   Criminal Cases Review (Insanity) Act

1999   Youth Justice and Criminal Evidence Act. Introduced a referral order for the youth court for young people convicted for the first time and its primary aim is to prevent re-offending. A youth offender panel will work with the young offender to establish a programme of behaviour for the young offender. Introduced reforms to the process of giving evidence to help young, disabled, vulnerable or intimidated witnesses give evidence in criminal proceedings such as use of screens, live link CCTV and the use of pre-recorded interviews; changes to the conduct of trials in rape cases

2000   *National Standards for the supervision of offenders in the community,* revised version came into force on 1 April 2000

2000   Criminal Justice and Court Services Act. Created the National Probation Service for England and Wales and the Children and Family Court Advisory and Support Service. Community orders were renamed: probation order became a community rehabilitation order. Extended the use of electronic monitoring and stricter enforcement. Measures to prevent unsuitable people from working with children. Sex offenders not to be eligible for the Home Detention Curfew scheme. Introduced new powers for the compulsory drug testing of offenders and alleged offenders at various points in their contact with the criminal justice system and allows a court considering the question of bail to take into account any drug misuse by the defendant

2000   Powers of Criminal Courts (Sentencing) Act. This was a consolidation Act that brought together all existing legislation on sentencing

2001   Sir Robin Auld's *Review of the Criminal Courts in England and Wales.* A comprehensive review of criminal procedure and the criminal courts

2001   Anti-terrorism, Crime and Security Act. In response to the 11 September terrorist attacks on New York and Washington. Introduced powers to cut off terrorist funds, allow government departments and agencies to collect and share information on terrorist activities, and provisions to improve the security of nuclear facilities that may be targeted by terrorists and enhanced police powers when detainees in police custody refuse to cooperate with the police as to their identity

2001   Criminal Justice and Police Act. Introduced on-the-spot penalties for disorderly behaviour and measures to prohibit the consumption of alcohol in designated public places

2001   Criminal Defence Service (Advice and Assistance) Act. Sets out the extent of the duty of the Criminal Defence Service to provide advice, assistance and representation

2001   International Criminal Court Act. The International Criminal Court (ICC) in The Hague, was established to try individuals for genocide, crimes against humanity and war crimes

2001   White Paper *Policing a New Century: A Blueprint for Reform*

2002   Police Reform Act. The Home Secretary will be required to produce an annual National Policing Plan. The Police Complaints Authority is replaced with a new body, the Independent Police Complaints Commission (IPCC)

2002   White Paper *Justice for All*

2002   Proceeds of Crime Act. Provides for powers to confiscate from convicted defendants the financial benefits criminals have made from their criminal activity. Confiscation orders are available following a conviction

2003   White paper *Respect and Responsibility – taking a stand against anti-social behaviour*

2003   Courts Act. Abolished Magistrates' Courts Committees (MCCs), and established courts boards. This Act abolishes commission areas and petty sessions areas and replaces them with local justice areas. It establishes a new HM Inspectorate of Court Administration

2003   Crime (International Cooperation) Act. Implements European Union police and judicial cooperation and provides for a database to store criminal information from all participating countries; cooperation to locate banking accounts and information relating to criminal investigations. Implements measures for combating terrorism. Implements the mutual recognition of driving disqualifications

2003   Anti-social Behaviour Act. It provides sanctions and powers for police, local authorities and housing associations to tackle anti-social behaviour in local communities and in social housing, including provisions aimed at dealing with noise nuisance. It provides a means for schools, local authorities and youth offending teams to work with the parents of children. Powers to tackle the problem of premises used for drug dealing; young people with air weapons, banning the possession of imitation guns and air guns in public; new powers of the police to impose conditions on public assemblies, deal with illegal raves and to deal with unauthorised encampments

2003   European Union (Accessions) Act. The Accession Treaty provides for the accession of 10 new states to join the existing 15 countries in the European Union on 1 May 2004

2003   Criminal Justice Act. Wide-ranging reforms to all aspects of the criminal justice system

2003   Sexual Offences Act. Redefines main sexual offences

PART A

Introduction to criminal justice

CHAPTER 1

What is criminal justice?

Main topics covered

➤ The criminal justice system in England and Wales

➤ Criminal justice defined: functions and form

➤ Principles of criminal justice

➤ Systems approach and criminal justice sub-systems

➤ Paradigms and models of criminal justice

➤ Recent legislation and current policy developments

INTRODUCTION

There are three distinctive criminal justice systems with separate procedures and agencies in the United Kingdom: England and Wales, Scotland, and Northern Ireland. The organisation and jurisdictional limits of criminal justice in England and Wales are determined by constitutional distinctions within the United Kingdom and increasingly by the need to respond to issues of crime in the outside world, especially in the light of the acts of terrorism in New York City and Washington DC on 11 September 2001. Membership of the European Union has also meant that on some constitutional, policy and everyday regulations we are no longer an isolated island in the sea of criminal justice. To varying extents the agencies of criminal justice in the United Kingdom have had to comply with aspects of harmonisation, integration and greater cooperation with our European partners (25 member countries in 2004).

Within the United Kingdom different government departments are responsible for criminal justice in the three jurisdictions – the Home Office for England and Wales, the Justice Department in Scotland, and the Northern Ireland Office. Other government departments such as the Department for Constitutional Affairs and the Attorney General's Office are involved in the administration of criminal justice. Local councils have a statutory duty to establish a Social Services Department employing qualified social workers to deal with children in trouble with the criminal law. Criminal investigations are not made exclusively by the police but also by many other agencies such as investigators for the Department of Trade and Industry, the

Serious Fraud Office, HM Customs and Excise and various local government bodies such as the Environmental Health and Trading Standards Departments. More details on the responsibilities of the different agencies are given below.

1.1 CRIMINAL JUSTICE IN ENGLAND AND WALES

Agencies

In England and Wales criminal justice agencies such as the police, prisons and probation are funded primarily by central government. Policy is established in part by civil servants who advise ministers and by legislation enacted by Parliament. For administrative purposes agencies are divided into regional areas. The main agencies are briefly described below:

- *Police*. There are 43 regional police forces each under the direction of a chief constable and, except for the Metropolitan Police and the City of London police, local police authorities. Forces vary in size, the biggest being the Metropolitan Police with 26,800 uniformed officers, and the smallest with just over 1,000 police. Across England and Wales in 2004 there were 138,000 police supplemented by 16,000 Specials, 4,000 Police Community Support Officers and 53,000 civilian employees. The police made 1.9 million arrests in 2000. The Home Office is the government department responsible for the police.

- *Prosecutors*. The Crown Prosecution Service was established in 1985 and is divided into 42 areas. The Attorney General is answerable in Parliament for the Crown Prosecution Service which is headed by the Director of Public Prosecutions, a senior lawyer. The CPS completes approximately 1.4 million cases a year in the magistrates' court and 125,000 in the Crown Court.

- *Criminal Defence Service*. The Criminal Defence Service oversees the system of legal support for those accused of a crime by advice, assistance and representation in court through a combination of full-time public defenders and contracted private sector lawyers.

- *Courts*. Most criminal cases have to go to the magistrates' courts, although more serious cases are ultimately dealt with in the Crown Court. Officials in these courts include judges, recorders, magistrates, magistrates' clerks and ushers. The criminal courts come under the authority of the Department for Constitutional Affairs which is responsible for the appointment of magistrates and judges.

- *Probation*. The Probation Service is responsible for preparing pre-sentence reports for courts, supervising community orders and helping prisoners adapt to community life following release. Legislation in 2000 established the National Probation Service .

- *Prisons*. The Prison Service is an executive agency, with policy direction from the Home Office, and is organised into 15 regional areas, with responsibility for 138 prisons; it held a record number of 75,000 inmates in 2004. With probation, it constitutes the proposed National Offender Management Service (NOMS) with the responsibility for managing offenders from sentence to resettlement in the community.

- *Youth Justice.* The Youth Justice Board is a central board that monitors the work of the youth justice system and the work of the Youth Offending Teams (YOTs). Established across England and Wales by 2000, YOTs are local authority multi-agency teams that coordinate the effort of the agencies and volunteers working with young offenders.

- *Serious and Organised Crime Agency (SOCA).* A high powered national policing agency is to be established in the UK in 2006 to deal with the increased threat from global organised crime and terrorism. SOCA will have around 5,000 agents drawn from the merger of the National Crime Squad, National Criminal Intelligence Service, Special Branch, Serious Fraud Office and elements of the customs and immigration services. The focus will be on drug and people trafficking and will provide an integrated approach to deal with the threat of cross-jurisdictional crime and international crime organisations.

Smaller agencies and bodies

- *Coroners.* Officials who investigate suspicious or unusual deaths.

- *Criminal Injuries Compensation Authority.* Compensates the victims of some forms of crime. In 2002, victims of violent crimes received £210 million in compensation for criminal injuries.

- *Forensic Science Service.* Independent scientific support service for the investigation of crime and the evaluation of evidence. In 2003 it had a database of 2 million DNA samples.

- *HM Inspectorates.* There are different inspectors who are semi-autonomous of Government who inspect and report on the work of the police, courts, probation, prison and the CPS. They report to the Government and Parliament on the efficiency and effectiveness of the specific service for which they have responsibility.

- *Parole Board.* This decides on the release and recall of prisoners where the sentence has an indeterminate aspect.

- *Victim Support.* An independent agency that organises 1,500 volunteers to provide support for victims of crime and also runs the Court Witness Service.

Civil society and the private sector

As well as the professions and officials in these agencies, many private citizens are involved in criminal justice. These include lay visitors to police stations, neighbourhood watch groups, victim support volunteers, members of juries, Independent Monitoring Boards in prisons, and over 30,000 lay magistrates.

There is also a growing army of employees in private security firms, of which Group 4, Pinkerton's, Securicor and Wells Fargo are the best known. There are also many smaller businesses, such as private detectives, locksmiths, bailiffs and credit investigation and information services. Although it is extremely difficult to estimate the total number of employees in this sector some have estimated the number to be as high as 400,000. The total number of private security guards outnumbers the police. Thus the private sector plays a major and growing role in crime prevention. It is also becoming increasingly involved in other sectors of the system. In November 1991, Group 4 signed a contract to run the first private prison, the Wolds Remand Prison in Humberside: others include Blakenhurst, a local prison; Doncaster opened in 1994; Altcourse, a Category A local prison; Parc, a local male prison; Lowdham Grange, a category B prison; and Buckley Hall for category C prisoners.

Finally, the legal professions are a vital part of criminal justice. Barristers and solicitors are the two branches of this powerful professional group, which is independent of government. Barristers are primarily court advocates whereas solicitors advise clients on a variety of matters and deal with clients prior to trial. The majority of advocacy in the Crown Court is done by barristers and the higher courts have only recently been open to solicitors as advocates. Both solicitors and barristers have the right to appear and represent clients (that is they have rights of audience) in the magistrates' court, where much of the work is undertaken by solicitors. A member of the public cannot directly seek advice from a barrister without first instructing a solicitor. A survey by the Law Society (1996) showed that of solicitors in private practice, 19 per cent dealt with criminal matters. In 2002 there were 9,698 practising barristers, most of whom will have represented criminal clients in their career; and some 2,800 members of the Criminal Bar Association in 2004 specialise entirely in criminal cases.

Expansion of the criminal justice system in the late twentieth century: personnel and costs

Whether we assess growth by expenditure, output or number of employees, the agencies constituting the criminal justice system in England and Wales have undergone change and general expansion over the last 50 years. Recent numbers involved (in 2001) are set out in Table 1.1.

In addition to the quantitative growth of this occupational sector, a qualitative change is also occurring as pressure mounts for greater professionalisation through degree level entry and an increasing emphasis on training. This is most evident in the police, prison and court services. The demand for greater professionalism reflects the greater complexity of the work of criminal justice employees in the twenty-first century. It is recognised, for example, that officials need to be responsive to the changing demands of society and the increasing complexities of the system. Social change and community demands have resulted in continual reviews and a re-examination of the function and practice of many agencies and professions. Further changes can be expected as the implications of greater European and international cooperation are examined. The introduction of new technology has increased demands for a more highly trained and flexible workforce.

The volume of recent legislation, government reports and commissions on aspects of criminal justice, which will be referred to throughout this book, reflects this state of change. Throughout the 1990s and into the twenty-first century we have seen a steady flow of legislation on matters concerning criminal justice (see the chronology section). Virtually every aspect of the system has recently undergone, or is currently undergoing, change, partly as a result of new problems such as ter-

Table 1.1 Employees and volunteers in the criminal justice system 2001

Police	
Police officers	131,548
Special constables	16,484
Civilian employees of the Police Service	53,370
Traffic wardens	3,570
PCSO	4,000
Private security guards	400,000
Forensic Science Service	1,600
Crown Prosecution Service	6,000
Victim Support volunteers	1,700
Judiciary	
Lay magistrates	30,361
District Judges	177
Magistrates' court staff	10,795
Judges, Recorders and Assistant Recorders	1,771
Corrections	
Prison Service staff	47,080
Probation Service	14,606
Independent Monitoring Boards	1,762

rorism and the expansion of 'electronic crime', partly because of the consequences of EU harmonisation and partly because of the steady rate of reform introduced by the New Labour Government since 1997.

The law and order budget has grown steadily in recent decades to a total cost of £12.7 billion in 2002, the major expense being the police (as is seen in Table 1.2).

The criminal justice system in England and Wales is extensive and widespread but what is it for? To answer these questions the subsequent sections of this chapter will examine the definitions of criminal justice, its principles, models and flow

Table 1.2 Costs: Percentage distribution of criminal justice system costs 2001/2

Police	55%
Prison	13%
Home Office (includes Youth Justice Board, CCRC, Victim Support)	9%
Criminal Defence Service	7%
Probation Service	4%
CPS and Serious Fraud Office	3%
Magistrates' court	3%
Crown Court	2%
CICA	2%
Other	2%

Source: Criminal Justice System Annual Report 2001–2

charts of the system of justice and finally look at some of the key policy directions as illustrated by legislative changes since 1990.

1.2 CRIMINAL JUSTICE DEFINED: FUNCTIONS AND FORM

How can a criminal justice system be defined and described? Criminal justice is about society's formal response to crime and is defined more specifically in terms of a series of decisions and actions taken by a number of agencies in response to a specific crime or criminal or crime in general. Following the recognition of a crime-like incident, or in seeking to prevent lawless behaviour, criminal justice agencies become involved. There are four key sub-systems of criminal justice:

- *Law enforcement*: involving the police and prosecuting agencies.
- *Courts*: making decisions about pre-trial detention, adjudication on the guilt of the defendant, deciding on the sentence for those convicted and ensuring that the rights of the defendant are respected.
- *Penal system*: involves probation, prisons and other agencies that punish and incarcerate and/or seek to monitor, control and reduce offending behaviour.
- *Crime prevention*: involves the above agencies, which deal with individual offenders, along with a wider group of agencies, some private, others governmental, which plan crime-free environments or seek to change the conditions that lead to criminal behaviour.

People are exposed in everyday life to images and realities of crime and criminal justice as victims, witnesses, professionals, offenders and as onlookers. We develop ideas about and images of the way the different agencies, such as the police, prosecutors, courts, prisons, probation, local authorities and private security agencies, respond to crime or its perceived threats. We are made aware through the media, official statements and political debates about the issues of crime and justice. In an effort to become more analytical in our approach to these issues, ideas and images, it is possible to conceptualise the criminal justice system in the following terms:

- *Substantive law*. The content of the criminal law provides the starting point of the criminal justice system by defining behaviour that is to be regulated through the use of the criminal law.
- *Form and process*. Who is given the task of responding to crime and what procedures must they follow?
- *Functions*. What are the intended consequences and aims of the system?
- *Modes of punishment*. What sentences are available to the courts?
- *Criminal justice paradigms*. What are the dominant ways of thinking about issues of crime, criminals and justice?

When we look at other countries we can see differences in the definitions of criminality in the criminal law, the procedures in the courts, the types of sentences, and the ways of thinking about crime and punishment (penal paradigms). The purpose of the criminal justice system will be very different when a secular society is contrasted with a religious one. It becomes apparent that cultural factors are a major influence on the operation of a criminal justice system.

The O J Simpson trial generated immense interest about the system of criminal justice in the United States of America and led to discussion as to whether this type of case would be dealt with in the same way in this country. A trip around the world would show that many aspects of law, procedure and punishment vary considerably. In Scotland the age of criminal responsibility starts at 7, while in Finland it is 15. In France the law demands that a bystander must intervene to help a person being attacked. The legal system in California found O J Simpson responsible for killing his wife in the civil court while the criminal court found him not guilty, as in the case in England and Wales of Tony Dietrick, who was found responsible in the civil court for the death of Joan Francisco (*The Times*, 25 March 1998: 1). Barbados, Jamaica and Trinidad & Tobago have threatened to leave the Commonwealth because the Privy Council in London reprieved all death penalty cases. Nearly all the former colonies of the Caribbean retained the Privy Council as the final Court of Appeal. South Africa abolished the death penalty in 1995 at a time when many US states were about to implement it. In Saudi Arabia beheading is regarded as an appropriate mode of punishment, and two nurses found guilty of the murder of an Australian colleague were subject to bartering for their lives. People living in different jurisdictions are subject to different sets of laws. In Saudi Arabia there is no concept of rape within a marriage but alcohol is prohibited by law.

We use these illustrations from around the globe, first, to demonstrate the many variations in the way issues of crime, guilt and punishment are approached in different jurisdictions; secondly, so that students of criminal justice should be conscious of this diversity of approach (it follows that an awareness of different legal systems is required for those who wish to understand the complexities of other jurisdictions and the differences in the definitions of crimes and criminal procedures); thirdly, to show that beyond the legal details are issues of morality, politics and ethics that might require a strong stomach and a willingness to understand that issues of criminal justice raise many fundamental questions about the nature of humanity and society.

Content of the criminal law: what is penalised?

In most countries, particular kinds of behaviour are criminalised through the criminal law, formulated in some countries by a penal code. As discussed in Chapter 2, there is no simple way of defining what behaviour is criminal, and this may vary between different countries and over time. Nevertheless, in most Western societies similar kinds of behaviour are considered to be criminal including homicide, rape, arson, kidnapping, robbery, burglary, assault, theft, fraud and motoring offences. Thus according to Knut Sveri, 'if a person does something which is considered to be a crime in Sweden, it will practically always be considered to be a crime in New York' (Sveri 1990).

Form and process: criminal procedure and criminal justice agencies

Different countries have very different ways of investigating and prosecuting criminal cases, based on different principles and rules. Varying procedures and regulations govern such matters as the investigation of crime, the arrest and interrogation of suspects, prosecution decisions, bail procedure, trial procedures, rules of evidence and the role of the jury, if there is one. There are also differences in how courts decide on the guilt or otherwise of defendants.

In part, this is because other countries have different agencies dealing with these matters. In France an investigating magistrate, the *juge d'instruction*, conducts investigations into serious crime and embraces a policing, prosecutorial and judicial role, in contrast to the United Kingdom where the police, prosecutors and judiciary have distinct responsibilities. In Germany the public prosecutor, the *staatsanwalt*, has overall responsibility for pre-trial proceedings and advises the examining judge on bail and remand decisions. There is no equivalent in England and Wales to the Scottish Procurator Fiscal who also has an investigating and prosecuting role, and can issue a fiscal fine. Across the United States of America, each of the 50 states has its own penal code and each county within a state has its own criminal justice agencies such as district attorneys and sheriffs, in addition to the state and federal agencies.

It is important to appreciate how criminal justice agencies define and interpret their role and legal responsibilities. The criminal law does not enforce itself. To understand a system we need to consider how law enforcers, prosecutors, lawyers, magistrates, judges, probation officers and prison officers perceive their job and their function within the system. How they work will be affected not only by their official role but by political, financial, organisational and cultural influences. While Parliament and judges may create and interpret the criminal law, they do not implement it on a day-to-day basis. An appreciation of the everyday world of those who translate the law as described in books into the law in action is therefore essential to an understanding of how criminal justice agencies operate.

Functions and aims of the criminal justice system

In exploring what a criminal justice aims to do, it is necessary to distinguish between the goals of the system as a whole, and the functions of the different agencies who make up the system. Agency-specific functions are shown in Figure 1.1. Cross-system goals include the following:

- *Public protection*: by preventing and deterring crime, by rehabilitating offenders and incapacitating others who constitute a persistent threat to the community.
- *Justice and the rule of law*: upholding and promoting the rule of law and respect for the law, by ensuring due process and proper treatment of suspects, arrestees, defendants and those held in custody, successfully prosecuting criminals and acquitting innocent people accused of a crime.
- *Public order*: maintaining law and order.
- *Punishment*: sentencing criminals with regard to the principles of just deserts.

Figure 1.1 Agency-specific functions

Police

- Investigating crime
- Preventing crime
- Arresting and detaining suspects
- Maintaining public order
- Protecting the public from terrorist threats
- Traffic control
- Responding to criminal and non-criminal emergencies

Some of these tasks are also carried out by private and other public law enforcement agencies such as Customs and Excise and environmental health and trading standards departments of local authorities.

Prosecution

- Filtering out weak cases
- Preparing cases for prosecution
- Prosecuting cases in the magistrates' courts
- Preparing cases for trial in the Crown Court by liaising with barristers for the prosecution before and throughout a trial

Criminal Defence Service

- Defending those charged with criminal offences

Courts

- Handling and processing cases efficiently
- Deciding on bail, remands, and mode of trial
- Protecting the rights of the defendant
- Deciding on guilt
- Passing sentence
- Hearing appeals against conviction and sentence
- Providing a public arena so that justice can be seen to be done

Prisons

- Holding persons remanded in custody by the courts
- Holding sentenced offenders
- Maintaining proper conditions for those held in custody
- Preparing inmates for release
- Attempting to rehabilitate offenders

Probation

- Preparing pre-sentence reports
- Providing bail facilities for and information to the courts on offenders' appropriateness for bail
- Working with offenders given community orders
- Running probation centres
- Supervising released prisoners and pre-release work with inmates in custody

- *Denunciation*: registering social disapproval of censured behaviour of criminal acts.

- *Victim services*: aiding and advising the victims of crime.

- *Public confidence*: maintaining public confidence so that the public system of criminal justice is perceived as dealing effectively and fairly with the threats to the public from criminals such that citizens do not feel the need to engage in private acts of vengeance and vigilantism.

Mode and distribution of punishment

Finally, variations between systems include differences in the modes and distribution of punishment, recognising that societies punish offenders in diverse ways. If one point of distinction in defining a criminal justice system is to establish what is punished, another is to describe the types or mode of punishment used.

The main penal sanctions or court sentencing options are imprisonment, fines, community penalties, discharges, admonitions and cautions. The death penalty for murder was abolished in this country in 1965 and has also been abolished in most European countries, although it is still in use in some states in the United States of America and in African and Asian countries.

The most noticeable difference between countries, however, is not merely in the mode of punishment but in the distribution of punishment, that is the range of sentences routinely given for particular offences. What is acceptable to a Swedish, UK or US court in terms of typical sentencing practice varies greatly.

In different cultures, ideas as to what constitutes an appropriate punishment will differ. A good illustration of this is provided in the extract from the *Daily Telegraph* (Figure 1.2), which looks at differences within Australia between the European and Aboriginal attitudes towards punishment and distinctive examples of the criminal justice paradigm.

1.3 PRINCIPLES OF CRIMINAL JUSTICE

Principles of criminal justice

Unlike many other countries, England and Wales have no written penal code or definitive statement of the principles of criminal justice. Nevertheless some important principles guide criminal justice procedure. A crucial feature of criminal justice in England and Wales is the adversarial principle, which determines how guilt should be established. A central aspect of this is that the individual has rights, whether as a suspect, defendant or convicted person.

Adversarial justice

The main principle that underpins the system of criminal justice in England and Wales is adversarial justice. The ideas of the burden of proof and the standard of proof are vital. The burden of proof requires the police to identify a suspect from the evidence available and, if there is sufficient evidence against him or her, to prosecute that person and establish his or her guilt. An adversarial system does not seek to establish what happened or the truth about an incident: that is sometimes left to inquiries. The adversarial system requires the police and prosecutor to identify a person, called a suspect. The logic of adversarial justice, however, requires that the police and the prosecutors will not continue to prosecute a case, even if they are

Figure 1.2 Tribal elders punish Aborigine car thieves

Six Aborigines have been beaten for stealing cars after Northern Territory police let their elders handle the matter in a traditional way.

The six, aged 15–25, were beaten with rubber hoses in front of the local council chambers in an Aboriginal community near Darwin.

Since the incident three months ago, only one minor offence of theft has been committed in the town.

It was not the first time Aborigines in the Territory have been handed over to elders by the Australian justice system for tribal punishment.

Earlier this year, Mr Brian Martin, the Chief Justice of the Territory, asked the Department of Correctional Services to monitor the tribal 'payback' spearing through both thighs of Wilson Jagamara Walker, an Aboriginal convicted of manslaughter. Mr Martin's decision was influenced by petitions from the man's tribal council and a group of senior women at Yuendumu, 150 miles southwest of Alice Springs, who warned him that innocent members of the man's family would be speared instead of him if he was jailed.

Taking this into account, the judge released Walker on a bond and asked that correctional services report on whether the spearing took place.

However, the judicial outcome remained unclear after officials said that the victim's family had decided not to proceed with the spearing even though Walker was prepared to submit to the punishment.

Mr Martin gave Walker a three-year suspended jail term and allowed six months, which expires in August, for the payback to occur. In the ritual, the convicted man will be speared through the thighs in front of the tribe by the younger brother of a man he stabbed to death in Alice Springs in a family feud last year.

Walker, who has accepted the tribal law and is said to be happy with the judge's decision, is now being cared for by relatives at an isolated settlement. He is said to be ready to return to Yuendumu for the spearing when preliminary tribal ceremonies have been completed.

Mr Kevin Kitchener, a barrister with the North Australian Aboriginal Legal Aid Service, said: 'Maybe we should go back to the old traditional ways. They seem to work.' Mr Kitchener, who related the beating incident to a conference on Aboriginal justice issues in Townsville, Queensland, said the youths had been surrounded in the street by Aboriginal male adults. They had not been seriously hurt because the adults knew how to beat them without causing permanent injuries.

'It sounds barbaric', he said, 'but the instant justice had an important further deterrent effect. They know that if they get into trouble again the same thing will happen. But next time women will be wielding the rubber hoses, which will give them an even greater sense of shame.'

Mr Kitchener said the day before the public beating another group of Aboriginal youths had been arrested in Darwin for similar offences.

'They told friends they were very glad to be facing white man's justice – not one of them wanted to face Aboriginal punishment,' he said.

by Geoffrey Lee Martin in Sydney

Source: *The Daily Telegraph*, 18 June 1994: 13. © Telegraph Group Limited, London, 1994.

convinced that they know who committed a crime, until they have sufficient evidence to show beyond reasonable doubt that the person accused of the crime did it. They will have to convince the magistrates in a summary trial, or a jury in the Crown Court. There is no burden on the defendant to establish his or her innocence as this is not a question raised in an adversarial courtroom in England and Wales.

'Beyond reasonable doubt' is a high standard of proof and this not only protects the innocent against wrongful conviction but also protects the guilty where the evidence is not available or exists but is not admissible. The adversarial system does not presume that all people arrested are innocent, otherwise no one would be arrested or remanded in custody. The presumption of innocence is a rule that governs the conduct of the trial stage. It means in effect that the prosecutor must convince a jury or magistrates of the fact that the person accused of the crime did it, by reference to evidence rather than assertion. The trial procedure is based on the assumption that the defendant is innocent and it is up to the prosecutor to demonstrate by evidence that the person is guilty beyond reasonable doubt. The trial and the system of appeals never establishes the innocence of the accused; a person's acquittal does not mean he or she was innocent in the commonsense meaning of the word.

The image of adversarial justice is of ranks of bewigged and articulate barristers using argument and evidence and cross-examination to establish the guilt or otherwise of the offender accused of a crime. This image is unrealistic as most defendants admit their guilt for an offence rather than have it established by trial. Thus in 2002 in magistrates' courts 782,400 (81 per cent) cases resulted in convictions because the defendant pleaded guilty. In only 56,700 summary cases did defendants contest their guilt by trial. In the same year in the Crown Court 66 per cent of 74,900 defendants pleaded guilty and therefore did not have a trial (*Criminal Statistics England and Wales 2002*, pp. 64, 67).

It is therefore arguable whether the adversarial nature of criminal justice is the dominant feature of a system in which only a small proportion of defendants exercise their right to trial. However, it is still accurate to describe the system as adversarial because the possibility of a trial, and the onus of having to prove beyond reasonable doubt the guilt of an offender, affects many parts of the system – particularly the way in which the police and prosecutors conduct their business. The police will need evidence that might be exposed to the full glare of a trial. A prosecutor's reputation will be adversely affected if he or she allows a case to proceed that does not meet the standards set in the Code for Crown Prosecutors for evidential sufficiency, which means the evidence must be admissible, credible and reliable such that it is likely to convince a jury that the person was guilty beyond reasonable doubt.

In adversarial systems, therefore, a trial does not establish whether the accused is innocent of the offence he or she has been charged with, but whether the evidence is sufficient, beyond reasonable doubt, to establish guilt. Criminal appeals examine the same issue, a point explained by Professor Michael Zander in the context of a Court of Appeal decision that overturned the conviction of Winston Silcott for the murder of PC Blakelock during the Broadwater Farm riot of October 1985.

In a letter to *The Times*, Zander explains the key logic of the adversarial system:

Guilt or Innocence?

Sir, In writing about compensation for Winston Silcott (August 3) Janet Daley says, 'He has now been declared innocent of one particular crime'. This commonly held view is incorrect.

Mr Silcott, whose conviction for another murder still stands, had his conviction for murder in the case of PC Blakelock quashed by the Court of Appeal. This no more represents a declaration of innocence than does acquittal by a jury.

A jury acquittal means that in the jury's view the prosecution have not proved beyond reasonable doubt, or that even if guilt has been established they are unwilling to convict. The quashing of a conviction by the Court of Appeal means that for one of a large number of possible reasons the conviction cannot stand. Very often the reason is that the judge directed the jury wrongly on law. In the Silcott case, the reason related to documents which the Court of Appeal considered had been tampered with.

Many people, including many commentators in the media, have confused these issues.

The question of whether someone is innocent is not one that is addressed in a criminal trial in our legal system (emphasis added).

(*The Times*, 12 August 1994: 15)

In the same way as the trial questions whether guilt has been established on the basis of evidence presented, an appeal after conviction considers whether the trial process was flawed. In neither case does the court ask 'Is the defendant innocent?'

Principles, other than adversarial, can be found in policy statements by parliamentary bodies such as the Select Committee on Home Affairs and in the written aims of separate agencies in the system (see Chapter 4). General statements can also be found in policy documents such as white papers or as preambles to legislation. The Home Office and the Department for Constitutional Affairs have overall responsibility for many aspects of the criminal justice system, but, unlike other more centralised systems, a policy document from these departments is not regarded as a definitive statement of policy to be followed slavishly. This is partly because this would conflict with other principles such as the independence of the judiciary, professional autonomy and divisions of responsibility for the management and funding of criminal justice (see Chapter 4).

In contrast to our system, some countries have penal codes that contain clearly stated principles. An example of this is Finland where the basic principles of the criminal justice system have been set out in the Penal Code of 1889. Although these have been amended over the century, the Finnish Ministry of Justice identifies the fundamental principles in Finnish criminal law and procedure:

Today, the fundamental principles in criminal law include the principles of legality, equality, predictability and proportionality. Among the consequences of the strict interpretation given the principle of *legality* in Finland is that the court may not impose forms of punishment that are not specified for the offence in question. *Equality* demands that all cases falling within a specific category are dealt with in the same way. *Predictability* demands that it is possible to assess, in advance, the certainty and level of punishment for a given act. Predictability increases if the law is simple and legal practice is uniform. *Proportionality* requires that the sanction for an offence is in proportion to its blameworthiness. This principle, which also requires that consideration be taken of all official and unofficial penal and non-penal consequences of an offence, establishes the maximum punishment. It is not seen to prevent mitigation of punishment where this is deemed reasonable.

In Finland, as in all of the Nordic countries, it is generally felt that punishments primarily have, and should have, a general preventive effect. General prevention can be enhanced by two components, the *certainty* and *severity* of punishment. Finnish criminal policy emphasizes certainty, but not severity. General prevention also involves the maintenance of standards of morality through the public disapproval

> that punishment directs at criminal behaviour. Individual prevention, as a primary goal of punishment, has been rejected. The coercive rehabilitation of offenders was found to be based on flawed arguments and to raise problems with legal safeguards and the control of discretion.
>
> (Joutsen 1990: 2)

Rule of law

Without a penal code or its equivalent the principles that govern criminal justice in England and Wales evolve from the system of parliamentary sovereignty and the principles of the rule of law. The system of parliamentary sovereignty means that Parliament is the supreme authority and the final arbiter of legality as defined by the enacted laws of the land. In recent years, since the Treaty of Rome, Parliament has not been the only source of rules and regulations and some aspects of the sovereignty of the British Parliament have been ceded to European institutions.

The basic principles of the rule of law were articulated by A V Dicey, who wrote:

> No man is punishable or can be lawfully made to suffer in body or goods except for a distinct breach of law established in the ordinary legal manner before the ordinary courts of the land.
>
> ... no man is above the law, but ... every man whatever be his rank or condition, is subject to the ordinary law of the realm and amenable to the jurisdiction of the ordinary tribunals.
>
> ... the general principles of the constitution (as for example the right to personal liberty, or the right to public meeting) are with us as the result of judicial decisions determining the rights of private persons in particular cases brought before the courts.
>
> (Dicey 1959: 188–95)

The rights of the defendant, and the victim and the public at large, are derived from the provisions enacted by Parliament and interpretations of the ordinary courts. A primary principle of the rule of law is that everyone is subject to the law including those who enforce it. They can claim no special status unless given by the law and must always be answerable to the law.

In England and Wales official objectives are typically expressed in Home Office documents, such as *Criminal Justice: A Working Paper* (Home Office 1984). In the foreword the then Home Secretary, Leon Brittan, specified four objectives for criminal justice, which would contribute towards sustaining the principle of the rule of law:

> A fair and effective criminal justice system marks the distinction between a civilised society and anarchy. If it works well, we as citizens can live our lives peacefully, and enjoy the rewards of our labours; if it works badly, many of us – particularly the elderly and the vulnerable – will have our lives marred by the fear, and sometimes the experience, of crime....

We needed a strategy...

The central objectives of this strategy are to sustain the rule of law:

a. by preventing crime wherever possible;

b. when crimes are committed, by detecting the culprit;

c. by convicting the guilty and acquitting the innocent;

d. by dealing adequately and appropriately with those who are guilty and by giving proper effect to the sentences or orders which are imposed.

Principles of criminal justice, whether set out in penal codes, legislation or policy documents, attempt to capture a complex set of issues in grand statements which are supposed to guide the policies and actions of participants in the system. However, the world of human behaviour is not so easily captured into a few phrases and reality is necessarily more complex. The presumption of innocence, for example, sounds simple but raises complex questions. One of these is how many guilty criminals we are prepared to allow to escape apprehension and punishment in order to ensure that no innocent person is unjustly arrested and punished. We could punish those whom we are absolutely certain have committed an offence, but victims may feel aggrieved when cases fall on seeming technicalities and the release of too many apparently guilty persons could encourage vigilantism. Then the chances of justice being done would be even less likely.

Principles of criminal justice are abstractions which portray what ought to happen. Anecdotal insights, be they from police officers, solicitors, barristers, probation officers or recidivists, are frequently stories of the way the system failed to work as it is supposed. Empirical studies by criminologists and social scientists in recent years have given credence to some of these insights by revealing the gap between principles and reality.

It is very important for a student of criminal justice not to treat the principles as facts, but to regard them instead as criteria by which to judge the performance and practices of a criminal justice system.

1.4 SYSTEMS APPROACH AND CRIMINAL JUSTICE SUB-SYSTEMS

We have used the term 'criminal justice system' and must now look at what this implies. The term 'system' is often used to describe a designed unit such as a central heating or a recording system, or a natural phenomenon such as the solar system. It has also been used by social reformers who applied the term to the education or welfare systems and talked in terms of social engineering. The word 'system' conveys an impression of a complex object with interconnected parts and subdivisions with a flow from beginning to end.

Would it be accurate to describe criminal justice as a system? Certainly, looking at the flow charts in Figures 1.3–1.5, it could well appear that there is a system at work which has a beginning and a number of predictable stages. The agencies in the criminal justice system are interdependent. One agency's output is another agency's input. Those who leave the courts with a custodial sentence become the intake into the prisons at the back-end of the system. The role of each agency depends on its particular function in the overall scheme of things. For instance, policing cannot be fully understood without an awareness of the role of the police in the overall context of the system. The system may therefore be seen as greater than the sum of its parts.

It is also useful to view criminal justice as a system when considering planning, organisation and policy. During the 1980s, for example, there were a number of attempts to encourage a systems approach towards criminal justice. The Home Secretary, Leon Brittan, in evidence to the Home Affairs Committee of the House of Commons, declared:

> ... on taking office I decided that we needed a strategy which would enable us to establish and pursue our priorities and objectives in a deliberate and coherent way ... Our principal preoccupation is, and I believe it ought to be, the criminal justice system which, incidentally, I wish to see treated in all that we do as a system.
>
> (Home Affairs Select Committee, 23 January 1984)

There are several implications of regarding criminal justice as a system. It recognises that agencies are interdependent. Hence, the work of the prison and probation services depends on the work of the courts who, in turn, depend on the filtering role of the Crown Prosecution Service, the generation of cases by the police and initially by the activities of lawbreakers. It is very important for financial and resource planning and is particularly crucial when considering reforms to recognise the interdependency of the system. Thus reforms proposed for one part of the system will often have an impact on other agencies not directly involved in the proposed changes.

This can be seen by considering how the prison population can be affected by changes in the law. In the last 50 years, the advent of the motor car has created the need for more regulation by the criminal law, as cars not only provide opportunities for theft, but also necessitate regulation of driving if others are not to be endangered or inconvenienced. This increases the number of people brought to court, which in turn affects the number in prison. Motoring offences have resulted in a rise in the number of receptions into prisons of those convicted of serious motoring offences such as causing death by dangerous driving, along with many fine defaulters initially convicted of a motoring offence.

A systems approach also encourages inter-agency consultation and cooperation. One recommendation from the Woolf Inquiry into the series of prison riots during 1990 was the need for greater cooperation and liaison between agencies in the criminal justice system. Thus prisons cannot be effectively managed without the fullest cooperation of all agencies responsible for dealing with offenders. The report recommended that a Criminal Justice Consultative Council (CJCC) be set up. This was done in 1991 and includes senior members of most of the agencies. Since then 24 local committees have been formed. The aim of establishing Area Committees was to encourage better communications between agencies and to improve strategic planning by identifying common areas of concern, receive reports, collect and distribute information on agency and cross-agency activities, disseminate information regarding available resources and be a forum for addressing strategic developments that affect all agencies (see Chapter 4).

Greater cooperation between criminal justice agencies and external organisations was also encouraged during the 1980s and the idea of joined up government has stimulated greater coordination in areas such as youth justice since 1997. With respect to crime prevention, many partnerships were set up, encouraged by the Home Office, involving links between official criminal justice agencies, local government and the voluntary and business sectors.

How systematic is criminal justice in England and Wales? It must be recognised that the multiple and competing aims of the system mean that different goals may be simultaneously pursued by different participants. These aims are not easy to reconcile, either in the system as a whole or within specific agencies. For example, should the judge give a sentence that deters the future lawbreaker or one that rehabilitates past lawbreakers?

These multiple aims also affect how those working in agencies see their role, and how, over time, they have developed their own ways of working within conflicting constraints. Thus agencies have developed what can be described as a distinctive working culture or professional ideology. One example of these kinds of conflicts can be found in the implementation of parts of the Criminal Justice Act 1991, which enacted curfew orders and electronic monitoring but did not provide details as to how or when they were to come into effect. These new sanctions were not popular with some sections of the probation service who regard themselves as a profession whose aim is to help or care for offenders, rather than to supervise or control them. So the central problem of describing criminal justice as a system is to recognise the practical implications of these conflicting goals.

Another problem may arise where agencies are expected to cooperate with each other. There may, for example, be competition between agencies over the allocation of responsibilities or funding. Different working cultures which derive from different perceptions of the goals of the system may lead to mistrust between agencies. This may mean that they are reluctant to cooperate with each other and may inhibit the exchange of information, which affected the initial relationship between the police and the Crown Prosecution Service when it was established in 1985. Differing models, as described below, may be followed: the police, who have traditionally been seen as following a crime control model, may have difficulties in communicating with lawyers whose role derives from the due process model, or with social workers, who may be more committed to a rehabilitative model.

A certain level of conflict is designed into the system by the *adversarial* nature of criminal trials. It is the duty of the prosecution to prove the guilt of the accused 'beyond reasonable doubt', whereas it is the duty of the defence lawyer to plant that 'reasonable doubt' in the minds of the magistrates or the jury and so secure an acquittal. This adversarial nature of criminal trials has important and pervasive consequences for other parts of the system. It affects the way the police, prosecutors and the probation service perceive and discharge their respective roles.

As we have seen, the trial seeks not to establish the truth, but provides a process for the conviction or acquittal of the accused which affects the kind of evidence the police must secure. The logic of the adversarial style of trial explains why the defence lawyer may cross-examine victims of crime, for example in rape cases, in a way that appears at times to be brutal and insensitive.

Flow charts of the criminal justice system

The interrelationships between agencies and stages in the system can be represented in flow charts which provide a helpful snapshot of the process to enhance understanding of the jigsaw of interrelationships in the system. Figures 1.3–1.5 illustrate the flow and stages of the criminal justice system from crime to prosecution, in the courts, and in the penal system.

Figure 1.3 Criminal justice flow chart 1: from crime to prosecution (for routine cases involving adults)

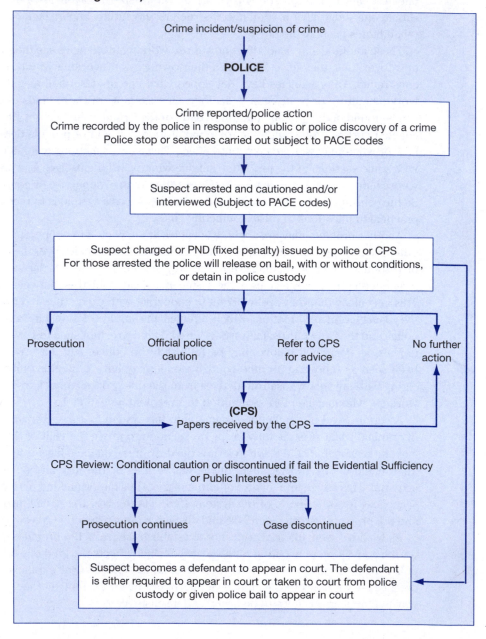

Figure 1.4 Criminal justice flow chart 2: the criminal courts – from first court appearance to conviction (for routine cases involving adults)

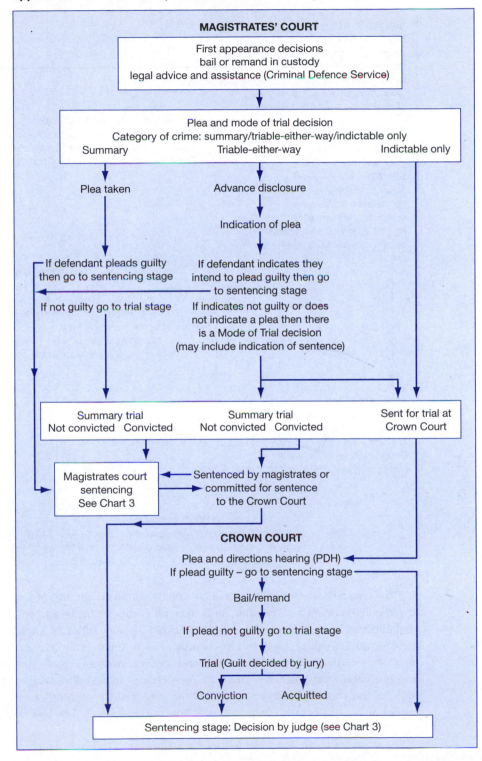

Figure 1.5 Criminal justice flow chart 3: interrelationship of agencies in the penal system (for routine cases involving adults)

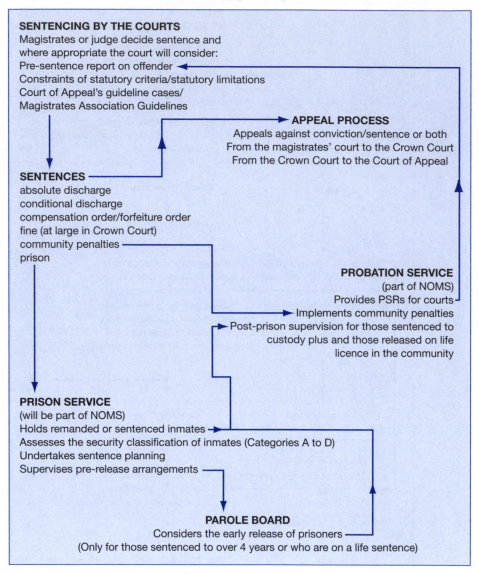

Flow charts, however, provide a misleadingly simplistic picture of a system that involves encounters between human beings, all coming into the system with their own motives, be they criminals, victims or criminal justice officials. Each encounter involves an individual story, and has significance in the overall drama of society's response to crime. The drama, morality and social consequences of crime and punishment cannot be portrayed easily in such charts. In addition, while they show some of the ways in which agencies and the stages of the system interrelate, they cannot always reflect the complexities of how one decision, taken by one agency at a particular point in the system, affects later decisions.

Some prefer to see criminal justice as a process – through which a case or a defendant passes. In this process all stages, each governed by a set of discrete rules, are interrelated and affect the eventual outcome. Whether a defendant pleads guilty or not guilty, for example, affects not only whether he or she is convicted, but whether and how evidence must be prepared, whether he or she is given bail, and it will almost certainly affect any sentence. At the same time, defendants' decisions about whether or not to plead guilty and, if so, when to plead guilty, will be affected by what might happen at later stages.

1.5 PARADIGMS AND MODELS OF CRIMINAL JUSTICE

In what ways are issues of crime and justice thought about in public debates and in everyday life? Are criminals regarded as an evil minority or just as ordinary people? Should the police be more concerned with strategies to prevent crime or to capture criminals? Should we spend more money on probation to help offenders or more on prison to punish them? Are the courts effective in ensuring fair trials and preventing miscarriages of justice? Should the phrase 'miscarriage of justice' apply only to those who are wrongly convicted of a crime they did not commit, or should it also apply to those who committed a crime but were not convicted through a lack of evidence caused by witness intimidation? Should it even apply to those who avoid conviction although they have committed a criminal act? These questions and issues will depend on a number of assumptions and views about the nature and extent of the problems of crime and the justice and injustices associated with the way the agencies who operate on behalf of society go about their business.

In this book we have included chapters about images of, and the extent of, crime and in this opening chapter we introduce the reader to some of the key principles of criminal justice, current policy shifts brought about by legislation, models of criminal justice, and flow diagrams that provide ways of thinking about the criminal justice system in England and Wales, or elsewhere. The sum of these different institutional arrangements and ways of thinking about crime and criminal justice is referred to as the criminal justice paradigm.

Models of criminal justice

Models of criminal justice are essentially different perspectives on, or different ways of looking at, criminal justice, derived from the work of writers from a variety of legal, sociological, or administrative backgrounds. They provide a way of looking at criminal justice in terms of some general characteristics, principles or themes of a system and help the person new to a system to come to terms with its complexities and to make some sense of it. But it should be remembered that, like all models, they are scaled-down versions of the real thing and will not capture all its complexities.

Herbert Packer first identified two alternative models – a crime control model which stressed the role of criminal justice in terms of the efficient controlling of crime (the conveyor belt), and a due process model (the obstacle course), which stressed the importance of the rule of law and procedural safeguards (Packer 1968). These ideas were extremely influential, and later writers identified further models: e.g. Michael King, who outlined six such models (King 1981).

Table 1.3 Models of criminal justice

Social function	Process model	Features of court
1 Justice	*Due process model*	(a) Equality between parties (b) Rules protecting defendants against error (c) Restraint of arbitrary power (d) Presumption of innocence
2 Punishment	*Crime control model*	(a) Disregard of legal controls (b) Implicit presumption of guilt (c) High conviction rate (d) Unpleasantness of experience (e) Support for police
3 Rehabilitation	*Medical model (diagnosis, prediction, and treatment selection)*	(a) Information collecting procedures (b) Individualisation (c) Treatment presumption (d) Discretion of decision-makers (e) Expertise of decision-makers or advisers (f) Relaxation of formal rules
4 Management of crime and criminals	*Bureaucratic model*	(a) Independence from political considerations (b) Speed and efficiency (c) Importance of and acceptance of records (d) Minimisation of conflict (e) Minimisation of expense (f) Economical division of labour
5 Denunciation and degradation	*Status passage model*	(a) Public shaming of defendant (b) Court values reflecting community values (c) Agents' control over process
6 Maintenance of class domination	*Power model*	(a) Reinforcement of class values (b) Alienation of defendant (c) Deflection of attention from issues of class conflict (d) Differences between judges and judged (e) Paradoxes and contradictions between rhetoric and performance

Source: King (1981: 13)

The *first model*, originally developed by Packer, is the *due process* model, which represents an idealised version of how the system should work derived from the ideas inherent in the rule of law. It encompasses the principles of the defendant's rights found in textbooks and constitutional documents. It incorporates principles conveyed in well-known phrases such as the presumption of innocence, the defendant's right to a fair trial, equality before the law and that justice should be seen to be done. These phrases embody principles that underlie and allow us to interpret the many rules surrounding both the trial and the pre-trial processes. They protect defendants in order that the innocent may be acquitted and only the guilty convicted.

With the Human Rights Act 1998 this model has come to the foreground of public attention as the implications for basic aspects of policing, criminal procedure and sentencing were subject to considerable scrutiny and challenges from the human rights and due process perspective.

The *second model* is the *crime control* model identified by Packer and earlier explored by Jerome Skolnick in his book *Justice Without Trial* (Skolnick 1966). This stresses the role of the system in reducing, preventing and curbing crime by prosecuting and punishing those who are guilty of offences. It also stresses the importance of protecting citizens and serving the public by crime reduction. Thus the police and prosecution agencies may interpret their role primarily as crime fighters responsible for ensuring that the guilty are brought to justice. However, problems arise if this aim is pursued regardless of rules protecting the rights of the suspect. Fabricating evidence or neglecting to use search warrants could be seen as justifiable in order to ensure that an offender whom the police 'know' to be guilty is found guilty. This problem underlies many laws governing police procedure, seen most recently in legislative reforms of the 1980s. The Police and Criminal Evidence Act 1984 introduced the procedure under which the police tape recorded interviews with suspects in police stations, and the Prosecution of Offences Act 1985 led to the establishment of a prosecution agency independent of the police – the Crown Prosecution Service.

For many decades it has been accepted that offenders may not be wholly responsible for their own actions but that their criminality may spring from individual characteristics or social factors. These may be psychological disturbance or problems related to their family circumstances or the social environment. It may make little sense to punish such offenders without at the same time attempting to deal with these underlying issues. This is reflected in King's *third model*, that of *rehabilitation*, which has affected many parts of the criminal justice process. Under this model one of the major considerations at each stage is how best to deal with the individual offender, assuming that their criminality can be reduced by taking a rehabilitative approach. Thus it might be more desirable for the police to divert some offenders, especially young offenders, from the system, in circumstances where they feel that no benefit will be served by prosecution. The police have powers to caution offenders and refer them to social work agencies which may also help adult offenders. Social workers and probation officers become involved at the sentencing stage, by preparing pre-sentence reports on the offender's circumstances and outlining sentencing options, which may involve counselling and treatment rather than punishment.

Rehabilitation therefore individualises decisions, requiring that the needs of the offender be taken into account. It gives all agencies far greater amounts of discretion. This may well conflict with other goals – for example, with those of due process which seek to ensure that all offenders are treated equally; or with the crime control model which stresses the need to punish the guilty.

King's *fourth model* reflects the pressure on criminal justice officials to implement rules and procedures within the many constraints imposed by limited resources and public pressure to solve crimes. Agencies must therefore establish measures of *bureaucratic efficiency*. They must ensure that defendants are tried and sentenced as speedily and efficiently as possible. If defendants spend too long in prison before they come to trial, if trials take too long and are too costly, or if it is argued that too many defendants are acquitted or that there are miscarriages of justice, agencies and courts will come under considerable criticism. The cost effectiveness of law enforcement and court administration has become a major concern of the government since the 1990s.

Balancing the interests of due process with those of crime control and bureaucratic efficiency is not always easy. It is difficult, for example, to subject abstract principles such as justice to tests of cost effectiveness. How many defendants should be acquitted? How many should be tried rather than plead guilty? There are no straightforward answers to these questions – no yardstick against which to assess the efficiency of the system. Indeed, in some instances the interests of justice may conflict with those of efficiency – as can be seen in the example of not guilty pleas. If the defendant pleads not guilty, the prosecution and the defence have to prepare a case which may involve collecting evidence, summoning witnesses and preparing the many documents involved in a trial. If the defendant pleads guilty, much of this work can be avoided. Guilty pleas are, therefore, cost-effective and save the time of victims, witnesses, police, courts and the Crown Prosecution Service. But any pressure on defendants to plead guilty could deprive them of their right to trial. However, if more defendants insisted on their right to trial the system could become overloaded and more costly.

On the other hand, the police might not have sufficient admissible evidence to proceed against a person they suspect is guilty. The due process model would result in no action being taken. However, there may be some concern about the resources expended on an investigation with no result. The tension between these models will result in a difficult decision on whether to charge the person and hope that he or she pleads guilty or to drop the case.

Some would argue that offenders should be publicly tried and sentenced in order to reflect the community's moral disapproval of offending behaviour. This is reflected in the *fifth model* identified by King – the *denunciation and degradation* model. In this model, public trial and punishment are necessary to underline the law-abiding values of the community. Some sociologists have argued that the criminal justice system serves an important social function in reinforcing social values. While this may conflict with the aims of rehabilitation, it can be argued that such public punishment and expression of society's disapproval can in itself be rehabilitative, as it may induce feelings of shame in offenders – a prerequisite for rehabilitation. John Braithwaite argues in favour of reintegrative shaming – offenders should feel ashamed of their offences but shaming should not be so extreme that it stigmatises offenders to a point where they cannot be reintegrated into the community (Braithwaite 1989).

Exploring the potentially repressive nature of criminal justice systems also raises questions about who makes the law and whose interests are served by the criminal justice system. This is reflected in King's *sixth model*, the *power* model. Some, using a Marxist or conflict perspective, argue that criminal justice systems essentially reinforce the role of the powerful – those who make the laws and who are served by the many agencies of the system. Thus criminal law and its enforcement are influenced by the interests of dominant classes, elites, races or gender, depending on the particular version of domination used. The state is regarded in this model as acting in the interest of the dominant group who use the criminal law to further these interests. Advocates of this approach point to the over-representation of those from poorer sections of the community as defendants in the criminal justice system.

To King's six models of criminal justice we would add two more models. A *seventh* would be the *just deserts* model. Combining elements of retribution for offenders with a notion of proper respect for the treatment of the accused or defendant, this model stresses the importance of punishing offenders in terms of their blameworthiness and the seriousness of their offence, not through crude revenge or incapacitation, but in response to the wrongfulness of their act. This brings together the principles of respect for the offender as a human being with certain rights, the need to establish the offender's culpability for the offence so as to punish only the guilty, and the right of society to exact retribution from those who have done wrong. This links punishment and crime to issues of morality and control.

An *eighth model, managing offender behaviour*, is a second model added by us to recognise the focus on instrumental-offender strategies that are broader than rehabilitation and, while encompassing efforts to change behaviour, also monitor and control criminals depending on the level of risk and record of offending. Intensive supervision and surveillance programmes for juveniles and electronically monitored curfews are examples of a strategy of intervention that relies on surveillance and supervision to reduce crime. Here we see the crime control model being extended beyond policing into the correctional stage, blending rehabilitative practice with surveillance and control.

How useful are these models of criminal justice? To an extent they focus on and magnify one feature of the system. They do, however, illustrate different ways of looking at the system and indicate very different influences on policy and practice. Most of these models have been developed by different academic disciplines such as criminology, sociology or law and, more recently, from systems analysis utilised by experts in management and auditing techniques. Not surprisingly these disparate disciplines provide different snapshots of bits of the system from their own perspective. Lawyers focus mainly on procedures before and during trial. Sociologists put emphasis on the informal influences that can lead to inequalities and injustice. Criminologists focus on crime statistics and explanations of crime. Systems analysts trace the aggregate flow of cases through the system, management consultants look at problems of accountability and effectiveness, while accountants examine the cost effectiveness of the entire system and agencies within it. This has led to the development of management by objectives and the use of auditing techniques in the criminal justice system.

These different models reflect the many different influences that come to shape practice and policy in criminal justice. A different emphasis is seen by the Human Rights Act 1998, which highlights the *due process model*. These shifts in emphasis are at times determined by events such as the terrorist bombing of the commuter trains in Madrid in 2004 leading to a greater concern with *crime control.*

In this last section of this introductory chapter on criminal justice we will look at recent changes brought about by legislative reforms as an indicator of the way British law makers perceive the need for change to the criminal justice system. Underpinning these reforms will be shifts in the way different aspects of the system are being balanced in the light of changing circumstances, such as attempts to control new crimes (cross-European crime), modernisation and efficiency, efforts to protect human rights, and a shifting political and economic environment, be it greater public concern about crime in the United Kingdom or the consequences of greater integration across the enlarged European Union of 25 countries. These changing circumstances and concerns are embodied in the history of recent legislation in the United Kingdom.

1.6 RECENT LEGISLATION AND POLICY DEVELOPMENTS

'The first five Criminal Justice Acts of the century were spaced out over nearly 50 years, from 1925 to 1972, whereas the last five have come in less than 20 years since 1972 and the current Act is the third in only five years.' Wasik and Taylor wrote this in 1991: subsequently there has been a major piece of criminal justice legislation in every year since 1993.

Some legislative reforms focus on one aspect of the system. The Proceeds of Crime Act 2002 attempts to deal with money obtained illegally and money laundering, be it associated with drug dealing, terrorist groups, organised crime, or tax and social security fraud. One consequence has been to change the way solicitors deal with clients they suspect as having obtained money illegally. Other statutes have a broader impact, such as the Criminal Justice Act 2003, resulting in changes across many aspects of the criminal justice process.

This section aims briefly to outline recent developments since 1990, highlighting how these reflect the many conflicting goals and models of the system and their effect on policy, starting with the Criminal Justice Act 1991.

Criminal Justice Act 1991

The Criminal Justice Act (CJA 1991) was preceded by an unprecedented amount of research, planning, consultation and training. An experiment on unit fines was carried out in magistrates' courts in Hampshire, and extensive training was given to those who were to enforce the Act. Yet despite the research and consultation that went into the Act, within seven months of its implementation the Home Secretary announced that amendments were to be made to it.

The CJA 1991 was hailed as a far-reaching systematic reform of sentencing, although it reflected many existing shifts in penal philosophy and sentencing policy. The underlying themes of this change were expressed in the 1990 White Paper, *Crime, Justice and Protecting the Public* (Home Office 1990a) and included the need for more consistency in sentencing policy and for sentences to be proportionate to the offence. In addition it introduced what has come to be known as a 'twin track' approach to sentencing, making a clearer distinction between property offences and violent crime. The former were to be dealt with by a greater use of punishment in the community, while the latter, with a view to crime prevention, could result in longer prison sentences. The overall framework for sentencing otherwise was provided by a philosophy of 'just deserts': punishing in accordance with the current offence, rather than past crimes or possible future ones.

Vociferous criticism was made of the unit fine and another aspect of the sentencing reforms introduced by the CJA 1991. Section 29 had prevented judges and magistrates taking into account past convictions when sentencing except in limited circumstances. Furthermore, they could only take into account two offences when assessing seriousness for a person convicted of multiple incidents. Thus the burglar convicted of 20 burglaries would actually be sentenced on the basis of the worst two burglaries. Sentencers felt unable to reflect the frequency and history of offending in their disposals.

Criminal Justice Act 1993

Most of the provisions of the CJA 1991 came into effect on 1 October 1992. By Easter 1993, Kenneth Clarke, the then Home Secretary, announced that the unit fine system was to be abandoned. Legislation to this effect was added to the Criminal Justice Bill already before Parliament. Thus the CJA 1993, which dealt primarily with measures to combat anti-terrorist acts, drug trafficking and insider dealing, was used to amend the CJA 1991. Section 65 abolished the two main planks of the 1991 Act: unit fines and s. 29. The new Act provides that sentencers must take account of means when fining, and adjust fines up or down as appropriate, but without imposing a framework for doing so. In addition, the court can now consider all offences before the court and offenders' previous convictions or any failure to respond to earlier sanctions can be used by the courts when deciding on a sentence.

Criminal Justice and Public Order Act 1994

This Act reformed many aspects of the criminal justice system. Details of its provisions will be given in relevant chapters. Below are its main provisions:

- the introduction of a secure training order for 12–14-year-old persistent offenders. The first half of this order was to be spent in secure training units, and the second half to be spent under compulsory supervision in the community;
- allowed a court to draw inferences from a defendant's silence during police questioning or in court;
- bail not to be granted to defendants charged with or convicted of homicide or rape or who have a previous conviction for such an offence. Section 26 provided that persons accused or convicted of committing an offence while on bail need not be given bail (see Chapter 9);
- pilot projects for curfew orders and electronic monitoring;
- with regard to discounts for guilty pleas, it required the courts to take account of the timing and circumstances of a guilty plea;

- tougher powers against trespassers and unauthorised camping were directed at new age travellers and rave parties of more than 100 people;
- changes to the laws in relation to obscenity to incorporate child pornography produced on computers and some restrictions on the classification of video recordings were directed against what are commonly known as 'video nasties';
- redefined rape to include the offence commonly known as 'male rape', and lowered the age of consent for homosexual acts from 21 to 18.

Police and Magistrates' Courts Act 1994

This made a number of changes to the organisation of the police and magistrates' courts, including proposals for reorganising police authorities and the introduction of devolved budgets and performance-related criteria in the administration of them (see Chapter 6).

Crime and Disorder Act 1998

An array of measures were introduced that permit intervention at an early stage and allow for a response to anti-social and criminal behaviour of children, including: a local child curfew scheme, parenting orders, action plan orders, and police repri-mands and final warnings. Youth offending teams were established on a multi-disciplinary basis to coordinate crime prevention and responses to youth crime.

New sentences for young offenders were introduced: the reparation order and the detention and training order replaces the secure training order. Secure training centres for those aged from 12 to 14 were brought under the authority of a new Youth Justice Board. Tougher community protection laws with respect to sex offenders and anti-social behaviour and a new category of racially aggravated offence was created.

In the courts, procedural changes included speeding up the process of dealing with cases by imposing time limits, and ended committal proceedings for indictable-only offences. Reform of the CPS allows lay employees to conduct pre-trial procedure such as bail hearings.

Access to Justice Act 1999

The Legal Service Commission was established to oversee the reformed legal aid scheme and the Criminal Defence Service (CDS) was introduced to secure the pro-vision of advice, assistance and representation, according to the interests of justice, to people suspected of a criminal offence or facing criminal proceedings.

Youth Justice and Criminal Evidence Act 1999

The Act introduced a new sentencing disposal for the youth court. A referral order is a new sentence of referral to a youth offender panel. Referral is available for young people convicted for the first time and its primary aim is to prevent re-offending. The youth offender panel works with the young offender to establish a programme of behaviour for the young offender to follow. The programme is guided by the following three principles of restorative justice: making restoration to the victim; achieving reintegration into the law-abiding community; and taking responsibility for the consequences of offending behaviour.

The Act further introduced measures designed to help young, disabled, vulnerable or intimidated witnesses give evidence in criminal proceedings: physical measures to reduce the stress of giving evidence at trial (such as informal dress, screens, live link CCTV and the use of pre-recorded interviews); restrictions on the freedom of defendants to cross-examine their alleged victims personally; further restrictions on what evidence about an alleged victim's sexual behaviour can be considered relevant in a trial for a sexual offence; and further restrictions on publishing information that might reveal the identity of a witness.

Criminal Justice and Court Services Act 2000

This created the National Probation Service for England and Wales and the Children and Family Court Advisory and Support Service. It aims to prevent unsuitable people from working with children, with a statutory ban enforced by criminal sanctions; and increases the maximum penalties for offences relating to indecent photographs of children and raises the age of the child protected from under 14 to under 16.

Community orders were renamed: probation orders became community rehabilitation orders, community service orders and combination orders. The Act enables greater use of electronic monitoring and stricter enforcement and ensures that sex offenders subject to the notification requirements of the Sex Offenders Act 1997 should not be eligible for the Home Detention Curfew scheme. New powers were introduced for the compulsory drug testing of offenders and alleged offenders at various points in their contact with the criminal justice system and a court considering the question of bail is allowed to take into account any drug misuse by the defendant.

Powers of Criminal Courts (Sentencing) Act 2000

This is a consolidation Act which brings together, under one Act of Parliament, legislation which is previously found in a number of different statutes.

Anti-terrorism, Crime and Security Act 2001

In response to the 11 September 2001 terrorist attacks on New York and Washington, new powers to counter the threat to the United Kingdom were enacted to cut off terrorist funding, and government departments and agencies are allowed to collect and share information required for countering the terrorist threat, streamline relevant immigration procedures, protect the security of the nuclear and aviation industries, improve the security of dangerous substances that may be targeted or used by terrorists and enhance police powers when detainees in police custody refuse to cooperate with the police as to their identity.

International Criminal Court Act 2001

The International Criminal Court (ICC) is situated in The Hague, to try individuals for genocide, crimes against humanity and war crimes. The Security Council may refer a situation to the ICC; alternatively a government can refer a situation to the Prosecutor or the Prosecutor can initiate an investigation.

Criminal Justice and Police Act 2001

This Act introduced penalty notices as a way of responding to a range of low-level anti-social offending associated with disorderly conduct such as consuming alcohol in a public place. Penalty notices may be issued on the spot or at a police station for a range of disorder offences.

Criminal Defence Service (Advice and Assistance) Act 2001

The Act set out the extent of the duty of the Criminal Defence Service to provide legal advice, assistance and representation for an individual and includes: the duty solicitor scheme at magistrates' courts; assistance to a prisoner who has been permitted to be legally represented in disciplinary proceedings; assistance to a detained person whose case is referred to the Parole Board.

Police Reform Act 2002

The Home Secretary is required to produce an annual National Policing Plan, and a new system for handling complaints against the police is introduced. The Independent Police Complaints Commission (IPCC) replaces the Police Complaints Authority.

Proceeds of Crime Act 2002

The Act contains powers to confiscate from convicted defendants the financial benefits of their crime and attempts to prevent money laundering by organised crime, drug cartels and terrorist groups.

European Union (Accessions) Act 2003

The Accession Treaty provides for the accession of 10 new states to join the existing 15 countries in the European Union on 1 May 2004. Nationals of eight of the new states will be given the same freedom of movement and rights to work in the United Kingdom as are enjoyed by nationals of the existing member states.

Crime (International Cooperation) Act 2003

The Act implements police and judicial cooperation within the European Union by adopting the mutual legal assistance provisions of the 1985 Schengen Convention, the Convention on Mutual Assistance in Criminal Matters 2000, and other agreements on terrorism and driving offences.

The Schengen Convention was designed to facilitate the free movement of persons by removing internal border controls. A series of measures to enhance police and judicial cooperation was then agreed to compensate for the lifting of controls. The Schengen Information System provides for a database to store criminal information from all participating countries

The Act implements the obligations for participating countries to respond to requests for assistance with locating banking accounts and to provide banking information relating to criminal investigations. It implements measures against terrorism and the mutual recognition of driving disqualifications.

Courts Act 2003

This Act abolished Magistrates' Courts Committees and established court boards. It abolished commission areas and petty sessions areas and replaces them with local justice areas. It establishes a new HM Inspectorate of Court Administration and provides for the functions and rights of entry and inspection of the Chief Inspector and inspectors.

Anti-social Behaviour Act 2003

The Act deals with serious anti-social behaviour and extends the powers of the police and local authorities and housing associations.

It introduces new powers for tackling the problem of premises used for drug dealing; young people with air weapons, banning the possession of imitation guns and air guns in public without good reason; new powers for the police to impose conditions on public assemblies, deal with illegal raves and to deal with unauthorised encampments.

It provides powers for local authorities and those working with them to tackle anti-social behaviour in local communities, extending landlords' powers to deal with anti-social behaviour in social housing and includes provisions aimed at dealing with noise nuisance. It develops the sanctions that are available for use against anti-social behaviour and extends the range of agencies that can use them.

Criminal Justice Act 2003

Many of the reforms proposed by the Auld and Halliday reports on the reform of the court and sentencing are enacted. A generic community sentence in introduced – custody plus, custody minus and intermittent custody – and for the first time the aims of sentencing are set out in a statute. Changes are made to pre-trial and trial process and the law governing evidence and juries.

CONCLUSION

In this chapter we have suggested that in order to understand how a criminal justice system operates it is necessary to identify its many aims, to be able to describe its procedures, modes of punishment and the behaviour criminalised and to appreciate the interdependencies between agencies, which at a minimum allow us to call it a system. We have also indicated, through the models of criminal justice, many of the influences and principles that guide criminal justice agencies and placed these into the context of the political, economic and cultural factors that shape participants' views and actions, whether offenders, judges, police or probation officers. Finally we have illustrated how models of criminal justice help us to come to terms with the tensions between the formal goals, principles and the real practices that go on in the world of those who enforce, interpret and implement the criminal law. That world is complex, given its many manifestations, aspirations and everyday encounters, and no one theory, model or principle will do justice to that reality. This book will attempt to reflect these many issues as we look at specific agencies and stages of the system.

Review questions

1 Identify and outline the characteristics of the eight models of criminal justice defined in Chapter 1.

2 Visit a local magistrates' court for a morning session and then work through the eight models of criminal justice and give examples of each model based on your observations from your visit.

3 Identify current issues and controversies affecting criminal justice (e.g. a current case, issue or debate in Parliament, statement by politicians or other public figures) and consider:
   (a) to what extent these reveal the conflicting goals of the criminal justice system;
   (b) how these would be approached by the different models of criminal justice outlined above.

Further reading

Ashworth, A (2003) *The Criminal Process* (4th edn), Oxford University Press: Oxford
King, M (1981) *The Framework of Criminal Justice*, Croom Helm: London
McConville, M and Wilson, G (2002) *The Handbook of the Criminal Justice Process*, Oxford University Press: Oxford

CHAPTER 2

What is Crime?

INTRODUCTION

What is crime? This is not such an easy question to answer as it might at first appear because a number of different meanings are associated with the words crime and criminal. In this chapter we will look at the differing ways in which criminal behaviour is defined and perceived, from the legal conception of crime used to establish a person's liability for criminal conduct to the social and popular images and concerns about crime. These images filter into everyday consciousness and affect the public's notions about activities which ought to be forbidden or allowed – in other words, about whether conduct should be criminalised or not. Popular opinion in turn may affect policy making when politicians increasingly wish to demonstrate accountability and response to public views. The views and concerns of the public also influence the way that the professionals in the criminal justice process think about crime, whether probation officer, police officer or judge.

2.1 DEFINING CRIME

Legally, a crime is any act or omission proscribed by the criminal law and thus punishable by the state through the criminal justice process. The criminal law and its associated punishment are used against a very wide range of behaviour – from murder, rape and assault to driving with excess alcohol, parking on a yellow line and failing to comply with a plethora of health and safety regulations. While few would dispute that murder is and should be an offence, not all members of the public would think of someone who drives with excess alcohol in their blood as a criminal.

The public have a commonsense view of what they regard as crime. Behaviour which people disapprove of is often described as criminal to emphasise its seriousness and unacceptability. These commonsense images tend to be associated with the deliberate infliction of physical harm, often involving a confrontation between an offender and a victim. Dishonesty, cheating or theft are also a key part of these commonsense notions of crime. Everyday conceptions of the criminal carry connotations of the wrongdoer who should be stigmatised. Stigma means that a person is not considered normal, or is deviant and should be censured as a person who behaves badly.

Yet not all activities proscribed by the criminal law are necessarily regarded as crimes, or their perpetrators as criminal. In the workplace, for example, employees may regularly fiddle the books or engage in petty pilfering. These activities are described euphemistically as perks or fiddles rather than as theft or fraud. Members of the public may inflate insurance claims or fail to disclose their full earnings to the Inland Revenue without regarding themselves as criminals, or being viewed as such by others. Drivers may regularly infringe road traffic laws without considering their behaviour as deviant. Different groups therefore may have different conceptions of where to draw the line between acceptable behaviour and crime.

Even where individuals are injured and killed as a result of illegal actions they may not always be regarded as victims of crime. Some injuries and deaths in the workplace are caused by neglect of health and safety regulations. Yet these are regularly dealt with as accidents rather than as crimes, and those responsible are rarely sanctioned as criminals (Wells 1988; Croall 2001). This may be because there is no immediate confrontation between offender and victim and because those responsible intended no harm. Many are also physically injured within the home, by the actions of their spouses, lovers, parents or children. Yet domestic violence was for many years not widely perceived as being as serious as other violent crime – partly because it takes place in the private sphere of the home.

Although there is considerable overlap between legal and everyday conceptions of crime there is therefore no necessary equation between the two. Public tolerance of different activities changes over time and legal categories are subject to change. The criminal law in our society is not based on a fundamentalist or absolutist conception of morality but shifts according to changes in public attitudes. This is reflected in political pressures to change legislation that defines crime. Thus over the last 50 years the way in which the law has dealt with drunk driving, homosexuality, prostitution, marital rape and criminal damage has changed. Changes in the public's tolerance of activities leads to campaigns to criminalise some behaviours and to decriminalise others. Parts of the Criminal Justice and Public Order Act 1994 aimed to curb the activities of new age travellers and organisers of raves, while lowering from 21 to 18 years the age at which men may lawfully perform homosexual acts in private.

Hence the legal conception of crime is subject to change and depends, in a parliamentary democracy, on political as well as moral considerations. However, if the criminal law did not express and reflect public morality and concerns about harm to the community the public would have little regard for the law – it would lose its legitimacy. Furthermore, it would be seen as unduly oppressive – as an instrument of social control and political domination. Such laws are unlikely to inspire public trust, confidence or legitimacy. They would be difficult to enforce and would undermine confidence in the criminal justice process.

Three aspects of the concept of crime

To avoid confusion between the more technical and legal conception of crime used by lawyers and its everyday usage, we suggest the following definition of a criminal:

> **A person whose behaviour is in breach of legally prescribed rules which renders that person liable to criminal proceedings.**

As a starting point this definition is useful because it focuses on the three elements that are indispensable if we are to understand and explain crime. They are: behaviour, breach of rules and the possibility of enforcement and punishment.

Behaviour

Criminal law is essentially concerned with the regulation of behaviour. This may involve prohibitions on some kinds of behaviour such as stealing another person's property or harming them deliberately. Some criminal laws may require a specific action, such as having insurance when driving a car, or complying with regulations. In some instances it is the combination of behaviour with a particular situation that defines a crime such as the offence of being drunk in a public place. In others it is the combination of status with behaviour such as the purchase of alcohol by someone under 16 years of age.

Illegality covers a multitude of actions, responsibilities, circumstances and statuses and hence the diversity of acts that may be characterised as criminal is considerable. Thus it is impossible to offer a simple explanation of why someone acts criminally. Furthermore, people do not act in an identical fashion. Some people are more prone to self-indulgence, others are more violent in character.

The causes of criminal behaviour are complex and multiple. They are multiple because crime does not relate to only one form of action. For instance, the causes of domestic violence by a woman may not be the same as when committed by a man. The causes that lead a teenager to commit arson may be very different from those that lead an old-age pensioner to fraud. Therefore, we should not expect to find a single cause for all types of criminality.

Furthermore, the complexity is apparent when we look at the range of factors used to explain delinquency. Contributing to the debate are criminologists, sociologists, psychologists, penologists, economists, biologists, geneticists, psychiatrists, town planners, architects, social workers, doctors, nutritionists, teachers and theologians. The potential list of causes is long: biological predisposition, lack of bonding between parent and child, inconsistent parenting, irresponsible parenting, failure at school, truancy, labelling, violent videos, hyperactivity, over-stimulating foods, drugs, glue, alcohol, masculinity, testosterone, repressed sexuality, underdeveloped super ego, lack of discipline, peer influence, television, lack of moral training, racism, lack of legitimate opportunities and too many illegal opportunities.

Some accounts of criminal conduct seek to identify the cause, or causes, that lead to behaviour that is distinctively deviant and untypical, such as the murders committed by Frederick and Rosemary West in their home at 25 Cromwell Road, Gloucester or Ian Huntley in Soham. In contrast, other theories of criminal behaviour focus on the types of motives that might affect anyone such as greed, envy, lust and jealousy as causes of bad behaviour. We will discuss some of these explanations later in this book as well as the importance that the theories about the causes of crime have in determining society's responses in terms of both the prevention and punishment of crime.

Rules

The rules which determine whether or not behaviour is criminal are found in legislation passed by Parliament or in decisions of the courts. These form the starting point for understanding crime as they provide the legal definition of criminal acts. As we have seen, these rules may change over time, and the number of potentially illegal acts may increase as new areas and types of behaviour are criminalised. For example, under the Firearms Amendment Act 1996, pistol owners were required to hand over to the police, before midnight on 30 September 1997, any hand guns over .22 calibre they possessed or face up to 10 years' imprisonment. In 1997, what had become known as stalking was made an offence by the Protection from Harassment Act. The development of the Internet and behaviour associated with it led to the formulation of offences dealing with the storage and retrieval of obscene computer images of children. Equally, however, conduct can cease to be criminal by virtue of legislation, such as abortion and homosexual acts.

There are two sources of law in England and Wales: legislation and law based on decided cases. Legislation consists of Acts of Parliament (statutes) and statutory instruments (often called subordinate legislation). Case law is law that has been built up over the years by decisions of the courts in individual matters: these may include decisions on the meaning of statutes. The law of England and Wales is thus based on the accumulation of previous cases and is described as a common law system, which distinguishes it from European systems which are based on codes established by legislation. Although the sources of the law are as above, since the enactment of the Human Rights Act 1998 all statutes and indeed the common law has to be interpreted in line with the Act, so that in a sense European human rights jurisprudence is now affecting the English law. Although many offences are now governed by, or were created by, statute, the general principles of criminal law are still matters of the common law, which also governs some of the most serious crimes: for example, murder. The idea that the common law evolves from the piecemeal interpretation of the law by judges is an integral part of the legal tradition in England and Wales. Nevertheless in order for behaviour to be defined and recognised as criminal it must be in breach of some rule laid down in case law or legislation.

Enforcement and criminal proceedings

Behaviour is not self-defining nor are rules self-enforcing. Laws do not have an impact unless they are enforced, or unless there is the anticipation of enforcement.

How, then, is behaviour interpreted as breaking the rules? By whom and how are rules interpreted and applied? The criminal law specifies who can enforce the law and what procedures are necessary to investigate and prosecute crime, adjudicate on guilt and decide on an appropriate sentence. Enforcement is the responsibility of specialist agencies or organisations specifically given the right to enforce the law, such as the police, Customs and Excise Officers and Crown Prosecutors. Although the basic procedures and guidelines for law enforcement are set out in statutes and case law, it is inevitable that these cannot cover every situation. That is why it is important to understand that many factors in addition to legal rules influence the way the criminal law is put into action.

Resources are required to fund the agencies and organisations that enforce the law. To learn how these agencies operate it is necessary to establish how they deploy these resources and how they interpret their formal goals and objectives. Professional loyalties, training and commonsense notions of crime and the crime problem will influence the way officials decide on priorities and interpret their responsibilities. Also, as officials in criminal justice agencies do not normally come from outside the society in which they work, many of the taken-for-granted prejudices of the wider culture also influence how they see their role.

Edwin Schur wrote, 'Once we recognise that crime is defined by the criminal law and is therefore variable in content, we see quite clearly that no explanation of crime that limits itself to the motivation and behaviour of individual offenders can ever be a complete one' (Schur 1969: 10).

The three elements that constitute a criminal act – behaviour, rules and the enforcement of rules – are further refined by the concept of criminal liability. Not all actions by a person that might appear to be in breach of the criminal law are necessarily criminal because there may be an excuse or acceptable reason for their behaviour. In commonsense terms and in a legal sense they may not be blameworthy or culpable. Establishing the culpability of a defendant is therefore central to the criminal process and explains the central role of the trial as the mechanism of establishing criminal liability.

Legal liability and the elements of a crime

One of the most fundamental principles of criminal law is that a person should not be punished unless he or she has both committed the act or omission in question and is blameworthy. This means that in order to be considered culpable, it must be established that an offender has not only committed an offence but is responsible for it. These two aspects are usually referred to as the *actus reus*, the guilty act, and the *mens rea*, the guilty mind. Both the act and the intention are generally required before someone is deemed to be guilty of a crime.

Some crimes, called crimes of strict or absolute liability, do not require a guilty mind. These include offences such as speeding, drinking and driving, and applying a false trade description to goods. These types of crimes tend not to attract the same level of blame or culpability as offences that involve intention and are largely concerned with commerce and public welfare. To illustrate the concepts of *actus reus* and *mens rea*, it is useful to analyse the offence of theft, which is now defined by s. 1 of the Theft Act 1968:

> **A person is guilty of theft if he dishonestly appropriates property belonging to another with the intention of permanently depriving that other of it.**

It can be seen that two different elements make up the offence: first, the act of appropriating property belonging to another person; and, secondly, the mental element of dishonesty and the intent to permanently deprive another person. If either of these elements is missing, the offence is not committed.

Someone is guilty of murder if that person kills another person either intending to do so, or intending to cause him or her serious harm. Killing means causing the death of. So, if a person shoots someone dead the pulling of the trigger and the consequent death constitutes the *actus reus*. The *actus reus* relates to the events and consequences. Despite the fact that someone died, the person with the gun might not be guilty of murder. In addition to the act, *mens rea* is necessary: the person who fired the gun must have intended to kill or cause really serious injury. If, for example, the gun was fired by mistake while it was being cleaned at home, or the victim was shot accidentally while straying onto a grouse moor, the person who fired the gun would not be guilty of murder: they did not have the relevant intent.

The significance of the concept of intent can be illustrated by the problem of dealing with those who take cars but abandon them after use. The takers never intended to keep the car, thus they cannot be guilty of theft, having no 'intention to permanently deprive'. Therefore a different offence had to be created if this conduct was to be punished as a crime. The offence, now in s. 12 of the Theft Act 1968, is 'taking a conveyance without the owner's consent'. This provision states:

> . . . a person shall be guilty of an offence if, without having the consent of the owner or other lawful authority, he takes any conveyance for his own or another's use or, knowing that any conveyance has been taken without authority, drives it or allows himself to be carried in or on it.

Different offences relating to similar behaviour – for example, assault – may reflect different levels of intent and seriousness of injury. This can be illustrated by examining the different crimes relating to offences of violence, the seriousness of which is determined both by the injury inflicted and the level of intention, thereby combining an assessment of *actus reus* and *mens rea* in determining culpability.

Common assault is the least serious, and can be tried only in the magistrates' court; it is punishable by up to 6 months' imprisonment. It is defined as the intentional or reckless causing of another to fear immediate unlawful violence. More serious is the offence of occasioning actual bodily harm under s. 47 of the Offences Against the Person Act 1861 (OAPA 1861). This can be tried either in the magistrates' court or the Crown Court and is punishable with a maximum sentence of 5 years' imprisonment. It is not necessary to establish that the accused intended the kind of injury that occurred. Actual bodily harm means any physical harm.

Another offence, higher up the ladder of seriousness, although attracting the same maximum penalty, is the offence under s. 20 of the OAPA 1861, of unlawfully and maliciously wounding or inflicting grievous bodily harm. Grievous bodily harm means really serious harm. More serious still, triable only on indictment, and attracting up to life imprisonment, is the offence under s. 18 of the OAPA 1861, of malicious wounding or causing grievous bodily harm with intent to do grievous bodily harm.

The most serious offence known to the criminal law is murder, which is punishable with a mandatory life sentence. This means that once a conviction is recorded, only a life sentence can be passed by the judge. However, the law has long recognised that deaths can be caused, even intentionally, in many different circumstances, not all equally blameworthy. This is reflected in three categories of homicide: murder, manslaughter and infanticide. Murder is described as unlawful killing involving intention to kill or cause grievous bodily harm. Murder can be reduced to manslaughter (for which the sentence is variable) because of 'provocation' by virtue of s. 3 of the Homicide Act 1957. This recognises that, under pressure, people may lose control and provocation relates to a 'sudden temporary loss of self-control'. This provision has recently been the subject of much criticism. Particularly problematic has been the situation of women who have been systematically brutalised by partners and have planned to kill them. Decisions where such women have been prosecuted have underlined the requirement that the defence of provocation will be successful only if there is a sudden explosion of emotions so that the person is temporarily out of control as a result of a particular trigger such as a remark or incident. Sarah Thornton, who was prosecuted for murder, stabbed her husband while he was in a drunken stupor and did not succeed with the defence that she had been provoked. Kiranjit Ahluwalia was convicted of the murder of her husband and sentenced to life imprisonment in 1989 despite claiming she was 'provoked' by 10 years of abuse at his hands.

Murder is also reduced to manslaughter when killing takes place as a result of diminished responsibility, defined as an abnormality of mind which impairs the mental processes, or under a suicide pact. Both these circumstances are referred to as voluntary manslaughter, where the intent was to kill but in less blameworthy circumstances. Some abused women have succeeded in arguing that they should be convicted of manslaughter rather than murder as a result of diminished responsibility brought on by the abuse. Kiranjit Ahluwalia's conviction was thus reduced to manslaughter on appeal in 1992.

Manslaughter includes all other forms of unlawful killing when there was a lesser degree of intent than that required for murder. Manslaughter is therefore committed when death results in the course of an unlawful act – for example, burglary – and in other circumstances where death was not actually intended. Many different combinations of circumstances can be envisaged and have come before the courts: the defendants who threw a brick from a motorway bridge to deter a 'blackleg' (*R v Hancock and Shankland* (1986)) and the defendant who played 'Russian Roulette' with tragic consequences for his stepfather (*R v Mahoney* (1985)).

The role of the law is to develop rules that reflect moral blameworthiness. But, as the following case illustrates, it is not always easy to apply these principles in cases involving the deliberate commission of a dangerous act resulting in death. In one case the Court of Appeal, seeking to clarify the application of principles, listed the kinds of situation in which this type of offence, sometimes called involuntary manslaughter, arises (*R v Sulman and Others* (1993)). This particular case arose after a patient died following a negligently conducted operation. There had been negligence – did that create a criminal offence? Negligent inattention in the sense of mere inadvertence does not create criminal liability; the degree of fault has to be gross negligence, such as:

- indifference to a known risk;
- foresight of a risk which is nevertheless undertaken;
- appreciation of the risk, and an intention to avoid it, but coupled with a high degree of negligence in the attempted avoidance;
- inattention to a serious and obvious risk.

Infanticide is also recognised as a special case by the law, which provides that a different offence, less culpable than murder, is committed where a woman kills her child in the first year of its life, when the balance of her mind is affected by the birth.

Another situation recognised by the law is where death occurs as a result of a road accident. Legislation has taken a variety of approaches to these situations, the current position being that it is an offence to cause death by dangerous driving. Dangerous driving is defined as driving at a standard far below that of a competent and careful driver and where it would be obvious to such a driver that driving in that way would be dangerous.

The problem of basing criminal culpability on the offender's intention and not on the result of the offence can be seen in the increasing number of cases in which pedestrians or other car users are killed by a driver subsequently convicted of careless driving. While careless driving can kill, in many cases it has either no adverse consequence or only a trivial one. Outraged relatives have been appalled when drivers who have killed a member of their family have been given non-custodial sentences or even a fine. Whilst the fact that death results does not change the nature of the offence, in 1999 the Court of Appeal indicated it could be taken into account in sentencing (*R v Simmonds* [1999]). In response to public concerns about deaths resulting from road 'accidents' where drugs or alcohol had been taken by a driver, new offences with higher penalties were introduced in the Road Traffic Act 1991.

Culpability under the criminal law stretches from those who deliberately set out to commit criminal acts such as a planned robbery, through those who behave recklessly and cause harm, to those who have no intention at all but nevertheless are guilty of a crime of strict liability. Failure to take steps to prevent harm can result in guilt: an offence of omission. The Court of Appeal upheld the decision of North Shield's magistrates' court who convicted Mark Greener under the Dangerous Dogs Act 1991 because he did not take sufficient steps to prevent his Staffordshire Bull Terrier from straying into a nearby garden and biting a young child's face (*Greener v DPP* 1996).

Criminal defences

In criminal trials the defence may argue that although the defendant did commit the act he or she had an excuse for so doing. These excuses reflect an acceptance that in certain circumstances the defendant could not help acting in a particular way, was somehow forced into the action, or could not control his or her behaviour and is therefore not to blame. The *mens rea* element of the criminal trial focuses on blameworthiness or moral culpability and the defence counsel may use arguments known as criminal defences in an attempt to show that the defendant was not responsible or blameworthy for the act he or she did indeed commit.

There are two categories of people who cannot be liable for criminal offences because they are not seen as responsible for their acts:

- children under the age of criminal responsibility;
- those certified as insane within a legal – rather than a medical – definition.

In the first category, children under 10 in England and Wales are, by law, deemed unable to commit offences: in other words they cannot be criminally liable. This is often referred to as being *doli incapax*. The mentally ill are not held responsible in law for their actions and if they do stand trial at all will be found not guilty by reason of insanity (see Chapter 7).

There are, however, other situations where, although the accused cannot escape liability because of age or mental incapacity, circumstances may provide a complete defence. If the defence is accepted the person is found not guilty. These circumstances are as follows:

- *Duress:* where people are compelled by threats or circumstances to do something criminal. The threat or danger must be severe – such as death or serious personal injury. This would excuse all offences other than murder and treason. In these circumstances, although the act is deliberate and intended, the offender is regarded as not responsible for the act committed.
- *Automatism:* where a person is not in control of his or her physical actions, such as during an epileptic fit.
- *Self-defence:* defendants are seen as not blameworthy when, in responding to another person's aggression, they cause injury in the process of defending themselves. The scriptures might require a person to turn the other cheek; the law does not.

In other situations, the defendant may be held less responsible or blameworthy, by relying on partial defences. A partial defence, as its name suggests, will partly exonerate the defendant. Whereas a successful complete defence means that the defendant is found not guilty of any offence at all, a partial defence means that, if successful, the defendant will be found not guilty of the major offence but guilty of a lesser offence. The situation arises only in the case of murder, where a successful defence of diminished responsibility or provocation will result in the accused being found guilty of manslaughter rather than murder.

A situation commonly found in criminal acts is that the defendant was affected by alcohol or drugs. The mere fact of being drunk is not a defence, even although it is recognised that drinking may reduce inhibitions. It may, however, be a defence where the alcohol or drugs had the effect that the offender was not able to form the intent required for the commission of the crime, such as murder or wounding 'with intent'.

Sentencing mitigation

Even where a legal defence – which removes all blame – is not available or has not been accepted by the jury or magistrates, other factors may reduce culpability. After a defendant has been found guilty or has pleaded guilty, the defence may offer a plea in mitigation to the court. This will introduce factors suggesting that the seriousness of the offence is not as great as it might be, or that the offender is less blameworthy.

Mitigation may relate to the offence: that the offender played a limited part, was led into the offence by others, or that it happened almost by accident. Defendants may claim they forgot to renew a licence or their motor vehicle insurance. Mitigation might also relate to the personal circumstances of the offender. It may be argued that an offender is in such difficult circumstances that he or she should not be blamed or punished any more than has already happened because he or she might have lost his or her job or have been deserted by his or her family. If you sit in court for any length of time you might be surprised to hear the same mitigation repeated, such as the number of recently convicted people who are starting a job next week or whose girlfriend has just discovered she is pregnant. This part of the criminal process allows the convicted person the opportunity to minimise their culpability for the offence and so increase their chance of a more lenient sentence.

The court must take all these factors into account in passing sentence, which may mean that individual sentencing decisions are unpopular. Some sentencing decisions cause outrage and public anxiety and have been widely criticised in the press, Parliament or on the radio and television. It is important to appreciate that members of the public may have very different perceptions of criminal responsibility from those of the court. Questions of crime and criminal responsibility generate many strong opinions and public conceptions may well conflict with legal concerns. Public views of crime are not necessarily informed by the somewhat narrow legal conceptions of culpability and blameworthiness outlined above, nor do the public always appreciate the technicalities of requirements to prove intent or to focus on the act rather than the result. Public discussion tends to be more general than legal discussion.

2.2 LEGAL CATEGORIES OF CRIMINAL OFFENCES

Legal categories also indicate in a variety of ways the level of blame and the level of severity accorded to a particular crime. This is in part achieved by the way the crime is defined, as discussed above, partly by the maximum sentence able to be imposed by courts and partly by the procedural and organisational categories into which all offences are divided. Criminal offences are divided into three categories as follows:

- summary offences
- offences triable on indictment only
- offences triable either way, i.e. summarily or on indictment.

The latter two categories together constitute the category of indictable offences. These divisions define the procedures and, in particular, the methods and place of trial for each type of offence. The categorisation is made by statute.

Cases triable only on indictment must be tried at the Crown Court. An indictment is the formal document used in a Crown Court trial setting out the charges against the defendant. The magistrates' court has power to hear summary offences and offences that are triable either way where a decision has been made to try them summarily, that is in the magistrates' court. In 2002, 1.93 million defendants were proceeded against in magistrates' courts, of which:

- 518,000 were indictable
- 624,000 were summary non-motoring
- 788,000 were summary motoring.

The time and place at which the alleged offence was committed can also affect where it is heard. Magistrates' courts can try only offences committed in their area and normally proceedings for summary offences must be started within 6 months of the commission of the offence. Indictable offences may be tried in any Crown Court and there is generally no time limit for the commencement of proceedings except in a few cases such as some Customs and Excise offences where there is a 20-year time limit.

Classification of offences: summary and indictable

Summary offences are comparatively less serious crimes. Most motoring offences are summary, including driving with excess alcohol, but there is a wide variety of other summary offences, including common assault, assaulting a police officer, and taking a motor vehicle without the owner's consent. All summary offences are made so by statute.

Generally speaking, the maximum penalty for a summary offence is 6 months' imprisonment or a £5,000 fine or both, but many summary offences carry much lower maximum penalties, and many are not imprisonable at all. The maximum financial penalties are determined in accordance with a range of levels established by Parliament. Level 1 offences currently carry a maximum fine of £200 and level 5 offences carry a maximum fine of £5,000.

The offence of being drunk and disorderly, for example, is a level 3 offence with a maximum fine of £1,000. These five levels were introduced by the Criminal Justice Act 1982 and they mean that as inflation erodes the value of money, fine maxima can be simply adjusted by legislation altering the value of the levels: the CJA 1991 set the maximum at £5,000.

Offences triable only on indictment are very serious matters, including murder, rape, blackmail, robbery, and wounding with intent. For those convicted of murder the only sentence available to the court is life imprisonment. Maximum penalties for other offences are laid down by statute and may include a discretionary life sentence or a simple term of years. For example, 14 years is the maximum custodial penalty for blackmail and burglary of a dwelling, while 10 years is the maximum for burglary of a non-dwelling. Financial penalties for offences tried on indictment have no limit but fines are rarely imposed for such serious offences.

Triable-either-way (TEW) offences include theft, burglary, assault occasioning actual bodily harm, and unlawful wounding. This category covers many offences where the offence's relative seriousness can vary tremendously depending on the facts. Theft, for example, includes stealing a bottle of milk from a doorstep, shoplifting and stealing from an employer. The seriousness of these matters is affected by the value of the theft and all the circumstances surrounding it, including the relationship between thief and victim.

Criminal damage is another offence where the circumstances can vary tremendously. The offence is committed when someone knowingly or recklessly inflicts damage on the property of another person and it is generally a TEW offence. However, in criminal damage cases not involving threat to life or arson and where the value of the damage inflicted is £5,000 or less, the charge is regarded as summary with a maximum penalty of 3 months' custody or a £2,500 fine. When the value of the damage is over £5,000 the offence remains triable either way.

Successive Acts have attempted to reduce the number of TEW offences, in part to reduce costs and to spread the work more efficiently between the courts. An offence which was reclassified in response to changing legislative and public perceptions of seriousness was taking a vehicle without the owner's consent, an offence under s. 12 of the Theft Act 1968. This, in its original form, was a TEW offence. In the Criminal Justice Act 1988 it, along with common assault and driving while disqualified, became triable in summary proceedings only. The early 1990s saw an increase in public concern about offences involving a number of widely reported incidents where such cars were used to commit robberies, or resulted in the deaths of the drivers or bystanders. Vivid newspaper reports about ramraiders fuelled political disquiet. In response Parliament created a new indictable offence, 'aggravated vehicle-taking', to cover the situation in which a car, taken without the owner's consent, was involved in an accident or crime. Changing views of what should be criminalised, and changing definitions of what is criminalised can cloud our understanding of crime. The first problem is how to measure the amount and type of crime that is committed.

2.3 MEASURING CRIME

We have seen above how difficult it is to define crime and establish that an offence has been committed – difficulties which also affect how crime can be measured. Before behaviour is dealt with and therefore counted as crime, it must be considered to be 'criminal' and be brought to the attention of a law enforcer, who must then establish whether it is indeed against the criminal law and what kind of offence it is. It was pointed out in Chapter 1 that criminal justice can be viewed as a process with many factors affecting how an incident or a suspected offender proceeds to a criminal conviction. Official statistics reflect different stages of this process, producing different figures as cases proceed. Therefore criminal statistics must be interpreted with considerable caution, although they are often taken as a barometer of crime from which the media, politicians and the public shape their ideas about crime. This in turn affects criminal justice policy. It is important to realise, however, that these statistics are likely to be at considerable variance with the actual incidence of crime and that all attempts to calculate the crime figure are no more than estimates. Thus the Home Office *Digest 2: Information on the Criminal Justice*

System in England and Wales commented that 'no-one knows the true extent of crime in this country' (Barclay 1995: 1).

Recent years have seen an 'explosion' (Maguire 2002) of information about crime and the criminal justice system, with statistics now being routinely available on the Internet, along with more detailed studies of particular kinds of crime. The main sources of information about crime include the official criminal statistics, based on records of crimes reported to and investigated by the police and victim surveys which ask samples of the general population about their experiences of crime. The following section will explore these sources of information and look at how they are created, what their main limitations are and how they can be best interpreted. Later sections will consider what they tell us about trends in crime, different groups of offences and information about offenders.

Home Office statistics on crime

The government publishes many different statistics on crime and the criminal justice process, the most definitive of which is the Home Office publication *Criminal Statistics England and Wales*. These statistics contain a wealth of information about the amount and kinds of offences dealt with by the police and the courts. They give details, for example, of the following:

- numbers of offences recorded by the police, along with breakdowns of different categories of offences (this may differ from the numbers of offences reported to the police because the police, for reasons which will be explored below, may not record all offences reported to them);
- numbers of offenders cautioned and convicted for offences, broken down by offence category, age and sex;
- numbers of court proceedings and sentences – again broken down by offence category, age and sex;
- increases and decreases in all of these categories.

More detailed information on specific offences such as different kinds of theft and fraud and less serious offences are given in the *Supplementary Criminal Statistics* which also show statistics by police area. Other publications such as *Crime in England and Wales* incorporate information from police records and the British Crime Survey (BCS) which will be described below. The Home Office's Offender Index holds data on individuals convicted of serious offences. Computerised in 1991, the index adds nearly half a million new pieces of data each year. Each record includes a name with initials, gender, date of birth, ethnicity and, if known, a CRO (Criminal Records Office) number.

Official statistics refer to many different categories of offences. The main statistics refer to notifiable offences recorded by the police. This covers most serious crimes including indictable offences along with some summary offences. While notifiable offences are often seen as more serious, many involve relatively small sums of money or damage, whereas some summary offences – such as, for example, driving after consuming alcohol or drugs – are counted as relatively serious (Maguire 2002). Considerations such as this have led to periodic changes in which offences are considered to be notifiable – leading, for example, to the inclusion in 1997 and 1998 of some summary offences (e.g. common assault and assault on a constable), which increased the number of offences in the category of violence against the person and produced an apparent increase in 'violent crime' (Maguire 2002).

The criminal statistics bring together data from many agencies including the 43 police forces and they provide much detailed information about crime and the activities of the criminal justice agencies. Nevertheless, many offences are not included. They omit, for example, offences recorded by police forces outside the ambit of the Home Office such as the British Transport Police, the Ministry of Defence Police and the UK Atomic Energy Authority Police. Many other offences are dealt with by agencies other than the police, some of whom may not prosecute some offences where they feel that there are more appropriate courses of action. Thus the Inland Revenue, Customs and Excise and Department of Social Security deal with a variety of offences, many of which are not prosecuted, as do the many regulatory agencies involved with public health, pollution or trading standards offences. Many of these are summary offences and statistics are available only for numbers of convictions.

In addition, many potential offences may not be defined as criminal or reported to the police. Some kinds of offences are less likely to come to the attention of the police than others, including the following:

- Offences which are not readily detectable by the police, victims or the public. These include offences which take place in private – for example, domestic violence, sexual offences and some offences in the workplace.

- Offences with no discernible victim, often called victimless crimes – for example, prostitution, pornography, illegal gambling or drug abuse. These involve an exchange of illegal commodities between consumers and suppliers who are unlikely to report themselves to the police.

- Offences where victims are unaware that they have been a victim of a crime. Many frauds, for example, depend on victims not noticing that they have been defrauded. Other offences, such as the failure of businesses to comply with health, safety or environmental regulations, involve dangers which cannot readily be detected.

Many offences are therefore not included in the criminal statistics. Criminologists have long recognised that there is a large hidden or 'dark figure' of crime and that official crime rates reflect only those crimes reported to the police. Variations in crime rates therefore could be the result, not of differences between the real rates of offending, but of variations in reporting.

Even when crimes are reported to the police, they may not subsequently be recorded and counted as crimes 'known to the police'. In some cases the police may decide to take 'no further action' or decide that 'no crime' has been committed. This may happen, for example, where police are called to an incident such as a pub brawl and resolve it without arresting or charging someone, or where items are reported missing but it is unclear whether they are lost or stolen. Police therefore have a high amount of discretion, as will be seen in Chapter 6, and not all incidents reported to them are considered as 'crimes' or worth recording or investigating as such. In addition, different Police organisations may use different recording practices. Changes in reporting and recording practices can produce apparent increases in different kinds of crime.

In an attempt to systematise how the police record crime a National Crime Recording Standard (NCRS) was introduced in April 2002, which effectively asks the police to take at face value what a person reports (Maguire 2002). This has had the effect of increasing the figures for some kinds of crime, making rises and falls difficult to interpret although they are taken account of in the latest estimates of crime trends (Simmons and Dodd 2003).

Statistics relating to offenders also have limitations. Many offenders escape detection as the police clear up only a proportion of crimes reported. Some crimes are easier to detect than others, which accounts for variations by offence in the clear-up rates given in the statistics. For example, many victims of assault know their assailant, leading to almost automatic clear up. If a fraud is discovered its perpetrator may be self evident. In 2002/3, the 1.4 million crimes 'detected' represented 23.5 per cent of crimes recorded by the police – a similar rate to 2001/2 (Simmons and Dodd 2003). The proportion of offenders detected becomes even smaller when the large volume of unreported crimes is taken into account. Thus only a very small proportion of offenders are ever caught.

Moreover, not all known suspects and offenders are subsequently brought to court as the police or the Crown Prosecution Service may decide not to proceed with a case (see Chapters 6 and 7). The police have discretion and may decide to take no further action, to caution offenders rather than bring a formal charge, not to proceed with the case because they consider they have insufficient evidence, or to proceed with the case and pass the papers on to the Crown Prosecution Service.

In effect, therefore, official statistics tell us which crimes the public choose to report and how those crimes are dealt with by the police. The data produced by the police will tell us as much about the method of policing as it does about the amount of crime. The report on the first British Crime Survey commented that:

> Variations over time or place in recorded crime rates can reflect the processes by which the statistics are compiled as much as the condition they are intended to depict.
>
> (Hough and Mayhew 1983)

This is illustrated in Figures 2.1 and 2.2 showing the drop in numbers at each stage of the process. Part 1 of Figure 2.1 shows that of the BCS estimated crime figures of over 12 million, the police recorded less than 6 million in 2002. Fewer were cleared up. Part 2 of the table illustrates attribution for indictable offences and the redirection at different stages.

Figure 2.2 further illustrates the large gap between recorded and detected crime, the number of persons proceeded against and the number of offenders found guilty or cautioned, for indictable offences. Additionally, it illustrates the steep rise in recorded offences from 1950 to 2000, which will be discussed later in the chapter.

Figure 2.1 Flows through the criminal justice system, 2002

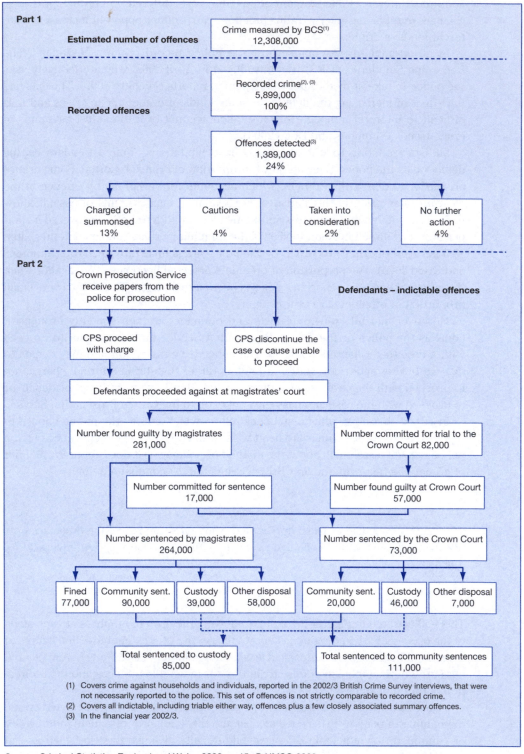

Part 1

Estimated number of offences

Crime measured by BCS[1]
12,308,000

Recorded offences

Recorded crime[2], [3]
5,899,000
100%

Offences detected[3]
1,389,000
24%

| Charged or summonsed 13% | Cautions 4% | Taken into consideration 2% | No further action 4% |

Part 2

Crown Prosecution Service receive papers from the police for prosecution

Defendants – indictable offences

CPS proceed with charge

CPS discontinue the case or cause unable to proceed

Defendants proceeded against at magistrates' court

Number found guilty by magistrates
281,000

Number committed for trial to the Crown Court 82,000

Number committed for sentence
17,000

Number found guilty at Crown Court
57,000

Number sentenced by magistrates
264,000

Number sentenced by the Crown Court
73,000

| Fined 77,000 | Community sent. 90,000 | Custody 39,000 | Other disposal 58,000 | Community sent. 20,000 | Custody 46,000 | Other disposal 7,000 |

Total sentenced to custody
85,000

Total sentenced to community sentences
111,000

(1) Covers crime against households and individuals, reported in the 2002/3 British Crime Survey interviews, that were not necessarily reported to the police. This set of offences is not strictly comparable to recorded crime.
(2) Covers all indictable, including triable either way, offences plus a few closely associated summary offences.
(3) In the financial year 2002/3.

Source: Criminal Statistics England and Wales 2002, p. 15, © HMSO 2003

Figure 2.2 Recorded crime, persons proceeded against and 'known' offenders, 1950–2002

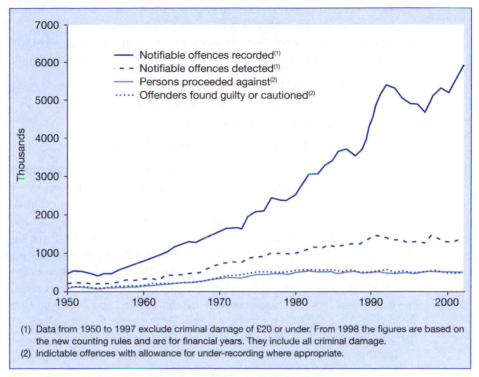

Notifiable offences recorded[1]
Notifiable offences detected[1]
Persons proceeded against[2]
Offenders found guilty or cautioned[2]

(1) Data from 1950 to 1997 exclude criminal damage of £20 or under. From 1998 the figures are based on the new counting rules and are for financial years. They include all criminal damage.
(2) Indictable offences with allowance for under-recording where appropriate.

Source: Criminal Statistics England and Wales 2002, p. 14, © HMSO 2003

Finally, the statistics may tell us about the numbers of different offences reported to the police, but little about how serious these offences are or the situations in which they occur. Many offence groups include vastly different kinds of offences. Thus categories of theft include very minor thefts along with serious ones, and frauds may involve very trifling sums or millions of pounds. In addition, as Maguire points out, a long-standing criticism of official statistics is that they cannot indicate changing patterns of crime – there may, for example, be changes in the kinds of typical thefts or robberies which are not reflected in broad classifications (Maguire 2002). More information about these kinds of issues can be found in crime surveys, which will be described below.

British Crime Survey

One way of finding out more about crime is to ask the public what kinds of crime they have been the victims of and whether or not they have reported this to the police. This is done in what are called victim or crime surveys such as the British Crime Survey (BCS) which was first carried out in 1982. The BCS normally relates only to England and Wales – separate surveys have been carried out in Scotland and Northern Ireland. The 2002/3 survey estimated that a total of 12.3 million crimes were committed against adults living in private households, with around 44 per cent being reported to the police (Simmons and Dodd 2003).

This survey has become a regular feature of the criminological scene, with further surveys during the 1980s and 1990s; and since 2001/2 surveys have been annual with 40,000 interviews of people aged 16 or over taking place each year. Respondents are selected randomly and asked how often they have been a victim of a specific offence in a specified time period. The scope of the questionnaire is extensive with 200 questions to elicit information on many aspects of crime, including the following:

- what kinds of crime people have been victims of;
- what proportions of these offences are reported to the police;
- why some offences are not reported;
- what kinds of crime people are most worried about.

This information can be compared with police statistics to ascertain the difference between crimes known to the police and those experienced by victims. This data can be charted over time to give a more accurate picture of crime trends. Thus the BCS estimated that the crime rate in the 1980s rose at a slower rate than that suggested by recorded police statistics. Between 1981 and 1991, for the subset of crimes covered by the BCS, the police recorded a 96 per cent increase in crime, in contrast to a 49 per cent increase reported in the survey. However, between 1991 and 1993, the British Crime Survey indicated an 18 per cent rise in crime compared with a 7 per cent increase recorded by the police, and between 1993 and 1995 recorded crime fell by 8 per cent, whereas BCS figures for equivalent offences rose by 2 per cent (Home Office 1994; Mirrlees-Black *et al.* 1996).

In addition to the comparisons with police figures referred to above, the survey can give useful information about unreported crime. The 2002/3 survey (Table 2.1) showed the proportion of incidents reported to the police.

Table 2.1 Proportion of incidents reported to the police

Theft of vehicle	97%
Burglary with loss	87%
Robbery	53%
Bicycle theft	50%
Theft from vehicle	47%
Wounding	46%
Common assault	34%
Theft from the person	33%
Vandalism	31%

High rates of reporting car theft and burglary reflect the higher losses typical of these kinds of crime along with the need for victims to report these offences for insurance purposes. The main reason why victims do not report a crime to the police is that they consider the incident to be too trivial and in many cases there is no loss. In addition victims often feel that the police cannot do much about it. These reasons accounted for 69 per cent of cases in 2002/3 with a further 28 per cent considering that the incident was a private matter which they would deal with themselves (Simpson and Dodd 2003).

Crime surveys can also provide information about which kinds of crime people are most worried about and about the risks of victimisation for different groups such as the young and ethnic minorities and how these risks vary by neighbourhood. The survey can thus capture information on aspects of crime which escape official attention and indicates the types of crime that give the public most concern. Numerically, crimes associated with motor vehicles, such as vandalism to a vehicle and theft of, or from, motor vehicles, account for 24 per cent of all notifiable offences (Home Office Statistical Bulletin, 7/98: 1). This does not, however, cause as much anxiety as other types of personal crime such as robbery and burglary which are less numerous.

While producing much valuable information, the BCS has important limitations. It includes only private households and therefore does not include crimes committed in organisations and businesses (such as shoplifting and theft by employee) and thus greatly underestimates the amount of theft committed. Many of the offences or incidents reported to the interviewers do not conform easily to legal classifications of crime and are therefore difficult to compare with police statistics. For example, if someone reports an assault, how is it to be classified? Respondents' information may be inaccurate. They may forget some incidents or exaggerate others. In some circumstances they may be unwilling to reveal offences to interviewers that cause them embarrassment. Respondents may misunderstand a question or the meaning of a word. Victim surveys cannot cover crimes of which victims are unaware, such as consumer fraud or those which have no direct victims – for example, drug offences. Some groups, many of whom may be at risk from crime, are under-represented. Crimes against children are not included as only those aged 16 and above are normally included. Others, such as the homeless, are less likely to be on the personal address files which are the basis of the sample. Despite these limitations, however, the BCS has become an invaluable source of information about the extent of some crimes.

2.4 CRIME TRENDS

What can be deduced from these official sources of data about crime? A major question of interest to governments, the media and the public alike has been whether crime can be said to have 'risen' or fallen in any given period of time. Any estimates have, however, to be treated with caution bearing in mind variations in reporting and recording practices. It is also dependent on which years are taken for comparison (Maguire 2002). Figure 2.2 dramatically shows the rise in recorded crime from 1950 to 2002. The total of over 5 million offences recorded in 2002 compares with 2.5 million in 1980, 1.6 million in 1970, 0.5 million in 1950 and an annual recorded figure of 100,000 which was relatively stable between 1876 and 1920.

While in general the BCS indicates a much higher rate of crime than police figures, it also suggests that increases in crime have been less dramatic than these figures suggest – Maguire (2002), for example, points out that for the sub-set of offences which are comparable between the BCS and police figures, the number of recorded crimes increased by 52 per cent whereas those reported to the BCS rose by only 22 per cent. The surveys showed that the level of offending for some crimes peaked in the mid 1990s and was followed by falls in the second half of that decade.

Figures from 2002/3 confirm this trend with the total number of crimes, after accounting for the effects of the new NCRS, having fallen by around 3 per cent. It is further reported that burglary has fallen by 39 per cent between 1997 and 2002 and vehicle related thefts by 31 per cent in the same period. Violent crime has, on the other hand, risen by 2 per cent even after the effects of recording changes (Simmons and Dodd 2003). In April 2004 the police recorded crime statistics showed that the serious violent crimes of homicide and serious wounding rose by 13 per cent between the last quarter of 2002 and the same period in 2003. The BCS showed that the category of robbery increased by 28 per cent in 2001/2 (Crime in England and Wales 2001/2: 47). It is apparent, therefore, that it is not always accurate to speak in terms of 'the crime trend', as trends seem to be crime specific.

A number of considerations thus have to be borne in mind when interpreting overall rises and falls in crime rates. Taking the twentieth century as a whole, the population itself has grown and a less dramatic growth is indicated when population figures are taken into account. Methods of recording crime have also changed, as have categories and definitions of crime, with new crimes emerging. Furthermore, the Home Office has helped to promote more reliable and consistent data collection methods. Crime statistics may also be affected by the growth of the police – if there are more police to record and investigate crime, this will produce higher rates of recorded crime.

Changes in the crime rate can also be affected by wider changes in society as a whole. For example, mass car ownership in the twentieth century resulted in the creation of new offences, such as reckless or dangerous driving, along with driving without a licence or insurance. Motor cars parked in streets have created many opportunities for theft, both of the cars themselves and of accessories such as radios and spare parts. In 1997, vehicle crime accounted for around one-quarter of all notifiable crimes recorded by the police. Economic factors such as rising unemployment, a growth in casual employment and a decline in manufacturing industries have had a major impact on society and, argue many, on patterns of crime. More recent years have seen the growth of new offences related to consumerism such as thefts of computers and mobile phones. It is therefore important to consider different kinds of crime, rather than looking at crime as a whole.

2.5 TYPES OF OFFENCE

Looking at different kinds of crime can correct some of the misleading images which result from the tendency of the press, for example, to focus on more dramatic and newsworthy offences. Table 2.2 indicates the percentages of different kinds of crime reported to the police in 2002. This illustrates that violent crime, which includes sexual offences, often represented as a major crime problem, accounts for a relatively small proportion of the total, with property crime including different kinds of theft, vehicle crime and burglary dominating the figures. Some of these categories will be explored below.

Table 2.2 Police recorded crime by type of crime, 2002/3

Burglary	15%
Theft of/from vehicles	17%
Other thefts	23%
Other property offences	19%
Violent crime	17%
Drug offences	2%
All other offences	7%

Based on Simmons J and Dodd P (eds) (2003) *Crime in England and Wales 2002/3* Home Office Statistical Bulletin 07/03, p. 15

Violent crime

Violent crime, which in many statistical breakdowns includes homicide, assaults and sexual crimes, accounted for 17 per cent of recorded crime in 2002/3. There has been an increase in violent offences reported from the 1980s, which is often attributed to an increased willingness to report offences, particularly domestic violence, although this is generally recognised to be under-reported (Mirrlees-Black *et al.* 1996). Of the violent offences reported to the most recent BCS in 2002/3, 61 per cent were common assaults involving at most minimal injury, with 49 per cent involving no injury to the victim whatsoever – indicating that much of what is counted as violent crime is not as serious as often imagined. Some features of the main categories of violent offences are summarised below.

■ *Homicide.* A general category covering the offences of murder, manslaughter and infanticide and attracting a lot of public attention. Many of the most notorious criminal incidents that enter public consciousness relate to horrific cases, such as the Moors murderers Ian Brady and Myra Hindley, Peter Sutcliffe (the Yorkshire Ripper) and Frederick West, the Gloucester builder who committed suicide in prison in 1995 while awaiting trial for the murder of 12 people. Much public concern was aroused by the brutal killing of 2-year-old James Bulger, murdered in Bootle on 12 February 1993 by two 10-year-old boys, Robert Thompson and Jon Venables. The case of Harold Shipman, the Manchester doctor who was found to have killed hundreds of his elderly patients, continues to affect homicide figures; and, most recently, the murder of Holly Wells and Jessica Chapman in Soham in April 2003 and the subsequent trial and conviction of Ian Huntley in December 2003 dominated the media with some papers offering 'pull out supplements' once the case had been completed. However, stranger murders of children are relatively rare. Between 1977 and 1996 there were on average seven deaths a year of victims under the age of 16 where the suspect had been identified and was not known to the victim. Typically homicide is a crime in which relatives and acquaintances rather than strangers kill each other. In the 10 years between 1987 and 1996 there were on average 686 homicides a year and most victims were male. A total of 1,048 deaths were initially recorded as homicide in 2002/3 with 172 being victims of Harold Shipman – following the official enquiry a number of deaths not initially recorded as homicide were entered as homicides during 2002/3. Once these are accounted for there is no significant increase in the number of homicides (Povey and Allan 2003).

■ *Domestic violence.* In the 1995 BCS, 1.3 per cent of all women surveyed reported domestic violence compared with 0.7 per cent of men (Mirrlees-Black *et al.* 1996). Women were more likely to have been attacked by their current or ex-partners (accounting for 80 per cent of reported incidents), whereas while 47 per cent of assaults on men were by current or ex-partners, half were by other household members and other relatives. There has been some fall in reported domestic violence with 2002/3 figures suggesting a 0.7 per cent risk for women, compared with a 0.4 per cent risk for men (Povey and Allan 2003). More difficult to calculate is the number of children and the elderly who are also affected by violence in the home.

■ *Assaults.* The picture which has emerged from victim and crime surveys is that many reported assaults take place in and around leisure sites such as pubs and clubs with the category of officially recorded assaults dominated by fights, largely between young men, who form the highest risk category. Figures for assault have undergone some changes with common assaults now being those which involve no injury (39 per cent of BCS violence) and those involving minor injuries (22 per cent of the total in 2002/3) being counted as 'less serious wounding' (Povey and Allan 2003).

■ *Violence in the workplace.* Violent offences may also take place at work – the 1988 BCS found that for those who worked, nearly one-quarter of violent incidents were associated with work, with welfare workers, nurses, production and site managers, entertainment managers and security workers emerging as most at risk. Shop workers may also face violence, as, of course, do the police and prison officers who deal with violent offenders.

While small in proportion to other forms of recorded crime, it is important to recognise that many violent incidents are not recorded, particularly where victims and offenders know each other – only one-third of domestic violent offences reported to the BCS in 1995 were reported to the police compared with two-thirds of muggings (Mirrlees-Black *et al.* 1996). In addition, while many violent incidents do not result in injury, threats of violence and harassment, where no actual assault takes place, can for some people be more psychologically damaging than occasional incidents of actual violence. This might happen particularly within families, among neighbours or with persistent racial harassment which may involve verbal abuse, threats of violence, vandalism and daubing racist slogans on the homes or businesses of members of minority ethnic groups. To the catalogue of violence could also be added 'road rage' and reckless or aggressive driving.

Sexual offences

The offences recorded by the police in this category include rape, indecent assault on males and females, indecency between males, unlawful sexual intercourse with a girl under 16, incest, abduction, bigamy and gross indecency with a child, and offences to do with procuring people for sexual purposes such as prostitution.

Offences in relation to prostitution, other than procurement, including kerb crawling, are summary offences and are not included in the statistics recorded by the police. In 2002/3 a total of 48,654 sexual offences were recorded by the police with just over half of these, 24,811, being indecent assaults on women and 1,880 were cases of gross indecency with a child. Many victims and offenders are known to each other – one survey carried out by the Home Office found that nearly two-thirds of rapes, three-quarters of indecent assaults on males and two-thirds on females involved family members. About one-quarter of rapes involved strangers, with one-third involving spouses, lovers, parents and other family members and another one-third involving acquaintances (Watson 1996). In general, sexual offences form a very small proportion of crime recorded by the police – accounting for 5 per cent of all police recorded violent crime and 0.8 per cent of all police recorded crime in 2002/3 (Povey and Allan 2003).

Property crime

As seen in Table 2.2, property crime dominates officially recorded crime. Theft, which together with handling stolen goods accounts for around half of all recorded crimes, includes shoplifting, theft by an employee and theft from the person – many of these may involve relatively trivial amounts although their net cost is considerable. Property crimes also include the following:

- *Burglary.* The BCS estimated that, in 2002/3, 3.4 per cent of households experienced an actual or attempted burglary with some experiencing more than one – this rate is similar to previous years but has shown a major decline since the 6.5 per cent figure for 1993 (Simmons and Dodd 2003). There has been some change in the most common items stolen. In 1995 these were jewellery, video equipment and cash (Mirrlees-Black *et al.* 1996), whereas the 2002/3 BCS indicates an increase in burglaries of computer equipment and bags, credit cards and mobile phones (Simmons and Dodd 2003).

- *Vehicle theft.* This category includes thefts of, and thefts from, cars. Thefts from cars, which include the theft of external items such as wheels and badges and the theft of audio equipment, accounts for the largest proportion in this category. Thefts of cars include so-called joyriding and thefts of cars for economic gain – with the latter having been estimated to have risen in the early 1990s (Webb and Laycock 1992). There has, however, been a consistent decrease in vehicle-related theft since 1997 (Simmons and Dodd 2003).

- *Fraud and forgery.* This accounts for around 3 per cent of recorded crime, although it is generally assumed to be undercounted – many frauds are not detected by victims and the frequent use of one credit card may only be counted once (Coleman and Moynihan 1996; Maguire 1997). The largest category of recorded frauds involves stolen credit cards although much business and financial fraud is either not detected or dealt with by agencies other than the police.

Organised and white collar crime

Any snapshot of recorded crime must also acknowledge the extent of many forms of crime which are less likely to appear in official statistics. These include organised and white collar crime – sometimes referred to as 'economic' or 'business' crime. Taken together, these kinds of crime would add enormously to the extent and impact of officially recorded offences as the following examples indicate:

■ *Professional and organised crime.* In contrast to one-off, occasional and opportunistic crimes the term 'professional and organised' refers to the structured and business-like approach of those involved, for example, in local and global businesses involving drugs, money laundering and a host of illegal enterprises (Levi 2002). Thus organised crime involves the sale of illegitimate goods and services or the illegal sale of otherwise legitimate goods in order, for example, to avoid revenue – there are major trades, for example, in 'bootleg' or 'contraband' cigarettes and alcohol. Other illegal trades include arms dealing, pornography, gambling, sex, stolen goods and 'people trafficking' (the transportation of illegal immigrants). The growing profits of the drugs industry, which need to be 'laundered', have also led to the involvement of organised criminals in major financial frauds and the manufacture of counterfeit goods such as designer clothes, sports equipment, audio and video cassettes.

■ *White collar and corporate crime.* In contrast to the category above these crimes are committed by people already engaged in legitimate enterprises in business or the professions who use their position to commit offences such as financial or pensions frauds. The collapse of major international corporations such as Enron and Worldcom amidst revelations of a host of fraudulent business practices and the association of major household names in pensions 'miss-selling' have recently highlighted these kinds of offences. These crimes can also affect the public service: the Healthcare Financial Management Association, for example, once estimated that 'tens of millions of pounds are being lost by prescriptions frauds and false claims of payment by doctors, dentists, pharmacists and opticians (*The Guardian*, 24 June 1997: 8). Frauds on the European Union are also said to be widespread, and to involve both legitimate and illegitimate business enterprises. While it is notoriously difficult to estimate the extent of these kinds of crime, many argue that, if known, their cost would far outstrip the costs of burglaries, robberies and other forms of property crime (Croall 2001). The category of corporate crime also includes breaches of health, safety and consumer legislation on the part of companies which, while such offences may endanger and on occasion take lives, are not included as notifiable offences but are counted as summary offences.

Offenders

The Criminal Statistics give details of the age and gender of offenders found guilty of or cautioned for offences. Young men tend to dominate the figures. When proportions of the population are taken into account, the highest rate of offending in 2002 was for young men aged between 18 and 20 (6,834 per 100,000 population). Eighty per cent of all known offenders (those found guilty or cautioned for indictable offences) were male. For females the highest rate of offending was for those aged between 15 and 17. It should also be borne in mind that many young offenders caught for the first time may not be formally cautioned, but are given an informal warning and that 'young offender crime' such as vandalism and criminal damage is considerably under-reported. The 'gender gap' between male and female offenders has been a consistent feature of the statistics, not only in England and Wales but across Europe and America. Female offenders also show a different pattern of offending, being less involved in violent offences and proportionately more involved in theft. While it has been argued that some of this difference could be due to a greater reluctance on the part of criminal justice agencies to take action against girls or women, most now accept that girls and women do commit fewer offences than boys and men.

Statistics do not give breakdowns of offenders by ethnic groups and information on this matter is somewhat inconclusive, having been gathered by a number of different research studies using only partial information. Broadly speaking, figures indicate that black people tend to be arrested, convicted and imprisoned in higher proportions than would be expected from their overall proportion of the population, with Asians being under-represented (Smith 1997). However, these figures are extremely difficult to interpret and could be affected by a variety of factors. For example, black people tend to be more concentrated in areas where more street crime occurs, and, compared to the white population, the black population has higher proportions of young people, who, as we have seen, feature prominently as offenders. Thus it might be expected that higher proportions of black youth would appear as offenders although many argue that there is also discrimination against black people at different stages in the criminal justice process (see, for example, Chapter 6).

These breakdowns may, of course, be affected by unreported crime. Fewer offences of domestic violence, white collar and organised crime are likely to be reported or detected so it could be argued that males over 21 are under-represented in the statistics. Although the majority of convicted offenders are from lower socio-economic backgrounds, the relative absence of white collar offenders from reported crime means that we cannot necessarily conclude that the majority of offences are committed by lower class individuals. On the other hand, acts of vandalism are estimated to be one of the least reported offences and, as seen above, many young people may be dealt with informally or diverted from the system (see also Chapter 8).

CONCLUSION

This chapter has explored many dimensions of crime. We have identified the three interrelated elements that are vital to understand crime: behaviour, rules and their enforcement. The legal conception of crime defined in terms of *actus reus* and *mens rea* focuses on the need of the criminal justice system to establish the blame or degree of blame with respect to behaviour either proscribed or required by the criminal law. Hence the importance of criminal defences such as self-defence or duress which might absolve a person of an act otherwise deemed criminal, and the mitigation statements put forward for those convicted in order to diminish their culpability for an offence. The different legal categories of crime have been explored and we have also seen that everyday conceptions of crime may differ from legal definitions affecting which behaviour people consider to be 'criminal' and that what is legally a crime changes over time.

This means that crime is not easy to define and the second part of the chapter has indicated that it is also not easy to measure with precision. The vast amount of information now available about crime based on police statistics and victim surveys can give only a partial picture of the real extent of crime. In effect it may tell us more about what the public define as crime and what the police and other agencies choose to process.

Exploring how these statistics are created has several implications for a consideration of criminal justice agencies and policy. In the first place, it shows that the actions of the public and the police have an important impact on the crime figures. It is therefore important, in examining the role of criminal justice agencies, also to examine how they contribute to overall estimates of the extent of crime and how offenders are selected for subsequent stages. There is considerable discretion at all stages in the process. In addition, the public can be affected by the images of crime portrayed in the media. If, for example, they learn that there has been an increase in a particular kind of crime, they may be more likely to report it. They may come to be more afraid of this kind of crime and take action to prevent it.

The analysis of crime figures also shows that public pressure and policy may be directed against a limited and atypical group of crimes – those which receive most attention in the media. Many offences are relatively trivial; many more never reach the attention of the police and many offenders remain undetected. Therefore those going through the criminal justice system may be a small and unrepresentative group of offenders. This raises important questions in relation to the role of criminal justice. How far can it seek to prevent crime, when it deals with only a proportion of those who commit it? A common response to a moral panic or a seeming spate of offences reported in the media is often to institute tougher penalties. However, if so many offenders remain undetected, how effective are these strategies likely to be? Should the system not focus on attempting to catch more offenders rather than punishing the ones that are caught? Or should it aim to do both? How much can sentencing policy really affect the volume of crime? These considerations underlie the current emphasis on crime prevention which will be discussed in Chapter 5. The impact that sentencing makes on crime is discussed in Chapters 12 and 13 and depends on whether it can deter some criminals, incapacitate others or rehabilitate those capable of change.

However, the criminal justice system exists not only to reduce crime – from the 'just deserts' and denunciatory perspectives it is important to punish wrongdoers regardless of their numbers. This directs us to the harm which crime causes. So far we have examined crime as an objective definable measurable concept but have not yet considered its impact on those most specifically affected: the victims. The impact on individuals is the focus of the next chapter.

Review questions

1 How would you define a criminal?

2 List the ways in which the criminal law reflects a concern with blameworthiness.

3 List the factors involved in the process of attrition charted in Figure 2.1.

4 List the main factors which could account for an increase in crimes reported to the police during the twentieth century.

5 Discuss the factors which might explain why men are convicted of more offences than women and young offenders are convicted in different proportions to adults.

6 See also Appendix 1, Practical Exercises 1 and 2.

Further reading

Coleman, C and Moynihan, J (1996) *Understanding Crime Data: Haunted by the Dark Figure*, Open University Press: Buckingham

Croall, H (1998) *Crime and Society in Britain*, Longman: London

Maguire, M (2002) 'Crime Statistics: The "data explosion" and its implications', in Maguire, M, Morgan, R and Reiner, R (eds) *The Oxford Handbook of Criminology* (3rd edn), Clarendon Press: Oxford

Muncie, J, McLaughlin, E and Langan, M (eds) *Criminological Perspectives*, Sage: London

CHAPTER 3

Victims and the impact of crime

INTRODUCTION

The victim is often described as the 'forgotten' player in the criminal justice process. This is in part because of an adversarial system of justice and the requirement to establish the guilt of an offender. Hence the victim is an essential part of this process: without victims to act by way of reporting crime, providing information and giving evidence in court, the system of criminal justice will not work. The system requires the prosecution to establish guilt beyond reasonable doubt, and this is difficult for many crimes without the active participation of the victim. Individual victims suffer financially, physically and emotionally from crime; and families, communities and society as a whole are also affected. The first section of this chapter will focus on this impact, drawing from the victim surveys described in Chapter 2. The risk of becoming a victim is not evenly spread throughout society and the following section will explore how the risks of crime vary according to geographic and socio-economic factors along with gender, age and race.

The latter decades of the twentieth century saw what has been described as the 'rediscovery' of the victim, with a range of studies revealing victims' needs for help, support, advice and practical help, and their dissatisfaction with their experiences of the criminal justice process. For some victims, particularly victims of violent and sexual crimes, the experience of reporting crime and giving evidence could amount to secondary victimisation. In what has been described as a victim 'movement', outlined in the third section of the chapter, a range of groups called for more attention to be paid to these issues. This led to the development of a number of policies and to a Victim's Charter. We will look at the ways in which the victim has become more 'centre stage' in recent years, with policies that aim to help victims deal with the consequences of crime and also to make their participation in the criminal justice system more tolerable.

Subsequent sections of the chapter will look at how victims are compensated, at the various ways in which they are supported and at their role in the criminal justice process – in relation to, for example, reporting crime, giving evidence and their role in sentencing and restorative justice. The chapter will conclude by considering some of the issues raised by these developments. How far do they represent a real improvement for victims? To what extent do victims, like offenders, have 'rights' in relation to criminal justice? To what extent can or should the criminal justice process incorporate the victim?

First it is important to look briefly at the concept of the victim which, like the concept of crime, requires some exploration. We have seen that victims play a key role in defining crime and victimisation must also be defined. In order to be considered or consider themselves as a victim, citizens have to be aware that they have suffered harm from an incident which they consider to be criminal. Thus in both commonsense and legal terms the notion of victim is linked to notions of crime and it is also subject to different social conceptions. If, for example, victims have been seen to have provoked an offence they will be seen as less 'deserving' than if they are perceived to be 'innocent'. These notions are also related to social perceptions of the situations in which a crime occurs and the characteristics of offenders and victims. The elderly person set upon by an attacker or the child victim of a murder are perceived to be vulnerable and innocent, whereas the woman appearing to invite rape by her dress or demeanour, or the victim of an assault who has been involved in provoking a fight are seen as less deserving of sympathy.

'Blaming the victim', by assuming that he or she provoked the crime, has been one theme in victimology (the study of victims). Early victimologists hypothesised that some groups, such as children, the elderly, the weak or the depressed, were particularly prone to being victims and others argued that some victims precipitated offences, particularly in cases of murder and rape (see, for example, von Hentig 1948; Walklate 1989). Amir, for example, surveying police records, stated that 19 per cent of rapes were 'victim precipitated' in that women had initially agreed to sex but later changed their mind or had not resisted strongly enough (Amir 1971).

Later victimologists focused more specifically on how people's lifestyles were related to victimisation, arguing, for example, that victimisation was related to the amount of time spent in public places where crimes were more likely to occur. If these situations can be identified then high-risk lifestyles can be better avoided and the cost and impact of crime reduced.

3.1   THE COST AND IMPACT OF CRIME

All members of the public are affected by crime. They pay for crime through taxes which pay for the criminal justice system, taxes which may be even higher to compensate for tax evasion. They also pay higher insurance premiums to protect themselves from the financial losses incurred by property crimes. Prices in shops include an amount to take account of theft by customers and employees and the costs of the health service also increase as a result of violent crime.

It is not easy to calculate the costs of crime. A Home Office study (Brand and Price 2000) estimated the cost of selected notifiable offences including violence, sexual offences, robbery, burglary, thefts, fraud and forgery and criminal damage, with numbers and estimated costs based on information from the BCS and commercial victimisation surveys. Costs included those incurred in anticipation of crime such as security expenditure and insurance administration, those incurred as a consequence of criminal events, such as stolen property and damage along with emotional and physical impacts and health services and those incurred in responding to crime including costs to the criminal justice system. According to these calculations the most costly property crimes are vehicle thefts with costs amounting to £4,700 per offence, with burglary costing an average of £2,300 and criminal damage around £500. Personal crimes involved higher costs with homicides costing around £1 million and other violent incidents around £19,000 per incident.

The total cost of crime to England and Wales in 1999/2000 was estimated as around £60 billion, although this does not include the impact on the victim's, or the public's quality of life. In this estimate 20 per cent is made up by the cost of the criminal justice response to crime, with around £19 million representing the cost of property stolen or damaged and nearly £18 billion representing the direct emotional and physical impact on victims. This is not a full figure as the study excluded a number of offences such as drug trafficking, handling stolen goods, public order offences, fare evasion and many summary offences.

While this figure is not complete, it does indicate the many ways in which crime affects victims and society as a whole. Crime not only has financial costs but affects our daily lives – people worry about crime and take steps to avoid it. Houses must be locked and protected and many people are scared to go to certain areas through fear of being mugged, raped or assaulted. Valuable items are postcoded and car windows have numbers etched on them. Indeed, what has been called the 'fear of crime' is seen by some as out of proportion to actual risks of crime, with the 2002/3 BCS providing some interesting information about the public's concerns about crime (Fletcher and Allan 2003). Many respondents felt that crime is rising, despite the falling rates of some crimes outlined in Chapter 2. Those who read tabloid newspapers were more concerned, and felt that crime was rising more than those who read broadsheet newspapers. Many avoid walking in the streets at night – 13 per cent of respondents felt very unsafe walking alone in their area, with women being more worried about violent crime than men and women over 60 years of age being most worried. Twenty-nine per cent of the sample said they never walked in their local area after dark. The effects of the fear of crime can, however, be exaggerated. It was found that those showing most concern did live in areas with higher crime rates, and not all of those who avoided walking in the streets at night were worried specifically about crime – some had no inclination to go out and others drove. The fear of crime was cited as a reason by one-fifth of respondents who went out at night less than once a month.

Crime affects individual victims financially, physically and emotionally and its impact varies according to the circumstances of the offence and the situation of the victim – some victims are not greatly affected by offences, with more severe effects being found among victims of wounding, burglary, and vehicle theft (Nicholas and Wood 2003). While some property offences involve trivial amounts, others involve considerable financial costs, particularly those involving cars. In 2002/3 the average financial loss to individuals from domestic burglary was £500, with around half of victims estimating their losses at between £1,000 and £5,000, and one-fifth at below £100. Burglary also has emotional effects as it can give rise to feelings that privacy has been invaded and to anger and annoyance. In the 2002/3 BCS 83 per cent of burglary victims reported an emotional reaction, which was more likely if entry had been gained. Anger and annoyance were the most common reactions with fear, loss of confidence and difficulty sleeping being reported by around one-quarter of victims. Thirty-seven per cent felt 'very much' affected by burglary. In addition to financial losses and injury, many offences cause inconvenience – reports have to be made to the police, lost goods replaced or damaged items and houses repaired.

Offences may also have indirect effects. Victims' families may be affected – most particularly in cases of murder and serious injury, but also in cases of burglary. Children in houses which have been burgled have been found to suffer from sleeplessness and bed wetting (Morgan and Zedner 1992). Witnesses to crime, particularly violent crime, may be emotionally affected and also have to suffer the inconvenience of giving statements to the police or attending court. In more general terms the quality of life of entire communities may be affected by high rates of crime, which may lead to the general 'decline' of an area.

3.2 WHO ARE THE VICTIMS OF CRIME?

While all of us are affected by crime and are at risk of being its victims, risks and effects are spread differentially amongst the population. Geographical location, lifestyles, socio-economic factors, gender, age and race and ethnicity all affect patterns of victimisation. These factors are interrelated. For example, neighbourhoods tend to contain people of similar socio-economic status, and different groups have different lifestyles – young people are likely to go out more than older people, which affects their risk of being a victim of street crime. A brief exploration of some aspects of differential victimisation follows.

Geographical area

Risks of victimisation tend to be higher in urban than rural areas. Less than 3 per cent of people in rural areas were victims of burglary compared with 5 per cent in non-rural areas according to the 2002/3 BCS, and similar patterns were also found in relation to vehicle-related theft and violent crime (Aitchison and Hodgkinson 2003). Figure 3.1 shows the percentage of household victims of certain kinds of crime in inner city, urban and rural areas and Figure 3.2 shows BCS victimisation rates for household and personal crime by region. This illustrates that household crime is highest in the Yorkshire and Humberside region and lowest in Wales. While variations between regions in relation to personal crime are not great, it is highest in London which has the highest rate of recorded crime per 1,000 population and lowest in Wales.

Figure 3.1 **Percentage of household victims of burglary, vehicle-related crime and adult victims of violent crime by area type, 2002/3 BCS**

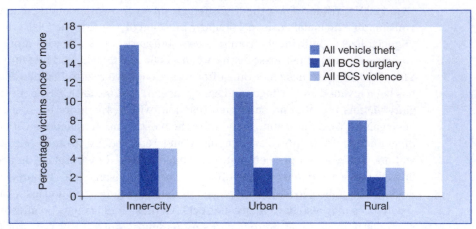

Source: Aitchison, A and Hodgkinson, J 'Patterns of Crime', in Simmons, J and Dodd, T *Crime in England and Wales 2002/3* Home Office Statistical Bulletin 07/03 July 2003, p. 97

Figure 3.2 **BCS victimisation rates by region 2002/3**

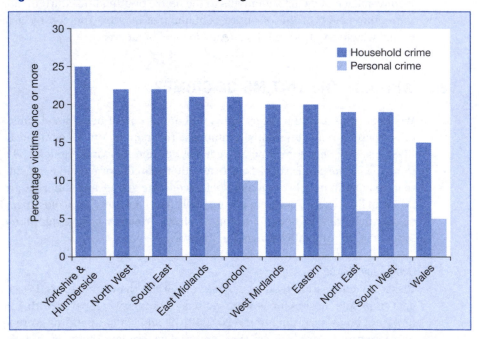

Source: Aitchison, A and Hodgkinson, J 'Patterns of Crime', in Simmons, J and Dodd, T *Crime in England and Wales 2002/3* Home Office Statistical Bulletin 07/03 July 2003, p. 93

Geographical area is also linked to socio-economic status, and the ACORN (A Classification of Residential Neighbourhoods) classifications used by the BCS incorporate measurements of economic, demographic and housing characteristics of areas, classified by postcode. These indicate that risks of burglary are highest in 'rising' and 'striving' areas, the former being characterised by young, professional couples and singles and the latter being council estates with higher numbers of elderly, single parents and unemployed residents along with multi-ethnic, low income areas. These latter areas also show a high risk of vehicle thefts, along with 'rising' areas (Aitchison and Hodgkinson 2003).

This reflects a variety of factors. Some kinds of houses are more ready targets for burglars – burglary is higher, for example, in flats than in houses, in terrace-type houses than in detached houses, and in rented accommodation. While lower income groups have high rates of victimisation, the more affluent may also make attractive targets especially to car thieves, as they have more worth stealing.

Lifestyle

Lifestyle (or what some call 'routine activities') also affects the risk of victimisation. As pointed out above, those who go out more often or travel through areas characterised by high rates of crime are more at risk. Young men aged between 16 and 24 are most at risk of violent crime, much of which takes place in or around places where people have been drinking. Lifestyle is also strongly related to factors such as socio-economic status, age, gender and ethnicity.

Socio-economic status

While the above figures indicate that 'rising' and 'striving' areas carry high risks of victimisation many argue, on the basis of closer analysis of patterns of victimisation and considerations of its impact, that 'survey data has constantly identified that those most likely to be victimised by crime in Britain are often the most marginalised social groups living in the poorest areas' (Davies *et al.* 2003: 13). Hope has argued that 'more than one-half of all property crime – and more than one-third of all property crime-victims – are likely to be found in just one-fifth of the communities of England and Wales' (Hope 1997: 148).

Gender

We have already seen some variations in victimisation rates by gender. Young men are more likely to be the victims of public and street violence whereas women are more likely to be victimised in the home. Overall men are more likely to be victims of violent crime with 5.3 per cent of male respondents to the last BCS reporting victimisation compared with 2.9 per cent of women (Povey and Allan 2003). A major thrust in the victim movement was the attention drawn by women's groups to the high rates of violence against women in the home. This has been recognised as more difficult to capture in standard victim surveys as victims may not wish to reveal this to interviewers. One survey, based on a sample of 1,000, indicates that 24 per cent of married women and 59 per cent of divorced or separated women had been hit by their spouses (Painter and Farrington 1998). Some forms of violence are what can be described as gender specific, with women being subject to a continuum of sexual offences ranging from verbal harassment through to physical and sexual threats and sexual assaults.

Age

Age is related to victimisation in different ways with both 'innocent' children and the elderly being perceived as particularly vulnerable victims. While cases of robbery or mugging against elderly victims receives much public attention – understandable in terms of the callousness of the crime – the elderly have lower rates of victimisation from violent crime than younger age groups. The chance of being a victim may be a result of different lifestyles, and any effects of age on victimisation also interact with socio-economic status and geographical location – as Pain (2003) points out, old people are not a homogeneous group and affluent old age pensioners living in the country have a low risk of being a victim. On the other hand, elderly people by virtue of being elderly can be the victims of 'elder abuse' in the home and in institutions and of stone throwing and harassment in local neighbourhoods (Pain 2003). They may also be targeted by investment frauds and the predatory sales tactics of, for example, the suppliers of burglar alarms where salespeople prey on their fear of crime (Croall 2001).

While young people are often more associated with committing crime they are also major victims. A range of studies have revealed considerable victimisation amongst school students (Anderson *et al* 1994; Hartless *et al* 1995), often excluded from national surveys such as the BCS. Much crime in this age group, which includes bullying, theft and violence, involves young people stealing from other young people as the recurrent stories of youth being 'mugged' for mobile phones and designer clothes indicates. Young people may be scared to report these crimes as it can lead parents to curtail their activities, and they fear that they may be treated by the police as suspects rather than victims.

Race and ethnicity

Racial or minority ethnic status may also affect victimisation. More recent sweeps of the BCS have taken 'booster samples' of minority ethnic groups, finding that both Afro-Caribbeans and Asians are more at risk of household and personal offences than whites. By 2000, rates for Afro-Caribbeans and whites for household crime had converged, whereas Indians, Pakistanis and Bangladeshis had a greater risk. Black respondents reported higher rates of personal crimes (Phillips and Bowling 2002). Many of these differences can be explained by socio-economic factors, although for some, especially Asian groups, it remains significant and these groups also perceive more crime to be racially motivated.

Some offences are specifically directed at ethnic minorities and are described as 'racially motivated' (Phillips and Bowling 2002). These can include verbal harassment and abuse, damage to property, stone throwing and various offences involving racist grafitti, throwing stones, eggs or other items at people or their property. While individual incidents may be trivial, their accumulation can have a serious impact on victims, not always recognised in surveys which record individual incidents. Reports of racially motivated offences have increased considerably since figures were first collected but this probably reflects an increase in reporting and recording. British Crime Survey information indicates that rates fell slightly to 1999, when 2 per cent of black, 4 per cent of Pakistani and Bangladeshi and 4 per cent of Indian respondents reported racial victimisation. The volume of racist incidents is higher in areas with concentrations of ethnic minority populations and in the North of England, and there have also been findings that attacks are most frequent in areas with small but growing ethnic minority populations (Phillips and Bowling 2002).

3.3 THE REDISCOVERY OF THE VICTIM

Having moved from being the 'forgotten player' in the criminal justice process, many argue that victims now occupy 'centre stage' of criminal justice policy, such has been the growth of strategies and policies to support victims and to address their needs in the criminal justice process. First, from approximately 1960 to 1975, compensation schemes for crime victims were developed. Secondly, from 1975 to 1980, following women's campaigns on the part of the victims of rape and domestic violence and the rise of support services for the victims of violent and property crimes, a range of support services grew up including shelters for female victims of domestic violence, specialist suites in police stations for the victims of rape, and a range of voluntary staffed support services under the auspices of Victim Support. This organisation, whose role will be described below, has, in addition to providing support services, conducted research and acted to advocate policies in relation to victims. Thirdly, from the 1980s there were repeated calls for justice for victims and improvements in their experiences of criminal justice.

The increasing use of victim surveys along with studies of particular groups of victims revealed more about the impact of crime along with the considerable problems which many victims encountered following a crime (see, for example, Shapland *et al.* 1985, Maguire and Pointing 1988). Victims reported, for example, that they needed immediate help in coping with practical matters, such as repairing damage from a burglary or making insurance claims, along with, in the most serious cases, help to overcome emotional problems. They also reported frustration at not being given information about the progress of their case and what would happen next. Many felt confused and uncertain about what was expected of them when giving evidence in court, which could be an intimidating experience, as they could face cross-examination from the defence in an attempt to discredit their evidence – problems also found amongst witnesses. Inside and outside the courtroom, victims could also be brought face to face with the offender. If the case did not go to court, particularly if it was discontinued, victims could feel 'let down' and were often not informed about why decisions had been made; and victims reported disappointment where they felt, particularly in relation to a discontinuance or what they saw as a lenient sentence, that the impact of the offence was not being taken seriously. In some cases, victims feared retaliation from offenders and felt that they were offered inadequate protection.

Children could be seriously victimised in the home with, following high profile cases, the revelation of the extent of physical and sexual abuse against children in the home and in institutions. Organisations such as 'Childline', set up following these cases, highlighted the problems of detecting, prosecuting and obtaining convictions in these cases. Giving evidence in court, especially against parents or those previously close to them, could be particularly harrowing for children who were obliged to give evidence in open court and be examined by strangers.

These issues led to a range of different policies and strategies and by the start of the 1990s more support was available for victims and there was some official recognition of victims' needs. There was, however, no coherent strategy, and the implementation of policies was limited by what Shapland (1988) described as a tendency for agencies in the criminal justice process to resist change to protect their 'fiefdoms'; and Newburn (2003) comments that political parties pursued half-formed and half-hearted policies in relation to victims. The 1990s saw increasing recognition of victims and the pace of change accelerated towards the end of that decade, with some major changes and initiatives which will be described below.

What are the main needs of victims? In 1995, Victim Support produced a paper 'The Rights of the Victims of Crime' (Victim Support 1995), which argued that the state should exercise responsibilities grouped under five main principles:

- *Compensation*: victims should be entitled to compensation which leaves them in approximately the same financial position as they were in before the crime.

- *Protection*: victims and witnesses should be protected in any way necessary including psychological protection by, for example, protecting their privacy.

- *Services*: victims have the right to respect, recognition and support, to receive services from an organisation dedicated to their needs and to be treated with respect by all the agencies they come into contact with.

- *Information*: victims have the right to receive information about the progress of their case, the procedures being followed and about their role in the process and their rights. This includes receiving an explanation of any decisions and the opportunity to give a statement about the full financial, physical and emotional consequences of the crime.

- *Responsibility*: victims should be free of the burden of decisions relating to the offender, decisions which lie with the state.

The Government had also recognised the needs of victims. A Victim's Charter was published in 1990, with a second following in 1996 (Home Office 1996). This spells out what victims should expect from the criminal justice process, including the following:

- the name and phone number of a police officer responsible for their case;

- a 'Victims of Crime' leaflet when they report a crime;

- to be informed about suspects being caught and the progress of the case including being informed about decisions to drop charges, the trial date and result;

- to have the chance to explain how they have been affected by the crime;

- to be told when an offender in prison is to be released;

- to be treated sensitively when giving evidence in court and to be given support from the Witness Service;

- to be paid travel and other expenses for attending court;

- to be offered support by Victim Support and, where appropriate, by the Criminal Injuries Compensation Scheme (CICS).

This list illustrates the range of services now available to victims and its publication saw the introduction of new strategies. The expectations in the Charter, however, are not legislative requirements and in practice may not always be implemented; and they are described as 'service standards' rather than 'rights' (Davies *et al*. 2003; Newburn 2003; Zedner 2002). Nevertheless, there has been a range of legislation addressing victims' issues, which will be outlined below, along with considerations of its effectiveness.

3.4 COMPENSATING VICTIMS

One of the rights advocated by Victim Support is compensation and victims can be financially compensated in two ways: first by the state through the Criminal Injuries Compensation Scheme (CICS); and, secondly, by offenders, through the imposition (at the time of sentencing) of compensation orders.

State compensation

In the early part of the twentieth century there was no formal means by which the victims of crime could be compensated by the state, and a range of penal reformers, including, prominently, Margery Fry from the Howard League for Penal Reform, argued that victims' needs should be recognised by the introduction of a state compensation scheme. The Criminal Injuries Compensation Board was set up in Britain in 1964. This did not recognise a 'right' of victims to compensation and restricted compensation to 'deserving' victims – for example, those who had failed to report crimes to the police, could be seen to have provoked a crime, or were related to offenders were not deemed eligible (Newburn 2003). The impetus for this scheme came largely from penal reformers and political parties and did not arise from any campaigning by or consultation with victims themselves (Davies *et al.* 2003; Newburn 2003).

The CICS is now well established and has compensated a large number of victims. From an initial 500 applications for awards following its introduction, increasing amounts have been paid to a growing number of applicants. There were approximately 22,000 applications in 1979–80, almost 66,000 by 1992–3 rising to 78,000 in 1999–2000. There have been recurrent attempts to reduce the cost of the scheme and, while in 1995 awards totalled £175 million, this had fallen to £116 million by 1999–2000, paid out to 40,000 victims. The scheme has several limitations and covers only violent offences. Victim Support and other commentators have pointed out that victims are not always informed of the scheme's existence, there are long delays, some victims are excluded and awards are too low (Davies 2003). Zedner (2002) points out that the minimum award is set at £1,000 which effectively excludes large numbers of victims of minor assaults and robberies; and compensation to families of a fatal injury amounts to £7,500. Where victims cannot work after 28 weeks they may be recompensed for loss of earnings, excluding those who are unable to work for less than that period. In a recent report Victim Support argues that it discriminates against some victims (Victim Support 2003). If, for example, victims are dependent on means-tested benefits such as income support and an award takes their savings over certain thresholds, their benefits can be reduced or cut.

Compensation orders

Compensation orders, first introduced in 1972, can be ordered by the court and form part of the sentence. From 1988 courts have been required to consider a compensation order in cases involving death, injury, loss or damage and to provide reasons in cases where an order is not made. Payment is now deducted at source from state benefits. Orders are widely used – in 1999, for example, 43 per cent of offenders sentenced for violent offences, 27 per cent for burglary, 45 per cent for robbery, 31 per cent for fraud and forgery, and 51 per cent for criminal damage were ordered to pay compensation. Failure to pay compensation can result in imprisonment. The Home Office issues magistrates with a table of injuries which indicates typical amounts of compensation.

This type of compensation is limited. As only a small number of offences result in the conviction of an offender, they are restricted to a small proportion of victims and awards are also limited by offenders' ability to pay. Where offenders have small incomes or are reliant on state benefits, victims may receive small amounts over a long period of time – which may prolong the financial and emotional effects of the offence (Davies 2003; Reeves and Mulley 2002). Victim Support has called for victims to be compensated immediately by the courts, with offenders having to pay instalments to the court (Reeves and Mulley 2002). While many victims therefore do receive compensation it applies to only a small proportion of victims and may not fully recompense them for the impact of offences.

3.5 VICTIM SUPPORT

There is now an extensive network of support available for victims. Victim Support provides a range of services, and criminal justice agencies and women's groups have addressed the needs of particular groups of victims such as rape victims and women who have suffered from domestic violence.

The activities of Victim Support have already been referred to and they now offer help to over one million crime victims per year. Victim support schemes were first set up in Bristol in 1974 and were nationally regulated by the National Association of Victim Support Schemes (NAVSS) which received financial support from the Government. By 2000, there were 386 schemes throughout England, Wales and Northern Ireland staffed by over 17,000 volunteers. Victim Support, as it is now known, is a charity which, in addition to providing individual support for victims, aims to influence the provision of services for victims and campaigns on matters relating to compensation and provision for the victim in court.

The major role of victim support is to provide services, on a voluntary basis, to individual victims at the local level. Each victim support scheme is run by a management committee and a coordinator collects details of victims from the police. Under local agreements the police give the local victim support scheme information about victims, including their name and address, unless the victim asks them not to. These details are then distributed to a pool of volunteers who contact victims either by letter, telephone or doorstep visits.

Schemes provide help with practical matters or the provision of information. The emphasis of victim support has mainly been on short-term help and support on a 'good neighbour' principle by providing a shoulder to cry on (Gill and Mawby 1990). The original emphasis was mainly on victims of burglary, robbery or theft, although it has now expanded its work to include more long-term work with the victims of sexual and violent crime, the families of murder victims and some schemes include a service for those involved in serious motor accidents. It also now runs a Witness Service and aims to provide a comprehensive service to all victims of crime, and to ensure that victims have access to services and that they can talk freely to an outsider. It also emphasises working closely with criminal justice agencies and is politically neutral, factors which have arguably contributed to its success (Newburn 2003).

In addition to Victim Support a range of services address the needs of particular groups of victims, particularly women and children. As seen above, an important part of the victims' movement was played by women's groups who also initiated support mechanisms. In 1972 Erin Pizzey established the first refuge for victims of domestic violence in Chiswick. Rape crisis centres were also developed during the 1970s, and by 1988 there were 40 such centres. These, staffed mainly by volunteers, offer a help line and a 24-hour counselling service. A Home Office Circular (69/1986) to chief police officers offered advice on achieving better treatment for victims of rape and domestic violence, including the provision of private facilities for the examination of victims, reference to advice and counselling services, and police training. Many police forces developed specialist units to provide a better service for women and child victims, and some set up special interview suites in police stations staffed by trained teams of female officers.

It also expressed an overriding concern with the safety of victims of domestic violence and the need to reduce any risk of further violence. In addition the CJA 1988 contained tougher provisions to ensure the anonymity of rape victims. The woman's identity is safeguarded, subject to the oversight of the courts, from the moment of allegation, whether or not any proceedings follow, and for the rest of her life. Other measures, described below, have now been introduced to assist rape victims in court.

3.6 VICTIMS AND CRIMINAL JUSTICE

Criminal justice agencies require cooperation from victims to provide information and evidence and yet the relationship between victims and the criminal justice process can be problematic. Criminal justice agencies deal primarily with offenders, and may not take victims' interests or needs into account. As seen above, victims may require protection and support and desire information about the progress of their case. Yet, as Davies (2003: 103) comments:

> realistically ... the police and criminal justice system have nothing tangible to offer the victim. There are no guarantees that property will be returned, that the offender/s will be caught or that justice will be done. Worse still ... the victim is at risk of becoming re-victimised by the police and the courts.

Complex issues also arise when considering the appropriate role of the victim in a criminal justice process which has as its primary aim establishing the elements of the offence and securing a fair balance between the conviction of those guilty of a crime and the rights of defendants to fair proceedings at all stages. Addressing victims' needs and involving the victim in the process may conflict with defendants' rights, particularly in relation to giving evidence and sentencing. This section will look at the role of the victim in some key areas of criminal justice, starting with the first stage at which victims come into contact – reporting crime.

Reporting crime and the role of the police

It was seen in Chapter 2 that not all victims report crime to the police and that many feel that the police would do little or might not take them seriously, yet the police are reliant on victims to report crime and to provide information which may help them construct a case against an offender.

We have seen that some victims experience particular difficulties, including victims of rape and domestic violence. In addition, victims of racially motivated crime have complained that the police fail to take account of racial motivation. Indeed once new instructions were issued reporting rates for many of these crimes increased. Nevertheless, some victims remain reluctant to report some crimes and, in general terms, the police and victims may have different priorities. While the primary concern for the police is detecting and prosecuting the offender, victims may want reassurance, protection, advice and information.

Following the Victim's Charters, the police role has now widened. They are expected to provide victims with more information and a leaflet about support services and compensation and to refer victims to victim support, which in itself is heavily reliant on the police for referrals. The provision of such information has been found to vary, and the ability of the police to provide support and advice may be limited by the demands of their other work. Reeves and Mulley (2000) give the example of the treatment of rape victims. Some police stations have set up a 'chaperone' system in which one specialist officer deals with the victim. After a period of time, however, the victim may still need support and help, whereas the dedicated officer must move on to other cases.

Following the second Victim's Charter, a pilot project described as 'One Stop Shop' (OSS) was developed in six police force areas. Under this initiative, victims of selected crimes could opt into a scheme in which they were kept informed by the police about whether a suspect is cautioned or charged, whether the charge is altered, the date of the trial, verdict and sentence.

Another major initiative arising out of the Victim's Charter was the introduction of pilot schemes of Victim Statements (VS), in which victims have a chance to describe the physical, emotional, financial and other effects of the offence. These are initiated by the police and passed on to the CPS. The information could be of use to the Police and CPS by, for example, signalling cases where victims or witnesses require protection. There has, however, been some confusion about the purpose of the VS which should, argue Reeves and Mulley (2000), be clearly distinguished from the 'victim impact statements' used in the sentencing of offenders in the United States and over which there remains, as will be seen below, considerable controversy. In 2001 a Victim Personal Statement Scheme was introduced which, according to a Practice Direction, was to play a limited role in sentencing – the statement could be used to provide information about the impact of the offence, but victims' or relatives' views about sentencing are not considered to be relevant. So far it is not clear what effects these initiatives will have; however, some argue that they may falsely raise victims' expectations, and that victims may not be clear exactly what benefit they wish to gain from opting into these schemes (Newburn 2003; Zedner 2002).

Victims in court

Without victims to act as willing witnesses the successful prosecution of criminals is difficult. The burden and the standard of proof tilts the system of justice in favour of the defendant. It is not as in a civil case where the judge has to decide which side to believe. In criminal cases the defendants do not have to explain themselves, as they are presumed innocent, and therefore the active role in a case is given to the prosecution to explain what happened, to identify who was culpable and to demonstrate this beyond reasonable doubt. This is difficult and in many cases impossible without victims willing to act as witnesses in court, which means undergoing the process of adversarial justice whereby the victim's version of events is frequently challenged by the defence. For many this adds to the outrage of being a victim.

Giving evidence and being subjected to cross-examination can be intimidating and it can be time consuming, incurring loss of earnings, and emotionally stressful as it involves reliving an unpleasant experience. It has also been seen that these problems are particularly marked for victims of violent and sexual offences whose credibility may be challenged. Despite the many improvements which have been made, Newburn (2003) cites a recent study by Spencer and Stern (2002) who found that around two-fifths of witnesses felt so intimidated by appearing in court and being cross-examined that they would not wish to give evidence again.

Victim support has also been involved with the provision of schemes to help victims in court, arising out of victims' complaints about their experiences. Initially a number of pilot schemes were set up. One such scheme was described by Rock (1991), who found that the main role of volunteers was to offer 'companionship and solace' during the long periods of waiting and confusion. All Crown Court centres now have a witness service run by Victim Support which includes advice about what might happen in court and victims and witnesses should receive a leaflet about their roles.

Rape victims and child witnesses have had their particular difficulties recognised. Child witnesses may have their evidence pre-recorded on video tape, be cross-examined by TV link from outside the court and may not be cross-examined by the accused personally. Rape victims are prevented from being asked about their sexual experience with people other than the defendant. The Youth Justice and Criminal Evidence Act 1999 contained a range of further provisions for such witnesses including screening witnesses from the accused, giving evidence by a live link, the removal of barristers' and judges' wigs and gowns, the opportunity to give evidence in private, video recording of cross- and re-examinations of witnesses, examination through intermediaries and aids to communication for young or incapacitated witnesses. While few dispute that some victims should be assisted in this way, there are issues about how far the protection of witnesses and providing them with assistance may interfere with defendants' rights to question those making accusations against them – a fundamental right in the adversarial system of justice. Moreover, many defendants may find the court an intimidating setting in which to present their version of events.

Victims and sentencing

There is considerable controversy over what, if any, role victims should play in sentencing, other than being compensated through compensation orders. Other proposals for bringing the victim into the sentencing stage have been made. In the United States of America, for example, there are provisions in some states for victim impact statements to precede the court's consideration of compensation and sentencing. In some cases victims may state an opinion about the sentence. In California the courts and the parole boards must listen to representation by victims, their relatives or legal representatives at the time of sentencing or in hearings regarding early prison release. As seen above these should not be confused with the victim statements currently being piloted in England and Wales.

These ideas have some strengths but they also raise significant issues as Ashworth (2000) points out. Victims are, he argues, those who have been wronged by the crime and allocution allows them to express their thoughts, which may assist their recovery, although there are other ways of doing this. In addition, the criminal justice system needs the cooperation of victims and it may be appropriate to make them feel that they have a role – in this sense victim participation can act as a 'sweetener'. On the other hand, he asks how many victims want this degree of involvement and points out, as does Victim Support, that it is the state's responsibility to make decisions about offenders. Other arguments against the use of impact statements are that it may be difficult to test the accuracy of the claims made and that it is questionable whether the court should take account of what may be the unforeseen effects of the offence on victims. While therefore it may be appropriate to use victim statements when deciding on compensation or reparation, it is less appropriate to use them in other aspects of sentencing. Indeed, he argues, it is wrong in principle, as sentencing should be a matter of public interest and it would be unfair – in terms of consistency of sentencing – if sentences varied because some victims are vengeful and others forgiving. Furthermore, it is unfair for the response to the crime to depend on whether or not a victim chooses to be involved and victims cannot be expected to know about the range of sentences available.

Mediation and restorative justice

Victims have also been involved in the growth of schemes falling under the general heading of restorative justice which are linked to mediation and reparation. Restorative justice involves a variety of strategies which aim to bring the offender and victim together, sometimes in 'conferencing' schemes, with a view to encouraging the offender to recognise the harm done by the offence and to make some direct reparation. There has also been a growth in mediation schemes, which involve meetings between offenders and victims, by which some form of compensation might be agreed. This may be an alternative to the formal trial process, it may be part of a community sentence, or it may be carried out while the offender is in custody. The Crime and Disorder Act 1998 introduced a new reparation order which can be a sentence on its own or combined with other disposals and it requires the young offender to make reparation to the victim. The Youth Justice and Criminal Evidence Act 1999 set up youth offender panels in which victims may be involved and which also contain restorative principles. There have, however, been difficulties in involving victims and victim participation rates are low, although this may be due to the patchy implementation of schemes (Newburn 2003; Zedner 2002). A further problem with the participation of victims in restorative justice is that the extent to which it benefits primarily offenders or victims can be questioned. It can, as Reeves and Mulley (2000) argue, become a 'burden' as it is not clear how much victims genuinely want to be involved and many schemes are primarily directed towards educating and rehabilitating offenders.

The probation service has become more involved in working with victims and with some of these schemes. Apart from its role in advising victims of serious crime about the release of life sentence prisoners, it has been encouraged to develop a more victim-oriented approach in pre-sentence reports and group work with offenders and victims. Yet, despite the significance of this new role for Probation Officers, little advice, guidance or preparation and no new resources were given for this work, and there are variations in how the Victim's Charter has been implemented (Davies 2003). A Thematic Inspection Report for the Home Office (*The Victim's Perspective: Ensuring the Victim Matters*, Home Office 2000) indicated that restorative justice is little developed. Only five services had a policy addressing restorative justice and only eight ran mediation/reparation projects. Many have pointed to the potential conflict between a victim-oriented and offender-oriented focus – probation officers have traditionally worked with offenders, and incorporating a victim orientation requires a cultural change.

Despite the often expressed view that victims are now at the centre stage of criminal justice policy, there remain many issues to be resolved in relation to the implementation and scope of many of the policies outlined above. Many argue, for example, that there still is no cohesive policy towards victims (Davies 2003; Newburn 2003) and also that victims still have few enforceable 'rights'. Moreover, many of the above policies have been unevenly implemented, with many victims still unaware of their entitlements to compensation and support; and reports by victims of feeling intimidated by their experiences of criminal justice are still common.

This was recognised in a Home Office review of the Victim's Charter in 2001 which argued that victims should have more rights; and the Home Office *Justice for All* White Paper of 2002 contains proposals which might lead to a more coherent strategy. These include the following:

■ appointment of an Independent Commissioner for victims and witnesses;

■ National Victims Advisory Panel to champion victims' interests;

■ victim liaison officers to join Youth Offending Teams;

- more measures for vulnerable and intimidated witnesses;
- extension of specialist support to the victims of road accidents and their families;
- a victims' code of practice spelling out what they have a 'right' to expect;
- a national strategy for victims and witnesses to better meet their needs;
- a 'right' of complaint to the Parliamentary Ombudsman for victims and witnesses.

Further problems lie in the implementation of the provisions of the Victim's Charter and subsequent policies, many of which have added to the responsibilities of criminal justice agencies such as the police, the CPS and the probation service. 'Integrating a victim's perspective' (Crawford and Goodey 2000) into the criminal justice process involves a major rethinking of the roles of agencies, which in turn involves a cultural change within them. Traditionally our adversarial criminal justice system has focused on offenders as suspects and defendants, and additional responsibilities to victims may conflict with the logic of adversarial justice.

Victims' interests may also, as Reeves and Mulley (2000) argue, be 'hijacked' by the criminal justice agenda. Emphasising the assumed needs or interests of victims can be used by those who argue for more severe sentences – thus Ashworth (2000) points to the dangers of victims being used in the 'service of severity'. He also argues that they can be used in the 'service of offenders': for example, when they are involved in restorative justice schemes, which, as seen above, Victim Support also identify as a potential burden for victims. There are dangers, therefore, of what Ashworth describes as 'victim prostitution' and there are also dangers of victims being used by politicians keen to demonstrate that they are doing something about crime.

On the other hand, there might be scope to follow some other jurisdictions to allow greater rights to victims such as the right of appeal against a court decision on conviction or sentence.

CONCLUSION

We have seen, therefore, that crime has a considerable impact on its individual victims, on communities and on the quality of life of all citizens, an impact which may fall particularly heavily on specific groups and is also likely to have a widespread consequence on communities at large in terms of feeling safe in their neighbourhoods. This directs our attention to the need to look carefully at where crime has a more severe impact and at strategies aimed to prevent crime, which will be the subject of Chapter 5, and at the role that sentencing can play in reassuring the public and in reducing criminality in Chapter 11, and Chapter 12 on sentencing and penal policy.

We have also seen that, having formerly been largely neglected by the criminal justice process and in legislation, much greater attention is now paid to the needs and interests of victims, and the issue of victims' 'rights' is now being widely incorporated. Victims are now seen as an important part of the criminal justice process. Despite the large volume of legislation and policies dealing with victims, however, there are still major issues to be addressed, including the culture of criminal justice agencies which may not fully recognise the needs of victims, and the balance, in an adversarial system, to be drawn between the rights of defendants and those of victims, and the appropriate role of victims in the sentencing process. These agencies and procedures will be more fully explored in subsequent chapters.

Review questions

1 What do victim surveys tell us about which groups of people are most likely to be the victims of crime and which are least likely?

2 List the different ways in which victims can be supported at each stage of the criminal justice process.

3 Discussion question: Consider how far victims should have 'rights' in the criminal justice process. Can these conflict with offenders' rights?

4 Look at the Victim Support website and identify a current policy issue affecting victims.

Further reading

Crawford, A and Goodey, J (eds) (2000) *Integrating a Victim Perspective within Criminal Justice: International debates*, Ashgate: Aldershot

Davies, P, Francis, P and Jupp, V (2003) *Victimisation: Theory, Research and Policy* Palgrave/Macmillan: Basingstoke

Newburn, T (2003) *Crime and Criminal Justice Policy* (2nd edn), Longman: London.

Zedner, L (2002) 'Victims', in Maguire, M, Morgan, R and Reiner, R (eds) *The Oxford Handbook of Criminology* (3rd edn), Clarendon Press: Oxford

Governmental, political and administrative context of criminal justice in England and Wales

Main topics covered

➤ Law and policy making

➤ Government and administration

➤ Political context

➤ 'Globalisation': cross-jurisdictional and international responses to crime

➤ Europeanisation of criminal justice policy

➤ Implementing criminal justice policy

➤ Monitoring, accountability and complaints

INTRODUCTION

Protecting the public is a major theme in political rhetoric that legitimates, or justifies, the very existence of government. While the provision of schools, hospitals and roads is important, they become secondary when citizens fear for their safety in the communities where they live. As Thomas Hobbes pointed out in the seventeenth century in *Leviathan* (1650), there are limits to the extent to which individuals can protect themselves and therefore one of the major responsibilities and purposes of government is to provide security against threats to personal safety from others. Thus criminal justice systems are expected to protect both the citizen and their property; and at the beginning of the twenty-first century the sense of personal security and fear of crime requires a governmental response that encompasses a global as well as a domestic perspective.

In a democratic society there may be differences of opinion as to how public protection, and the process of reassurance that goes with this, can best be achieved. Since the late eighteenth century we have seen a steady growth of interest in all aspects of criminal justice. With this have come innovative modes of intervention:

■ the development of professionals such as the police, psychiatrists and social workers;

- new institutions such as borstals, youth courts and detention centres;
- use of technologies for crime prevention, investigation and offender monitoring such as fingerprints, electronic tagging, DNA and CCTV;
- a succession of paradigms about how best to curb crime, deal with criminals, maintain law and order, and provide due process to ensure justice for those accused of a crime.

It is evident that ideas about these issues are subject to change and today's plethora of legislation, which would have been inconceivable by Parliaments and Governments for much of the twentieth century, illustrates that we live in a society where the response to crime is a major feature of government and politics. One aspect of the section on politics includes a look at the approach of the New Labour Government, in power since 1997 after 18 years of conservative governments (1979–1997). Reforms include those to the hallowed and traditional role of the Lord Chancellor, new rules on detaining terrorist suspects, measures to prevent criminals living off the proceeds of crime, and interventions and experiments to curtail crime by use of neighbourhood curfews on children on the street after 9 pm. New Labour cannot be accused of complacency as every aspect of criminal justice has undergone review and reform.

In this chapter we will identify the main features of the administrative, political and policy-making context of the criminal justice system in England and Wales. Key players are to be found in Whitehall and Westminster but we will be looking beyond the United Kingdom to the increasing internationalisation of crime policy, particularly the growth in European cooperation, and further fuelled since 11 September 2001 by fears of international terrorism.

We will examine issues to do with the implementation of criminal justice policy such as the problems of coordination between agencies, the increasing role played by private industry and the continuing and considerable role played by the lay and voluntary sector. Pragmatic and political issues are raised by the system for evaluating and monitoring the effectiveness of agencies through such innovations as performance indicators. Despite greater efforts to clarify objectives and assess performance, the issue of accountability is still relevant as it affects public confidence in the system and whether they feel it works to protect people's safety and property. The political and public reaction to crime policy will involve issues of how crime is represented in the media and the attitudes of the public to issues of crime and punishment. This leads on to the role that the public may play in responding to crime, through initiatives such as Crime and Disorder Reduction Partnerships. The public might also become involved as victims of crime and we will discuss some of the recent reforms that focus on victims (see also Chapter 3). Ideas change and policy experiments and initiatives do not wait for legislation but enter the fray of public discourse. Fashions change about the proper way to respond to crime, and new theories, policies and slogans may become encapsulated in crime strategies and new policy directions.

4.1 LAW AND POLICY MAKING

Who makes crime policy?

The most fundamental statement of criminal justice policy is to be found in legislation. Acts of Parliament provide both the starting point for defining many crimes and also the criminal justice agencies' powers and responsibilities in their response to crime.

In the United Kingdom, central government plays the dominant role in legislative reforms. Laws may start out as ideas in ministerial speeches, parliamentary statements and election manifestos. After a period of 18 years in opposition the newly formed Labour Government set out its approach to crime in the Crime and Disorder Act 1998. At other times the government may be responding to a new or newly perceived problem as a result of a single incident which reflects wider public anxiety. Following the stabbing of headmaster Philip Lawrence outside his school in Maida Vale in 1995 the law was changed to prohibit children under 16 from buying knives. The murders of Jessica Chapman and Holly Wells in Soham in 2003 prompted calls to change police vetting procedures and raised questions about the misuse and misunderstandings of the Data Protection Act. The murder of Stephen Lawrence in 1993 was responded to by far-reaching analyses of policing, discussed in Chapter 6, and led to a change to the law to allow for a retrial, previously regarded as infringing the double jeopardy rule (Criminal Justice Act 2003).

Where legislation is approaching the planning stage, the government may issue a Green Paper, a general discussion document inviting comment on particular ideas or proposals. Subsequently, a White Paper may be published which gives firm detailed proposals taking account of the feedback from the Green Paper. The White Paper is the most definitive statement of the government's policy and usually forms the basis of subsequent bills although many bills are introduced without this preliminary process of deliberation. All bills must go through a number of stages in both the House of Commons and the House of Lords before being transformed into an Act of Parliament. This process is not a formality and parliamentary debate may lead to amendments to the original details set out in the bill.

Policy can emerge in forms other than legislation and can be influenced not only by ministers or other politicians. Permanent officials in government departments will also have a departmental view on such issues as prison reduction and police powers. Policy statements are not always embodied in statute and innovations such as the introduction of the office of the Prison Ombudsman and providing cautioning *in lieu* of prosecution by the police had no statutory basis but emerged from decisions within the Home Office. Documents published by the Home Office are most influential on a range of matters concerning the police, probation and prisons. The Lord Chancellor's Department is important on matters relating to the judiciary and the courts.

Whitehall – a term that refers to both ministers and civil servants – is not the only source of policy statements. The work of the Home Affairs Committee at Westminster is important as are the views of the non-elected members of the House of Lords who include senior members of the judiciary, the Lords of Appeal who sit in the Upper House. During Michael Howard's term as Home Secretary senior members of the judiciary in the House of Lords spoke strongly against proposals in the Crime (Sentencing) Bill that proposed mandatory prison sentences for those re-convicted of serious violent or sexual offences, drug trafficking and for those convicted for a third time for burglary of a domestic dwelling. They were very critical of Michael Howard when Home Secretary and claimed he was pandering to public opinion in introducing tougher penalties that would increase the prison population.

It would be simplistic to think that policy making is restricted to Whitehall and Westminster. Policy is also found in the many documents defining the role and approach of the various agencies and professional and voluntary bodies that make up the criminal justice system. The process of policy making is very complex and reflects the fact that government is only one of a number of key players in the system. Other influential players in the process of consultation are professional groups, pressure groups and lay participants who have a unique role in criminal justice in this country when compared with others. The Magistrates' Association, for instance, has played an important role in developing sentencing guidelines.

Professional bodies are of considerable influence in England and Wales and include the following:

- Association of Chief Police Officers (ACPO)
- Police Federation (represents the ordinary police officer)
- National Association of Probation Officers (NAPO)
- Prison Officers' Association (POA)
- Prison Governors' Association
- Bar Council and the Criminal Bar Association (represent barristers)
- Law Society (represents solicitors)
- Justices' Clerks Society.

The most powerful of professions on matters of criminal law, procedure and pro-secution are the lawyers represented by the Bar Council, Criminal Bar Association, Law Society and the judiciary (judges) both individually and through bodies such as the Council of Circuit Judges and the Judicial Studies Board. The judiciary, although small in number, is powerful in defence of the principle of the independence of the judiciary, and is regularly consulted about new legislation. Lawyers' views are sought and listened to by the major government departments such as the Office of the Attorney General, responsible for the Crown Prosecution Service, and the Department for Constitutional Affairs which is responsible for constitutional matters, the appointment and training of judges, and the administration of the courts through the Court Service.

Parliament and the Select Committee on Home Affairs

A system of select committees was introduced in 1979 allowing for committees of the House of Commons to monitor the work of government departments. The aim was to provide a forum by which parliamentary committees could monitor and scru-tinise the work of government departments. The Select Committee on Home Affairs has over the years held public hearings and issued reports on a number of criminal justice topics such as improving the machinery for investigating complaints against the police (1981), administration of the prison service (1981) and the state and use of prisons (1987). Similar topics have been revisited over time: police disciplinary codes and complaints procedure (1997–8), and the use of custody in 1998. The committee's agenda is heavily influenced by the legislative proposals and reports of the Home Office. In 2002, it published reports on the Police Reform Bill, the Criminal Justice Bill and the Extradition Bill and produced a report *The Government's Drugs Policy: Is it Working?* In 2003, it published reports on the Sexual Offences Bill and the Asylum and Immigration (Treatment of Claimants, etc.) Bill. In 2004 it reported on asylum applications and conducted an inquiry into the Government's proposal to introduce a national system of identity cards. It also returned once again to a topic that has arisen several times since 1979 and is no doubt related to the activities of the pressure groups such as NACRO, that is the rehabilitation of prisoners and the effectiveness of prisons in reducing re-offending.

The committee can ask interested witnesses to give evidence before it and senior civil servants and agency heads may also be required to give evidence. The 1997 inquiry into police disciplinary codes and complaints procedure heard evidence from Paul Condon, the Metropolitan Police Commissioner, Barbara Mills, head of the Crown Prosecution Service, as well as from the Police Federation, Police Superintendents' Association, Police Complaints Authority, and the pressure group Liberty. In 1997 Frederick Crawford, chairman of the new Criminal Cases Review Commission, gave evidence about the work of the commission, and the then Lord Chancellor, Lord Irvine, gave evidence about the work of the Lord Chancellor's Department. The committee can set its own agenda and may develop its own particular perspective on issues. Its prison reductionist agenda has been apparent for some time regardless of the party in government. In 1998 the committee inquired into the use of custody and alternatives to prison sentences with the aim of seeking 'to reduce the prison population' (Home Affairs Committee, Press Notice, 31 July 1997).

In January 1998 the committee published a critical report of the existing procedure for dealing with complaints against the police, outlined in Chapter 6. Its 43 recommendations included proposals to improve the system of dealing with corruption by police officers and to reform the complaints and disciplinary system. The report sought a change to the rules in disciplinary hearings involving police officers, moving away from the existing standard of proof, beyond reasonable doubt, as used in criminal court cases, to the civil court standard based on the balance of probabilities. Furthermore, at present an officer acquitted in a criminal case will not face subsequent disciplinary charges. While open to criticism on the ground of double jeopardy the report recommended the possibility of further action when an officer is found not guilty in court. Other recommendations related to holding disciplinary meetings in public and making it easier to sack police officers guilty of serious misconduct. The Home Secretary accepted the report and produced reforms to the way the police complaints and disciplinary system works (see Chapter 6).

Established parliamentary lobby groups also work within Westminster. The Parliamentary All-Party Penal Affairs Group (PAPPAG) started in 1979 and is aided by a clerk, Paul Cavadino, who worked as the senior information officer for NACRO.

This lobby group has led the prison reductionist argument in Parliament with considerable success. For example, the introduction of statutory criteria for the use of custody for those under 21 in the Criminal Justice Act 1982 led to a substantial drop in the use of custody for offenders under 21. Other campaigns have not been so successful such as attempts to reform the mandatory life sentence for murder. Reformers have persuaded Parliament to take a lead on some criminal justice issues such as the abolition of the death penalty against the wishes of the majority of the voting public. Since the Murder (Abolition of the Death Penalty) Act 1965, the House of Commons has held 14 debates and votes between 1969 and 1994 and each time there was a clear majority against the restoration of capital punishment. Public opinion has consistently shown about a 70 to 30 per cent divide in favour of the death penalty, but, despite this, MPs have consistently voted against its restoration. This is possibly because the government of the day has not regarded this issue as a matter of government or party political policy but left it to a 'free vote' in which MPs are asked to follow their conscience.

4.2 GOVERNMENT AND ADMINISTRATION

Home Office

The Home Office is the single most important government department with respect to criminal justice policy. As a source of ideas and funding, its role is pivotal in determining reforms of the criminal law and the direction of criminal justice policy. The Home Office has responsibilities for the police, prisons, probation, reviewing the criminal law, crime prevention and victim support. It has other non-criminal duties regarding the fire service, immigration control, dangerous dogs, national security, licensing of gambling and sales of alcohol, passports and applications for British citizenship.

While it is wrong to suggest that there is only one source of influence on criminal justice policy in England and Wales, the Home Office is the government agency with an overall view of the system. Issues of public confidence in the system of justice in terms of effectiveness, efficiency and fairness would normally be regarded as the responsibility of the Home Office, although the Lord Chancellor's Department and the Attorney General have an interest in such matters.

The Home Office has responsibilities regarding the criminal justice system in the following areas:

- legislative reform of the criminal law;
- public safety and responding to public disasters;
- sentencing policy;
- policy, funding, training and the efficiency of the police service, including setting performance indicators and vetting senior appointments;
- policy for the probation and prison services;
- forensic services (an executive agency of the Home Office since 1991);

- appointments to the Parole Board and responding to its recommendations about the release of those sentenced to over 4 years and those serving life sentences for release on licence;

- appointment of the Prisons and Probation Ombudsman;

- exercising the prerogative of mercy;

- dealing with foreign jurisdictions on matters of common policy, for example Europol, and individual decisions regarding the extradition of suspects and the transfer of convicted prisoners;

- mentally disordered persons subject to restriction orders;

- producing annual statistics on the work of the criminal justice agencies and commissioning and conducting research into policy developments;

- providing information to Parliament in response to parliamentary questions about activities under its control and providing information for government inquiries and Royal Commissions on criminal justice topics;

- promoting crime prevention policy;

- funding Victim Support schemes;

- conducting the British Crime Survey.

The responsibilities and duties of the Home Office have changed over time. For example, the administration and control of prisons between 1877 and 1963 was the responsibility of the Prison Commission. In 1964 prisons came under the direct control of the Prison Department in the Home Office. The Permanent Secretary at the Home Office at that time, Charles Cunningham, believed the advantage of amalgamating the prison service into the Home Office was that it would bring the key law enforcement and crime control agencies under one roof to allow for a more integrated approach to crime prevention and permit better planning of the forces available to the state to combat crime. The idea of coordinating the work of criminal justice agencies and involving the voluntary and business communities in multi-agency approaches will be discussed later in this chapter, and it is clear that in the 1980s the Home Office gave a lead on this issue in the field of crime prevention.

However, by the 1990s it was also clear that government was attempting to devolve and diversify responsibilities for the day-to-day running of criminal justice agencies and the courts. In 1993 the prison service became an executive agency. This signalled the beginning of a fundamental change in the administration of powers and budgets and management responsibilities.

Home Secretary

The Home Secretary, one of the major political figures in government, is responsible for promoting criminal law reform and has a general responsibility for the criminal justice system. During the 18-year period of Conservative governments, from 1979 to 1997, influential figures were appointed to the post: William Whitelaw, Leon Brittan, Douglas Hurd, David Waddington, Kenneth Baker, Kenneth Clarke and Michael Howard. In 1997, Jack Straw became the first Labour Party Home Secretary since Merlyn Rees in 1979, followed by David Blunkett in 2001. It is a demanding office to hold, and regarded as potentially disastrous for those who have further political ambitions, despite being one of the three great Offices of State, along with the Chancellor of the Exchequer and the Foreign Secretary. Only two twentieth-century Home Secretaries, Winston Churchill (1910–11) and Jim Callaghan (1967–70), went on to become Prime Minister.

Some of the momentum for reforms that laid the foundations for new agencies in the system of criminal justice came from influential nineteenth-century Home Secretaries. Robert Peel (1822–7 and 1928–30) played a vital role in the foundation of the Metropolitan Police Force. Lord Palmerston (1852–5) introduced a number of penal reforms during his period at the Home Office, abolishing transportation and substituting the sentence of penal servitude (The Penal Servitude Act 1853), and introducing reform schools (The Reformatory Schools Act 1854). Palmerston's responsibilities on matters of policing meant that a political row blew up when the political refugee Louis Kossuth was exiled to London. He was a radical who led the independence movement to free the Magyars from the Austrian Empire. His activities were investigated by plain-clothed policemen and he was implicated in a plot to manufacture arms and send them to Hungary for use in an uprising. Parliamentary questions, threats of prosecution and press coverage, particularly in *The Times*, led to the type of high-profile public controversy that most Home Secretaries can expect to cope with.

Home Secretaries are vulnerable to the type of political rows that get front page press coverage. They are expected to respond to public disquiet following major crime stories such as those about Jack the Ripper in 1880 or Peter Sutcliffe in Yorkshire a century later. Murders particularly attract media coverage, no more so than when the victims are numerous (Fred and Rosemary West) or vulnerable, such as patients murdered by their doctor (Harold Shipman), or are children (Thompson and Venables; and Ian Huntley). Very emotive issues have to be considered, such as claims for the restoration of the death penalty, deaths in custody, and appropriate responses following miscarriages of justice, corruption within the police force, disasters such as those at Hillsborough and Dunblane, prison escapes such as those by the Great Train Robber Ronnie Biggs, the KGB spy George Blake and IRA terrorists. They also have to consider what to do with terrorist or murder suspects who are wanted for crimes in jurisdictions where they are likely to receive the death penalty. The European Convention bars extradition of those who might be executed. So when the radical Muslim cleric Abu Hamza Al-Mazri was arrested by police acting on US extradition order for terrorism-related charges ie helping al-Qaeda – the UK could not surrender him if the death penalty was a possibility. Such issues of great moral concern and public interest require the Home Secretary to provide leadership at times of heightened public anxiety about the safety of UK citizens from both domestic and overseas threats. In addition to the potential political rows following major crime and related incidents, the Home Secretary has a minefield to tread in the area of civil liberties. Unlike other government departments where the minister is responsible for the broad issues of policy, the Home Secretary has discretionary powers to make decisions affecting individuals in a number of ways, such as in deportation cases.

The Home Secretary exercises the prerogative of mercy on matters of reprieves and pardons. In the period before the death penalty was abolished in 1965, the Home Secretary made decisions as to whether to reprieve condemned persons or let them hang. Chuter Ede, the Home Secretary in 1950, decided that the case against Timothy Evans was strong enough to allow him to hang for the murder of his wife and daughter. A later Home Secretary in 1966, Roy Jenkins, decided that a posthumous pardon was the right course of action, given the possibility of the involvement of John Reginald Christie who lived at the same address as Evans and was subsequently hanged for the murder of at least six women whose bodies were found in the house at 10 Rillington Place in 1953. There were many other high-profile cases involving the death penalty and much subsequent public discussion and disquiet, particularly in the cases of Derek Bentley, James Hanratty and Ruth Ellis. Ellis was the last woman to be hanged in this country on 13 July 1955, provoking the headline in the *Daily Mirror*, 'Should Hanging be Stopped?'

Despite its abolition, death penalty cases continue to involve the Home Secretary and in 1992 Kenneth Clarke announced that he had rejected the application for a posthumous pardon for Derek Bentley who was hanged aged 19 in 1953 for the murder of PC Sydney Miles. Bentley and an accomplice, Christopher Craig, had broken into a warehouse in Tamworth Road, Croydon. They had been seen climbing over the gate and the police were alerted. As the murder was a joint enterprise, the execution was legal although by today's standards considered harsh as Craig, who was by law too young at 16 to be executed, had pulled the trigger that had killed the police officer. Craig was released from prison in 1963 but the campaign by Bentley's sister to get him pardoned continued and the case was submitted to the newly formed Criminal Cases Review Commission in 1997 and was heard by the Court of Appeal in 1998 when the conviction was overturned.

Department for Constitutional Affairs

The Department for Constitutional Affairs (DCA) emerged in June 2003 not so much as a fully fledged Department of Justice as is found in the United States of America and Europe but as a consequence of a number of influences, one of which was the desire to reform the office and role of the Lord Chancellor. Announced as part of a cabinet reshuffle, the new Department was given the task of taking on responsibility for constitutional matters as well as the work of everyday matters concerning the judiciary: the appointment of new judges and overseeing the effectiveness and efficiency of the courts. The new department provided part of the answer to the problem of a Lord Chancellor who combined many roles: head of the judiciary, senior member of the executive with a place in the Cabinet, and a role equivalent to the Speaker in the House of Commons. In short the role brought together an office holder who was at one and the same time a key player in the judicial, executive and legislative branches of government. With European jurisprudence in mind and the principle of the 'separation of powers' it is thought desirable for the protection of liberty that the three aspects of government be kept clearly demarcated as they are in the constitution of the United States of America. Reform of the Lord Chancellor's Office also reflected New Labour's wish to be seen as a modernising party willing to forsake English tradition in the cause of efficiency, fairness and innovation. Lord Irvine, Lord Chancellor from 1997 to 2003, had also been presented in the press and by the Opposition as controversial, especially on matters of choice of wallpaper and salary increases.

The first head of the DCA, Lord Falconer, combines the offices of Secretary of State for Constitutional Affairs and Lord Chancellor. His role is to reform the administration of the courts system in line with the Courts Act 2003 whereby the old Petty Sessions and Magistrates' Courts Committees are abolished with the creation of a single, unified court service in England and Wales. Responsibility for the magistrates' courts is no longer to be with the Home Office. The DCA will play its part in working alongside the Home Office, Immigration Appellate Authority and the Legal Service Commission, which administers civil legal aid. A major reform which is part of the DCA's workload will be to set up an independent Judicial Appointments Commission for appointment of judges, free from the claim that they are political appointments.

The DCA also has broader responsibility for matters of constitutional reform. To meet the separation of powers principle the DCA will be responsible for creating a new Supreme Court to replace the system whereby the current Law Lords no longer operate as a committee of the House of Lords. Thus the DCA, although established with little consultation and out of a desire to meet many demands for change, has been given the task of reforming the Lord Chancellor's Department and identifying the residual powers of the Lord Chancellor, a post not yet abolished, so that the tasks of government may be carried out with a clear demarcation between the powers of government, Parliament and the judiciary.

In the next section we will explore the political dimensions and context of the representation and polarisation of opinion around matters of crime and justice in England and Wales.

4.3 POLITICAL CONTEXT

Politics

Policy cannot be divorced from politics and crime is a salient issue on the political agenda in the United Kingdom. As seen in the earlier section of this chapter, the Home Secretary plays a high-profile role in the politics of law and order and in influencing policy developments. Politicians quite properly talk about issues which worry the public and there can be little doubt that crime is a major election topic.

But who do the politicians listen to? We can see from the previous section of this chapter that, on the issue of the restoration of the death penalty, politicians chose to disregard public opinion. However, they cannot completely ignore the public mood among voters and the fact that they can afford to do this at all illustrates the nature of the system of parliamentary government. Political office, and hence influence on decision making, depends on the fortunes of political parties in which voters primarily focus upon deciding which political party they wish to see in office. The democratic process means that politicians are at the centre of a number of influences and ideas about how best to respond to crime.

Politicians can provide leadership on issues such as hanging but will follow the public mood on other matters. They also have to negotiate their position within the party and the annual party conference. Politicians are answerable to their party

activists and even ministers may feel embarrassed by the need to explain themselves and their policies to the annual party conference. William Whitelaw, a
Conservative Party Home Secretary (1979–83), regarded as a liberal on sentencing
matters, wrote that he 'dreaded and disliked the prospect of the law and order
debate, for the atmosphere was so strangely hostile and so different from that
accorded to one's colleagues' (Whitelaw 1989).

There was a time when crime policy was not at the centre of party political disagreement with a cross-party consensus about many aspects of criminal justice
policy, but in the 1950s and 1960s crime issues started becoming more politicised.
There are those who blame right-wing politicians for exploiting the fear of crime
issues by presenting their opponents as soft on crime. Another factor was the level
of public interest in the death penalty. The moves towards abolition in 1957 and
1965 involved parliamentary debates that generated considerable media coverage
and public interest. What it highlighted, of course, was the strong division between
parliamentary opinion as represented by MPs who voted for abolition and the public
who then, as now, wish to retain the death penalty. It seems likely that public
interest in matters of law and order may well have been stimulated initially by the
high profile given to the death penalty debate, as well as by the steady rise in the
recorded crime from 1950 to 1990.

In the 1979 General Election, the Conservative Party was able to represent the
Labour Party as soft on crime and the criminal. (See the poster reproduced in Figure
4.1.) In recent elections the Labour Party has sought to change its image as being
the softer party on matters of crime. In 1994 the Labour Party spokesman for Home
Affairs, Tony Blair, popularised the slogan that a Labour Government would be
'tough on crime and tough on the causes of crime'.

Figure 4.1 Conservative Party publicity on crime in the 1979 General Election

MUGGING UP 204%*
CRIMINAL DAMAGE UP 135%†
ROBBERY UP 88%†

Labour's record on crime is criminal. Crime is one of the few things in Britain that is booming under Labour.

In England and Wales last year, over 800,000 more crimes were recorded than in 1973. That's a rise of almost 50%. And yet since Labour came to power, police strength has risen by a mere 7%.

Perhaps if Labour had been more concerned with creating wealth rather than re-distributing it, they might have found it easier to be able to afford to increase policemen's pay. But it's not just more pay our policemen need.

The Government have a duty to be seen to support law and order, to protect people and property.

It certainly doesn't make the police's job any easier when some Labour Ministers are seen associating themselves with potentially violent situations, as they did at Grunwick last year.

The police are doing a difficult job, in difficult times-and they need the support of all the people-and that includes Government Ministers.

Many policemen feel there's only one way they can make the Government understand their plight.

And that's by leaving the force.

IS IT SAFE TO VOTE FOR ANOTHER LABOUR GOVERNMENT?

VOTE CONSERVATIVE X

*Figure for London between 1973–1977. † Home Office Annual Criminal Statistics for England and Wales between 1973–1977

Political controversy is likely to continue even though the ideological gap between the parties has narrowed dramatically on the issue of crime. There has been, for example, considerable political disagreement over the extent to which rising crime can be attributed to greed or badness on the part of individuals, to family problems or problem families, or whether it is related to wider social factors such as unemployment. The Conservative Party expressed the following view during the 1987 General Election:

> The origins of crime lie deep in society in families where parents do not support or control their children; in schools where discipline is poor and in the wider world where violence is glamourised and traditional values are under attack.

Suggestions of a link between crime and unemployment, poverty or deprivation were dismissed as, in effect, excusing crime. In 1988 Margaret Thatcher commented that:

> If anyone else is to blame it is the professional progressives among broadcasters, social workers and politicians who have created a fog of excuses in which the mugger and burglar operate.
>
> (Loveday 1992: 302)

The link between poverty and crime was rejected in a Conservative Political Centre pamphlet in 1994. David Hunt, the Employment Secretary at the time, wrote:

> some of the so-called cultures springing up in our country reject all decency and civilised values ... the bulk of thieving today, of course, has nothing to do with poverty. It is the result of wickedness and greed.
>
> (*The Guardian*, 21 March 1994)

New Labour and criminal justice reforms

Between 1997 and 2004 the Home Office has launched over 120 consultation papers, introduced 44 bills and commissioned major reviews of the criminal justice system such as the Auld Report on the courts and Halliday on sentencing. Centuries-old traditions have been swept away such as the Petty Session administrative units of the magistrates' courts and the role of the Lord Chancellor. New criminal justice roles have been created, with Police Community Support Officers (PCSOs), Serious Organised Crime Agency, Youth Offender Teams and Community Safety Officers, and initiatives to combat crime from neighbourhood curfews, anti-social behaviour orders and parenting orders. New bodies have been established such as the Sentencing Guidelines Council and the Youth Justice Board. The names of community penalties have been changed at least twice with a probation order becoming a community rehabilitation order in 2000 and under the CJA 2003 becoming a community order with supervision requirements. Proposals were made in 2003/4 to change prisons and probation to Correctional Services and subsequently to the National Offender Management Service.

Today the political spectrum is changing so that the 'right wing tough on crime, and left wing soft on crime' polarity no longer applies. No one would regard New Labour as soft on crime with record numbers being sent to prison. David Blunkett's views on crime and asylum seekers do not match the old Labour Home Secretaries' such as Roy Jenkins who introduced laws perceived as liberal, with laws on abortion, abolition of the death penalty, and homosexuality. New Labour can claim liberal credentials by its introduction of data protection and freedom of information laws, the Human Rights Act 1998, the reclassification of some Class B drugs and the speed with which it complies, unlike other European Governments, with rulings from the European Court of Human Rights. The left–right model on responses to crime no longer applies.

Is this capacity for reform and the pace of innovations a result of change for its own sake or to achieve a new approach to criminal justice? We will present two views about New Labour and the nature of all this change and whether it results in a fairer and more effective system of justice or whether it demonstrates confused and undirected change in the quest for modernisation.

Tony Blair's vision for dealing with crime is spelt out in his speech to the Labour Party conference 2002:

'Partnership is also citizenship for the 21st Century.

I don't have the toughest job in Government. David Blunkett does.

On asylum, where big reform is needed urgently.

And on crime.

I still hear from time to time this nonsense that crime is not a real Labour issue, and all we have to do is deliver on poverty and opportunity.

Of course we have to do that.

But try telling a 92 year old pensioner, a Labour supporter for the last 70 years, that she'll have to wait for the Tories to get tough on the young thugs who battered her. That's not a conversation I'm prepared to have.

. . .

We're the first Government since the war under which crime has fallen not risen. Does that reassure everyone?

No.

There is less of a chance today of being a victim of crime than at any time for 20 years. Does everyone believe it?

No.

We have increased the numbers of police to record numbers, toughened the law on everything from rape to benefit fraud. Does that mean everyone feels safer?

No.

Why? Because the problem is not just crime. It is disrespect. It is anti-social behaviour. It is the drug dealer at the end of the street and no-one seems to be able to do anything about it.

This is not only about crime.

It is about hard-working families who play the rules seeing those who don't, getting away with it.

The street crime initiative has been one of the most successful exercises in partnership between Government and police in living memory. Not my words, but those of the Chief Constables.

But what was fascinating was not the initiative itself, but what it uncovered.

Outdated identity parades taking weeks if not months to organise.

Defendants who didn't answer to their bail and never got punished for it. Police officers told it was a breach of civil liberties to check whether defendants were obeying bail conditions.

It's not civil liberties.

It's lunacy.

Drug addicts with previous offences routinely bailed though everyone knew what they would be doing between bail and trial.

Magistrates unable to remand persistent young offenders in custody because no places existed in prison or secure accommodation.

The whole system full of excellent people, worn down and worn out.

Step by step David and his team, working with the police, are putting it right.

. . .

For 100 years, our Criminal Justice System like our welfare system was based on a messy compromise between liberals and authoritarians.

The liberals tended to view crime as primarily about social causes and the welfare system primarily about giving to the poor.

The authoritarians wanted harsh penalties and as ungenerous a benefit system as possible.

The compromise was a Criminal Justice System weighted in favour of the defendant but with harsh penalties for the convicted; and a passive welfare system with mean benefits.

In short, the worst of all worlds.

In its place, a new contract between citizen and community.

We give opportunity to all.

We demand responsibility from all.'

(Speech by Tony Blair, Prime Minister,
Labour Party Conference, Blackpool, October 2002)

A contrasting analysis of the nature of change under New Labour is provided in the following extract by Andrew Rawnsley about the proposals set out in the Queen's Speech on the legislative agenda for Parliament in 2002/3.

Never mind the quality, feel the quantity

'Measured in one crude way, this government has been an exceedingly busy government. Indeed, it has been a hyper-active government, even a manic government. In the last parliamentary session – not many people know this – Ministers broke all records by passing into law more pages of legislation than in any previous session. At the Charter 88/Observer conference on democracy last weekend, Robin Cook predicted that his Stakhanovite Cabinet colleagues would set another new record for output in the next legislative shift.

Whether you are impressed by the volume of the words they disgorge on to the statute book depends on whether you think government should be celebrated for its quantity rather than its quality. Mr Cook, even though the Leader of the House is foreman of the law factory, seemed to harbour his own doubts about whether the best laws are thick laws.

...

The self-proclaimed themes of this Queen's Speech will be reform of public services and cracking down on crime. Where have we heard that before? We have heard it in every other speech that Tony Blair has put into the mouth of his regal ventriloquist's dummy. What does change from year to year is what they mean by public service reform. Sometimes, the shifts are of emphasis as Ministers jump from promoting one initiative to another...

...

The most gargantuan deluge of new legislation will spew forth from David Blunkett's fiefdom – yet again. Having hogged parliamentary time in the last session, the Home Office will do the same again in this session, as it has in so many parliamentary sessions over the past 20 years.

I suppose it's not surprising that the department of law enforcement is so pathological about wanting to give itself more and more laws to enforce. What it finds acutely challenging is creating laws that actually work. For the construction of legislation which is useless, the Home Office is the most serial offender in Whitehall.

I wish Mr Blunkett luck with his latest slew of legislation designed to reduce antisocial behaviour. The antisocial behaviour orders, announced in their time with as much fanfare as will be the new crackdown on people who drop chewing gum on the pavement, have not been deployed in anything like the numbers Ministers hoped for.

The number of drug abstinence orders used by the courts can be counted on the fingers of one hand – two hands, at best. The number of child curfews imposed since they became law can be counted on the fingers of a man with no hands. One of the very earliest anti-crime measures passed by this government was three strikes and you're out (in non-baseball language, three offences and you're jailed). This promised an automatic prison sentence for repeat offending burglars. No court has ever used it.

The Government is so frantically creating new powers that Ministers neglect to ask themselves whether those powers are usable by those to whom they are given. Ministers have had to hand over the mental health legislation to a standing committee of MPs from whom it will eventually emerge in much shrivelled form. Only belatedly has it been grasped that the power to detain mentally ill people who are suspected of being dangerous can't be used if psychiatrists won't co-operate with identifying the suspects.

(*The Observer*, 10 November, 2002: Copyright Guardian Newspapers Limited 2002)

Pressure and interest groups

Political parties are not the only representative groups to engage in debates about crime. A number of other bodies representing professional interests also contribute to discussions of crime policy. They may participate officially in Royal Commissions, appear on current affairs programmes or contribute newspaper articles. These bodies include, as we stated earlier in the chapter, the Police Federation, ACPO, NAPO, POA, the Bar Council, the Law Society, and the Justices' Clerks Society. Voluntary groups such as the Magistrates' Association and Victim Support also contribute in this way.

Pressure groups also have an important role in shaping attitudes about penal policy. The Howard League for Penal Reform, the Prison Reform Trust and the National Association for the Care and Resettlement of Offenders (NACRO) have played a key role in changing opinions. NACRO, for example, carries out research, sponsors projects, runs conferences and provides much useful information to its members, along with schools, colleges, journalists, policy makers, politicians and academics. NACRO aims to ensure that the case for improved prison conditions and less frequent use of custodial sentences is put effectively both in Parliament and in the mass media.

In a study of the impact of pressure groups on penal policy, Ryan (1978) describes the history of the Howard League and the considerable influence exercised by its representatives Margery Fry and George Benson MP, during the 1950s and 1960s, in Whitehall and Westminister. It was an acceptable pressure group: reliable, practical and trusted. In contrast, Ryan outlines the fate of RAP (Radical Alternatives to Prison), which did not have status as an acceptable pressure group in its campaign to abolish all prisons. The differences in resources, contacts, access and the degree of ideological congruence between lobbyist and officials are important if a group is to have an influence on public policy.

The mass media has considerable influence on the way policies are presented. The opportunity for making political gains is evident if a good sound bite or slogan can be found. In the 1979 General Election campaign the Conservative Party, on advice from Saatchi and Saatchi, ran a poster campaign on the theme of crime and whether it was safe to vote for Jim Callaghan's Labour Government. The poster, shown in Figure 4.1, made use of official statistics to highlight the growth of mugging, robbery and criminal damage.

Media

Some people find out about crime and form views on the basis of their own experiences or those of their family, friends or neighbours. In large part, however, their views are also influenced by information in newspapers or on television. This may include coverage of individual cases, and some may follow discussions on crime by politicians and commentators.

Most people are influenced to some extent by the mass media – newspapers, television, books or films. This is because the majority of the public have limited first-hand knowledge about crime or the criminal justice system unless they are victims or perpetrators. Newspapers and television coverage of crime stories will influence people's knowledge about crime and may enhance their fear of becoming a victim. Media coverage in itself may affect people's behaviour – women and the elderly, for example, are often scared to walk the streets at night for fear of being raped or mugged, and parents may be frightened to let their children out of the house alone through fear of kidnapping, sexual assault or murder.

Crime is, of course, a popular subject in the mass media and, as many point out, crime, especially sexual crime, sells newspapers (see, for example, Schlesinger and Tumber 1994; Soothill and Walby 1991). Crime dramas are also extremely popular, as seen in the high ratings given to TV detectives such as Inspectors Morse, Taggart, Wexford or Barnaby. Few, of course, believe that drama gives a real picture of crime or policing – otherwise the murder rate in Oxford, Glasgow, Kingsmarkham or Midsomer Common would be the subject of national concern and police clear-up rates would be vastly improved!

A new type of television documentary such as Crime Watch UK has become popular in recent years in which the police provide information and CCTV photographs to encourage the public to telephone in with information about crimes and suspects. Police videos are broadcast on television that show drivers at their worst, as in Police, Camera, Action! Thus information blends with entertainment.

High-profile cases provide a fascination that might be untypical and could lead people to draw general conclusions based on limited knowledge gleaned from such cases as the trials of Ian Huntley and Maxine Carr. They, Derek Bentley and Myra Hindley have become household names because of the interest taken by the mass media. But the focus on these selective and unusual cases may not provide for a reliable impression of the crime problem. This selectivity means that a very unrepresentative picture of crime may be given by the media. From all the possible news stories about crime, the media can select only a small number. This selection will depend on decisions as to whether or not such stories are newsworthy. What makes a story newsworthy is likely to be its novelty or dramatic elements. Thus cases reported in newspapers are likely to be unusual or have elements capable of providing drama or titillation (Chibnall 1977; Soothill and Walby 1991). Most researchers would appear to agree, for example, that sexual and violent crimes, which play on the public's fear, are more likely to be reported than more common kinds of crime such as theft or vandalism (Ditton and Duffy 1983). In addition, these kinds of crime are also selectively reported with an overemphasis on, for example, serial killers or rapists (Soothill 1993). Many have argued that the reporting of rape tends to focus on the 'sex fiend' who attacks women in public places, whereas in reality women are more likely to be raped in private places, by people they know (Soothill 1993).

Newspaper reports also tend to simplify crime stories, providing little by way of extended analysis (Schlesinger and Tumber 1994). News reports about crimes are necessarily abbreviated accounts of events, focusing on those aspects considered likely to attract the public's attention. This is also the case when the criminal statistics are reported. Although these are complex documents requiring careful interpretation, reports in the media tend to focus on simple questions about whether some kinds of crime have risen or fallen.

The media may also set in train what is called a moral panic about a particular kind of crime (Cohen 1980). This happens where a spectacular incident or series of incidents – for example, a riot, a series of child abuse cases, or someone being killed by joyriders – alerts the public to a particular problem. The media may effectively create a new form of crime, as the example of 'road rage' demonstrates. 'Road rage' was a term coined to describe violent incidents between motorists triggered by a dispute over such things as parking, driving styles or accidents.

The press are blamed by some criminologists for generating public anxiety in order to sell newspapers. However, many of these stories are newsworthy not just because they are printed in the papers but because they capture a fascination about a bizarre or horrific event that would be in itself of public interest. Deviancy, as the sociologist Emile Durkheim pointed out, provides a community with a concrete example of unacceptable and censored behaviour and thus gives a collective focus to re-evaluate and rethink its values. The press might also justify their coverage as campaigning newspapers when the criminal justice system appears to let victims down or wrongly convicts an innocent person. Campaigning programmes on the television and reports in the press have helped to clear innocent people and convict guilty ones. Frustration with the lack of action in the murder inquiry following the death of the black teenager Stephen Lawrence, discussed in Chapter 6, led the *Daily Mail* to take the unprecedented step of printing the names of five men they believed responsible for his death under the headline, 'Murderers'. The *Daily Mail* commented:

> We are naming them because, despite a criminal case, a private prosecution and an inquest, there has still been no justice for Stephen. . . . One or more of the five may have a valid defence to the charge which has been repeatedly levelled against them. So far they have steadfastly refused every opportunity to offer such a defence.
>
> (*Daily Mail*, 14 February 1997: 1)

4.4 'GLOBALISATION': CROSS-JURISDICTIONAL AND INTERNATIONAL RESPONSES TO CRIME

The nightmare pictures of aeroplanes flying into the World Trade Centre, killing 3,000 civilians in New York City and Washington, DC on 11 September 2001 meant the beginning of the twenty-first century has seen a growing consciousness of the global threat of crime. The global terrorist threat is not the only concern as the potential for Internet-based fraud becomes more apparent and the networks of organised crime from Russia to China operate on a worldwide scale to illegally move drugs, weapons and people around in a world where there is greater mobility and opportunities to exploit. Free movement of people in the enlarged European Union means that criminals have a wider market to deal in and more places to hide both themselves and their assets.

In response a number of regional and world developments have emerged and a greater insight into both the nature of crime and of other criminal justice systems as law enforcement agencies try to share information, and attempt to harmonise with and accommodate each other's systems and procedures. International agreements on extradition and cooperation between jurisdictions was evident after September 2002.

The mood of interdependency was captured in a speech by the Prime Minister, Tony Blair:

The paradox of the modern world is this:
We've never been more interdependent in our needs; and
We've never been more individualist in our outlook.
Globalisation and technology open up vast new opportunities but also cause massive insecurity.

...

Interdependence is obliterating the distinction between foreign and domestic policy.
It was the British economy that felt the aftermath of 11 September.
Our cities who take in refugees from the 13 million now streaming across the world from famine, disease or conflict.
Our young people who die from heroin imported from Afghanistan.
It is our climate that is changing.

...

Interdependence is the core reality of the modern world.
It is revolutionising our idea of national interest.
It is forcing us to locate that interest in the wider international community.

(Speech by Tony Blair, Prime Minister,
Labour Party conference, Blackpool, October 2002)

International cooperation

One reform that preceded the terrorist attack on the United States of America in 2001 came about as a result of world abhorrence at the genocide in Rwanda and Kosovo. This led to the foundation of the International Criminal Court (ICC). This will be a permanent court, situated in The Hague, to try individuals for genocide, crimes against humanity and war crimes. Not all countries have agreed to be subject to the ICC but the United Kingdom did with the passing of the International Criminal Court Act 2001. The Act provides for international cooperation in terms of identifying, arresting and extraditing suspects, collecting evidence; and it enables cooperation with ICC investigations into the proceeds of crimes.

The Anti-terrorism, Crime and Security Act 2001 established new powers to: cut off terrorist funding; allow government departments and agencies to collect and share information required for countering the terrorist threat; streamline relevant immigration procedures; protect the security of the nuclear and aviation industries; improve the security of dangerous substances that may be targeted or used by terrorists; and enhance powers when detainees in police custody refuse to cooperate with the police as to their identity.

Other forms of cooperation include bilateral agreements between two countries to combat crime and these indicate the greater cross-jurisdictional awareness among governments of the need to cooperate to deal with a problem that is not restricted within national boundaries. Successful criminals have exploited the differences in the law and legal procedures to avoid detection or, if discovered, prosecution.

Bilateral international cooperation has been given a lead by the United States of America. The UK/USA Drugs Agreement of 1988 provides for cooperation in the investigation of drug-trafficking offences, the freezing and confiscation of the proceeds of drug-related crimes, providing for the exchange of documents and banking evidence, allows for the transfer of prisoners with their consent to give evidence, and carrying out requests to search and seize property. On 27 February 1997 Poland and the United Kingdom signed a mutual cooperation agreement to work together to deal with the illegal distribution of weapons, drugs and organised crime. This allows for swifter extradition orders, intelligence gathering on illegal arms and drug sales and powers to confiscate the proceeds of crime that have been moved between the jurisdictions. Poland signed a similar agreement with the United States in 1996.

International cooperation involved the Forensic Science Service (FSS) conducting DNA tests in 1992 in response to the Russian Government's approach to check the remains of a group of people, thought to be those of the Romanov family, the Russian royal family that disappeared, presumed murdered, on the night of 16 July 1918, or soon after. Using bone material the FSS concluded that the DNA test supports the view that the family found in the mass grave was the Romanovs.

International cooperation is increasingly evident between the 176 member countries of Interpol. Within the National Criminal Intelligence Service (NCIS), Customs and Excise manage a network of Drugs Liaison officers (DLOs) who work with their counterparts in Europe and around the world. The success of the policing of Euro 96, when between one-quarter and half a million foreign football supporters came to England, was due in part to the role played by the NCIS who helped to plan the policing of this event by putting together a team of experts on football hooliganism from different forces across the country, and liaison officers from each of the competing countries, as well as relying on information from Interpol.

The NCIS will also be involved in the efforts to combat international crime gangs, which were set out in the White Paper, *One Step Ahead: A 21st Century Strategy to Defeat Organised Criminals* (2004). The paper contains details about the Serious Organised Crime Agency (SOCA), announced by the Home Secretary in February 2004. SOCA will have hi-tech and financial specialists; new powers are proposed to combat criminal activity; and there is discussion of ways to make better use of existing legislation such as tax, immigration and planning laws.

4.5 EUROPEAN INFLUENCES ON CRIMINAL JUSTICE POLICY

The European Union in 2004 expanded to a total of 25 states with the accession of the Czech Republic, Estonia, Cyprus, Latvia, Lithuania, Hungary, Malta, Poland, Slovenia and Slovakia. The increasing interdependency of the European states has meant that many policy developments are no longer the sole responsibility of Parliament in the United Kingdom; and today policy is shaped by a need to take account of other jurisdictions, most notably those in the European Union. Apart from the gradual process of European harmonisation, the exploitation of relaxed border controls and new forms of crime have prompted the governments of Europe to take initiatives to combat cross-jurisdictional crimes such as drug trafficking and international fraud. Cross-jurisdictional cooperation has become essential given the limitations of crime policy based on the nation state and its restricted geographical boundaries.

Countries take it in turn to hold the presidency of the European Union for a 6-month period and crime issues feature large in the rhetoric of each country's agenda for the period. Jack Straw, as Home Secretary, declared that, 'Organised crime is no respecter of borders and it is crucial that we recognise that reality' (*Daily Telegraph*, 29 December 1997: 2). The areas of primary concern were identified as paedophiles, drug trafficking, money laundering, electronic fraud, and industrial and political espionage. Priority was given to improving arrangements for the extradition of suspects, introducing video links to interview suspects and witnesses, and greater powers to intercept messages sent via the Internet, referring to the cyber-criminals such as terrorist groups and paedophiles who use modern technology, especially coded e-mail messages, to organise their criminal activity.

In 1995 all members of the European Union agreed to the establishment of Europol. The United Kingdom became the first country in the European Union to ratify the Europol Convention in December 1996, which provided for a pan-European law enforcement organisation for the exchange and analysis of crime intelligence responsible for drug trafficking, unregulated dealing in nuclear and radioactive substances, illegal immigrant smuggling, motor vehicle crime and terrorism.

In January 1997 Michael Howard, the Home Secretary, met the Russian Interior Minister in Moscow to discuss greater co-operation to deal with organised crime. He commented:

> Serious, dangerous criminals do not respect national borders. ... Organised criminals run their operations across the whole of Europe, including Russia. We need to find their ring-leaders and bring them to justice. The UK has helped set up Europol – for the exchange and analysis of criminal intelligence which will help catch and convict international villains.
>
> (Home Office press release, 25 January 1997)

The Crime (International Cooperation) Act 2003 implements police and judicial cooperation between EU countries in response to the attacks of 11 September 2001, with the purpose of ensuring that all EU member states have effective terrorist legislation in place. There is also agreement regarding a database storing criminal information from all participating countries and procedures for sharing banking information and tracing illegal money. On another level is the mutual recognition of driving disqualifications so that motorists resident in one member state of the European Union who are disqualified from driving in another member state will also be disqualified in their state of residence.

Another aim is the approximation of the laws and regulations of the member states, which means in the future there will be other EU-wide agreements and cooperation, and where possible the harmonisation of laws as is currently the case with crimes concerning counterfeiting the Euro.

4.6 IMPLEMENTING CRIMINAL JUSTICE POLICY

Coordinating criminal justice

Developments within the international community to improve cooperation on matters of crime have helped bring attention to the need to do more to promote better coordination within the criminal justice system in England and Wales. This has many parts and, like the 12 blind men describing different parts of the elephant (see Preface to second edition), has many different agencies with distinctive functions and styles of operating. This fragmentation leads to 'discorrespondence' in two senses of the word: in that agencies do not always communicate effectively with each other; and that the work of different agencies does not always fit together to provide for an efficient system. The origins of the fragmentation are complex and are concerned with the distinctive constitutional, political and cultural histories of the agencies and professions, each having a unique agenda of interests and concerns. The judiciary in England and Wales come from a strong profession with deep traditional roots that are well embedded in the system of power and influence in this country. Thus when issues of policy such as a proposal for a sentencing commission is perceived as threatening the independence of the judiciary we can be sure that much pressure will be brought to reformulate the proposal. Traffic wardens, in contrast, do not have this degree of influence.

Coordination between agencies has also been a problem because of the principles inherent in our adversarial system, which puts the offender in centre stage with defence counsel and probation officers taking a pro-defendant line and the police and prosecutors doing their best to convict the accused. The combative nature of the contest encourages strategies among the participants, such as appealing to prejudice, lack of frankness regarding the facts, and undermining the confidence of a witness, which may have more to do with winning the case rather than discovering the truth, with public interest and justice sometimes taking second place. Different working cultures add to the difficulties of getting better cooperation between the agencies.

Until the 1950s governments took an interest in but did not seek directly to intervene on routine matters best left to judges and other professional groups. A more interventionist role for government on matters of crime control was revealed in the White Paper, *Penal Practice in a Changing Society*, published in 1959:

> The Government's responsibility does not end with ensuring that the efficiency of the police is maintained and that the courts are equipped with adequate machinery. Behind these front lines of defence the counter-attack on crime must be mounted. It is to the development of the means of dealing with the individual offender who has been sentenced by the courts to some form of detention that this Paper is principally directed.
>
> (Home Office 1959: s. 16)

It has fallen to the Home Office to take on the task of organising and planning an approach to crime control that is more comprehensive than maintaining law-enforcement agencies and punishment options. This task involves the need to develop strategies at a number of levels, provide adequate funding and, most diffi-cult to achieve, coordination between the differing agencies involved both on the 'front line' and in the 'counter-attack on crime'.

Since Leon Brittan's period at the Home Office (1983–5) there has been a more concerted effort to generate greater attention to inter-agency consultation and regard for the general objectives of the criminal justice system as a whole. This has involved two developments in which the government has come to take a more central and corporatist role to crime and widened its approach by moving from a reactive to a preventative approach to crime; and, secondly, by taking the initiative to coordinate the activities of the different criminal justice agencies, which because of their own institutional histories have tended to regard themselves as not part of a system.

The problems of coordination are threefold: first, getting agencies performing the same tasks to work together (for example, will the Metropolitan Police cooperate with an investigation originating from the Merseyside Police?); secondly, getting the different agencies in a region to work more cooperatively together (for example, the probation and prison services having an integrated post-release supervision pro-gramme for prisoners before and after release); and, thirdly, ensuring that the regional work of the agencies operates within a framework of priorities that reflect national and, nowadays, internationally established objectives.

One solution to improve the collaboration between the agencies that in the past have worked with different regional areas was to introduce co-terminosity, that is have similar district and regional alignments across all the agencies. To this end the 13 CPS areas were brought into line with the 42 police forces in England and Wales (the London area CPS to cover the work of the Metropolitan and the City of London police).

Awareness of the way that administrative boundaries provide potential hin-drance to crime prevention and investigation is revealed in a survey of 39 police forces in England and Wales: *Tackling Cross Border Crime* (Porter 1997). Its main recommendations were to encourage neighbouring forces to establish collaborative arrangements, such as regional crime groups to share intelligence on crime and criminals, and appointing inter-force liaison officers and joint operation teams.

Another report, *Getting to Grips with Crime – A New Framework for Local Action* (Home Office 1997b), led to a new statutory duty on the local authority to take into account the impact of crime when making decisions on planning, housing, social service and locating schools. The intention is to make the police and local authorities jointly responsible for crime prevention; and the Home Office sets targets for crime reduction. Targets are set and the police and local authorities will be expected to provide leadership for a cooperative community-wide approach to crime (see Chapter 5).

At the national level the *National Criminal Intelligence Service* (NCIS), referred to in Chapter 6, was established in 1992 to coordinate the approaches of law enforcement agencies. It provides nationwide and international intelligence to law enforcement agencies by collecting and analysing information about serious and organised crime. The Police Act 1997 provided for another new agency, *National Crime Squad*, discussed in Chapter 6, to deal with crime across police areas in England and Wales.

The *Criminal Justice Consultative Council* (CJCC) was established in 1991 to promote a greater awareness between agencies of their common purpose. The first recommendation of the Woolf Report on prison unrest in 1990 was the need for closer cooperation between the different parts of the criminal justice system and proposed a national forum and local committees. The CJCC was given the task of improving communications, cooperation and coordination by improving consultation and information sharing. To help to do this it publishes an annual report. It was set up with 23 area committees and membership is drawn from the judiciary, police, social services, criminal justice agencies and government departments. In 1997 the chairman, Lord Justice Rose, said that the CJCC provided a unique opportunity to promote 'a greater awareness between agencies of their common purpose'. It has looked at video evidence, fast-tracking cases involving child witnesses, race issues, and standardising definitions in child abuse cases.

More recent attempts to provide greater coordination is evident in the joined up approach to dealing with offenders. The proposal in 2004 to merge prison and probation services was concerned to deal with the criminal from sentence to resettlement but the merger of two agencies with a history of different traditions and cultures, blending different styles of dealing with offenders has yet to be advised. Another way of achieving a more coordinated approach is to have coterminous boundaries between all the agencies so that a regional police force does not have to deal with different CPS offices and probation regions.

The Courts Act 2003 requires the new Courts Boards to cover the geographical area for which they are responsible, and they should be, wherever possible, coterminous with CJS areas, which are based on areas defined in the Police Act 1996.

Finally, if the agencies are to work better together on common tasks in agreed geographical localities it would also be helpful if they shared common IT systems but this proves to be easier said than done. Common electronic case files was one of the ambitions of the Auld Report, with files being sent onwards from one agency to another. However, attempts to wire up a single agency has proved difficult, as was seen with a huge project to put all the nation's magistrates' courts on one computer system. The cost of the scheme, called Libra, has risen from £146 million to almost £400 million and as yet is not a success.

The Criminal Justice Information Technology (CJIT) unit of the Home Office has been developing an integrated information system to enable criminal justice professionals in criminal justice organisations, defence lawyers and barristers to share electronic case file information in the form of case-specific documents (such as charge sheets), information in other formats (such as video clips) and information of wider interest (such as court listings). These files must be secure and it is also intended to be capable of providing automatic updates (for example, court results) into linked online systems and should allow victims of crime to track the progress of their case.

Lay participation

An unprecedented role in criminal justice in England and Wales is played by unpaid volunteers who contribute in many different ways. There are over 30,000 lay magistrates who play a vital role in pre-trial procedure and in making decisions about guilt and sentencing – seen in Chapter 10. It was seen in Chapter 3 that Victim Support is a charity that provides practical and emotional support to victims of crime. There are special constables and lay visitors (custody visitors) to police stations and independent monitoring boards for each prison. Custody visitors are independent members of the local community appointed by the Police Authority to visit police stations to observe, comment and report on the welfare of people detained in police custody; conditions in which they are held; and the operation of the rules governing their detention.

Independent watchdogs based in all prisons and immigration removal centres will now be known as Independent Monitoring Boards. All prisons and immigration removal centres have boards of volunteers who monitor conditions and report to ministers and the general public. Previously known as Boards of Visitors in prisons and Visiting Committees in Immigration Removal Centres, they are currently constituted by 1,740 volunteers.

Another role for volunteers is as an 'appropriate' adult because of the requirements of the Police and Criminal Evidence Act 1984. This requires an appropriate adult to be present before the police can begin interviewing a young person in custody. Normally this would be a family member to act in this role but for some young people this is not always possible, so volunteer appropriate adults are used. Their role is to ensure that the rights, interests and welfare of young people, aged 10–17 years old, in custody are safeguarded. Appropriate adult volunteers must be aged 18 or over and cannot be employed by the police.

The significance of lay participants has to be understood in terms of a political culture in which society has not wanted to become over-reliant on state functionaries and professional elites. This aspect of civil liberties is often misunderstood by those who question the representativeness of magistrates. They represent decision makers who do not have to take orders from government or follow the strictures of professional interest. They represent the laity and are expected to bring a common sense to the process of decision making. This may not make better decisions but it might at important times represent another point of view independent of the latest orthodoxy as laid down by government or professions.

There are over 30 Independent Monitoring Boards in England and Wales, one for each prison and young offender institution. These were established under the Prison Act 1952, and each has on average 15 lay members who receive no payment. They are independent of the prison service and must provide an annual report to the Home Secretary on the running of the prison; they must visit the prison regularly and hear complaints from prisoners and have a general concern for the treatment of inmates. The report from the Board of Visitors at Whitemoor Prison correctly predicted future security problems before the escape from their maximum security unit in 1994. The 1997 annual report of the Board of Visitors at Wormwood Scrubs Prison referred to allegations of abuse and assaults of inmates by prison officers, leading to the trial and conviction of prison officers. The Chief Inspector of Prisons made an unannounced inspection of Wormwood Scrubs in 1999 and amongst the options in his report was the possibility of closure or privatisation because of the failure to respond to a previous visit and a critical report about the standards in the prison.

Lay or custody visitors to police stations are volunteers aged between 18 and 70, but Justices of the Peace, retired police officers and people convicted of a serious crime cannot be appointed. Lay visitors have the right to visit police stations to check on the treatment of people held in custody. They may arrive unannounced, and usually in pairs, and the police must allow them immediate access to custody areas of the police station. They will typically ask the custody officer how many detainees are being held and are then shown around the cells, escorted by an officer. Cells that are occupied will be opened and the officer will tell the detainees the reason for the visit and ask whether they will talk with the visitors. If they agree they will be asked questions such as how long they have been held by the police, have they contacted a solicitor, do their relatives know they are here, and whether they have received food and drink. If any of the detainees are drunk, violent or hostile the visitors may talk to them through the grill in the cell door. Lay visitors are expected to talk with all those detained in police custody and they prepare a report. The report is sent to the secretary of the lay visitor panel and a copy to the officer in charge of the police station. If they find anything wrong in their visits they should talk directly with the officer in charge of the station and expect an immediate response.

Under new management: privatisation and agency status

The political economy of crime control changed in a very obvious sense in the 1990s, during which a shift from the public to commercial sector took place. Some prisons are now run by Group 4, Securicor, Wackenhut Corporation and UK Detention Service Ltd; and a private security industry at least the size of the police service provides security for paying clients. Business interests are evident in other ways such as sponsorship of Safer City and Crime Concern projects. Finance and auditing methods have changed for those agencies remaining within the public sector. The prison service is now an executive agency with control over the budget allocated to it. The police service must now charge the economic costs for activities such as maintaining order at football matches.

In addition to the greater privatisation and commercialisation of the sector and the devolution of budgets there has been an associated change in the culture of management in which a more aggressive accounting approach is adopted by management, with performance indicators used to assess efficiency. The Conservative Governments of the 1980s were determined to tackle what was regarded as a corporatist and overly intrusive system of government that generated a bureaucratic and costly approach to public sector funding and management. By 1990 reform ideas were emerging by which the public sector agencies had to cope with objectives that could be measured by performance indicators relating objectives to funding.

The police and prison service were to undergo radical organisational and managerial reforms. The prison service had been involved in a long-running battle with the Prison Officers' Association over the way prisons were managed. In 1978 the *Committee of Inquiry into the United Kingdom Prison Service* (Home Office 1979) was set up following 'a long period of deteriorating industrial relations, especially in England and Wales' (para. 1). A new pay structure was established under the Fresh Start programme in 1987 but industrial conflict was to continue. In this historical context the late 1980s and 1990s saw the introduction of initiatives to save money and undermine traditional styles of doing business that included: private prisons, new funding initiatives such as the Private Finance Initiative (PFI) to raise capital from the private sector, financial targets, Key Performance Targets, and structural reforms that included redesignating the prison service as an executive agency, and the contracting-out of prison escort work. They bore the hallmarks of the new management culture.

Management and administration of the courts

Sir Robin Auld's Review of the Criminal Courts in England and Wales, 2001 recommended that a single centrally funded agency, as part of the Lord Chancellor's Department (now the Department for Constitutional Affairs), should replace the Court Service and the Magistrates' Courts Committees (MCCs) – these are the benches, the basic unit of local magistrates' court organisation. In the White Paper *Justice for All, 2002* the Government accepted the recommendation for a single courts organisation. The Courts Act 2003 abolished the MCCs and replaced them with courts boards.

A new executive agency, part of the Department for Constitutional Affairs, will replace the Court Service and the 42 MCCs. This agency will have local community links through the courts boards and these will consist of: at least one judge; at least two lay magistrates; at least two other members who appear to have knowledge or experience of the work of the courts in the area; and at least two members who appear to be representative of local people in the area. The DCA will take over responsibility for the magistrates' courts; there will no longer be a need for the MCCs. The Act abolishes petty sessions areas and replaces them with local justice areas. Lay magistrates will be appointed nationally rather than to local petty sessional divisions.

The Crown Court and county courts are organised into 6 circuits and 18 groups. A Circuit Administrator heads each circuit. Below circuit level, Group Managers are responsible for the Crown Court centres and county courts within their areas. Group boundaries are aligned to the 42 criminal justice system (CJS) areas.

4.7 MONITORING, ACCOUNTABILITY AND COMPLAINTS

By the 1990s the new management culture went hand in hand with new ideas about monitoring performance and the accountability of the services. The political agenda on accountability had moved on from the political issues raised about who controls police work and how it is to be accountable to the local community to monitoring in a very different sense in terms of auditing performance targets set centrally but delivered locally. The agencies had to meet specific criteria established by key performance indicators (KPIs) and respond to a new breed of HM Inspectors who monitored regimes in prisons and the performance of the probation and the police services. Key performance indicators provide targets by which agency performance can be measured. For the probation service, KPI 1 aims 'to lower the actual reconviction rates for all types of order and achieve rates lower than those predicted'. This is monitored by the Home Office.

Key performance indicators: police

Police forces must monitor their performance against five performance targets set by the Home Secretary. The Home Secretary's key objectives for policing were issued in 1995 and the KPIs used to assess these are as follows:

Policing objectives and KPIs (in brackets)

1 To maintain and if possible increase the number of detections for violent crimes (KPI: number of violent crimes detected per 100 officers).

2 To increase the number of detections for burglaries of people's homes (KPI: number of burglaries of dwellings detected per 100 officers).

3 To target and prevent crimes which are a particular problem in partnership with the public and other local agencies (no KPI).

4 To provide high visibility policing so as to reassure the public (KPIs: public satisfaction with the levels of foot and mobile patrols/number of police officers available for ordinary duty per 1,000 population/proportion of uniformed constables' time spent in public).

5 To respond promptly to emergency calls from the public (KPIs: percentage of 999 calls answered within the local target time/the percentage of responses within the local target time to incidents requiring immediate response).

The local forces will establish their own targets. For instance, in the case of objective 5 they will have to decide their local target time for answering 999 calls, and the time to reach the incident in the case of an emergency call requiring an immediate response. They will then, at the end of the year, calculate what proportion of calls are answered within that target time. Most forces aim to answer a 999 call within 10 to 15 seconds. In Cambridgeshire in 1995/6 they sought to answer 999 calls within 12 seconds and did this in 80 per cent of all such calls. In responding to emergencies that required immediate response, they set themselves a target of 10 minutes in urban areas and 18 minutes in rural areas, targets which were met in 72 per cent of call outs.

Key performance indicators: prisons

While the police force have targets against established KPIs set locally, prison service targets are set centrally. The *Prison Service Annual Report and Accounts* shows the performance of the prison service with respect to KPIs (detailed below). Thus one objective, keeping prisoners in custody, is measured by the number of escapes from prisons and escorts. In 1999/2000 the prison service set itself the target that no Category A prisoner would escape. It met this target. To assess how well the prison service met the objectives of helping to prepare prisoners for their return to the community they used a KPI which looked at the number of prisoners completing accredited programmes in reducing re-offending. The target for 1999/2000 was aimed at getting 3,600 prisoners to complete accredited programmes. In that year 4,664 offending behaviour programmes were completed (*Prison Service Annual Report and Accounts 2000*: 11).

Prison Service objectives and KPIs (in brackets)

1 To keep prisoners in custody (KPI: number of escapes from prison and escorts). The Category A target set at zero was met in 1999/2000 but the target rate for other escapes at 0.05 per cent was not met.

2 To maintain order, control discipline and a safe environment (KPI: number of assaults on staff, prisoners and others which result in a disciplinary adjudication. KPI: rate of positive random drug testing).

3 To reduce overcrowding: provide decent conditions for prisoners and meet their needs, including health care (KPI: number of prisoners held in units of accommodation intended for fewer prisoners). In 1999/2000 the target of the percentage of cells designed for one prisoner holding two was set at not exceeding 18 per cent; this they failed to meet, with 18.9 per cent in such cells.

4 To provide positive regimes which help prisoners address their offending behaviour and allow them as full and responsible a life as possible (KPI: number of hours which, on average, prisoners spend in purposeful activities). In 1999/2000 the target of allowing each prisoner on average at least 24 hours per week was not met. The average was 23.2 hours.

5 To help prisoners to prepare for their return to the community (KPI: number of prisoners completing programmes accredited as offender behaviour programmes). The 3,600 target was met (see above).

6 To deliver prison services using the resources provided by Parliament with maximum efficiency (KPI 8: average cost of a prison place and the amount of staff sickness). The amount of staff sickness target was not met but the cost per place per prisoner was met, with the average cost per prisoner in 1999/2000 being set at not exceeding £27,392.

Her Majesty's Inspectors

There is a system of inspection for magistrates' courts, prisons, police and probation. Her Majesty's Inspectors provide independent expert advice to the Secretary of State. They may publish detailed reports on specific inquiries conducted and are required to produce an annual report for Parliament on the efficiency and effectiveness of the organisations for which they have responsibility.

■ Her Majesty's Inspector of Constabulary was established in 1865. It is not primarily a policy-making body and its main function is monitoring, although it offers a source of consultation and advice on objectives, performance indicators, and on senior police appointments. It helps to disseminate good practice throughout the 43 forces in England and Wales. The annual report provides a source of information on the overall picture of police work in England and Wales such that in 1996/7 we learn that the police responded to just under 19 million incidents, 7 million 999 calls and made 1.75 million arrests. The report provides basic information about the size of the 43 forces and their performance against the Home Secretary's objectives. Home Office policies on policing and local targets are set out in the police authority's policing plans.

■ The probation service inspectorate was established in 1936. The current system of inspection was established in 1985 and given a statutory role in the Criminal Justice Act 1991. The first annual report from Her Majesty's Inspectorate of Probation was published in 1994. It covers all of the 54 probation areas in England and Wales. The Chief Inspector is Graham Smith. The inspectorate looks at all aspects of the work of probation officers, including their role in the magistrates' and Crown Courts.

■ Her Majesty's Inspector of Prisons reports on specific aspects of operations within a prison following a visit as well as on general issues affecting prisons. The focus is on management practice, spreading good practice and identifying bad practice. In December 1995, David Ramsbotham was appointed Chief Inspector of Prisons, followed in August 2001 by Anne Owens.

■ Her Majesty's Magistrates' Courts Service Inspectorate (MCSI) started in 1995 and was given statutory authority by the Police and Magistrates' Courts Act 1994. It reports to the Lord Chancellor's Department. Its task is to inspect and report on the organisation and administration of magistrates' courts for each magistrates' courts committee area. It is not involved in considering the judicial process or decision making. The Chief Inspector in 1996 was Rosemary Melling. The Courts Act 2003 established a new HM Courts Service Inspectorate.

Complaints: Prisons and Probation Ombudsman

The Prison Ombudsman was set up in 1994 following the recommendations of the Woolf Report 1991. The report referred to the importance 'of a proper balance between security and control on the one hand and humanity and justice on the other' (Home Office 1991a: para. 10.44). It went on specifically to recommend an independent complaints adjudicator to investigate individual grievances and act as the final avenue of appeal against findings of disciplinary hearings (para. 14.347). The government accepted the need for an independent element in the complaints procedure and the 1991 White Paper *Custody, Care and Justice* (Home Office 1991c) stated, 'there should be an independent avenue of appeal against disciplinary findings once avenues within the prison service have been exhausted' and 'appeals against decisions made in response to complaints should also be considered by the same independent body' (para. 8.8).

In 2002 the role was extended to include complaints from those serving community sentences under the probation service or under post-release supervision or parole or licence and on matters concerned with pre-sentence and other reports.

Complaints must first have been aired through the internal complaints system of either the Prison Service or the National Probation Service. The Prisons and Probation Ombudsman will take a fresh look at the complaint and decide whether it has been dealt with fairly. If the Ombudsman upholds the complaint, he will make recommendations to the Prison Service or the National Probation Service to put things right.

The Ombudsman is able to investigate nearly all matters for which the prison service is currently responsible with respect to individual prisoners, including contracted-out prisons and contracted-out services within a prison.

The Prison Ombudsman only takes complaints from prisoners or their legal representative acting on their behalf; he does not act on complaints from relatives, neighbours or friends. The range of complaints typically cover food, assault, loss of property and complaints against adjudication decisions. Prisoners are not denied the right to go to court – they can still sue in the civil courts and can still seek judicial review. Most complaints are from long-term prisoners.

Of the complaints referred to it in 2002–3, 3,132 were about prison (an increase of 15 per cent on the previous year); only 192 were about the probation service (but this report concerned the first full year of operation). Of the prison complaints, 33 per cent were upheld in whole or in part or resolved locally. Of those concerning probation, 25 per cent were upheld in whole or in part.

Those that are investigated and upheld will lead to a recommendation for action that is sent to the prisoner and the prison service. They are not made public. The Prison Ombudsman's remit is not to investigate prisons as a whole, as that is the responsibility of the prison inspectorate; he deals solely with grievances from individual prisoners who have written to him.

The Prison Ombudsman may make the following types of recommendation. For instance, if there is negligence regarding a prisoner's property that gets lost, he may recommend compensation. If there is a complaint about a transfer from one prison to another, he may suggest returning the prisoner to the original situation or, if it is too late, may recommend a written apology from the prison service. He may recommend changes in the security classification or review of a prisoner's security classification.

Independent Police Complaints Commission (IPCC)

From 1 April 2004 a new system for dealing with police complaints in England and Wales was introduced. The new system, operated by the Independent Police Complaints Commission, is designed to raise standards, cut delays, increase public confidence and transform the way police forces handle complaints from the public. It is intended to ensure that complaints are handled in an open, efficient and fair way. The Commission consists of 18 independent commissioners who cannot have worked for the police. They and their staff are organised in four regional offices and will be involved in running or supervising investigations and from these identifying areas for improvements and best practice. Much emphasis in the new system is placed on the rights of complainants to be kept informed of progress. The previous system, under the auspices of the Police Complaints Authority (PCA), where complaints were conducted by the police themselves (see also Chapter 6) was criticised as being lacking in independence and objectivity. However, the PCA had been critical of police work in some very high-profile cases inquiries. For example, the inquiry conducted for the PCA by the Deputy Chief Constable of Kent, Robert Aylingon, into the police handling of the investigation of the murder of the black teenager, Stephen Lawrence, aged 18, in Eltham in April 1993, found that the Metropolitan Police Force was insufficiently thorough in its investigation.

Complaints about the police do not prevent individuals who have been subject to unlawful acts at the hands of the police from using the civil court procedure to seek compensation. In serious miscarriages of justice compensation may be awarded against, or offered by, the police. In 1997 George Lewis received £200,000 in compensation after serving 5 years of a 10-year sentence for burglary and robbery after the police, he claimed, had concocted the evidence. The police officer involved, Detective Constable John Perkins, was a member of the West Midlands Crime Squad and had been cited in 23 cases where fabricated evidence had led to convictions, including the arrests and imprisonment of those convicted of killing Carl Bridgewater.

CONCLUSION

The government, administration and political aspects of criminal justice are likely to continue to grow in complexity, if for no other reason than we will be encompassing a more worldwide view of the crime problem and crime responses as a result of world terrorism, membership of the European Union and the global significance of the Internet and movement of people as tourists and migrants. The public will look to the political leadership to provide solutions and this is bound to lead to demand for more effective crime prevention strategies and more responsibilities on the police. These topics are looked at in the next two chapters.

Review questions

1 Below is a list of Home Secretaries over the last 50 years. Use the index to identify the Home Secretary when the following occurred:
   ■ introduction of detention centres
   ● execution of Derek Bentley
   ■ abolition of the term 'borstal training'
   ■ introduction of the term 'Young Offender Institution'
   ■ publication of the Woolf report.

Home Secretaries

1940–1945	Herbert Morrison	1974–1976	Roy Jenkins
1945	Donald Somervell	1976–1979	Merlyn Rees
1945–1951	James Chuter Ede	1979–1983	William Whitelaw
1951–1954	David Maxwell-Fyfe	1983–1985	Leon Brittan
1954–1957	Gwilym Lloyd-George	1985–1989	Douglas Hurd
1957–1962	Richard (Rab) Butler	1989–1990	David Waddington
1962–1964	Henry Brooke	1990–1992	Kenneth Baker
1964–1965	Frank Soskice	1992–1993	Kenneth Clarke
1965–1967	Roy Jenkins	1993–1997	Michael Howard
1967–1970	Jim Callaghan	1997– 2002	Jack Straw
1970–1972	Reginald Maudling	2002–2004	David Blunkett
1972–1974	Robert Carr	2004–	Charles Clarke

2 The Criminal Justice Consultative Committee, established in 1991, has the task of improving awareness and cooperation between the different agencies in the criminal justice system. In what ways could the work of this committee be extended? Answer this by indicating which of the following *key words* and phrases indicate the type of coordinating role you would think desirable for the criminal justice system in England and Wales. Think initially in terms of the impact of greater

cooperation between agencies working in the same field such as policing. Secondly, how might these key words apply to cross-agency cooperation between different functioning agencies, for instance probation and prisons.

> *Information exchange*
> *Consultation*
> *Data-sharing*
> *Cross-agency computerisation of data*
> *Joint operations*
> *Exchange of personnel*
> *Establishing common definitions*
> *Agreeing to cross-agency common objectives*
> *Mergers of local units into regional units*
> *Merger of regional units into nationwide units*
> *Merger of national units into European-wide agencies*
> *None of these.*

3 On pages 92/3 we have reprinted extracts from a speech by the Prime Minster, Tony Blair, and on pages 93/4 we have reproduced extracts from an article by Andrew Rawnsley. Read their extracts and answer the following.

- How do these two accounts differ in terms of the nature of reasons and impact of the change made by the New Labour Government on crime?
- Do you think the New Labour approach can be regarded as right or left wing?
- What are the key themes that the Prime Minister sees as underpinning the reforms the New Labour Government is making?
- Does the Offender Management Model of criminal justice apply to New Labour's policies?
- Do other models apply to the changes introduced by New Labour since 1997?

4 The Private Security Industry Act 2001 established the Security Industry Agency. Explore their website and list the types of firms regulated.

Further reading

Newburn, T (2003) *Crime and Criminal Justice Policy* (2nd edn), Pearson: London
Ryan, M (2003) *Penal Policy and Political Culture in England and Wales: Four essays on policy and process*, Waterside Press: Winchester
Windlesham, Lord (1993/2001) *Responses to Crime* (4 vols), Clarendon Press: Oxford

PART B

Criminal justice process: law enforcement

Crime prevention and reduction

INTRODUCTION

How central to a criminal justice system is the goal of preventing crime? The formal process of adversarial justice described in this introductory book about the criminal justice system in England and Wales is based on responding to the offender as suspect, defendant, convicted, sentenced and sometimes as prisoner. The central concern of this system is justice and fairness under the rules of adversarial justice to ensure the guilty are convicted and the innocent acquitted, with the convicted being given a deserved penalty. This is not to ignore the desired outcomes of re-habilitating, incapacitating or deterring offenders, but these offender-instrumental aims are secondary and in part speculative as the impacts of deterrence and re-habilitation are unpredictable. There are those who deny the system as having any deterrent effect or who maintain that rehabilitation does not deliver as 'Nothing worked' (see Chapters 11 and 12). We have also seen in Chapter 2 that most crimes are not reported and, of those that are, the majority do not result in a conviction. Furthermore, there are criminologists who have claimed the factors determining the crime rate are outside the control of the formal system and are determined by econ-omic or cultural forces. The tenfold increase in the crime rate from the 1950s to the 1990s does not suggest that the criminal justice system was working in that period to reduce crime. Of course this might in part be a consequence of growing affluence and/or cultural attitudes changes since the 1960s; or the lenient and liberal sen-tencing approach of the judges in the 1970s may in part have been responsible for the growth in crime (Davies 1997). Whatever it did, the criminal justice system did not appear able to do much about the growth in crime in the second half of the twentieth century.

Crime reduction became an issue that was initially thought about as an addition to the criminal justice system rather than a central aspect of it: more locks, more publicity, more private security, and anti-theft devices, that is interventions not concerned with the adversarial process of justice. Where government looked to the formal system the debate on crime policy tended to swing between claims to be tougher on crime (e.g. more police, less bail, tougher penalties) or doing more to change offenders' behaviour in a rehabilitative sense (e.g. counselling, therapy, education, training, drug-use reduction, anger control strategies). In the 1980s new initiatives outside the formal process emerged with community-focused initiatives such as Safer Cities and Neighbourhood Watch.

What started as peripheral activity has become central in the approach of the New Labour Government since 1997 (described in Chapter 4). It has put crime reduction as central to the aims of the system. This is evident in: the focus on pre-criminal intervention, which has upset the civil liberties lobby (both left and right), with such schemes as neighbourhood child curfews, parenting orders and anti-social behaviour schemes; reform to the traditional divide between the prison (punishment and containment of criminals) and probation services (rehabilitative focus), in a reform that sees them merge to become part of the National Offender Management System (NOMS), overseeing the offender from sentence to resettlement; new Police Community Support Officers (PCSOs) to focus on street low-level anti-social behaviour, and new orders to ban alcohol in city centres and 'joined up' initiatives proliferate, such as the Crime and Disorder Reduction Partnerships (CDRPs) – a combination of police, local authorities, organisations and businesses who have banded together to develop and implement strategies for tackling crime and disorder on a local level. There is change to the political rhetoric and the focus on reducing crime is now centre stage.

Whether crime has reduced is yet to be seen, but the new emphasis on crime reduction led us to suggest in Chapter 1 that we need an additional model of criminal justice, one that takes account of this new focus on controlling offenders in a way that is more systematic and comprehensive than the rehabilitative model.

5.1   WHAT IS CRIME PREVENTION?

Crime prevention is defined as

> '**any action taken or technique employed by private individuals or public agencies aimed at the reduction of damage caused by acts defined as criminal by the state**'
>
> (Hughes in McLaughlin and Muncie 2001: 63).

It therefore includes everyday actions which we all take, such as locking doors or concealing money to redesigning buildings to make them more secure, redesigning products to make them more difficult to steal or to use after they have been stolen, or redesigning the urban environment. Crime prevention strategies aim to reduce crime, and more recently the government has increasingly used the phrase 'crime reduction', although this can be used more or less interchangeably with 'crime prevention' (Pease 2002). Many of the strategies involved in crime reduction operate at the level of local communities and the term 'community safety' is also widely used; there has also been a growth in the number of 'community safety officers' who are responsible for implementing many crime prevention strategies. This term is more problematic – as will be seen below, it can have wider meaning than being restricted to the prevention of crime (Pease 2002; Hughes 2002).

What is unusual is that in the crime prevention literature the formal criminal justice agencies are seen as having a role in their secondary capacities, police liaising with communities; but clearly the police, courts, prisons and probation are all activities that have some impact on crime prevention.

As seen above, there are many different forms of crime prevention. One typology identifies primary, secondary and tertiary approaches.

- *Primary crime prevention* refers to strategies aiming to prevent crime before it happens and involves all the social, physical and other strategies to prevent crime. It may involve target hardening, by making a target more difficult to steal (e.g. by installing better locks on doors). It also involves the process of socialisation whereby we attempt to make a person a responsible member of society by instilling the dominant moral values of society. Crime prevention is often presented as a matter of nuts, locks and bolts but another means of crime prevention lies in childhood acquisition of moral perspectives and the development of responsible citizens who respect the law; institutions teaching appropriate behaviour and good civic values: such as the family in promoting respect for others and their property, schools instilling sound civic values. Becoming a member of civil society is a complex process and the more agencies and groups in the community, such as the church or neighbours, significant others, media influence, peers, who reinforce the values that underpin a society, the less the likelihood of crime. Of course we must not forget that the criminal justice system also plays a part here, particularly in the denunciatory function of affirming and reinforcing the dominant moral code as a justification for punishing those who infringe against it.

- *Secondary crime prevention* identifies 'at risk' people and situations. It involves policies which target people considered to be at risk of becoming offenders – such as young people in areas known for high levels of offending; or situations where crime is likely to occur. Thus a variety of educational and sports schemes aim to divert youth in high crime areas from criminal activity. The focus is on 'at-risk' neighbourhoods, schools and families. An important role is played by health, educational, welfare and medical staff to spot those at risk of committing a crime, or of being a victim. Thus nurses question children who come into hospital with signs of violent injury. Teachers check on pupils they suspect of being truant. Interventions to reduce the likelihood of disturbance and potential for crime led to the ability of police and local authorities to ban alcohol in areas where public nuisance is associated with the public consumption of alcohol. Another recent innovation is the curfews for children aged under 10 – now extended to 15. In designated areas police will pick up unaccompanied children on the streets after 9 pm and take them home to their parents. Most important is the general role of the police as an effective deterrent against those thinking of committing crime. In 2003 a White Paper was published outlining proposals for tackling anti-social behaviour, *Respect and Responsibility – taking a stand against anti-social behaviour*. The proposals resulted in the Anti-Social Behaviour Act 2003 (ASBA 2003) which introduced several secondary crime prevention measures to help to deal with younger offenders and their parents and social nuisances such as graffiti. It provides a means for schools, local authorities and youth offending teams to work with the parents of children who are behaving anti-socially. The ASBA 2003 extends the measures that can be taken to remove graffiti, and restricts the sale of aerosol paint to children.

■ *Tertiary crime prevention* deals with known criminals and crime situations. It aims to prevent those already convicted of crime from continuing with their criminal careers, mainly through the sentences of the court. Parenting orders and drug abstinence orders are new court orders. A more integrated approach to dealing with known offenders has been introduced with a number of policies demanding greater cooperation and even mergers of agencies dealing with offenders, set out in *Reducing Crime, Changing Lives*. The object behind the proposed National Offender Management Service (NOMS) is to ensure that offenders are managed throughout the whole of their sentences, whether in custody or in the community by merging prison and probation services. This will require new arrangements for case management based on a common system operating in custodial and community settings. Other examples of more joined-up approaches to responding to known offenders is seen in Youth Offender Teams, Local Criminal Justice Boards, Crime and Disorder Reduction Partnerships and Drug Action Teams.

Van Dijk and de Waard (1991) developed the threefold typology explained in Figure 5.1 and focused on three different targets of the offender, victim and potential crime situations.

Another classification was suggested by Graham and Bennett (1995): criminality prevention, situational crime prevention and community crime prevention. Another way of looking at different forms of crime prevention is to distinguish between policies which focus largely on the situational aspects of crime, and those that attempt to target the broader social aspects of crime. Thus many refer to situational and social crime prevention.

■ *Situational crime prevention*, sometimes referred to as 'physical' crime prevention, involves altering the situational or spatial characteristics either to make offending more difficult or detection easier (Crawford 1998).

■ *Social crime prevention* is based more on the social factors associated with crime such as living conditions, relative deprivation and social disorganisation. This may include what is often described as 'community crime prevention' and may involve community regeneration.

While primary crime prevention is often equated with situational crime prevention, the relationships between these different forms are more complex – a combination

Figure 5.1 Typology of crime prevention

	Primary: *General interventions*	**Secondary:** *Focus on at-risk groups and situations*	**Tertiary:** *Responding to known criminal activities and offenders*
Offender	School socialisation on civic responsibilities Educational and deterrent strategy of a media campaign about the effects and possible consequences of drink and driving	Youth employment training project in high crime area Curfews on those suspected of anti-social behaviour	Restorative justice mediation between offender and victim Electronic tagging of offender
Situations	All cars manufactured with anti-theft devices Gun control laws	CCTV in city centre areas where rowdy behaviour is predicted Identity checks on people coming into the country to combat terrorism Identity cards to reduce likelihood of credit card fraud	CCTV situated outside public houses where there have been disturbances
Victims	Media campaign to warn the public to be aware of growing incidence of a particular crime such as credit card fraud	Surveillance of homes of those who have received threats or are likely targets of artifice burglary such as homes for the elderly	Repeat victims of burglary offered security advice and grants for locks

Source: Adapted from Van Dijk and de Waard (1991)

of these different ways of classifying crime prevention is suggested by Crawford (see Figure 5.2).

5.2 THE THEORETICAL BASIS OF CRIME PREVENTION

Crime prevention policies are implicitly or explicitly based on theories about why crime occurs. These can focus on different elements of crime. Some theories focus on offenders – seeking to establish, for example, if there are any characteristics which distinguish offenders from the rest of the population and whether offenders are 'predisposed' to commit crime. Alternatively, crime can be related to a variety

Figure 5.2   A Process/Target Two-Dimensional Typology of Crime Prevention

	Primary	Secondary	Tertiary
Social	Education and socialisation, public awareness and advertising campaigns, neighbourhood watch	Work with those 'at risk' of offending: youths, the unemployed, community regeneration	Rehabilitation, confronting offending behaviour, aftercare, diversion, reparation
Situational	Target-hardening, surveillance, opportunity reduction/removal, environmental design, general deterrence	Target-hardening and design measures for 'at risk' groups, risk prediction and assessment, deterrence	Individual deterrence, incapacitation, assessment of dangerou sness' and 'risk'

Source: Crawford *Crime Prevention and Community Safety: Politics, policies and practices* (Longman: London), p. 19

of social factors such as social deprivation, high rates of unemployment, or the effects of social change. A different approach is to explore the situations in which crime occurs – it is easier, for example, to commit a crime successfully in situations in which there is less chance of being observed or being caught. As Pease (2002) explains, crime can be related to psyche, structure or circumstance. While it is not possible to explore these theories fully, a brief exploration is important to understand the theoretical basis of crime prevention.

A major feature of what is known as 'positivist' criminology, which developed from the late nineteenth century, was the attempt to establish scientifically the 'causes' of crime, in order to develop a 'cure'. Offenders were believed to have some form of 'pathology' and researchers looked for characteristics which differentiated offenders from the rest of the population. Early criminologists focused on biological characteristics: the Italian criminologist Cesare Lombroso studied the physical characteristics of convicts in prisons, and claimed that criminal men were distinguished by what he called 'physical stigmata', which included long arms, shifty glances, droopy eyelids, bushy eyebrows, large ears, twisted noses and abnormal mouths and skulls (Lombroso 1897). His theories were later discredited, particularly as many similar characteristics were found in the general population, but they stimulated further research relating criminality to physical and genetic characteristics. A variety of factors were related to crime, such as body shapes, and later research looked at the possibility that chromosome abnormalities or biochemical factors such as vitamin deficiencies or food allergies were also associated with crime. While attributing crime to biological characteristics has produced much interesting research, it has had limited applicability as few characteristics clearly differentiate offenders from so-called 'non-offenders'. Moreover, as seen in Chapter 2, crime is a form of behaviour which contravenes rules made by society. Even if we could assume that people could inherit a propensity to behave aggressively, such aggression could have legitimate and illegitimate outlets. Criminality involves issues of morality, a choice between right and wrong, learnt within the social environment. Thus it is virtually impossible to establish the extent to which characteristics are a result of genetic inheritance or socialisation.

Another line of enquiry has been to explore psychological factors. Criminal behaviour, like any other form of behaviour, is learnt during the socialisation process and learning theories have considerable potential in establishing how criminality is learnt. Other psychological approaches have focused on links between personality traits such as extraversion, neuroticism, psychoticism and crime (Eysenck 1977), while others have looked at the possible relationship between criminality and mental illness. While these factors are related to some individual offences, mental illness, for example, is found only in a minority of offenders and, in addition, the majority of people considered to be suffering from mental illness do not commit crime.

Individuals are also affected by their immediate environment, particularly the family, and much research has explored the relationship between offending and family background. Parental discipline has been seen as important, with inconsistent and erratic discipline in the home having been found to be more likely to be associated with crime than lax or strict discipline (West and Farrington 1973, 1977). Much attention has recently been paid to the quality of parental supervision, and one Home Office study found that supervision was strongly related to offending, with higher numbers of those who were not closely supervised admitting offending. Around one-third of boys who were closely supervised had offended compared with over half of those who were not closely supervised (Graham and Bowling 1995). The structure of families may also be important – some studies have found that fewer offenders come from families living with two natural parents, but there is no evidence to suggest that divorce, separation or single parenthood are criminogenic in themselves, as these are widespread throughout society and not always related to crime (Utting *et al.* 1993; Graham and Bowling 1995). The quality of relationships within the family is particularly important (Graham and Bowling 1995) and the conflict surrounding separation or divorce may be more significant than family breakdown (Rutter 1985); a single-parent home may provide the child with a more caring and affectionate environment than one in which two parents are constantly in dispute and have little time to pay attention to their children (Utting *et al.* 1993).

Sociologists have focused on the relationship between crime and the wider social structure and to the adverse effects of social and economic change. To Emile Durkheim, for example, writing at the end of the nineteenth century amidst rapid social change, social and economic changes following the Industrial Revolution had led to the decline of communities and religion which provided people with guidance about morality and standards of behaviour. This could lead, he argued, to the development of anomie, or normlessness, in which individuals lacked such guidance. In addition, the growth of materialism led to people developing what he called 'boundless aspirations' which often could not be met (Durkheim 1970). These ideas were taken up by the American sociologist Robert Merton. In American society, he argued, goals of material success predominated, and socially approved norms provided guidelines to achieve these goals by legitimate means such as hard work and educational achievement, but not all who work hard would achieve the goals. This strain could produce anomie, in which the norms of hard work are no longer relevant, especially to those at the bottom of the ladder (Merton 1938). Many theories developed out of this anomie paradigm, and while its original formulation had many limitations, the view that crime can be interpreted as a 'solution' to the problems of blocked aspirations has continued to influence sociological approaches.

Subcultural theory focuses on groups, often of young people, within which particular kinds of crime are seen as normal and where status may derive from delinquent or criminal activity, examples of which include groups of joyriders, juvenile thieves or drug takers. These subcultures can be seen to emerge out of the strain faced by young people confronted with the difficulties of achieving culturally approved goals such as employment, material success or consumption. Participation in crime may be a 'deviant solution', particularly in the presence of what has been described as the structure of illegitimate opportunities of a particular neighbourhood (Cloward and Ohlin 1960). In areas with an existing criminal subculture, youth can learn how to engage in activities such as burglary or theft. Without this knowledge, and suitable outlets for stolen goods, such participation would be far less likely. Delinquent subcultures can therefore be interpreted as providing an achievable, if criminal, aspiration for youth who have failed to achieve different cultural goals transmitted through the media. In contemporary culture which places a high value on young people's consumption of, for example, designer goods and clothes, the latest technology and expensive leisure activities such as clubbing, those deprived of these opportunities through, for example, lack of resources or employment, may turn to crime and the consumption of drugs to participate in this 'high life' (Collison 1996).

Crime can therefore be associated with economic deprivation and, while there is no simple relationship between crime and absolute deprivation or levels of income or unemployment, it may be related (as Lea and Young (1992) suggest) to relative deprivation. If people expect and feel entitled to achieve a certain standard of living, they will feel more frustrated if they are denied the opportunity, particularly if they can see others succeeding. This may be exacerbated by the impact of the major social changes of the twentieth century which have led to the decline of traditional industries and, for many, permanent employment. In communities affected by these changes young people can no longer expect stable full-time employment, which affects their ability to undertake financial and other commitments, such as buying a house or getting married. Many of the communities most affected are also geographically isolated, some in peripheral estates outside towns and cities. This has led to what some see as a situation in which groups and whole communities are effectively excluded from participation in society.

Theories which focus on individual offenders and the social structure suggest many avenues for reducing crime. As will be seen in later chapters, for a large part of the twentieth century the belief that individual offenders could be rehabilitated or 'cured' was a crucial part of criminal justice policy. This criminological 'project', however, came to be questioned as it was found that many rehabilitative programmes had less effect than was assumed and that, as some research suggested, 'nothing works'. Sociological approaches were also questioned by the continuing rise in crime rates despite the development of the welfare state and rising affluence – all of which should theoretically have reduced crime. New approaches were sought which moved away from looking at how offenders might be 'predisposed' to crime and instead focused on trying to stop crime before it happened – on 'prevention' rather than 'cure'. This involved looking at the third factor identified above: the situations or circumstances in which crime occurred.

This involved a different approach to offenders' motivation and it was argued that individuals make rational choices whether or not to commit an offence. They may weigh up, for example, the gain they might derive from the crime against their chances of being caught and punished. Thus crime depends on this evaluation of risk and the opportunities provided by the situation (see, for example, Clarke 1980). Faced with an open till in an empty shop, a potential thief is more likely to steal than if the shop is crowded and has publicised video surveillance. Much crime, it was argued, is therefore opportunistic, rather than being related to individual pathologies or subcultural motivation.

This led to more attention being paid to the relationship between crime and what Felson has described as 'routine activities' (Felson 2002). Simply put, this involves looking at crime as involving a triangular relationship between an offender, a victim and a location – change one and the crime will not take place. As Pease (2002: 950) explains:

> In a pub (location), someone (offender) assaults someone else (victim) in an argument about whose turn it was to be served. The offender could be banned, the victim may choose to drink in another pub, or the licensee may be encouraged to change bar arrangements or train staff so as to make such disputes less likely. Each option could resolve the problem.

Crime prevention was also related to the work of Oscar Newman (1972) who argued that the physical design of estates and public buildings can hamper the community's surveillance of social space and thus reduces its ability to control crime. High-rise buildings and estates that are built so that windows do not overlook public spaces, and buildings with many corridors and exits, help to create conditions conducive to crime because they do not provide the opportunity to be able to see or respond to anti-social behaviour. Thus redesigning housing schemes may produce more 'defensible space' – space which people occupy and feel responsibility for. This prevents crime as it means that strangers can be more readily observed and, therefore, deterred. In any situation in which a crime may occur, levels of surveillance are crucial. Surveillance can be increased informally by altering the design of buildings to ensure greater surveillance by employees or residents, or formally by employing security guards or installing video cameras.

5.3 THE GROWTH OF CRIME PREVENTION

While people have always taken steps to prevent victimisation, institutional responsibility for crime prevention was, until the mid-twentieth century, largely restricted to police crime prevention units; and the police have always had crime prevention as part of their role, albeit a small and often unrewarded one. Crime

Prevention Panels were set up in 1966 although it was not until the 1980s that crime prevention 'took off' (Tilley 2002) as a major part of governmental policy. Since then there has been a large volume of research, a large number of different policy initiatives, CCTV has become widespread and partnership arrangements between criminal justice agencies and local authorities have been institutionalised. There were many reasons for this rapid growth (Hughes 2002; Crawford 1998; Tilley 2002; Newburn 2003). Rising crime rates created an 'overload' for the criminal justice system, and increased its costs. There was also a rising political and public concern about crime to which governments wished to respond. In the face of the growing recognition of the limits of the criminal justice system to reduce crime, crime prevention offered an attractive, and relatively inexpensive, means of reducing crime. As Tilley (2002: 16) comments: 'where cure appears unavailable, and containment is very expensive, prevention looked extremely attractive in the face of a high profile problem like crime'.

A major role in the rising focus on crime prevention was played by the development of the Home Office Research and Planning Unit, under Ron Clarke. In an influential publication this Unit detailed the potential of a variety of measures (Mayhew *et al.* 1976) which had had some success, and in 1983 the Crime Prevention Unit was set up. Many different research projects, focusing largely on situational crime prevention, were undertaken to establish which strategies affected which crimes in specific circumstances. It was also recognised that crime prevention necessarily involved a range of agencies other than the police, and was best achieved through 'multi agency' working and collaborative partnerships. At governmental level also, crime prevention was encouraged. In 1983, the Home Office Standing Conference on Crime Prevention was strengthened by having a Home Office Minister in the Chair, and a circular in 1984 stated clearly that:

> The primary objective of the police has always been the prevention of crime. However, since some of the factors affecting crime lie outside the control or direct influence of the Police, crime prevention can not be left to them alone. Every individual citizen and all those agencies whose policies and practices can influence the extent of crime should make their contribution. Preventing crime is a task for the whole community.

This, argues Crawford (1998: 36) was a crucial symbolic milestone and following this central government policy became clearly fixed around the partnership approach.

By the late 1980s many new initiatives had been launched. In 1988 Crime Concern, a charity funded partly by the Home Office and partly by private enterprise, was launched. This organisation has been responsible for a large number of crime prevention projects in conjunction with both commercial and public organisations. The Crack Crime campaign was also launched in 1988. In 1993 a National Board for Crime Prevention was established to bring together representatives of central and local government, business, voluntary agencies, the media, the police and the probation service.

A major development was the Safer Cities programme, launched in 1988. This started with the Five Towns Initiative in Bolton, North Tyneside, Croydon, Swansea and Wellingborough which was followed by a larger programme, Safer Cities, incorporating a total of 20 projects funded by the Home Office (Tilley 1993). Safer Cities had three stated goals:

1. to reduce crime;
2. to lessen the fear of crime;
3. to create safer cities where economic enterprise and community life can flourish.

It incorporated not only crime prevention but a concern with other related aspects of community safety. It included the growing concern for crime victims and recognised that crime was related to economic enterprise and community life. If crime rates are high in a particular area and the population has a high fear of crime, people will avoid public places, local shops and community activities.

The *Annual Safer Cities Progress Report of 1992/3* stated that, up to 1993, more than 3,300 crime prevention and community safety measures had been initiated involving £20.4 million Home Office funding. This report also indicated the variety of activities undertaken as part of the Safer Cities programme, which included:

- projects to improve security in homes, businesses and public facilities;
- helping young people as potential offenders, offenders and victims of crime;
- schemes to tackle domestic violence and other women's safety issues;
- action on car crime and racial harassment.

(Home Office 1993: 7)

While representing a major development in crime prevention and incorporating many multi-agency groups, the safer cities initiative had limitations – it was somewhat 'ad hoc' and was implemented only in selected areas (Newburn 2003) and projects often lacked resources. Taken together with other developments of the 1980s it did not represent a national strategy for crime prevention and, while partnership working was encouraged, there was no clear idea of which agency should take the lead in developing local community safety strategies.

In 1991 the report of a review carried out by the Standing Conference on Crime Prevention, of the development of crime prevention through the multi-agency or partnership approach, was published. The Morgan Report, named after the Chair of the Committee, made several important recommendations. Local authorities, argued the report, should be given statutory responsibility, working with the police, for the development of community safety and crime prevention. Voluntary groups and businesses should also be involved. New legislation should be monitored by a national body and a community safety strategy group should be set up at the highest tier of local government. There should be a local action group to formulate objectives and a strategic plan, consulting many local and neighbourhood-based groups. This would have provided a coherent structure (Crawford 1998), although it was never fully implemented partly due to the then Conservative Government's reluctance to enhance the role of local authorities. It did, however, highlight the importance of partnership working and underline the role which local authorities and local agencies could play (Tilley 2002). In the event many local community safety partnerships were formed.

Government strategy in the early to mid-1990s was largely dominated by a concern with tough penal strategies, although it continued to advocate the partnership approach and encouraged people to be 'active citizens' by becoming involved in Neighbourhood Watch schemes; and there were plans to increase the use of voluntary special constables (Newburn 2003). There was also encouragement for the use of CCTV, and, in 1995, the National Board for Crime Prevention became the National Crime Prevention Agency, whose task was to focus on and coordinate the national agenda, to disseminate good practice and to develop strategies for preventing and reducing crime. It had representation from the Home Office, the Police, Crime Concern and other individuals but no representatives from local government. It was not an independent body as envisaged by the Morgan report, nor did it have any agenda-setting powers compared to other National Crime organisations such as those in Sweden, France or the Netherlands (Crawford 1998).

The Labour Party had made a manifesto commitment to implement the recommendations of the Morgan Committee; however, the new Labour Government's Crime and Disorder Act 1998, while setting up structures for Crime Prevention, did not give local authorities a 'lead' role but emphasised principles of partnership and collective responsibility between local authorities and chief police officers to work in cooperation with probation committees and health authorities to implement a 'strategy for the reduction of crime and disorder in the area'. Before doing so the responsible authorities, known as Crime and Disorder Partnerships, are required to carry out a review of the levels and patterns of crime and disorder in the area; prepare an analysis of the results of that review; publish a report of this analysis; and obtain views of relevant authorities. Strategies should contain 'objectives to be pursued by the responsible authorities, and long term and short term performance targets'. The Act also requires local authorities, police authorities, joint authorities, National Parks Authorities and Broads Authorities to take crime consequences into account in their practices and policies. Local Partnerships have to undertake this work in a 3-year cycle, and are advised by, amongst others, the Home Office Crime Reduction website which includes a 'knowledge base', 'toolkits' made up from evaluated best practice, a discussion forum and a strategy statement (Pease 2002). By November 2000, 376 statutory Crime and Disorder Partnerships in England and Wales were implementing their first 3-year strategy to reduce crime and disorder (Phillips 2002).

Partnerships must set 5-year targets, with annual milestones for the reduction of vehicle crime, burglary and robbery under the Government's Crime Reduction Programme (Newburn 2003). Performance monitoring regimes have been put in place. All nine regional government offices now have Regional Crime Reduction Directors, high-ranking civil servants, whose task is to facilitate, inform and catalyse increased and improved attention to crime reduction in their areas (Tilley 2002). This is in line with the managerialism characteristic of many areas of criminal justice and social policy. According to Tilley (2002: 23) they involve 'new rules, roles, committees, tiers of authority, accountability mechanisms and reporting hierarchies'. He cites the example of one large city which has a six-tier multi-agency management and reporting hierarchy which includes a 'responsible authority group' (including the probation service, health authority and other invited agencies), below which is an 'executive partnership group', below which are found divisional 'community safety coordinating groups', below which are sub-divisional 'partnership groups', below which are 'local action partnerships', below which are 'task groups'. Community safety officers and departments are now part of the local authority structure and are being professionalised through a process of training and accreditation. A National Community Safety Network had around 200 members by 2000 (Hughes 2002) and there is a growing research literature, aimed at producing 'evidence based' community safety policies.

Some indication of how these partnerships work, along with some of the problems which they have faced, is provided by a Home Office Research project into three crime and disorder partnerships (Phillips 2002); a number of points are summarised below:

- Membership includes a police basic command unit commander, the chief executive and officers of key local authority departments such as housing, education, social, environmental and legal services, the assistant chief probation officer, the youth offending team manager, police/local authority liaison officers, community safety officers and representatives from the voluntary sector.

- The primary function of groups is to coordinate the compilation of the crime and disorder audit and to formulate a strategy and action plan to reduce crime and disorder in the locality. It was found that health authorities were more difficult to engage due to a lack of resources and a lack of clarity about their role. Businesses were also found to have a limited role.

- There were indications of improvements in intra-agency networking and raising the profile of crime reduction within some agencies and the partnership process was felt to have facilitated information exchange. Unlike previous multi-agency partnerships they were not seen as police 'take overs' but the leading roles of the police and local authorities could make some smaller voluntary and community organisations feel marginalised.

- There were some potential areas of conflict over how to define the crime problem, which areas to prioritise and over appropriate preventative solutions. Many partnerships resolved this by developing broad generic aims which could appeal to all rather than detailed action plans and included a range of situational and social measures although some partners were less willing to be involved than others. All faced time and resource limitations.

- The setting of nationally determined 5-year targets placed pressure on the partnerships and could conflict with what they saw as local priorities. There is a danger, argues Phillips, that the pressure of performance management may encourage partnerships to opt for the 'quick wins' associated with situational crime prevention rather than longer-term measures.

Crime prevention (and its associated structural framework) has therefore grown considerably in a short space of time – what therefore does it consist of and how can it be evaluated? The following sections will look at some of its major forms, and at some issues of evaluation.

5.4 SITUATIONAL AND SOCIAL CRIME PREVENTION

Situational crime prevention

As seen above, situational crime prevention measures focus on the circumstances in which crime takes place, rather than on offenders. Measures commonly involve 'the design of products, services, environments or systems to make them crime resistant' (Ekblom in Muncie and McLaughlin 2001: 263). It may involve making sure that an area is subject to surveillance by, for example, householders, residents or employees and its methods include simple strategies such as the use of anti-climb paint on drainpipes to prevent burglars or vandals. What is sometimes described as 'opportunity reduction' (Crawford 1998) can take three main forms:

1 Increasing the effort involved in crime, often known as 'target hardening', examples of which are installing speed humps on roads to prevent speeding, or introducing physical protection to targets such as locks and bolts.

2 Increasing the risks of detection, which involves increasing surveillance by, for example, redesigning buildings, introducing concierges or installing CCTV cameras.

3 Reducing the rewards of crime by, for example, making sure that a stolen item can be traced through property marking, or 'target removal', an example of which is replacing coin operated meters or boxes with those which require a swipe card (Crawford 1998).

There have now been many 'success stories' associated with situational crime prevention and, as Pease (2002) argues, the literature demonstrating their effectiveness is now extensive. An early example of the success of such measures was not related to crime but to the reduction of suicide by the replacement of toxic town gas with non-toxic natural gas (Crawford 1998; Pease 2002). This led to a fall in suicide rates in England and Wales from 5,700 to under 3,700 between 1963 and 1975, at a time when suicide rates were increasing across Europe. Suicide by domestic gas virtually disappeared whereas it had previously accounted for 40 per cent of suicides. An important feature of this is that those wishing to commit suicide are highly motivated and might be assumed to look for alternative methods – thus showing the potential of preventative measures. Other 'successes' have included the following:

■ The introduction of steering locks in cars has been found to reduce car theft although it may displace car theft to cars without steering locks. In West Germany, where steering locks were introduced in all cars, rates fell dramatically, whereas in Britain, where they were introduced only to new cars from 1971, theft may have been 'displaced' to cars without steering locks.

■ Improved street lighting provides a good example of the more subtle effects of crime prevention measures (Pease 2002). Some have claimed that improved street lighting reduces the incidence of assault, auto crime and threats, with Painter (1988) having claimed a 75 per cent decrease in a period of 6 weeks. Theoretically, argues Pease, it could be assumed that this 'works' by increasing surveillance and would be most effective at night, whereas it also appears to reduce crime during daylight! Its effect, therefore, may lie more in an increased pride in the community and community cohesion, although not all research confirms its effect on crime reduction (Crawford 1998). It does, however, appear to reduce people's fear of crime and increase feelings of safety.

■ The Kirkholt Project: an extremely influential project was targeted at repeat victimisation from burglary on a housing estate in Kirkholt near Rochdale, which had a rate of burglary double that which would be expected, and high rates of repeat victimisation. A range of interventions included the installation of window locks and strengthened doors, the removal of coin-fed meters, neighbourhood watch schemes and support for burglary victims. Repeat victimisation declined by 80 per cent within 7 months and within 3 years burglary rates had fallen by around one-quarter. The scheme became a model, although it was subsequently difficult to establish which of the many measures might have contributed to the decline of burglary (Crawford 1998; Pease 2002).

These examples demonstrate the considerable promise of situational crime prevention but also indicate some of the difficulties of evaluating it. It is difficult, for example, to pinpoint the factors which have led to a reduction in crime and further difficulties are raised by the problem, common to all forms of crime prevention, that crime may have been displaced elsewhere. Displacement can take several forms, outlined by Crawford (1998):

■ Spatial or geographic displacement – the same crime is committed in a different place.

■ Temporal displacement – the same crime is committed against the same target at a different time.

■ Tactical displacement – the same crime is committed against the same target but in a different way or by a different means.

■ Target displacement – the same type of crime is committed but a new target is selected, for example increasing bank security may have led to robbers moving to post offices and then to garages or other, easier targets.

■ Type of crime displacement – a change in nature of criminal activities, for example moving from robbing post offices to street mugging.

■ Perpetrator displacement – new offenders fill the vacuum.

Displacement is clearly a major problem in evaluating crime prevention schemes and often features in criticisms of them. It may not, however, always be negative; as Crawford argues, it can be malign if it involves a shift to more serious offences, but it can also be benign if lesser consequences result.

Other limitations of situational crime prevention include issues concerning how sustainable improvements may be (Pease 2002) – there may be, for example, an initial reduction followed by an 'escalation' (Crawford 1998) in which one set of measures is overcome by offenders which necessitates the introduction of a further set of measures. The introduction of increased security measures may also adversely affect the quality of life in an area, and perversely heighten people's concern about crime rather than reducing it. (Other issues surrounding situational and other forms of crime prevention will be discussed later in the chapter.) Nevertheless most accept that many forms of situational crime prevention do reduce some offences in some circumstances and, as Pease (2002) argues, looking at their sustainability and identifying precisely 'how' they work are important issues for the future.

Social crime prevention

As seen above, social crime prevention targets those considered most likely to commit crime and to intervene before crime occurs. While generally regarded as less well developed, and more expensive and difficult to implement than situational crime prevention, many schemes have attempted to target 'at risk' groups, mainly young people, and to enhance crime prevention within communities – sometimes known as 'community crime prevention'.

Young people are often the targets of social crime prevention as they feature so prominently among offenders and there has always been a general belief that the pursuit of a criminal career can be prevented by 'nipping it in the bud'. A wide range of research has attempted to identify factors that place young people 'at risk' of offending – including family background, early experiences, parenting, living conditions, school and peer group influences and employment (Crawford 1998). As seen above, parental supervision is seen as crucial as are relationships within the family. Many policies now claim the benefits of 'early intervention' – as the further a young person moves towards crime, intervention may have little success (Pease 2002). Early intervention involves a range of schemes including, for example, supporting 'good' parenting by working with families and improving parental supervision, targeting schools by focusing on school discipline, tackling truancy and reducing school exclusions as around 42 per cent of offenders of school age sentenced in the youth court have been excluded from school (Crawford 1998). A large number of schools now attempt to tackle 'bullying', often seen to be associated with youth crime and disorderly behaviour.

While some success is claimed for many of these schemes, they are difficult to evaluate. Links between 'poor' parenting and offending are not always clear cut and, as Crawford (1998) asks, how can this be defined? At what point should intervention into young people's lives take place? Intervention also carries dangers of labelling some groups which may have the effect of increasing rather than decreasing their offending. While focusing on parents may have benefits it can also be part of a 'tougher' stance towards youth offending by, for example, the introduction of 'parenting orders'.

Other forms of social crime prevention involve what is sometimes referred to as 'community crime prevention' – involving individuals and institutions in a community or neighbourhood and mobilising community resources. Some of these have been influenced by Wilson and Kelling's (1982) influential 'broken window' theory, which argues that communities may 'tip' into high crime areas following an increase in, for example, incivilities, graffiti and rowdy behaviour. It is, however, sometimes unclear in what sense the word 'community' is being used – does it refer, for example, to some rather idealised notion of 'community', to a geographical neighbourhood, or to an aggregate of individuals and organisations within this neighbourhood? An example of how communities can become involved is provided by Neighbourhood Watch.

Neighbourhood Watch emerged in the early 1980s, based on the principle that the police and the community can work together to prevent crime. Based on local areas, schemes involve the public looking out for and reporting anything suspicious – being the 'eyes and ears' of the police. By 1988, as many as 14 per cent of households were members (Mayhew *et al.* 1989) and by 1996 there were 150,000 Neighbourhood Watch schemes with 5 million members.

The organisation of individual schemes varies enormously; however, they normally involve groups of residents with a local coordinator. Members produce and distribute newsletters and leaflets giving general crime prevention advice, often supported by local businesses. Some schemes encourage property marking and security surveys and members are asked to display their membership by the now familiar stickers on doors.

Despite its popularity the success of Neighbourhood Watch has been limited. One problem is that schemes are easier to set up and operate more effectively in areas in which they are least needed. Thus the British Crime Survey found that schemes were most common in affluent suburban areas, with members being drawn from high status and higher income groups (Mayhew *et al.* 1989). The population in multi-racial areas and poorest council estates, on the other hand, were least likely to join. This survey also found that areas where membership was lower also tended to be those where burglary risks were higher. This may have the effect that schemes divert police resources from high-crime to low-crime areas (Heal and Laycock 1986).

In addition, membership of a Neighbourhood Watch scheme may in reality mean very little and involvement often falls off after initial launch meetings (Bennett 1990). Three-quarters of members interviewed by the British Crime Survey had put stickers or posters in their windows but 21 per cent had neither attended progress meetings nor knew the name of their coordinator. Many members found it difficult to pinpoint any specific benefits of schemes although there are some indications that burglary risks were lower after joining Neighbourhood Watch. Displacement, discussed above, is also a problem of Neighbourhood Watch as a successful scheme might prevent crime in one group of streets, but crime may rise in an adjoining area without a scheme. It might well be that the benefit of schemes such as Neighbourhood Watch is to reassure the community that someone is trying to do something about crime.

5.5 THE 'SILVER BULLET': CCTV

A major feature of crime prevention has been the use of CCTV in a variety of areas including high streets, shopping malls, housing estates, organisations, schools, hospitals and individual retail establishments. From a mere two local authority schemes in 1987, there were around 440 town centre schemes by 1998. The government provided £37 million to fund the introduction of schemes between 1994 and 1997, and during that period it took up around 78 per cent of the crime prevention budget. A further £170 million was made available in 1999 (Coleman and Norris 2000). As Norris and Armstrong (1999) point out, it is now virtually impossible in Britain to move through public and private space without being subject to surveillance – as they comment:

> As consumers we are monitored by the routine use of cameras in retail outlets; whether in the supermarket, department store or corner shop. When we leave the store our image, in all probability, will be captured by high street, town centre and shopping mall camera systems. On our journey home, traffic cameras will monitor our compliance with speed and red light restrictions and, if we travel by rail, cameras at stations and along platforms will ensure a record of our presence. In other roles, whether it be as workers on the factory floor or at the office, as students, from kindergarten to university, as hospital patients, football fans or even customers at a local restaurant, cameras are probably watching over us. Put simply, in urban Britain ... in almost every area to which the public have access we are under surveillance from CCTV.
>
> (Norris and Armstrong 1999: 1)

It is widely believed that CCTV performs a number of functions and its use was highlighted in 1993 by the filming of the abduction of Jamie Bulger, the small child later killed. Its use may reduce the fear of crime by making people feel safer. A survey of losses from shops and retailers in 1994/5 showed a decrease in cheque fraud, down 53 per cent. This might be explained as customers switch to plastic cards. It is interesting to note that fraud using plastic cards was down 60 per cent and might reflect the methods of the use of CCTV (Brooks and Cross 1996). It is assumed that it can act as a deterrent to crime, as it means that an offence may be captured on camera and the perpetrator identified. It is thus seen as having the ability to prevent crime and to assist detection; and great faith was placed in this so-called 'silver bullet' to reduce crime. As the Home Secretary stated in 1995:

> CCTV catches criminals. It spots crimes, identifies law breakers and helps convict the guilty. The spread of this technology means that more town centres, shopping precincts, business centres and car parks around the country will become no-go areas for the criminal ... CCTV is a wonderful technological supplement to the police.
>
> (cited in Coleman and Norris (2000: 151).

CCTV is now ubiquitous and its use has grown particularly in the following areas (see, for example, Norris and Armstrong 1999):

- *In residential areas.* Many will be familiar with 'concierge' systems which monitor communal areas of housing estates and multi-storey blocks. It can be used to monitor those coming into areas to protect residents' safety but can also be used to monitor residents – against, for example, anti-social behaviour, vandalism and drug dealing in residential estates.

- *In schools.* Schools were previously vulnerable to intruders and vandals, and there were also concerns about assaults on teachers within schools. Many schools now have CCTV equipment. This can protect against intruders, verify the identity of people coming to collect children and identify the cause of possible accidents. CCTV cameras in schools can also be used to monitor the behaviour of pupils, checking, for example, for drug dealing in playgrounds.

- *On the road.* Since 1992, speed cameras, which have caused considerable controversy, have been employed and used in the enforcement of traffic legislation, as well as for popular entertainment shows. Vehicle licence plates can be recorded to assist catching thieves of stolen cars and also to assist combating terrorism.

- *In car parks and petrol stations.* There has been a considerable increase in video surveillance of car parks which has been claimed to have dramatically cut the numbers of vehicles stolen and vandalised. In addition, most major petrol stations now have CCTV installed to prevent robbery and theft.

- *Railways and trains.* Most stations now have CCTV monitoring and during the 1990s London Underground installed CCTV across its 250 stations. Drivers also have 'track to train' systems which allow them to receive pictures of the platform at each station and see pictures of the side of the train to monitor door and passenger safety (Norris and Armstrong 1999).

- *In shops.* Most shops, whether small corner shops or large supermarkets, chain and high street stores have CCTV. These protect against shoplifting, assaults on staff and robberies. In large stores they are also used covertly to monitor staff behaviour – to prevent theft but also to control behaviour – one Parcel Force employee was sacked after being filmed playing frisbee during working hours (Norris and Armstrong 1999).

- *In hospitals.* Publicised cases of babies being stolen and staff and patients being victimised by threatened and actual violence highlight the importance of security in hospitals and this is now widespread.

- *In town and city centres.* During the 1980s and 1990s, CCTV spread to public as well as private spaces – starting with, in 1985, a system covering the promenade in Bournemouth. The government funding referred to above led to a situation in which all major cities had city centre schemes by around 1996, and many smaller and medium-sized towns by 1998.

(Norris and Armstrong 1999)

Like other crime prevention measures, the success or otherwise of CCTV is not easy to evaluate. Any reduction in crime may be the result, not of CCTV, but of other factors – crime rates, for example, fluctuate in any event, and the police might patrol areas covered by CCTV more intensively (Coleman and Norris 2000). Displacement is also a problem. Its success may also be affected by the kind of systems in use and the extent to which, even if a crime is on camera, an operator is watching and can do anything about the offence. Research results have been somewhat contradictory, with some showing a reduction in crime after the installation of cameras, whereas others show little reduction, and yet others have indicated displacement. A variety of factors may affect the extent to which CCTV might work. For example, in order to be deterred by surveillance, a potential offender has to be aware of it, yet many people may not be aware of the system in operation. Discussing apparently contradictory results between studies in Airdrie, in Scotland, and Glasgow, Ditton and Short (1999) point out that Airdrie is a small town and the existence of cameras was well known. In addition, if offenders were filmed they could be readily identified. In Glasgow, however, many were unaware of the cameras and offenders were less easy to identify. Coleman and Norris (2000: 168) conclude that the 'criminological evidence is far from straightforward: the effects are neither universal nor consistent', and Ditton and Short (1999: 217) argue that 'open-street CCTV can "work in limited ways" ... in different ways in different situations'. As with forms of situational crime prevention, CCTV also raises issues of the intrusiveness of surveillance, which will be discussed below.

5.6 ISSUES IN CRIME PREVENTION

Crime prevention has therefore been a growth industry involving a 'mixed economy' of government, private sector, local authorities, criminal justice agencies and private citizens. There is a growing recognition that crime prevention should be taken into account by a wide range of agencies, and is not an activity restricted to criminal justice. This consciousness of crime prevention can nevertheless be spread wider than it is at present. There have been successes but there are also a number of issues associated with this growth. Some critics claim that successes are often short term and limited to situational crime prevention while leaving the social structural roots of crime relatively untouched. In addition, there are a number of concerns about the overall impact of crime prevention strategies.

As seen above, the Crime and Disorder Act 1998 requires a range of local bodies to consider crime and disorder by, for example, considering the impact on crime prevention in the designing of new homes, the provision of public transport, lighting and the licensing of pubs and clubs. Nevertheless, there remain areas where such a consciousness of crime prevention could usefully be developed and some talk of the 'greening' of crime prevention where the potential for crime could be incorporated into many more aspects of design and organisation (Pease 2002; Tilley 2002). As Pease points out, central government is not included in these requirements, nor is the private sector; and crime reduction practitioners report frustration at commercial practices such as the reluctance to add photographs to cheque guarantee cards. Pease argues that product designers should be required to look at the 'criminogenic capacity' of a product. Crime prevention should also be considered by a number of 'place managers' such as landlords whose neglect of property may assist burglary and drug dealing, licensees whose poor management allows pubs to be used for the sale of stolen goods and transport companies whose poorly lit stations and badly constructed bus shelters may encourage theft and vandalism. The implications of the growth of e-commerce should also take crime prevention into account.

Whatever the future developments of crime prevention may be, many point to some of the dangers inherent in some of the current strategies. Some, for example, point to the danger of creating a 'fortress society' organised around crime reduction (Crawford 1998; Tilley 2002) which may produce an adverse effect on the quality of life and on social relationships. Locks, bolts, bars and entry phones in housing developments may deter intruders but may also limit normal social interaction. An extreme form is the 'gated community' with 'perimeter' security. These kinds of schemes and the ever present surveillance from CCTV may, as seen above, increase people's fear of crime and feelings of insecurity.

Moreover, some measures may exacerbate social divisions. Tilley (2002), for example, talks of the creation of a society divided into safe and unsafe areas with whole groups of people, perceived to pose a danger, being excluded. There are also dangers of stigmatising communities, families and groups of young people picked out for their risk of becoming involved in crime. Social divisions may also be exacerbated by the ability of financially better off citizens to pay for security, whereas those with fewer resources cannot so do. Security, argue some, has become a 'commodity'. Moreover, the crime 'displaced' from the more affluent may be displaced onto those who are already the subject of repeat victimisation (Crawford 1998; Hughes 2002).

Other criticisms hinge around the faith placed in the 'technological fix' of situational crime prevention and the consequent neglect of the social conditions which may themselves be associated with crime. This limits the potential effectiveness of crime reduction measures while also diverting attention from these social conditions. This may be exacerbated by the tendency to prioritise crime reduction in areas of social policy. In what is described as the 'criminalisation of social policy', critics argue that community safety can be associated with the marginalisation of fundamental public issues except in so far as they are related to their criminogenic qualities (Hughes 2002).

Further criticisms of crime prevention and community safety policies relate to the relatively narrow range of crime which they encompass. The focus has largely tended to be on public, street crime, and more recently on a range of incivilities and disorderly behaviour – largely amongst young, working class youth. Other forms of crime may be relatively neglected such as the large amounts of violence in homes and workplaces, organised crime and white collar and corporate crime. The term 'community safety' has become associated with a relatively restricted range of crimes whereas in theory the notion of community safety could embrace a wider range not only of crime but of other harms, such as pollution, transport and other threats to safety. Some have accordingly called for a broader, 'pan hazard' approach to community safety which deals with a wide range of harms (Hughes 2002).

Finally, crime prevention has been regarded in the past as a bolt-on to the mainstream activities of the criminal justice system. Two things have changed this. The New Labour strategy that insists that all criminal justice agencies work together to concentrate on the objective of reducing crime and that it is not just the business of local communities or a matter of designing out crime. This new direction in crime prevention is also reinforced by a mood of optimism about the impact of a new style of policing adopted in the United States of America.

5.7 ZERO TOLERANCE POLICING

The crime prevention project was in part a frustration with the growth in crime and the feeling that nothing seemed to be working in terms of reducing and preventing crime. However, during the 1990s across the Atlantic could be heard a new mood of optimism that policing could play a more proactive and effective role in preventing crime. This emerging approach to crime prevention was called zero tolerance policing. It was an old idea that had gone out of fashion, the essential idea being that the police are the community's main weapon against crime and that if the police were more active and interventionist and did not tolerate, in the sense of ignoring, so much crime, then crime would fall. The phrase 'zero tolerance' was coined first within the New York Police Department (NYPD) to indicate that there would be no tolerance of police officers' involvement in drug taking and corrupt behaviour. If the NYPD could be cleaned up, then why not New York City? This more aggressive approach to policing low-level street crime, allowing more local autonomy to police commanders, using local neighbourhood intelligence and crucially not ignoring the minor acts of anti-social behaviour, was associated with William Bratton in Boston and NYC, Ed Davis Lowell in Massachusetts and the ideas of James Q Wilson and George Kelling and the broken windows thesis (*The Atlantic*, March 1982, pp 29–38).

William Bratton was appointed Police Commissioner of New York in 1994. Seven thousand extra police had been hired since 1990 under an initiative by Mayor David Dinkins to cope with the image of New York City as a place where crime was out of control. Bratton reformed the system of management so that it was more decentralised. Responsibility and accountability were pushed downward, empowering local commanders but with instructions to concentrate on types of crime that were conducive to public anxiety, including those that the police had been ignoring or tolerating in the past. The police were told to have a more visible profile on the streets and not to ignore minor infringements. Performance targets were introduced for local precincts. Considerable success is claimed for this method of policing. William Bratton writes, 'Over the past three years, the City's crime rate has dropped by 37 per cent. The homicide rate alone has plummeted over 50 per cent' (Bratton 1997: 29).

The emphasis of zero tolerance policing was not only to reduce crime but also to restore citizen confidence in New York as a safe place by showing that the police and not the criminals are in control of the streets. Part of the idea is to 'Prevent anti-social elements developing the feeling that they are in charge' (Dennis in Bratton 1997: 3). Norman Dennis wrote:

> Zero-tolerance policing is based on three ideas. One is the simple principle, 'nip things in the bud'. Prevent anti-social elements developing the feeling that they are in charge. Prevent a broken-down and ugly environment of neglect becoming a breeding ground for crime and disorder.
>
> (Dennis 1997: 3)

Tolerating minor crimes, such as disorderly behaviour, encourages the boundaries of anti-social behaviour. The broken windows thesis (Wilson and Kelling 1982) states that if minor incivilities, such as drunkenness, vandalism, begging, litter, graffiti and disorderly behaviour, go unchecked then an atmosphere is encouraged in which more serious crime will flourish. Incivilities encouraged a more general fear of crime. Graffiti might be seen by some as the exploration of artistic talent, whereas others might see it as a sign of urban disorder which drives away the respectable citizens and attracts anti-social elements.

> Subway stations became a shanty town for the homeless and aggressive begging increased, exacerbating a climate of fear, compounded by a significant and notorious decline in the quality of life as a whole.
>
> (Dennis 1997: 33)

The need to include community consultation was central to the project. The police are not able to control crime alone and need the cooperation of the public, and to do this they had to show they were acting in the interest of the public. Community partnership became part of the approach in New York City.

CONCLUSION

We have seen, therefore, that crime prevention has become a crucial area for many criminal justice agencies, working in partnership with a wide range of other groups. This grew out of a recognition that the criminal justice system was limited in its capacity to reduce crime. However, it has many other functions and (as seen above) tertiary crime prevention refers to work with offenders after conviction. Moreover, an essential part of crime reduction is the detection and prosecution of offenders; and the next chapter will look at the agency responsible for this – the police.

The debate about the effects of the zero tolerance approach to policing, and its failure to prove as popular in the United Kingdom as in the United States, reminds us that responding to crime in a democratic and free society is not the responsibility of any one agency. Professionals, lay groups and the community at large, as well as central government and local authorities, have a responsibility for responding to crime and seeking to prevent it. A truly comprehensive response to crime is unlikely to insist that the answer is found in any one solution, be it CCTV, reducing unemployment or working with criminals and potential criminals. A comprehensive approach would also recognise the crime prevention role played by the law enforcement agencies and the courts in curtailing the activities of the more active criminals and in reassuring the law-abiding public that, if caught and convicted, the criminal will be adequately punished. The public are undoubtedly aware that much crime is not solved and that many criminals evade prosecution. The problem in recent years is that some aspects of the criminal justice system have been seen by some sections of the public as colluding in helping offenders avoid punishment for their crimes. The phrase 'zero tolerance' captures a new and more aggressive public mood in which more is expected from the criminal justice system, and the police in particular, in its response to crime. In the next chapter we will examine the nature of policing in England and Wales at the beginning of the century.

Review questions

1 Read this extract from a speech by the Prime Minister at the Labour Party conference in Blackpool in 2002. Which of the measures listed in the speech do you think will have most effect on reducing crime and which in your opinion is likely to have least effect?

> Later this year we will introduce the Criminal Justice and Sentencing Reform Bill. It will re-balance the system emphatically and in favour of the victims of crime.
> Old rules will be swept away; court procedures simplified;
> Sentencing built round the offender as well as the offence, with
> Those on drugs getting treatment or custody.

More police on the beat. More Community Support Officers.

Instant fines for anti-social behaviour.

Parents of truants who refuse to cooperate with the school will be fined or lose benefit.

Anti-social tenants and their anti-social landlords who make money out of abusing Housing Benefit, while making life hell for the community, should lose their right to it.

Those who assault teachers or nurses should go to jail.

And from early next year, wealthy drug dealers or organised criminals with money in their bank account or a home or an asset of any sort but no lawful means of support will have it taken from them unless they show it was come by lawfully not through crime.

2 There are 376 Crime Reduction Partnerships in England and Wales. Use the map in the following website to find your local CDRP and identify its strategy for reducing crime. http://www.crimereduction.gov.uk/regions_map.htm

3 Read the extract below on the broken window's account of the causes of crime in a community. Answer the following questions:
   - What type of crime are the authors describing?
   - What is the sequence of causes that makes crime in the community more likely?
   - In terms of crime prevention how could this type of crime be prevented or reduced?

... at the community level, disorder and crime are usually inextricably linked, in a kind of developmental sequence. Social psychologists and police officers tend to agree that if a window in a building is broken and is left unrepaired, all the rest of the windows will soon be broken. This is as true in nice neighborhoods as in rundown ones. Window-breaking does not necessarily occur on a large scale because some areas are inhabited by determined window-breakers whereas others are populated by window-lovers; rather, one unrepaired broken window is a signal that no one cares, and so breaking more windows costs nothing. (It has always been fun.)

Philip Zimbardo, a Stanford psychologist, reported in 1969 on some experiments testing the broken-window theory. He arranged to have an automobile without license plates parked with its hood up on a street in the Bronx and a comparable automobile on a street in Palo Alto, California. The car in the Bronx was attacked by "vandals" within ten minutes of its "abandonment". The first to arrive were a family – father, mother, and young son – who removed the radiator and battery. Within twenty-four hours, virtually everything of value had been removed. Then random destruction began – windows were smashed, parts torn off, upholstery ripped. Children began to use the car as a playground. Most of the adult "vandals" were well-dressed, apparently clean-cut whites. The car in Palo Alto sat untouched for more than a week. Then Zimbardo smashed part of it with a sledgehammer. Soon, passersby were joining in. Within a few hours, the car had been turned upside down and utterly destroyed. Again, the "vandals" appeared to be primarily respectable whites.

Untended property becomes fair game for people out for fun or plunder and even for people who ordinarily would not dream of doing such things and who probably consider themselves law-abiding. Because of the nature of community life in the Bronx – its anonymity, the frequency with which cars are abandoned and things are stolen or broken, the past experience of "no one caring" – vandalism begins much more quickly than it does in staid Palo Alto, where people have come to believe that private possessions are cared for, and that mischievous behavior is costly. But vandalism can occur anywhere once communal barriers – the sense of mutual regard and the obligations of civility – are lowered by actions that seem to signal that "no one cares".

We suggest that "untended" behavior also leads to the breakdown of community controls. A stable neighborhood of families who care for their homes, mind each other's children, and confidently frown on unwanted intruders can change, in a few years or even a few months, to an inhospitable and frightening jungle. A piece of property is abandoned, weeds grow up, a window is smashed. Adults stop scolding rowdy children; the children, emboldened, become more rowdy. Families move out, unattached adults move in. Teenagers gather in front of the corner store. The merchant asks them to move; they refuse. Fights occur. Litter accumulates. People start drinking in front of the grocery; in time, an inebriate slumps to the sidewalk and is allowed to sleep it off. Pedestrians are approached by panhandlers.

At this point it is not inevitable that serious crime will flourish or violent attacks on strangers will occur. But many residents will think that crime, especially violent crime, is on the rise, and they will modify their behavior accordingly. They will use the streets less often, and when on the streets will stay apart from their fellows, moving with averted eyes, silent lips, and hurried steps. "Don't get involved." For some residents, this growing atomization will matter little, because the neighborhood is not their "home" but "the place where they live". Their interests are elsewhere; they are cosmopolitans. But it will matter greatly to other people, whose lives derive meaning and satisfaction from local attachments rather than worldly involvement; for them, the neighborhood will cease to exist except for a few reliable friends whom they arrange to meet.

Such an area is vulnerable to criminal invasion. Though it is not inevitable, it is more likely that here, rather than in places where people are confident they can regulate public behavior by informal controls, drugs will change hands, prostitutes will solicit, and cars will be stripped. That the drunks will be robbed by boys who do it as a lark, and the prostitutes' customers will be robbed by men who do it purposefully and perhaps violently. That muggings will occur.

Source: James Q Wilson and George L Kelling (1982) 'Broken Windows: The police and neighborhood safety', *The Atlantic Monthly*, March, pp 29–37

4 Look at Figure 5.1 and identify whether the crime solutions discussed in the extract from Wilson and Kelly above are:
   – *primary/secondary/tertiary*; and
   – focused on *offender*, *situation* or *victims*?

Further reading

Pease, K (2002) 'Crime Reduction' in Maguire, M, Morgan, R and Reiner, R (eds) *The Oxford Handbook of Criminology* (3rd edn), Clarendon Press: Oxford pp. 947–979.

CHAPTER 6

The police

INTRODUCTION

Policing attracts much public interest. Police dramas and documentaries nightly fill up television schedules and detective fiction and crime stories regularly feature in publishers' bestseller lists. But these popular images are often very far from the reality of policing. Police dramas feature murder, violent and organised crime, and investigations involve following up clues, dramatic car chases and almost always the police catch the offender and bring him or her – or them – to justice. In reality, as we have seen, clear up rates are more modest, murders are rare, many crimes are solved because the victim identifies the perpetrator, or they are discovered by chance, and in the life of an average police officer car chases and violent encounters with suspects are, perhaps fortunately, rare. The routine work of policing is less dramatic than television portrays, but is no less important for everyday life in the community. In addition, the police perform a wide range of essential roles – they are at the forefront of the 'wars' against terrorism and serious crime and have to respond to major incidents and disasters as well as dealing with a host of non-criminal problems such as missing persons.

There are other, less positive, images of policing. In riots and demonstrations the police can be seen in pitched battles with demonstrators and there have been allegations of incompetence as well as improper behaviour: planting evidence, 'fitting up' suspects and violence by the police. These different images illustrate some of the problems in defining the role of the police. Are they better described as a force or a service? Is it possible to talk about consensus policing or are the police essentially a paramilitary force waging a war against crime and disorder?

The conflicting demands of due process, crime control, bureaucratic efficiency and offender management strongly affect how the police are organised and evaluated. They are expected to find and bring to court those suspected of having committed an offence, but while doing so must stay within the law, and the requirements of the adversarial system of justice. The police must have powers to investigate crime but the public must be able to proceed without undue interference. Policing must be cost effective, but this is difficult to measure – how, for example, can the value of due process be measured? Having more police on the beat may make the public feel happier, but it might be costly and have little effect on crime. The police have also been affected by the managerialist policies affecting all parts of the criminal justice process, with an emphasis on national and local plans, targets for specific offences and 'intelligence led' policing. While collecting evidence and bringing offenders to justice is often perceived as the major role of the police, as seen in Chapter 5, they also play a major role in crime prevention and in managing offenders and suspects, such as in crime and disorder partnerships, and in diverting potential or actual young offenders from crime or the criminal justice system.

There have been major reforms to police work in the last three decades. A key piece of legislation affecting police powers was the Police and Criminal Evidence Act 1984 which brought together and rationalised many disparate rules, including providing a clearer set of procedures for stopping, searching and detaining and questioning suspects. Major changes to police organisation and management followed the Sheehy Report of 1993 and the subsequent reform enacted in the Police and Magistrates' Court Act 1994. Responses to concerns raised about 'institutional racism' in the MacPherson Report of 1999 have driven further legislative and practice changes. The Police Reform Act of 2002 introduced new procedures regarding the supervision of police forces and a new independent system for handling complaints against the police. This broadened the circumstances in which senior officers can be removed, and made changes to police powers.

This chapter will examine many of these issues and explore the current organisation of policing in England and Wales. It will start by looking at the role and development of the police. It will then examine how the police are organised and how accountable they are. Legislation regulating how the police exercise their powers will be considered, followed by an outline of different forms of police work and community policing. The police have considerable discretion and how they exercise this will be explored along with issues identified in relation to the particular issues of policing of minority ethnic communities. Many discussions of the police automatically refer to the police in the public sector, but it is important to recognise, as seen in Chapter 1, that there is a vast and growing private security sector, its members carrying out an increasing number of police tasks. This chapter will look primarily at the work of the public police service.

6.1 THE ROLE AND DEVELOPMENT OF POLICING

Policing in its general sense is a part of social control and can be carried out in many different settings, only some of which involve the organisation known as 'the' police. To Reiner (2000: 7) 'policing' is:

> an aspect of social control processes which occurs universally in all social situations in which there is at least the potential for conflict, deviance or disorder. It involves surveillance to discover actual or anticipated breaches and the threat or mobilization of sanctions to ensure the security of the social order.

Policing may be carried out without involving any specialist organisation – it takes place, for example, in schools and workplaces. As seen in Chapter 5, surveillance may involve CCTV or can be incorporated into the design of city spaces and buildings; thus preventing crime need not involve 'the police'. In pre-industrial societies policing was carried out by an assortment of constables or watchmen, gamekeepers or by individuals employed to protect property. In contemporary societies many organisations carry out policing functions – government departments such as the Inland Revenue or the Department of Trade and Industry have investigatory agencies who may prosecute offenders; and the Health and Safety Executive, Trading Standards Officers and Environment Agency also 'police' compliance with health and safety legislation, consumer protection and pollution control. There are a large number of security firms and many large companies have security departments. Citizens, as seen in Chapter 5, are involved in Neighbourhood Watch Schemes or may join the Special Constabulary and there are vigilante organisations. Indeed there has been an enormous growth in what are often described as private police organisations, such as Group 4. These are distinguished from the 'public police', most commonly described as 'the police', who are tasked with the investigation of crime, the arrest and detention of suspects and preparing cases to pass on to the CPS. 'The police' are distinct in that they can legitimately use coercive force; and organised state police forces emerged along with the modern state.

The police are responsible for law enforcement, for investigating crime, arresting suspects and deciding whether or not to pass the case on to the CPS. This reflects their key role as enforcers of the criminal law. They are also the guardians of the Queen's Peace and preserving law and order in society. This involves a peace keeping role characterised by patrolling the streets and dealing with local disputes and disorder along with a more 'militaristic' role in dealing with major disturbances and demonstrations. They are expected to play a role in reducing crime, and reassuring the public. In addition they perform roles which are less involved with crime but rather with what has been described as 'social' or emergency service in which they trace missing persons, inform citizens about the death or injury of relatives, deal with accidents and a host of other non-criminal incidents. Some of the many different roles of the police, whose main functions are outlined in Chapter 1, are:

- *Crime control and investigation*: 'crime fighting' – detecting and identifying suspects and compiling a case against offenders.
- *Crime reduction*: patrolling and playing a role in crime and disorder partnerships; giving advice about crime prevention (see Chapter 5).
- *Order maintenance*: dealing with crowds at, for example, sporting events and demonstrations.

- *Peace keeping*: maintaining the 'Queen's Peace' which involves dealing with neighbours' disputes and minor skirmishes.

- *Social service*: dealing with reports of missing persons and other non-criminal issues which are reported to them.

- *Emergency*: providing an emergency service and responding to disorder, accidents and other emergencies.

- *State security*: protecting public figures, state buildings and intelligence work in relation to terrorist and other perceived threats to the state.

In practice, these roles are interrelated and not all incidents the police are called to are immediately identifiable as either 'crime' or 'public order' – they are incidents requiring some form of action. Imagine, for example, a situation in which officers are called to investigate complaints about noise and disturbance in a street. In this situation they will principally be concerned to calm the situation which might be achieved by their very presence or might involve making arrests. If they behave too aggressively, however, they might exacerbate the situation. In other circumstances they may proffer advice and help or refer parties to another agency. Thus in many situations roles are combined, when the police are dealing with 'potential crime' situations. Studies of calls to the police have found that potential crime situations account for 53 per cent of all calls, with 20 per cent involving social disorder, 18 per cent involving information or services and traffic matters accounting for 8 per cent of all calls (Morgan and Newburn 1997). Much police work therefore does not involve dealing with serious crime and is much more mundane than the 'crime fighting' or 'detecting' images suggested in the media.

There can be conflicts between these different roles. Bowling and Foster (2002), for example, discuss the potentially opposing 'liberal' and 'military' models of policing. The British Police have been noted for an emphasis on consensus policing emphasising their role as peace keepers providing a *service*, who use minimum force and stress community safety. On the other hand, the police are expected to provide a rapid and efficient response to major disturbances which may emphasise their military role, and describing them as a *force* emphasises 'harder' policing styles using vocabulary such as the 'war on crime'. The style adopted may affect other roles – if, for example, the police are seen as a 'force' from outside imposing order, people may be less likely to provide them with the information which is so vital for collecting evidence for prosecution.

The adversarial system of criminal justice may create further dilemmas. As seen in Chapter 1, this system does not seek to establish the truth, but requires that a case is proved beyond reasonable doubt through the provision of legally admissible evidence. Thus the test of success for the police becomes whether an investigation leads to a prosecution and finding of guilt. In some of the cases which have been labelled as 'miscarriages of justice' it has been alleged that the police have tampered with evidence or improperly gained confessions in order to provide evidence to support their view of the defendants' guilt. If no other source of evidence is available they face the possibility that a guilty person will escape justice. In high-profile cases arousing public outrage, especially those involving terrorism, pressure to get a result may lead to the use of illegally obtained evidence. The Police and Criminal Evidence Act 1984 recognised these pressures by enacting a range of measures from disciplinary proceedings to the inadmissibility of evidence to make such temptations easier to resist.

Development of policing

Some of these issues can be seen in a brief account of the development of policing in England and Wales particularly since the inception of the 'new police' in the nineteenth century, before which there was no one public organisation responsible for policing.

In 1829, the Metropolitan Police Improvement Act set up the Metropolitan Police Force. Initially this consisted of 1,000 officers controlled from No. 4 Whitehall Place – backing on to Scotland Yard. Similar forces were set up in municipal corporations and counties and, following the County and Borough Police Act 1856, there were 239 forces operating in England and Wales. These early police forces concentrated largely on patrolling the streets. In 1842, following two attempts on the life of Queen Victoria, a small detective branch was set up, consisting of two inspectors and six sergeants. By 1877 it had expanded to 250 men. A Fenian bombing campaign during the 1880s led to the formation of the Special Irish Branch, later to become the Special Branch, specialising in counteracting subversive political and industrial activity. As the police force grew and new technology became available, new specialist functions emerged. In 1901 the system of classifying fingerprints was introduced, and in 1910 the Metropolitan Police first caught a criminal using radio telegraphy. In 1920 the police acquired two motor vans – the birth of the flying squad. Women officers were introduced in 1919, although women, often police constables' wives, had been employed as 'matrons' to deal with female convicts and matters involving children. Until 1973, women were organised in a separate department and paid less than male officers. After 1973 the women's organisation was abolished and the force was integrated.

From their inception, the 'new police' were unpopular. The working classes saw them as a potentially oppressive force, popularly described as a 'plague of blue locusts', 'blue devils', or 'crushers'. The middle and upper classes saw a threat to their liberty from so-called government spies. Gradually, however, opposition from both groups was overcome and the police gained legitimacy. This success was due, according to Reiner (2000) to the policies adopted by early commissioners which created the distinctive style of English policing. Crucial to these policies, devised in an attempt to secure the support of the public at large, was the emphasis on the independence of the police from any particular class or political influence.

Reiner identifies several key elements of these early strategies. In the first place, a quasi-military command structure incorporated elements of rank, authority and discipline. This bureaucratic organisation, which included training and a career structure to attract high-quality recruits, distinguished the 'new' police from their disorganised and often corrupt forerunners. In addition, the importance of upholding the rule of law was stressed, thus protecting citizens from any abuse of police powers. A policy of minimum force sought to allay fears of the working classes that the police would be unduly oppressive. This led to one of the most distinctive features of British policing – the absence of firearms in everyday duties and a reluctance to use paramilitary tactics more common in the United States and many European countries. In addition, the police were to be non-partisan and impartial in their enforcement of the law, favouring the interests of neither one class nor the other. This impartiality was underlined by denying police officers the vote until 1887, and they are still not allowed to affiliate to political parties or have a trade union. The Police Federation represents police officers of the rank of constable (up to chief inspector) but they are not allowed to take industrial action.

The reluctance to expand the detective branch arose out of a deep-rooted suspicion of the plain clothes officer. Hostility was reduced as the new police gained a reputation for being relatively effective in preventing and detecting crime. Finally, argues Reiner, their legitimacy increased as a result of changes in society itself. By the 1950s there was less class conflict than before, the working classes had become more incorporated into society and were relatively homogeneous – thus the public as a whole tended to have a shared conception of what they expected from the police.

By the 1950s, generally depicted as a golden age of consensus policing, the legitimacy of the police was established. This was symbolised by the popular Dixon of Dock Green television series which portrayed a friendly local bobby whose knowledge of his patch helped him to prevent crime, catch local villains, and help many members of the local community. Dixon was followed by very different TV heroes in such programmes as The Sweeney and the Professionals in the 1970s and 1980s, and the popular series of the early 1990s Between the Lines dealing with police discipline and complaints.

From the 1950s the legitimacy which the police had established was challenged on several fronts. The urban disturbances of 1981, which led to the Scarman Report, were in part attributed to the frequent use in multi-racial areas of stop-and-search powers. Increasing evidence emerged of cases where the police were found to have tampered with evidence, secured false confessions and abused their powers. Other complaints concerned how suspects were dealt with in custody. This raised the issue of how accountable the police were – both in terms of individual complaints and police policy. What happened to change the image of the police, in Reiner's words, from 'plods to pigs'? (Reiner 2000: 59).

The key factors which led to increased legitimacy, according to Reiner, can also account for its decline. Revelations about corruption on the part of police officers during the 1960s and allegations about improper behaviour severely dented the image of the police as a disciplined force, showing that they could readily break the law in order to enforce it. The 1970s and 1980s saw the increasing use of riot shields and other modern hardware in the control of industrial disputes and urban unrest, replacing the 'pushing and shoving' strategy used in demonstrations during the 1950s and 1960s. The accidental killing of innocent citizens by armed police officers attracted much criticism, especially from their traditional supporters, the middle classes. The traditional political impartiality of the police was also questioned during the general election of 1979, when they campaigned vigorously for stronger law and order policies. Finally, society itself had changed. Whereas during the so-called golden age the working class was a more homogeneous community, by the 1980s it was increasingly fragmented and divided with the growth of unemployment, the increasingly multi-racial nature of urban communities, and the growth of what some describe as an underclass. This made it more difficult for the police to satisfy the now conflicting expectations about how areas should be policed.

Police relationships with the public were also affected by the consequences of changes in the nature and organisation of policing. Like any organisation the police face pressures for efficiency and must respond to changes in crime which may lead to the use of more sophisticated technology. These pressures also produced specialisation. This necessitated organisational changes which vitally affected relationships between the police and local communities.

A simple example of this is the effect of expansion in cars, traffic and car owner-ship. The increasing volume of cars on the roads necessitated the development of techniques of traffic control and the enforcement of road traffic legislation. Specialist traffic control using increasingly sophisticated technology followed. As car ownership spread, many groups, particularly the middle classes, previously unlikely to encounter the police in their law enforcement role, became the subject of police attention. Cars also became an essential tool in law enforcement and patrolling, and had a fundamental impact on the job of the police constable. The car chase has become a symbolic feature of policing in both popular imagery and police folklore. And, of course, as well as increasing the mobility of criminals, cars have provided multiple opportunities for crime – from vandalism to serious car theft, ramraiding, joyriding and 'car jacking': for some joyriders part of the thrill is the chase with the police. Violence resulting from motoring incidents has even led to the coining of a new term for such crimes: 'road rage'.

Similar points could be made about other technological developments – com-puters have radically changed the nature of policing as have developments in communications. The beat officer of 40 years ago could not instantly call on the police computer, let alone the local station, to provide instant back-up. Information had to be gathered directly from the public. While undoubtedly these developments have increased the ability of the police to respond quickly to emergencies, to call for help, and to sift through large amounts of information, they have had important con-sequences for relations between the police and public, and for the basic role of the police officer.

This can be seen in contrasting the work of officers during the period of the so-called golden age of policing, when officers were allocated a beat and were responsible for patrolling it, often on foot. This meant that officers got to know the local community – they would make purchases from shopkeepers, visit local cafés and come into contact with many residents. The intelligence they gathered from these natural social contacts may have helped when they came to investigate a crime. Armed only with a truncheon and a whistle to call for help, the constable had to rely on his or her own wits to handle troublesome situations. Communication with the station was made through the police box and incidents had to be handled on the spot.

This form of policing could, however, be seen as inefficient. One officer could cover only a limited area, whereas two officers, in a car, receiving their information from a radio link with the station, could cover a much larger area and arrive at inci-dents much quicker. The lone officer on patrol is also unlikely to catch many criminals – no self-respecting burglar is going to break in when they see a constable walking down the road. The growth of many specialised functions also fundamen-tally changed the job of the basic constable on the beat, who became less involved in detecting crime and proportionately more involved with the more mundane elements of police work such as dealing with drunks, vagrants or handling minor local incidents.

This affected relationships between the police and the public. Whereas the old style beat officer encountered many members of the public while pounding the beat, officers in cars had less immediate contact. The public were less likely to know or have encountered these officers, and information tended to come from the police station rather than from the public. The ability to call instantly for back-up meant that officers were less reliant on their own personal skills to handle situations and the cars and radios in themselves became symbols of authority.

In addition, pressures for efficiency led to a stress on law enforcement as opposed to service or preventative roles – to the more readily measurable aspects of police work such as arrest rates, clear-up rates and response times, often described as fire brigade policing. This meant that other, less easily measurable, tasks became seen as less significant. The 1970s and 1980s also saw the rise of what is often called paramilitary policing. A spate of urban disturbances and industrial disputes prompted the development of specialist squads trained to deal with riots and crowd control. These units, including the Special Patrol Group, were increasingly armed with the hardware used for disturbances in Ulster and abroad. Their tactics caused enormous controversy, especially during the miners' strike of 1984. Some were also used as a back-up for crime-fighting initiatives, which involved the intensive use of stop-and-search powers. These kinds of tactics were found by the Scarman Report to have been partly responsible for local resentments which contributed to the breakdown in relations between the police and public preceding the Brixton disturbances of 1981.

All of these factors illustrate the many tensions in the role of the police and there are different views about which roles they should prioritise. An Audit Commission report, for example, recommended that the police should adopt a more proactive, 'intelligence led' approach involving targeting the most prolific offenders and using 'intelligence' gathered from informers and surveillance. This may conflict with public opinion which consistently indicates a preference for more 'bobbies on the beat' and foot patrols (Morgan and Newburn 1997), although this may not be very effective in preventing or investigating crime – one study, for example, estimated that a patrol officer in London was likely to pass by a burglary only once in every 8 years and even then might not catch the offender (Clarke and Hough 1984). Research commissioned for the Audit Commission found that while the public were generally satisfied with police performance in relation to emergencies, motoring offences, traffic and riot control they were dissatisfied with their performance in relation to detecting burglaries and foot patrols. Other studies indicate a public preference for more community-based policing. This may, however, conflict with police officers' own preference for what to them is 'real police work' and is associated with action, arrests and catching serious offenders (Morgan and Newburn 1997).

6.2 ORGANISATION AND ACCOUNTABILITY

Policing in England and Wales is carried out by 43 forces and in 2002 involved a net annual expenditure of £8,385,909,749 (Mawby and Wright 2003). The number of police officers has risen to record levels in recent years with a total of 129,603 officers in 2002. The number of female police officers has also increased to a total of 22,784 in 2002 and there were 3,362 minority ethnic officers. In addition there were 58,022 civilian staff and 11,598 special constables. The different forces differ in size, with the eight metropolitan forces, in Greater Manchester, City of London, Merseyside, the Metropolitan Police, Northumbria, South Yorkshire, West Midlands and West Yorkshire, accounting for 46 per cent of the total police strength. Scotland has eight regional police forces with a different legal tradition and accountability structure and the Police Service of Northern Ireland replaced the former Royal Ulster Constabulary in November 2001.

Police officers are distributed between various ranks, a feature introduced to maintain discipline. The rank structure was felt by the Sheehy Report to contain 'too many chiefs and not enough indians' and the number of ranks was reduced by the Police and Magistrates' Courts Act 1994. From 1995, the rank structure is as shown in Figure 6.1.

Figure 6.1 Rank structure

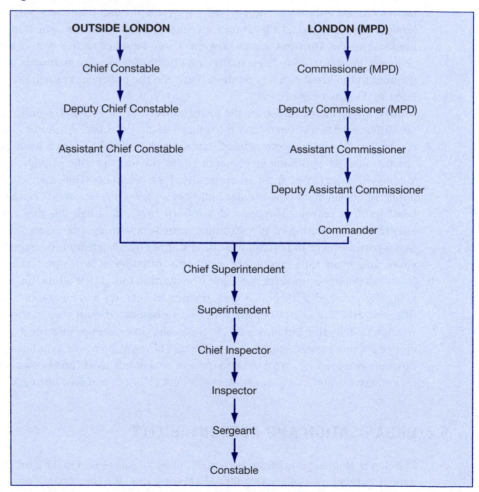

Each force is divided into geographical areas or divisions and, while there is considerable variation in organisation, there will typically be a force headquarters which houses strategic managers and support departments, and a number of Basic Command Units (BCUs), which deliver policing services within a geographical area. Mawby and Wright detail the structure of a typical provincial force – summarised in Figure 6.2.

Basic Command Units are seen as a central element of this structure and, since April 2001, they have been subject to Inspection by HMIC and to a range of performance indicators. The responsibility for working with the Crime and Disorder Partnerships outlined in Chapter 5 is placed with BCUs although it is often passed to Local Policing Units or 'sectors' which have responsibility for local areas, with some officers being responsible for maintaining links with the local community on 'beats' and 'micro-beats' (Mawby and Wright 2003).

Figure 6.2 The structure of a typical provincial force

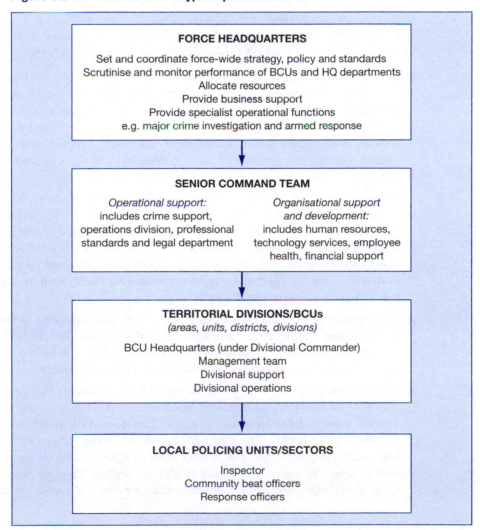

FORCE HEADQUARTERS

Set and coordinate force-wide strategy, policy and standards
Scrutinise and monitor performance of BCUs and HQ departments
Allocate resources
Provide business support
Provide specialist operational functions
e.g. major crime investigation and armed response

SENIOR COMMAND TEAM

Operational support:
includes crime support, operations division, professional standards and legal department

Organisational support and development:
includes human resources, technology services, employee health, financial support

TERRITORIAL DIVISIONS/BCUs
(areas, units, districts, divisions)

BCU Headquarters (under Divisional Commander)
Management team
Divisional support
Divisional operations

LOCAL POLICING UNITS/SECTORS

Inspector
Community beat officers
Response officers

Source: Adapted from Mawby and Wright (2003) *Handbook of Policing*, p. 176

The Metropolitan Police have a number of specialist squads and departments dealing with forensic investigations, intelligence, serious crimes and terrorism. These squads can all call on specialist departments such as the forensic science laboratories, the fingerprint branch, the photographic branch and the national identification bureau. There are also the traffic police, the Thames division which patrols the River Thames 24 hours a day, a mounted branch and an air support unit which assists with traffic and crowd control along with the royalty and diplomatic protection department, the special escort group and an art squad. Not all forces have such a large number of branches. While the police in England and Wales are organised primarily on a local level, the increasingly international and organised nature of serious crime has led to the development of nationally and internationally organised policing (Mawby and Wright 2003). These are particularly important as what is often called serious crime, which includes organised crime, operates across regional and national borders – often described as 'cross-border' or transnational crime. The drugs industry and serious crimes such as organised art theft, people trafficking, counterfeiting and money laundering are now global enterprises requiring much more cooperation between regional and national police organis-ations. Some of these were referred to in Chapter 4 and they include:

■ *National Crime Squad.* Regional Crime Squads were set up in 1964 to deal with offences transcending the local boundaries of any one force, such as drug traf-ficking. In 1998 these were amalgamated to form the National Crime Squad (NCS) whose work involves targeting serious and organised crime such as drug traf-ficking, immigration crime, illegal arms trafficking, money laundering and counterfeit currency – around 75 per cent of its work involves drugs. Officers are seconded to the squad, which had 1,176 officers in 2002.

■ *National Criminal Intelligence Service* (NCIS). This body also seconds officers not only from the police but from the Home Office, HM Customs and Excise and local authorities. In 2002 it had 287 police officers and 482 civilians, some of whom are 'analysts'. It has links with Interpol and its work covers strategic overviews of organised crime; gathering operational intelligence on the 'top few' criminals; providing specialist services; coordinating intelligence; and producing the National Intelligence Model (NIM).

■ *Interpol* is the oldest international police network which passes criminal intelli-gence between different countries. It has 176 members. The *United Nations Convention Against Transnational Organised Crime* was signed in 2000 to promote cooperation in respect of transnational organised crime.

■ *Europe-wide police arrangements* include the Trevi Group, originally set up to deal with counter-terrorist measures, and the Schengen Group, which was set up following relaxed border controls in the European Union and provides for increased police cooperation, information systems and the ability of officers from one country to pursue offenders outside their own jurisdictions. *Europol* was set up following the Maastricht Treaty in 1993 to replace Trevi to develop infor-mation exchanges between law enforcement agencies in EU member states.

To whom are the police accountable?

A key issue in looking at police organisation is to whom are they answerable, or accountable. As we have seen, a major characteristic of the British police has been their independence from direct political control. This can, however, lead to a situation in which they could be seen to have too much autonomy from both central government or local communities. At the same time too much control from the centre is often criticised as leading to centralisation, thereby reducing the influence of local communities. Outside London, local police authorities (LPAs) are responsible for a variety of functions. Disciplinary and complaints procedures deal with individual matters, and the police are ultimately accountable to the law and the courts.

The Police Act 1964 set up a tripartite structure involving, outside London, chief constables, the Home Secretary and police authorities which were composed of two-thirds elected representatives from local councils and one-third justices of the peace. The Metropolitan Police area does not have a police authority and the Commissioner is directly answerable to the Home Secretary. By the 1990s these bodies were subject to criticism that they were large, some having as many as 46 members, and that their links with the local community and the extent of their powers were uncertain. While they were, for example, responsible, under s. 5(1) of the Police Act 1964, for 'the maintenance of an adequate and efficient police force for the area', exactly how they should do this was ambiguous. Two key roles were the appointment of a chief constable and approving the budget. The Home Secretary, however, approved the appointment of chief constables and in practice police authorities had little control over how budgets were spent or over police policy. While they could ask for a report from the chief constable, this could be refused if it would contain operational matters which it would not be in the public interest to disclose. A study by the Policy Studies Institute found that policy developments such as crime prevention, crimes against women and children, and the diversion of administrative tasks from uniformed officers to civilian employees was increasingly determined by central government, and that local police authorities had little influence over these developments (Jones and Newburn 1994a). This study also found that police authorities took too narrow a view of their role, lacked relevant information and expertise and were too large and cumbersome to carry out effective discussion.

The Police and Magistrates' Court Act 1994 changed this structure. In controversial proposals the government sought to make chief constables more responsible for budgets and to exert more control over their appointment. Many of the original proposals, which might have led to greater centralisation, were dropped, and the Act set up a new structure, aspects of which are summarised below (Leishman *et al.* 1998; Mawby and Wright 2003).

- The primary duty of the police authority is 'to secure the maintenance of an efficient and effective police force for its area'.

- Each local police authority consists of a maximum of seventeen members consisting of three magistrates, five independent members and nine locally elected councillors.

- Independent members are selected through a complex procedure involving existing members of police authorities and the Home Office.

- Local police authorities are no longer committees of local authorities but free-standing authorities.

- Financial management is the responsibility of the chief constable, with authorities having a monitoring role.

- Each authority must develop a local policing plan, drafted by the chief constable, who must be consulted about any changes which the police authority, who retain 'ownership' of the plan, wish to make.

- The Home Office determines the cash grant to police authorities and approves the appointment of Chief Constables and the Home Secretary is empowered to amalgamate forces.

- The Home Office is also responsible for setting national objectives for policing, which must be taken account of by local police authorities.

Changing policy views on the correct balance between local and national policing have been evident in legislation. Part of the intention of the Police and Magistrates' Court Act 1994 was to strengthen the role of local police authorities. Despite this, considerable local variations have been found in local policing plans, and later legislation has moved more power to the centre with an apparent shift from political to managerial accountability and greater emphasis on national policing objectives and key performance targets (Bowling and Foster 2002). The latest legislative changes, in the Police Reform Act 2002, introduced the National Policing plan for 2003–6 which sets out the government's strategic priorities for the police service. These are to deliver improved police performance and greater public reassurance with particular regard to the following priorities:

- tackling anti-social behaviour and disorder;

- reducing volume, street, drug-related and violent and gun crime in line with local and national targets;

- combating serious and organised crime operating across force boundaries;

- increasing the number of offences brought to justice.

Local communities may affect policing via Police Community Consultative Groups (PCCGs) set up after the Scarman report. These consist of members of the public, usually invited from a number of relevant organisations, and a number of local officers. They have no formal power, and tend to be drawn from a very small section of society, with few representatives from groups who are likely to suffer most from any abuse of police powers or from the adverse effects of policies (Morgan 1989), although the Crime and Disorder Act 1998 requires local authorities and the police to consult with 'hard to reach groups'. While they have played some role in improving police communications with surrounding communities (Morgan and Newburn 1997), they are generally seen as relatively ineffective with little information on the basis of which to affect or effectively criticise police policies. As Bowling and Foster (2002) point out, they involve consultation, which is not full accountability.

Legal accountability

The police are not above the law. They must operate within the same laws as the public and within additional rules specific to the police. The rules both give power to the police and limit their actions. The Police and Criminal Evidence Act 1984 (PACE) and the codes made under its authority, outlined below, are there to protect the citizen from the abuse of police powers, and also to set out what is acceptable behaviour on the part of the police, and so protect them.

In order to convict, a court must be sure that an offence has been committed and that the evidence to prove this is admissible in court. PACE affects what is admissible in court by giving the courts the power – in some cases the duty – to exclude evidence that has been obtained in contravention of some of its major provisions. Thus the courts and the judiciary play a role in police accountability. Abuse of powers in the early stages could ultimately prevent a conviction being obtained.

Yet despite safeguards, courts do convict on illegally obtained evidence, if the judge and jury are convinced that it is reliable and relevant evidence. In court, in some cases the reality often is that it is a police officer's word against a defendant's. Given that the police are trained to present evidence in court they are likely to appear more credible witnesses, especially where they enjoy public confidence.

Aggrieved citizens can complain to the police force in question, and internal discipline within the police also protects the citizen. Prior to 2002, all complaints were recorded and, if not dealt with informally, were investigated under the auspices of the Police Complaints Authority (PCA). Complaints were investigated by an officer within the force but serious complaints, or those against a senior officer, involved the appointment of an officer from another force. This structure attracted criticism, particularly on the grounds that it was largely the police investigating themselves. This was justified on the basis that professionals such as the police, along with doctors and lawyers, are the only people with the necessary knowledge and expertise to investigate complaints. Many who complained expressed dissatisfaction with the process and there was considerable support for an independent system. In 2000 the government announced the creation of the Independent Police Complaints Commission (IPCC) to increase public confidence, accessibility, openness and independence and improve communication between the police and the public. This may well increase public confidence but commentators such as Bowling and Foster (2002) question the extent to which it will be able to resolve some of the problems which contribute to the low rate of substantiation of complaints. Many complaints, for example, involve incidents which have not been observed, meaning that it is the complainant's word against a police officer's, and they also refer to a 'blue wall of silence' that covers up police misconduct.

6.3 POLICE POWERS AND THE POLICE AND CRIMINAL EVIDENCE ACT 1984

As we have seen, the exercise of police powers is subject to rules and guidelines, and the extent of police powers has occasioned considerable controversy since the inception of the 'new police'. On the one hand, the police clearly need powers to stop people on the street if they are suspected of a crime, to enter people's houses if they suspect that they are hiding stolen goods or firearms and to arrest people they suspect of a crime. They need to be able to interview suspects in the police station and may have to hold suspects in cells. On the other hand, individual citizens need to be able to go about their everyday lives without risking being stopped on the street, having their homes ransacked by the police and being arrested and taken to the police station. Suspects must be protected from torture, brutality and the extraction of false confessions. Special protection may be afforded to vulnerable groups such as the young and mentally ill. Legislation on police powers therefore must balance conflicting needs and reflects the constant tension discussed in this book between disparate approaches to criminal justice, most notable in this area between crime control and due process.

The Royal Commission on Criminal Procedure (RCCP) set up in 1978 found that the law on police powers was piecemeal and haphazard. Different provisions enabled the police to stop and search, and powers of arrest were included in 70 different statutes. In addition the Royal Commission felt that crime investigation should be separated from prosecution and accordingly recommended the setting up of a separate Crown Prosecution Service. The subsequent Police and Criminal Evidence Act 1984 (PACE) sought to modernise and rationalise the law governing police powers and to reform aspects of the law relating to criminal evidence. One of its major innovations was to provide for the tape recording of interviews in police stations. Other safeguards for suspects included provisions requiring the police to keep records of their dealings with suspects at all stages. PACE, as it has become universally known, fundamentally changed many aspects of policing.

The Act provides for the creation of Codes of Practice to deal with the minutiae of implementation. Codes can more easily be amended than Acts of Parliament. The Codes themselves, which in their latest form were implemented on 1 April 2003, and are supplemented by Annexes and Notes for guidance to aid interpretation, cover the following areas:

- Code A Powers of stop and search
- Code B Search of premises and seizure of property
- Code C Detention, treatment and questioning of suspects
- Code D Identification procedures
- Code E Tape recording of interviews with suspects
- Code F Visual recording with sound of interviews

The operation of PACE has been considered in the context of reviews of the criminal justice system, such as in the Runciman Commission. The Codes made under PACE have been regularly updated and amended in the light of developing practice and new technology. Additionally, in May 2002 the Home Secretary announced a joint review, specifically of PACE, by the Home Office and the Cabinet Office. The purposes of that review were to focus on simplifying procedures, reducing administrative burdens on the police and speeding up justice. Some of the Review's recommendations have been incorporated into the Criminal Justice Act 2003 in relation to changes to police powers. A new power is made to create codes of practice that relate to specific areas for specific periods or to apply to particular offences or descriptions of offender.

Whilst the Codes are not part of direct legislation and whilst breaches of a provision of a Code by the police does not of itself constitute an offence, they can be the basis of a complaint against the police which may lead to a disciplinary matter or, in appropriate cases, criminal proceedings or a civil claim. Additionally, and importantly, significant transgression of any Code provision may mean that evidence obtained as a result might be excluded in any subsequent trial (see Chapter 10).

The Act sets out the powers of the police in various circumstances, and provides safeguards for suspects as to when the powers can be exercised. In some cases an officer can act only after authorisation from a senior officer (for example, in delaying access to legal advice). In certain situations reasons for a procedure must be given to a suspect – for example, the reason why an officer wishes to stop and search a suspect. On other occasions the police officer must formally explain the individual's rights – for example, when someone is arrested they must be informed of their right to remain silent and the consequences of so doing.

There is also a requirement for written records. Custody records must show all the details of a suspect's stay in police detention, and may be analysed by the defence. Any irregularities would support their argument for the exclusion of evidence.

Two highly significant areas covered in detail by PACE are those setting out the powers of the police in relation to the searching of persons and property, and in the detention and questioning of suspects. Whilst such powers are vital in the investigation and prevention of crime, they also provide opportunities for significant intrusions of individual freedoms. Finding the correct balance is not easy. These two areas are considered below: first an outline of the main powers of search.

Search powers: PACE

The main provisions dealing with powers of search in PACE are as follows, although some items – for example, correspondence between the suspect and their solicitor, confidential personal records, such as those held by a doctor, and certain confidential trade documents – are not permitted to be taken in a search.

Stop and search (ss. 1–7)
Stop and search allows an officer to stop and search a person or a vehicle in a public place where there are reasonable grounds for suspecting that there are stolen goods, or weapons or articles for use in offences such as theft or burglary and criminal damage. Detention for a reasonable period is allowed, and the person searched must be told reasons for the search and of his or her right to a copy of the search record. Stopping cars to check whether they are carrying offenders, or witnesses, is provided for in s. 4.

Search warrants (s. 8)
An officer can obtain a search warrant from a magistrate when it is reasonable to believe that there would be evidence relating to an offence (for example, drugs or

stolen property) on the premises to be searched. With such a warrant, the officer may enter and search the specified premises, and remove any such evidence.

Entry for searching and arrest (s. 17)

This power provides that an officer can enter property in order to carry out an arrest for the following reasons:

- with a warrant, for an arrestable offence;
- for recapturing escaped prisoners;
- for arrestable offences (that is any offence for which the sentence is 5 years or more and certain other specified offences);
- to save someone from injury or prevent damage to property.

Entry and search after arrest (s. 18)

Entry and search after arrest allows a police officer to go into an arrested person's home or business premises to collect evidence about an offence, subject to getting the authority of an inspector.

Search on arrest (s. 32)

Search on arrest allows an officer to search a person who has been arrested, or the premises where the suspect was found, for evidence, or for things that might help them escape, or with which they might harm themselves.

Searches of detained people (s. 54)

Section 54 sets out the responsibilities and powers of the custody officer and other officers in relation to search of people in police detention. The police must make a record of the arrested person's possessions. They are entitled to search for, and remove things, that might allow the person to harm themselves or someone else, or for things that might be used to escape. They must explain why such items are being removed.

Intimate searches (s. 55)

This section limits the situations in which intimate searches can be carried out to searches for things that can harm the suspect, or injure other people, and drugs. The search can be carried out only by an officer of the same sex.

Further provisions in relation to stop and search are contained in the Criminal Justice and Public Order Act 1994, which allows certain exceptions to the 'reasonable suspicion' provision. Under these provisions the police will have powers to act when senior officers believe incidents involving serious violence may take place or to prevent terrorism. These powers will last for up to 24 hours, but may be extended if serious violence does break out. While introduced to allow the police to prevent serious violence, some fear that the abandonment of reasonable suspicion might lead to some groups being unduly harassed.

Arrest, detention and interview

Perhaps even more difficult can be achieving the correct balance in identifying when a person should be able to be arrested, detained and questioned, and how such a person should be treated. Such powers are the ultimate interference with liberty.

Sections 24–33 of PACE deal with powers of arrest. First, the Act lays down the circumstances in which any individual, including a police officer, store detective or ordinary person carrying out a citizen's arrest, can arrest a person. They may arrest anyone who is, or whom they reasonably suspect to be, committing an arrestable offence, and anyone who has committed or who can reasonably be suspected of having committed an arrestable office. Additionally, police officers have wider powers of arrest including the power to arrest someone when they believe that person is about to commit an arrestable offence. An arrestable offence is defined as one for which the penalty is fixed by law (for example, murder), or, which carries a sentence of 5 years' or more imprisonment, or, as in the case of taking a vehicle without consent, is specifically made arrestable by statute.

Further, the police have specific powers of arrest where a breach of bail occurs or is anticipated; for specific offences listed in PACE; and where the 'general arrest conditions' are satisfied. The 'general arrest conditions' allow the police to make an arrest, whatever the offence, to prevent injury, property damage, or where a person has given a suspicious name or address.

Although these provisions provide the police with wide powers, they are not limitless and any officer infringing them may be liable to civil or criminal proceedings or disciplinary action. Perhaps most importantly they risk losing an otherwise promising case as evidence obtained after a wrongful arrest may be excluded by the court. Where an arrest is improperly made the police may also be liable for damages to the wrongfully arrested person.

Provisions about the suspect's rights on arrest and at the police station were also consolidated by PACE. On arrest, any person arrested on suspicion of committing a crime is entitled to be:

- told that he or she has been arrested and why;
- arrested without excessive use of force;
- cautioned;
- taken to a designated police station for interview and not interviewed before arrival at the police station except in urgent cases. The Criminal Justice Act 2003 provides for an alternative procedure to what has become seen as an unwieldy process, taking up much police time. From January 2004 police officers can bail those they have arrested to attend a police station at a later date without first taking them to a designated police station (street bail). This procedure will be used for minor offences where the offender's identity is certain and the offender is not in a particularly vulnerable category.

At the police station PACE and the Codes provide a comprehensive and detailed framework for the treatment of suspects and arrestees at the police station. Those in custody are the responsibility of the custody officer, a police officer not involved in the investigation. This officer is wholly responsible for all aspects of the period of custody, for any incidents which occur, and for the custody record. The Act provides a complex timetable for the review of detention before charge to ensure that arrested people are not kept in custody for long periods without charge.

On arrival at the police station the custody officer must ensure that persons arrested are informed about their rights. These include, first, a right to inform someone that they have been arrested. Secondly, any persons arrested have the right to contact and consult a legal adviser in private. If they do not wish to or cannot contact a solicitor, or do not have one, free advice is available from a duty solicitor who can be contacted round the clock. Thirdly, arrested persons have the right to have access to PACE and the Codes. This is to a certain extent window dressing, as few arrested persons are likely to pore over the minutiae of the Codes, but it is an important reminder to suspects and the police of their provisions.

Prior to 1995, throughout the period of arrest and interview suspects had the 'right to remain silent' and were reminded of this in a caution given on arrest, before any interview, and on charge. Thus they should have been advised that:

> You do not have to say anything unless you wish to do so but what you say may be given in evidence.

The right to silence was redefined by the Criminal Justice and Public Order Act 1994. This, contrary to some assertions, does not remove the right, but affects the use that can be made of silence in the trial. Before 1995 juries were told that they should not assume a defendant was guilty because he or she failed to answer an accusation at the time of arrest or when interviewed at a police station. Under the 1994 Act, the jury will be told that they can, in certain circumstances, make 'adverse inferences' from silence. For example, a jury might take the view that a defendant did not answer the questions asked of him because he could not think of a plausible excuse. Where appropriate the jury should, however, be reminded that there are other reasons why someone might not answer: fear, bewilderment or drunkenness, for example.

The words of the caution needed to reflect the change. The caution introduced in 1995 is as follows:

> You do not have to say anything. But it may harm your defence if you do not mention when questioned something which you later rely on in court. Anything you do say may be given in evidence.

Additionally, where a suspect is asked about his or her presence, at or near the scene of a crime, or, why he or she is in possession of an item, a warning must be given about the implications of failing to respond. Vulnerable groups are given extra protection by PACE in that young people should not be interviewed in the absence of an appropriate adult, usually a parent or social worker; and a similar provision protects the mentally ill. Those who do not speak English fluently, and the deaf, should have appropriate translators present at interview and foreign nationals must be told of their right to contact their embassy or High Commission.

Code C deals with the detention, treatment and questioning of suspects and seeks to provide that all people should be dealt with quickly and not be detained any longer than necessary. It places the overall responsibility for the control, recording and supervision of the custody period with a custody officer: a police officer, usually with the rank of sergeant or above, who has overall responsibility for ensuring the correct treatment of those held at the police station. Many of the detailed provisions of this code set constraints on police conduct. They must keep a record of what happens to an offender during detention and provide information to suspects about their rights. Other provisions relate to the minimum level of comfort that should be provided to all suspects. Rules limit the time a suspect can be kept in police custody before being charged. The most important of these matters are described below.

- The custody record is made a fundamental part of the custody process, in which must be written everything that affects the suspect while in the police station, including time of release, comments made by the suspect at various stages, and a list of the suspect's property. The suspect's lawyer has the right to examine this record at the police station or during any subsequent court proceedings. An examination of the record may reveal that procedures were not correctly followed, or indeed establish that they were, as the suspect will be asked to sign the custody record, for example, to indicate that legal advice has been offered. If the suspect refuses to sign when asked, that refusal must also be recorded. Any interview with the suspect must be recorded in full. This will usually be by means of tape recorded interviews (governed by Code E) which replaced the old system of 'contemporaneous notes' as they were more susceptible to fabrication by the police or unfounded challenge by those interviewed. Interviews should be carried out only at designated police stations, except when an interview is urgent – for example, to get information about an imminent attack on a person.

- When an interview forms part of the evidence against a defendant, he or she is entitled to a balanced summary of the recording, and can demand a copy of the tape. While the taping of interviews protects the accused, it may also prevent unfounded complaints against the police and allegations of false confessions.

- The Code states that suspects should be held usually in single cells, which should be adequately heated, cleaned, lit and ventilated, with adequate clean bedding and access to toilet and washing facilities. They should be offered two light meals and one main meal in a 24-hour period, and a reasonable number of drinks. Medical assistance should be called if necessary.

Perhaps the most significant provisions relate to the continuing assessment of whether an arrested person can be charged or released. Under the Criminal Justice Act 2003 a range of options is provided, depending on the state of the evidence and investigation:

- charge with an offence;
- release without charge and without bail, which concludes the case unless new evidence comes to light;
- release without charge on bail for further enquiries to be made;
- release without charge and on bail for the police to take legal advice from the

Crown Prosecution Service. Where this course is taken, the suspect must be informed that this is the position.

Detention in a police station without charge usually arises to allow the person to be questioned to obtain evidence. Once sufficient evidence has been obtained, and the suspect has said what he or she wishes to say, the questioning must stop and the suspect charged. After charge, suspects may:

- be released on bail to attend court for the start of proceedings against them;
- be released and required to return later to the police station;
- be kept in police custody and taken to the next sitting of the magistrates' court.

Whether it is necessary to keep the suspect any longer, or indeed whether the police have enough evidence to charge, must be considered at the following times (sometimes referred to as the PACE or detention clock):

- 6 hours after detention was first authorised,
- then at not more than 9-hourly intervals from when the detention was first authorised, up to a total of 36 hours.

Further detention must be authorised after 24 hours. Any longer period must be authorised by an officer of the rank of superintendent or above. This further period can extend the period to 36 hours, and then only if necessary for the effective investigation of an arrestable offence.

- If the police want to interview the suspect further they must apply to a magistrates' court for permission to hold the person for any longer time. A court can authorise an extra 36 hours of detention, on two occasions. The overall maximum period of detention is 96 hours.
- Telephone and video reviews may be undertaken so that senior officers do not always have to be physically present at the relevant station.
- People suspected of terrorist offences can be detained for a total of 14 days without charge. The fact that different rules apply to terrorist suspects indicates an important area where due process and crime control or prevention are given differing importance than in other offences.

PACE was introduced amidst fears that it would vastly increase police powers at the expense of the civil liberties of defendants. The police feared that it would result in much extra paperwork and that its many safeguards would hamper their efficiency. Research since the Act indicates that neither of these sets of concerns has been borne out. There is little evidence, argue Morgan and Newburn (1979), to suggest that police efficiency has been hampered and the police have come to accept practices such as the routine taping of interviews, which initially attracted resistance. In a review of research, Brown found that the new powers have been used considerably and that, on the whole, custody officers do ensure that suspects are aware of their basic rights. There has been an increase in the demand for legal advice by suspects, although the quality of this advice is uneven. It has been estimated that suspects are protected by the tape recording of interviews in police stations and that the use of unacceptable tactics to secure confessions has declined

(Brown 1997). While these procedures in the station have given suspects better protection, there are more problems outside the station where it remains difficult to determine the extent to which stop-and-search procedures are carried out with 'reasonable grounds'. This is more difficult to review objectively, as these decisions are difficult to monitor independently 'after the event', and, as will be seen later in the chapter, are heavily determined by the context in which they are made and the informal working rules of police officers 'on the street' (Brown 1997).

Figure 6.3 **Aspects of the use of police powers under PACE in England and Wales in 2002/3**

- The police stopped and searched a total of 895,300 persons and/or vehicles.

- Thirteen per cent of searches led to an arrest.

- The most frequent reason (41 per cent) for stops and searches was to look for drugs which has replaced looking for stolen property as the most frequent reason. Thirty-six per cent were searches for stolen property and other searches were to look for firearms, offensive weapons, and articles which could be used in burglary or theft – 'going equipped'.

- 633 persons were detained for more than 24 hours and subsequently released without charge.

- A total of 172 intimate searches were carried out – mainly for drugs.

- Thirty per cent of stops in England and Wales took place in the Metropolitan Police area.

Source: Compiled from Ayres, Murray and Fiti (2003) *Arrests for Notifiable Offences and the Operation of Certain Police Powers under PACE* Home Office Statistical Bulletin, 17/03

6.4 POLICE WORK

It can be seen from the above that there are many different aspects of policing. The police have an increasing array of technological aids to assist investigation and, as seen above, have to cope with organised and serious crime which operates at a national and global level. Government policies and national policing plans have to be complied with, managerialism has introduced targets and performance indicators and the Audit Commission and others emphasise the importance of 'intelligence led policing'. At the same time the police are expected to take into account the requirements of and to involve local communities. This section will explore some of the many dimensions of police work.

Investigating crime and new technologies

The police have a unique role in investigating crime and, apart from a few specialist agencies, handle most crime investigation in this country. Thus most prosecutions depend on the routine information collected by uniformed officers and the detective work of their non-uniformed colleagues in the criminal investigation departments, the CID.

Criminal investigations over the years have stimulated the development of technical and expert services such as forensic services. Since 1995 there has been a national DNA database run by the Forensic Science service for the Association of Chief Police Officers.

Today's police have access to computer information systems such as those storing details of all car registrations, and more recently they have employed psychological profiling in murder cases. The most widely accepted form of forensic evidence is the fingerprint test. The idea was developed by Edward Henry, Inspector-General of the Nepal Police, who noticed its use in nineteenth-century India and the Metropolitan Police introduced it in 1901. Its use led to the conviction of two brothers – the Strattons – for murder in 1905. The basic premiss of the fingerprint is that no two sets are the same. Each fingerprint is based on the ridges made by the barely visible papillary lines on the skin's surface and each print can be classified in terms of the patterns of arches, whorls and loops that are displayed and the distinctive characteristics in a fingerprint – split, lake, island or end of ridge. Fingerprinting until recently was widely regarded as foolproof and conclusive of guilt by police and juries. But doubt was raised about the ability of fingerprints to determine individual identity, in the case of Neville Lee, who was arrested solely on the basis of a fingerprint left in blood in a lavatory cubicle after a brutal rape of an 11-year-old girl in Clumber Park near Worksop in August 1991. He was arrested by the Nottinghamshire police and detained in custody for 6 weeks before another sexual attack in the same park led to the arrest of a person who confessed to the rape of which Lee had been accused.

Computers are used in police investigations and prosecutions to search a national fingerprint database using the National Automated Fingerprint Identification System (NAFIS). The widespread use of mobile phones has had a bonus for police investigation in that users can be tracked by global positioning satellites. New digital technology allows for enhanced quality face recognition such that suspects' details can be used to scan public spaces where there are CCTV cameras. The greater use of this technology has implications for its use as evidence and hence the development of the PACE Codes with respect to video and CCTV evidence. The development of specialist forensic science has given the police new techniques to analyse crime scenes, such as the use of blood pattern analysis, and forensic archaeologists and botanists to determine the timing of events – what pollen was on the tyre tread, which may show whether, and when, a car has visited a crime scene.

The use of DNA profiling is regarded as reliable as fingerprinting to check the unique characteristics of an individual. Developed by Dr Alec Jeffries, the technique is now used in criminal and civil cases around the world. The DNA technique involves comparing a number of bands in the suspect's DNA with those of the DNA from body fluid or tissue involved in the crime. A calculation is then made on the probabilities of another person having a similar match. The Criminal Justice and Public Order Act 1994 allowed the police to take DNA samples, such as hair or mouth swabs, without consent of the accused, from offenders charged with, or convicted of, recordable offences – broadly those that are imprisonable. The national DNA database, which was started in April 1995, by 2004 held 2.1 million samples from individuals and 215,000 profiles from crime scenes, after a total investment of £182 million in the system up to March 2004.

While fingerprints and DNA profiling are familiar, at least in concept, to most people, other identification evidence can be important, such as voice analysis or earprint identification as used in the conviction of Calvin Sewell for burglary in February 1998 (see Figure 6.4).

Forensic evidence, based on scientific procedure, provides valuable evidence for investigators and prosecutors in contrast to the unpredictability of human witnesses. Scientific evidence can be used in all manner of circumstances, as in the case of Tracie Andrews. She was convicted of the murder of her boyfriend who, she claimed, was a victim of a road rage attack. Examination of a hat, which she said had nothing to do with her, showed hairs belonging to her mother's cat. But the faith in scientific evidence has been shown to be unjustified in dramatic cases such as the Birmingham Six convicted in 1975 for the murder of 21 people in 1974 after a bomb

Figure 6.4 Earprint identification

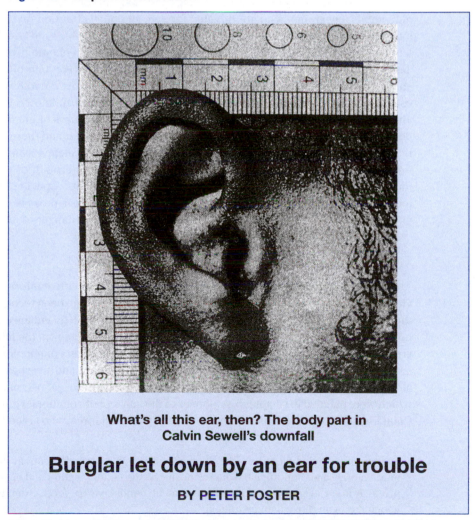

**What's all this ear, then? The body part in
Calvin Sewell's downfall**

Burglar let down by an ear for trouble

BY PETER FOSTER

Source: The Times, 21 February 1998. © Times Newspapers Limited, 1998. Photo © Photonews Service, 1998.

was left in a public house in the central shopping district. The conduct of the test to show that the suspects had been handling explosives was later to prove unreliable.

An extension to the use of DNA techniques is a process called 'familial searching' which led to the conviction in April 2004 of Craig Harman for the manslaughter of Michael Little, a lorry driver. He died after a brick was thrown through his cab window. DNA evidence led to the identification of a close relative of the offender and thence to the defendant.

Information technology is also employed in what is often called intelligence led policing, which relies on the use of information to develop and maintain a detailed and up-to-date picture of patterns of crime and criminality (Tilley 2003). Under the National Intelligence Model (NIM) developed by the NCIS, such information can be used to intervene in and to disrupt networks and remove prolific offenders at local and cross-border levels and can target serious and organised crime. While it is not yet clear whether NIM will be widely adopted, it has so far enjoyed considerable support. Tasking and coordination meetings and analysts can identify 'hotspots' and individuals and groups who are targeted for special police attention on the basis of intelligence about who is actively involved in crime and who is networked with whom. Intelligence led policing also involves the use of new technology to establish 'harder' links between offenders and crime scenes and between one offender and another. A Forensic Led Intelligence System (FLINGS) carries a database of links established through physical evidence between known and unknown individuals and scenes. While popular, Tilley (2003) queries the effectiveness of intelligence led policing as there is little systematic independent evaluation of it and there are potential ethical and operational problems in employing the covert means which it entails – particularly a risk of violating privacy. However, in the aftermath of the Soham murders, it is evident that the concern about the human rights aspects of data protection and privacy laws meant that police checks used to screen those working with children failed to identify information revealing the potential danger of Ian Huntley.

Community policing

An important source of 'intelligence' at the local level is the wealth of information provided by victims, witnesses and the general public and it has long been recognised that the relationship between the police and community is vital to enhance not only police–community relations but the effectiveness of the police. From the late 1970s a growing number of initiatives described, somewhat loosely, as community policing, emerged, including the more familiar policing tasks of patrolling and investigating crime along with strategies aimed at crime prevention and reducing the fear of crime, many of which were outlined in Chapter 5. A pioneer of the concept of community policing was Chief Constable John Alderson of the Devon and Cornwall force, who argued:

> community policing would exist in its purest form where all elements in the community, official and unofficial, would conceive of the common good and combine to produce a social climate and an environment conducive to good order and the happiness of all those living within it.
>
> (Alderson 1978)

In Alderson's version the community constable was seen as a 'social leader' working with the community and the emphasis is firmly placed on preventative rather than reactive policing. In theory, community policing is based on ideas that the police should consult and seek cooperation with the public and in 'general notions of creating a tranquil and safe environment' (Bennett 1994b: 6).

In practice, community policing encompasses a wide variety of different schemes and Bennett identifies five models or styles (Bennett 1994a). First, many schemes involve area-based policing, known variously as neighbourhood, zonal, team or sector policing, in which a small team of managers, supervisors and officers are allocated to a local area. As seen above, this is a major element in most forces. Bennett's second model of community policing refers to the multi-agency approach, in which the police work in partnership with local authorities and voluntary agencies – some examples of which were outlined in Chapter 3 in respect of police working with victims, and Chapter 5 in relation to Crime and Disorder Partnerships. Bennett's third theme, crime prevention, includes the neighbourhood watch schemes also discussed in Chapter 5. Bennett's fourth model identifies schemes which involve police contact with the public. This may be through foot patrols or setting up shops on estates and high streets away from the police station. It may also involve the police knocking on doors to contact the public directly. Fifthly, community policing refers to the consultation mechanisms outlined above and the introduction of lay visitors to police stations.

Despite the many potential benefits of community policing it has not proved easy to implement. Full implementation would, argue many, involve a total reorganisation of police forces in which prevention and service roles take precedence over law enforcement and public order roles. Yet within the police, law enforcement and investigation are often seen as 'real' police work, with community policing being accorded lower status, community-based officers having been described derogatively as 'hobby bobbies'. Some have discerned a tendency for community police functions to be 'bolted on' to existing organisations and seen as an addition to, rather than the main purpose of, organisations (Bennett 1994a).

In addition, given the vast number of tasks which the police are expected to perform, there may simply not be enough officers to allocate to beats on a semi-permanent basis. In times of emergency they may be called off the beat to deal with football disturbances, public order incidents or other duties. This means that the community cannot rely on consistency of cover. In addition, community constables spend much time on administrative duties and in the police station, and relatively small amounts of time on 'community contacts' (Bennett and Lupton 1992). Moreover, in organisations where community policing has a low status, officers may be keen to move on from such roles, meaning that few gather sufficient experience. In general, community policing has been found to be more successful in smaller, suburban middle-class communities than in inner city areas where the greatest problems have occurred, and which arguably stand to benefit more from it (Fielding *et al.* 1989; Tilley 2003). As Tilley (2003: 331) comments, 'communities most in need of community policing seem to have taken to it least enthusiastically'.

6.5 FRONT-LINE DEFINERS OF CRIME: POLICE DISCRETION

Legislation such as PACE, local and national policing plans and emphases on community or intelligence led policing all provide the context within which the police carry out their work at a day-to-day level. A major feature of this work is that the police have considerable discretion at all stages of the criminal justice process – quite simply, they cannot enforce all the laws all the time. To attempt anything approximating full law enforcement would result in extremely large numbers of police officers exercising surveillance over the population by means of video cameras and intensive patrolling. This would be extremely costly and would lead to what would be regarded as a police state. The police therefore have neither the numbers, resources nor technological expertise to enforce all laws fully. How this discretion is exercised from chief constables to beat police officers is a major determinant of how well any policies or strategies will work. Many criticisms of the police involve the use of discretion and many laws and rules seek to limit its impact.

Chief constables must determine the style of policing and priorities for their area within their given budget and national and local policing plans. Some may favour an emphasis on community policing, others may target particular offences. These general policies are implemented by areas and divisions who may also interpret policy in the light of what they see as the most pressing problems of their area. In the police station yet more discretionary decisions are involved. How suspects are dealt with, interrogated, and charged are all decisions made at this level, along with decisions about cautioning or proceeding with charges. Police officers on the streets have discretion in deciding where to patrol, what to investigate, whether and how to intervene in incidents, or whether to stop and search members of the public. Unlike many other organisations where those at the top exercise the greatest amounts of discretion, police officers on the street have to make difficult decisions on the spur of the moment. This is illustrated in comments made by the then Commissioner of the Metropolitan Police, Sir Paul Condon, who, in a speech in October 1993, said that many key decisions have to be taken by some of the most junior officers. He went on to say, 'they are expected to be counsellors, negotiators, mediators, managers, advisers, experts, parental figures, law enforcers and humble servants, ready to make contentious decisions, some involving life or death'.

There have been many studies of aspects of police discretion exploring how decisions are made and how tasks are prioritised. Clearly the law constrains the use of discretion, but a variety of non-legal or extra-legal factors are also important, and there may well be a gap between the law in action and the law as described in books.

In general, while legal factors form a backcloth against which decisions must be made, the law is often ambiguous and requires interpretation – what situations, for example, amount to 'reasonable suspicion'? As seen in previous chapters, the police must judge when actions are to be defined as criminal. The immediate situation affects the way an incident will be dealt with. Outcomes may be affected by apparently trivial circumstances such as the weather, the officer's mood, or the time of day. For example, at the end of a long shift, an officer may not want to be delayed by the amount of paperwork which could result from an arrest.

Alternatively, on a wet, cold night they might want to get back to the station and might even look out for people to arrest (Cain 1973). Many studies of police have found that a wide variety of factors affect how they react to specific incidents such as drunken brawls, disturbances by youths or disputes between neighbours. As seen in Chapter 5 and earlier, particular offences, offenders, groups or neighbourhoods may be specific targets of special attention as a result of national priorities or local consultation.

Whether a person is likely to be seen as 'suspicious' depends also on cultural cues. The police have a set of expectations about what kinds of people belong in a certain area, and when and in what circumstances one would expect to find them. Behavioural cues like walking slowly or quickly may also affect judgments of 'suspiciousness' – and these are also culturally determined. The local knowledge and experience of the officer is likely to be important here, as is the local police culture which defines certain areas and groups as representing trouble, and which also provides guidelines for appropriate responses. This can be seen particularly in relation to the decision to stop and search.

The decision to stop and search

The significance of the words 'reasonable suspicion' in relation to stop-and-search powers has already been indicated. The PACE Codes state that this must not be based on someone's race or hairstyle, on the fact that they are members of a group or community that have a higher than average record of committing that type of offence, nor on the fact that they are known to have previous convictions for possession of an unlawful article. These guidelines, however, like the law, are limited. Decisions to stop and search are made on the spot, and rely on the individual officer's judgment of the situation. In deciding who to stop, officers will be guided by a host of cues which relate to their conception of what is 'normal' and what is suspicious, taking account of their knowledge of the area, their knowledge of what the most common kinds of crime are and the circumstances in which they are committed and their assumptions about which individuals and groups constitute the 'usual suspects'. They are encouraged to learn, as part of their training, to identify such situations, and indeed the public is reliant on them to prevent crime by apprehending suspects. No one factor, be it age, colour, style of dress or the circumstances in which they find someone, can be responsible for any one stop. The complexity of this situation is thus difficult to capture in guidelines, and informal considerations may take precedence over formal ones. This may not, however, emerge in subsequent written reports.

In the police station

The Police and Criminal Evidence Act 1984 also deals with the exercise of police discretion in the police station, where individual suspects are interviewed and decisions are made about how to proceed with a case. As we have seen, it introduced requirements for the taping of interviews and custody records. Nevertheless, as in any job, ways are often found to circumvent formal rules, and informal practices may become the norm. The PACE Codes cannot, for example, control the informal interviews which police have with suspects outside the police station, in the car or in the cells (Leng *et al.* 1992). Such conversations are not officially defined as interviews. In addition, in recorded interviews, the fear of the suspect and the attitude of the officer cannot be fully reproduced on tape. Thus even although confessions which are involuntary, or produced in oppressive circumstances, are inadmissible, these factors may still mean that tactics used by skilled and experienced officers may 'put words into' a suspect's mouth.

These considerations do not imply that the police act illegally – many practices are essentially a way around the perceived constraints of law. To the police, obtaining evidence to secure a conviction of someone they have good reason to believe is guilty is part of their job. Nor does it mean that laws such as PACE are entirely without effect as they may curtail blatant abuses of police powers, as was indicated above (Brown 1997).

Police culture

The exercise of discretion is strongly affected by what is often described as the occupational culture of the police. This includes the informal rules which affect how the police behave in any particular incident or situation. Many occupations have associated cultures, within which members use a special language, and share a similar view of the world and their occupation. Anyone starting a job very quickly learns the distinction between how things should be done and how they really are done. These informal rules are learnt during what sociologists call occupational socialisation where a recruit learns the norms and values associated with the occupation. The expectations associated with the job and what constitutes success are part of such a culture, as are attitudes about the role of the occupation. This is particularly the case where the occupation faces hostility or misunderstanding from the public – as may be the case with the police. In this case the culture may have a justifying role, justifying the job that members do.

In some occupations this culture is stronger than others – policing is not a 'nine to five' job from which officers can switch off when they leave the station. It makes heavy emotional demands on officers, involves high levels of stress, danger, and is a vocation as well as a job. Police work involves shift work reducing the time officers spend with 'civilians'. This makes for closer relationships between officers and a stronger culture than in many jobs. The job may also affect how the police carry out their work – for example, the police must display authority in order to handle some situations, especially where large numbers of people are involved. Police can 'handle' situations only if the public respect the authority of the police. This may affect decisions about suspects to the extent that those who appear to challenge authority may be more likely to be stopped, arrested or charged. Authority is reinforced by the symbols of the job – cars, radios and uniforms all signify the authority vested in the role of police officer (Holdaway 1983).

All these factors give rise to a strong occupational culture within the police, described by many authors (Reiner 2000; Holdaway 1983; Foster 2003). While it is impossible to make sweeping generalisations, certain themes appear to characterise police culture in Anglo-American societies:

■ *A sense of mission*: police officers feel that their job is important and they often see themselves as forming a 'thin blue line', protecting society from disorder. A key part of this mission is catching criminals.

- *'Real police work'*: law enforcement is seen as 'real' work in contrast to much-hated desk or paperwork and also when compared with some community work.

- *Action*: this involves action seen most clearly in the imagery of the car chase. Car chases, according to Holdaway, are often the subject of animated conversations in dull moments in the canteen and they form an important part of the police folklore.

- *Machismo*: there is a strong element of machismo within police culture which may affect attitudes to some kinds of work and to female officers who may be treated protectively and assumed not to be able to cope with elements of the job – not a 'suitable job for a woman' having been a pervasive attitude (Heidensohn 1992).

- *Racism*: as will be seen below, many studies have found strong elements of racism within police culture, with derogative language being used to describe not only people of colour but also members of groups such as the Irish, Scots and inhabitants of areas associated with high crime rates.

These are some of the major characteristics of police culture although it should also be recognised that there are in practice many variations (Foster 2003). Detectives may have a perspective and a culture very different from uniformed officers and may need to adopt very different styles to perform their job adequately (Hobbs 1991). Different stations within a particular area may have very different cultures, affected by the policy of the division (Foster 1989). Some officers may value their role within the community, whereas others may see themselves more as crime fighters. Rural policing may be very different from urban policing, with rural police being more involved in all the tasks of the police simply because of the time it may take to call in the specialists from the town (Cain 1973). Those involved in public order duties, especially those in special patrols, may also come to look forward to a 'piece of action' (Jefferson 1990). Whatever the variations, an understanding of police culture is important when policy reforms and new laws are considered. Cultures where 'real police work' is strongly related to law enforcement may resist efforts which may be perceived to curtail their powers and discretion or to foster more community-oriented schemes. This is not to say that attitudes cannot change and it is important not to paint too static or simple a picture.

Police and ethnic minority communities

A major issue affecting policing and policing policy is the relationship between the police and ethnic minority communities, highlighted by, amongst other indicators, 'flashpoints' of urban unrest. The exercise of discretion can, where insufficiently regulated, lead to discrimination, and there have been recurrent allegations that some ethnic minorities have been subjected to 'over policing', evidenced by higher rates of stops, searches and arrests than would be expected, which has led to higher rates of dissatisfaction with the police amongst some communities. The victimis-ation of different ethnic groups, outlined in Chapter 3, raised concerns that the police were reluctant to acknowledge that some offences were racially motivated, and indeed may be more likely to suspect some groups of being perpetrators rather than victims. The small numbers of ethnic minority officers within the police has also been perceived to be a problem. The extent to which this can be accounted for by racism within the police has been subjected to considerable investigation, culminating in the MacPherson Report in 1999 which found what it described as 'institutional' racism and made several recommendations for reform.

Concerns about relationships between the police and minority communities date back to the 1960s; since then a wide range of reports have detailed what Bowling and Phillips (2003) describe as oppressive policing of minority communities. The declining relationship between police and black people was highlighted by the Scarman Report which followed the 'riots' in Brixton and other English cities in 1981. The Brixton disturbances followed an aggressive street policing strategy described as 'Operation Swamp '81', when high numbers of black youths were stopped on suspicion. The Scarman Report of 1982 identified widespread resentment against the police amongst black youth and was critical of many aspects of policing. Its many recommendations included improvements in police community relations, such as the community policing strategies outlined above, employing more ethnic minority police officers, identifying racial prejudice among police recruits, and improvements in training and supervision. This report did produce many changes, and stimulated a large body of research. However, the 1980s saw further instances of urban unrest – in particular the riots on the Broadwater Farm estate in Tottenham in which PC Keith Blakelock was stabbed to death. While later urban disturbances were not specifically linked to the issue of race, disturbances in the summer of 2001 in the North of England, in Burnley, Bradford and Oldham, followed a series of attacks on Asian youths by white youths and, yet again, as Bowling and Phillips (2003) recount, subsequent reports called for more ethnic minority police officers and better communication between the police and the community. All these instances draw attention to the factors which may be important in affecting police relationships with ethnic minority communities.

To Bowling and Phillips (2003: 534) the 'use of stop and search powers by the police has been the most controversial issue in debates about policing ethnic minorities'. As seen above, while PACE Codes govern the use of stop and search powers the concept of 'reasonable suspicion' can be contested and can give rise to concerns about discrimination and the use of stereotypes in determining what circumstances might merit a stop. From the 1980s onwards, research has indicated that black people have a higher chance of being stopped than might be expected. Research in the 1980s by the Policy Studies Institute in the Metropolitan Police area found that proportionately nearly twice as many black males aged 15–24 were stopped as white youth, with Asian youth being stopped less (Smith and Gray 1985). More recent studies confirm this picture. In England and Wales in 2001/2 the rate of stops per capita (a figure which takes into account the proportions of different groups within the population) for white people was 13 per 1,000, while for black people the figure was 106 and for Asian people 35. This has been popularly interpreted as indicating that 'black people are eight times and Asian people three times more likely to be stopped and searched by the police in comparison with their white counterparts' (Bowling and Phillips 2003: 536). Black people are also more likely to be stopped under the stops and searches under s. 60 of the Criminal Justice and Public Order Act 1994 and are less likely to be given a reason for being stopped.

It has also been found that black people are more likely to be arrested than might be expected. In the 1980s, after examining statistics for arrests in the Metropolitan Police area, Monica Walker concluded that 'black people must have four and a half times the chance of being arrested for a burglary ... (compared to white) ... to account for their over representation' (Walker 1987). In 2001/2 black people's rate of arrest was five times higher, and Asian people's two times higher, than that for white people, relative to their proportion in the general population (Bowling and Phillips 2003). Black people were over-represented in arrests in 1999/2000 for all offence categories, but the disproportion was greatest for offences of fraud, forgery, drugs and robbery (Phillips and Bowling 2002). There is also some evidence, cited by Bowling and Phillips, that the police may be overcharging some ethnic minority suspects as the CPS terminated more cases involving ethnic minorities on the grounds of insufficient evidence. Black youth also have lower rates of cautioning and are more likely to be referred to multi-agency panels – a finding which may reflect black youths' reluctance to plead guilty and their more hostile attitude to the police (Phillips and Bowling 2002).

It is very difficult to interpret these statistical indicators and to attribute them, as some critics do, to direct racism on the part of the police. It was seen above, for example, how many factors the police have to take into account when making a decision to stop, and the area, the circumstances of the stop and indicators of a variety of factors such as age, gender, income, employment are all important – for example, young people are more likely to be stopped than older people and males more than females. The many factors involved in the decision to stop and search make it very difficult to statistically establish any 'race factor' (Holdaway 1997). If more black people live in and are more likely to be on the street in areas which attract heavier policing, they will be more likely to be stopped. Attempts to assess 'stop rates' controlling for the relative proportion of ethnic groups on the street indicate that black people's rate of being stopped is not necessarily higher than white and rates vary across different areas. Consideration of these factors also suggests that it cannot be assumed that stop rates for different groups should be the same, making it difficult, therefore, to see these figures as indicating large amounts of racism on the part of individual officers.

Nevertheless, there are also indications that the attitudes of individual police officers and police culture mirror the racism prevalent in wider society and that decisions to stop may be affected by racist stereotypes. As the BBC documentary in October 2003 'The Secret Policemen' demonstrated only too clearly, some police officers display strongly racist attitudes. This does not in itself mean they exercise discrimination on the street or that they are reflective of the majority of the police – the Policy Studies Institute (PSI) studies, for example, found little evidence that racist attitudes led to discrimination on the street. What is more likely is that there may be indirect discrimination, which exists where the policies or practices of an institution are applied evenly, but have an unequal impact on different groups. Thus when the police prioritise lower class, high-crime areas containing a large proportion of ethnic minority residents, more lower class and black people become subject to stops, searches or arrests and search. Wider social inequalities such as unemployment, poor housing conditions and family breakdown further compound the disadvantages of black youths as they enter the criminal justice system – as they may then be less likely to be cautioned or warned and more likely to be taken to court.

Moreover, many studies have documented the existence of racism within the police culture. Research conducted by the PSI found that police officers did use derogatory language when describing black people, and that the 'canteen culture' contained many racist elements (Smith and Gray 1985). Reports from the Chief Inspector of the Constabulary have cited unacceptable levels of prejudice and sexist and racist behaviour on the part of the police as a disincentive for both women and ethnic minority individuals to join the police (*The Guardian*, 14 June 1994).

In addition, there is now considerable evidence that being a member of a group associated with crime can become grounds for 'reasonable' suspicion. For example, research indicates that factors such as style of dress and types of car can all arouse suspicion – which can be negatively associated with African/Caribbeans (Phillips and Bowling 2002). One recent study reported officers who were said to 'subscribe to the philosophy that, if you see four black youths in a car, it's worth giving them a pull as at least one of them is going to be guilty of something or other' (Cashmore 2001: 652, cited in Bowling and Phillips 2003: 537).

These kinds of attitudes have also been found to affect how the police deal with the victims of racist violence, in respect of which there have been recurrent complaints that the police are reluctant to acknowledge a racial motivation and in many instances have failed to take incidents seriously enough. These were highlighted particularly in the Stephen Lawrence case, detailed below.

Racist attitudes within the police may also lead to discrimination against and the alienation of ethnic minority recruits in the police. As seen above, the Scarman Report recommended the recruitment of more ethnic minority officers and efforts have been made to redress the low representation of such officers. Numbers have increased, from 0.7 per cent in 1986 to 3.0 per cent in 2002 (Bowling and Phillips 2003), but they remain under-represented with around 7 per cent of the economically active population being from ethnic minority populations. Research has indicated that such officers experience a variety of problems fitting in with police culture including coping with racist attitudes and developing social networks with other officers. They are more likely to leave the police and cite these experiences and dissatisfaction with how racism has been dealt with by senior officers as reasons for leaving (Holdaway and Barron 1997). They are also under-represented in senior ranks and take longer to be promoted. Recruitment targets were set in 1998, not only for the police but also for the probation and prison services, which recommend positive action to achieve equality of representation including strategies to encourage local people within communities to join the police and conducting targeted recruitment campaigns. Potential recruits may, however, be put off by the experiences of existing ethnic minority officers.

Many of these issues were highlighted by the case of Stephen Lawrence, the black teenager who was stabbed to death in Eltham, South East London on 22 April 1993 by what was widely accepted to be a group of hostile and abusive white youths (Newburn 2003). No one was successfully charged with murder although there was an unsuccessful private prosecution against five suspects in 1996. The conduct of the investigation was widely criticised by the victim's family and subsequently more widely by interest groups and the media. The police had initially assumed that Lawrence and his friend Duwayne Brooks had initiated the violence and failed to follow up leads to find the perpetrators. Following considerable representation, the New Labour Government in July 1997 set up the MacPherson Inquiry, whose terms of reference were 'to inquire into the matters arising from the death of Stephen Lawrence ... and to identify the lessons to be learned for the investigation and prosecution of racially motivated crimes' (cited in Newburn 2003: 90). The Inquiry reported in 1999 (MacPherson 1999) and, in addition to revealing deep-seated racism within the police, made a number of important recommendations.

The Inquiry documented the police denial of any racial motive for the murder, along with the racist stereotyping of Duwayne Brooks. There was, according to MacPherson (para. 2.10), 'no doubt whatsoever but that the first MPS investigation was palpably flawed and deserves severe criticism'. The use of inappropriate and offensive language was criticised along with the insensitive and patronising handling of Mr and Mrs Lawrence. It found that the 'investigation was marred by a combination of professional incompetence, institutional racism and a failure of leadership by senior officers' (para. 46.1). This incompetence, according to Newburn (2003), included a 'lack of direction and organisation in the hours after the murder, little or no pursuit of the suspects, inadequate processing of intelligence, ill thought out surveillance and inadequate searches'. It defined institutional racism as follows:

> **The collective failure of an organisation to provide an appropriate and professional service to people because of their colour, culture or ethnic origin. It can be seen or detected in processes, attitudes and behaviour which amount to discrimination through unwitting prejudice, ignorance, thoughtlessness, and racist stereotyping which disadvantage minority ethnic people.**
>
> (para. 6.34)

It also commented on the absence of confidence and trust in the police among ethnic minority communities as a result of a failure to respond to racist violence, the use of stop-and-search powers, and the high numbers of deaths of black people in police custody; and the Inquiry concluded that the black community was 'over policed ... and under protected' (MacPherson 1999: 312).

The MacPherson Report made 70 recommendations, which included the following:

- making it a 'ministerial priority' to increase trust and confidence among ethnic minority communities;
- the application of freedom of information and anti-discrimination legislation to the police;
- the monitoring and assessment of police performance;
- improved reporting and recording of racist incidents and crimes;
- improvements in the investigation and prosecution of racist crime;

- improvements in arrangements for family liaison;
- improvements in the treatment of victims and witnesses;
- improved training and discipline;
- improvements in procedures for dealing with complaints;
- improvements in the use of stop-and-search powers;
- improvements in relation to the recruitment and retention of ethnic minority police officers.

The Report was not without criticism. The definition of institutionalised racism means that it is subjective and dependent on an interpretation and only requires an assertion to be made. MacPherson defines a racist incident as 'any incident which is perceived to be racist by the victim or any other person' (MacPherson 1999: 328). This 'unwitting racism' means that members of the host culture, especially police officers, must not offend the cultural sensitivities of people from other backgrounds or they risk being labelled as racist.

Police interactions with ethnic minorities become difficult if encounters are interpreted from a racially sensitive perspective so that a discriminatory motive is imputed to comments made by police officers. Robert Skidelsky writes with reference to the MacPherson Report:

> Thus from the fact that Police Constable Joanne Smith described Duwayne Brooks, who had been with Stephen Lawrence when he was stabbed, as 'irate and aggressive' – he called her 'a f***** C***' – the Report deduces that: 'Mr Brooks was stereotyped as a young black man exhibiting unpleasant hostility and agitation'
>
> (Skidelsky in David Green 2000: 3).

Skidelsky continues to make a point concerning the priorities that are being established by the MacPherson Report. He continues:

> When officers arrived on the scene of the crime to find Stephen Lawrence dying, none of them knew how to give him first aid. This, one would have thought, is a far more serious defect than their lack of training in race relations.
>
> (Green 2000: 4)

Michael Ignatieff sees this as a tragedy which has reduced 'institutional incompetence' to an issue of police racism. He wrote:

> As with the Scarman report after Brixton, we seem unable to come to any awareness of these issues without a convulsion of guilt ridden confusion. What is most dismaying, looking back on Lawrence, is that it becomes a story about just one thing – race. But the central issue was not race, it was justice. Why were we talking about institutionalised racism, when the issue was institutionalised incompetence? Why were we talking about 'race awareness' when the issue was equal justice before the law?
>
> Everyone talked as if the Lawrence family and a larger fiction called the 'black

community' had been 'let down'. The 'black community' is no more of a reality than the 'white community'. To suppose this is to believe that skin trumps all other identities, that we are only our surfaces. In reality the Lawrence family were denied justice, and because they were denied justice, all of us have good reason to feel anger and shame that we cared so little about institutions which operate in our name.'

(Green 2000: 21)

Overall the Report and its recommendations, a large number of which were accepted, is widely agreed to have made a significant difference to contemporary policing. Newburn (2003: 91), for example, argues that the 'climate of policing has changed since Lawrence', and Reiner (2000: 211) that the MacPherson report has 'transformed the debate about black people and criminal justice'. To Bowling and Phillips (2002), it revealed that the failings of the police were systemic and resulted from insufficient accountability by recommending lay oversight into all areas of police work. Particularly significant were its recommendations for a fully independent complaints system and bringing the police into the ambit of race relations law. Additional grounds for optimism to them are the visible support on behalf of the police to improve policies in relation to racist violence and their response to ethnic minority crime victims, along with the acceptance of a commitment to recruit more ethnic minority officers.

Some policies have changed – Bowling and Phillips, for example, cite a 'MacPherson' effect in relation to the use of stop-and-search powers – as overall stops have declined and there appears to be a decline in the significance of race as a factor affecting stops for all categories except stops of black people in cars – although the rate of decline for black people is less than for white. Whether this is a progress or not depends in part upon at what price race relations supersedes other goals of policing, such as reducing crime. The warning from the Police Federation has been that the unintended consequence of MacPherson has been that police officers have become reluctant to use their powers of stop and search for fear of accusations of racism in some areas. This causes particular difficulties when police and community crime reduction programmes are trying to target young people carrying weapons in communities with a high proportion of ethnic minorities. This is a problem for policing crimes such as black on black murders associated with the control of illegal drug trade, and robbery to steal mobile phones. In 2000/1, data on phone robbery from London and Birmingham showed that 90 per cent were male, one-third of all offenders cautioned were aged 15 and 16, and that 71 per cent of suspects in the Metropolitan police area were black. In the West Midlands 54 per cent were black (Trends in Phone Robbery 2002, Home Office, p. 41). In these areas a clamp-down on street robberies involving mobile phones is likely to lead to the problem of at least some community spokesperson claiming the police are picking on and stereotyping young black males as robbers.

The Home Office, in April 2000, produced a Code of Practice on Reporting and Recording Racist Incidents and ACPO produced guidance on Identifying and Combating Hate Crimes in 2000. Additionally, the Metropolitan Police has created a Racial and Violent Crimes Task Force and Community Safety Units in all London boroughs, whose officers are especially trained to investigate 'hate crimes'. While these policies have had some impact there remains a risk that this will be seen as a specialist area and as not applying to other areas of policing (Bowling and Phillips 2003).

While there has been some change, it has been described as slow (Newburn 2003), and other critics from the civil liberties perspective point to the potentially racist impact of the Immigration and Asylum Act 1999 and the Anti-Terrorism Crime and Security Act 2001, which may lead to further targeting of people from racial and ethnic minorities. The problem is that, as illegal immigrants and asylum seekers are foreigners and the current major threat to public safety is from Islamic terrorists, the question has to be asked how the police are to do their job of protecting the public and avoid accusation of being racist, if, as is inevitable in these matters, the focus will be on questioning new migrants and the Islamic community.

CONCLUSION

This chapter has shown how the police are organised and looked at different ways of assessing their role and function. It has also outlined the main laws governing police investigation along with how the police are made accountable. These rules and guidelines, however, provide only a backcloth against which the police operate on a day-to-day level, which is inevitably affected by their own perception of their job, the occupational culture and how they interpret the many rules and guidelines. This is important for a number of reasons. Should the police, for example, perceive their main role as one of crime control, then they may be tempted to neglect due process in the interests of making sure that those guilty of crime are brought to court and found guilty. They may, as we have seen, downgrade the service or preventative aspects of their role. Discussions of police policy must therefore recognise the significance of discretion in police work and the role of the police culture and its influence on police work.

This chapter also raises questions about the role of the police, vital to our understanding of the criminal justice process as a whole. What is their main role? Should they be seen as and assessed primarily as 'crime fighters' or as crime preventers and public protectors? Should they work more with local communities or spend more time in the war against serious, organised and transnational crime? What might be the unintended effects on police community relations of moves towards the greater use of technology and intelligence led policing? One of the functions of the police not yet explored is their role in determining whether a suspect is prosecuted or diverted out of the criminal justice system. This will be discussed in Chapter 7.

Review questions

1 Outline the range of tasks carried out by the police service.

2 What are the main ways in which the police are rendered accountable? How and why have these arrangements recently been changed?

3 Look at the way in which the police are portrayed in the media through police dramas, documentaries or news stories. How does this reflect the different roles of the police?

4 Identify the possible infringements of PACE and Code C in the following:

> At 10 pm Alan is seen at the scene of a suspected burglary with a video camera thought to come from the burgled house. PC Bob asks him where he got the camera. Alan does not reply whereupon, without more ado, he is bundled into the police van and taken to the police station.
>
> At the police station, Alan is placed in a cell with three other people, and told he will be seen when the officer has time. The only light in the cell is broken. Four hours later Alan has not been interviewed. He wants to sleep but cannot as the only bed is occupied. Alan is very cold, and asks the custody officer for a cup of tea. He is told that there has been a problem in the canteen and he can have a glass of water. This arrives one hour later. At 6 am Alan is interviewed about his possession of the camera and suspected involvement in the burglary. He asks to see a solicitor, but is told the duty solicitor has just left and is not likely to want to come back before morning. Alan states that he stole the camera. Alan is 16.

To help you answer consider the following:
- Was Alan arrested properly?
- Should anything have been said when he was taken to the police station?
- Should anything have been said to him when he got to the police station?
- Were the conditions in his cell acceptable?
- Should he have been asked if he wanted to contact anyone?
- Should he have been given refreshments?
- Should he have been given anything else?
- Was the time during which he was kept at the police station acceptable under the Code?
- Should he have been allowed to speak with a duty solicitor?
- Should anyone else have been present during the interview?

5 Read the extract below and answer the following questions about the relevance of these nine principles published in 1829 to policing in the twenty-first century.

> The following set of principles, which lay out in the clearest and most succinct terms the philosophy of policing by consent, appeared as an appendix to *A New Study of Police History* by Charles Reith (London: Oliver and Boyd, 1956). Reith was a lifelong historian of the police force in Britain, and this book covers the early years of Metropolitan Police following the passage of Sir Robert Peel's 'Bill for Improving the Police in and near the Metropolis' on 19 June 1829. Reith notes that there are particular problems involved in writing police history, owing to the loss or destruction of much early archive material, and, probably for this reason, the principles appear without details of author or date.
>
> However, it seems most likely that they were composed by Charles Rowan and Richard Mayne, as the first and joint Commissioners of the Metropolitan Police. Rowan was a military man and Mayne, fourteen years his junior, a barrister. Rowan retired in 1850 leaving Mayne as sole Commissioner until his death in 1868. The sentiments expressed in the 'Nine Principles' reflect those contained in the 'General Instructions', first published in 1829, which were issued to every member of the Metropolitan Police, especially the emphasis on prevention of crime as the most important duty of the police.
>
> Reith notes that Rowan and Mayne's conception of a police force was 'unique in history and throughout the world because it derived not from fear but almost exclusively from

public co-operation with the police, induced by them designedly by behaviour which secures and maintains for them the approval, respect and affection of the public' (p. 140).

The Nine Principles of Policing
1. To prevent crime and disorder, as an alternative to their repression by military force and severity of legal punishment.
2. To recognise always that the power of the police to fulfil their functions and duties is dependent on public approval of their existence, actions and behaviour and on their ability to secure and maintain public respect.
3. To recognise always that to secure and maintain the respect and approval of the public means also the securing of the willing co-operation of the public in the task of securing observance of laws.
4. To recognise always that the extent to which the co-operation of the public can be secured diminishes proportionately the necessity of the use of physical force and compulsion for achieving police objectives.
5. To seek and preserve public favour, not by pandering to public opinion; but by constantly demonstrating absolutely impartial service to law, in complete independence of policy, and without regard to the justice or injustice of the substance of individual laws, by ready offering of individual service and friendship to all members of the public without regard to their wealth or social standing, by ready exercise of courtesy and friendly good humour; and by ready offering of individual sacrifice in protecting and preserving life.
6. To use physical force only when the exercise of persuasion, advice and warning is found to be insufficient to obtain public co-operation to an extent necessary to secure observance of law or to restore order, and to use only the minimum degree of physical force which is necessary on any particular occasion for achieving a police objective.
7. To maintain at all times a relationship with the public that gives reality to the historic tradition that the police are the public and that the public are the police, the police being only members of the public who are paid to give full time attention to duties which are incumbent on every citizen in the interests of community welfare and existence.
8. To recognise always the need for strict adherence to police-executive functions, and to refrain from even seeming to usurp the powers of the judiciary of avenging individuals or the State, and of authoritatively judging guilt and punishing the guilty.
9. To recognise always that the test of police efficiency is the absence of crime and disorder, and not the visible evidence of police action in dealing with them.

Source: Civitas website: www.civitas.org.uk

Answer the following points:
(a) To what extent has the crime problem changed since that time? Identify new crimes not known to the police in 1829.
(b) To what extent do you think the public's expectations about the police have changed since 1829?
(c) What have been the main changes to the organisation and routines of police work since 1829?
(d) Consider each of the nine principles in turn and state whether you think they are valid today.

Further reading

Bowling, B and Foster, J (2002) in Maguire, M, Morgan, R and Reiner, R (eds) *The Oxford Handbook of Criminology* (3rd edn), Clarendon Press: Oxford
Newburn, T (ed) (2003) *Handbook of Policing*, Willan Publishing: Cullompton

Reiner, R (2000) *The Politics of the Police*, Harvester Wheatsheaf: London

Wright, A (2002) *Policing: An introduction to concepts and practice*, Willan Publishing: Cullompton

Zander, M (2003) *The Police and Criminal Evidence Act 1984* (4th edn), Sweet and Maxwell: London

CHAPTER 7

Prosecution, caution and diversion

Main topics covered

➤ Cautioning

➤ Prosecution

➤ The Code for Crown Prosecutors

➤ Private prosecutions and other prosecuting agencies

➤ Mentally disordered offenders

INTRODUCTION

Once the police are reasonably sure they have identified a suspect, they have several options. They may decide to take no further action at all, or give an informal warning, or decide to issue a formal police caution, or refer the case to some form of mediation. They may instead decide to pass the papers to the Crown Prosecution Service. Many criminal cases are therefore diverted from the criminal justice process without any public trial or hearing. The decision to prosecute is a vital one and we will look at the rules and guidelines surrounding this decision, at the agencies responsible for it, and at the issues raised for criminal justice.

Prosecution and diversion raise many issues which can again be highlighted by looking at the different perspectives on criminal justice. Under a crime control approach, for example, it is clearly important that guilty offenders are convicted and punished and the system would be seen to lack any deterrent potential if this does not happen. Principles of due process also require that the defendant should have the opportunity to be publicly tried and enabled to refute any allegations of guilt. In addition, the notion that all are equal before the law underlies the principle that justice should be seen to be done. Diversion of some at the expense of others might produce a situation where critics from a class domination perspective could argue that some groups of offenders enjoy advantages. In addition, it is important to proponents of a denunciatory approach that offenders ought to be publicly tried and punished for the system to perform its function of expressing society's disapproval of particular behaviour. Victims also may feel aggrieved if they do not see those who have harmed them publicly held to account. If suspected offenders are diverted from the system it implies that the police and prosecutors are essentially making judicial decisions which should be made formally in the public forum of the criminal courts to ensure just deserts.

There are strong arguments that all suspects should be prosecuted (Gross 1979). Such an approach, however, would pose considerable problems. The process of prosecution and trial is costly. Police officers, prosecutors and the legal profession must collect evidence and produce and contest it in court, which also occupies the time and resources of court personnel. Diverting offenders from the formal process can therefore produce considerable savings and reduce delays. In addition, there may be many circumstances in which diversion is desirable. It can also be argued that the stigmatising effects of public trial and punishment could propel some offenders into more crime. For young offenders particularly it may be desirable in the interests of rehabilitation to avoid prosecution and eventual punishment. Some offenders, such as the very young or the mentally disordered, may be considered to be not fully responsible for their own actions, making trial and punishment inappropriate.

In recent years a number of policies have encouraged diversion although not, as we shall see, without some criticism. This chapter will focus on five main aspects of prosecution and diversion. It will first look at the considerations surrounding the cautioning of offenders. It will then explore the decision to prosecute, and describe the agency responsible for the majority of prosecutions, the Crown Prosecution Service (CPS), and will outline the Code for Crown Prosecutors. It will go on to look at some other agencies involved in prosecution and then at the treatment of one group for whom diversion is often seen as appropriate: the mentally ill. The arrangements for these offenders are clearly distinguishable from others and we will outline the options available to the court and in the pre-trial stage to divert these offenders from being prosecuted.

7.1 CAUTIONING

Before looking at formal cautions given in lieu of trial and sentence, it is important to recognise that some cases are diverted from the system with no formal action being taken. Whereas an official caution is recorded and can be referred to on subsequent appearances, cases which result in no further action (NFA) or an informal warning are not recorded. While precise numbers are not officially recorded, on the basis of research it has been estimated that as many as 25 per cent of known offenders are so dealt with (Sanders 2002).

No further action may be taken in a variety of situations. An individual officer may do nothing because the matter is too trivial and making an 'issue' of it could create further problems out of proportion to the incident. In other cases there may be a formal reason why the police cannot proceed with a prosecution: for example, where they cannot provide sufficient evidence for the court, or where the offender is too young. In other situations they may feel that no useful purpose will be served by taking matters any further, particularly where offenders are elderly or mentally ill.

No further action may also reflect the use by the police of what Sanders describes as speculative arrests, which might occur where the police arrest people to encourage them to give information (Sanders 2001). Arrest may in effect be a strategy to assist further investigation and may not be intended to lead to prosecution.

The officer may, instead of doing nothing, give an immediate informal caution or warning. This might happen with trivial offences, such as where an officer observes young people riding bicycles on the pavement, and issues a few words of warning (Evans and Wilkinson 1990). This is only appropriate in less serious matters and is completely within the discretion of the officer. In some offences involving the main-tenance of vehicles, an officer can issue a Notice to Rectify advising the motorist to correct the defect within a number of days, to avoid prosecution. Only if this is not done will prosecution result. A further option is the formal warning, a system which operates in some areas where a written warning is given in lieu of prosecution after the suspect has been reported for a possible offence. These alternatives are used for a variety of minor infringements – road traffic matters and very minor public order matters being the most common.

The most significant alternative to prosecution is the formal caution, which is used in a wide range of offences of varying seriousness. The issue of a police caution is a regulated and recorded procedure whereby a potential defendant admits guilt without evidence being fully gathered and is formally warned by a senior police officer 'not to do it again'. Cautions are recorded at the local Criminal Record Office, retained for 3 years and may be quoted in court at the time of sen-tence. Although cautions are given most often to young defendants, including young adults, they are available for defendants of any age. The use of cautioning with young offenders was given statutory authority in the Children and Young Persons Act 1969, and further changes were made by the Crime and Disorder Act 1998 which introduced reprimands and warnings as a form of cautioning for those under 18.

Cautions can be referred to in court, and, as they constitute a significant diver-sion from prosecution, the system is regulated. A number of guidelines have been issued, including the Attorney General's guidelines entitled *Criteria for Pro-secution* issued in 1984, and Home Office Circular 14 in February 1985 which encouraged the greater use of cautioning. In 1990, Home Office Circular 59 was issued to promote national standards for cautioning. Home Office Circular 18 in 1994 recommended limiting multiple cautions or cautions for serious offences. The Code for Crown Prosecutors also gives guidance on the use of cautioning. In some circumstances chief constables issue internal guidelines indicating which offences are appropriate for a caution. The most important prerequisite for a caution is that the offender accepts guilt. In order for a caution to be administered the following conditions must be fulfilled:

- there must be sufficient evidence to warrant a prosecution;
- the offender must admit guilt;
- either the person being cautioned, or, in the case of a child or young person, the parent or appropriate adult, must consent to such a disposal after being warned that the caution may be cited in future court appearances.

A number of criteria guide the decision of whether to initiate a prosecution, including the following:

- the nature and seriousness of the offence;
- the likely penalty if the offender was convicted by the court;
- the offender's age, personal circumstances and state of health;
- the offender's character and previous criminal history;
- the offender's attitude to the offence, including practical expressions of regret;
- the view of the victim.

The 1990 circular indicates that 'courts should only be used as a last resort, particularly for juveniles and young adults', and that where the criteria for cautioning are met there should be a 'presumption in favour of not prosecuting'.

The cautioning rate is the number of cautions as a percentage of the totals of all those found guilty by the courts. Cautioning grew in use throughout the 1980s to over 300,000 offenders cautioned annually, with an average increase of 6 per cent per year from 1985 to 1992. Since then the number has fallen and in 2002 a total of 225,400 offenders were cautioned. The usage still varies considerably with age and sex, with females more likely to be cautioned. In 2002 cautioning rates for males and females were respectively 27 and 44 per cent of all those either convicted or cautioned for indictable offences. Younger offenders are more likely to be cautioned than older, with rates declining by age (Criminal Statistics England and Wales 2002).

The 1990 standards were in part a response to the diversity in cautioning rates (see, for example, Evans and Wilkinson 1990; Ashworth 1994a). This variation still persists. In 2001 eight police forces had cautioning rates for indictable offences which exceeded 40 per cent, whereas four had a cautioning rate of less than 20 per cent. Leicestershire had the lowest rate at 9 per cent and Dyfed-Powys the highest at 54 per cent (Criminal Statistics England and Wales 2002).

This illustrates the element of discretion underlying these decisions. For example, guidelines do not specify precisely what account needs to be taken of particular factors and the police may use the decision to caution or prosecute in a

Figure 7.1 Offenders cautioned or sentenced 1975–2002

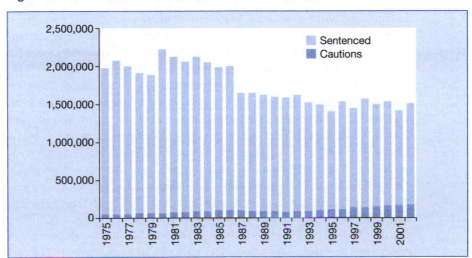

Source: Compiled from *Criminal Statistics England and Wales*, 1975 to 2002.

way that accords with their working rules. Thus officers may simply feel that some offenders deserve prosecution, and cautions may avoid unnecessary paperwork. Indeed, while cautions should only be given where there is sufficient evidence to prosecute, Sanders points to research indicating that some suspects were cautioned because there was insufficient evidence to prosecute – thus a caution can be used to clear up a case which might otherwise not have been prosecuted (Sanders 2002). Thus, argues Sanders, the low visibility of cautioning can enable the police to use cautions as a bargaining tool.

The exercise of discretion also raises issues of possible bias. Girls are more likely to be cautioned than boys although this may well reflect the point made in Chapter 2 that they tend to commit less serious offences. Ethnic minorities have been found to be cautioned less, which may reflect findings that ethnic minority suspects are more likely to contest a case – as seen above, a caution can be given only if guilt is admitted. In addition, there have been some indications that black juveniles are less likely to have cases referred to the multi-agency panels which exist for juveniles, a difference which remained even after admission of guilt was taken into account. This, speculate Phillips and Bowling (2002), might reflect the more hostile attitudes pertaining between black youth and the police.

There is also some concern that cautioning may have a built-in class bias. Many of the criteria relating to offenders' circumstances may unintentionally advantage better-off offenders or young people from middle-class homes. Ashworth indicates how the criterion concerning attitude to the offence may work in this way. This criterion includes consideration of whether the offender has made some practical demonstration of regret, such as an apology to a victim, or an offer to put matters right, for example by voluntary compensation. Thus, he comments, 'wealthy offenders might be able to buy themselves out of prosecution by offering payments to their victims, whereas impecunious offenders cannot' (Ashworth 1994a: 138–9).

In addition, the regulatory agencies, such as the Inland Revenue or local authority consumer protection departments, which are responsible for the prosecution of offences involving white collar or business offenders, often, as will be seen in a later section, follow a policy of not prosecuting offenders and extensively use both informal and written cautions. Indeed these agencies regularly caution offenders on many occasions before a prosecution is considered and the extent to which offenders have sought to rectify matters is part of this decision (see, for example, Croall 2001; Ashworth 1994a; and below).

The police are responsible for the decision to give a caution. The CPS may send the papers in the case back to the police with a recommendation that one is given. If a caution is given this normally means an end of the matter and the police and the Crown Prosecution Service will take no further action. However, it is possible for a private prosecution to be taken out against an offender who has been cautioned by the police. Thus Mr Hayter instituted a private prosecution in Basildon against two youths who had assaulted his son. The police were of the view that a caution was the appropriate means of dealing with the matter, and both boys agreed after having legal advice. In the cautioning process, both were told that it did not prevent an aggrieved person bringing proceedings, and that is what Mr Hayter did. Although it was argued that the prosecution should not continue, the Queen's Bench Division of the High Court (QBD) decided that the case could continue (*Hayter v L and Another*, 1998).

Under the CJA 2003 a conditional cautioning procedure is introduced. This was recommended by both the Runciman Commission in 1993 and the Auld Review in 2001 and will be made available to prosecutors and police. When introduced, this system, aimed at 'facilitating the rehabilitation of offenders' and 'ensuring reparation' to victims, will be available for adult offenders, and will mean that those who fail to comply can be brought to court. Thus the system provides an opportunity for both a warning to be given and the offender to actually do something to show a change of heart. Demonstrating this change will ward off court proceedings. Conditions that can be attached to a caution will be set out under a Code of Practice to be issued under s. 25 of the Act. This Code will also specify procedures to be employed when giving conditional cautions. The conditions available are likely to involve those cautioned making financial or other recompense to the victim or undertaking activities designed to help the offender change his offending behaviour. The following requirements must be met before a conditional caution can be issued:

- the police or investigation officer must have evidence that the offender has committed an offence;
- there must be sufficient evidence to charge, and the prosecutor (not the police) must decide it is appropriate to caution;
- the offender must admit the offence (as with unconditional cautions);
- the offender must have the effect of the caution explained and, in particular, that failure to comply with the conditions may result in prosecution;
- the offender must sign a document setting out the terms of the caution.

Thus the conditional caution is intended to be more proactive than the unconditional caution, whilst still removing many – usually first-time – offenders from the court process.

Cautioning and young offenders

Cautioning was originally predominantly used in relation to young people as a means of diverting young offenders from the court system in the hope that they would behave better without the stigma of being labelled a criminal. Arguments critical of its use focused upon the problem of net widening, suggesting that the apparently more benign approach might be responsible for increasing the number of youngsters caught in the net of the criminal justice system. Other critics looked at the high proportion of crime committed by young offenders (see Chapter 8) to suggest that it was not an effective means to control delinquency.

These arguments about the use of cautioning with young offenders came under fire in 1996 in the Home Office document *Misspent Youth*, which provided evidence that pointed to the limited effectiveness of repeat cautioning, the problems of inconsistent usage and to the fact that cautioning does not 'nip offending in the bud' (Home Office 1997b, para 5.10). The Crime and Disorder Act 1998 replaced the system of cautioning for young offenders with 'police reprimands' and 'final warnings'. Under the Act, when an offence is committed by a young person, the police can take no action at all, or give a police reprimand, or give a final warning, or start a prosecution. Normally for a first offence the police would decide upon one of the following:

- a police reprimand if the offence was not very serious;
- a final warning if it was more serious;
- a decision to prosecute.

For a second offence, if a reprimand had already been given, a further reprimand could not be given and the young person would be given a final warning, or prosecuted.

After any final warning the commission of a further offence would automatically result in criminal proceedings unless 2 years had elapsed from the warning and the new offence was minor. A final warning would usually involve offenders and their families in a community intervention programme aimed at trying to change offenders' behaviour to prevent further offences being committed.

The rights of both defendants and victims are affected by cautions. A caution can be given only following an admission of guilt. This raises the question of the extent to which defendants may be under pressure to admit guilt which they otherwise deny in order to avoid the stress of a court appearance. The low visibility of cautions raises concerns about how far defendants' rights are observed at this stage, especially since a caution may have a bearing on subsequent sentence.

There may also be a conflict between the benefits of diversion and the interest of victims. When offenders are cautioned, victims are deprived of the opportunity to obtain compensation (Ashworth 1994a). While some areas have provisions for offering mediation between offenders and victims as a form of diversion, this practice, which will be discussed more fully in Chapter 14, is by no means widespread.

Once the police have decided that a prosecution rather than any other form of action is appropriate, the papers are referred to the CPS for consideration.

7.2 PROSECUTION

The vast majority of prosecutions are undertaken by the CPS, but a number of other agencies also have responsibility for undertaking criminal prosecutions. These include the agencies responsible for enforcing laws regulating many aspects of business, trade and commerce. Their work will be outlined following an examination of the CPS. Private bodies and individuals may also prosecute but this accounts for only a very small number of prosecutions.

The process of prosecutions is formally started either following the arrest and charge of a suspect by the police, or after a summons has been issued by a magistrates' court. The court issues a summons after receiving information from the police or other prosecuting bodies or from individuals about an alleged offence; this is referred to as 'laying an information'. There are many more summonses issued than people arrested and charged (see Table 9.4). A large number of prosecutions for 'summary only' offences such as motoring offences are started this way. The CJA 2003 introduces refinements to the process for the introduction of written changes and requisitions requiring attendance at court, and provides mechanisms for custody officers to seek advice from the CPS on the correct charge to be made.

Custody officers will have the following options when dealing with an arrested person:

- to charge and bail;
- to charge and keep in custody until next court;
- to release without charge or bail, bringing the proceedings to an end unless new evidence comes to light;
- to release without charge on bail pending further investigations;
- to release without charge on bail for advice from the DPP as to the sufficiency of the evidence and the nature of the charge.

Where advice is sought from the DPP (i.e. the CPS), the following decisions may be taken and the suspect must be informed:

- there is insufficient evidence to charge;
- there is sufficient evidence to charge but it is not in the public interest to proceed (see CPS Code of Practice);
- charge;
- advise a caution (including conditional caution, and warnings and reprimands): which the police must then give: they will no longer have the ability to decide not to caution.

The Crown Prosecution Service

Before the creation of the CPS in the 1980s, the police and the Director of Public Prosecutions (DPP) were responsible for prosecution. The office of the DPP was set up by the Prosecution of Offences Act 1879, and its task was to institute, undertake or carry on criminal proceedings, and to give advice and assistance to chief officers of police and other persons responsible for the prosecution of offences. The DPP was responsible for prosecuting cases of murder, along with those involving national security, public figures and police officers.

The police were responsible for the prosecution of routine offences in magistrates' courts, and there were 43 prosecution authorities in England and Wales. They were advised by solicitors, who were either employed or consulted by them, and who conducted more complex cases in the magistrates' courts. Cases in Crown Courts were conducted by barristers on behalf of the police.

The police were therefore both investigators and prosecutors, a dual role which caused considerable concern. It was argued, for example, that the crime control function of investigation could clash with the interests of due process in ensuring that prosecutions be undertaken only on the basis of sufficient evidence. The potential conflict was noted by Royal Commissions in 1929 and 1962 and the Royal Commission on Criminal Procedure, known as the Phillips Commission, which was set up in 1978 and reported in 1981. It pointed out that there was no uniform system of prosecution in England and Wales, and that there was a strong civil liberties case for an independent agency, other than the police, to review and conduct the prosecution of criminal cases. It argued that a new prosecuting agency would encourage greater consistency in approach to prosecution. It stressed that the roles of investigating crime, collecting evidence and arresting suspects were likely to interfere with the impartial review of a case and decisions about whether prosecution was necessary or likely to be successful. The dual responsibility for policing and prosecution could lead to the abuse of the rights of the arrested person by the police, born out of an anxiety to convict those whom the police believed were guilty. There were also concerns from an efficiency viewpoint about the number of weak cases, where the evidence was insufficient to lead to a conviction, being taken to court and then thrown out as a result of a judge-directed acquittal, which was both costly and time consuming.

Following a debate in the House of Commons and the Bonan Working Party whose report was published in August 1983, a White Paper proposed the setting up of a Crown Prosecution Service. The Prosecution of Offences Act 1985 established the CPS and specified its functions, which included taking over the conduct of all criminal proceedings instituted by the police. As seen in Chapter 6, the introduction of the CPS was closely linked with the Police and Criminal Evidence Act 1984 (PACE).

There was much debate over whether the service should be a centralised national service or a local one or combine elements of both. In the end a national service was created: the CPS therefore represents a single independent and nationwide authority for England and Wales. It is independent of the police and has the power to discontinue prosecutions. Unlike prosecution agencies in other jurisdictions it has no powers to institute proceedings or to direct the police to carry out any further investigations. Its introduction had substantial constitutional significance for a number of reasons. For the first time there was a single state prosecuting authority charged with making decisions of a quasi-judicial nature which could ultimately affect the rights and liberties of the individual. It also created a new legal interest group directly linked to government. These lawyers, although civil servants, were expected to be independent of government control, although little was put in place to guarantee this, save the *Code for Crown Prosecutors* and the existing *Codes of Professional Conduct for the Legal Professions*.

The introduction of the CPS as a body with a duty to review cases at every stage of a prosecution inevitably caused problems. Some of these sprung from initial rivalry between the police and the CPS and misunderstandings about their respective roles. The necessary bureaucratic changes also produced problems – major delays followed changes in the system for transmitting files to court and prioritising cases. The Royal Commission on Criminal Justice in 1993 commented that the service was hastily conceived and inadequately resourced. A report in 1990 by the Public Accounts Committee on a Review of the Crown Prosecution Service (House of Commons 1990) found that estimates of how much the system would cost were initially too low and that many problems were caused by understaffing and inadequate resourcing.

The powers of the CPS to discontinue cases also caused friction with the police and frustration on the part of victims and courts. As we shall see below, the rate of cases discontinued continues to cause concern, although one of the roles of the CPS was to reduce the number of trials aborted on evidential grounds. Other critics saw the CPS as a threat to civil liberties, as it intermingled judicial and executive functions.

The organisation and functions of the Crown Prosecution Service

In England and Wales the CPS, with a budget in 2002/3 of £453 million, has become the main agency responsible for the prosecution of offenders. It started in 1986 as a result of the Prosecution of Offences Act 1985 and its establishment was part of a complete reform of the laws governing police investigation (PACE 1984) (see Chapter 6) and the prosecution of offences. By the end of March 2003 it employed 7,046 people, including 2,267 lawyers and 4,711 caseworkers and administrators dealing with (in 2002/3) 1.44 million cases sent by the police leading to 1.08 million prosecutions in the magistrates' courts and 80,000 in the Crown Court. They are responsible for carrying out the major tasks of the CPS which are as follows:

■ to review cases to decide whether to continue or discontinue them;

■ to liaise with the police on matters of evidence and agreeing charging standards;

■ to liaise with barristers who represent the prosecution in the Crown Court;

■ to present cases in the magistrates' courts at all pre-trial and trial stages.

Their role as civil servants and crown employees is tempered by the *Code for Crown Prosecutors* and by their professional ethics as lawyers, with a primary duty to the court. The head of the CPS is the Director of Public Prosecutions (DPP). Ken Macdonald was appointed DPP in November 2003.

The work of the CPS is divided into different geographical areas. Between 1986 and 1998 there have been three reorganisations of the CPS. These have sought to create a balance between areas so that they have similar case loads while, where possible, having boundaries that are coterminous with other agencies, especially the police.

The Phillips Commission (1978/81) originally conceived the CPS as a locally accountable organisation and recommended dividing the country into 43 areas reflecting the 43 police force areas. However, when introduced in 1986 the CPS was organised into 31 areas, in an attempt to equalise workloads. In 1992, reorganisation to achieve a more cohesive national structure led to these being re-divided into 13 areas.

In April 1997 the Labour Party produced a policy document, *The Case for the Prosecution*, suggesting another reorganisation into 42 areas, each with a Chief Crown Prosecutor, with one to cover the entire area of the Metropolitan and City of London forces. Outside of London the boundaries are the same as for the police. The document underlined the need for an independent service but with opportunity for closer liaison with the police. After the Labour Party was elected, the new Attorney General announced that this policy statement would be put in force. However, in June 1997 the Glidewell review of the CPS was initiated with wide-ranging terms of reference covering the organisation and structure of the CPS with a view to enhancing the efficient prosecution of crime within existing resources. Specific questions were re-examined in connection with falling conviction rates, downgrading of charges and CPS relations with the police. The report, in 1998, recommended the boundary and administrative reforms outlined above.

Once an accused person has been charged or summoned the papers are forwarded to the appropriate branch of the CPS which deals with cases from the police station where the offence originates. On receipt of these papers the CPS is under a duty to review the case in accordance with two criteria involved in the decision to prosecute. These two criteria, which will be discussed in detail below, are (a) that there is sufficient evidence to continue the case, and (b) that it is in the public interest to continue.

When the accused is brought to the magistrates' court in custody, the CPS normally receive the papers on the morning of the first hearing and are expected to represent the prosecution on adjournments and applications for bail. Once papers are received the CPS is entirely responsible for the conduct of the case. This includes deciding which charges should be proceeded with, what evidence is relevant and admissible and whether or not it is sufficient – in effect, whether there is a reasonable prospect of success. It also includes assessing whether or not it is in the public interest to continue with the prosecution and, if so, ensuring that the case is prepared and ready for trial.

By 1998, as mentioned above, the CPS was waiting to implement the range of reform proposals emanating from the new Labour Government, incorporating the ideas from the Glidewell Review (1997/8) and the Narey report on the *Review of Delay in the Criminal Justice System* (Home Office 1997c). The Narey report made sweeping recommendations for all stages of the criminal justice system and may reflect a more systems-based approach to criminal justice involving greater cooperation and liaison between agencies. The recommendations affecting the CPS included the following:

- an enhanced role for CPS staff without legal qualifications to review files and to present non-contested cases in the magistrates' courts;

- an end to the discontinuance of cases on the public interest ground that it considers the case as not serious;

- greater local autonomy;

- closer cooperation with the police on the preparation of prosecution files to reduce delay – this includes a permanent CPS presence in police administrative support units with the aim of prosecuting, as soon as possible after the charge, those cases where a guilty plea is likely;

- closer liaison with the courts and improved communications between the CPS and the magistrates' courts through daily telephone contacts on hearings listed for the next day.

The use of non-legal staff to take over some of the duties of legally qualified staff was enacted in the Crime and Disorder Act 1998. It allowed non-lawyers to review cases with regard to decisions whether to continue prosecution and also allowed a right of audience to present criminal proceedings in magistrates' courts, although they are not allowed to represent the prosecution at the trial stage. They will therefore have the right to conduct much more of the pre-trial stages in the magistrates' court such as hearings regarding bail. The Act defines the trial as starting at the stage when the plea is taken. However, it may be that structural changes are not the only ones in prospect: before its election the Labour Party was proposing a District-Attorney-style prosecutor. This would involve greater local contact but without the direct democratic accountability that is achieved in the United States of America by the election of a District Attorney. The idea is to raise the local profile of the Chief Crown Prosecutor so that he or she becomes 'a named and known' individual.

7.3 THE CODE FOR CROWN PROSECUTORS

The Code for Crown Prosecutors is a public statement of the guidelines to be applied to the decision on whether to prosecute an offender. In June 1994 the Code was revised to clarify it. The Fourth edition of the Code, taking account of the Human Rights Act 1998, was issued in 2000 and the Fifth in November 2004, dealing with the CJA 2003. Two statements explain the CPS approach.

> One of the most important tasks of the CPS is its review function. This means that we consider the evidence supplied by the police, and any other relevant information, and make a decision . . . in accordance with . . . the Code . . . At all times, we exercise an independent judgement about the case presented, on the basis of the tests set out in the Code . . .
>
> The decision to prosecute . . . is a serious step. Fair and effective prosecution is essential to the maintenance of law and order . . . a prosecution has serious implications for all involved – the victim, a witness and a defendant. The Crown Prosecution Service applies the Code . . . so that it can make fair and consistent decisions about prosecutions.
>
> (CPS Annual Report 1993/4: 6)

The Code is the cornerstone of the CPS's review and decision-making role and embodies values and principles of the CPS. First issued under s. 10 of the Prosecution of Offences Act 1985, it restates principles concerning the fairness, objectivity and independence of the CPS, and gives guidance about cautions, charges, mode of trial, acceptance of guilty pleas and restarting prosecutions which have been abandoned. The 2004 Code recognises the role of the CPS in post-conviction matters and in conditional cautions. The bulk of the Code is concerned with the two tests involved in the decision to prosecute: evidential sufficiency; and public interest.

The evidential sufficiency test is applied first; if the case does not pass this test, no matter how serious, important, or publicly notorious, it will not go ahead. Only if the case passes the evidence test will the second test, public interest, be applied.

The purpose of the evidential test is twofold. First, on a financial and practical basis, there is no point in proceeding with a case which will inevitably be 'thrown out' by the court because there is not enough evidence. To proceed in such cases would be very wasteful of limited resources. Secondly, it follows the general principle underpinning the whole criminal justice system, that people should not be put at risk on insufficient evidence, and that the duty of providing sufficient evidence is always on the prosecution. Some might argue that in certain cases the high public interest in a prosecution – even if it is doomed to failure – overrides the lack of evidence: that it is important to air the matter, even the lack of evidence, in the public domain.

Evidential test

The CPS must be satisfied that there is a 'realistic prospect of conviction' on the available evidence. The test must be applied in respect of each defendant and each charge. A realistic prospect of conviction means that – in the view of the CPS – the magistrates or jury, properly advised on the law, are more likely than not to convict. This involves considering the availability, admissibility and reliability of evidence. In reaching a view, the CPS must consider whether any of the available evidence is admissible and reliable:

In considering admissibility the CPS will consider whether the evidence:

- is likely to be excluded by the judge because it has been illegally obtained – for example, by breaches of PACE and its Codes;
- is confession evidence likely to be excluded because of a breach of PACE, s. 76, where the confession has been obtained by improper means;
- emanates from witnesses who are legally incompetent (cannot give evidence); who are unwilling and cannot be compelled to give evidence; or who are children to whom special rules and considerations apply.

In considering reliability the CPS will consider the following:

- the defendant's age, understanding and intelligence in considering any confession;
- whether a defendant's explanation is credible as a whole;
- whether the witness's credibility is affected by background matters;
- if identification evidence is involved, whether the evidence is strong enough, bearing in mind the special difficulties with identification evidence.

Public interest test

This refers to criteria by which the CPS may, even after satisfying the evidential sufficiency criteria, decide not to proceed with a case. The use of the phrase 'public interest' is somewhat misleading as what is deemed to be in the public interest involves no consultation with the public, but relates to notional standards encompassing concepts of 'fair play', whether a prosecution is 'worth while' and so on. Why this was called a public interest criteria is difficult to discern. Until the revision of the Code for Crown Prosecutors (CCP) was published in June 1994, the criteria indicated a series of points which favoured dropping the case against a defendant; the public benefit being to save money. It assumed that only certain cases needed to go forward for the public interest to be served. This assumption generated concern from victims and the public. Lord Shawcross, a former Attorney General, is quoted to justify this criteria:

It has never been the rule in this Country – I hope it never will be – that suspected criminal offences must automatically be the subject of prosecution. Indeed the very first Regulations under which the Director of Public Prosecutions worked provided that he should ... prosecute 'wherever it appears that the offence or the circumstances of its commission is or are of such a character that a prosecution in respect thereof is required in the public interest'. That is still the dominant consideration.

(Shawcross 1951)

The criteria in the CPS Code now indicate public interest criteria both in favour of and against prosecution. As a general rule more serious cases are less likely to be discontinued but the criteria must be applied in each case. The factors for and against prosecution must be weighed carefully. It is in this context that the greatest discretion lies, and where most concern or confusion is caused. Thus it is stated that the factors for and against prosecution are not exhaustive, must be considered where appropriate and that all factors do not apply in all cases. Prosecutors are specifically expected to consider the interests of the victim, of young offenders, the possibility of a police caution, and guidelines for dealing with mentally disordered offenders. The criteria are summarised in Figure 7.2.

Particular reference is made in the Code to young offenders. Whilst the CPS must consider the interests of the youth when deciding whether to prosecute, the Code takes account of the fact that cases involving young offenders will usually be referred to the CPS only after a reprimand and final warning have been given unless the case is serious. Thus the public interest test is already usually met in youth cases.

The criteria used by the CPS are broadly similar to those used in sentencing. In other words, the offences which will be perceived as less serious by a court, thus attracting the lowest sentence, are unlikely to be prosecuted at all. This may have a number of implications for the criminal justice system. First, the 'bottom layer' of offences will be removed with the possible consequent downgrading of remaining incidents. Secondly, the CPS is applying a quasi-judicial function 'second-guessing' possible sentences. Thirdly, the public interest in the denunciatory effect of bringing a range of offences to court is weakened.

The Code also sets out guidelines in relation to what charges should be made – for example, which offences a defendant should be charged with. This can on occasion cause disquiet, where, for example, it appears that a defendant is being charged with a lesser offence than that merited by the facts of the incident. Charges should therefore be chosen, according to the Code, to reflect the seriousness of the offence, and to enable the case to be presented in a straightforward way.

In August 1994, the first charging standards were published, resulting from cooperation between the CPS and police to encourage consistency and understanding between the two agencies and those dealing with the courts. The first standards related to an area where most confusion and inconsistency is likely – that of assaults:

■ Common assault will be the appropriate charge where the injuries include no more than grazes, scratches, abrasions, bruises, swellings, 'black eye', or superficial cuts.

Figure 7.2 Public interest criteria used by the CPS

Factors militating against prosecution

■ The likelihood of a small or nominal penalty

■ The defendant has already been sentenced and the new matter would be unlikely to add to it

■ The offence was committed as a result of a genuine mistake

■ The loss or harm was minor and the result of a single incident, particularly if caused by misjudgment

■ There has been a long delay since the offence – except where the offence is serious; the delay was caused by the defendant; the offence has only just come to light; or there has been a long investigation

■ A prosecution will adversely affect the *victim's* physical or mental health (having regard to the seriousness of offence)

■ The *defendant* is elderly, or at the time of the offence suffering from significant mental or physical illness, unless the offence is serious or there is a possibility of repetition

■ The defendant has put right the loss (but defendants should not be seen as 'buying' their way out of prosecution)

■ Details could be made public which in the public interest should not be revealed

Factors militating in favour of prosecutions

■ The likelihood of a significant sentence of confiscation or other order

■ Use of a weapon or violence threatened

■ Offence against a person serving the public (for example, a police officer or nurse)

■ Defendant committed the offence in a position of authority or trust

■ Defendant was the prime mover in the offence

■ Premeditated or group offence

■ Offence committed in presence of child

■ Victim particularly vulnerable, put in fear, or suffered personal attack, damage or disturbance

■ Offence motivated by racial, sexual, religious, disability or political discrimination

■ Marked difference between ages (real or mental) of defendant and victim or element of corruption

■ Defendant has relevant previous convictions

■ Commission of offence whilst subject to court order

■ Likelihood of repetition

■ Widespread offence in area or impact on public confidence

Source: CPS Code for Crown Prosecutors 2004

■ Assault occasioning actual bodily harm (ABH) will be appropriate where there is loss of, or a broken tooth, temporary loss of sensory functions, extensive bruising, displaced broken nose, minor fractures, minor cuts, or psychiatric injury more than fear.

■ Examples of grievous bodily harm (GBH) are injury resulting in broken limbs, permanent disability, or more than minor, permanent visible disfigurement.

It should be emphasised that these charging standards are statements of prosecution practice, and the aim of publishing them is to foster a greater consistency of approach between agencies and areas. By 1998 further charging standards had been issued in relation to driving and public order offences (including football offences and drunk and disorderly behaviour).

The work of the Crown Prosecution Service

The following data shows the workload for the CPS in 2002/3 in the magistrates' courts and the Crown Court (from the CPS *Annual Report 2002/3*):

Total CPS caseload and discontinuance 2002/3

- 1.8 million magistrates' court cases were dealt with
- 12.6 per cent of magistrates' court cases were discontinued
- 80,000 Crown Court cases were dealt with

Cases completed in the magistrates' courts in 2002/3

- 978,000 defendants pleaded or were found guilty

Cases completed in the Crown Court in 2002/3

- 72,000 defendants were convicted
- 62 per cent of those who pleaded not guilty were convicted.

In assessing the effectiveness or otherwise of the CPS we need to consider its working relationship with the police. As we have seen, the police also consider the sufficiency of evidence and make decisions on whether to take any further action or to caution. In theory, therefore, the police should initially have sifted out cases which do not merit prosecution. Therefore, as Ashworth points out in relation to discontinuances on public interest grounds, these could either be interpreted as 'police failures' or 'CPS successes' (Ashworth 1994a: 182).

Thus to understand the developing relationship between the police, CPS and the courts we must recognise that:

> prosecution decisions are taken not in a laboratory atmosphere but in a working context that brings the CPS into contact with the police, with victims, and with magistrates ... any attempt to explain practical decision making must take account of the organisational and operational contexts in which the decisions tend to be made.
>
> (Ashworth 1994a: 193)

It is apparent that, while the CPS is independent of the police, it is reliant on police information. And, given that the police have already sifted out cases, the CPS may have a tendency to assume that cases passed to it merit prosecution. In addition, developing working relationships and shared assumptions about which cases should be prosecuted may result in a reluctance on the part of the CPS to go against police advice, thus reducing discontinuance rates. Some research conducted in the early days of the CPS was critical of this tendency, and pointed out that the police tended to provide information which would support their decision to prosecute (Leng *et al.* 1992).

In addition, the evidential sufficiency criteria essentially ask the CPS to predict the likely outcome of a case. This may change, however, as a case proceeds because vital witnesses may refuse to give evidence, or new evidence may come to light. The CPS does not know in advance what the defence is likely to be except in the Crown Court. Weak evidence may not, however, lead to a case being dropped, especially where defendants indicate at an early stage that they intend to plead guilty. Thus the CPS may feel that a weak case is worth proceeding with and one writer comments that 'it is the experience of prosecutors that weak cases commonly produce a guilty plea' (Leng *et al.* 1992: 136). Other factors such as the attitude of local courts may also affect prosecution decisions in that prosecutors may second guess the likely attitude of the courts. This can produce local variations. The local CPS also builds up a working relationship with the local police, who in turn may come to anticipate the decision of the prosecutor. Figures on discontinuances, therefore, may reflect the operation of these informal factors. The statistics on the number of cases that are dropped or subsequently acquitted could be taken to indicate a failure of the review process. But the reasons why cases are dropped may not, as seen above, be evident at the start of a case, and may emerge only during the trial.

Rising numbers of cases discontinued in the early 1990s raised questions about the benefits of prosecution and diversion. In 1993, for example, a total of 193,000 cases were discontinued. If these figures are taken alongside the large numbers of cautions and the under-reporting of crime it means that fewer and fewer cases are being taken to court. This could be seen as reducing any deterrent, denunciatory or crime control potential of the criminal justice system. In addition, defendants who are repeatedly asked to attend court and then told that the case has been dropped may have a valid grievance: not least those who wished to clear their name positively in court. Such defendants do have the right to seek repayment of costs incurred by them – for many this, combined with the relief of having the case dropped, is sufficient. For others there remains a lingering grievance against 'the system'.

On the other hand, many cases are dropped in accordance with the criteria, because of a 'missing legal element', which indicates that they should never have been commenced at all (see Figure 7.3). As we have seen, official policy has encouraged diversion, and it is clearly stated that it is not in the interests of efficiency or public interest to prosecute all cases. The CPS was indeed intended to reduce the number of weak cases coming to court. Other critics have argued that the CPS does not discontinue enough cases on public interest grounds and is therefore not sufficiently independent of the police (Leng *et al.* 1992).

Studies show that the CPS does discontinue cases on public interest grounds as well as on the grounds of evidential insufficiency. This can be seen in a survey of discontinued cases carried out by the CPS (Crown Prosecution Service Survey, January 1994) of 11,000 cases in November 1993. Prosecutors across the country were asked to record the reasons for discontinuance under four main headings: insufficient evidence, public interest, prosecution unable to proceed, and defendant producing documents in court for the first time. Forty-three per cent of cases dropped or discontinued were through the application of the 'insufficient evidence'

Figure 7.3 Results of CPS Discontinuance Survey (1993)

Insufficient evidence (43%)

- 11% of the cases discontinued related to insufficient evidence about the identity of the accused – for example, a witness identified a man she said she had seen committing a burglary, but she had seen him in poor lighting and had not had a good view of him (there was no other evidence to link the man with the offence)
- 13% of the cases dropped due to insufficient evidence were dropped because there was a legal element missing – for example, a defendant was charged with theft of a car radio cassette even though there was no evidence that it was stolen property
- 19% of the cases had an essential legal element missing

Prosecution unable to proceed (17%)

- 13% were because of a missing witness
- 2% related to offences already taken into consideration
- 2% case not ready and adjournments refused

Defendants produced driving documents in court for the first time (9%)

Public interest (31%)

- 9% were convicted or sentenced on other matters
- 6% a nominal penalty was anticipated
- 4% staleness
- 3% complainants' attitude
- 2% defendant's age
- 1% defendant mentally ill
- 6% other

Source: Compiled from CPS *Annual Report 1993/4*: 15–16.

criteria and 31 per cent through the application of the 'public interest' criteria. Forty-one per cent of all cases discontinued during the month of the survey were minor motoring offences. Figure 7.3 summarises the main reasons why cases were discontinued.

The most common single factor leading to discontinuance on public interest grounds was that the defendant had been convicted or sentenced for other offences, and in a further 6 per cent the court was expected to impose only a nominal penalty, such as an absolute discharge. An example of staleness was a case where a defendant was summoned for having no driving licence, test certificate or insurance. The CPS did not receive the papers until almost 33 months after the offences were committed. Examples of discontinuance using other criteria include that of a woman charged with being drunk and disorderly and subsequently admitted to a psychiatric hospital. Consistent with the spirit of the Home Office Circular on Provision for Mentally Disordered Offenders the CPS decided that the wider public interest did not demand a prosecution. In another case, an 82-year-old motorist collided with a parked car without causing injury. The motorist surrendered his licence to the Driver and Vehicle Licensing Agency so the CPS decided that it was no longer necessary to prosecute.

Other cases are not proceeded with or fail because of the non-attendance of witnesses. William and Valerie Wicks were jailed in November 1994 for 4 weeks for contempt of court after refusing to give evidence against a person charged with causing grievous bodily harm to Mr Wicks. The attack on Mr Wicks was witnessed by his wife (*Daily Telegraph*, 19 November 1994: 6). In another case an expert witness went on holiday instead of giving evidence at a rape trial. The defendant was acquitted, and Dr Kusum Agrawal (the police doctor involved) was fined £3,000 by an Old Bailey judge (*The Times*, 21 January 1995: 8).

A final issue to be raised is what role victims can or should play in the prosecution process. Recent attention to the victim in the criminal justice process lay behind the criterion that victims' interests should play a part. But to what extent does this conflict with other criteria? What, if any, role should victims play? If the victim does not wish to proceed with a case, and is unwilling to give evidence, then the prosecution may be unsuccessful. Thus the victim's role in the provision of evidence may be crucial, as in the Wicks case referred to above. In addition, as with cautions, a failure to prosecute may deprive the victim of compensation, although some diversionary schemes provide for mediation between victim and offender (see Chapter 14). Any further role for the victim is problematic as it could be argued that to take the victim's attitude into account might conflict with any public interest there may be in prosecuting the offender to ensure that they are duly punished.

7.4 PRIVATE PROSECUTIONS AND OTHER PROSECUTING AGENCIES

Private prosecutions may be started by, for example, department stores to deal with shoplifting on their premises, or individuals who feel that an issue should be dealt with by the courts, as when, in January 1998, 72-year-old Roy Edney of Harrow started proceedings against Bath rugby player Kevin Yates, alleging that he had bitten off a lump of skin from another player's ear during a match. Sometimes aggrieved victims and their families take up a prosecution, as with the Hayter case cited above and with the murder of Steven Lawrence, because they feel that the police or the CPS have taken insufficient action. The right to start a private prosecution is subject to limitations:

- the magistrates may refuse to issue proceedings;
- the Attorney General can stop what are called 'vexatious litigants' from bringing cases;
- the DPP has a power to take over prosecutions and end them.

Prosecution by regulatory agencies

While the CPS is responsible for the majority of prosecutions (75 per cent in the magistrates' court and 95 per cent in the Crown Court), many other agencies also undertake criminal prosecutions. These include: local authority departments responsible for consumer protection and environmental health; the Health and Safety Executive; agencies responsible for pollution; Driver and Vehicle Licensing Authority (DVLA) for the non-payment of motor vehicle tax; and the TV Licensing Records Office for non-payment of a TV licence. The RSPCA may prosecute those accused of neglecting or mistreating animals; and the National Society for the

Prevention of Cruelty to Children may do the same with regard to the maltreatment of children. The Department of Social Security (DSS) also prosecutes in relation to social security frauds. General taxation matters are the responsibility of the Customs and Excise and Inland Revenue departments, and many more government departments are responsible for investigating frauds and other offences involving business, trade and financial services. These include the Serious Fraud Office and the Department of Trade and Industry. It was seen in Chapter 2 that many of these offences are not included in the criminal statistics, and statistics on how many offences are prosecuted in relation to known offences are not generally available, although some can be found on the websites of the agencies concerned along with details of prosecutions. Research into these agencies indicates that they prosecute only a very small proportion of known offenders. It has already been seen that they use the caution extensively and prosecution is often seen as a last resort (see, for example, Croall 2001).

It is interesting to examine briefly how these agencies proceed, as their attitude to prosecution is very different. In his study of the origins of the factory inspectorate, established by the Factory Act 1833, which regulated the labour of children and young persons in mills and factories, W G Carson made the following observation:

> We ... need to understand the social origins of an enforcement agency which, from its very inception, has not seen itself as being busy about the business of catching criminals. In adopting this historically explicable stance, the Factory Inspectorate has played its own inadvertent part in perpetuating a collective representation which portrays crime as being concentrated in circumscribed and morally peripheral segments of the community.
>
> (Carson 1974: 138)

Different attitudes to prosecution are strongly related to the perceived role and function of these agencies. Many see themselves not as industrial police officers with a primary duty to prosecute the guilty, but as agencies responsible for improving standards of business, trade or commerce by ensuring that businesses comply with regulations. Securing compliance is therefore seen as their primary aim, and prosecution is only one of many tools to achieve this. Therefore they tend to pursue what are often described as compliance strategies, which can be compared with a prosecution strategy (see, for example, Croall 2001; Croall 2003). Under a compliance strategy, the prevention of offences is seen as paramount, with education, advice and persuasion being seen as preferable to prosecution. Prosecution is likely to be seen by many agencies as costly and counter-productive, as it may lead to poor relationships between agencies and businesses.

Cost-effectiveness underlies many of these strategies. In many areas prosecution involves high costs. Many offences in the world of business and finance are very complex, and investigation may involve gathering enormous amounts of evidence and interviewing many witnesses. Fraud trials, for example, can be lengthy and involve extremely complex evidence. Fraud trials are also seen as risky – the chances of conviction may be lessened by the complexity of the case and the ability of defendants to contest it. If there is a chance for the matter to be resolved without trial an out-of-court settlement becomes an attractive prospect. For local authority departments, if a prosecution is unsuccessful, they may have to bear the costs of prosecution themselves, thus reducing the resources they have for investigation.

In addition, many agencies have options other than doing nothing, cautioning or prosecuting. Some, such as environmental health departments, may be able to grant or withhold licences from offending businesses, thus effectively threatening their viability. Others, such as the Inland Revenue, can impose sanctions or fines without taking offenders to court. Yet others can disqualify those who need licences to operate, such as financial service employees. Many would argue that these powers constitute a greater deterrent than prosecution, which may be followed by only a small fine.

Prosecution may only result if compliance is not forthcoming after a series of other measures. A prosecution may therefore reflect enforcers' attitudes that defendants are more blameworthy and deserve prosecution. In addition, the threat of prosecution may be used as a bargaining counter in persuading offenders to comply (Hawkins 1984). In some cases, however, these considerations can be overridden where, for example, there has been considerable public interest in a case and where prosecution may be considered necessary given the seriousness of the case. This may happen following major incidents in which there has been large-scale pollution or where members of the public have been killed or injured.

Discussing the circumstances in which prosecution of financial offences is more appropriate the former Head of the Serious Fraud Office (SFO), Rosalind Wright, lists a number of situations in which criminal proceedings are more appropriate. These include situations in which there is evidence of serious dishonesty; there is a high level of public concern and a need for urgent action; the nature of the offence requires strong deterrence and there is little cooperation. Regulatory action, action short of prosecution, is more appropriate in situations where the offence is seen as 'technical' or lies in a 'grey area'; regulatory penalties seem sufficiently severe and are publicly known; regulators can take urgent action; there is no motive of personal gain; regulation is more likely to succeed and the main issue relates to the protection of markets rather than serious dishonesty (Wright 2000). She argues:

> the very public nature of many of our prosecutions and the press attention paid to them can provoke fundamental changes in attitudes and practices amongst businessmen ... The mere fact that a solicitor or accountant has been investigated or charged with a criminal offence ... can send shock waves through the profession (Wright 2000).

Regulatory agencies play a major diversionary role, and in addition some have powers to sanction offenders. Some argue that this means that justice is being done in private rather than in a public hearing. To others, these powers represent an important and cost-effective means of diverting offenders from the full process of trial and conviction and there have been suggestions that prosecution agencies such as the CPS should have similar powers. In Scotland, for example, there is a system known as the Fiscal Fine, which the Royal Commission on Criminal Justice 1993 has recommended should be considered in England and Wales. In 2001 a total of 18,855 offenders in Scotland were dealt with by a Fiscal Fine and a further 20,333 by a Fiscal Warning (Scottish Executive 2003).

7.5 MENTALLY DISORDERED OFFENDERS

There are strong arguments for diverting mentally disordered offenders from the criminal justice system before trial and before punishment. At the same time, however, mentally disordered offenders may constitute a danger to themselves and others and may arouse fears on the part of the public. In order to protect the public, therefore, it may be seen as necessary to commit them to hospital, or, if this is not possible, to some form of containment, even where their offences are not so serious as to merit a prison sentence. Thus due process may conflict with a protectionist stance which raises issues concerning the rights of mentally disordered offenders.

The approach to the mentally disordered offender, as it is with the younger offender, is affected by notions of responsibility and liability. The criminal law, as we have seen, depends by and large on the concept of a 'guilty mind' and harm to create criminal liability which provides the justification for intervention and punishment. It is important to recognise that the mental state of the defendant is considered at three stages in the criminal justice process. In the first place, there is the issue of whether someone is culpable for an act committed while they were suffering from some kind of mental disorder. A second question arises in establishing whether a person is mentally fit and able to undergo a trial. Finally, there is an issue as to whether someone who was mentally disordered at the time of the offence, or has subsequently become mentally disordered, can or should be punished.

Responsibility for the offence

The criminal courts do not regard as culpable or blameworthy for an offence a person who is deemed 'not guilty by reason of insanity', or where the court accepts the statutory defence of diminished responsibility, or where the state known as automatism is established, as described below:

Insanity is governed by the M'Naghten Rules, formulated after the trial in 1843 of Daniel M'Naghten who, suffering from a delusion that he should kill the then prime minister, Sir Robert Peel, killed his secretary by mistake. The rules provide that a defendant is not guilty by reason of insanity if 'he was labouring under a defect of reason because of a disease of the mind so that he did not know the nature and quality of his act, or if he did know it, did not know it was wrong'. If found not guilty by reason of insanity, the court may make a hospital order, a guardianship order, a supervision and treatment order or an absolute discharge. There is a right of appeal against such a verdict.

This definition has caused many difficulties, principally surrounding what is to be counted as a disease of the mind. For example, in the case of *Sullivan* in 1984 it was held that a minor epileptic seizure fell within the definition of insanity. In addition, courts have distinguished between defects of reason caused by internal factors, such as medical conditions, which can give rise only to an insanity defence or verdict and external factors, such as a blow to the head or medication, which can give rise to a non-insane automatism defence.

Automatism describes a condition where a person is not strictly in control of his or her actions. If a criminal act is not voluntary the defendant is not responsible for the *actus reus*. Where automatism is caused by something deemed to be a disease of the mind the verdict should be not guilty by reason of insanity. If the automatism is caused by any other reason – for example, an injury – the defendant should be acquitted. As described above, there has been much unease about the line between non-insane and insane automatism, first because of the possible stigma attached and, secondly, because of the consequent disposal.

Diminished responsibility is a special defence only to murder and is defined in s. 2 of the Homicide Act 1957, under which a person who kills, or is a party to the killing of another, cannot be convicted of murder if found to be 'suffering from such an abnormality of mind as substantially impaired his mental responsibility for his acts or omissions'. The abnormality in question may arise from arrested or retarded development, an inherent cause or disease or injury. The onus of proving such an abnormality is expressly placed on the defence. Diminished responsibility is only a defence to murder, and if the *actus reus* is established the accused using such a defence will be found guilty of manslaughter instead. Diminished responsibility is therefore a partial defence, which reduces the level of culpability of the defendant and avoids the mandatory life sentence.

Before reaching a trial, defendants may be found unfit to plead. It is inherent in a criminal trial that a defendant must be 'fit to plead' – that a defendant knows and understands any charges and is able to instruct a lawyer. A defendant is held to be unfit to plead if he or she is either physically or mentally incapable of instructing legal advisers, following the proceedings or objecting to jurors.

The procedure of establishing fitness to plead is governed by the Criminal Procedure (Insanity) Act 1964, as amended by the Criminal Procedure (Insanity and Unfitness to Plead) Act 1991, which provides that the issue can be addressed by the court at any time up to the beginning of the defence case. Unfitness must be determined on the evidence of two or more doctors. If found unfit, the trial proceeds to establish whether or not the defendant has committed the *actus reus* – this is to avoid a mentally ill person being sentenced without proof of an offence. If the defendant is found fit to plead, the trial is carried on in the normal way, and any issues of mental disorder are raised in defence or mitigation. In cases where defendants are found to be both unfit to plead and have committed the *actus reus*, the court may make a hospital or guardianship order, a supervision order or impose an absolute discharge.

Police and the mentally disordered

In responding to a breach of public order or breach of the peace the police may find they have arrested a mentally disordered person. On other occasions a theft or violent crime may result in the police arresting and detaining someone who is mentally disturbed. In the main they will be taken to the police station. A Home Office Research Study commented, 'Up to two per cent of detainees are treated by the police as mentally disordered or mentally handicapped. In London, the figure may be nearer four per cent. Up to one-third are brought to the police station as a place of safety rather than on suspicion of committing an offence' (Brown 1997: 213).

If the police know or suspect that they have a person with a mental disorder or a mental disability they must, under PACE, get an appropriate adult to attend the police station to be present at the interview. The arrested person may be regarded as unfit for interview. Often there is no interview. 'Custody officers often summon the police surgeon in the first instance and, acting on the doctor's advice, do not then call for an appropriate adult in many cases' (Brown 1977: 213). Mental health and social work specialists are also called in as an appropriate adult as they are able to respond quickly to calls from the police.

The police are unlikely to take further criminal proceedings with those they arrest that are certified as mentally ill. Usually no criminal charges are involved and the local health medical authorities are informed. In one Home Office study of 2,739 people arrested by the police, 18 were considered mentally ill and in need of care and control in a 'place of safety' (Mental Health Act 1983, s. 136). Of the remaining 2,721, the researchers estimated that a further 37 showed signs of serious mental illness. Of these, 52 per cent were arrested for breach of the peace or public order offences and they were much more likely to be released without further action (46 per cent) than detainees arrested for similar offences who were not considered mentally ill (11 per cent) (Robertson *et al.* 1995).

Orders available to the courts for mentally disordered offenders

The courts have a number of options in dealing with mentally disordered offenders. These raise the issue of the rights of mentally disordered offenders, who may find themselves being deprived of their liberty for longer periods of time than if they were not mentally disordered, arising from the inevitable tension between the desire of the court to protect the public and the rights of offenders. In addition, diagnosing what form of mental disorder an offender is suffering from is not always straightforward, as is assessing how amenable the condition is to treatment. There are four types of mental incapacity defined in s. 1 of the Mental Health Act 1983.

Mental disorder is defined as 'mental illness, arrested or incomplete development of mind, psychopathic disorder and any other disorder or disability of mind'. More specifically, *mental impairment* is defined as 'a state of arrested or incomplete development of mind (not amounting to severe mental impairment) which includes significant impairment of intelligence and social functioning and is associated with abnormally aggressive or seriously irresponsible conduct on the part of the person concerned'. *Severe mental impairment* is defined as 'a state of arrested or incomplete development of the mind which includes severe impairment of intelligence and social functioning and is associated with abnormally aggressive or seriously irresponsible conduct on the part of the person concerned'. A *psychopathic disorder* is defined as 'a persistent disorder or disability of mind (whether or not including significant impairment of intelligence) which results in abnormally aggressive or seriously irresponsible conduct on the part of the person concerned'.

The main options for the court when dealing with a mentally disordered offender are as follows:

- Supervision with treatment if the court is satisfied on the evidence of an approved medical practitioner that the mental condition of the offender requires and may be susceptible to treatment but that the condition does not warrant a full hospital order.

- Mental health hospital or guardianship orders can be made if the court is satisfied, first, that the defendant is suffering from:

  (1) a mental illness

  (2) a psychopathic disorder

  (3) mental impairment

  (4) severe mental impairment (see definitions above)

  and, secondly, that either the condition makes it appropriate for detention in a hospital for treatment (which, in the case of a psychopathic disorder and mental impairment is likely to improve the condition) or the offender is 16 or over and the condition warrants a guardianship order and the court feels such an order is the most suitable disposal.

  A hospital order lapses after 6 months but can be renewed and the detainee can be discharged at any time by the hospital managers or the medical officer responsible for the case. For a hospital order to be made the condition must be treatable – which is not required for a guardianship order. The order lasts initially for one year but is renewable. Hospital or guardianship orders cannot be made by an adult magistrates' court on a young person under 18. Both the Crown Court and the magistrates' courts can make interim hospital orders on the evidence of two registered medical practitioners initially for up to 12 weeks, but this may be renewed for periods of up to 28 days at a time for a maximum of 6 months.

- An order under s. 37(3) of the Mental Health Act 1983: where a person has been charged and the court would have power on conviction to make a hospital order, a magistrates' court may, if satisfied that the accused did the act, make a hospital order without a conviction. This section does away with the requirement for a finding that the *actus reus* was accompanied by the requisite *mens rea*.

- Restriction order under s. 41 of the Mental Health Act 1983: this power is not available to magistrates and can be exercised only by the Crown Court. The order provides for detention for a defined or indefinite period, so that the offender cannot be discharged from hospital without the permission of the Secretary of State or the Mental Health Review Tribunal. It may be imposed where it is felt necessary to impose such an order to protect the public from serious harm taking into account the nature of the offence, the history of the offender and the risk of future offending. Where magistrates, taking the same considerations into account, feel that a restriction order is necessary, they may commit the offender to the Crown Court.

- Hospital and limitation direction: created by s. 46 of the Crime (Sentences) Act 1997 for those suffering from a psychopathic disorder, a court can impose a sentence of imprisonment and direct that the person be sent to a hospital.

In December 2000, there were 2,937 restricted patients in hospitals with 1,170 in high security hospitals. Over the 1990s there was a stable number of approximately

1,200 in high security hospitals; however, the number in other hospitals doubled over the decade from 819 in 1990 to 1,767 in 2000 (Johnston S *et al.* 2001: 3). Restricted patients admitted in 2000 were admitted to hospital in relation to the following types of mental disorder: 840 for mental illness; 36 for mental illness with other disorders; 36 for psychopathic disorder; 28 with mental impairment; 3 had mental impairment with psychopathic disorder; and 4 for severe mental impairment (*Home Office Statistical Bulletin* 22/01: 14). The type of offences committed by the restricted patients admitted to hospital in 2000 were: 61 murder, 31 other homicide, 227 other violent offences, 71 sexual offences, 83 burglary, 81 robbery, 82 arson, 12 theft and handling stolen goods and 315 other offences (HOSB 22/01: 15).

De-institutionalisation and care in the community

The Mental Health Act 1959 brought about a major revision in the treatment of the mentally ill. The policy of placing mental patients into mental hospitals had its origins in the county asylums of the late eighteenth century and early nineteenth century. The new approach was called 'community care' and was based on a new respect for the rights of the mental patient and a wish to avoid the use of the gloomy institutions that, in some places, held regimes that were brutal and uncaring. It was also believed that rehabilitation was more likely to take place in the more normal world of the community rather than the closed worlds of total institutions (Goffman 1961). Advancement in pharmaceutical drugs meant that new methods of treatment were available for the control of behaviour and the cure of patients. It was a policy that was also cheaper if measured in monetary terms. The number of beds available for psychiatric patients fell from 140,000 in 1959 to 37,000 in 1998.

While few would dispute that it is desirable to divert mentally disordered offenders from the criminal justice process or refer them for treatment rather than punishment, there are some concerns about the orders outlined above. Particularly problematic is the definition of different kinds of mental disorder. These definitions are somewhat narrow and may not accord with psychiatric diagnoses. The definition of psychopathy has raised special problems, as there is little agreement over what kind of underlying condition produces the behaviour which amounts to its definition. In essence, argues Peay, it is 'a legal category defined by persistently violent behaviour', rather than being a clearly defined mental disorder (Peay 2002: 1146).

A person's mental condition may change and indeed be affected by the process of being arrested or institutionalised, making predictions of whether and how the condition will respond to treatment extremely problematic. It is difficult, therefore, to state with any certainty how long a mentally disordered offender should be held in hospital. Given the fear that released offenders may re-offend this may lead to longer periods of hospitalisation than would be merited either by considerations of the offence or the needs of the offender for treatment.

However, tragedies have shown that these fears are not imagined; fears which have been exacerbated by the current policy of treating mentally disordered offenders in the community. In December 1992 Jonathan Zito, a musician aged 27, was waiting for an underground train at Finsbury Park Station in London when he was stabbed in the face and killed by Christopher Clunis, a diagnosed schizophrenic. Clunis had a long history of violence which included stabbing a person in the neck. He had been released from prison to a mental hospital, from which he had been discharged in 1992.

Community care and public safety

A report from the Royal College of Psychiatrists (17 August 1994) revealed, in a survey of an 18-month period from July 1992 to December 1993, that 34 people were killed by newly released mental patients. William Boyd of the Royal Edinburgh Hospital investigated 22 of the 34 killings and discovered that all the perpetrators had been in the care of psychiatric services in the 12 months preceding the killings. Of the 22, 17 had histories of violence. Fifteen of the killings were committed by men, most of whom had been diagnosed as schizophrenic or paranoid psychotic. Nine of the 15 men had convictions for violent behaviour. The seven women in the study were mostly suffering from depression and six of them killed their own children.

Since the Clunis incident a number of changes of practice have been introduced to avoid the problem of dangerous mentally ill people being left unsupervised in the community. The Mental Health (Patients in the Community) Act 1995 introduced provisions that make it easier to return a mental patient to hospital. The Act gives the supervisor the power to take and convey the patient to any place where the patient is required to reside or to attend for the purpose of medical treatment. There is a new system in which each patient has a 'responsible medical officer' (a doctor), a 'key worker' (care/social worker), a 'key plan' and should be put onto a 'supervision register'.

While it is recognised that only a small proportion of offenders are considered to be mentally ill and that the vast majority of mentally disordered people do not commit crime, the view that mentally ill people are neither more nor less dangerous than other offenders has also been challenged by recent reports. In October 1997 the Zito Trust published the results of its survey on homicides by people released from institutions and who were being supervised in the community. Between 1990 and 1997 there were 141 homicides, that is two a month on average, resulting in the death of 44 strangers, 23 acquaintances, 3 health professionals, 13 co-residents, 34 family members and 33 children under the age of 16 (Zito Trust 1997).

There is a problem of balance between patients' rights and the public's right to be protected from dangerous people. Doctors take as their priority the care and treatment of their patients. Community control by medically trained staff is a problem as they are likely to put patients' rights before the needs of the criminal justice system. When they wish to take action there is often a problem of lack of beds in the medium security wards available to the local health authority. There is also the problem of monitoring mentally ill patients released from secure accommodation. Lack of contact with their case workers and failure to take medication have been cited in inquiries into deaths caused by psychiatric patients.

Coordination of services and sharing of information were identified as problems in the inquiry led by Louis Blom-Cooper, a former chairman of the Mental Health Tribunal, into the case of Jason Mitchell. In December 1994 Mitchell was released into the community from St Clements Hospital in Ipswich on the advice of the consultant psychiatrist. He was staying in a halfway house when he broke into the home of a couple, both aged 65, and killed them before going to his father's home nearby in Bramford in Suffolk where he beheaded and dismembered him. The inquiry found that records from his time in a young offender institution, identifying him as a potential killer, had been lost and a later report on his attitudes revealing a violent disposition was ignored by doctors. In July 1995 he was given three life sentences and sent to Rampton hospital.

The balance between patients' rights and public safety has been the focus of much concern. The then Health Secretary, Frank Dobson, announced in 1998 that the policy of 'care in the community' had not been a success and a review was in progress, and added that 'Care in the community has become a discredited policy'. Future plans are for seriously disturbed psychiatric patients to be kept in secure units to protect the public. The plans include building new homes or converting old buildings into care centres for the mentally ill. Paul Boateng, then a Health Minister, stated: 'There will be no return to grim Victorian asylums. But the old mantra, "community good, hospitals bad" is dead' (BBC, 17 January 1998).

As a result of concerns about the way in which people with mental health problems are treated – not only those whose problems led to or contributed to offending – an expert committee was set up by the government to review the Mental Health Act 1983 and reported in 1999. At the same time as the committee reported, the government issued proposals for consultation. This was followed by a White Paper, *Reforming the Mental Health Act*, and a draft bill. In November 2003 the Health Secretary, John Reid, stated: 'The government is fully committed to reforming mental health legislation. We must make significant improvements to patient safeguards, provide a modern framework of legislation in line with modern patterns of care and treatment and human rights law, and protect public safety by enabling patients to get the right treatment at the right time' (Department of Health Press Release, 26 November 2003, 2003/0481).

The Bill contains a single definition of mental disorder and provides a framework for the consideration of the needs of individuals including those whose condition makes them a danger to others. It also 'breaks the automatic link between formal treatment and detention in hospital'. Whilst trying to provide for the most appropriate form of treatment, whether in hospital or in the community, the object of the intended legislation is also to safeguard patients' rights.

Thus it can be seen that, in considering the issues involved in offending by those who are mentally ill, the various approaches to criminal justice can be seen in tension with each other – due process and the rights of individuals, in contrast to crime control and crime prevention – which may mean intervention in anticipation of offending for those perceived as dangerous to others.

CONCLUSION

In this chapter we have examined the pre-trial decisions by which some offenders are diverted out of the criminal justice system. Some are diverted because of their status either as young offenders or because they are mentally disordered; others are diverted because of decisions made by the police and the CPS. Many of the issues involved in these decisions and the policy that drives them have their roots in our concepts of criminal responsibility. Diversion also demonstrates the conflict in goals of the criminal justice system: to treat all equally before the law, to provide a cost-effective system, and to ensure judicial decisions are made openly, fairly and even-handedly.

It is, for example, clearly cheaper and less wasteful of resources to divert offenders who for various reasons might not be convicted, or if convicted would receive only a nominal penalty or some form of treatment rather than punishment. It may even be seen as desirable in the interests of equity and efficiency to allow prosecutors greater powers to impose sanctions for some offences without taking offenders to court. To prosecute all offenders uses up valuable resources which might be better used for the investigation and prevention of crime.

At the same time, however, this means that justice is being done in private rather than in public, which in turn means that it is less publicly accountable and that equal treatment cannot be guaranteed. Diverted defendants have less chance fully to dispute allegations, and treatment programmes which may seem more desirable than punishment may involve more control than punishment. In addition, as we have seen, it may be in the public interest to see offenders publicly tried and punished as well as giving victims the chance to obtain compensation and the satisfaction of seeing justice being done. Another consideration from a crime control perspective is the potential threat to the public of dangerous offenders, be they sometimes young or mentally ill, being released back into the community. Many of these considerations also affect pre-trial processes. Chapter 9 describes the procedures they will go through before they reach the trial stage.

Review questions

1 Identify the main considerations underlying the decision to caution or prosecute and relate these to the models of criminal justice.

2 What criteria do the Crown Prosecution Service use in deciding whether to continue with a prosecution?

3 What are the main arguments in favour of a 'compliance' as opposed to a criminal approach for business offenders?

4 Why should the mentally ill be treated differently in the criminal justice system?

5 At what stages are those suffering from mental incapacity dealt with differently from others?

6 What are the main orders available to the courts in respect of the mentally ill?

Further reading

Ashworth, A (1994) *The Criminal Process*, Clarendon Press: Oxford
Peay, J (2002) 'Mentally Disordered Offenders', in Maguire, M, Morgan, R and Reiner, R (eds) *The Oxford Handbook of Criminology* (3rd edn), Clarendon Press: Oxford

CHAPTER 8

Youth justice

Main topics covered

➤ Youth and crime

➤ Youth justice system

INTRODUCTION

It was seen in Chapter 2 that a large proportion of crime is committed by young people, and many of the crime reduction measures described in Chapter 5 are targeted primarily at young offenders. Indeed when the crime problem is discussed it is often youth crime that is seen as *the* problem and a wide range of criminal justice policies are specifically focused on youth and juveniles. It is important therefore to look at the different ways in which young people are involved in crime. Most jurisdictions have different systems for dealing with young offenders, to attempt to divert them from the more formalised systems of courts and to develop criminal justice policies that seek to prevent further offending. Systems of youth justice have been based on a balance between the need to punish or control young offenders and to encourage them to take responsibility for their actions, and the need for strategies which take account of the many problems which may have led to an involvement in crime – a welfare-based approach. For much of the twentieth century, approaches to young offenders showed a mixture of these different approaches.

The Crime and Disorder Act 1998 made radical changes to the system, some of which have already been referred to, and 'youth justice', according to some commentators, provides a very clear example of the Labour Government's approach of being 'tough on crime, tough on the causes of crime' (Newburn 2003). The new approach reflects our eighth and new model of criminal justice (see Chapter 1) whereby the offender becomes the focus of a wide range of intervention strategies that combine rehabilitative and punishment aspects with intensive monitoring in an effort to control and limit the opportunities for criminal activity. A good example of this is the intensive supervision and surveillance programme (ISSP) aimed at the persistent young offender – estimated to be responsible for 25 per cent of all youth crime – and combines supervision for at least 25 hours a week with specified activities, curfews and electronic monitoring.

This chapter will start by looking at the problem of youth crime and the different ways in which young people are involved in crime. It will go on to look at how the welfare and justice approaches have affected policies towards young offenders and at the way in which youth justice systems attempt to both control offenders and respond to their welfare. It will outline the main changes made to the system and look at the structure of youth courts and at the sentencing of young offenders.

8.1 YOUTH AND CRIME

It is interesting to place contemporary concerns about youth crime in a historical context. While it is common to hear politicians and the media commenting adversely on the 'state of youth today' and the need to take action against unruly, disorderly and criminal youth, concerns about such activities have been prominent throughout the centuries. A newspaper editorial in 1843, for example, contained the following statement: 'morals are getting much worse. When I was young my mother would have knocked me down for speaking improperly to her'. Similarly, the Howard Association in 1898 commented that 'the manners of children are deteriorating ... the child of today is coarser, more vulgar, less refined than his parents were' (both examples from Muncie 1999: 50).

Social change, the effects of alcohol and the adverse influence of popular entertainment such as 'penny dreadfuls', football and music halls were all held to be responsible for hooliganism during the nineteenth century. Today 'video nasties', violence on television and in films, and drugs and alcohol are seen as having an adverse effect. A social commentator and advocate of boys' clubs commented in 1917, 'their vulgarity and silliness and the distorted, unreal Americanised view of life must have a deteriorating effect and lead to the formation of false ideals' (cited in Muncie 1999: 50).

These echo many of today's concerns, even although the level of criminality was far less. The twentieth century saw recurrent moral panics about young people, their expressive subcultures and involvement in illegal leisure pursuits, such as the consumption of illegal drugs, involvement in petty crime and in subcultures which were associated with fighting and violence. The term 'moral panic' was used in relation to highly publicised confrontations between the Mods and Rockers of the 1960s. Research indicated, however, that many self-styled mods and rockers were not involved in these activities (Cohen 1980). Throughout the latter part of the twentieth century there were subsequent panics about skinheads, lager louts, yob culture, football hooligans, rave culture; and, more recently, about persistent young offenders and anti-social behaviour.

Young people in recent years have often therefore been seen as 'out of control' or lacking in self discipline or lacking respect for authority. This reflects in part the many changes in the dominant culture such that a clear civic culture and moral consensus is less obvious in the early twenty-first century. It is also in part related to the nature of youth and its associated lifestyle, especially as it developed in the latter part of the twentieth century. Young people are more likely to spend their leisure time in public; 'hanging about' and looking for diversion, fun and excitement are normal for most young people. This may lead to them being victims of crime as well as perpetrators and it was seen in Chapter 3 that young people are often victims as well as villains. Changes in lifestyle and youth culture since the end of the Second World War have meant that young people are drawn to expressive subcultures, encouraged by the commercialisation of style for teenagers; and this search for novelty and the public nature of young people's leisure can be seen by older people as a threat. The sight of large groups of young people hanging about can be seen as intimidating and lead to complaints to the police. Young people are more likely to come into contact with the police on the streets than other groups.

Nevertheless, concerns about youth crime cannot be dismissed solely as a moral panic and, as Newburn (2002) points out, young people aged between 10 and 17 are responsible for around one-quarter of all recorded crime, and some young people go on to engage in criminal careers. The citizens of many neighbourhoods have real concerns about the effects of unruly behaviour on their quality of life and make frequent complaints to the police and to community representatives. The following section will explore aspects of young people's involvement in crime.

Young people's involvement in crime

It was seen in Chapter 2 that young people predominate amongst offenders and that males aged between 18 and 20 have the highest rate of known offending. This stands at 6,834 per 100,000 population compared with 1,050 per 100,000 for the population as a whole. Figure 8.1 shows the rates per 100,000 population for both males and females, indicating what is conventionally described as the peak age of known offending. For men, this rose to 19 in 2002, having, according to the official statistics, been 18 since 1988 (Home Office: Criminal Statistics 2002). The peak age for females is currently 15 years, at 1,483 per 100,000 population. Figure 8.1 also shows how these rates have fluctuated over the years, with, in 2002, the overall rates for males going down for 10–11-year olds, 12–14 year-olds and 15–17-year-olds, but rising for 18–20-year-olds and those over 21.

It is also important to recognise that perceptions of the relationship between age and crime may change with age as a consequence of the different types of crime associated with different age groups. Young people's offending is often more public and visible, whereas older people have more opportunity to commit crimes at work or in the home, which may have a lower chance of detection. Some indication of this is provided by self report studies, which indicate that 14–15-year-olds tend to be involved in fights, buying stolen goods, theft and criminal damage, 16–17-year-olds are less involved in criminal damage, theft and buying and selling stolen goods, whereas 18–21-year-olds show a declining involvement in shoplifting and criminal damage and an increasing involvement in fraud and workplace theft as they move towards offences which have a lower chance of being caught (Flood-Page et al. 2000).

Young people show different patterns of involvement in crime. Self report studies indicate, for example, that high numbers of young people report committing offences but for many this is only a transitory involvement in less serious forms of crime (Anderson et al. 1994). Many young people engage in vandalism, petty theft or get involved in fights but this may be seen as a relatively normal part of growing up and does not lead to a criminal career. Some activities, which to the observer may

Figure 8.1 Offenders[1] found guilty of, or cautioned for, indictable offences per 100,000 population by age group 1992–2002

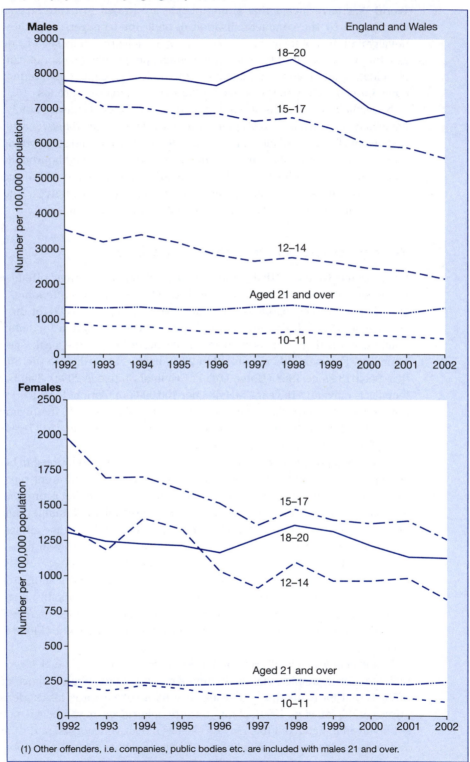

(1) Other offenders, i.e. companies, public bodies etc. are included with males 21 and over.

Source: *Criminal Statistics England and Wales* 2002, p. 23.

be criminal, may be perceived as fun or exciting, as may experimenting with some forms of drugs and alcohol. Thus while many report having used an illegal drug in their lives, far fewer report doing so regularly and persistently. It has also been recognised that many young people grow out of crime as they mature, find legitimate work and get married. Indeed the delayed entry of some young men into employment, with high rates of youth unemployment and the consequent decline in numbers getting married, could in itself contribute to the higher peak age of crime and to the rates of 18–30-year-olds committing crime.

A minority, however, may be involved in more serious offending – committing more offences and more serious offences – being what is often described as persistent offenders. A high proportion of all youth crime may be attributable to a small group and the factors associated with their offending may be very different. Whereas young people across the social spectrum report being involved in some forms of crime, those reporting more serious involvement tend to be more concentrated in lower class areas and have also been found to have more chaotic lifestyles involving family, school or housing problems (Hagell and Newburn 1994).

Some indication of this can be found from studies of young people, which include self report material, such as the Youth Lifestyle Survey (YLS), first carried out in 1992/3 (Graham and Bowling 1995) and most recently in 1998/9 (Flood-Page *et al.* 2000). This survey interviewed 4,848 people aged between 12 and 30 in England and Wales and asked them about their involvement in 27 different offences. Some of its findings are summarised below:

- Offending was found to be common – 57 per cent of men reported committing at least one offence during their lives and 26 per cent in the last year. Figures for women were lower, with 37 per cent reporting having committed an offence in their lives, and 11 per cent in the last year.

- Those aged between 14 and 21 committed most offences.

- A small number (8 per cent in total: 12 per cent of men and 4 per cent of women) were counted as 'serious' or 'persistent' offenders because they had either committed three or more offences in the last year of one of a group of more serious offences such as violence, burglary, car theft or robbery.

- Ten per cent of offenders were responsible for nearly one-half of all the crimes reported by the sample.

- Young people's crime is primarily property crime – three-quarters of all offences were property or fraud offences – and violent offences constituted one-fifth of male offences and one-tenth of women's.

- Those aged over 21 reported a declining number of offences, particularly for criminal damage and violence. Involvement in property crime did not fall so sharply and some reported their first crime of fraud or workplace theft at ages 26–30.

- Those reporting offending over a long period came from all areas; however, serious and persistent offenders were twice as likely to come from inner city than from rural areas.

- Serious and persistent offenders were also twice as likely to be unemployed than employed or in education.

It was seen in Chapter 5 that a variety of factors have been associated with crime, particularly youth crime, and criminologists have studied the association between involvement in offending and a host of factors including individual characteristics, family factors and wider social factors. Given the importance of the family in young people's early lives, particular attention has been paid to a range of circumstances within families. As they grow up, however, young people spend more time out of the home, at school and with their friends; and performance and attendance at school are also associated with offending, as is the presence of friends who are also involved in crime. Social structural factors may affect employment and leisure opportunities – with those who cannot participate in employment and desired leisure facing temptations to engage in crime. A wide range of factors therefore affect young people's participation in crime – and many have looked at what are now described as 'risk factors'.

Again the latest YLS provides a good illustration of a combination of factors. The study identified a group classified as 'offenders' which excluded those who had committed one or two minor crimes, and a group of serious or persistent offenders, and explored which factors were most strongly associated with offending. While these were present for both male and female offenders, because of the smaller number of female offenders the figures are most reliable for boys. For 12–17-year-old boys the 'risk factors', in order of importance, were:

- having used drugs in the last year
- being disaffected from school
- hanging around in public places
- having delinquent friends or acquaintances
- poor parental supervision
- persistent truancy.

A broadly similar picture emerged for those aged 18 and over, with heavy drinking emerging as a strong factor and not having any educational qualifications being the second most important predictor. Family influences, on the other hand, appeared to be less important.

These factors cannot be said directly to lead to participation in crime. Those already likely to be involved in crime could, for example, also start truanting and seek out the company of likeminded youth – thus leading to a mutually reinforcing situation. Thus crime may lead to truanting rather than the other way round. Nevertheless, the strength of these associations demonstrates, as the authors argue, the importance of directing policies towards families and looking closely at how to prevent young people becoming disengaged and excluded from school.

Whatever the reason, the number of young people involved in grave crimes (crimes that could attract 14 years in prison if committed by an adult) such as murder, manslaughter, wounding with intent, rape, robbery and burglary has increased from 6 convictions in 1970 to 561 in 2000. This inevitably brings them into contact with the youth justice system and leaves open the question of whether there is a moral panic about youth crime – moral panic is defined as an over-exaggerated response to a problem – or whether the response, panic or not, is justified:

However, against this backdrop of a general fall in crime, there has been a steady rise in recorded violent crime since 1991. The number of juveniles cautioned or convicted for violence, drug offences and robbery has also risen, although this accounts for only around one-third of indictable juvenile crime. There are almost 3,000 young people in prison, half as many again as there were ten years ago, although the numbers levelled off from 1997 onwards. Only 21 per cent of the public are 'very' or 'fairly' confident that the criminal justice system is effective in dealing with young people accused of crime.

(Audit Commission, 2004)

8.2 YOUTH JUSTICE SYSTEM

The law distinguishes between different age groups in an effort to recognise differences in maturity and understanding. Section 107 of the Children and Young Persons Act 1933 (CYPA 1933) defined:

- a child as a person under the age of 14,
- a young person as someone who has attained the age of 14 and is under 18,

and 'a young adult', not defined by statute, is a term used to describe those aged 18 to 20.

Children under 10 years of age are deemed by the law to be incapable of telling right from wrong and therefore incapable of doing wrong – in legal terms *doli incapax*. As they are not regarded as responsible they cannot be put on trial, punished or regarded in law as blameworthy. In a trial at the Old Bailey in January 1998, described later in this chapter, two 10-year-old boys were accused of rape in a West London school. A third boy was not prosecuted because he was 9 years old at the time of the offence.

The age at which children are regarded as responsible for their actions in law varies across Europe such that in Cyprus, Ireland and Switzerland it is 7, and in Scandinavian countries it is 15. In the case of *T v United Kingdom*, it was argued that setting the age of criminal responsibility as low as 10 breached the Human Rights Act 1998. The European Court of Human Rights said that, although there was no common standard amongst the member states as to the age of criminal responsibility and even though England and Wales had a low age, the age of 10 was not so young 'as to differ disproportionately from the age-limit followed by other European States'.

Apart from legal liability for a crime, the age of an offender will also affect where and how the young person is dealt with in the criminal justice system.

It has been accepted for many years that special procedures are needed to deal with young offenders, and a series of different arrangements has developed. These arrangements reflect conflicting views over how such offenders should be dealt with. In general, two broad approaches can be contrasted. On the one hand, what is often described as a welfare approach seeks to protect children and young persons from the potential stigma of a criminal prosecution and encourages courts to take the welfare of the child or young person into account at all stages. Under this approach, diversion is encouraged and prosecution should be a last resort; and when taken to court, special procedures should protect young people from the harshness of a criminal trial and ensuing punishment. The rehabilitative approach was of particular relevance for young offenders, who were seen to be potentially more likely to respond to measures involving help, treatment, discipline and education. On the other hand, many of these measures have been criticised as ineffective, too soft, or as insufficiently deterrent or punitive, and have attracted recurrent calls for tougher measures.

The range of measures, therefore, has tended to reflect a mixture of approaches, and very serious incidents involving young offenders renewed these conflicts. When the toddler James Bulger was abducted and murdered in Liverpool by two children in 1993, a shocked public was exposed to the views of the experts, whose opinions ranged from the call for more treatment to the demand for the punishment of the offenders. In January 1998 an Old Bailey rape trial involved two 10-year-old defendants who were eventually acquitted of raping a 9-year-old victim. The prosecution and trial of these boys highlighted concern and horror at the serious allegations, together with concerns over the way that such young defendants should be tried. Great efforts were made to make the courtroom less intimidating. A report in *The Times* described the scene:

> Court 12 at the Old Bailey has been transformed like a stage set into a modern primary school classroom. The only thing missing is a sandpit, a lump of Play-doh or a large frieze showing the letters of the alphabet ... Four square tables have been arranged in the middle of the room ... just as at school. The four barristers have dispensed with their wigs.
>
> (*The Times*, 16 January 1998: 1)

The Criminal Justice and Public Order Act 1994 was enacted amidst concerns about increasing rates of offending by the young and introduced a number of tougher measures. Publicity given to cases where young offenders were sent to holiday camps or abroad as part of their sentences attracted criticism that offending youngsters should not be given advantages not enjoyed by their law-abiding counterparts. This reveals the conflicting pressures on youth justice policy – on the one hand, to punish young offenders and ensure that they are made to recognise the seriousness of their offences and, on the other, to take action against what are often seen to be the causes of their behaviour – adverse family or social circumstances. In addition, the juvenile justice system has been subject to considerable criticism as being too disparate and lacking coherent policies and has, like many other areas of criminal justice policy described in this book, been subject to auditing processes and the increased effect of managerialism, seen particularly in the reforms introduced in the Crime and Disorder Act 1998, described below, which focus more specifically on identifying risk factors and developing policies which more clearly target these.

Special provision for juveniles

Before the nineteenth century, juvenile offenders were treated in the same way as adults and could be sent to adult prisons, hanged or transported. Throughout the nineteenth century, however, there was a gradual development of measures specifically directed at young offenders, influenced by arguments that juveniles could be 'saved' and rehabilitated. This led to the development of special institutions such as reformatories, whose very name indicated an emphasis on reform through education and training. Reformatories catered for those with criminal convictions and the industrial schools for children in need of care as manifested by truancy, vagrancy or who were in the care of adults with criminal or drunken habits. They were established by the Reformatory Schools Act 1854. At this time a separate prison for boys was opened at Parkhurst on the Isle of Wight.

The Children Act 1908 set up the juvenile court and formally separated cases involving juveniles from adult courts. It also abolished the use of imprisonment for juveniles. A mixture of welfare and punitive philosophies can be seen in the comment of the minister responsible for introducing this Act, Herbert Samuel, who stated that the 'courts should be the agencies for the rescue as well as the punishment of juveniles' (cited in Gelsthorpe and Morris 1994: 951). Other institutions for juveniles also reflected a welfare and punishment approach – special institutions were set up as part of the prison system, the first being in Borstal in Kent. The Borstal system, as it came to be known, emphasised a mixture of discipline and training. Some Borstals stressed education, being strongly imbued with the values and traditions of English public school education, and later some adopted a therapeutic approach (see, for example, Hood 1965).

Further moves towards a more welfare-based approach included the Children and Young Persons Act 1933 which established a special panel of magistrates to deal with juvenile offenders and stipulated that the court should have regard to the welfare of the child. In addition, the court could act in the place of parents, *in loco parentis*, and take such steps as necessary to ensure that the welfare of the child was being met (see, for example, Gelsthorpe and Morris 1994). Approved schools, established in 1933, were residential schools for primarily delinquent boys and girls. They included naval and agricultural colleges and were mainly run by charitable groups or local authorities. They had to be approved by the Home Office. They were later abolished by the Children and Young Persons Act 1969. In 1948 local authorities were enabled to take into care those children considered to be 'in need of care and protection'. The same year, however, saw the introduction of detention centres and attendance centres which reflected a more punitive approach (Morris and Giller 1987). Detention centres were institutions in which young offenders could be sentenced to a short period of custody, in a regime intended to be tough and disciplinary. Much emphasis was laid on physical education although there were also elements of education and training. Attendance centre orders required juveniles to attend a centre, run mainly by the police, for a number of hours per week, often on a Saturday afternoon. They aimed to deprive delinquents of their leisure time and were often used in an attempt to take football hooligans off the terraces. Discipline was a key feature of early attendance centres which mixed elements of physical education with more practical pursuits.

Diversion

The argument that there is little point in punishing juveniles whose delinquency may be related to family or other problems continued to influence policy. Some went so far as to suggest that juveniles should be removed from the criminal justice system entirely, and dealt with by a family council or tribunal which would deal with all children with family or social problems. These proposals were resisted, although they did form the basis of the Scottish Children's Hearings system in which children who offend are referred to a Children's Panel which is not a court of law and deals with offending and non-offending young people. These ideas strongly affected the next important piece of legislation dealing with young offenders, the Children and Young Persons Act 1969 (CYPA 1969). This Act, often seen as representing the peak of the welfare approach, was based on a mixture of welfare and diversionary policies and made several radical and controversial changes (Morris and Giller 1987).

The benefits of diversionary policies were stressed and it was proposed that all offenders under 14 should be dealt with by care and protection rather than by criminal proceedings. The police were encouraged to use cautions for juvenile offenders and only refer them to court following consultation with the social services. The expanding role of the social worker was also reflected in provisions for care orders, which, after being given by magistrates, were to be implemented by social workers. Social workers rather than magistrates, therefore, would make the key decision as to whether the young person would be sent to a residential institution or left at home. Community homes, which were to house all children in care whether or not they had committed an offence, replaced the approved schools which dealt only with delinquents. It was also intended to phase out Borstals and detention centres and to replace them with a sentence of intermediate treatment – again run by social services.

In the event, many sections of the CYPA 1969 were never implemented and it attracted considerable controversy and opposition among observers of and practitioners involved in the system. Magistrates, for example, felt that too much power had been lost to social workers and that they were powerless to determine what might happen to an offender. Rising rates of juvenile crime attracted criticisms that the system was too soft and was unable to cope with serious juvenile offenders.

Diversion increased in the years following the CYPA 1969 with an enormous rise in numbers cautioned by the Juvenile Liaison Bureaux set up by the police. In the 1980s there was a growing recognition of the limitations of custodial or institutional treatment. Not only was such treatment costly – with detention in some institutions costing more than boarding schools – but the vast majority of juveniles coming out of such institutions went on to re-offend. Recidivism rates for detention centres, for example, were as high as 80 per cent. Many also argued that institutions for juveniles acted like schools of crime where offenders perpetuated a delinquent or criminal subculture. Concern was also aroused by evidence of violence and bullying within institutions. Treatment in the community, therefore, was seen as being preferable and as no less effective in terms of reconviction rates.

The Criminal Justice Act 1982 introduced criteria to restrict the use of care and custodial orders and requirements for juveniles to be legally represented. Custodial orders were only to be made in cases where it could be established that the offender had failed to respond to non-custodial measures, where a custodial sentence was seen as necessary for the protection of the public or where the offence was serious. Borstals were abolished, removing any element of indeterminacy from the system. Until then offenders had been sentenced to a period of Borstal training, with the date of release of up to 3 years to be decided by those running the system. Borstal was replaced by a fixed-term youth custody order and the Act also abolished the use of imprisonment for offenders under the age of 21. New sentences were then introduced and abolished with bewildering speed. From 1983 a determinate sentence of youth custody was introduced for offenders aged 15 and under 21, with a maximum sentence for those aged under 17 of 12 months (raised to 2 years in 1994). A sentence of custody for life was introduced as the equivalent to life imprisonment when the offender was aged 17 and under 21. Detention sentence orders for males were changed so that the usual sentence ranged from 21 days to 4 months instead of 3 to 6 months. The Criminal Justice Act 1988 abolished the detention sentence order and youth custody. The new term for youth custody was to be detention in a young offender institution.

Diversionary policies continued throughout the 1980s with a series of Home Office circulars stressing that prosecution should be used as a last resort for young offenders. There was also encouragement for the greater use of informal warnings instead of cautioning to avoid net widening (Gelsthorpe and Morris 1994). The use of cautions for second and third offences was encouraged along with the development in some areas of caution plus schemes, which incorporate a caution with some form of supervised activity in the community. The open-handed use of cautioning was to come in for criticism as to its effectiveness. Cautioning for younger offenders was revised by the Criminal Justice Act 1998 into a more restricted use of reprimands and warnings.

From the 1970s until the mid-1990s diversion policies worked in the sense that they kept children (10–13), young people (14–17) and young adults (18–20) out of the courts and out of custodial institutions during a period when crime was rising steadily. Figure 8.2 shows the percentage of male offenders aged 10 to 14, who received various sentences or orders for indictable offences during the ten-year period 1992/2002. You will notice the steep rise in Community sentences from 1999 and the second graph in the figure shows how these Community sentences are broken down by type of sentence. Figure 8.3 shows the pattern for male offenders aged 15 to 17 years of age.

Since the mid-1990s the main trend in sentencing has been the greater use of community penalties (64 per cent in 2002) with males aged 15–17. The use of immediate custody remained relatively stable (15 per cent in 2001 and in 2002) for males aged 15–17 at 15 per cent of that age group sentenced; for offenders aged 12–14 the custody rate was 7 per cent, the same in 2001 and 2002. In the 10–17 age range 500 females were given custody in 2002 in contrast to 5,700 males (Criminal Statistics in England and Wales 2002: 89–90).

By 1990 a new mood had set in and there was a growing disillusionment with diversionary and welfare approaches to young offenders. This reflected a growing concern about a number of related issues; and criticisms involved a perceived reluctance of the system to respond to younger offenders, the type of sentences given by

Figure 8.2 Percentage of male offenders aged 10 to 14 sentenced for indictable offences who received various sentences or orders 1992/2002

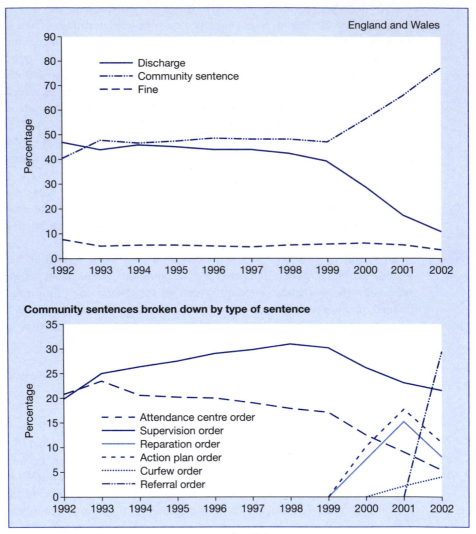

Community sentences broken down by type of sentence

Source: *Criminal Statistics England and Wales* 2002, © HMSO

the courts, the lack of control and the leniency of the treatment of delinquents. There was a view that the system had moved too far in the direction of concern for the welfare of the young offender. It was felt that the wish to avoid labelling young offenders had resulted in a diversionary approach where youngsters felt they could get away with most things, and that the public was not being protected from dangerous or persistent young criminals. There were concerns, for example, about persistent young offenders who committed further offences while on bail, about the lack of secure facilities to hold such offenders, and about the absence of public protection provided by the system.

The then Conservative Government introduced a number of measures to deal

Figure 8.3 Percentage of male offenders aged 15 to 17 sentenced for indictable offences who received various sentences or orders[1] 1992/2002

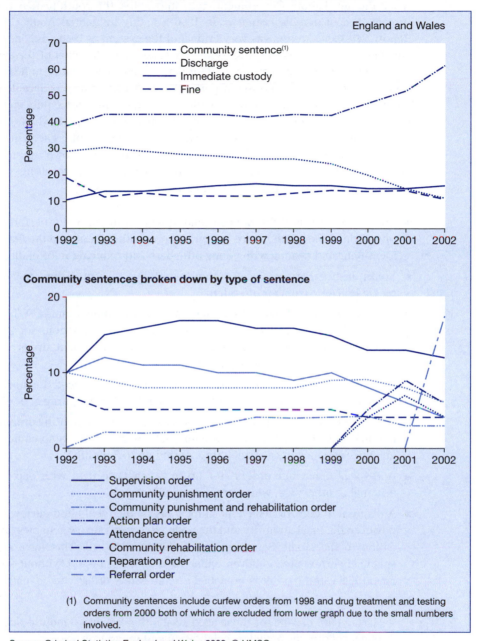

Source: *Criminal Statistics England and Wales* 2002, © HMSO

with these concerns. The Criminal Justice and Public Order Act 1994 introduced a secure training order for persistent offenders aged from 12 to 14. The Crime (Sentences) Act 1997 extended the use of community sentences for younger offenders and allowed for electronic tagging of 10–15-year-old offenders.

The Crime and Disorder Act 1998

When the new Labour Government came into office, the youth justice system was subject to considerable criticism. In 1996 a highly influential Audit Commission Report, *Misspent Youth*, was very critical of the system as being expensive and inefficient. It stressed the need for some consistency in the aims of the system, for greater inter-agency cooperation and for appropriate performance indicators for all agencies and better monitoring of performance. This had a considerable influence on the new Government and in November 1997 the Home Office published a White Paper, *No More Excuses*, and a number of consultation papers which promised a radical overhaul of the youth justice system. The Government, as seen in Chapter 5, were also influenced by the Wilson and Kellings 'broken windows' argument which proposed early action against disorderly behaviour. The resulting Crime and Disorder Act 1998 included the introduction of the following:

- Youth Justice Board for England and Wales: to monitor the performance and operation of the youth justice system, by preventing crime and the fear of crime, identifying and dealing with young offenders and reducing re-offending.

- Youth Justice Service: local authorities, police and probation to combine to tackle crime by younger offenders.

- The introduction of multi-disciplinary Youth Offending Teams (YOTs) in every local authority area including representatives from probation, social services, police, health authority, local authority education department, drugs and alcohol misuse teams and housing departments.

- A system of pre-court reprimands and final warnings replaced the more informal process of police cautioning of younger offenders for the purpose of diversion.

- Disposals based on supporting parents in their control (Parenting orders): to help parents control their children. Parents can be required to attend counselling and guidance sessions once a week for a period up to 3 months.

- Anti-social behaviour orders (for up to 2 years) to deal with bad behaviour, criminal or otherwise, which are discussed below.

- A disposal to control behaviour in local areas: the local child curfew: this gives power to the local authority and the police to set up curfew schemes, after application to the Home Secretary, for children under 10. This means that in a specified curfew area children under 10 should not be out without supervision late at night. If the order is breached a 'child safety order' can be made.

- New kinds of community order:
  - *Action plan orders*: for those aged 10–17, that will last 3 months and combine elements of punishment, rehabilitation and reparation.
  - *Reparation orders*: available for 10–17-year-olds, which the courts have to consider when a compensation order is not imposed. This order can require the offender to make direct recompense (or reparation) to the victim and may include mediation or apologising.

- A new custodial disposal: Detention and training order (DTO): for those aged 10–17 years of age. This replaced the sentence of detention in a young offender institution and the secure training order. It is intended for serious offences where custody is justified and, for the younger age groups, additional criteria are met. In relation to 10 and 11-year-olds the criterion is 'for the purpose of protecting the public' although this disposal has not yet been made available for this age group; for 12–14-year-olds the DTO can only be used with respect to persistent offenders. One-half of the term of a DTO is spent in custody and the other half under community supervision. Offenders can be detained in a young offender institution, secure training centre, youth treatment centre or local authority secure unit supervised by the Youth Justice Board.

These provisions, and the discussions surrounding them, display elements of both punishment and welfare, along with the influence, through requirements for action plans, clear objectives and performance reviews, of managerialism. Some of the provisions of the Act have been widely criticised and seen as overly punitive, particularly those relating to parenting orders and curfews, and the introduction of anti-social behaviour orders (ASBOs). These orders seek to tackle disorderly and anti-social behaviour. They are civil orders which can, however, involve criminal enforcement following non-compliance. There may also be a conflict between some policies, such as ASBOs which could work to exclude offenders and the more inclusionist approach of the policies adopted by YOTs. There have also been fears that, while parenting, curfew and anti-social behaviour orders target what are seen as relevant risk factors, these do not tackle the root causes and that 'good' behaviour cannot be imposed by seemingly coercive measures. At the same time, however, there remain strong elements of welfare philosophies. The emphasis, for example, on early intervention, on addressing the 'causes' of youth crime, on looking at families and, in particular, the emphasis on restorative justice illustrates the persistence of welfare principles; and the Act has led to greater funding for the youth justice system. Youth justice policy continues, therefore, to contain an at times uneasy balance between welfare and punishment (Newburn 2003). In Scotland also, where the system instituted in 1969 was based on an overtly welfare philosophy, there have been criticisms that it cannot cope well with persistent young offenders and the system is currently undergoing an extensive review. There are also problems with young people aged between 16 and 18 who may be tried in adult courts. Youth Court pilot schemes have been set up which, while being presented as 'tough options', retain a commitment to welfare-based policies and social inclusion (McNeill and Batchelor 2004).

The Youth Justice system is increasingly seen as having a pervasive approach – as defined by our new eighth model of criminal justice – with interventions tailored to:

- the young person at risk of offending;
- the young person who commits a first or second offence or is behaving anti-socially;
- a person who is charged by the police after committing further offences or is charged with a more serious offence;
- the young person bailed or remanded in custody;
- the young person in court;
- convicted and sentenced young offenders.

The pre-court stages have been considered further in Chapter 7. In this chapter we consider the court and sentencing stages.

Youth courts

Youth courts were set up by the Criminal Justice Act 1991 and replaced and extended the jurisdiction of the old juvenile courts. They now deal with the majority of offenders aged 10 to 17, although some in this age group may be dealt with in the adult magistrates' court or in the Crown Court. The situations in which this occurs are as follows:

■ Where defendants are charged with homicide (murder or manslaughter) they must be sent to the Crown Court for trial (MCA 1980, s. 24);

■ Defendants aged from 14 to 17 when charged with other grave crimes – defined as any offence which carries a maximum term of imprisonment of 14 or more years, plus indecent assault on women, causing death by dangerous driving and causing death by careless driving whilst under the influence of drink or drugs – may be sent to the Crown Court for trial if the magistrates' powers of punishment do not seem sufficient (Powers of Criminal Courts (Sentencing) Act 2000, s. 91). A Practice Direction (Crown Court: Trial of Children and Young Persons) (2000) sets out the arrangements for trial of young offenders in the Crown Court, after concern was raised about the effect of the Crown Court trial process on young defendants in the case of *T and V v United Kingdom* 1999. The practice direction (guidance from the Lord Chief Justice) advises that the defendant should be able to visit the court in advance, should be able to sit with parents or other supporters, that robes and wigs should not normally be worn and that care should be taken to ensure that they understand what is going on.

■ Young defendants may be dealt with in an adult magistrates' court if charged in association with another defendant, aged over 18, when both are to be dealt with in the adult court.

They may also be referred to the Crown Court for sentence. Guidelines from the Court of Appeal indicate that where, in the case of an adult, the sentence for the offence would be 2 or more years' imprisonment, it is appropriate for the youth court to refuse jurisdiction and commit the defendant to the Crown Court for trial.

The youth court has more informal procedures than adult courts, and special rules protect young people from publicity and contact with older defendants. Members of the public other than those directly concerned are not allowed to be present at a youth court hearing, and although members of the press are allowed to attend, they may not publish any information which can identify a young defendant. The CYPA 1933 empowers the court to restrict any reporting of cases revealing the name, address or school of a defendant or containing any particulars which could lead to the identification of any child or young person concerned in proceedings. This provision applies to witnesses as well as defendants, and may be applied in the adult court. Most magistrates' courts have a separate court room set out appropriately for youth courts, so the young person is seated on the same level as the magistrates, rather than in the dock, and make arrangements to minimise the chances of young defendants being in contact with adult offenders. Defendants are addressed by their first names, and although they plead guilty or not guilty a finding of guilt rather than a conviction is recorded. For defendants under 16 the court must require a parent or guardian to attend also. For those over 16 the court may require the parent or guardian to attend. Where a child or young person is in the care of the local authority, a local authority representative can be required to attend.

In Inner London, magistrates are appointed directly to the youth court panel. In other areas a youth court panel is made up of magistrates especially chosen from the bench because of their special knowledge of, or interest in, young people. As a result of this interest many magistrates sit in both the youth court and the Family Proceedings Court which deals with care proceedings. The bench dealing with a youth court hearing will be composed of two or more (usually three) members of the youth court panel. District judges can now try young people alone. A lay bench should contain at least one male and one female magistrate. They have a wide discretion in the youth court but are guided by CYPA 1933, s. 44 which states that every court shall have regard for the welfare of the child or young person and, where proper, take steps to remove him or her from undesirable surroundings and ensure that adequate provision is made for training and education.

Sentencing young offenders

Before sentence is passed, the offender, either individually, or through a lawyer, parent or guardian, must be allowed to make representations and the court has to consider all available material concerning the offender, his or her background, education and medical history. It is usual to have reports from social or probation services, and often a school report.

The sentences applicable to a young offender vary according to the court in which they are being sentenced. Very often, where a conviction is recorded in an adult court, a young offender will be remitted to the youth court for sentence. Just as applies to adult offenders, young offenders can be given absolute or conditional discharges, community and compensation orders. Some special provisions relating to the sentencing of young offenders are set out below.

Absolute and conditional discharge

An absolute discharge can be imposed when the court feels it is inappropriate to inflict punishment because the offender is morally blameless. A young person receiving a conditional discharge receives no immediate punishment because the court feels it is 'inexpedient to inflict punishment'. A period of up to 3 years is set and, as long as the young person does not commit a further offence during this period, no punishment will be imposed. If the young person re-offends during this period, they can be brought back to court and resentenced.

Fine

The maximum fine payable by an offender under the age of 14 is £250, and for an offender aged 14 to 17 is £1,000. Where the offender is under 16 the court is under a duty to order that payments are made by the parent or guardian unless they cannot be found and it would be unreasonable for them to be ordered to pay. For offenders over 16, magistrates have discretion to make such an order.

Community orders

Under the CJA 2003 youth community orders will replace the previous community penalties available to some young offenders, such as community punishment and rehabilitation orders. For those aged 16 or 17 a community order can require the young offender to undertake an activity; prohibit activities; impose a curfew, electronic monitoring, residential requirement, drug, alcohol or mental health treatment requirement, and an attendance centre requirement. Youth community orders for children and young people include action plan orders, attendance centre orders, supervision orders, exclusion orders and curfew orders.

Attendance centre order. This sentence is available only for offences punishable with imprisonment in the case of an adult. The offender must not have received previous detention. The police normally run attendance centres. The regime typically involves discipline, physical training and social skills. The order is normally for a minimum of 12 hours and can last up to 36 hours depending on the age of the offender and the seriousness of the offence.

Action plan order. This sentence, introduced by the Crime and Disorder Act 1998 for 10–17-year-olds, provides for supervision for 3 months by a probation officer, social worker or members of the youth offending team. Before the courts impose it a report from the local youth offending team will be produced. Following consultation with the young offender, a detailed plan of action will be recommended and should be tailored to address the offending behaviour.

Drug treatment and testing order (DTTO). This is used for young offenders who have drug misuse issues that require treatment. It can only be used with young people who are 16 years of age or older and the young person must agree to comply with the order before it can be made. The order lasts between 6 months and 3 years. Under the Criminal Justice Act 2003 a DTTO may be an additional element for action plan orders or supervision orders. The order requires the young person to provide samples to test whether they have been using drugs.

Intensive supervision and surveillance programme (ISSP). This programme includes up to 25 hours a week of intensive supervision. Other conditions and requirements can be part of the programme, which was enhanced in 2003 increasing the total length available from 6 to 12 months and extending the intensive supervision aspect from 3 to 6 months for very persistent offenders. Participation in an ISSP could require an offender to undertake drug treatment, curfews or residence requirements which might require a young person to live in local authority accommodation for the period of the sentence.

Parenting order. When a young person or child is before the court a parenting order may be considered. These can be given to the parents or carers of young people who offend, truant or who have received a child safety order or anti-social behaviour order or sex offender order. It lasts for 3 months, but can be extended to 12 months. It requires a parent or carer to attend counselling or guidance sessions. The parent or carer may also have conditions imposed on them such as attending their child's school, ensuring their child does not visit a particular place unsupervised or ensuring their child is at home at particular times. A failure to fulfil the conditions can be treated as a criminal offence and the parent or carer can be prosecuted.

Reparation order. Reparation orders are designed to help young offenders understand the consequences of their offending and take responsibility for their behaviour. They require the young person to repair the harm caused by their offence either directly to the victim (this can involve victim–offender mediation if both parties agree) or indirectly to the community. Examples of this might be cleaning up graffiti or undertaking community work. A Youth Offending Team (YOT) oversees the order.

Referral order. This was introduced by the Youth Justice and Criminal Evidence Act 1999 with effect from April 2002. All young people who plead guilty to a first offence (that is they have no previous convictions) in court must receive a referral order, unless they are given an absolute discharge, or the offence is so serious that a custodial sentence is required. Once a referral order is made, the young person is required to attend a youth offender panel. This is made up of a YOT officer and two volunteers from the local community. The panel, with the young person, their parents or carers and the victim agree a contract lasting between 3 and 12 months. The contract can include attending programmes to address offending behaviour, repairing the harm done by their offence or a variety of other actions. If the offender agrees, a conviction is not recorded; otherwise they are referred back to the court for sentencing. The conviction is spent once the contract has been completed.

Supervision order. A supervision order is similar to the supervision (formerly probation or rehabilitation) element in adult community penalties. It can last up to 3 years. A range of conditions can be attached to a supervision order when the sentence is used for more serious offences. These are called 'specified activities' and can last for up to 90 days. A young person receiving a supervision order is also required to take part in activities set by the Youth Offending Team which could include reparation either to the victim or the community and programmes to address their offending behaviour, such as drug treatment.

Custody

Detention and training order (DTO). This is the most used custodial sentence for young offenders, introduced as a generic custodial sentence for 12–17-year-olds by the Crime and Disorder Act 1998, although powers exist to extend this to 10–12-year-olds. For 15–17-year-olds the test is simply that the offence is so serious that only custody is justified. For 12–14-year-olds, in addition the young person must be a persistent offender. The length of the sentence can be between 4 months and 2 years. The first half of the sentence is spent in custody whilst the second half is spent in the community under the supervision of the Youth Offending Team. The court can require the young person to be on an intensive supervision and surveillance programme (ISSP), which is discussed above, as a condition of the community period of the sentence.

Dangerous and serious offenders might be sentenced under section 90 or 91, applying only to offences such as murder or rape or those offences for which an adult would receive a sentence of 14 years or more. This sentence can be given by a Crown Court only and the entire sentence is completed in custody. The release date for a young person sentenced under section 90 is decided by the Home Secretary. The release date for section 91 sentences is set automatically.

For dangerous young offenders there are new custodial provisions in the Criminal Justice Act 2003, with two sentences being introduced: 'detention for public protection' and 'extended detention'. These are for young people convicted of specified sexual or violent offences.

Detention for life can be given where a child or young person is convicted of a serious offence and the court is of the opinion that there is significant risk to members of the public of serious harm by the commission by him of further specified offences. An indeterminate sentence, release is dependent on the recommendations of the Parole Board but they remain on licence for life.

For children there are secure units run by local authorities. They have high staff to student ratios: some have 30 adults looking after 8 children at a cost of £4,000 per week (in 2003).

CONCLUSION

Youth crime is widely perceived to be a major issue, although, as we have seen, much of it may be transitory and trivial. Nevertheless, a minority of young people are responsible for a large amount of recorded crime, and citizens can feel considerably threatened by youth crime. Measures to deal with youth crime have, over the years, developed a sometimes uneasy balance between the perceived need to control and punish young offenders and not to be seen as 'soft' on youth offending and the recognition that involvement in the formal systems of courts and prisons can have a damaging effect on young offenders and possibly exacerbate not only their involvement in crime but the problems which may have contributed to that in the first place. How much to control, punish, divert and how much to intervene in young people's lives are therefore major issues which youth justice systems must tackle. The long-term impact of the major changes introduced in 1998 remains to be evaluated fully, but they demonstrate the complexity of the issues surrounding the control of youth crime. Recent reforms involving intensive measures to prevent further offending, particularly focusing on younger offenders, that included parents, schools and local communities led us to conclude that there was a need for a new model of criminal justice.

Review questions

1 Why have separate systems of justice for young people been seen as desirable?

2 Outline the main features of the welfare and punishment approaches to dealing with young offenders and illustrate them with some examples from the history of juvenile justice.

3 Identify the various orders available for young offenders and consider whether they represent a punishment or welfare approach.

4 Look at the different levels of crime prevention set out in Chapter 5 (see Figure 5.1).
   (a) Have recent orders, such as parenting orders, neighbourhood curfews, and anti-social behaviour orders been aimed at the primary, secondary or the tertiary level of crime prevention?
   (b) Thinking of the three levels of crime prevention, how does or might the family and parenting play a part in reducing crime amongst younger people?

5 Do you think that youth crime is a moral panic and an exaggerated response based on media presentation of news stories about youth? In answering this question, consider: newspaper coverage of crime stories, crime statistics since 1950 (see Chapter 2), and other sources.

Further reading

Audit Commission (2004) *Youth Justice 2004: a Review of the Reformed Youth Justice System*, Audit Commission: London.

Flood-Page, C, Campbell, S, Harrington, V and Miller, J (2000) *Youth Crime: Findings from the 1998/99 Youth Lifestyles Survey*, Home Office Research Study 209, Home Office Research, Development and Statistics Directorate Crime and Criminal Justice Unit: London

Muncie, J (1999) *Youth and Crime*, Sage: London

Newburn, T (2003) *Crime and Criminal Justice Policy* (2nd edn), Longman: London

Newburn, T (2002) 'Young People, Crime and Youth Justice', in Maguire, M, Morgan, R and Reiner, R (eds) *The Oxford Handbook of Criminology* (3rd edn), Oxford University Press: Oxford

PART C

Criminal justice process: criminal courts

CHAPTER 9

Criminal courts, judiciary and pre-trial procedure

Main topics covered

➤ Magistrates' courts

➤ Crown Court

➤ Judiciary

➤ Summons, bail and remands in custody

➤ Indications of plea and mode of trial decisions

➤ Case management

INTRODUCTION

Following a decision to prosecute there are various stages to be undergone before an eventual conviction or acquittal can be arrived at. These stages are in part administrative: to ensure resources and paperwork are available at the right time in the right place; and part judicial: to ensure that the interests of justice, including those of the defendant are met. Criminal cases are dealt with in either magistrates' courts or the Crown Court. Nearly all start in the magistrates' court, and before a full trial or hearing the magistrates may have to decide whether or not the accused is to be held in custody while awaiting trial. In some cases the accused has to decide whether to have the case heard by magistrates or before a judge and jury. As with the decision to prosecute or caution, many issues are involved with conflicting pressures between the goals of due process, crime control and cost efficiency.

In a trial the defendant, according to the principles of due process, is presumed innocent until proved guilty. But before the trial stage, a defendant may be placed in custody, to ensure that they are present to answer the case against them, or to ensure that they do not interfere with evidence or with witnesses, or to protect the public. Crime control interests, therefore, may require that the defendant's liberty be restricted before they have been convicted. Other procedures seek to ensure that defendants' interests are protected, particularly in respect of their rights to legal representation, to know the case against them, to have jury trial where appropriate and to not being tried on insufficient evidence. In addition, the organisation of criminal proceedings seeks, by including lay persons in both the magistracy and the jury, to involve representatives of the community as well as professionals and experts. As we have seen, however, due process may be lengthy and expensive and pressures for efficiency have resulted in changes in these procedures. This has led to fears, particularly from a class domination perspective, that too much power lies with the police and other professionals and that defendants' rights are being eroded.

Different courts in the English legal system deal with different kinds of cases and proceedings. The criminal justice system is concerned with criminal cases which can be contrasted with civil cases. In criminal cases, a prosecution is conducted on behalf of the state or the Crown (or, occasionally, privately) against a defendant in order to establish whether or not that defendant is guilty of a crime. Guilt may be proved by evidence in a trial or accepted after a guilty plea, following which a conviction is recorded. This will normally be followed by a form of punishment referred to as a sentence.

Civil cases, in contrast, are mainly concerned with the settlement of disputes between two or more parties, often involving arguments over such matters as rent, boundaries, contracts, negligence, commercial disputes, family disputes on the break-up of marriage and inheritance. In civil cases a claimant sues another person – called the defendant – with a view to obtaining a judgment. A judgment may result in the court ordering the defendant to pay money as damages to compensate the plaintiff. Alternatively the court may issue an order or injunction requiring the defendant to do or to refrain from doing something. In other cases the court may make a declaration, or change the status of an individual – for example, by granting a divorce. The typical explanation of the difference between criminal and civil proceedings is that a criminal case is concerned with the relationship between the state and the individual, and a civil case is involved with regulating relationships between individuals.

Different courts deal with different types of cases: the county court can deal only with civil cases – it has only civil jurisdiction. Other courts – for example, the High Court and magistrates' courts – have jurisdiction in both civil and criminal matters. Magistrates' jurisdiction over civil law matters is limited to licensing matters and family proceedings.

A case may be transferred from one court to another. Nearly all criminal cases start in the magistrates' court and some, as will be seen below, are then passed to the Crown Court. Other cases may be heard by different courts because one or other party has appealed against the decision of the first court. Courts are therefore classified not only on the basis of the type of matter they deal with, but also in accordance with their jurisdiction to hear cases 'at first instance' or on appeal. Two criminal courts – the magistrates' courts and the Crown Court – deal with trials; they therefore have first instance criminal jurisdiction. The administration and organisation of the criminal courts, including how the work is allocated between these two tiers, has been criticised on many occasions and the most recent proposals for change were made in the Auld Review of the Criminal Courts (Auld 2001). This report proposed fundamental changes to the structure of the Criminal Courts, including the creation of a unified criminal court, divided into three divisions, to deal with serious, minor and mid-range offences. Whilst the three-tier recommendation was not accepted, a Unified Courts Administration was provided for in the Courts Act 2003, coming into effect in April 2005 to remove some of the administrative anomalies and delay consequent upon a divided system.

The two levels of criminal courts will now be explored in more detail, starting with the magistrates, those voluntary workhorses of the system, along with their professional colleagues, the 'District Judges (magistrates' courts)' who were formerly known as stipendiary magistrates, and then going on to examine proceedings in the Crown Court, before the thoroughbreds of the process, the judges. This chapter will then go on to consider crucial pre-trial decisions such as whether to remand on bail or in custody and the mode of trial decision, before going on to examine the process of establishing guilt, in Chapter 10.

9.1 MAGISTRATES' COURTS

Upon visiting a magistrates' court – all of which are open to the public, except when dealing with family matters or young people – it will be found that between 9.45 am and 10.00 am, when business normally starts, the lobby of a typical urban court resembles a station ticket office during the rush hour. Defendants are looking for their names on lists pinned to the wall and lawyers and probation officers are seeking out their clients. Ushers and clerks are attempting to impose order by checking lists to see which defendants have arrived. Victims, witnesses, reporters and the interested public are also attempting to find out what is happening, which is not always immediately evident. To the uninitiated the high turnover of defendants making short appearances may give an impression of confusion with little being achieved.

Although there have been recent changes, discussed below, to remove delay and increase the throughput of cases – for example, by 'fast track' procedures – only very trivial or straightforward cases can be dealt with on the defendant's first appearance. Most defendants are making their second or third trip to the court after an adjournment. They are therefore appearing at different stages of the pre-trial and trial process; some for remand or bail hearings, others to enter a plea or decide whether a case is to be heard in the magistrates' court or in the Crown Court. Other defendants will be returning for a summary trial to take place. Even that may not be the end of the matter as proceedings may be adjourned again to await a pre-sentence report before a sentencing decision. A magistrates' court is presided over either by lay magistrates, who are also known as justices of the peace (hence JP), who usually sit as a bench of three, or by a District Judge (magistrates' courts) sitting alone. Lay magistrates are advised on matters of law by a legally qualified clerk. A senior magistrate chairs the bench and speaks on its behalf but all three magistrates have equal power. A specially trained panel of magistrates sits in the youth court.

In a summary trial, magistrates decide on guilt in cases where the defendant contests guilt, that is pleads not guilty. A contested case will involve a trial, which in a magistrates' court is known as a summary trial. Most defendants plead guilty and are sentenced by the magistrates, as are those who have been found guilty following a trial. Nearly all criminal cases start in the magistrates' court and most, approximately 95 per cent, end there.

All magistrates' courts are advised by a team of clerks who, since 1 January 1999, must be professionally legally qualified as a barrister or solicitor. These include the

Figure 9.1 Decision making by magistrates

During the course of a case, the magistrates may make decisions about:

- whether to issue a search warrant
- whether to adjourn a case to another day, and how long the adjournment should be
- remanding the accused in custody
- remanding the accused on bail with or without conditions
- in Triable Either Way cases, where the case should be tried
- whether to hear a case in the absence of the defendant
- granting a warrant to arrest the defendant
- whether someone is guilty or not, in a trial
- asking for reports on a convicted defendant
- the sentence to impose if someone is found guilty, including imposing disqualifications, for example, from driving or from owning an animal
- sending cases to other courts, for example, to another magistrates' court so that a number of matters can be dealt with together, or to the youth court if a young person has been charged with an adult
- sending cases to the Crown Court for sentence or for trial
- whether to impose a different or further sentence if someone breaks an order of the court
- enforcement of fines.

Clerk to the Justices who has overall responsibility for the administration of and legal advice to the court or group of courts. They are supported by a team of legal advisers (court clerks) who are responsible for advising the bench on matters that arise during the day's proceedings and for ensuring the smooth running of the work of the court. At the end of March 2001 there were around 1,800 magistrates' courts' legal advisers in England and Wales. The role of the court clerk and Justices' clerk is seen as very important: in that he or she should be able to provide independent advice to the magistrates. The clerk should advise magistrates on legal matters and matters of mixed law and fact, which includes guidance on their powers of sentence, and the formulation of reasons for decision making. Clerks, whilst being able to assist the bench by reminding them of evidence given to the court, should not take any part on questions of fact, such as whether the court believes a witness, whether to find a defendant guilty or not guilty; nor advise on the actual sentence to impose. Legal advice given to magistrates should be given or repeated in open court, so that both prosecution and defence know the legal advice on which the magistrates made their decision.

District Judges in the magistrates' courts, who were formerly called stipendiary magistrates, sit in larger urban courts, or are appointed to a group of courts (such as in the Thames Valley), and have exactly the same sentencing and decision-making powers as lay magistrates. However, they sit alone and can exercise all their powers alone. They are paid, and are professional lawyers with at least 7 years' experience as a barrister or solicitor. At 1 January 2002 there were 95 such District Judges in post. Lay magistrates are unpaid, sit part time, and are not required to be legally qualified, although they undergo training and appraisal. On 1 April 2003 there were 28,344 lay magistrates in England and Wales: 14,392 were men and 13,952 were women. Magistrates are appointed by local panels, which include experienced magistrates, under the jurisdiction and direction of the Lord Chancellor and Secretary of State for Constitutional Affairs. Individuals may put their own name forward for appointment; others are nominated by existing magistrates, charitable bodies, political parties, trade unions or other organisations. The appointment panels who, as far as possible, represent a cross-section of the community, then interview suitable candidates. They therefore attempt to balance the bench in terms of sex, age, political affiliation, ethnic origin, and background.

The overriding consideration for appointment is that the candidate is suitable in terms of integrity and local standing. Thus anyone who is an undischarged bankrupt or has a conviction for a serious offence or a number of minor offences is unlikely to be appointed. Certain categories of people employed in enforcing the law are ineligible to apply, even when retired. This includes police officers, members of the special constabulary, traffic wardens, civilians working for the police, and members of the armed forces.

An applicant will not be appointed to a district if he or she has a mother, father, son, daughter, brother or sister who is a police officer, special constable, traffic warden or JP in that district. No one may be appointed with a close relative who works for the Crown Prosecution Service or the magistrates' courts in that district, or is a retired police officer, traffic warden or special constable. Members of Parliament, those adopted as political candidates, and full-time political agents in that district cannot apply to be JPs.

These restrictions are based on the need to keep those who adjudicate on the law separate from those who make or investigate it. A key feature of criminal justice in England and Wales is that magistrates are generally lay, as opposed to professional or expert. They are therefore clearly distinct from other participants in the adversarial system such as the police, prosecution or defence and from other professionals such as probation officers. The magistracy is therefore independent of any other interest, and its members are there to represent the wider community. Magistrates are expected to have six key qualities:

- good character and personal integrity;
- ability to understand and communicate effectively;
- social awareness and an understanding of the rule of law and of local communities, and respect for and experience of those of different backgrounds;
- maturity and sound temperament, including confidence, courtesy and decisiveness;
- sound judgment: using objectivity
- commitment and reliability: including a willingness to undertake training and between 26 and 35 sittings per year.

Whilst few would doubt that these are the desired attributes of magistrates, the constitution of the magistracy has occasioned some criticism. It has been argued, for example, that it makes little sense for such vital roles as the adjudication of guilt and the sentencing of the offender to be carried out by amateurs, who cannot be expected to appreciate the finer points of criminal liability, let alone the complexities involved in making sentencing decisions. It could therefore be argued that criminal justice should be in the hands of full-time professionals.

On the other hand, leaving these decisions in the hands of professionals and experts could be seen as leaving too much power in the hands of experts, power which the involvement of lay persons in the system can check. Magistrates themselves clearly value their independence and argue that their experience and common sense are valuable assets in making the system work (see, for example, Parker *et al.* 1989). Others are critical of the composition of the magistracy on the grounds that they are not elected and are not representative of the general population. The magistracy is often perceived to be dominated by middle-class, middle-aged white professional groups. Women are well represented, and the magistracy is 'approaching ethnic representativeness of the population at a national level but with substantial local variations, so that, in areas where there are large minority ethnic communities, such as in London, the local bench may not reflect that' (Auld 2001: 119). A high proportion is retired from full-time employment and such people tend to sit more frequently because of this than their working colleagues. To attempt to combat some of these concerns, in October 2003 the Department for Constitutional Affairs, following a recommendation in the Auld review of the Criminal Courts (Auld 2001), instituted a strategy for recruitment to increase diversity in appointments to the magistracy.

Critics have also focused on the social class profile of magistrates. Recent figures on the class composition of magistrates are difficult to obtain (see Dignan and Wynne 1997), but it is felt to be 'disproportionately middle class and almost certainly financially well-off compared to the population at large' (Auld 2001: 119, quoting Morgan and Russell).

Being a magistrate takes up a considerable amount of time. Many people are not able to leave young children, the office, the schoolroom or the factory floor for extended periods. This inevitably means that some groups, such as middle-class housewives or the relatively affluent self-employed, are over-represented and others, such as manual workers, are under-represented. Furthermore, the latter are less likely to be proposed, or to be seen as having 'local standing' – a point which also militates against the appointment of the unemployed, the young and recently settled members of ethnic minorities.

The issue of representativeness is not, however, easy to resolve. What would a more representative magistracy achieve and just what, or who, should it represent? A representative magistracy on the grounds of demographic characteristics alone may not make different decisions in relation to either guilt or sentencing from the

Table 9.1 Overview of the magistracy in England and Wales by age, gender and ethnic background

Total	Under 40	40–49	50–59	60–69	Male	Female	White	Black	Asian	Other
28,344	919	4,662	12,764	9,873	14,392	13,952	26,548	609	845	255
%	3.7	16.5	45.0	34.8	50.8	49.2	93.7	2.1	3.0	0.9

Source: Department for Constitutional Affairs (data as at 1 April 2003)

current magistracy. Women magistrates appear no more sympathetic, for example, to female offenders, who often come from very different socio-economic backgrounds (see, for example, Eaton 1986), and there is also little evidence of any direct bias on the grounds of social status in respect of business offenders (see, for example, Croall 2001).

Should magistrates in some way represent the views of the community? Should they be elected? In California judges have to go through an election or re-confirmation process. This means that they must campaign for office as if a politician. This could itself be seen as undesirable as the magistracy should be free from political commitments – they are supposed to make decisions on behalf of the whole community, not just those who vote for them. Should the magistracy be selected on the basis that they represent the views of the population on punishment? Representativeness in terms of community values could, for example, see a magistracy in which a large proportion would welcome the restoration of capital punishment. A 1993 survey of social attitudes confirms previous findings from opinion polls in that 74 per cent of respondents thought that, for some crimes, the death penalty was appropriate (Jowell *et al.* 1994: 78).

The magistracy represents a lay element in the system which means that the public, albeit a somewhat selected group, play a part in the administration of justice and sentencing. A professional magistracy, which, as we have seen, would place more power in the hands of professionals, would also be less representative in terms of social class.

Other cricitisms of the magistracy have focused on their lack of formal training, and lack of transparency in decision making. Although magistrates have for many years undergone initial and refresher training the 1990s saw the introduction of a new form of training – the Magistrates' New Training Initiative (MNTI) – to meet specified competences. As a result of MNTI, for the first time magistrates had to be appraised by their peers. For those who sat as chairmen, special emphasis was placed on competences in structured decision making and the giving of reasons. The introduction of the Human Rights Act 1998 in October 2000, saw an increased need for all decisions in the magistrates' courts to be accompanied by full and public reason giving.

9.2 CROWN COURT

The Crown Court is presided over by a judge. Usually this will be a circuit judge, a full-time judge appointed by the Lord Chancellor from the ranks of barristers and solicitors to the circuit bench. In 2002, in 78 Crown Court Centres there were:

- 605 judges
- 1,310 recorders (this figure includes those previously appointed as assistant recorders: a post abolished in 2000).

Recorders are part-time judges drawn from the ranks of barristers and solicitors of a number of years' standing. A High Court judge presides over the most serious criminal cases.

The Crown Court system was introduced by legislation in 1971 and replaced the older system of assizes and petty sessions. Technically there is one Crown Court in England and Wales sitting at a number of locations or Crown Court Centres. Although the Crown Court has a limited civil jurisdiction on appeals, the vast majority of its work is on criminal matters. It is a first instance court which deals with more serious matters than the magistrates' court and also hears appeals against conviction or sentence from the magistrates' court.

Criminal cases come to the Crown Court in three main ways. Some have been previously sent or committed to the Crown Court for trial from a magistrates' court. These may not always lead to trials, as defendants may change their mind at the last minute and plead guilty. Other cases have been sent on from a magistrates' court for sentence and yet others involve appeals against decisions of guilt or sentence at a magistrates' court.

The Crown Court, High Court and Court of Appeal all have appellate jurisdiction which means the right to hear an appeal. Most appeals against conviction and sentence from the Crown Court go to the Court of Appeal, Criminal Division. A few appeals on points of law will go to the High Court, which is divided into Divisions; the Queen's Bench Division deals with appeals on criminal matters. The Court of Appeal has a wider appellate jurisdiction hearing both criminal and civil matters, and the Criminal Division of the Court of Appeal is the usual venue for appeals from the Crown Court. An appeal from the Court of Appeal goes to the House of Lords, which is the highest domestic appeal court. In certain cases there is an appeal to the European Court of Justice.

The number of cases dealt with in the magistrates' courts and the Crown Court is given in Tables 9.2 and 9.3. Table 9.2 shows the total number of cases; the cases not continued by the CPS; and the outcomes in the magistrates' court. It shows the high proportion of guilty pleas and the small percentage of cases determined by trials. Table 9.3 shows the Crown Court caseload in recent years and indicates the number of cases committed for trial from the magistrates' courts. It also gives the number of appeals that were sent to the Crown Court, either against conviction or sentence, and the number of cases sent to the Crown Court from the magistrates' court for sentencing.

Table 9.2 Magistrates' courts: numbers of cases and outcomes 2001/2, 2002/3, and 2003/4

	2001/02	%	2002/03	%	2003/04	%
Total cases brought	1,221,534		1,274,852		1,274,615	
Discontinuances (inc. bind overs)	197,799	16.2	197,680	15.5	175,779	13.8
Arrest warrants etc	73,084	6.0	80,477	6.3	72,078	5.7
Discharges	758	0.1	1,006	0.1	2,225	0.2
Dismissals finding no case to answer	1,675	0.1	1,745	0.1	3,053	0.2
Dismissals after trial	14,913	1.2	15,452	1.2	15,997	1.3
Proofs (of guilt) in absence	114,509	9.4	126,518	9.9	152,757	12.0
Guilty pleas	781,878	64.0	811,583	63.7	800,525	62.8
Convictions after trial	36,918	3.0	40,391	3.2	52,201	4.1

Source: Compiled from *CPS Annual Report 2003/4*

Table 9.3 **Crown Court caseloads 2001/2, 2002/3, 2003/4**

Category	2001/02	%	2002/03	%	2003/04	%
Committed for trial	84,335	73.3	94,546	75.2	95,234	75.1
Appeals	11,841	10.3	11,504	9.2	11,418	9.0
Committed for sentence	18,838	16.4	19,659	15.6	20,191	15.9
Total	115,014		125,709		126,843	

Source: Compiled from *CPS Annual Report 2003/4*

The jurisdiction of magistrates' courts and the Crown Court

Jurisdiction for criminal cases – that is, where cases can be tried – is determined by a number of factors. The first is the type of offence. Criminal offences are divided into three categories as follows:

- summary offences
- offences triable on indictment only
- offences triable-either-way, i.e. summarily or on indictment.

The latter two categories are referred to as indictable offences. Cases triable only on indictment must be tried at the Crown Court. An indictment is the formal document used in a Crown Court trial setting out the charges against the defendant. The magistrates' court has power to hear summary offences and offences that are triable-either-way where a decision has been made to try them summarily, that is in the magistrates' court. In 2002, 1.93 million defendants were proceeded against, of which:

- 518,000 were indictable
- 624,000 were summary non-motoring
- 788,000 were summary motoring.

The time and place at which the alleged offence was committed can also affect where it is heard. Magistrates' courts can only try offences committed in their area and normally proceedings for summary offences must be started within 6 months of the commission of the offence. Indictable offences may be tried in any Crown Court and there is generally no time limit for the commencement of proceedings except in a few cases such as some Customs and Excise offences where there is a 20-year time limit.

Classification of offences: summary and indictable

Summary offences are comparatively less serious crimes. Most motoring offences are summary, including driving with excess alcohol, but there is a wide variety of other summary offences, including common assault, assaulting a police officer, and taking a motor vehicle without the owner's consent. All summary offences are made so by statute.

Generally speaking, the current maximum penalty for a summary offence is 6 months' imprisonment or a £5,000 fine or both, but many summary offences carry much lower maximum penalties, and many are not imprisonable at all. The maximum financial penalties are determined in accordance with a range of levels established by Parliament. Level 1 offences currently carry a maximum fine of £200 and level 5 offences carry a maximum fine of £5,000. The offence of being drunk and disorderly, for example, is a level 3 offence with a maximum fine of £1,000. These five levels were introduced by the Criminal Justice Act 1982 and they mean that, as inflation erodes the value of money, fine maxima can be simply adjusted by legislation altering the value of the levels: the CJA 1991 raised the maximum to £5,000. A few summary offences, such as some pollution offences, carry much higher penalties. The Criminal Justice Act 2003 when fully in force will provide for a different approach to custodial sentencing in the magistrates' court, with a theoretical greater maximum sentence (see Chapter 11).

Offences that are triable only on indictment are very serious matters, including murder, rape, blackmail, robbery, and wounding with intent. For those convicted of murder the only sentence available to the court is life imprisonment. Maximum penalties for other offences are laid down by statute and may include a discretionary life sentence or a simple term of years. For example, 14 years is the maximum custodial penalty for blackmail and burglary of a dwelling, while 10 years is the maximum for burglary of a non-dwelling. Financial penalties for offences tried on indictment have no limit but fines are rarely imposed for such serious offences.

Triable-either-way (TEW) offences include theft, burglary, assault occasioning actual bodily harm, and unlawful wounding. This category covers many offences where the offence's relative seriousness can vary tremendously depending on the facts. Theft, for example, includes stealing a bottle of milk from a doorstep, shoplifting and stealing from an employer. The seriousness of these matters is affected by the value of the theft and all the circumstances surrounding it, including the relationship between thief and victim.

Criminal damage is another offence where the circumstances can vary tremendously. The offence is committed when someone knowingly or recklessly inflicts damage on the property of another person and it is generally a TEW offence. However, in criminal damage cases not involving threat to life or arson and where the value of the damage inflicted is £5,000 or less, the charge is regarded as summary with a maximum penalty of 3 months' custody or a £2,500 fine. When the value of the damage is over £5,000 the offence remains triable either way. Where the offence is racially or religiously aggravated the offence is again made more serious.

Successive Acts have attempted to reduce the numbers of TEW offences, in part to reduce costs and to spread the work more efficiently between the courts. During the discussion of the Criminal Law Bill 1977 proposals were made to change the classification of some offences including criminal damage and theft. These changes were criticised on the grounds that they reduced the defendant's right to a trial by jury. In respect of theft, it was felt that anyone threatened with a conviction for dishonesty must retain this right, however trivial the offence. An offence which was reclassified in response to changing legislative and public perceptions of seriousness was taking a vehicle without the owner's consent, an offence under s. 12 of the Theft Act 1968. This, in its original form, was a TEW offence. In the Criminal Justice Act 1988 it, along with common assault and driving while disqualified, became triable in summary proceedings only. The early 1990s saw an increase in public concern about offences involving a number of widely reported incidents where such cars were used to commit robberies, or resulted in the deaths of the drivers or bystanders. Vivid newspaper reports about ram raiders fuelled political disquiet. In response Parliament created a new indictable offence, 'Aggravated Vehicle-Taking', to cover the situation in which a car, taken without the owner's consent, was involved in an accident or crime.

As we will see below with TEW offences a decision has to be made as to where the case will be tried. Table 9.4 shows whether offenders were summoned, or were on bail or in custody. Table 9.2 gives the breakdown of the number of cases completed in the magistrates' courts.

Table 9.4 **Arrest or summons: offenders in the magistrates' court 1998, 2000 and 2002**

	Number of persons proceeded against (in thousands)					
	1998		*2000*		*2002*	
Indictable offences						
Summoned	53	[9%]	36	[6%]	51	[8%]
Arrested and bailed	451	[75%]	432	[76%]	462	[76%]
Arrested and held in custody	95	[16%]	100	[18%]	99	[16%]
Total	599	[100%]	568	[100%]	611	[100%]
Summary non-motoring offences						
Summoned	380	[61%]	423	[64%]	408	[61%]
Arrested and bailed	212	[34%]	207	[32%]	233	[35%]
Arrested and held in custody	28	[5%]	26	[4%]	24	[4%]
Total	620	[100%]	655	[100%]	665	[100%]
Summary motoring offences						
Summoned	750	[82%]	708	[82%]	695	[80%]
Arrested and bailed	145	[16%]	135	[16%]	152	[18%]
Arrested and held in custody	20	[2%]	16	[2%]	18	[2%]
Total	915	[100%]	859	[100%]	865	[100%]
All offences						
Summoned	1,183	[55%]	1,167	[56%]	1,154	[54%]
Arrested and bailed	808	[38%]	774	[37%]	846	[40%]
Arrested and held in custody	143	[7%]	142	[7%]	141	[7%]
Total	2,134	[100%]	2,082	[100%]	2,141	[100%]

Note: In 2002, 78,000 of those summonsed, 119,000 of those bailed and 13,000 of those arrested and held in custody failed to appear at some stage in the magistrates' proceedings.

Source: Compiled from Home Office *Criminal Statistics England and Wales, 2002*

9.3 JUDICIARY

The role of magistrates as triers of facts and sentencers is discussed above. In Crown Court procedure, the content and style of a trial are different to take account of the split in functions between those who decide on the guilt of the offender – the jury – and the person who decides on the sentence – the judge. In the Crown Court, the presence of, and separation of functions between judge and jury creates the need for special procedures and rules. Before these are considered in relation to the trial, we should put the trial process into the context of the judge's overall work, described below by the then Lord Chief Justice:

> **What do judges do?**
> Many people believe that when judges sit in the morning from 10.30 to 1 pm and in the afternoon from 2 to 4.30 pm, they have a very cushy life. First of all, as any juror would confirm, sitting in court for 5 hours in the day is very exhausting in itself. It cannot be compared to attending an office or other workplace for 5 hours. Time in court requires concentrated attention on the evidence and the submissions. There is no scope for day-dreaming, telephone calls, cups of coffee, badinage with a fellow employee or even visits to the lavatory. But on top of that, what the public see of a judge's work between 10.30 and 4.30 is only the tip of the iceberg. He has to read all the papers and consult any legal authorities before coming into court. He also has to deal with paper applications, and find time to write reserved judgments. Most judges have in addition a number of extra-mural commitments, for example, Presiding Judges on the Circuits have much administrative work to do, others as members of the Parole Board, the Judicial Studies Board, Area Committees of Court Users and there are many other commitments.
>
> (Lord Taylor 1993)

Court proceedings are the most visible part of judges' duties. In a trial the role of the judge is to direct the jury on the law, determine questions of the admissibility of evidence, determine sentence if the defendant is found guilty and generally to be 'in charge' of the proceedings. For trials to be regarded as fair it is important that judges are regarded as independent and not subservient to political or other interests. Lord Taylor also explains the importance of the independence of the judiciary.

> To maintain not only the fact of judicial independence but its appearance, judges have to be cautious in their social activities and must avoid politics. The result of all this care to guard judicial independence is that litigants can be confident the judge will try their case on its merit and as the judicial oath requires: Without fear of favour, affection or ill-will.
>
> (Lord Taylor 1993)

During the trial the judge's function is to direct the jury on the law. The jury must accept these directions, but any views the judge has or expresses on the facts can be disregarded by the jury. The judge is entitled to comment on the facts, and a very important part of the judge's role is to help the jury assess the relevance of evidence, and to marshal what is often a large body of material into some order. It is often very difficult, therefore, to gauge when the judge oversteps the line and begins to usurp the jury's function by determining or appearing to determine issues of fact. If, however, the judge does exceed his or her function, convicted defendants may use this as a ground for appeal.

The judge's influence is paramount where it is argued that evidence (usually but not always prosecution evidence) should not be admitted in the trial. This could be an argument that the evidence fell within a category which is not admitted, or an argument asking the judge to exercise his discretion to make a judgment to exclude certain evidence. For example, the judge in a criminal trial has the power to exclude (that is, prevent) evidence being put before the jury where its prejudicial effect outweighs its value as evidence. In addition to this general discretion the judge has discretion under s. 78 of the Police and Criminal Evidence Act 1984 to exclude evidence whose admission would be unfair in all the circumstances, including the manner in which the evidence was obtained. This section is often relied upon in cases involving breaches of the Codes of Practice under PACE (see Chapter 6).

Judges have often been criticised as being out of touch, an impression fostered by media reports of judges who are unaware of current popular music or sporting icons. In recent years attempts have been made to address this impression, partly by the appointment of some younger judges. Criticism of the racial composition of the judiciary was addressed by the then Lord Chancellor, Lord Irvine, in a speech to a Minority Lawyers Conference in London in November 1997. He said he wished to encourage ethnic minority applicants for appointment, and also made the point that he would like to remove some of the perceived secrecy about judicial appointments. Increasingly this has been done by advertising judicial vacancies including in minority ethnic press, providing feedback to disappointed candidates and making information about appointments public. In 2002/3 there were 93 vacancies for appointments as recorder (a part-time judge, often seen as the first step on the judicial hierarchy). Table 9.5 shows the breakdown by race and gender of applicant interviewees and appointees.

9.4 SUMMONS, BAIL AND REMANDS IN CUSTODY

The court process starts with the attendance of the defendant. Most will have been summonsed, normally by post, as is the case, for example, with minor motoring

Table 9.5 Judicial appointments – race and gender

	Male	Female	White	Black	Asian	Other/not known
Applicants: total 589	483	106	538	9	19	23
Interviews: total 376	315	61	343	5	13	15
Appointments: 93	81	12	87	2	2	2

Source: Dept of Constitutional Affairs: *Judicial Appointments Annual Report 2002/3*

offences. Some will have been arrested and may have been held overnight in police custody, or released on police bail to attend court. Yet others may have been remanded in custody and arrive from a prison. Cases are not normally completed on their first appearance and most are adjourned. This is necessary to allow both the prosecution and the defendant time to prepare their case, to seek legal or other expert advice or to contact witnesses.

Both the police and the courts can make decisions about holding an accused person in custody prior to conviction. The police must decide whether to release arrested persons with or without bail or to detain them in police custody. In 2002 the police arrested and detained in custody 7 per cent of those who were prosecuted. They released on bail a further 40 per cent. Most (54 per cent) of those prosecuted were summonsed.

Following their first appearance in the magistrates' court, defendants may be released to await trial or may be remanded on bail or in custody by the magistrates. Similar decisions have to be made by the judge if the case goes to trial in the Crown Court. In 2002, 24 per cent of offenders prosecuted were granted bail by the magistrates, 4 per cent were remanded in custody and 72 per cent were released with no conditions (*Criminal Statistics England and Wales* 2002: 132).

Less serious cases will simply be adjourned and defendants will be notified of the date of the next hearing. In more serious cases, however, defendants will be remanded either on bail or in custody. Remands can only be for a fixed period of time, and remand length varies in relation to whether or not the accused is held in custody. There are fixed limits to the length of time that a person can be detained by the police at a police station and by the magistrates when remanding an alleged offender in custody.

As seen in Chapter 6, PACE governs police powers in relation to detention without charge. Under a strict timetable, a suspect may only be held for questioning for a limited time before being charged. If the time limit is reached the suspect must be charged or released. PACE also provides that once a suspect has been charged they may be released by the police on bail to attend the magistrates' court at a specified time. The time limits are extended in the case of those suspected of terrorist offences. Under the Criminal Justice and Public Order Act 1994, for the first time, the police could impose conditions of bail generally in the same terms as a court. In January 2004, s. 4 of the Criminal Justice Act 2003 was implemented, allowing police officers to admit suspects to bail (street bail) without first taking them to the police station (as an efficiency measure).

Defendants may be detained by the police without charge initially for 24 hours. If, in the opinion of the police, the offence is a 'serious arrestable offence', then the period of detention by the police may be extended for a further 12 hours on the authorisation of a senior officer of superintendent rank or above. Under the CJA 2003 this period will be extended to 36 hours for any arrestable offence: the 'serious' qualification is removed. After 36 hours accused persons must be presented at a magistrates' court, who may return them to police custody for a further 36 hours. After this time they must again be returned to the court, when the magistrates may decide on a further period of remand. The maximum total period of remand without charge in police custody is 96 hours. Thereafter the suspect must be charged or released. After charge, further decisions on remand in custody or bail are made and, if remanded in custody, the accused will be held in a remand wing or centre in a prison service establishment.

Unconvicted defendants may not be initially remanded in custody by magistrates for more than 8 days at a time. They may be remanded for up to 28 days, however, if they have been previously remanded in custody for the same offence and are present in court. A convicted defendant can be remanded in custody for up to 3 weeks for reports. In order to prevent repeated custodial remands, custody time limits were introduced following the creation of the Crown Prosecution Service. These provide a maximum time limit for proceedings where the defendant is in custody. When the limit is reached, leave to extend the period must be applied for or the defendant must be given bail. Under the Prosecution of Offences (Custody Time Limits) Regulations 1987 the limits are 70 days between first appearance and summary trial or committal proceedings, unless the decision to have summary trial is reached earlier than 56 days, in which case the limit is 56 days. The maximum period for holding a defendant in custody between committal to the Crown Court and trial is 112 days.

Bail

The operation of the bail system in England and Wales is governed by the Bail Act 1976. If a person accused, convicted or under arrest for an offence is granted bail, he or she is released under a duty to attend court or the police station at a given time.

Bail may be granted subject to certain conditions, which aim to ensure that the defendant appears for the next hearing. The court may ask for a *surety* (someone who will pledge to pay an amount of money set by the court should the defendant not turn up) or may require a *security* (the deposit of a sum of money). In other circumstances, the court may require that the accused lodge their passports with the police to ensure that they do not flee the country, or the court may decide to restrict defendants' movements by imposing a curfew order, or insisting they report daily to a police station, or ban them from making contact with witnesses or victims.

Those who are granted bail must appear at the time and place specified, which they will be given written details of. If they do not surrender to custody, they are guilty of an offence, except when they are prevented from so doing because of, for example, an accident. A warrant may be issued for their arrest and if found guilty of the offence of failing to attend they risk a fine of up to £5,000 from the magistrates' court or up to 3 months' imprisonment. The police may also arrest someone on bail if they have reasonable grounds for believing that any conditions are not being met or that the accused is unlikely to surrender.

Criteria for bail

The criteria for granting and refusing bail are also dealt with by the Bail Act 1976. In general there is a presumption in favour of bail for unconvicted defendants but there are some important exceptions. Bail need not be granted to defendants charged with imprisonable offences, if:

- the court or the police (for police bail) think there are substantial grounds for believing that, if released, the defendant:
  - will fail to return to court
  - will commit an offence
  - will interfere with witnesses, for example by contacting them about the court proceedings, or otherwise obstruct the course of justice;
- the defendant is already on bail at the time and is charged with a new indictable offence;
- it is necessary for the defendant's own protection or, if a young person, for his or her welfare;
- the defendant is already in custody on other matters;
- the defendant has already absconded in the present proceedings;
- it has been impracticable to obtain information in order to make a bail decision.

In deciding whether grounds exist for refusing bail and in deciding whether to impose any conditions on the bail, the court or police will consider:

- the nature and seriousness of the matter and the probable sentence;
- the character and previous convictions of the defendant;
- neighbourhood ties such as family, job, property;
- any previous bail record (has the accused always attended court when asked?);
- strength of the evidence against him or her;
- any other relevant information.

Where someone is accused of offences involving rape, murder or manslaughter and has already been convicted previously for such an offence, bail will only be given in exceptional circumstances. For convicted offenders bail can be withheld if it is necessary to hold the person in custody to allow a report to be compiled.

Concerns about bail

As a result of increasing concern about the possibility of dangerous offenders being released on bail, the Bail (Amendment Act) 1993 gave the Crown Prosecution Service limited rights to appeal (in cases such as offences carrying a sentence of 5 years or more) against a bail decision made in a magistrates' court; this right is extended to all imprisonable offences by the CJA 2003. The case of Andrew Hagans in 1992 highlighted the public disquiet caused by releasing convicted violent offenders charged with another serious violent offence.

Andrew Hagans was released from prison in July 1991. He was 25 years old and had 28 convictions, mainly for violent and sexual offences. At the age of 15 he was placed under supervision after holding three women at knife-point and indecently assaulting them. A year later he was again placed under supervision for 3 years for burglary with intent to rape. On 4 August 1991, 3 weeks after release from prison, he was arrested and charged with raping a woman in Cheltenham. After a week on remand in jail he was given bail by the magistrates' court, despite strong opposition from the police. The condition of his bail was that he lived in a bail hostel and did not go to Cheltenham. Sixteen days later Hagans was in Gloucester where he raped and murdered 23-year-old Anna McGurk. In June 1992 he was jailed for life at Bristol Crown Court.

The concern over the link between drug use and offending on bail is reflected in a provision to be introduced under the CJA 2003: s. 19 provides that where a person is shown to have Class A drugs in his body, the court believes that the drug caused or contributed to the offence and the suspect has refused to undergo drug assessment or has failed to take follow-up steps, then bail may be withheld unless the court is satisfied there is no real risk of offending.

When bail is refused the court must consider whether it ought to be granted on subsequent occasions. This does not mean that the accused can make repeated applications on the same grounds. After bail has been refused for any of the stated reasons, other than insufficient information, only one further bail application is usually allowed and the court does not have to hear further applications unless there has been a change in circumstances. A remand in custody on the basis that there is insufficient information is not a refusal of bail as such and does not count as a bail application, so the accused may still make two applications.

Some concern has been expressed about the length of adjournments, especially where defendants are remanded in custody. This clearly causes immense stress to defendants, let alone the cost to the taxpayer. In addition, those remanded in custody and subsequently acquitted are not entitled to any compensation. In 2002 the average waiting time for trial for defendants committed for trial to the Crown Court was 15.8 weeks, and 12.8 weeks for those in custody awaiting trial (*Judicial Statistics* 2002: 75).

The issues underlying the granting of bail again illustrate the conflicting models of, and pressures on, the criminal justice system. As we have seen, there is an assumption that a defendant, who has not yet been proved guilty or sentenced by the court, should have a right to bail. Placing defendants, who may yet be found not guilty, in custody involves depriving possibly innocent persons of their liberty, disrupting their lives and possibly endangering their employment opportunities. The high cost of custodial remands also causes concern. The average daily prison population in 2001 included 11,237 remand and unsentenced prisoners (17 per cent of the total).

On the other hand, it is important from the point of view of due process, just deserts, crime control and denunciation that those who are suspected of a crime appear in court to be tried and sentenced. In 2002, 82,600 defendants bailed by the magistrates subsequently failed to appear and 127,800 failed to appear in response to a summons. In the Crown Court 4,800 (9 per cent) of those granted bail by judges failed to appear (*Criminal Statistics England and Wales 2002*: 137). Remands in custody are also necessary from a crime control perspective as the public require protection from offenders who may commit further offences while awaiting trial.

Whether or not fears of excessive numbers of offences committed by those on bail are justified, they led to the provisions in the Criminal Justice and Public Order Act 1994 to remove the right to bail for a person charged with a further indictable offence while on bail.

Remands in custody

Remanding defendants in custody raises important issues concerning civil liberties. Around 14–15 per cent of untried prisoners are subsequently acquitted or not proceeded against, and a further one-third will not receive custodial sentences (Morgan and Jones 1992). In a letter to *The Times*, Stephen Shaw, Director of the Prison Reform Trust, wrote:

> Some 40 per cent of those who are remanded in custody are eventually found not guilty or are given a non-custodial sentence. Clearly there are individuals who could, and should, have been granted bail.
>
> (*The Times*, 17 September 1991)

This argument reflects a view that some defendants are being unfairly dealt with – especially those who are eventually acquitted. It could be argued that depriving a person of their liberty before trial amounts to the police or the courts pre-judging guilt. On the other hand, however, as we have seen, conflicting arguments surround the granting of bail. If a person has been accused of a very serious offence, the interests of public protection require that they should be prevented from committing a 'further' offence. If they should re-offend, the public might well query why they were released back into the community. Also, as argued above, due process is not well served if defendants abscond and do not appear to answer any charges.

The other part of the argument concerns those who, having been remanded in custody, are subsequently given non-custodial sentences. Yet the principles underlying bail or custody decisions are different from factors shaping sentencing decisions. Remand in custody is not a punishment for an offence not yet proved; it is a preventative measure, to prevent further offending, interfering with witnesses or evidence or absconding. In the case of remand, as we have seen, public protection may be a paramount interest, and full information about the risk posed to the public by a defendant may not be available. Defendants may, before sentencing, provide sufficient mitigation to limit their culpability by giving information which may not be available at the time of the decision on remand.

Time spent in prison on remand will be deducted from any eventual sentence. Furthermore, the fact that a defendant has had a 'taste of prison' may be a factor militating against an eventual custodial sentence. This is certainly an argument much used by defence counsel. On the other hand, it would not justify the use of such a 'taste of prison' as a tactic by magistrates to deter the offender before guilt has been proved. This again illustrates how difficult it is to examine any one stage of the criminal justice process in isolation from other stages. While theoretically separate, decisions on remands in custody and sentencing are necessarily interrelated.

While remand prisoners enjoy certain privileges compared to sentenced prisoners, there is considerable evidence that conditions in remand prisons can be severe – thus adding to the stress and frustration of those awaiting trial and sentence (Morgan and Jones 1992). However, although remand prisons and centres are among the most overcrowded, they do allow more freedom and they are usually nearer the defendants' home as they are often in urban areas. This may explain the finding of a survey asking defendants why they opted for trial at a Crown Court, in which 24 per cent responded that they wished to serve part of an expected sentence on remand. So despite the poorer conditions found in many remand wings, the extra privileges of being on remand and the proximity to where they lived were an inducement for those who expected to be found guilty. Yet again we see how decisions which are theoretically separate are interdependent and how informal considerations influence these decisions.

Whether or not it is felt that too many, or too few, defendants are granted bail, it is clear that the decision whether to remand on bail or in custody is a crucial one both for individual defendants and for the system as a whole. Accordingly, a number of initiatives have been suggested to assist magistrates in their assessment of which offenders are most suitable for bail. These include the use of information schemes which aim to provide more information about defendants on their first appearance. Bail can be denied if, at an early stage of the proceedings, there is insufficient information to make a decision. This may happen when the individual refuses to give a name and address, or where the court doubts the reliability of the information given. In these cases bail information schemes have proved successful in enabling the courts to make decisions based on reliable and accurate information. Bail support schemes, involving a mixture of advice, counselling and surveillance, have also been suggested to cut down the numbers remanded in custody awaiting trial.

Bail hostels, run by the probation service, are available in some areas, providing accommodation for defendants awaiting trial. This provides a fixed address suitable for those of no fixed abode or where 'home' accommodation is considered to be related to the offending. Hostels provide a measure of freedom mixed with some supervision and enable those remanded to attend work. Many have argued for the provision of more of these hostels.

We can see from this discussion of remand that not only do the conflicting pressures on criminal justice operate on pre-trial proceedings, but also that one stage cannot be treated in isolation from others. Whether or not the accused is remanded in custody or on bail is only one of many decisions taken before trial and magistrates also deal with cases that have moved further on in the process. One crucial decision with triable-either-way offences is the mode of trial decision.

9.5 INDICATIONS OF PLEA AND THE MODE OF TRIAL DECISIONS

In summary cases and those that can be tried on indictment only, there is no choice as to where the case will be dealt with. For triable-either-way (TEW) cases a decision has to be made about which court will hear the case. This is called the mode of trial decision. Decisions over where these midway offences are tried and who makes that decision have been the subject of controversial reform or attempted reforms for many years. The issues demonstrate the tensions between bureaucratic efficiency, due process and increasingly the management approach to criminal justice. A cost-effectiveness model suggests that as many defendants as possible should be tried in the cheaper and quicker venue of the magistrates' court, and that defendants should not have the choice of going to the Crown Court when the case is trivial or where their choice is made for tactical reasons. Due process suggests, at least to some people, that everyone at risk of conviction of a serious cat-egory of crime, including offences that might damage their reputation, should have the option of trial by jury. This argument assumes that jury trial is better or safer than trial by magistrates. The mode of trial or venue decision has important conse-quences in terms of the courts' organisation and in terms of the perception of justice.

Prior to the implementation of the Criminal Procedure and Investigations Act 1996 (CPIA 1996) the mode of trial decision was made before any plea was entered and without regard to any subsequent plea, but, since s. 49 of the Act came into force in October 1997, the situation is reversed and the defendant is asked about any plea in advance of a decision on venue.

Before any decision on plea can be made, the defendant needs to have some knowledge of the case against him. The Magistrates' Court (Advance Information) Rules 1985 provide that for any TEW offence, if asked, the prosecution must give the defendant a copy of, or summary of, the statements or other evidence on which they intend to rely. This rule does not apply to summary offences, although often the CPS will voluntarily provide information in those cases. When the advance disclosure is provided, accused persons and their solicitors may well wish to have time to con-sider it, in order to make decisions about whether they wish to plead guilty or not. In those circumstances, the defendant may ask for an adjournment for that to take place. In other cases, defendants will be clear about which course they wish to take, and may not even wish to see the papers before pleading guilty immediately.

Once the court is satisfied that the defendant has had an opportunity to consider the evidence, or does not wish to take advantage of this process, the defendant will be asked to indicate a plea of guilty or not guilty. The defendant will be told, in the event of a guilty plea, that the magistrates will deal with the case, but that they nevertheless may come to the conclusion that their sentencing powers are insuf-ficient and may send the case for sentence to the Crown Court. If a defendant indicates a guilty plea, then the magistrates move immediately to the sentencing stage. If the defendant pleads not guilty or is unwilling to indicate a plea, then a mode of trial decision is required. This takes the following form:

- The prosecution outlines the basic allegations, highlighting points relevant to its seriousness.

- The prosecutor gives a view as to where the case should be tried (see criteria below).

- The defendant, or their representative, may make their view clear as to the choice of venue, although that will probably not be necessary if the intention is to elect trial by jury in any event.

- The magistrates make their decision on whether they will accept jurisdiction, on the basis that, if the defendant were to be convicted, the case is within their powers of sentencing.

- If it is decided that the case can be heard in the magistrates' court, the clerk will tell the defendant that the magistrates are willing to deal with the case, but that the defendant has a choice whether to *consent to summary trial* or to *elect trial by jury*. At this stage defendants are warned that if they are tried in the magistrates' court and found guilty, the magistrates might send them to the Crown Court if they feel that their powers of punishment are insufficient.

■ If the defendant consents to a summary trial they will then be formally asked to plead not guilty. If they elect jury trial then the case will be adjourned for later committal to the Crown Court.

■ If the magistrates decide that their powers of punishment are insufficient or that the Crown Court is a more appropriate venue for other reasons, they will refuse to hear the case and will *direct* that it is sent to the Crown Court. The case will then be adjourned for committal proceedings to take place. No formal plea will be taken, and the defendant will not be given a choice as to venue.

For the purpose of the mode of trial decision, the court assumes that the prosecution allegations are correct, and assumes that the defendant has no previous convictions. The decision is based, in part, on whether the sentencing powers of the magistrates would be adequate. The normal maximum powers of the magistrates' court in sentencing is 6 months in custody or a fine of £5,000 for one offence, with an overall maximum of 12 months' custody for two or more TEW offences tried together. (The overall limits of the magistrates will increase to 12 months for a single offence under the Criminal Justice Act 2003.)

When magistrates make their decision on mode of trial they must consider, by virtue of s. 19 of the Magistrates' Courts Act 1980:

■ the nature of the case;

■ the seriousness of the offence;

■ the magistrates' powers of punishment (including compensation);

■ other circumstances making one venue more suitable than the other;

■ the representations of prosecution and defendant.

National Mode of Trial Guidelines were issued in October 1990 by the Lord Chief Justice and amended in January 1995 by the Criminal Justice Consultative Committee to give guidance to magistrates on the mode of trial decision and to encourage them to commit fewer cases to the Crown Court for trial. These list the factors that should be considered in mode of trial decisions in general and give particular guidance in respect of the most common offences. General guidance includes the following:

■ the decision should never be on grounds of convenience or expediency;

■ a difficult question of law or fact should be dealt with on indictment;

■ subject to the defendant's consent, the presumption is in favour of summary trial.

The guidance also lists specific factors that may make a case not suitable for summary trial, the overriding factor being the magistrates' powers of punishment. For example, for offences of violence that are TEW (ss. 20 and 47 of the Offences Against the Person Act 1861), the guidance states that summary trial should take place unless one or more of the following features are present:

■ use of a weapon of a kind likely to cause serious injury;

■ a weapon is used and serious injury is caused;

- more than minor injury is caused by headbutting, kicking, or similar forms of assault;
- serious violence is caused to someone working with the public, for example a taxi driver, publican, or police officer;
- a particularly vulnerable victim, for example very young or elderly;
- the offence has a clear racial motivation.

Appropriate guidelines are given for other offences. As jury trial is seen as a corner-stone of the criminal justice system, it is important that defendants are aware of their rights and can make an informed choice. The mode of trial procedure is there-fore mandatory for a TEW offence unless the defendant indicates a guilty plea. Table 9.6 shows the number of cases between 2001/2 and 2003/4 committed to the Crown Court either as a result of the magistrates' direction or because the defen-dant chose or elected to have the case dealt with there. It also shows cases that could only be tried at the Crown Court.

Defendants' choice may be influenced by a number of factors, and research pub-lished in 1992 indicated that 70 per cent of defendants who opted for jury trial did so on the advice of their lawyer (Hedderman and Moxon 1992). Almost one-third of defendants thought opting for Crown Court would delay the trial, whilst just over one-third thought it would be quicker. Rather unusually, 59 per cent of respondents in the survey thought that they would receive a lower sentence in the Crown Court, a perception which does not reflect the sentencing powers of the two courts. It may reflect a tendency for the Crown Court to give sentences at the lower end of their spectrum for TEW offences; and, as seen above, almost one-quarter of defendants were influenced by the consideration that they would, by delaying the trial, spend longer in remand prisons.

The most common reason given was the increased chance of acquittal (see Table 9.7). It is generally believed that juries are more likely to acquit than magistrates, and there is some justification for this view as the acquittal rates in the Crown Court have been found to be higher than in magistrates' courts (Vennard 1985). It is also generally believed that magistrates' courts tend to accept police evidence more readily (Ashworth 1994a). It may be, therefore, that defendants are encouraged to elect jury trial whenever the case against them is not very strong. However, the study also found that 70 per cent of those defendants who elected trial at the Crown Court pleaded guilty to all charges on the day of the trial.

Table 9.6 Mode of trial decisions

Crown Court: source of committals for trial 2001/2, 2002/3 and 2003/4						
	2001/2	*%*	*2002/3*	*%*	*2003/4*	*%*
Magistrates' direction	36,740	43.6	40,274	42.6	41,997	44.1
Defendants' elections	14,956	17.7	15,051	15.9	13,037	13.7
Indictable only	32,639	38.7	39,221	41.5	40,200	42.2
Total	84,335		94,546		95,234	

Source: Complied from CPS Annual Report

Table 9.7 Reasons defendants and solicitors gave for preferring Crown Court trial

Reason	Defendants (%)	Solicitors (%)
Better chance of acquittal	69	81
Magistrates on the side of the police	62	70
Lighter sentence	59	38
To get more information about the prosecution case	48	45
Would be sent to Crown Court for sentence	42	40
More likely to get bail	36	11
Crown Court quicker	34	6
Delay start of trial	28	19
Co-defendant wanted Crown Court	26	19
To serve part of sentence on remand	24	Not asked
Easier to get legal aid	19	4

Source: Hedderman and Moxon (1992: 20).

Since this research was carried out, important changes in the law have been introduced that were expected to affect the numbers of defendants committed to the Crown Court for trial. These are, first, the change described above so that defendants who plead guilty are dealt with in the magistrates' court, and, secondly, the so-called discount for a guilty plea set out in s. 48 of the Criminal Justice and Public Order Act 1994. This provides that courts in sentencing must take account of the fact that the defendant pleaded guilty, and consider reducing the sentence, but in particular will take account of the stage of proceedings at which the guilty plea was entered. This means that defendants' sentences will often be significantly reduced if they plead guilty at an early stage.

One of the reasons behind the series of reforms that now encourage defendants to indicate their intention to plead guilty at an earlier stage of proceedings than was the case before October 1997, was the aim to reduce the number of 'cracked cases'. These are cases in which preparations for a contested trial at the Crown Court have been made with witnesses, and evidence assembled and barristers briefed; and if, at the start or during the trial, defendants change their plea to guilty, then an enormous amount of effort, time and money is wasted. In 2002, of the 19,636 cracked trials, 12,444 (63.4 per cent) were as a result of a late guilty plea (Judicial Statistics 2002).

The cost of a Crown Court trial far exceeds that of a summary trial. It is perhaps unsurprising, therefore, that on the grounds of cost-effectiveness there have been successive attempts to reduce the number of TEW cases. As has been referred to above, these attempts include the following:

■ reclassification of offences as summary only

■ plea before venue procedure

■ 'discount' for early guilty plea

■ increasing sentencing powers of magistrates.

Case management generally has become an important issue for the courts and is discussed below. Cases that can be tried only at the Crown Court are 'sent' for trial under s. 51 of the Crime and Disorder Act 1998, which provides a rapid procedure with the minimum of bureaucracy so that cases are moved to the Crown Court where all the preparation for trial or guilty pleas can take place.

Where a case is TEW the procedure for transferring it from the magistrates' court to the Crown Court is known as committal proceedings. These are held for TEW cases where a decision has been made to send them to the Crown Court. Committal proceedings were originally intended to allow the lower court to examine cases and sift out those that had insufficient evidence. Committals eventually took two forms: one without considering the evidence, and the other which provided for the calling of witnesses and their cross-examination. The procedure was criticised in the Runciman Royal Commission, which stated:

> We accordingly recommend that, where the defendant makes a submission of no case to answer, it be considered on the papers, although the defence should be able to advance oral argument in support of the submission and the prosecution should be able to reply. Witnesses should not be called: the right place to test their evidence is the trial itself. We do not accept that they should be required in effect to give their evidence twice over. Quite apart from the time and trouble wasted by unnecessary duplication, we agree that there is a significant risk that some of them will feel so intimidated on the first occasion that they will be unable to give their evidence at the trial satisfactorily or perhaps at all. We believe that a hearing on the papers would be sufficient to enable the court to prevent from proceeding to trial cases too weak to deserve it.
>
> (Lord Runciman 1993: 90)

Since October 1997 committal evidence has been tested by an examination of the documents only. The requirement for witnesses to be called to give oral evidence was removed. To that extent the recommendations of the Royal Commission of 1993 were accepted. Committal proceedings for indictable only offences were abolished by the Crime and Disorder Act 1998.

Once committed to the Crown Court the case would formerly be listed 'for plea' so that an indication of the progress of the case could take place, but, as has been already seen, many cases were prepared for trial and a guilty plea was entered at the last moment. While it is unlikely that the problem of 'cracked trials' can be completely eradicated, some of the efficiency measures have been specifically aimed at reducing their number.

Introduction of the proposals in the Criminal Justice Act 2003 will have an impact on pre-trial procedures: for instance, committal proceedings will be abolished. Before the magistrates' court decides whether its powers of punishment are sufficient, the court will be informed about the defendant's previous convictions if any. This will enable the court to make a full judgment about whether its powers of punishment are sufficient both on the facts of the case and on the basis of the defendant's record. This means that if the court accepts jurisdiction there will be only a limited power to commit for sentence.

The most important change to be introduced is the right of defendants to ask for an indication of the sentence they would receive in the magistrates' court. Although the magistrates do not have to comply with the request, if they do, and as a result (because a non-custodial penalty is indicated) the defendant then changes the plea, the court is bound by that indication. This change in procedure offers inducements for the defendant both to plead guilty and to accept the magistrates' jurisdiction.

9.6 CASE MANAGEMENT

As has been made clear above, there are significant issues for and criticism of the criminal justice system in relation to efficiency: see the Auld Report. Much has been made of the possible conflicts between the due process model and the cost-effectiveness models of case management. The link between them is often asserted in the adage: 'justice delayed is justice denied'. If a defendant is rushed through proceedings without having opportunity properly to address issues, this poses significant questions of principle and due process. However, delay and cost from courts being idle or being unable to progress cases because of faulty communications, missing or incomplete papers, defendants who have failed to attend without good reason, or are not produced by the prison service, reports that are not prepared in time for the court hearing, or cases that take much longer or indeed a much shorter time than expected, are all matters that should be able to be addressed by systems organisation.

In October 1996 the Home Office set up a review of delay in the criminal justice system, which reported in February 1997, *Review of Delay in the Criminal Justice System* (Home Office 1997c). Its terms of reference were wide-ranging over all aspects of the system and not limited by existing legislation. Fundamental changes about case management in the magistrates' court were introduced, including: giving justices' clerks wider powers, and early listing of likely guilty pleas. These fast-track 'Narey hearings' take place soon after arrest in cases that are likely to be guilty pleas in the magistrates' court: notably for driving with excess alcohol. The introduction (discussed above) of the 'sending' procedure under the Crime and Disorder Act 1998, which replaced the previous committal procedure, was introduced by way of a pilot scheme in 1998 and 1999. Early evaluations of the scheme suggested a total annual saving of £15.7 million pounds, together with time saving and shortening of time in which cases were resolved (Ernst and Young 2000).

Administrative steps are used increasingly in the court to identify issues and ensure that only issues that are actually contested will be challenged. In magistrates' courts pre-trial reviews are automatically arranged a number of weeks before trial to verify that the case will proceed to a trial, and that all sides are prepared for the trial date. In the Crown Court a procedure called the 'plea and directions hearing' (PDH) is held at the first stage after a case has been 'sent' or 'committed'. This is administered by a judge, often at the time when the defendant is arraigned (i.e. the plea to the indictment is formally taken) so that it can be seen whether a guilty plea is expected at this stage, and administrative and legal matters are canvassed which will affect the time the trial will take and the state of readiness of the parties. The purpose of many of the questions on the Plea and Directions questionnaire is to save matters suddenly arising at trial and causing delay. Plea and directions hearings are now conducted in some courts by electronic means; and, increasingly, electronic mechanisms, such as electronic presentation of evidence and digital audio recording are used. The Xhibit project, concerned with the collation of case management information, is being piloted, to identify savings in costly court and lawyers' time and to improve communications (Moss 2004).

In long or complex cases the CPIA 1996 makes provision for preparatory hearings, as has been done in serious fraud cases, which allows the trial judge to make decisions on the case without the jury needing to attend, thus limiting sometimes lengthy debate in the absence of the jury in such cases, with consequent waste of court and juror time. There are rights of appeal from rulings made in these hearings and limits on what can be reported in the press, so the eventual jury in the cases will not be affected by media reports.

Forty-two Local Criminal Justice Boards were set up in 2003 to improve communications and effectiveness within the criminal justice system. One measure they introduced was the setting of a number of local timeliness targets which supported national public service agreements. The targets in the Crown Court relate to committals for sentence, committals for trial, trials and appeals and in the magistrates' courts covering separately youth and adult cases, divided between initial guilty pleas, trials and committals. The aim to reduce ineffective trials again underpins the national agreement to 'improve the delivery of justice by increasing the number of crimes for which an offender is brought to justice by 2005/6 . . . and a reduction in the proportion of ineffective trials'.

Thus concerns for efficiency have resulted in changes not only to court procedures, and in the allocation of work, but also in internal restructuring and in performance targets as in any other industry. The inherent tension is that for one of the end users at least – the defendant – this is not a 'service' that he or she wishes to be involved in, and for other end users such as the victim or public the concern is much more to do with ideas of justice and appropriate punishment than efficiency.

CONCLUSION

It can be seen from the above discussions that many important processes precede a full trial or hearing, and that complex issues are involved in pre-trial procedures. We have also seen the interdependency between different stages of the process. Although very different considerations and rules surround decisions to grant bail and the sentencing decision, in practice what happens at one stage affects the later stage. A remand in custody may affect the eventual sentence and become part of defendants' calculations on mode of trial or plea decisions.

The pre-trial processes show the conflict between the different goals and models of criminal justice, and further illustrate how difficult it is in practice to balance these competing pressures. The due process model stresses the rights of the defendant throughout the process. Yet the crime control model requires that those who are guilty of crime be brought to court, convicted and punished. Due process requires procedures to assure that defendants are able to take advantage of their rights. As seen above, the issues raised by bail or custodial remands are particularly difficult to resolve. It is clearly in the interests of due process that citizens are not deprived of their liberty until proved guilty. On the other hand, there is understandable concern that dangerous or persistent offenders may be allowed to return to the community and that many offences may be committed while offenders are on bail. Crime control and prevention aims nevertheless conflict with due process.

The cost of keeping offenders in custody is high, and bureaucratic and financial pressures also indicate that remands in custody should be kept to a minimum and that court adjournment periods should be kept as short as possible. Many of these issues are also seen in Chapter 10, which deals with the processes by which guilt or not is established.

The bureaucratic efficiency model of criminal justice underlines the need for speed, efficiency and cost effectiveness. The cost and speed of justice has become an increasingly important issue.

Despite the changes outlined above, a visitor to any magistrates' court would see many cases adjourned, almost without consideration because they are 'first time in', where a culture still exists that no progress is expected. Others will not be able to progress as expected because 'the defendant needs legal advice', or the prosecution papers are not ready, or available, or have not been shown to the defence in sufficient time for them to be considered. Current pressures to remove delay and reduce cost are beginning to take effect but dangers exist when pressures conflict with the due process issues which are fundamental to a fair criminal justice system.

Review questions

1 What are the advantages and disadvantages of having lay people make the decision on the guilt of the defendant?

2 List the three categories of criminal offences dealt with by the courts.

3 Describe the circumstances in which a mode of trial decision is made and outline its stages.

4 Gary Fowles appears at the magistrates' court after being arrested the previous night and held in police custody for burglary. He is 25 years old and lives with his girlfriend and their 6-month-old child. They have lived together in their council flat since the birth of their child. He works on a market stall selling CDs. He takes home approximately £150 per week. His girlfriend does not work.

He has previous convictions (see below) and is currently undertaking a 150-hour community punishment order (CPO)/community order with unpaid work requirement for a previous conviction of burglary. He has an absconding conviction.

Gary was arrested coming out of a house last night carrying computer equipment worth £500. He had entered through an unlocked door. He made a full confession to the police and is anxious to be released on bail to return to his girlfriend. He is willing to comply with any conditions the magistrates may impose, but cannot offer any surety.

He has the following previous convictions:

Date:	Conviction for:	Sentence:
2 years ago	Common assault	Fine of £150
1 year ago	Taking vehicle without consent	Fine of £200
6 months ago	Burglary	CPO (unpaid work) for 150 hours
6 months ago	Absconding (missed court appearance)	Fine of £20

Questions:
(a) Might the police or CPS object to bail?
(b) On what grounds might they object?
(c) If bail were granted, what conditions might be appropriate?
(d) What do you think the magistrates should do?

Further reading

Ashworth, A (1998) *The Criminal Process* (2nd edn), Clarendon Press: Oxford
Auld Report (2001) *Review into the Workings of the Criminal Courts in England and Wales*, Home Office: London
Sprack, J (2004) *Emmins on Criminal Procedure* (10th edn), Blackstone Press: London

CHAPTER 10

The trial and establishing guilt

Main topics covered

➤ Adversarial justice: the burden and standard of proof

➤ Role of the trial

➤ Juries

➤ Rights of the defendant in court

➤ Evidence

➤ Appeals system

➤ Criminal Cases Review Commission

INTRODUCTION

All aspects of the trial and adversarial justice in England and Wales have been subject to a very comprehensive and challenging review by Lord Justice Auld in a report published in 2001. Many of the report's recommendations have been incorporated into the reforms of the Criminal Justice Act 2003, which will have an impact across all aspects of the criminal justice system – for example, the role of judges and the laws of evidence – and will when implemented result in a culture shift for criminal justice in England and Wales. His report was detailed, comprehensive and is a compelling commentary on the issues facing the adversarial system at the beginning of the twenty-first century.

The criminal court was the primary focus of the Auld review and is the focus of this chapter. Court proceedings are the most public manifestation of the criminal justice process, the arena in which justice is very literally 'seen to be done'. This is especially true of the trial, generally assumed to be the stage in the process where the defendant has his or her day in court and the opportunity to assert innocence. The trial is a vital part of the adversarial system and, as we have seen, the right to trial by one's peers, represented by the jury system, is seen as a fundamental protection for the defendant against the power of the state. In the trial the defendant is presumed innocent until proved guilty beyond reasonable doubt. Rules of evidence, which seem technical and abstract, embody the principles of due process, and are there to protect the defendant from unfair or unsuitable allegations. In addition, the trial plays a key role in denunciation and just deserts – it is the arena in which society expresses its moral disapproval of wrongdoing and it is important in the interests of justice that accused persons who say they are innocent are tried in public.

As we have seen, however, only a minority of defendants exercise their right to a full trial, with many being diverted before prosecution and yet more pleading guilty. Indeed only a minority of defendants contest their guilt. Nevertheless, the court system is still subject to delays and is very costly. The system operates with only a small number of defendants pleading not guilty and going to a full trial. Is there a pressure on defendants and officials in the system to speed up the process? Are defendants pressurised into pleading guilty? Are defendants aware of their rights and of the protection offered to them by rules of evidence? One commentator from the United States of America has argued that the pressures of crime control and cost-effectiveness may lead to what is in essence a presumption of guilt, whereby defendants are processed through the system like cars on an assembly line (Blumberg 1967).

It is sometimes suggested that the adversarial system is too concerned with 'winning or losing' and not sufficiently concerned with truth and justice but in winning the 'game'. These metaphors of 'adversarial dialectics' are most pronounced as the protagonists manoeuvre to gain advantage over their opponents in terms of facts that they want the jury not to hear, and through the tactical deployment of the procedural rules of evidence. In the meantime victims, witnesses, jurors and public look on with astonishment as natural justice and common sense are apparently excluded as the game rules are manipulated. This criticism was taken seriously in Lord Justice Auld's *Review of the Courts in England and Wales* (2001), and his recommendations sought ways to restore public confidence in the trial.

Although so few defendants exercise their right to a trial, whether in the magistrates' court or the Crown Court, it is nonetheless regarded as the epitome of the adversarial process. This chapter will begin by looking in more depth at the role and function of the trial and at its participants. In criminal courts in England and Wales the guilt of the defendant is in most cases determined by representatives of the public: lay magistrates or the jury. In Chapter 9 we looked at the role and function of magistrates in summary trials and that of judges in the Crown Court. In this chapter we will look at the role of prosecution and defence in the trial, and we will outline the various arguments for and against the retention of the jury in the Crown Court. We will then examine the rules of evidence and procedure, which aim to ensure that defendants are dealt with fairly. As we have seen in previous chapters, however, the practical impact of all rules and procedures is affected by informal processes and working cultures. These will be explored before finally considering the implication for concepts of justice of the idea of plea and sentence negotiation – another topic which clearly illustrates the problems of balancing the *due process* and *just deserts* models of criminal justice with those of *bureaucratic efficiency* and *crime control* (four of the eight models of criminal justice introduced in Chapter 1).

10.1 ADVERSARIAL JUSTICE: THE BURDEN AND STANDARD OF PROOF

In England and Wales, the trial, indeed the criminal justice system as a whole, is based on what is called an adversarial approach. This describes not only the format and structure of a trial, but the role of the trial itself. The adversarial approach can be contrasted with legal systems in most European jurisdictions which have a more inquisitorial approach. In the latter the court enquires into the circumstances of an allegation in order to find the truth of what happened. An adversarial (or accusatorial) approach is based on accusation and challenge. Someone – the prosecutor in a criminal case, claimant in a civil – makes a claim or accusation which they then have to try to prove within the rules and procedures of the particular court. The opponent can deny or challenge the claim or can wait to see if the claim is sufficiently established. In an adversarial system, the court does not enquire into the truth of what happened but asks whether the prosecution has proved the allegation. This itself raises the following questions:

- What exactly has to be proved?
- Who has to prove it?
- To what extent must the allegation be proved?
- Who decides whether proof has been achieved: in other words who needs to be persuaded?
- What information can be placed before a court to prove the case?

These questions raise fundamental issues about the conduct and purpose of the criminal trial, but none is more fundamental to the concept of the adversarial procedure than the questions relating to the burden and standard of proof. The burden of proof is concerned with answering who has to prove the case, and the standard with answering 'to what extent'. In England and Wales the burden of proof lies with the prosecution and the standard of proof required is that the case must be proved beyond reasonable doubt. This means that the triers of fact – magistrates in the magistrates' court, the jury in the Crown Court – must be satisfied of the guilt of the defendant to that standard. Although the precise formulation of the standard may be varied by, for instance, the use of the phrase 'satisfied so you are sure', the famous time-honoured formulation 'beyond reasonable doubt' is still that most favoured in the courts. The rules concerning the burden and standard of proof are the most significant of all rules of evidence.

These two concepts must be examined closely as they underpin any criminal trial and set the parameters for determination of guilt. The phrase 'burden of proof' indicates where the onus of proving a case lies. In a criminal case, this burden lies with the prosecution. The only exceptions are where the defendant is seeking to rely on insanity as a defence, or where a statute states or implies that the burden is on the defendant. The fact that the prosecution has to prove its case – and every element of it – is reflected throughout the trial process. The defendant is 'innocent until proved guilty' is the popular statement of the rule and the defendant's right to remain silent during and before the trial is a natural concomitant of it.

However, certain statutes explicitly place the burden of proof on the defendant. Perhaps the clearest example of this is where someone is charged with not having a licence – for example, a driving or shotgun licence. The relevant statutes place the burden of proof to disprove the allegation on the defendant, who must show the court that he or she did have a licence. The rationale for this is that it is a matter specifically within the defendant's own knowledge, and easier to prove than disprove a situation. The fact that the burden is on the prosecution means that the defendant need, in principle, do nothing and wait to see if the case is made out against him or her. The role of the trial is to establish whether the case has been successfully proved.

10.2 ROLE OF THE TRIAL

A Crown Court trial has some of the appearance of a theatrical performance with costumes, ceremony, dramatic setting and seating for an audience. These dramatic qualities are also evident in the cross-examination of witnesses to see who will play their part well, and the speeches of counsel to win the sympathy of the jury. They play out their roles in line with the adversarial principles of the trial. In the Crown Court the prosecution and defence counsel present their arguments before a judge whose role is to ensure a fair trial, and the jury, who must decide on the guilt, or not, of the defendant. The real life drama of the trial lies in its public examination of and formal adjudication upon matters of human weakness and wickedness.

At a more prosaic level the trial seeks to establish the guilt, or otherwise, of the accused. Whether a trial takes place in the magistrates' court or the Crown Court, the key issues are the same and relate to the principle of the presumption of innocence and the application of the adversarial approach to justice. The rules are largely the same although differences do arise to take account of the different participants. In a summary trial the magistrates determine the facts, including guilt or innocence, apply the law and in most cases will determine sentence. In a Crown Court the jury determine the facts while the judge alone is concerned with sentence.

At the trial stage a presumption is made that the defendant is innocent, and it is the duty of the prosecution to try to establish guilt: the trial is based on the principle that the burden of proof is on the prosecution. The prosecution must provide evidence to establish the defendant's guilt 'beyond reasonable doubt'. If the jury or magistrates suspect a person has committed a crime, they should not convict unless convinced that the evidence clearly demonstrates guilt beyond reasonable doubt. It was seen earlier that in an adversarial system a trial does not set out to establish directly the truth of what took place or enquire into its causes but rather whether there is sufficient evidence to establish whether a person (the accused) is guilty of the offence. Hence, the trial is the quality control mechanism to try to ensure that only the demonstrably guilty are convicted and punished. Of course, in the end this is a matter of human judgment and it does not guarantee that the jury or magistrates will not make mistakes, but the legal principle influencing the procedure of the trial is that a person is innocent unless and until proved guilty by a verdict of the court. If acquitted, does that mean the defendant is – in reality – innocent?

As pointed out by Lord Donaldson, Master of the Rolls from 1982 to 1992, this does not follow. In a letter to *The Times* he wrote:

A 'guilty' verdict means that in the view of the jury the accused undoubtedly committed the offence. It is not only the innocent who are entitled to a 'not guilty' verdict. They are joined and, in my experience, are heavily outnumbered by the almost certainly guilty. This is as it should be because, as every law student is taught, it is far better that ten guilty men go free than that one innocent man be convicted.

(*The Times*, 19 August 1994: 17)

Thus jury members might well suspect from what they have heard that the person has committed a crime but they cannot be certain beyond reasonable doubt. They must therefore find the accused not guilty. Everyone is innocent until proved guilty in legal doctrine but this does not always reflect commonsense notions of responsibility for a crime. In Scotland, besides guilty and not guilty there is a third possible verdict of 'not proven'. A 'not proven' decision by a jury does not result in any punishment and means the prosecution may not reopen the case, but it might more accurately reflect the opinion of the jury on the evidence.

Rules of procedure and evidence have developed to try to ensure that only the guilty are convicted, and they take account of and reflect our adversarial system. Some rules seek to prevent the jury being misled or unfairly prejudiced by information which is not strictly relevant to the question of whether the defendant committed the offence in question. Thus rumour, gossip about the defendant or facts about the defendant's previous criminal behaviour is not normally allowed as evidence. Anyone who has been involved in the case or who knows witnesses or the defendant can therefore not sit on a jury. Other rules reflect our increasing understanding about human memory and observation and therefore limit or prevent the admission of certain types of evidence. In criminal cases it has for long been recognised that there is a need to limit the extent to which defendants' confessions can be used in evidence against them. Out-of-court confessions are in principle admissible – why would a defendant say something against his or her own interests unless it was true? Rules are necessary, however, to protect those who might have been induced or pressured by the police into making confessions. Section 76 of PACE provides criteria which must be met before a confession can be adduced in evidence. Confessions obtained as a result of pressure by the police will be ruled as inadmissible.

Strict rules of procedure also determine the order the proceedings should follow and determine how and when evidence can be presented and challenged. This means that trials are formal proceedings which use legal rather than everyday language, which can often be confusing for the lay participant or observer. This, however, ensures that the proceedings are regulated and that only appropriate and useful evidence is brought to the court. It also ensures that the defence has the opportunity to challenge evidence and witnesses in a systematic way.

Table 10.1 shows the number of cases resolved by the Crown Court. As seen in Chapter 9, most defendants, having reached Crown Court, enter a plea of guilty (58,624, or 73 per cent of the 79,796 cases that go to trial). Cases not proceeded with account for some 7 per cent of the total. Cases are not proceeded with for a variety of reasons – it was seen in Chapter 6, for example, that the CPS has a continuing

Table 10.1 Crown Court results 2002/3

Completed case results	Numbers	%
Guilty pleas	58,624	61
Conviction after trial	13,099	14
Acquittals after trial	6,573	7
Judge directed acquittals	1,500	2
Cases not proceeded with	13,440	14
Bind overs	1,231	2
Other disposals	1,766	2
Total	**96,233**	**100**

Source: Compiled from CPS *Annual Report 2002/3*: 30–31. Percentages are rounded to whole numbers

duty to review the case. Cases are not proceeded with for the following reasons. A defendant may already have been dealt with by the Crown Court for other offences, or it may be found that the defendant has a serious medical condition. In other cases, witnesses may fail to attend to give evidence, or the CPS may feel that the evidence is not sufficient to proceed. In these latter cases, no evidence is offered by the CPS and the judge will order a formal verdict of not guilty. The figure of cases not proceeded with has increased as a result of the 'sending' procedure introduced by the Crime and Disorder Act 1998 – committal proceedings are no longer used for indictable only offences. Under this procedure cases which can be tried only at the Crown Court are sent immediately from the magistrates' court: the first opportunity for review is therefore after the case has already arrived at the Crown Court. Thus it can be seen that changes in one part of the criminal justice system have impact in other areas. In Table 10.1 the numbers of 'other disposals' refer to situations where defendants fail to appear for trial, have died, or have been found unfit to plead as a result of mental illness. Bind-overs refer to cases where, without trial, the defendant is bound over to keep the peace.

A prosecutor in a magistrates' court will usually be employed by the CPS, or other prosecuting authority. In trials this will be a legally qualified employee, although 'lay presenters' or 'designated caseworkers' employed by the CPS may now appear in less complex matters. The introduction of non-professional presenters was made possible by the Courts and Legal Services Act 1990 and they can deal with cases which:

- are summary only, or are TEW cases suitable for summary trial,
- involve only adults, and
- the accused has pleaded guilty, or
- there has been an admission of guilt and there is no dispute as to the facts.

In a Crown Court trial the CPS will usually be represented by a barrister it has instructed. The duty of prosecutors is to present the evidence fairly, and to seek a conviction on the most serious offence warranted by the evidence. Their role is not to seek a conviction at all costs: they should prosecute not persecute. As seen in

Chapter 7, the Code for Crown Prosecutors also indicates that the prosecution must assess and balance all the arguments for and against prosecution in the particular case in accordance with the Code for Crown Prosecutors. Lawyers are bound by codes of conduct, which provide that they must never knowingly mislead the courts. Barristers and solicitors are deemed to be officers of the court, and must assist the court in the administration of justice. Although these general rules apply equally to the defence, the prosecution is charged, in furtherance of the concept of fairness, to disclose information that might be of assistance to the defence. This includes details of previous convictions of prosecution witnesses, and unused witness statements. Judith Ward's conviction for terrorist offences was overturned by the Court of Appeal in June 1992. In this case witness statements obtained by the prosecution which undermined its case had not been made available to the defence. The Court of Appeal strongly underlined the principle that the defence is entitled not only to information that the prosecution intends to use in the trial but also to any information collected by the police in the process of investigating a case which may assist the defence. The principle of prosecution disclosure was criticised in some quarters as giving the defence undue advantage. The Criminal Procedure and Investigations Act 1996 introduced a comprehensive regime of disclosure of evidence for both the prosecution and, in the Crown Court, the defence, so that defendants are properly able to meet the case against them, and the prosecution is not taken by surprise by an 'ambush' defence in the midst of a trial (i.e. those entered at the last minute, which make it difficult for the prosecution to check or investigate).

The lawyers dealing with the defence case will include a solicitor who is instructed directly by the defendant, will take initial instructions, and may represent the defendant in the magistrates' court. If the trial takes place in the Crown Court, the lawyer appearing there will usually be a barrister, although increasingly solicitors have 'higher rights of audience'. The role of the defence lawyer is influenced by the fact that the prosecution must prove the case, and that – strictly – the defence need do nothing. However, as a result of changes to the law introduced by the Criminal Justice and Public Order Act 1994 and the Criminal Procedure and Investigations Act 1996, there are grave dangers to some defendants who do not state their account or give an explanation. This is because the court may be able to draw an 'adverse inference' from the fact that a defendant does not give evidence – that is, make assumptions about the reasons why the defendant has not given an explanation.

Defence counsel must represent the defendant fearlessly, without regard to his or her own view of the case or his or her own interests. This latter point is reflected in the so-called cab-rank principle, which demands that a barrister must always represent a client when asked, provided the barrister is not otherwise engaged, they practice in the relevant court and is offered a suitable fee. This means that defendants with unpopular beliefs and those accused of even the most unpleasant crimes will be represented.

10.3 JURIES

In the Crown Court, the body charged with determining guilt or not is the jury. Defended by some as the bastion of democracy, castigated by others as an unwieldy anachronism that allows miscarriages of justice to take place, the jury has been part of the criminal justice system in one form or another since the twelfth century. Juries are currently composed of 12 men and women drawn from the register of electors for the area in which the trial is to take place. The qualification for jury service is now laid down in the Juries Act 1974 as amended by the Criminal Justice Act 2003. This means that anyone who is:

- between the ages of 18 and 70,
- ordinarily resident in the United Kingdom for at least 5 years since the age of 13,
- not mentally disordered,
- not disqualified,

is eligible to serve on a jury. Disqualified categories of persons include anyone who has received a custodial sentence of more than 5 years or a life sentence, or a community order or imprisonment within the last 10 years or is currently on bail. Prior to the Criminal Justice Act 2003 members of the legal profession were ineligible for jury service, on the basis that they had specialist knowledge which might affect or overly influence other jury members. This ineligibility (together with that of certain other groups) has now been removed to make juries more representative of the population. The principle suggested by the Auld review (Auld 2001) was that although certain disqualifications on the basis of criminal convictions or mental incapacity should continue, no one should be ineligible or excusable as of right. It is possible to seek excusal or deferral of jury service at the discretion of the Jury Summoning Bureau to take account of people's individual commitments.

The Jury Central Summoning Bureau was established in 2001 to coordinate and improve efficiency in calling jurors for jury service. They randomly select jurors electronically from the electoral roll, and also check that the individual does not have a criminal record. The group summonsed form the jury panel, from which 12 are selected. Selection is done in the court of trial by the random selection of names. The 12 selected will then try the case unless any of them are challenged by the prosecution or defence or asked to 'stand by' for the prosecution. This may be done if a juror is known to someone involved in the case or appears unable to understand the proceedings, by virtue of mental disability or language difficulties. Jurors who may be biased can be challenged also, but, as there is no normal power of jury vetting, by either side, it is unlikely that prejudices would be known. There is no power to create specifically a racial or gender balance, or indeed imbalance, on a jury, other than by the random selection process itself. There is a limited power of jury checking in cases involving national security, terrorism, or where there is reason to believe that disqualified persons are present on the panel.

Once jurors have been called and not challenged, they take the jury oath and a place in the jury box. The complete jury is then charged with returning a verdict on the charge or charges in the indictment. A jury is of course only required when the defendant pleads not guilty, so a plea is taken before the empanelling of the jury.

Once the jury is sworn in the trial can begin. The randomness of the jury selection process is often fiercely defended as its greatest strength. In principle, this ensures that no one grouping of opinion can dominate the outcome, and thus limits the ability of outside individuals or bodies to affect decisions. However, by definition this means that a randomly selected jury could all belong to one sex, one political party, one religion or one race.

In a criminal trial the function of the jury is to determine the facts of the case, including the most significant fact – whether the defendant is guilty of the charge on the basis of the evidence. The jury members will be told by the judge that it is their duty to seek to arrive at a unanimous verdict. Majority verdicts have been possible since 1967, but are acceptable only when the jury has been deliberating for a long period (at least 2 hours in straightforward cases; longer if the issues are complex) and has been directed by the judge that a majority verdict (a verdict of at least 10) is acceptable. The judge will stress, however, that although he or she is prepared to accept a majority view, the jurors should still strive to achieve unanimity. When a majority verdict of guilty is accepted, the foreman is asked to announce the number comprising the majority and minority (10:2 or 11:1). When the verdict is not guilty, no information is sought about the distribution of views among the jury. In Scotland the jury consists of 15 people and a simple majority verdict is acceptable.

In England and Wales if at least 10 of the jury members are unable to agree and there seems no prospect of agreement the judge will discharge the jury from giving a verdict. If the defendant has been convicted on other matters, the charge may be allowed to lie on the file or the prosecution may decide not to proceed. Normally, however, the defendant will be retried at a later date by a different jury. The judge may or may not be the same.

Proceedings within the jury room are entirely privileged which means that conduct in the jury room cannot be investigated nor should it be revealed to others (Contempt of Court Act 1981). Jurors are forbidden to discuss the case or their deliberations with anyone else, for fear of distorting the trial process. If they do they may be charged as being in contempt of court. The Royal Commission on Criminal Justice 1993, however, recommended that the Contempt of Court Act 1981 be amended so that properly authorised research can be carried out into the way juries reach their verdicts. This suggestion was repeated in the Auld Review of the Criminal Courts (Auld 2001) but as yet no changes in the law have resulted. The secrecy of jury deliberations also has the result that alleged irregularities in the jury's discussions cannot be a ground for appeal. This principle was recently re-affirmed in the case of *R v Connor and Mirza* in 2004 in which a juror complained that a verdict had been influenced by racism. The House of Lords reaffirmed that it was not possible to look at what goes on in a jury room unless all jurors agreed they had abrogated their functions by, for example, deciding their verdict on the toss of a coin. The reason for secrecy is to protect the jurors from retaliation and from interference. The British tradition of juries not giving reasoned answers as to why they convicted or acquitted an accused stands in contrast to the Human Rights Act 1998, which has made transparency and reasoned decisions an aspect of a fair trial.

Misconduct by the jury or a jury member outside the confines of the jury room can, however, be a ground for appeal. If the problem is discovered during the trial, it can be a reason for the judge to discharge the juror, or the whole jury. An example of where this might happen is when information inadvertently falls into the jury's hands about previous convictions of the defendant, where such matters were not admissible in the trial.

Table 10.1 shows the outcome of cases heard in the Crown Court, in terms of the number of guilty pleas, convictions after trial, acquittals, and cases not proceeded with, or dealt with by the defendant being bound over to keep the peace. Over 80 per cent of all cases in the Crown Court resulted in a conviction. Table 10.1 also shows the number of defendants acquitted by the jury after full trial, and the number acquitted at the direction of the judge. These judge-directed acquittals accounted for 2 per cent of all cases in the Crown Court in 2002/3.

The use of juries has been the subject of conflicting views among lawyers, politicians and the public at large. Some of the arguments advanced in favour of and against juries are set out in Figure 10.1.

The arguments in favour of the jury involve fundamental principles developed over the centuries. The right to a trial by jury involves the concept of being tried by one's peers. It is therefore essential to this principle that jury members be chosen from a random selection of the population. In this way lay members of the public are involved in justice. Fears of oppressive laws and governments also underlie the argument that juries can affect the law itself. In so-called 'equity' verdicts juries have acquitted on the grounds that they do not think that the law is right even where the accused has quite clearly committed the act. This was apparently the situation in 1986 when Clive Ponting was prosecuted under the Official Secrets Act and acquitted by the jury despite a clear directive by the judge that he had no defence. Jurors may not wish to see the defendant receive a harsher punishment than they

Figure 10.1 Debate on the jury

Arguments for retaining the jury
- Juries represent a cross-section of the population so the accused is tried by his or her peers.
- Juries enable the public's view of the criminal justice system to be reflected.
- Juries ensure that unpopular or 'unjust' laws cannot be enforced.
- There is no acceptable alternative.
- Jury members are not 'case-hardened' and are more likely to have an open mind.
- The jury system is the cornerstone of our criminal trial process.
- Fact assessment is a commonsense matter best left to lay people.

Arguments against retaining the jury
- Juries are not representative of society as a whole.
- Juries are not able to handle complex issues.
- Juries are subject to prejudice and irrationality.
- Jurors are not treated with consideration, and are expected to perform a difficult important function in uncomfortable surroundings and without preparation.
- Juries prolong the length and therefore the cost of trials.
- Juries acquit the guilty.
- Juries convict the innocent.
- Juries are too ready to believe the prosecution evidence.
- Juries are reluctant to believe the police.
- Juries are naïve and unaware of courtroom tactics to manipulate information.

feel is deserved – juries during the 1950s, for example, often acquitted drivers accused of manslaughter. As a result of this, a new offence of causing death by reckless or dangerous driving was introduced in 1956. On the other hand, juries are costly largely because they slow down the process of justice.

In a complex society, ensuring trial by a random sample of one's peers can also raise difficult issues. Should minority groups, for example, be able to ensure that a sample of their group is on the jury? Seeking, as some have argued, a racially balanced jury necessarily militates against randomness. It is often suggested that juries, especially in cases involving a racial incident, should be racially balanced, or that trials of rape or other sexual offences should be equally composed of men and women, or even have a predominance of women. It is difficult to reconcile these views with the principles of due process – that all defendants should be tried in the same way – or with the existence of the jury at all. To seek a specially composed jury for certain cases suggests that the ordinary random jury is not able to perform its task in the required way. If that is the case, then surely the whole jury system should be reformed, and not merely in certain cases. Another problem is that some crimes have become more complex – especially frauds, where trials are lengthy and the ability of the jury to follow often complex financial evidence has been questioned. Yet frauds inevitably involve complex issues and judges themselves are not necessarily financially qualified. There is a danger that the jury has become a scapegoat for other failings in the prosecution of serious frauds (see, for example, Levi 1987). After much pressure to reduce reliance on juries the Criminal Justice Act 2003 makes provision for trial without juries in cases of serious and complex fraud and also where there is a fear of jury intimidation. The last proposal deals with concerns that juries or individual members of the jury may be threatened or pressured into verdicts.

Other arguments involve not criminal intimidation or 'jury nobbling' through bribery or intimidation but concern over whether or not juries are likely to be swayed by eloquent arguments and to produce 'perverse' verdicts. As no research on real life juries has been permitted it is difficult to produce firm evidence. The only research possible has been with either mock or shadow juries. The former consisted of a jury randomly chosen from the public who watched films of trials. Shadow juries watch the trial as a real jury and proceed to act as a jury. In general these studies found that juries did proceed in a rational manner, rarely disagreed over verdicts and that shadow juries tended to agree with the real jury (McCabe 1988). It can readily be objected that these juries were not dealing with real life cases and were knowingly participating in a research activity – both of which might affect their discussions.

Another method is to question participants in the trial about how they viewed the verdict. Here, a slightly different picture emerges. Baldwin and McConville (1979) found that out of 114 acquittals, judges expressed satisfaction in 70 and dissatisfaction in 41 cases. In many of the latter there appeared to be some reasonable explanation of the result, such as a weakness in the prosecution case. It is normally the trial judge who criticises the jury for being perverse and yet one of the main arguments for the jury is that they are there to counterbalance the judge. Thus can there ever be a perverse acquittal? Lord Devlin argued, 'perversity is just a lawyer's word for a jury which applies its own standards instead of those recommended by lawyers' (Blackstone Lecture 1978, cited in Harman and Griffith 1979).

The approach to jury composition in England and Wales is in stark contrast with that in the United States of America, where jury selection and challenging potential jurors is a recognised and extensive part of the pre-trial process, especially in cases with emotive issues, as was seen at the jury selection in the trials of O J Simpson and Louise Woodward. In these cases, shadow or test juries and jury consultants were used extensively to assess not only which jurors would be more likely to be amenable to one side or the other, but also what arguments would be likely to find favour with them.

The trial of nanny Louise Woodward in 1997 in Massachusetts for the murder of Matthew Eappen, a baby in her care, occasioned much debate about the value of juries. The US system has significant differences in such matters as jury selection, access to jurors, the roles of participants and culture of the courts, which is illustrated by the amount of access to the courtroom by the media during a trial. Nevertheless, much of the press discussion focused on factors that, although possibly extraneous to the court decision, might have affected the jurors' minds, and are equally applicable in British courts. Similarly, when local or national concern about a case is intense, it is sometimes difficult for members of juries to put out of their minds impressions of the case or the defendants gained from the press. Some have advocated the abolition of the jury, replacing the jury with lay assessors, or allowing the judge to decide not only on the law, but also on guilt and innocence. Others fear the power which would be placed in the hands of legal 'experts' were the jury to be substantially altered.

Furthermore, recent research into the perceptions of 361 jurors in six English courts as to their understanding, confidence and satisfaction of the system they participated in showed that they had a generally positive attitude to the experience and to the role of juries in the criminal justice system (Mathews *et al.* 2004). Jurors also were favourably impressed by the professionalism and courtesy of court personnel and the concern they saw demonstrated for due process. Main criticisms centred on the use of legal terminology and some lack of clarity in the presentation of evidence. Interestingly, whilst the majority (57 per cent) of those questioned recorded that a positive aspect of jury service was the greater understanding of the criminal justice system, a large proportion of those questioned listed purely personal aspects as some of the positive aspects of jury service (meeting new people 40 per cent; personal fulfilment 22 per cent; and enhancement of self-confidence 8 per cent) (Mathews *et al.* 2004: 3).

Having identified some of the participants, we will now examine the principles and procedures to be followed in the trial, which, as we have seen, are guided by the due process model, and affected by – or created for – the adversarial system in England and Wales.

10.4 RIGHTS OF THE DEFENDANT IN COURT

A person suspected, arrested, prosecuted or convicted of an offence has rights under the law at each stage of the criminal justice system. These are there to protect the suspect or defendant against the greater power of the state as embodied by the police, the courts and the prison system, and are a key feature of the due process model. As seen in Chapter 1, the most important protection for the citizen is that no official is above the law and that all officials are accountable for their actions regardless of their rank. It was also seen in Chapter 6 how laws relating to police powers seek to balance the interests of the citizen with those of efficient law enforcement. Along with this general principle established by the rule of law, the citizen has specifically defined rights at each stage of the system. Many of these arise from the key principle that the prosecution must prove beyond reasonable doubt that the accused person is guilty of a crime and that it is not the duty of the suspect to help them to prove guilt. Prosecutions can be started by the accused being arrested and charged or by the laying of an information and the issue (by the court) of a summons or arrest warrant. Many minor offences, particularly road traffic offences, are started by the summons procedure. After the police or other prosecuting authority form a provisional view that an offence has been committed they will usually (and in the case of some driving offences, must) warn the person that they may be prosecuted. A decision will then be made whether to commence proceedings or to caution the suspect informally. If the decision is made to proceed to prosecution, a document is prepared called an 'information'. This informs the relevant magistrates' court of the details of the alleged offence, the name and address of the accused and the informing officer. Provided it appears in order, the court will then issue a summons based on the allegation, and it will be served on the defendant by post. The summons, as its name suggests, summons the defendant to court at a specified date and time to answer the charge. This procedure will be replaced by the 'written charge' and 'requisition' under the Criminal Justice Act 2003. The requisition requires the attendance of the defendant at a magistrates' court.

Having been charged by the police, the suspect now becomes a defendant and is entitled to certain rights even before the case is heard. These include the following rights:

- To know the nature and details of any charges.
- The opportunity to be legally represented by a solicitor or barrister.
- An entitlement to unconditional bail except where there are reasons for not granting bail.
- If remanded in custody defendants are entitled to apply again for bail on their next appearance if their circumstances have changed.
- To jury trial in TEW cases.
- To advance disclosure of the evidence in any TEW offence.
- To see unused prosecution evidence before Crown Court trial and be notified of witnesses interviewed by the prosecution but not called. The prosecution has a general duty to give the defence information of use to them, under the Criminal Procedure and Investigations Act 1996.

Defendants have the right to a fair trial in which they are entitled to challenge any evidence or witness used in the case against them. They are also entitled to call witnesses and evidence on their own behalf to counter the accusations of the prosecution. The defendant should expect to be found not guilty unless the case has been proved beyond reasonable doubt. The defendant should be assured that the usual established procedure for trial applies to him or her. In particular, defendants have the following rights:

- To seek legal representation, and to have legal aid if the interests of justice require.

- To have the assistance of a Mackenzie friend (someone to assist them if they are unrepresented).

- To challenge jurors, if they have a good reason (i.e. 'cause').

- Not to give evidence.

- To call evidence on their own behalf.

- To cross-examine (i.e. question) witnesses against them.

- Not to have previous convictions mentioned during the trial stage except in limited and well-defined circumstances.

- To argue that the prosecution has not made out a case to answer.

For many defendants the key to their protection is the assistance of someone who understands the issues and the legal system. This section will briefly outline a defendant's rights to legal representation. Where defendants have insufficient resources to pay for their own lawyer, they are entitled, if it is in the interests of justice, to free legal assistance. The scheme which was formerly known as the Legal Aid Scheme, administered by the Legal Aid Board, was replaced under the Access to Justice Act 1999 by a 'right to representation' funded by the Criminal Defence Service, established by the Legal Services Commission. The Criminal Defence Service, which started operating on 2 April 2001, is the quality control mechanism for criminal defence work, and also the funding body.

Much defence work is undertaken through the duty solicitor scheme, which is an important way in which those accused, arrested or appearing in court can seek legal advice and representation. The duty solicitor scheme has two aspects: the police station advice scheme for suspects being interviewed, and the court scheme to assist defendants, which covers most magistrates' courts. The scheme provides financial assistance, in that legal representation or advice is provided free of charge (without any means testing). The system depends on a rota of local solicitors. At the police station, PACE provided for a 24-hour duty solicitor advice scheme for those being questioned by the police whether arrested or attending the police station voluntarily. The solicitors involved will attend calls on a rota basis and will be members of a locally appointed panel.

At court, a defendant can seek advice from the member of the duty solicitor panel in attendance that day. The solicitor can give advice on straightforward matters to enable defendants to deal with cases themselves or can represent clients in court on simple matters such as bail applications and pleas in mitigation after a guilty plea. They can also apply for an adjournment to allow the client to apply for full legal aid for more complicated matters. The court scheme does not apply to very minor incidents such as most motoring matters. Whilst it is an important right that individuals should have access to free legal representation, and this access to justice, in appropriate cases concerns have been expressed that apparently wealthy individuals before the courts have been given legal aid at the taxpayers' expense. Table 10.2 sets

Table 10.2 Costs of cases supported by Criminal Defence Service 2002/3

Type of service	Total claimed (£000)
Representation in court	296,608
Advice and assistance to those who had been charged	41,251
Advice to those who had not been charged	168,762

Source: Legal Services Commission *Annual Report 2002/3* (HMSO)

out some of the costs of cases supported by the Criminal Defence Service in the year 2002/3 when 575,526 cases were supported by court representation.

10.5 EVIDENCE

Visitors to courts are often surprised by the significance attached to, and the time taken by, matters of procedure. This may be particularly noticeable at the pre-trial stage, but may loom large also at the trial stage. Procedure can have immense significance for the outcome of a trial and, even where it does not directly affect the outcome, a knowledge of the structure and format of legal procedure is necessary to understand the context and significance of criminal proceedings. Rules of evidence, which are in part procedural and in part substantive legal rules, very often play a decisive role. The significance of procedural rules is partly practical – cases should finish within a reasonable time and impose a recognisable pattern on the trial process. Procedural rules are also affected by jurisprudential considerations, such as the need to seek justice by the even-handed application of rules. The system has its critics and currently there is much legal and public debate over whether changes in the procedure of criminal trials could remedy perceived shortcomings. The adversarial system, in which two opposing sides contest the evidence, also affects the procedure of the trial with the emphasis on the oral testimony of witnesses in court.

This procedure and its justification was examined in the Auld Report: 'Our system of trial is dominated by the principle of orality, namely that evidence as to the matters in issue should normally be given by oral testimony of witnesses in court, speaking of their own direct knowledge.' The Association of Chief Police Officers (ACPO) presented an argument to Auld that '... the "adversarial dialectic" and the "principle of orality" have been elevated to ends in themselves rather than as a means to get at the truth' (Auld 2001: 516). Thus greater weight is typically given to what is said in court by a witness under cross-examination than to a written statement or oral or videotape statement made shortly after the event. The importance of hearing from a 'live' witness also justifies the exclusion of information described as hearsay because it is a statement about what another person had said and is not subject to direct examination in court. Auld quotes from John Spencer, 'that the weakness of the principle of relying solely or mainly on oral testimony is that it requires us: "to accept two remarkable scientific propositions: first, that memory improves with time; and secondly, that stress enhances a person's powers of recall"' (Auld 2001: 548).

The focus on partisan information is also considered in Auld. He quotes from Ian Dennis:

> ... witnesses will not generally be questioned by anyone involved in the proceedings in a spirit of free impartial inquiry. Partisan, controlled questioning is the norm, and free report by the witness is the exception. This point helps to explain why some witnesses find the process of testifying at best bewildering, because they are unable to tell their story in their own way, or at worst traumatic, because of 'robust' cross-examination which may have the effect of making them feel that they themselves are on trial.
>
> (Auld 2001: 526)

Thus the Auld Report proposed that English law of criminal evidence 'should, in general, move away from technical rules of inadmissibility to trusting judicial and lay fact finders to give relevant evidence the weight it deserves' (Auld 2001: 547). In other words it should allow more information into the trial and allow the judge, magistrates and jury to decide how relevant and significant it is. This was to lead to reform: the Criminal Justice Act 2003 will change important evidential rules relating to the use that can be made of hearsay and information about previous convictions of the defendant. The details of the rules of evidence are currently governed by technical rules, which we will outline in this chapter.

The main stages in procedure will be outlined below, but it is important to note that, as indicated above, there are some differences between the magistrates' court and the Crown Court. The differences in procedure between magistrates' courts and the Crown Court reflect a functional difference: while juries are not trained in any way for their role, even lay magistrates have considerable training and, of course, regular experience on the bench.

The structure of a trial in the magistrates' court highlights the adversarial nature of the trial process, with magistrates acting as independent arbiters, not investigators involved at first hand in the proceedings. Whether the offence is only triable summarily, or a decision has been made to try a triable-either-way offence summarily, the first stage is that the charges are read to the accused, and the defendant then pleads guilty or not guilty to each charge.

Where the defendant pleads not guilty, the prosecution outlines the case and calls evidence in support of it. After the prosecution evidence has been called and challenged, if desired, by the defence, the defence will call the evidence in support of its case. This can be challenged by cross-examination on behalf of the prosecution. Cross-examination of either side is seen as the essential way of testing the truthfulness of a witness. At the end the defence will make a closing speech, putting any argument on the facts and the law to the magistrates. The prosecution may reply only on matters of law. When all the evidence has been heard, and all arguments made, the magistrates will reach a verdict.

Where a lay bench is sitting, the members will usually retire to discuss their views. Where there is a disagreement, the majority view prevails, but normally magistrates will try to come to a unanimous decision. Whether the decision is unanimous or by a majority the verdict is announced without explanation. If the verdict is guilty the accused is said to have been convicted and will then be sentenced to some form of punishment, even if it is only a token form such as an absolute or conditional discharge. If the verdict is not guilty the accused is acquitted.

When a defendant decides to enter a plea of guilty, the prosecution outlines the facts and information is provided on the background of the offender including any previous convictions. The defence can make a plea in mitigation and then the court proceeds to sentence, often after an adjournment in more serious cases to receive a pre-sentence report (PSR).

Trials in the Crown Court have a similar format to trials in the magistrates' court, but some differences reflect the presence of the jury as the fact-finding body, and of the judge as the arbiter of legal issues and procedure such as the admissibility of evidence. The most significant differences are that both prosecution and defence make closing speeches after all the evidence, and that the judge will thereafter sum up to the jury. In the summing-up the judge will direct the jury members on the law and remind them of the evidence. The jury members will then retire to consider their verdict and return to court to deliver it when they have agreed.

The format and structure of the trial process is affected by the rules of procedure. The content is affected by the rules of evidence, discussed below.

As we have seen, defendants can only be convicted on the basis of evidence. A criminal trial is founded on the presentation of admissible evidence with a view to persuading the tribunal of fact, that is the magistrates or the jury, of the soundness or otherwise of the prosecution's case. A trial determines whether or not the defendant is guilty as charged on the basis of evidence. Rules of evidence determine what must be proved, what can and cannot be used as evidence, along with who must prove the issues and to what standard. These rules will be referred to later, but it is important first to consider what is meant by the word evidence.

> **Evidence is any material which tends to persuade the court of the truth or probability of some fact asserted before it.**
>
> (Murphy 1992: 1)

Thus evidence can take many forms, and can be described in different ways, either in terms of how it is presented to the court, in terms of the legal rules applicable, or in terms of the function it fulfils. In relation to how the evidence is given in court, it can include the following:

- Oral testimony of witnesses.

- Documentary evidence in, for example, business records and witness statements, and computer print-outs.

- *Real* evidence such as exhibits of items to be displayed in court – for example, a murder weapon, fingerprints and other forensic items.

- Evidence of video and audio tapes and photographs.

As far as identifying its nature and persuasiveness, evidence is often described in the following ways:

- Eye-witness evidence from an observer of the facts.

- Evidence of alibi, indicating that the defendant could not have been at the place claimed.

- A confession from the accused, usually obtained when they are interviewed by the police.

- Character evidence about a witness's history and background.

- Opinion evidence from an expert to interpret specialist matters to the court.

- Circumstantial evidence from which inferences can be drawn about matters relevant to the case.

Circumstantial evidence can be very weighty. It refers to deductions which can reasonably be made from the circumstances. For example, if there is evidence that a person accused of murder was in the habit of wearing a distinctive item of clothing, and that such an item was found at the scene of the crime, then that is some evidence of involvement.

Evidence legally categorised as hearsay (reference to a statement made out of court) is less reliable because its truth cannot be checked in court by cross-examination; and it will not usually be admissible. Rules relating to the admissibility of evidence mean that much material is not permitted to be put before the court.

The law of evidence is concerned with the rules governing these issues. It is a body of procedural or adjectival law, in contrast with what is termed substantive law – for example, the law of crime or contract. It should not be thought that rules of evidence constitute a dry body of regulations unrelated to the social context of law – the development of evidential rules over the years has reflected social and moral concerns with the protection of the defendant, the delimitation of police powers and notions of justice as well as purely theoretical legal concepts. Fears that evidence may be unreliable or concocted have strongly influenced the development of the law of evidence – the hearsay rule in particular has developed to minimise the danger of unreliable evidence. This rule has been continuously refined, especially in relation to confessions because of concerns over methods of police interrogation. In addition, as mentioned above, many rules develop out of fears that the jury might be unfairly prejudiced against the defendant.

These rules reflect the due process model of criminal justice. Recently, crime control concerns have gained some ascendancy: the fear that the prosecution is hampered by technical rules from proving guilt has found support in the argument that even lay participants in the trial can properly and fairly examine the value or weight to be given to different types of evidence.

The Auld Report suggestion, referred to above that 'the law should in general move away from technical rules of inadmissibility to trusting judicial and lay fact finders to give relevant evidence the weight it deserves' has been reflected in some of the provisions in the Criminal Justice Act 2003 (the admissibility of hearsay evidence, subject to safeguards, and the admissibility of evidence of previous convictions in certain situations) but whether these will be seen as less technical, only time will tell.

Evidence should not be confused with proof. Evidence is the means by which some fact is proved or disproved or rendered more or less likely. Neither should be confused with truth: as we have already seen the court aims to establish guilt beyond reasonable doubt in the light of the evidence presented at the trial.

When considering evidence, three basic principles need to be considered:

- relevancy,
- admissibility, and
- weight.

The relevancy of a piece of evidence is determined largely as a matter of common sense but tempered by legal rules for the protection of defendants. Nothing can be admitted in evidence unless it is relevant to a matter before the court. But some relevant evidence may be inadmissible because of a procedural rule. Such evidence is often excluded to protect the defendant or to prevent the jury being misled. For example, previous conduct of the accused is usually deemed irrelevant to the current charge, although the rules governing this are affected by the Criminal Justice Act 2003. This means that a jury or magistrates will not normally be told about any previous convictions of the defendant – at least not unless and until the defendant is found guilty.

The weight or cogency of evidence is not normally related to its admissibility, but to its reliability or credibility – how persuasive it is likely to be. A jury or magistrates, when assessing the weight to be attached to evidence of a witness in court, may, for instance, consider whether they believed the witness, whether the witness's memory was likely to be reliable, whether the witness had a reason to fabricate the evidence or to misinterpret an incident. They are thus assessing the weight to be attached to that evidence. Similarly, where two witnesses give conflicting evidence, the jury will need to assess the weight to be attached to each witness in order to determine whether they prefer one witness to the other. Oral witnesses may often give a version which contradicts documentary evidence – the jury will need to consider whether the documentary evidence is preferable to the oral evidence, which might be affected by how well the witness can remember an event that may have involved traumatic circumstances.

As we have seen, the criminal law determines that in order to prove theft, it must be established that the defendant:

> dishonestly appropriated property belonging to another with the intention of permanently depriving that other of it.
>
> (Theft Act 1968, s. 1)

If Mrs Smith is charged with stealing a frozen chicken from a supermarket, the prosecution must prove that Mrs Smith (and not someone else) is guilty as described above. The prosecution may be able to bring evidence from a store detective that Mrs Smith was seen taking the chicken from the display and hiding it inside her coat, and leaving the supermarket without paying for it.

In the absence of a credible explanation, the prosecution, if the above evidence is believed, will be able to show an appropriation of property (the chicken) belonging to the supermarket. What of dishonesty? That can be assumed or inferred from the action: who hides a frozen chicken in their coat if they are not dishonest? What of intention to permanently deprive? Intention is one of the most difficult elements to establish – as it is known only to the defendant. But intention too can be inferred from conduct.

The criminal law defines what must be proved; the law of evidence determines how that can be done, with rules concerning the admissibility of evidence and the burden and standard of proof. Many of our rules of evidence have been developed over the years, often by the courts, to protect the defendant in a criminal trial, and especially to ensure that the jury is not misled by weak or irrelevant evidence. Whilst many support these approaches, fears have been raised in some quarters that rules such as preventing a jury from knowing about the previous convictions of a defendant allow the guilty to go free. Again the crime control and due process models come into conflict and the restriction of information in the adversarial system stands in contrast to the wider focus in knowing what happened of the inquisitorial system. The Auld Review of the Criminal Courts (Auld 2001) suggested extensive changes to two significant areas of evidence: in relation to the previous convictions (the 'bad character') of the defendant and to the hearsay rule; and significant changes to these two areas are included in the Criminal Justice Act 2003. These matters are further discussed below.

As previously mentioned, defendants are not compelled to give evidence on their own behalf. However, there are circumstances where their failure to do so, or their failure to give explanations at an early stage, can be construed against them at trial. This means that, when defendants are on trial, evidence can be given to the court that when they were arrested for an offence they failed to answer questions in any of the following matters:

- why they were at the place where and when the offence was committed;
- why they had in their possession items (such as tools that could be used in burglary, or scales usable for drug dealing) relevant to the offence in question;
- why they had in their possession substances (such as acid that might inflict property or personal damage) that could relate to the offence;
- why at the place of arrest there were items (such as drugs) relevant to the offence;
- why there were bodily marks (for example, traces of dirt gained in a burglary, or cuts gained in a fight) that could relate to the offence.

In any of the above cases, or at trial, where a defendant:

- uses an excuse that could have been mentioned when first interviewed or charged, but was not, or
- does not give evidence at all, or
- fails to conform to the disclosure provisions of the Criminal Procedure and Investigations Act 1996,

then the court (that is, the jury or magistrates) can take that into account with other evidence in deciding whether or not they find the defendant guilty. In doing so they must consider whether the defendant could or should have explained. Was there a good reason not to explain at the time? Was the defendant hiding some other, non-criminal, behaviour? Were they too ill or too frightened or too drunk to explain? Did they not know enough about the accusation? The mere fact that a solicitor advises a client not to answer questions will not of itself be sufficient reason to prevent an 'adverse inference' from being drawn.

Presentation of evidence

These are rules governing the order in which witnesses are called and evidence produced. The prosecution starts the proceedings and the defence responds, or decides not to respond to the prosecution case. After outlining the case, the prosecution calls the prosecution witnesses in the order that enables the case to be presented most coherently. The defence are then entitled to call witnesses but need not do so. If the defendant is to give evidence, he or she will appear before any other defence witnesses. Each witness will be asked questions initially by the counsel who has called them. They may then be cross-examined by the opposing side, to elicit inconsistencies or weaknesses, and may also be re-examined by the original questioner. Although, as has been stated above, evidence can be in documentary or real form, the most common type of evidence is oral evidence given in the witness box and referred to as testimony. Most of the discussion below refers to testimony. In order to appreciate the process by which evidence is advanced, we will first examine the course of evidence and consider how the trial process takes place.

In the course of producing evidence, each side must be aware of what evidence is inadmissible. Hearsay evidence and evidence relating to the bad character of the defendant are common kinds of contested evidence. These have caused public confusion and criticism and will be subject to significant amendment when the Criminal Justice Act 2003 is fully brought into operation.

The hearsay rules come into effect when a witness states in court what someone else had told them. The rules are applied when a witness refers to a statement, comment or opinion made by another person. The other person may not be available to give evidence for a variety of reasons: for example, because they have since died or become ill or could not be traced – or because they are afraid to give evidence. Alternatively, the person may not in fact exist, or may have been lying or be unreliable. But the hearsay rules also apply to where witnesses are available, but where evidence is being given of what they said, by someone else. The reason for the hearsay rule is because, unlike the person in the witness box, the originator of the statement is not available to be cross-examined on the accuracy of the statement.

In criminal cases, hearsay evidence has been usually inadmissible. An important exception relates to confession or admissions of guilt made out of court. It has long been recognised that, as confessions constitute very powerful evidence against any defendant, the desire on the part of the police to obtain this evidence may result in defendants being pressured into making confessions. There is also an awareness that some people do confess when they are in fact innocent. A series of measures are in place to avoid this: PACE provides that confessions will only be admissible if the prosecution can show that they were not obtained by oppression, or in consequence of anything said or done that would render a confession unreliable (s. 76). If the way in which the confession was obtained is called into question, the prosecution must establish beyond reasonable doubt that it was not obtained in contravention of the Act. Breaches of the Codes of Practice under PACE are often relied on in arguments based on the potential unreliability of a confession.

In the case of *R v Paris and Abdullah* in 1992, the defendants were being interviewed by the police about the murder of a prostitute in Cardiff. One defendant denied being involved over 300 times before eventually confessing. The Court of Appeal ruled that the confession should have been excluded because it was obtained by using oppressive methods. It castigated the police officers for their manner of interview and the accused's legal representative who had been present at the interviews and allowed it to continue.

Other non-confession kinds of hearsay – for example, documentary evidence and other out-of-court statements where the original speaker is not available for a reason specified in the Criminal Justice Act 2003 – will be made more easily admissible in criminal proceedings subject to certain safeguards to allow the defence to challenge them. Another controversial area of evidence is in relation to the previous convictions of the accused. On the one hand, it could be argued that the knowledge that the accused has 'done it before' is an important piece of information of which the jury should be aware in that past behaviour is a guide to current issues before the court. On the other hand, this information may well influence the jury and lead them to a conclusion that might be influenced more by prejudice than by the evidence in the case. Prior to the changes under the Criminal Justice Act 2003 the jury or magistrates did not know about such information during the trial. The jury would not know, for example, in a rape case, if the defendant has been convicted of previous rapes. This is because it was thought that knowledge of previous criminal history would unfairly prejudice the jury against the defendant. Having committed a previous offence does not necessarily mean the defendant is guilty of the present one – the law deems the previous matter irrelevant to proof of the current one.

There are currently exceptions, however, with regard to the admissibility of previous convictions. The first concerns what is known rather inaccurately as the 'similar fact' rule. This could happen in cases where, for example, previous convictions are cited because they show that the same individual was responsible for a series of offences, perhaps because they have a distinctive pattern.

The conflicting views about these matters are demonstrated by the case of *R v Kevin Johnson* in 1994. The case turned on the identity of a masked intruder who had burgled, robbed and attempted to rape a woman. The victim and her boyfriend identified the voice of the defendant on tape as that of their attacker. The trial judge allowed evidence to be given of the defendant's two previous convictions for rape. In all the three cases reference was made to the rapist's 'gentleness' – thus the judge took the view that the previous convictions for rape could be put before the jury. The Court of Appeal held that the judge had erred in allowing the information of previous convictions to be used in evidence.

The second exception is where the defendant makes his or her own character an issue by falsely stating that he or she is of 'good character'. Also, if a defendant attacks the character of a prosecution witness or a deceased victim, or gives evidence against a co-accused, he or she can be cross-examined about his or her own character, including previous convictions, but this exception arises only if the defendant actually gives evidence. This exception, embodied in the Criminal Evidence Act 1898, was enacted as part of a fundamental change in the law. Until that time, defendants were not able to give evidence in their own defence as it was felt that such evidence was so obviously biased that it was of no value. When the law was changed allowing defendants to be witnesses for the first time, they were also protected by the prohibition on questions about previous convictions, as it was felt that this would be too prejudicial. In order, however, that the defendant should not shelter too easily behind this protection, a 'tit-for-tat' rule was included whereby defendants are safe unless they try to mislead the court about themselves or to malign prosecution witnesses.

The effect of hearing about the previous convictions of the defendant is well illustrated by the case of *R v Bills* (set out in Figure 10.2) where it appears that the jury members' minds were changed after hearing the defendant's previous convictions. This led to the unusual situation – and subsequent appeal – described.

Under s 101 of the Criminal Justice Act 2003, evidence of the defendant's bad character, including previous convictions, will be admissible if any one of a series of criteria exist, including that the evidence is relevant to an important matter in

Figure 10.2 Jury's change of mind

Jury changed verdict after hearing antecedents Regina v Bills

Before Lord Justice Russell, Mr Justice Hooper
[Judgement February 17]

Although there was no fixed rule of principle or of law that once the jury had been allowed to reconsider their verdicts, it could not be considered safe for them to reconsider when they had heard evidence of the defendant's previous convictions.

The Court of Appeal, Criminal Division, so held in allowing the appeal of Adrian Mark Bills against his conviction in April 1994 at Wolverhampton Crown Court (Judge Malcolm Ward and a jury) of wounding with intent to do grievous harm, contrary to section 18 of the Offences Against the Person Act 1861, for which he was sentenced to three and a half years' imprisonment.

Mr Patrick Darby, assigned by the registrar of Criminal Appeals, for the appellant; Mr Michael H J Grey for the Crown.

LORD JUSTICE RUSSELL, giving the judgement of the court, said that the defendant had been charged with an offence of wounding with intent to cause grievous harm, contrary to section 18 of the 1861 Act, but the jury had acquitted him of that offence and had convicted him of the lesser offence of unlawful wounding, contrary to section 20 of the 1861 Act.

After the trial judge had accepted that verdict, and while the jury remained in the jury box, prosecuting counsel dealt with the defendant's previous convictions which included other of-fences of violence such as assault occasioning actual bodily harm and robbery. The jury were then discharged. What happened thereafter was unique in the experience of the court.

It appeared that immediately upon leaving court a juror spoke to the court usher and told him that the jury foreman had given the wrong verdict. The judge was informed. He decided to reconvene the jury and invited them to explain themselves. They indicated that the wrong verdict had been returned. The judge clarified the three possible verdicts and the unanimous altered verdict of guilty of the more serious offence was given and recorded.

It seemed to their Lordships that the original verdict was plain and unequivocal and they were abundantly satisfied that no adequate explanation had been put forward as to the jury's change of mind. It could not be gainsaid that the jury had heard material which they had no right to hear, namely the previous convictions of the defendant.

Wherever the truth lay, that course of action had led to a verdict which was unsafe and unsatisfactory and the appropriate course would be to reinstate the jury's original verdict of guilty of the section 20 offence and to alter the sentence to one of 30 months.

Solicitors: CPS, Midlands.

Source: The Times, 1 March 1995; © Times Newspapers Limited, 1995.

dispute between the prosecution and defence, or to correct a false impression given by the defendant. This has been a controversial change, and has been introduced after long deliberation. Again the debate has been interpreted by its critics as reflecting the conflict between the crime control and the due process model. To others, including Auld, it is a change to allow more, rather than less, information about a case to be made available to the judge, magistrates and jury based on an inclusionary presumption rather than an exclusionary one. Auld writes:

> The need and form of reform of the rule against hearsay should be approached from the fundamental standpoints that rules of evidence should facilitate rather than obstruct the search for truth and should simplify rather than complicate the trial process. Inherent in a search for truth is fairness to the defendant and his protection from wrongful conviction – but it should not be forgotten that the present rule can operate unfairly against a defendant as well as the prosecution.
>
> (Auld 2001: 560)

Although the rules of evidence may be complex, the crucial task for those charged with determining the facts, who are usually lay people, is to assess the evidence submitted. This means they must decide whether they believe the evidence, and, if so, what it tells them about the facts in issue. This may involve weighing up the reliability of witnesses: whether they could observe, interpret and remember key incidents, whether they could identify participants, whether they had a reason to lie. Where witnesses give evidence they may support each other or conflict: could one or both be mistaken? Often, direct evidence of what a witness perceived gives only half the story: it is circumstantial evidence. What inferences or deductions can be made from those circumstances? Sometimes expert witnesses will be called to assist the court on matters outside the court's knowledge. Doctors, engineers, forensic scientists or psychiatrists might be called to explain the significance of evidence to the jury or to magistrates: this might result in the fact-finders being 'blinded by science' rather than being helped to determine the facts. In 2002 acute governmental and public concern arose when expert evidence in proceedings involving children was found flawed and the conviction of Angela Channing for killing her three children was overturned. The expert evidence upon which the trial court had concluded that Mrs Channing had been suffering from Munchausen's Syndrome by proxy was discredited. The Minister for Children, Margaret Hodge, indicated after this case that over 200 cases of child deaths where parents were convicted on the now discredited approach would be reviewed. The case had far-reaching effects, not only on criminal convictions, but in cases where children deemed at risk were taken into care or adopted on the basis of the same expert approach.

10.6 APPEALS SYSTEM

There are provisions for the defendant to appeal against most of the decisions made in the court process, and against decisions such as those relating to bail and legal aid, but the most significant areas for appeal are the two decisions that most directly affect the offender: the decision to convict and the decision on sentence. The prosecution has generally only limited rights of appeal in these matters: against conviction only on a point of law, which does not affect the acquittal; and on sentence against unduly lenient sentences in a limited number of more serious cases. The Criminal Justice Act 2003 does introduce a new provision allowing retrial after an acquittal for murder. This was introduced to reflect the ability of modern science to provide new evidence even some years after an event that was not available at the original trial.

A defendant convicted after a trial in the magistrates' court can always appeal to the Crown Court against conviction and/or sentence. After a guilty plea the appeal is only against sentence. The appeal must be lodged within 21 days or any extended period granted by the Crown Court. The appeal takes the form of a fresh trial in the Crown Court, but the format is that of a summary trial, so there is no jury: the verdict is reached by the judge sitting with two lay magistrates. Their powers are to make any order that the original magistrates had power to impose. This means that a defendant can be more severely punished by the Crown Court on appeal and is a factor that may deter some appellants. Alternatively, an appeal arguing that a procedural error took place goes to the Queen's Bench Division of the High Court.

Appeals from Crown Court trials are generally made to the Court of Appeal, Criminal Division, against either sentence or conviction or both. Before a person can appeal they must obtain permission to do so. This permission can be given by the trial or sentencing judge granting a certificate that the case is fit for appeal, or by the Court of Appeal granting leave to appeal. The former is rare, except where a novel point of law is involved and both sides accept that the matter would inevitably need resolution by a higher court, and the vast majority of cases are dealt with by the Court of Appeal first as applications for leave. The court will allow an appeal against conviction only if it is felt that the conviction is unsafe (Criminal Appeal Act 1995). If the appeal is allowed, the Court may quash, that is overturn, the conviction, convict the defendant on another lesser offence or order a retrial in the Crown Court. Where the appeal is against sentence (except where the prosecution has used the special procedure to appeal against an unduly lenient sentence) the Court may not impose a more serious sentence than the original sentence appealed against. Appeals from the Court of Appeal are made to the House of Lords by either side if leave is granted, or a certificate that a point of general public importance is involved. There are limited rights for the prosecution to appeal including on points of law, and again the Criminal Justice Act 2003 will provide an important change: allowing for appeals against acquittals in certain very serious cases on the basis of fresh evidence coming to light since the original verdict.

Despite the appeal system, there are occasions when an injustice may still occur and a 'safety-net' system was set up in 1997 to provide an additional mechanism of challenging court decisions. This is the Criminal Cases Review Commission.

10.7 CRIMINAL CASES REVIEW COMMISSION (CCRC)

Under the Criminal Appeal Act 1995 an independent 11-member body was established to review suspected miscarriages of justice. This was established in response to the Report of the Runciman Commission in the aftermath of several notorious miscarriage of justice cases, including that involving the Birmingham Six. The Commission recommended the establishment of an independent body:

- to consider suspected miscarriages of justice;
- to arrange for their investigation where appropriate; and
- to refer cases to the Court of Appeal where the investigation revealed matters that ought to be considered further by the courts.

The Commission was set up and started its work on 31 March 1997 with the duties set out above and also with the power to advise the Home Secretary on the granting of Royal Pardons. By the end of February 2004 the CCRC had received in total 6,563 referrals as set out in Table 10.3, which also shows the results of the cases. Many cases were ineligible to be heard by the Court, but of those submitted to the Court of Appeal nearly 70 per cent resulted in the conviction being quashed (that is overturned).

Some of the cases dealt with were historic or infamous cases, such as those involving Derek Bentley (whose conviction for murder was quashed in 1998), Ruth Ellis (whose appeal was rejected by the Court of Appeal in 2003) or Stephen Downing (whose murder conviction was quashed in 2002); others concern less public cases but provide a mechanism for righting wrongs that the 'normal' appeal system failed. Controversy has arisen over the handling of historic cases brought by relatives seeking a pardon for someone for murder. In the case of Ruth Ellis, the Court of Appeal questioned whether such investigations were any longer in the public interest. The majority of the work of the Commission relates to cases which do not attract a huge amount of media interest and Table 10.3 relates to examples of cases where procedures – due process – may have gone wrong.

CONCLUSION

In this chapter we have outlined the stages and participants in the trial and the principles and procedures followed, consistent with the due process model of criminal justice. It is clear that while the trial is central to the due process model, judgements about what is due process and how should due process and crime control be reconciled are difficult to make, leading to the controversy over changes such as to the right to silence, and the admissibility of hearsay evidence. Due process also demands an effective way of challenging decisions which, because dependent on

Table 10.3 **Total of CCRC case reviews (to 29 February 2004)**

Total applications:	6,563
Open:	221
Actively being worked on:	425
Completed:	5,917
Heard by Court of Appeal:	174 (Results: 118 quashed; 54 upheld; 2 reserved)

Source: Criminal Cases Review Commission 2004

human judgement, will inevitably be wrong on occasion. In general, pressures for cost effectiveness may also conflict with those for crime control, just deserts and due process.

We have discussed some of the reforms proposed by the Auld report in 2001, and introduced by the Criminal Justice Act 2003. The full impact of these measures is yet to be evaluated although there is no doubt that these will constitute a major shift in the everyday business of the criminal courts and the justice system in England and Wales.

Similar conflicts arise in the next stage of the criminal justice process, at least for those found guilty: the sentencing stage.

Review questions

Write short notes on the following:

1 Does the trial in England and Wales establish the innocence of the defendant?

2 Why do rules of procedure and evidence exist?

3 What is meant by the terms 'burden' and 'standard of proof'?

4 Is there an acceptable alternative to the jury system?

5 Below are six examples of evidence presented during a criminal trial.
   (a) Classify them using the following categories of evidence:
      Character evidence
      Eye-witness identification evidence
      Expert evidence
      Alibi evidence
      Computer evidence
      Real evidence
   (b) Classify them in terms of whether they are oral, documentary or an exhibit:
      (1) Mrs Green states in the witness box that she recognised the defendant coming out of the shop where the robbery took place.
      (2) A report from a professor of mechanical engineering is presented to the court, setting out the damage to a car and explaining the likely speed of impact.
      (3) A till roll from an electronic checkout machine is presented showing there was no entry in respect of items found in Mr Brown's shopping basket.
      (4) A quantity of white powder, found in the defendant's car, is produced.
      (5) Mr White says that the defendant has worked for him for 10 years and has always been a model of probity.
      (6) Miss Scarlet states in her evidence that Rhett, the defendant accused of arson, was with her the whole of the night during which the offence is alleged to have taken place.

6 What are the arguments for and against the admission of evidence about the previous convictions of the defendant in a criminal trial? Are there different arguments dependent on the type of conviction?

Further reading

Allen, C (2004) *A Practical Guide to Evidence* (3rd edn), Cavendish Publishing: London

Ashworth, A (2003) *The Criminal Process* (3rd edn), Clarendon Press: Oxford

Auld, Lord Justice (2001) *Review into the Workings of the Criminal Courts in England and Wales*, Home Office: London

Hannibal, M and Mountford, L (2002) *The Law of Criminal and Civil Evidence*, Pearson: Harlow

Mathews, R, Hancock, L and Briggs, D (2004) 'Jurors' perception, understanding, confidence and satisfaction in the jury system: a study in six courts', Home Office Research Findings 227.

Sanders, A and Young, R (1994) *Criminal Justice*, Butterworth: London

PART D

Criminal justice process:
penal system

CHAPTER 11

Sentencing aims and process

Main topics covered

➤ Aims of sentencing

➤ Types of sentence

➤ Sentencing procedure

➤ Factors influencing sentencing decisions

➤ Structuring sentencing decisions

➤ Sentencing Advisory Panel and the Sentencing Guidelines Council

INTRODUCTION

Sentencing is a key function of the criminal justice process and brings together the objectives of protecting the public, defining public morality in practice and at the same time providing justice for defendants and victims. Reconciling these different goals in a consistent manner is a challenge to any criminal justice system. The models of criminal justice explored in previous chapters indicate some of the issues to be addressed by an examination of sentencing decisions and policy. Should sentences aim to punish or rehabilitate the individual offender or protect society from the risk posed by particular offenders? Should sentencing perform a broader role of expressing the community's condemnation of particular kinds of behaviour as the denunciation model suggests? Can or should the criminal justice process attempt to reduce crime, either by devising sentences aimed at individual offenders or at potential offenders in the general population? Can any criminal justice system reasonably aim to do all of these things or should the purpose of sentencing be more restricted? Should sentences be individually tailored to the needs of, or risks posed by, an offender, or is consistency of disposal more important? As with other aspects of the process, a balance must be sought between the often conflicting pressures of different goals.

In this chapter we will focus on sentencing decisions and the mechanisms and procedures which affect the sentencing process. We start by examining the multiple aims of sentencing which affect the choice of sentence: a choice increasingly curtailed by statutory and other considerations.

The Criminal Justice Act 1991 (CJA 1991) was the first statute which set out to provide a coherent theoretical approach to sentencing. Since then, various amendments (both minor and radical) have been introduced, culminating in the Criminal Justice Act 2003 with a different set of goals – denunciation is out and deterrence is back, and a greater role is given to the rehabilitation and incapacitation of persistent offenders.

We will look at the range and pattern of sentences given by the courts. It is unlikely that there is a jurisdiction in the world in which judges and magistrates have the choice from as wide a range of penalties. Coming to grips with the range of penalties is not easy as, since 1998, when New Labour came into power, the pace of change has been considerable with the introduction of a range of new sentences and orders and the renaming of existing ones. Thus in 2000 probation orders were renamed community rehabilitation orders, community service orders became community punishment orders and the combination order was re-branded as the community punishment and rehabilitation order. Several new disposals have been introduced: action plan order, detention and training order, drug treatment and training order, drug abstinence order, referral order and reparation order.

The Criminal Justice Act 2003 (CJA 2003) introduced fundamental changes. When implemented, all community sentences will come under the generic term of a community order, with a range of possible requirements such as curfew, electronic monitoring, supervision, unpaid work and drug treatment. The Act also makes changes to shorter custodial sentences in allowing for intermittent custody (weekend gaol) and supervision after release of criminals sentenced to under 12 months in custody.

These changes have been driven by the desire for modernisation and greater effectiveness (see the Halliday report published in 2001, *Making Punishments Work*). What the subsequent impact on crime will be is as yet unclear. What is clear is that with such a wide range of choice there will be further concern about consistency amongst sentencers.

The choice amongst so many sentences and orders gives rise to a concern about disparities; when similar crimes, committed in similar circumstances, are given different sentences. To this end, over the last 30 years of the twentieth century a number of reforms were introduced to achieve a more uniform approach amongst sentencers. Thus statutory constraints, limits, maxima, minima and criteria were added to the existing appeal process. The appellate process was enhanced by Court of Appeal guideline rulings on different types of crime and the Attorney General's right of appeal against unduly lenient sentences. Added to this has been the widespread adoption of guidelines by the magistrates. Additional bodies have been created to give guidance and promote consistency. The Sentencing Advisory Panel was established by the Crime and Disorder Act 1998 and the Sentencing Guidelines Council by the CJA 2003.

The next section will examine other less obvious influences on sentencing decisions, some of which have caused concern on the grounds of alleged bias or inconsistency. The developments referred to above have been overtly driven by desires for consistency in sentencing: a goal not easily achieved in terms of individual circumstances of cases and complex life histories of offenders but made doubly difficult in the context of political pressures to respond both to crime control issues and an escalating prison population.

11.1 AIMS OF SENTENCING

In 2002, 1.4 million offenders were sentenced by the criminal courts in England and Wales (see Table 11.1). To discover more about why all these people were sentenced in the way that they were, we need first to distinguish between the aims of sentencing, the justification for sentences and the distribution of sentences.

The *aim* of sentencing is the purpose or objective that the sentencer or policy maker is seeking to achieve. Does the sentence aim to rehabilitate, punish, or deter an individual offender or mark the seriousness of offences in some way? The *justification* for sentencing involves considering why the aims are desirable, especially where sentences aim at some beneficial consequences. The justification for sentencing policy may be that it can reduce crime, prevent private vengeance, or mark unacceptable behaviour. The *distribution* of punishment allows us to examine who is punished, and how they are – or should be – punished. Should the convicted criminal in a particular case be executed, locked away or made to pay a penalty? How long should they be locked away for? How much should they be required to pay if fined?

A sentence might involve some form of *punishment*, and a key feature distinguishing criminal from other branches of law is that it involves the possibility of the state imposing a punishment on an offender. Such punishment, however, must follow a finding of guilt in accordance with due process. This distinguishes state punishment from private vengeance. One definition of punishment in this context is provided by H L A Hart (1968).

- Punishment must involve pain or other consequences normally considered unpleasant.

- It must be for an offence against legal rules.

- It must be of an actual or supposed offender for an offence.

- It must be intentionally administered by human beings other than the offender.

- It must be imposed and administered by an authority constituted by a legal system against which the offence is committed.

Through punishment it is often hoped to achieve one or more sentencing aims, often described as theories of sentencing. Six main theories are found in most jurisdictions, although the balance between different theories varies according to the prevailing sentencing policy of any individual system, which may place a greater emphasis on one aim or on a particular combination. The six theories are retribution, incapacitation, rehabilitation, deterrence, denunciation and restitution.

These theories affect what the sentencer hopes to achieve by a sentence and what considerations should be taken into account. Thus if the aim is to rehabilitate, the needs of the offender must be considered; if to protect the community through incapacitating dangerous offenders, the risk of future danger must be calculated. If the aim is to deter, an evaluation of what will make an impact on those considering criminal acts in the future must be made; if to denounce, the moral expectation of the community must be signalled; if to seek retribution, the right balance must be found between the seriousness of the offence and the severity of the sanction.

The theories can be distinguished in terms of what they wish to achieve. Three of the objectives are sometimes described as offender-instrumental in that they aim to

Table 11.1 Offenders sentenced in 2002

	Total no. of offenders	Indictable offences	Summary offences		% of those sentenced		
			Non-motoring	Motoring	Indictable	Summary non-motoring	Summary motoring
Magistrates' court							
Absolute discharge	18,900	2,700	55,700	10,500	1	1	2
Conditional discharge	96,000	44,600	42,500	8,900	17	9	2
Fine	970,400	76,600	379,100	514,600	29	78	86
Probation/CRO	56,000	32,700	11,400	11,900	12	2	2
Supervision order	9,800	6,400	2,800	700	2	1	0
CSO/CPO	42,500	20,200	10,500	11,800	8	2	2
Attendance centre	4,000	2,300	1,600	200	1	0	0
Combination order/CPRO	12,500	5,900	2,300	4,600	2	1	1
Curfew order	5,800	3,100	1,400	1,200	1	0	0
Reparation order	5,000	2,600	2,200	200	1	1	0
Action plan order	6,100	3,600	2,200	400	1	0	0
DTTOa	3,700	3,300	100	200	1	0	0
Referral order	19,200	10,400	5,800	3,000	4	1	1
Detention and Training Order	5,200	4,000	700	500	2	0	0
YOI	9,400	5,100	1,700	2,500	2	0	2
Prison	50,300	30,100	6,600	13,600	11	1	2
Otherb	25,400	10,300	8,000	10,100	4	2	2
Total	**1,343,400**	**263,700**	**484,600**	**595,000**	**100**	**100**	**100**
Crown Court							
Absolute discharge	100	100	0	0	0	0	0
Conditional discharge	2,500	1,900	500	0	3	21	2
Fine	2,400	1,800	300	200	3	13	25
Probation	7,800	7,300	300	100	10	13	16
Supervision order	700	600	0	0	1	1	0
CSO	8,300	7,800	500	0	11	19	6
Attendance centre	0	0	0	0	0	0	0
Combination order	2,800	2,700	100	0	4	3	4
Curfew order	500	400	0	0	1	2	1
Reparation order	0	0	0	0	0	0	0
Action plan order	100	100	0	1,000	0	0	0
DTTOa	0	0	0	0	2	1	4
Detention and training order	1,600	1,600	0	0	2	0	0
YOI	1,400	1,400	100	100	2	5	8
Prison	8,000	7,800	400	200	11	17	30
Sections 90–92 PCC(S) Act 2000	36,600	35,900	n/a	n/a	49	n/a	n/a
Otherb	3,000	2,800	100	0	4	4	6
Total	**76,200**	**73,000**	**2,400**	**800**	**100**	**100**	**100**

(a) DTTO is a Drugs treatment and testing order   (b) Other includes suspended sentences

Compiled from Home Office (2003) *Criminal Statistics England and Wales 2002*: 93.

affect the future behaviour of individual offenders. Rehabilitation aims to change future behaviour through counselling, treatment and training. Deterrence aims to make the potential offender think again through the anticipation of future sanctions. Incapacitation seeks to restrain offenders physically to make it impossible for them to re-offend. However, the impact on the offender is just one aspect of sentencing, for there is another audience: the public and its desire to see criminals punished and to be protected from physical injury and loss of personal property. This is reflected in the aims of retribution, denunciation and incapacitation. Restitution seeks directly or indirectly to recompense the victim for the harm suffered.

Thus sentences may be individualised, that is based on a consideration of their impact on individual offenders. This means that the circumstances of the offender and the risk they pose must be taken into account. On the other hand, sentences may be based primarily on the seriousness of the offence in that they aim to reflect public disapproval or attempt to punish in proportion to the seriousness of the offence. In addition, it is often seen as desirable that sentences should be concerned with justice for, and fairness to, individual offenders, as implied by the due process model. Thus if different sentences are given for similar offences to offenders with similar circumstances and background, they could be seen as unjust or unfair. This is known as sentencing disparity, and is more likely to happen, according to Andrew Ashworth, when the sentencer can draw on any one or any combination of the six theories to justify a decision. Different sentencers may have different aims and different conceptions of distribution, producing little consistency of approach. Therefore, unless a priority is established and agreed, individualised sentences will lead to disparities. Ashworth argues that 'unless decisions of principle are taken on priorities among two or more sentencing aims, the resultant uncertainty would be a recipe for disparity' (von Hirsch and Ashworth 1993: 258).

Turning penal aims into sentencing policy is not, however, easy, especially as most jurisdictions attempt to combine elements of the six theories so that sentencing policy simultaneously seeks to:

> **denounce the wrongful, deter the calculating, incapacitate the incorrigible, rehabilitate the wayward, recompense the victim and punish only the culpable.**
>
> (Davies 1989: 6)

In addition, different theories may be more influential at different times and the shifting balance between them is apparent not only in England and Wales but in other jurisdictions. These shifting penal paradigms will be examined in detail in Chapter 12. It is helpful, however, when exploring the influences on sentencing aims and practice, to look at policy pronouncements on these issues. In the 1990 White Paper, *Crime, Justice and Protecting the Public*, which led to the CJA 1991, the following balance between objectives was articulated:

> The first objective for all sentences is the denunciation of and retribution for the crime. Depending on the offence and the offender, the sentence may also aim to achieve public protection, reparation and reform of the offender, preferably in the community. This approach points to sentencing policies which are more firmly based on the seriousness of the offence, and just deserts for the offender.
>
> (Home Office 1990a: 6)

Although regarding the two goals of denunciation and retribution as primary, the statement makes it clear that they are not the exclusive aims of sentencing and it also refers to public protection, reparation and reform of the offender (Home Office 1990a: 6). Note the absence of a reference to deterrence.

Subsequent reports have lost any reference to denunciation and restored deterrence as an overt aim of sentencing (cf. Halliday 2001 and Auld 2001). The White Paper *Justice for All* (Home Office 2002, para. 5.8) referred to the purpose of sentencing in the following terms: sentences should 'first and foremost protect the public, act as a punishment and ensure the punishment fits the crime, reduce crime, deter, incapacitate, reform and rehabilitate, and promote reparation'.

The CJA 2003 was the first statute to spell out in detail the multiple aims of the sentencing system. The term incapacitation is subsumed under protecting the public. The goals in relation to adult offenders (set out in s. 142(1)) are:

(a) the punishment of offenders,

(b) the reduction of crime (including its reduction by deterrence),

(c) the reform and rehabilitation of offenders,

(d) the protection of the public, and

(e) the making of reparation by offenders to persons affected by their offences.

As we see above, the objectives of sentencing can change over time, with different priorities being given by policy makers. The courts have the task of translating those objectives into sentencing disposals. There is rarely agreement among policy makers about the ideal form of sentencing. Translating sentencing objectives into a range of penalties and disposals for the courts, and providing a framework of principles to apply, is no easy task because of the multiple aims we simultaneously seek to achieve through sentencing. While philosophical, criminological and legal principles are important they are not the only considerations. The CJA 1991 introduced the concept of unit fines. This was a method of calculating fines, in cases where it was decided by the court that a financial penalty was appropriate, to give a fairly precise reflection of both the seriousness of the offence, and the means of the offender. The repeal of this provision after a very short time shows the importance of not losing either the confidence of the judiciary or the public on such matters. Even if we devise a tariff of penalties and disposals within a just deserts framework, and ignore other claims, we would still have problems as the tariff cannot be derived from the scientific calibration of seriousness of a crime or the severity of a sanction as the tariff is not a fixed currency but moves with the public mood.

The CJA 1991 was passed following a period of unparalleled consultation and planning, yet it was subject to fundamental amendments by the CJA 1993 after only 6 months of operation. Since then, further alterations to the CJA 1991 have followed in the Criminal Justice and Public Order Act 1994, the Crime (Sentences) Act 1997, the Crime and Disorder Act 1998, the Youth Justice and Criminal Evidence 1999, the Powers of Criminal Courts (Sentencing) Act 2000, and the Criminal Justice Act 2003. Sentencing policy, perhaps more than any other aspect of the criminal justice system, is constantly being re-examined and reflected upon in terms of 'Does it work?' and 'Is it credible?'

The history of sentencing policy is a history of changing emphases on the six sentencing goals which we will now examine in turn.

Retribution

As we have seen, many theories see the purpose of sentencing as to reduce crime or change offenders' behaviour or attitudes. Retributionists do not use this rationale. The purpose of retribution is to seek vengeance upon a blameworthy person because they have committed a wrongful act. While some versions of retributive theory sought to justify punishment by talk of redressing the moral balance or atonement for wrongs committed, the more straightforward versions merely state that some acts are wrong and deserve to be punished, thus punishment is an end in itself.

This theory is sometimes referred to as an 'eye-for-an-eye', but if taken literally this would require the duplication of the offence as the punishment. Thus proponents of capital punishment use the phrase 'a life for a life'. However, punishment based on the literal duplication of the crime could be seen as unethical, especially where the crime was a particularly cruel murder. It is also impractical for most other crimes. For instance, what would be the eye-for-an-eye for offences such as burglary or handling stolen goods? Even more problematic would be deciding what punishment should be given to a serial killer, a rapist or a child molester. The eye-for-an-eye is more helpful as a metaphor to suggest that there should be some balance between the wrong done by the offender and the pain inflicted on that offender in the form of a punishment, popularly expressed as 'let the punishment fit the crime'.

In a retributive approach the calculation of punishment depends on two factors: first, culpability or blameworthiness. Retributionists insist that only blameworthy offenders should be punished. Therefore, as seen in earlier chapters, children and the mentally ill are absolved of blame for their criminal conduct and need not be punished. We have also seen that a crucial element in criminal liability is not only the *actus reus* but the *mens rea*. Thus before convicting for murder, the court must establish whether the defendant is blameworthy or, as in a case of self-defence, acted in an acceptable way and is therefore not culpable of murder. Also, as we saw in Chapter 2, different defences and mitigating factors are used to absolve the defendant, or reduce the level of culpability.

Once culpability is established the retributionist will look at the seriousness of the offence to determine the deserved penalty. In this respect retributive theory refers to commensurate punishment, a concept not used so much today because it implies a notion of equivalence. The term 'proportionate sentence' is preferred because this suggests that offences and penalties can be ranged from more to less severe without any suggestion that there can be an exact measurement of equivalence. Thus what is generally referred to as a tariff of penalties is notionally arranged in order of severity. There is no assumption, however, that they are somehow equivalent to the harm done by the offender.

Incapacitation or public protection

We have already seen how considerations of public protection influence all stages of the criminal justice process. These underlie the aim of incapacitation, the purpose of which is to impose a physical restriction on offenders which makes it impossible or reduces the opportunities for them to re-offend. The most common way of incapacitating offenders is through long periods of imprisonment justified on the grounds that they prevent persistent or serious offenders from re-offending. Thus the Prevention of Crime Act 1908 introduced a new measure of preventative detention to deal with 'habitual criminals' who made a career from crime. Section 10 of the 1908 Act allowed an addition of 5–10 years' detention on top of the original sentence for the current offence. The term applied to those who were persistently leading a life of crime and had three convictions since the age of 16. The extended sentence which replaced preventative detention in the Criminal Justice Act 1967, the discretionary life sentence and the retention in the CJA 1991 of discretionary parole for offenders sentenced for over 4 years in custody were similarly justified in terms of public protection. The Crime (Sentences) Act 1997 provides minimum sentences for repeat offenders in drug trafficking and a mandatory life sentence for some serious offences.

There are other ways of incapacitating offenders. Disqualification of drivers convicted of serious motoring offences aims to stop them driving; and company directors convicted of serious fraud and other business offenders may also be incapacitated by disqualifications or by withdrawing licences which make it impossible for them to carry on in business. Offenders convicted of mistreating animals can be banned from owning them. Normally incapacitation is linked to the type of crime committed but a generally incapacitative sentence is introduced by the Crime (Sentences) Act 1997 under which a driving disqualification can be imposed for any offence. More recent 'high tech' forms of control, including electronic surveillance by the use of electronic tags and curfew orders, have an incapacitative element. The common justification for these approaches is that they prevent a future offence from being committed and thereby protect the public.

In the United States of America, public protection was the justification given for the 'three strikes and you are out' policy of incapacitation of those criminals convicted of three felonies. In 1994, in some US jurisdictions legislation was introduced to make a mandatory prison term applicable after the third similar offence – whatever the mitigation. This same incapacitative logic is to be found in the justification of the reforms found in the Crime (Sentences) Act 1997.

Incapacitation and retribution are often contrasted in terms of sentencing aims and effects. Retribution relates to punishment for the wrong done, whereas incapacitation relates to the prevention of future wrong where exceeding any notion of proportionate sentencing is justified on the grounds that the offender is a continuing risk. The contrast is often articulated as 'deservedness versus dangerousness' (von Hirsch 1986), and both ideas are given as criteria for imprisonment in the CJA 1991 and the Powers of Criminal Courts (Sentencing) Act 2000. One of the major problems with incapacitation lies in how offenders are selected for extended periods of imprisonment or other forms of incapacitation. As this involves longer and more severe sentences than would be considered appropriate by other theories, it raises issues not only of fairness, but of how accurate predictions of the risk of further offending are likely to be.

Incapacitation seems to have been uppermost in Mr Justice Butterfield's mind when he sentenced Victor Farrant for murder and attempted murder in January 1998. On passing the mandatory life sentence for murder and 18 years for the attempt, committed within weeks of being released after serving 7 years of a 12-year rape sentence, the judge said:

> This murder was so terrible and you are so dangerous that in your case the sentence of life should mean just that – you should never be released. You have devastated the lives of many people. The opportunity to do so again should not be allowed to you.
>
> (*The Independent*, 30 January 1998: 13)

Rehabilitation

We have seen in previous chapters how the rehabilitative model affects not only the sentencing process – it permeates the entire criminal justice process. As a sentencing goal, rehabilitation is concerned with the future behaviour of an offender and aims to reduce the likelihood of future re-offending. Thus the use of welfare and treatment strategies targeted at individual offenders. The justification for this is that, if successful, fewer people will be future victims of offences committed by these offenders.

In the twentieth century the emergent social sciences appeared to hold out the hope that crime could be reduced humanely. It was believed that through the application of science the causes of crime, which was seen as a kind of illness, could be diagnosed and treated. Criminals, therefore, were in need of treatment rather than punishment. Rehabilitative sentences, therefore, must consider the needs of the offender rather than issues of morality, the seriousness of the offence or criminal responsibility. Thus sentences with a rehabilitative aim may be very different from those indicated by other approaches. Rehabilitation could justify a longer sentence than the seriousness of the offence might suggest to allow for a programme of treatment to be carried out, or alternatively might suggest treatment outside institutions although this would mean less protection for the public. Rehabilitative ideals have strongly influenced penal policy in many jurisdictions and led to the development of social work and psychiatry in the penal system and of special institutions to cater for offenders considered to be in need of psychiatric help. The claims for rehabilitation are now much more modest for reasons which will be explored in Chapter 12.

Rehabilitation thus necessitates a sentencing policy that allows for the sentence to fit the individual rather than the offence. To this end, rehabilitative sentencing policies require the following:

- *Monitoring and classification.* Pre-sentence reports are required by the courts to assess needs prior to sentencing and constant monitoring is required during a sentence to establish progress.
- *Individualisation.* A flexible range of sanctions and resources should be

available so as to be able to respond to the individual needs of each offender in the hope of changing their future behaviour. Some offenders will need counselling with regard to drug dependency; others will need social skills training.

- *Indeterminacy.* If the offender has committed a sufficiently serious offence, or is deemed a danger to the public, institutional containment in prisons or hospitals might be necessary. However, rehabilitative and treatment needs mean that the length of such incarceration should be flexible, to allow for the response of the offender, now classified as an inmate, client or patient, to a treatment programme. Thus sentences may be indeterminate, where the amount of time is not fixed at the time of sentence but is dependent on the progress of treatment.

Deterrence

The object of deterrence is to reduce the likelihood of crimes being committed in the future by the threat of punishment. It is based on the assumption that offenders, fearing punishment, will refrain from criminal behaviour. Deterrent policies may be aimed at individual offenders, thus we talk of individual deterrence, or it may aim to affect the behaviour of others who may be contemplating committing a crime, known as general deterrence. Deterrence is used in everyday life – it is, for example, the theory underpinning a threat issued to encourage people to comply with rules or refrain from infringing them, and is a principle well known to most parents: 'if you do that again I will ... (threat), or you won't ... (reward)'.

Deterrence, like rehabilitation and incapacitation, aims to reduce the likelihood of an offence being committed in the future. Thus they are described as 'consequentialist' theories as the focus is on the consequences of sentencing. Deterrent theory is not concerned with issues of fairness and justice but with the question of effectiveness. Does it work? This question can be looked at theoretically and empirically.

At a theoretical level the theory makes certain assumptions. It assumes that before engaging in criminal acts criminals calculate how unpleasant a sentence might be. This involves three other assumptions: first, that crimes occur as a result of individuals exercising free will and acting out of choice; secondly, that these individuals consider the consequences of their acts and the likelihood of being caught; thirdly, that the potential criminal regards the potential sentence as undesirable.

Objections might be made that many criminal acts do not match these assumptions. In particular, the most serious crimes such as homicide are not always carried out after calculation, but result from anger, fear or a momentary loss of control. Other, and possibly most, offenders do not expect to be caught – so the likely sentence is far from their thoughts. Some serious crimes may be affected – offenders may, for example, think about the repercussions when deciding whether to use a weapon in a robbery. At the other end of the offending scale, in road traffic matters, deterrence has apparently had some effect. Sir Paul Condon, the then Metropolitan Police Commissioner, is reported as commenting that 'fatalities on stretches of roads in West London are down by one-third since the introduction of law-enforcement cameras' (Condon 1994).

Although, as we have seen, deterrence was not given much credence in the 1990 White Paper, Court of Appeal judges continued to use it to justify sentencing decisions. In May 1993 the Court of Appeal reduced a 12-months custodial sentence for Nicholas Decino to 10 months. Mr Decino had a 10-months suspended sentence for burglary and possession of drugs activated after he was convicted of theft from a telephone kiosk. The Court of Appeal thought this was sufficiently serious to justify a prison term but made it run concurrently so that the total term would be 10, not 12 months. Lord Justice Beldam explained the sentence of the court:

> ... this was the kind of offence which was capable of depriving members of the public of the use of the public telephone which, to many people, was a lifeline. Of necessity telephone boxes were left unprotected. It was a matter of public policy to deter thefts from such boxes.
>
> (Law Report, *The Times*, 10 May 1993)

Denunciation

The denunciation model stresses the role of the criminal justice system in publicly expressing society's condemnation. Thus sentences can be used to underline the community's outrage at the particular offence and crime in general. Denunciation is concerned with the impact of the sentence on the community and how this in turn affects the demarcation of the moral boundaries of society. Thus by identifying what behaviour is unacceptable, societies define themselves.

Under denunciation theory, sentencing is an act of official disapproval and social censure. It shares with retribution a focus on the morality of the act, but unlike retribution it looks beyond what should happen to the offender and examines the impact of a sentence on the community. It thus brings to centre stage issues of morality and how community perceptions of crime and punishment may conflict with those of the state and the law.

> The impact of punishment is not a private matter between offender and victim, for it also involves the community's expectations about appropriate standards of behaviour ... The criminal provides us with a living example of our moral boundaries: by our outrage we come to recognise our shared fears, rules of communal living and mutual interdependency. We collectively define what sort of people we are by denouncing the type of people we are not.
>
> (Davies 1993: 15)

Thus one of the key functions of sentencing is to portray, however impressionistically, the public's mood about unacceptable behaviour, and to represent a collective expression of right and wrong in response to offensive behaviour. Judges, in passing sentence, sketch the official portrait of public morality but the community's response to sentencing decisions provides the fine detail. Sentencing decisions are on some occasions unpopular and judicial pronouncements are criticised as too avant garde or too dated.

This can be seen in cases where sentencing decisions have become the focus of public debate about the society we live in as they draw attention to the offence committed and the response. Of course, not all sentencing decisions evoke a moral debate; many, if not most, go unnoticed. However, occasionally sentences receive considerable publicity and criticisms of their appropriateness. In more routine cases the audience for the moral drama may only be the jury, victim and witnesses or their neighbours, friends and relatives. The message they receive may be distorted by their limited understanding of criminal procedure and law. But they will form an impression of the state of public morality, which, while affecting them only directly, will influence their perception of the type of community they live in.

Everyday morality is constructed, in part, in this way. In a more individualistic and pluralistic society, the attempt to express the community's view becomes more difficult but even more important as an effort to identify commonly held expectations about how we should behave towards each other. If unacceptable behaviour is not acknowledged and assumed morality is not reinforced by the courts, it might be concluded that there is no shared definition of unacceptable behaviour. This could enhance individualistic responses to crime and break down collective expectations, thus creating unpredictability and uncertainty and undermining the basis of citizenship. It is also likely to encourage people to take action themselves against crime by, for example, acts of vigilantism. This latter point has led to recent suggestions that there is possibly a further aim of sentencing – to maintain law and order and prevent such private responses to crime.

Restitution or reparation

Increasing concern with the interests of victims has led to a growth of interest in reparation and restitution which aim to compensate the victim of crime, either specifically or symbolically, usually through a financial payment or services provided. Thus an offender can be ordered to make financial compensation to individual victims, or to symbolically pay back society or the state for the harm done. Experimental reparation schemes have involved bringing offenders and victims together to attempt not only reparation, but also conciliation. Outside the sentencing sphere, the Criminal Injuries Compensation Authority administers a government fund whereby the state rather than the offender compensates the victim for harm done by violent crime. This, however, may be more akin to a state-based insurance scheme: it is not a sentence, although it seeks to make reparation.

The potential effect of reparation is greatest perhaps with property crime and in circumstances where victims are willing to participate and offenders can make some kind of meaningful reparation. Their application is less appropriate in cases of serious violent crime, where it is unlikely that the offender can make any meaningful reparation. A symbolic form of reparation underlies some other sentencing options, as it can be argued that there is a notion of reparation in community service, in that the offender is in some way giving something back to the community.

Having looked at the theories underlying sentencing, we will now outline the main sentences available to the courts and, in general terms, ask which of the sentencing aims may be fulfilled by them.

11.2 TYPES OF SENTENCE

Four main categories of sentence – discharges, financial penalties, community orders and custodial sentences – are available to the courts. All are available to both magistrates' courts and the Crown Court but the magistrates' court has an upper limit for financial and custodial sentences. In addition, the court may bind over a defendant, defer sentence or impose a range of ancillary orders. Table 11.1 on p. 294 shows the use made of these different types of sentences by the courts in 2002.

Discharges

There are two main forms of discharge. An absolute discharge in effect means that, although the conviction is recorded, nothing will happen to the offender. A conditional discharge means that if, for the duration of the order (a specified period of up to 3 years), offenders are not found guilty of any other offence, they will receive no punishment. If, however, during the period of the discharge, they are sentenced by a court for another offence, they may be sentenced not only for the new matter, but also for the offence for which they were originally discharged. Under the Powers of Criminal Courts (Sentencing) Act 2000 (PCC(S)A 2000) a court may impose a conditional or absolute discharge where it is of the opinion it is 'inexpedient to inflict punishment'.

A discharge is thus a sentence that does not seek to punish. The main sentencing aim that would appear relevant, therefore, is denunciation – merely acknowledging that an offence has been committed – but in the circumstances it is accepted that it is unnecessary to punish. The conditional discharge also has a deterrent purpose: 'Do this again and you will be punished.' It is used in a wide variety of circumstances, but most commonly for first offenders who commit a less serious offence.

Financial penalties

A fine is the most common penalty, and is the most likely result for summary offences and many triable-either-way (TEW) offences heard in the magistrates' court. Where a case is sentenced in the magistrates' court the maximum fine is governed by the statutory maximum for that offence. Summary offences range from level one (maximum £200) to five (maximum £5,000). Most TEW offences are governed by the overall magistrates' court maximum, currently £5,000 for adult offenders. However, a few trading and environmental offences carry a penalty of up to £20,000 or £50,000. In the Crown Court fines are 'at large', which means there are no limits. Fines must be assessed in relation to the seriousness of the offence, and it has long been a principle of sentencing that the level of fine imposed on an individual should take into account the offender's means and income, and the court will vary the fine accordingly. The fine, therefore, can be accurately adjusted in terms of proportionality, and is usually thought of as a deterrent or retributive sentence. Some would urge that a fine can also have an incapacitative effect in limiting an offender's opportunities, perhaps by preventing the offender from buying alcohol when the offence is drink related.

Compensation must be considered by a court when dealing with a case that has resulted in personal injury or property damage. It can be ordered instead of, or in addition to, another order (PCC(S)A 2000). If the court fails to order compensation in such circumstances, it must state its reasons. If a compensation order is made, it means that the offender should pay a stated amount to the person harmed by the offence. A compensation order is the prime reparative disposal.

Costs are also frequently ordered against offenders and may represent a substantial part of the financial effect of a court order. Costs may be awarded against any convicted offender, but rank after compensation and fines in order of payment: if the offender's means are insufficient to meet all three, compensation to the victim takes priority.

Community penalties

Sentencing reforms have been very pronounced in the area of community penalties ranging from changes in the names of orders to adding new orders and reorganising their availability and implementation. In 2000 probation orders were renamed community rehabilitation orders, community service orders became community punishment orders and the combination order was renamed as a community punishment and rehabilitation order. In addition, many new disposals were introduced: action plan order, detention and training order, drug treatment and training order, drug abstinence order, referral order and reparation order. A fundamental reform to community penalties is introduced by the Criminal Justice Act 2003. When implemented, all community sentences will come under the generic term of a community order with a range of possible requirements such as curfew, electronic monitoring, supervision, unpaid work, drug or alcohol treatment, mental health treatment, prohibited activities, and exclusion or an attendance centre or residential requirement. For young people a youth community order can include the following elements: curfew, exclusion order, attendance centre, supervision or action plan order.

The criteria for the imposition of a community sentence were first laid down by the CJA 1991, later, as we have seen, amended by the CJA 1993. These criteria have been reaffirmed in the CJA 2003. Consequently, a community sentence can generally be only imposed if:

■ the offence or offences being dealt with are serious enough to warrant its imposition,

■ the combination of orders is suitable for the offender, and

■ the restriction on liberty of the offender is commensurate with the seriousness of offending.

An exception to the first (seriousness) criterion was introduced by the CJA 2003 to deal with persistent minor offenders. This provides that, where a person who is over 16 is before the court for sentence and has previously been fined on at least three occasions, the court can impose a community sentence if it is in the interests of justice so to do.

A pre-sentence report must be obtained before assessing whether or not the offender is suitable for an order unless the court considers it unnecessary to do so. A pre-sentence drug test may also be ordered before a community sentence is passed.

The details of each type of community sentence are now provided for in the

Criminal Justice Act 2003, and are listed in Table 11.2 together with the parameters, such as minimum and maximum length, and special criteria for their imposition. (Previous names of the order are also given where appropriate.)

What will be called an unpaid work requirement requires that a person should perform

Table 11.2 Community orders under the CJA 2003

Name of requirement	Parameters	Requirements
Unpaid work (formerly community punishment order and previously known as community service order)	Range from 40 to 300 hours to be completed within 12 months	Court must be satisfied offender suitable and may add electronic monitoring
Activity	Up to 60 days' attendance and/or activities (may include reparation to victim)	Court must be satisfied (by consultation with probation service) order feasible and may add electronic monitoring
Programme participation (as previously attached to probation/rehabilitation orders)	Would be linked to supervision order and order to comply with direction by probation service	Court must be satisfied (by consultation with probation service) order feasible and may add electronic monitoring
Prohibited activity	For specified days or period	Court must be satisfied (by consultation with probation service) order feasible; may include prohibition on having firearms; may add electronic monitoring
Curfew	2–12 hours per day for a specified period up to 6 months	Must usually add electronic monitoring
Exclusion	Up to 2 years (can be from different places for different days)	Must usually add electronic monitoring
Residence		If hostel, must be after recommendation of probation service; must consider home surroundings; may add electronic monitoring
Drug rehabilitation/ Mental health or alcohol treatment	Drugs and alcohol minimum 6 months	Court must be satisfied dependent or requires such order; may add electronic monitoring
Supervision (formerly simple community rehabilitation order, formerly probation order)	Maximum 3 years	To promote rehabilitation; may add electronic monitoring
Attendance centre	12–36 hours but only once per day for up to 3 hours	Available only for under 25s; centre must be reasonably accessible; may add electronic monitoring

unpaid work for between 40 and 300 hours under the supervision of the probation service. This requirement, originally introduced as a community service order and subsequently as a community punishment order, satisfies simultaneously many penal objectives. It includes a symbolic element of reparation, if not to the individual victim, then at least to the community. It also involves denunciation, particularly if the imposition of the sentence is followed by a visible performance of the work, and the restriction on liberty is intended to have a punitive impact so as to deter and punish offenders. Others point to the rehabilitative effect of doing valuable work for the community. Other orders may concentrate solely on rehabilitation such as the supervision order (formerly probation or community rehabilitation order) or on a mixture of objectives.

Electronic monitoring is a relatively new technological approach to the monitoring of community sentences and is delivered by the private sector. Following trials of curfew orders, 5-year contracts were issued to the private sector in 1999. In the first year of the contract (28 January 1999 to 31 January 2000), electronic monitoring was used in 19,642 cases. Of these, 84.5 per cent (16,589) were prisoners on Home Detention Curfew, and 13.1 per cent (2,568) were curfew orders made under the Criminal Justice Act 1991 (others account for the remaining 2.4 per cent (471)). Completion rates are estimated at between 90 and 94 per cent.

Custodial sentences

As a result of successive legislative efforts to reduce the numbers of offenders receiving prison sentences, a prison sentence (which includes the suspended sentence) may be passed only where one of the following criteria is satisfied:

- the offence is fixed by law; or
- the offence is so serious that only a custodial sentence is justified; or
- the offender has failed to consent to a requirement in a community order where consent is required or failed to comply with a pre-sentence drug test.

Until the CJA 2003 is brought into force an alternative criterion for custody exists: that the offence is one of sex or violence and only a custodial sentence is sufficient to protect the public. The new Act will amend this provision to provide that serious offences specified in the Act can be followed by life imprisonment or indeterminate imprisonment where the public needs protection. It also provides for the imposition of extended sentences for the protection of the public, for up to 5 years for specified violent offences and up to 8 years for certain sexual offences. This latter provision attempts to deal with the situation where it is the risk of harm that the order seeks to prevent (i.e. an incapacitative approach) rather than punishment for what has been done (i.e. a proportionate retributive approach).

The CJA 2003 will introduce a completely fresh approach to custodial sentences, particularly for short-term prisoners, with the introduction of intermittent custody and custody plus, as well as changing magistrates' powers to imprison. Key points are as follows:

- Magistrates will be able to impose a sentence of up to 12 months' custody for a single offence (subject, as now, to the statutory maximum).

- All sentences of up to 12 months will be either 'custody plus' or 'intermittent custody'.

- 'Custody plus' involves serving time in prison of between 2 and 13 weeks, as specified by the court, followed by a period of licence for a minimum of 26 weeks. So, if magistrates impose 12 months' imprisonment for an offence, the maximum time they can order to be served in custody is 13 weeks. Where two or more offences are sentenced together the maximum custodial period goes up to 26 weeks. The court may impose one or more specific requirements to be observed during the licence period, just as when imposing a community penalty.

- Intermittent custody will allow the serving of a prison sentence over a longer period, intermittently: typically at weekends, allowing those in work to continue with their employment. Again there is a custodial period (14–90 days) followed by a licence period (in the community) of 28–51 weeks.

There has long been the possibility of suspending prison sentences. This means that the offender has to satisfy the criteria for prison but because of 'exceptional circumstances' the sentence can be suspended. Offenders do not go to prison unless they commit an offence during the period of suspension, whereby some or all of the sentence will then be served. It has long been felt that this sentence is anomalous. It signifies, in a symbolic denunciatory model, the seriousness of the offence, but in fact 'nothing happens'. The sentence could, of course, be seen as the ultimate deterrent sentence (if you offend again, you will go to prison), but the need for additional rehabilitation or punishment of offenders falling into this category has been recognised. Thus, under the CJA 2003, short-term (28–51 weeks) custodial sentences, which would otherwise be custody plus or intermittent custody, can be suspended. Requirements may be added to a suspended sentence that the offender does unpaid work, engages in an activity, undergoes drug rehabilitation etc., thus treating the suspended prison sentence very like a community order – which, in fact, from the public and offender perspective, it is.

A life sentence is the most severe penalty available. It is a mandatory sentence for those found guilty of murder, and thus the judge has no choice. It is also a discretionary maximum sentence for those convicted of serious indictable crimes such as manslaughter, arson, rape, robbery, aggravated burglary, causing grievous bodily harm, wounding with intent, supplying class A drugs and kidnapping. Under the Firearms Act 1968 crimes of assault, theft, arson and resisting arrest carry a maximum sentence of a life sentence if the offender is carrying a gun. The Powers of Criminal Courts (Sentencing) Act 2000 introduced automatic life sentences for second serious offences such as rape or grievous bodily harm (unless exceptional circumstances applied) and automatic minimum sentences for the third offence of trafficking class A drugs (7 years) and the third offence of domestic burglary (3 years) unless it was unjust so to do.

Custodial sentences can be justified by most of the major theories of sentencing. A prison sentence can be seen as a deterrent and it is still commonplace to argue that prisons should be austere places which should not provide comforts not generally available outside. The forbidding nature of prisons also underlines society's disapproval of inmates. The essential punishment involved in imprisonment is the deprivation of a person's liberty, and thus a prison sentence can be retributive, with the length of a sentence being determined by the seriousness of the offence. Prisons also take offenders out of society and thus protect the public and, as we have seen, they are the main form of incapacitative sentence. Furthermore, as will be seen in Chapter 12, a major influence on penal policy and on the development of prison regimes throughout the twentieth century has been the belief that offenders can be rehabilitated while in prison.

Sentencers also have various ancillary orders available, including orders allowing the confiscation of the proceeds of crime, the forfeit of money or property associated with offences and the destruction of items such as weapons or drugs. Other penalties relating specifically to motoring offences are worthy of note: the imposition of penalty points and disqualification from driving. Advertising campaigns, particularly over the Christmas period, focus on the potential harm caused by driving with excess alcohol, to enhance the denunciatory effect and stress the impact of the penalty, i.e. disqualification from driving, highlighting the deterrent element of the sentence.

Enforcement of sentences

Each type of sentence brings with it particular problems in relation to dealing with the offender who fails to comply. For some sentences the approach is simple: it is an offence to escape from prison and an escaped prisoner will be given an additional sentence. Committing an offence during the currency of a conditional discharge means that the offender can be sentenced for the original offence as well as the new offence.

Community penalties and fines pose particular problems. During the period of a community penalty two problems may arise:

- failure to comply, for example, by behaving badly, failing to attend for, or doing unpaid work poorly, or not attending supervision meetings;

- committing further offences during the period covered.

The courts' approach to a breach of the terms of any community order or of the commission of further offences during the period of an order was rationalised by the CJA 1993. For failure to comply with the terms of an order the offender can be ordered to pay a fine up to £1,000 or to perform up to 60 hours of a CSO. If the offender already has a CSO, the total hours must not exceed the maximum applicable. The court may revoke the community sentence and impose a different penalty for the original offence. For offenders under 21, an attendance centre order may be made. If the offender wilfully and persistently refuses to comply with the order, this may be taken as refusing consent to it and the court can impose a custodial sentence. For the commission of a further offence the order can be revoked and the offender dealt with in some other way. The order can also be revoked and dealt with in some other way for good progress.

The Criminal Justice and Court Services Act 2000 and the CJA 2003 introduced a new procedure for failure to comply with the terms of the order and provide for a formal warning procedure for minor breaches, followed, in the event of further non-compliance, with a return to court. The court can then amend the order by increasing the requirements, impose any other sentence it could originally have given for the offence or, where the failure to comply is 'wilful and persistent', can send the offender to prison – even where the offence itself was not imprisonable.

For the commission of a further offence the order can be revoked and the offender dealt with in some other way. The order can also be revoked and dealt with in some other way for good progress.

Enforcement of fines perhaps causes the most difficulty, not least because it is the most used sentence. Much time and cost are spent chasing recalcitrant payers: some who are well able to pay but are simply avoiding payment; others who are financially inept; others who are genuinely in difficulty or who find that their finances worsen after the imposition of the fine.

In 2002 just under a million offenders (970,400) were fined in the magistrates' courts. When imposing a fine magistrates must take into account the offender's means as measured in terms of income and expenses. However, circumstances may change and the offence and the sentence may lead to a worsening of the offender's financial situation: a drink driver might not be able to get to work after disqualification, or might lose their job; a man who assaults his wife might have to find alternative accommodation; an employee who steals from an employer will usually lose their job.

If the offender cannot pay immediately, time to pay can be, and usually is, allowed. If the offender still falls behind, a number of measures to obtain payment can be used:

- attachment of earnings, where a specified sum is deducted monthly or weekly from the earnings by the employer and sent to the court;
- distress warrants, allowing a bailiff to seize goods to the value of the outstanding fine, other than clothing, bedding or tools of the person's trade;
- deduction from benefit.

Since the Crime (Sentences) Act 1997 other measures for responding to fine default have been introduced:

- curfew with electronic monitoring;
- an unpaid work requirement;
- driving disqualification of up to 12 months.

Other measures available to deal with outstanding fines include:

- overnight detention in a police station in lieu of a fine;
- remission of fines, by reducing the original fine because of subsequent hardship or new information;
- writing off of fines as an administrative act of the court;
- imprisonment where the offence for which the fine was imposed is itself punishable by imprisonment and the offender is able to pay and refuses to do so.

In 2000 the average time served in prison for fine defaulters was 7 days for males and 5 days for females (*Prison Statistics England and Wales 2000*: 30). For a fine defaulter who is imprisoned for a separate offence the fine can be disposed of by serving days in lieu of payment. This is normally served concurrently so, in effect, no extra days are served in prison.

Despite difficulties of enforcement, the fine is by and large a simply administered sentence and gains revenue. Additionally, effectiveness of fine collection is easily measurable in terms of amount and percentage successfully recovered and the time scale involved. Thus fine enforcement can be identified as a measure of performance of courts and recovery agencies and has been identified for performance improvement in magistrates' courts. In 2004 a 'blitz' on fine defaulters called 'Operation Payback' was launched in 42 Magistrates' areas. The aim was twofold: first to draw attention to the problem of fine dodgers; and, secondly, to make a concerted effort to recoup some of the £354.4 million outstanding in financial penalties at the end of 2003.

The fine is an infinitely flexible punishment – as a result it can be used in a wide variety of cases and is popular with policy makers.

Distribution of sentences

In 2002 the magistrates' courts sentenced over a million offenders (1,343,400) and the Crown Court 76,200. Table 11.1 on p. 294 shows the numbers and the percentage distribution of sentences given to offenders for indictable, summary motoring and summary non-motoring offences. In total 1,419,600 were sentenced. The table shows the range of sentences available and the frequency of their use by judges and magistrates. Magistrates gave 96,000 offenders a conditional discharge, sent 53,300 adults to prison and 9,400 younger offenders to custody in young offender institutions. The Crown Court gave 2,500 offenders a conditional discharge and sent a total of 36,600 adults to prison and 8,000 to young offender institutions. Three-quarters of all offenders left the court with a fine, which is the most often used sentence (970,400 in the magistrates' courts and 2,400 in the Crown Court).

11.3 SENTENCING PROCEDURE

Between the determination of guilt and decision on sentence there are various stages to go through, including a hearing of the mitigation the defendant may wish to offer in an attempt to reduce the severity of the sentence. Only in the most serious and the most trivial of cases will sentencing be carried out immediately after the decision on guilt. There is, as we have seen, a mandatory life sentence in cases of murder, and for many petty offences a discharge or small fine is likely and can be imposed immediately.

If the sentence follows a trial, the facts will have been presented. If there has been a guilty plea, the facts must be presented to the court by the prosecution. Occasionally there may be a dispute over the facts which affect the plea; for example the defendant may admit to an assault with fists, but deny kicking the victim. If the dispute is likely to affect the sentence, the sentencer must either sentence on the basis of the facts most favourable to the defence, or there must be what is called a 'Newton' hearing. This is like a mini-trial, where evidence is taken, but only on the specific issue involved.

The defendant may ask for offences to be taken into consideration (TIC). This means that the court takes them into consideration when sentencing, although there has been no formal conviction. This procedure is often used where a number of related offences have been committed, but the police may have been unable to prosecute them successfully – for example, where the defendant has confessed to a number of thefts from cars, or several cheque frauds. They may also form part of the plea negotiations.

There is no statutory basis for the TIC procedure, but it is recognised by the courts. Lord Goddard described the process as:

> simply a convention under which, if a court is informed that there are outstanding charges against a prisoner, the court can, if the prisoner admits the offences and asks that they should be taken into account, ... give a longer sentence than it would if it were dealing with him only on the charge mentioned in the indictment.
>
> (*R v Batchelor* [1952], 36 Cr App R 64)

The effect of having offences taken into consideration does not mean that the defendant is convicted of them. Strictly, a defendant can be charged with the offence taken into consideration, but no additional penalty can be imposed. In practice, once an offence has been taken into consideration by a court, it is not the subject of later charges.

Whether or not there are offences to be taken into consideration, the court will then need to know whether the offender has any previous convictions and whether they are in breach of any existing orders.

The defendant, personally or through an advocate, may then put forward any mitigation in respect of the offence or their own circumstances. This is known as making a plea in mitigation, and is the opportunity for the defence to put the offending behaviour into the best possible light in order to gain the lightest sentence. This is the point at which financial information may also be given to the court. Financial details are relevant not only to show why a defendant may have committed an offence, but also because the court must take the means of the offender into account when imposing a financial penalty. Apart from the details of the case, such as that the defendant only took a small part, sentence mitigation will include factors such as that the defendant pleaded guilty, especially if the guilty plea was entered early (PCC(S)A 2000, s. 152), and that they were of previous good character (i.e. have no previous convictions). Defence counsel may argue, for example, that in some way the offender was pressured into committing the offence by financial or family problems. They may argue that, while they have admitted the offence and can offer no defence, nevertheless they did not intend the harm done and the offence occurred almost by accident, with no planning or forethought. This is especially the case where the offence is one of strict liability which does not require intent, or where the offence has involved an omission to do something. Thus defendants may claim that they simply forgot to renew a licence, but had always intended to do so or that they forgot to tell the Inland Revenue about their earnings from a part-time job. Others may claim that they did not anticipate driving home after going to the pub. As seen in Chapter 2, these mitigating factors attempt to reduce the culpability of the offender and thus seek to influence the eventual sentence.

Before proceeding to sentence the court may require further information about the offender's circumstances, including their physical or mental health. In many cases before the Crown Court and in the more serious cases in magistrates' courts a pre-sentence report is required. For adults, this is provided by the probation service and its preparation typically involves an adjournment of 3 weeks. The report contains information considered relevant by the probation officer and may cover such matters as home life, medical, psychiatric details, criminal background and schooling or employment. In the report the probation officer or social worker is asked to make an assessment of the seriousness of the offence, the risk of further offending and to consider the impact on the victim, although information on victims is often not available (see Chapter 3). In addition it should consider the possible sentences and the likely impact of such sentences on the offender. Before sentencing, the judge or magistrates will hear from the convicted person's defence counsel to remind the court of any mitigating circumstance and will also consider the pre-sentence report. This double exposure of mitigation before sentence has led to the criticism that it focuses too heavily on the circumstances, background and personality of the convicted person and insufficiently on the offence.

11.4 FACTORS INFLUENCING SENTENCING DECISIONS

Many factors influence sentencers' decisions. In respect of a particular case, the judge or magistrate must consider how serious the particular offence is in relation to other similar offences and assess whether or not the offence had any particular mitigating or aggravating factors. For example, if the offence has involved harm to a particularly vulnerable group such as the elderly this would be an aggravating factor, whereas absence of direct physical harm to a victim is more likely to be seen as a mitigating factor. Additionally, as seen above, the defendant may provide information about mitigating factors. Sentencers are also likely to take into account the previous convictions and record of an offender, and the recommendations in the pre-sentence report. Influences on sentencing can be grouped under the following headings:

- case-specific factors: case facts and offender circumstances and previous record of offending
- statutory constraints
- appellate process
- judicial training, guidance and guidelines.

Case factors refer to the individual case before the courts and sentencers must always address the information provided in the case papers available to them about the offender and the circumstances of the offence. However, the response to individual case facts is determined by legislation, the appeal process and guidelines that reflect the prevailing policy on sentencing.

First, there are the statutory requirements, i.e. responses to crime that are set out in legislation. We have a mandatory life sentence in the case of murder. All offences have statutory maximum sentences, such as 14 years for burglary of a domestic dwelling, even though this maximum is rarely, if ever, used. It provides an indication, however, of Parliament's view of the seriousness of the offence and so helps to set the sentencing tariff. There are a few minimum sentences for first offences, such as the 2-year disqualification for those convicted of causing death by dangerous driving under the Road Traffic Act 1988. Offenders convicted of driving with excess alcohol will receive a minimum period of 12 months' disqualification.

The Crime (Sentences) Act 1997 introduced a mandatory minimum 7-year sentence for a third conviction for drug trafficking in class A drugs. For serious violent and serious sexual offences such as murder, manslaughter, rape or robbery with a firearm, an offender aged over 18, convicted of one of these offences for a second time, will be given a compulsory life sentence unless there are exceptional circumstances.

Statutes can provide limitations on sentencing in other ways: for example, the limitation on sentences given to young offenders of different ages (see Chapter 8). They can also limit sentencing powers by providing statutory criteria for the use of certain powers such as custody. The statutory criteria for the use of imprisonment were first set out in the CJA 1991 with respect to adults, although this had previously applied since 1982 for young persons.

Magistrates are further curtailed by legislation which limits their powers to send a person to prison and imposes maxima on the fines they can give.

Other jurisdictions use legislation to indicate more precisely the power of sentences. In California the 1976 Uniform Determinate Sentencing Act specified the prison terms that a judge could give with respect to each criminal offence. Thus at that time, although subsequently amended upwards, the sentence for rape would be 3, 4 or 5 years. The judge would choose which of these three terms to give depending on the aggravating and mitigating factors of the case. The middle term would be used in typical cases. Thus a system of presumptive, or expected, sentences was established and these sentences were determinate, that is fixed in length by statute.

In the magistrates' courts, sentencing decisions have increasingly been influenced by guidelines issued by the Magistrates' Association (see Figure 11.1). These were originally issued in the 1970s in respect of motoring offences in an effort to curb complaints of inconsistency between benches. These had some success, especially for offences which could be easily compared – thus a speeding offence on the M1 is very similar to a speeding offence on the M25. Their use, after consultation with the Justices' Clerks' Association and the Lord Chancellor's Department, was extended in 1989 to most offences dealt with in the magistrates' courts. More guidelines were issued to clarify the implementation of the CJA 1991 and reflected not only the framework of that Act but also the move towards more structured decision making, discussed in the next section of this chapter. The guidelines were re-issued in 1993 to reflect the changes in the CJA 1993 (in particular, the abolition of unit fines) and again in April 1997. Changes in the law and adjustments to the tariff were reflected in the latest edition, published as a section in a new publication, *The Magistrates' Court Bench Book*, under the auspices of the Judicial Studies Board in 2004.

As can be seen, the guidelines indicate, by means of an arrow, the likely sentence for a typical or average case of its type. They also contain a list of factors that make a 'typical offence' more or less serious. Although the guidelines inevitably lead to greater consistency, their influence can be a source of concern when sentencers feel unable to give a sentence they think to be appropriate in an individual case. The concern is that the guidelines, which are merely advisory, become the basis of rigid tariff.

The guidelines change over time. The 1993 guidelines, for example, indicated a community sentence as the likely sentence or entry point for the offence of actual bodily harm. In 1997 custody was indicated.

A major influence on sentences in the Crown Courts in England and Wales is the appeal system. In 1907 the Court of Criminal Appeal was established to promote some degree of judicial self-regulation. Renamed the Court of Appeal (Criminal Division) in 1966, this deals with appeals from the Crown Court against conviction and sentence. Most appeals are, however, against sentence. In 2002, 7,718 offenders appealed to the Court of Appeal (Criminal Division): 5,804 appealed against their sentence and 1,914 against conviction; 1,302 were successful in their appeal against sentence (Department of Constitutional Affairs, *Judicial Statistics 2002*).

Since the 1980s the Court of Appeal has issued guidance to sentencers with a series of guideline cases. These include *Bibi* in 1980 on the use of custody, *Brewster* in 1997 and *McInerney* in 2002 on burglary offences; *Roberts* in 1982 and *Billam* in 1986 on rape; *Barrick* in 1985 and *Price* in 1993 on theft. For drug dealing a number of guideline sentencing cases include *Aramah* in 1983, *Aranguren* in 1994 and *Warren and Beeley* in 1996.

The Court of Appeal sentencing guidelines play a decisive part in fixing the appropriate tariff for an offence. Guideline cases are those where the appeal court has taken the opportunity to lay down detailed guidance to assist courts in sentencing. For example, in 1986 in *Billam*, the Lord Chief Justice both made a general statement of principle – that rape should be followed by a custodial sentence – and laid down a list of aggravating features which would call for a longer sentence than the norm, which he set at 5 years. Similarly, in the case of *Barrick*, which involved theft in breach of trust (e.g. from an employer), guidelines as to the length of a custodial sentence were given in terms both of the amount stolen, and the degree of trust broken. In the case of *Aramah*, and subsequent cases, guidelines were set out in terms of street value and class of drugs imported or supplied.

While these cases are an important and influential guide for lower courts in sentencing – and indeed for defendants and those advising them as to the likely sentence in a given case – they have limitations. First, the Court of Appeal can respond only to cases brought before it: therefore no systematic approach to offences or a certain range of offence can be made. Secondly, the cases that come before the Court of Appeal have, until recently, been a result of appeals against sentence on behalf of the defence.

The prosecution has only limited rights to appeal against unduly lenient sentences by virtue of the changes made in s. 36 of the Criminal Justice Act 1988. This gave the Attorney General the right to refer to the Court of Appeal sentences that seem unduly lenient. This system of reference is not an automatic right for the prosecution to appeal routinely on sentences. It applies to sentences for those convicted of offences that are triable only on indictment, so it does not apply to TEW offences. Despite this system of reference on unduly lenient sentences, the Court of Appeal tends to be concerned with lengthy custodial terms, as defendants receiving community sentences are not likely to appeal. It is comparatively rare, therefore, for short custodial or non-custodial sentences to be considered.

Figure 11.1 Magistrates' Association Sentencing Guidelines

| Public Order Act 1986 s.3
Triable either way – see Mode of Trial Guidelines
Penalty: Level 5 and/or 6 months | **Affray** |

CONSIDER THE SERIOUSNESS OF THE OFFENCE
(INCLUDING THE IMPACT ON THE VICTIM)

IS DISCHARGE OR FINE APPROPRIATE?
IS IT SERIOUS ENOUGH FOR A COMMUNITY PENALTY?
GUIDELINE: ➜ **IS IT SO SERIOUS THAT ONLY CUSTODY IS APPROPRIATE?**
ARE YOUR SENTENCING POWERS SUFFICIENT?

THIS IS A GUIDELINE FOR A FIRST-TIME OFFENDER PLEADING NOT GUILTY

 ## CONSIDER AGGRAVATING AND MITIGATING FACTORS AND THE WEIGHT TO ATTACH TO EACH

| **for example**
Busy public place
Football related
Group action
Injuries caused
People actually put in fear
Vulnerable victim(s)
This list is not exhaustive | **for example**
Provocation
Did not start the trouble
Stopped as soon as the police arrived
This list is not exhaustive |

If racially or religiously aggravated, or offender is on bail, this offence is more serious
If offender has previous convictions, their relevance and any failure to respond to previous
sentences should be considered – they may increase the seriousness. The court should
make it clear, when passing sentence, that this was the approach adopted.

TAKE A PRELIMINARY VIEW OF SERIOUSNESS, THEN CONSIDER OFFENDER MITIGATION

for example
Age, health (physical or mental)
Co-operation with police
Evidence of genuine remorse
Voluntary compensation

CONSIDER YOUR SENTENCE

Compare it with the suggested guideline level of sentence and reconsider
your reasons carefully if you have chosen a sentence at a different level.
Consider a reduction for a timely guilty plea.

DECIDE YOUR SENTENCE
NB. COMPENSATION – Give reasons if not awarding compensation

© The Magistrates A ssociation   Issued October 2003 for implementation 1 January 2004

Figure 11.1 *(cont'd)*

Offences Against the Person Act 1861 s. 47
Triable either way – see Mode of Trial Guidelines
Penalty: Level 5 and/or 6 months

Assault –
actual bodily harm

CONSIDER THE SERIOUSNESS OF THE OFFENCE
(INCLUDING THE IMPACT ON THE VICTIM)

IS DISCHARGE OR FINE APPROPRIATE?
IS IT SERIOUS ENOUGH FOR A COMMUNITY PENALTY?
GUIDELINE: ➡ *IS IT SO SERIOUS THAT ONLY CUSTODY IS APPROPRIATE?*
ARE YOUR SENTENCING POWERS SUFFICIENT?

THIS IS A GUIDELINE FOR A FIRST-TIME OFFENDER PLEADING NOT GUILTY

 ## CONSIDER AGGRAVATING AND MITIGATING FACTORS AND THE WEIGHT TO ATTACH TO EACH

for example	**for example**
Abuse of trust (domestic setting)	Minor injury
Deliberate kicking or biting	Provocation
Extensive injuries (may be psychological)	Single blow
Headbutting	*This list is not exhaustive*
Group action	
Offender in position of authority	
On hospital/medical or school premises	
Premeditated	
Victim particularly vulnerable	
Victim serving the public	
Weapon	
This list is not exhaustive	

If offender is on bail, this offence is more serious
If offender has previous convictions, their relevance and any failure to respond to previous
sentences should be considered – they may increase the seriousness. The court should
make it clear, when passing sentence, that this was the approach adopted.

TAKE A PRELIMINARY VIEW OF SERIOUSNESS,
THEN CONSIDER OFFENDER MITIGATION

for example
Age, health (physical or mental)
Co-operation with police
Evidence of genuine remorse
Voluntary compensation

CONSIDER YOUR SENTENCE

Compare it with the suggested guideline level of sentence and reconsider
your reasons carefully if you have chosen a sentence at a different level.
Consider a reduction for a timely guilty plea.

DECIDE YOUR SENTENCE
NB. COMPENSATION – Give reasons if not awarding compensation

© The Magistrates' Association   Issued October 2003 for implementation 1 January 2004

Figure 11.1 *(cont'd)*

Theft Act 1968 s.9 Triable either way – see Mode of Trial Guidelines Penalty: Level 5 and/or 6 months	**Burglary** (dwelling)

CONSIDER THE SERIOUSNESS OF THE OFFENCE
(INCLUDING THE IMPACT ON THE VICTIM)

IS DISCHARGE OR FINE APPROPRIATE?
IS IT SERIOUS ENOUGH FOR A COMMUNITY PENALTY?
IS IT SO SERIOUS THAT ONLY CUSTODY IS APPROPRIATE?
GUIDELINE: ➤   **ARE YOUR SENTENCING POWERS SUFFICIENT?**

THIS IS A GUIDELINE FOR A FIRST-TIME OFFENDER PLEADING NOT GUILTY

 ## CONSIDER AGGRAVATING AND MITIGATING FACTORS AND THE WEIGHT TO ATTACH TO EACH

for example	for example
Force used or threatened Group enterprise High value (in economic or sentimental terms) property stolen More than minor trauma caused Professional planning/organisation/execution Significant damage or vandalism Victim injured Victim present at the time Vulnerable victim *IF ANY of the above factors are present you should commit for sentence.*	First offence of its type AND low value property stolen AND no significant damage or disturbance AND no injury or violence Minor part played Theft from attached garage Vacant property *ONLY if one or more of the above factors are present AND none of the aggravating factors listed are present should you consider NOT committing for sentence.*

If racially or religiously aggravated, or offender is on bail, this offence is more serious
If offender has previous convictions, their relevance and any failure to respond to previous sentences should be considered – they may increase the seriousness. The court should make it clear, when passing sentence, that this was the approach adopted.

TAKE A PRELIMINARY VIEW OF SERIOUSNESS, THEN CONSIDER WHETHER THE CASE SHOULD BE COMMITTED FOR SENTENCE, THEN CONSIDER OFFENDER MITIGATION

for example
Age, health (physical or mental)
Co-operation with police
Evidence of genuine remorse
Voluntary compensation

CONSIDER COMMITTAL OR YOUR SENTENCE

Compare it with the suggested guideline level of sentence and reconsider your reasons carefully if you have chosen a sentence at a different level.
Consider a reduction for a timely guilty plea.

DECIDE YOUR SENTENCE
NB. COMPENSATION – Give reasons if not awarding compensation

© The Magistrates' Association   Issued October 2003 for implementation 1 January 2004

Figure 11.1 *(cont'd)*

| Criminal Damage Act 1971 s.1
Triable either way or summarily only. Consult legal adviser
Penalty: Either way – Level 5 and/or 6 months
Summarily – Level 4 and/or 3 months | **Criminal damage** |

CONSIDER THE SERIOUSNESS OF THE OFFENCE
(INCLUDING THE IMPACT ON THE VICTIM)

GUIDELINE: ➤   *IS DISCHARGE OR FINE APPROPRIATE?*
IS IT SERIOUS ENOUGH FOR A COMMUNITY PENALTY?
IS IT SO SERIOUS THAT ONLY CUSTODY IS APPROPRIATE?
ARE YOUR SENTENCING POWERS SUFFICIENT?

THIS IS A GUIDELINE FOR A FIRST-TIME OFFENDER PLEADING NOT GUILTY

GUIDELINE FINE – STARTING POINT C

 ## CONSIDER AGGRAVATING AND MITIGATING FACTORS AND THE WEIGHT TO ATTACH TO EACH

for example	for example
Deliberate	Impulsive action
Group offence	Minor damage
Serious damage	Provocation
Targeting	*This list is not exhaustive*
Vulnerable victim	
This list is not exhaustive	

If offender is on bail, this offence is more serious
If offender has previous convictions, their relevance and any failure to respond to previous sentences should be considered – they may increase the seriousness. The court should make it clear, when passing sentence, that this was the approach adopted.

TAKE A PRELIMINARY VIEW OF SERIOUSNESS, THEN CONSIDER OFFENDER MITIGATION

for example
    Age, health (physical or mental)
    Co-operation with police
    Evidence of genuine remorse
    Voluntary compensation

CONSIDER YOUR SENTENCE

Compare it with the suggested guideline level of sentence and reconsider your reasons carefully if you have chosen a sentence at a different level. Consider a reduction for a timely guilty plea.

DECIDE YOUR SENTENCE
NB. COMPENSATION – Give reasons if not awarding compensation

© The Magistrates' Association   Issued October 2003 for implementation 1 January 2004

The Sentencing Advisory Panel (SAP) was created by the Crime and Disorder Act 1998 and was introduced to provide a means to develop a more systematic approach to sentencing guidelines. It takes a particular crime such as rape or a sentencing factor such as discounts for guilty pleas and reviews the current approach and makes recommendations to the Court of Appeal. The Court may then incorporate its views and give legal effect to the recommendations. With the introduction of the Sentencing Guidelines Council (SGC) which came into effect in April 2004, SAP will make recommendations through the SGC.

The four factors identified above are recognised constraints on sentencing decisions. As with any other discretionary process, however, informal factors also play a role. As we have seen, sentences may be directed towards different aims and many different considerations affect the decision. How, therefore, do sentencers approach individual decisions?

In a detailed review of sentencing decisions in the Court of Appeal, David Thomas identifies a twofold sentencing process. In the first, or primary, sentencing decision, judges decide on the basis of the individual case whether a 'tariff' sentence, primarily a retributive deterrent sentence, is appropriate or whether the sentence should be individualised – that is, based primarily on rehabilitative grounds (Thomas 1979). Individualised sentences may also be based on incapacitative and deterrent considerations with respect to the individual offender before the court, and will depend on an assessment of the likelihood of their re-offending and the danger they may be to the public. The secondary decision is which sentence will be imposed. Factors affecting the primary decision include both the personal characteristics of the defendant such as age, sex and previous history along with relevant personal circumstances and the seriousness of the offence. Where sentences are individualised it is extremely difficult to discern whether or not they are consistent as so many factors may affect the individual case (Thomas 1979).

Sentencers themselves may have their own individual approach, or philosophy, based on a mixture of the theories of sentencing outlined above. They may also be affected by the attitudes and opinions prevailing on their own bench.

All these influences undoubtedly contribute to the variations found throughout the country which have caused so much concern. They may also, arguably, produce disparities not only when individual offenders are compared but when groups of offenders are compared. There has been criticism, for example, about the fairness of sentencing policy in relation to women and ethnic minorities. Concerns about the treatment of both unemployed and white collar offenders raise issues of how far socio-economic status affects sentencing decisions. The next section will look briefly at these issues.

Race and sentencing

According to Home Office figures, in June 2000 19 per cent of the male prison population and 25 per cent of the female prison population were from minority ethnic groups (Home Office 2002) compared with approximately 6 per cent of such groups in the general population. The higher proportion of ethnic minorities in female prisons, in contrast to males from ethnic minorities, is explained by the higher proportion of foreign nationals (8 per cent of the male prison population and 15 per cent of the female prison population) – often imprisoned for illegally importing drugs. Information collected from magistrates' courts decisions indicated that:

> for property offences the use of custody was similar for white (14%) and black offenders (12%) but above that for Asians (9%). However for violent offences ... the use of custody was higher for black offenders (28%) than Asian (20%) and white offenders (14%). Black offenders were more likely to be sentenced to a community sentence and less likely to be fined or given a conditional discharge than white or Asian offenders.
>
> (Home Office 2002: 13)

As we have seen in respect of earlier stages in the process, many other factors may account for this over-representation, indeed earlier stages of the process may affect sentencing outcomes. The legal and procedural factors which affect sentencing may account for many of the differences. Thus sentences are affected by the nature of the offence, the characteristics of individual offenders and whether or not defendants have pleaded guilty. We have already seen, for example, that more black offenders elect Crown Court trial and plead not guilty. This means that if convicted they would receive sentences that would not include a discount given for a guilty plea.

A Home Office research study of sentencing (Flood-Page and Mackie 1998: 116) highlights one of the difficulties of research into difference of sentencing patterns for racial groups:

> ... it needs to be borne in mind that the fairly crude ethnic breakdowns used in most studies (including this one) simplify a complex picture. Among the 'Asian' group are a number of ethnic minorities who differ in their socioeconomic position (e.g. Pakistanis and Bangladeshis suffer higher rates of unemployment than Indians and East African Asians) and there is some evidence that, while the proportions of Indians and Bangladeshis in prison is the same as in the general population, there are a disproportionately high number of Pakistanis in prison ... There are also important differences between black people of Caribbean origin (most of whom are British citizens) and Africans (some of whom are temporarily in the UK).

In their sentencing study based on 3,000 cases in 25 magistrates' courts and 1,800 in 18 Crown Court centres Flood-Page and Mackie conclude:

> Asian men were significantly more likely to be sentenced to custody than would have been expected on the basis of their offence and other factors. However, variables such as the type and number of offences, their plea, whether they were subject to a court order when they committed the offence, being mentally ill or whether the offence was premeditated explained more of the variations in custody rates than ethnic origin ...
>
> That ethnic minority males were not significantly more likely to receive custodial sentence than white males when other factors were taken into account was confirmed by further analysis. The differences in custody rates were explained by

variables such as the type and number of offences, their plea, whether they were subject to a court order when they committed the offence, being mentally ill or whether the offence was spontaneous.

(Flood-Page and Mackie 1998: 118–120)

Sentencing women

Hedderman and Gelsthorpe's study in 1997 found that women were more leniently treated than men. However, the situation was complicated because the courts fined women less frequently than men, and were more likely to impose a discharge. Overall comparisons are difficult because in general women tend to commit less serious crimes than men and to commit fewer – therefore more women who are convicted are first offenders. These factors have, therefore, to be taken into account as shown in the studies below. As a consequence, repeat female offenders were more likely to be given a community penalty for subsequent offences. In 1995 statistics show that twice as many men (9.5 per cent) as women (4.6 per cent) sentenced for indictable offences received a custodial sentence. Men were also more likely to be fined than women, with a higher proportion of women receiving a conditional discharge. Just under 30 per cent of both men and women received a community penalty though more women were given probation and more men CSOs (*Criminal Statistics England and Wales 1995*).

Home Office researchers who conducted a study of 3,000 sentencing cases in the magistrates' courts and 1,800 in the Crown Court commented:

Even allowing for their much lower rate of offending, females are much less likely to be prosecuted: in 1995, 59 per cent of women convicted or cautioned for indictable offences were cautioned, compared to 37 per cent of men ...

In this study a higher proportion of male first offenders received a custodial sentence than female first offenders in the Crown Court. So few first offenders received custodial sentences in the magistrates' courts sample that the difference was not significant. Men with previous convictions were four times as likely to receive a custodial sentence than women who were repeat offenders in magistrates' courts. In the Crown Court male repeat offenders were one-and-a-half times as likely to receive a custodial sentence as women.

Further analysis confirmed that men had a significantly higher probability of receiving a custodial sentence than women even when other factors were taken into account.

(Flood-Page and Mackie 1998: 121–2)

In respect of the sentencing of women one question is to ask whether they are sentenced more leniently or harshly. Another issue is to consider the differential impact of sentences on men and women. Answers reveal that issues of justice are hard to resolve and come down to whether it should be the offender or the offence that provides the primary focus when determining sentence. It may well be reasonable for sentencers to refrain from sending women to prison to avoid adverse effects on their children, but this is scarcely fair on fathers and their families.

However, significant changes to courts sentencing patterns for women offenders have been identified recently. Whilst women make up approximately 6 per cent of the prison population (clearly an under-representation as regards their proportion of the population as a whole) with an average of 4,299 women in prison in 2002, in the decade to 2002 the average population of women in custody rose by over 173 per cent compared with a 50 per cent rise in the number of male prisoners. Nearly half (40 per cent) of the sentences were as a result of convictions for theft or handling stolen goods whilst drug offences accounted for 13 per cent, and violence for 16 per cent (Home Office 2003).

Socio-economic status

The effects of both gender and ethnicity may also be related to the socio-economic circumstances of offenders. Thus it is more likely to be women in adverse socio-economic circumstances who end up in prison and, as seen above, many black offenders are unemployed. Thus the potential effect of socio-economic status on sentencing must be explored.

This can be seen in the situation of the unemployed, which provides a clear example of indirect and 'unintentional' discrimination. It is routinely stated in mitigation for offenders that they are in employment and that imprisonment would lead to the loss of such employment. Such employment is generally regarded as being a sign of good character (Cavadino and Dignan 1997) and a factor that might help promote good habits and so reduce the likelihood of future offending and thus appeal to sentencers seeking a rehabilitative approach. On the other hand, the unemployed, having less to lose, may be more likely to end up in prison. It is also more difficult to fine unemployed offenders.

The situation of the unemployed offender contrasts starkly with that of the middle-class and particularly the white collar offender. Many such offenders, for example, may plead in mitigation that they have much to lose – that a prison sentence would harm their innocent families and they might lose their house and their 'standing' in the community. Again, while it may be fair to take such factors into account, it may discriminate, albeit unintentionally, against offenders who have little to lose, let alone any 'standing' in the community (see, for example, Croall 2001; Levi 1989). Few studies have, however, found that social status or class alone affects sentencing outcomes. Indeed, judges, concerned to be fair and seen to be fair, may be conscious of any likely partiality on the grounds of class. Thus Mr Justice Henry, on refusing leave to appeal against a £5 million fine levied on one of the Guinness defendants, commented that:

> punishments are after all intended to be punitive and the court must ensure that a man's wealth and power does not put him beyond punishment.
>
> (*The Guardian*, 3 October 1990; quoted in Croall 2001: 131)

At the same time, however, few offenders could pay a massive fine and the ability of wealthier offenders to pay both large fines and substantial compensation may make a financial penalty more likely. In addition, they are better able to employ legal representation, which may affect how they present their case. Other factors may operate to reduce the severity of sentences for white collar offenders. The absence of direct victimisation in many white collar offences and in some the apparent lack of intent may also lead to less severe sentences (Croall 2001).

On a more general level, lower-class offenders may appear in court to be less likely cases for sympathy. As indicated above, sentencers may make judgments based on the demeanour and bearing of offenders and look for evidence of character, remorse and an acceptance of the courts' authority. Decisions earlier in the criminal justice process may also demonstrate a differential approach, where the police may be more likely to caution middle-class youths – a decision which may reflect home circumstances and the employment of parents (Cavadino and Dignan 1997).

Taken together, consideration of the effects of ethnicity, gender and socio-economic status on sentencing decisions reveals how difficult it is to determine whether any discrimination exists on the part of sentencers. Nevertheless, at the end of the criminal justice process there are differences in the proportions of some groups of offenders who receive different sentences. These raise important questions about the calculation of 'just deserts', which will be discussed in Chapter 12.

11.5 STRUCTURING SENTENCING DECISIONS

We can see from the above that a variety of factors directly and indirectly influence sentencing decisions and these tend to reflect two different goals in respect of sentencing policy and practice:

- the need for consistency so that justice is even handed and disparities are avoided (disparity occurs when similar case facts about the offence and the offender result in different sentences)
- the need for flexibility so that sentences can be matched to the individual circumstances of the case.

These concerns have generated a desire to achieve a more consistent approach to sentencing without creating too much of a straitjacket. Consistency has at least three dimensions: across place (is there consistency across different courts?), time (is the approach of the courts consistent with what they did before?) and cases (are similar facts of a case dealt with in the same way?). There have accordingly been various attempts to encourage a structured approach to sentencing decisions.

The 1990 White Paper which preceded the CJA 1991 pointed out that 'there is still too much uncertainty and little guidance about the principles which should govern sentencing ... The Government is therefore proposing a new and more coherent statutory framework for sentencing' (Home Office 1990a: 1). The White Paper goes on to argue that 'to achieve a more coherent and comprehensive consistency of approach in sentencing, a new framework is needed for the use of custodial, community and financial penalties' (Home Office 1990a: 5). The CJA 1991 sought to provide a firm basis for such consistency. Magistrates' training has increasingly focused on a structured approach following a systematic path to the sentence, ensuring that factors are considered in the appropriate order. Examples of the

Magistrates' Sentencing Guidelines are shown in Figure 11.1. Magistrates start by considering the seriousness of the offence, taking account of any aggravating or mitigating factors of the offence and of any previous convictions of the defendant. The second stage is to consider whether there is any mitigation in favour of the defendant, such as remorse or a guilty plea. The third stage requires a decision about the sentence, bearing in mind the entry point at the top of the guideline.

A number of initiatives have been introduced with the aim of achieving a more consistent or structured approach. The Judicial Studies Board is now responsible for collecting and disseminating statistics and for arranging Judges' Conferences and training sessions on sentencing. As already mentioned, initiatives from the Magistrates' Association led to the development of guidelines to foster a more consistent approach to sentencing.

Sentencing Advisory Panel and Sentencing Guidelines Council

The introduction of such bodies as guideline councils and sentencing commissions have been set up to achieve a number of aims: consistency in sentencing decisions, developing a policy framework in an expert setting, providing a barrier to populist political intervention of public opinion, and incorporating resource constraints.

The use of sentencing commissions has been popular in some states in the United States of America and Figure 11.2 shows the Minnesota sentencing grid to show how sentences are arrived at in that state. The two axes of the grid represent the main factors of seriousness of offence and the offender's previous criminal history. The bold line represents the in/out, or custody or not, presumption set out by the sentencing commission. Below the line incarceration is presumed; above it the judge may substitute a community penalty. But if they decide to give custodial sentence above or below the line, the range of sentences is set out for all categories of crime except for first-degree murder.

Sentencing commissions are another initiative introduced in recent years in several states in the United States of America as well as for sentencing in the federal courts. Michael Tonry, writing for the National Institute of Justice, commented:

> The Minnesota and Washington experiences suggest that the combination of sentencing commissions and presumptive guidelines is a viable approach for achieving consistent and coherent jurisdiction-wide sentencing policies. However, the experiences in Maine, New York, Pennsylvania, and South Carolina counsel that the sentencing commission approach won't necessarily succeed. Six jurisdictions are too few to support any but the most tentative generalizations about success and failure. Still, it is clear that most local legal and political cultures shape the environments in which the commissions work. Minnesota and Washington, for example, are both relatively homogeneous states with reform traditions. In neither state were criminal justice issues highly politicized. New York and Pennsylvania, by contrast, are heterogeneous states in which criminal justice issues are highly politicized and law-and-order sentiment is powerful. In some states, especially where trial judges are elected, judges may vigorously resist efforts to limit their discretion. Perhaps the

Figure 11.2 **Minnesota sentencing grid**

Severity levels of conviction offense		Criminal history score						
Structuring Criminal Sentences *Presumptive sentence lengths in months*								
		0	1	2	3	4	5	6 or more
Unauthorized use of motor vehicle Possession of marijuana	I	12*	12*	12*	15	18	21	24 23–25
Theft-related crimes ($150–$2,500) Sale of marijuana	II	12*	12*	14	17	20	23	27 25–29
Theft crimes ($150–$2,500)	III	12*	13	16	19	22 21–23	27 25–29	32 30–34
Burglary – felony intent Receiving stolen goods ($150–$2,500)	IV	12*	15	18	21	25 24–26	32 30–34	41 37–45
Simple robbery	V	18	23	27	30 29–31	38 36–40	46 43–49	54 50–58
Assault, second-degree	VI	21	26	30	34 33–35	44 42–46	54 50–58	65 60–70
Aggravated robbery	VII	24 23–25	32 30–34	41 38–44	49 45–53	65 60–70	81 75–87	97 90–104
Assault, first-degree Criminal sexual conduct, first-degree	VIII	43 41–45	54 50–58	65 60–70	76 71–81	95 89–101	113 106–120	132 124–140
Murder, third-degree	IX	97 94–100	119 116–122	127 124–130	149 143–155	176 168–184	205 195–215	230 218–242
Murder, second-degree	X	116 111–121	140 133–147	162 153–171	203 192–214	243 231–255	284 270–298	324 309–339

* One year and one day.

Note: Italicised numbers within the grid denote the range within which a judge may sentence without the sentence being deemed a departure. First-degree murder is excluded from the guidelines by law and continues to have a mandatory life sentence.

> only generalization that can be offered concerning political and legal culture is that
> the potential and the effectiveness of a sentencing commission will depend on how
> it addresses and accommodates constraints imposed by the local culture.
>
> (Tonry 1987: 59)

It seems, therefore, that the legal and political culture of the jurisdiction contributes
to the success or failure of such an approach. This point was reflected in the United
Kingdom in the consultation leading up to the CJA 1991, when the idea of a sentencing council was rejected. John Patten, a junior minister at the Home Office in
1991, identified the traditions of the criminal justice system as a reason why he
thought the idea of a sentencing council would not work in England and Wales. In
a letter to *The Times*, he wrote:

> Sentencing councils are the most fashionable nostrum these days for how much that
> advice (on sentencing) might be formalised. There seems to be almost as many
> recipes as there are cooks, producing councils, commissions or whatever; they vary
> in how much guidance or instruction should be given to the courts on sentencing
> and by whom it should be given.
>
> At the end of this road stands Minnesota in the United States. There, I am told,
> the local sentencing commission has produced tight numerical guidelines for prison
> sentences, which have taken the form of a 'sentencing grid'. Two axes determine the
> presumptive sentence. Along one side are the offence categories and along the other
> categories of 'criminal history'. So the ultimate sentence really depends on where
> the points along each axis occupied by the offender meet in the middle ...
>
> Those who ponder sentencing councils must not ignore that which is already in
> place, potentially providing so much of what they want to see, but in a way that
> works with the *grain of the criminal justice traditions* in this country. For there is
> a fast developing framework for judges and magistrates.
>
> In no particular order, first, there is the coherent statutory framework for sen-
> tencing in the new criminal justice bill, as we do not think that Parliament has said
> enough about the principles that govern sentencing decisions. Second, there is the
> power for the Attorney-General to refer cases to the Court of Appeal, where sen-
> tences are allegedly over-lenient. Third, the powerful effect of guideline judgments
> with the Court of Appeal is self-evident. Last, the work of the Judicial Studies Board
> seems to be of ever-increasing importance in training and guiding the sentencers in
> their work.
>
> (*The Times*, 5 February 1991; emphasis added)

The New Labour Government in England and Wales has established two sentencing bodies to provide advice and guidance: the Sentencing Advisory Panel and
the Sentencing Guidelines Council.

The Sentencing Advisory Panel (SAP) is an independent public body set up by the
Crime and Disorder Act 1998. It has 14 members and the inaugural chair was
Professor Martin Wasik. It initially provided advice direct to the Court of Appeal.
The prime aim is to achieve consistency in sentencing but other policy goals have
become apparent such as reducing the use of custody. In Scotland, where sen-

tencing has been characterised by a very strong tradition of judicial discretion and the Court of Appeal has not, unlike the situation in England and Wales, issued guideline judgments, a Sentencing Commission, headed by Lord MacLean, has been set up. This will examine: the scope to improve consistency of sentencing; the effectiveness of sentences in reducing re-offending; the arrangements for early release from prison and supervision of short-term prisoners on their release; and the basis on which fines are determined. It will also examine the use of bail and remand.

The Criminal Justice Act 2003 introduced another sentencing body, the Sentencing Guidelines Council. The SAP now submits its advice to the new body. The review by and recommendations of SAP have covered specific offences such as murder, burglary, sexual, racial and drug-related offences; and it has considered specific sentencing factors such as the discount for a guilty plea.

Essentially the perennial difficulty remains – a multitude of objectives and the conflict between the desire to individualise cases, taking account of personal circumstances, character and history, always unique to the offender, and the desire to have a consistent approach so that similar cases are dealt with in the same way, in the interests of fairness, just deserts and due process.

CONCLUSION

This chapter has indicated the many issues involved in sentencing decisions. In the first place, the different theories of punishment embody the different aims which sentencers may take into account. The present range of sentences available to the court reflect these different aims, and many sentences may be directed to achieve a combination of these aims. Before the CJA 1991 and other reforms attempted to impose greater consistency in sentencing policy, sentencers could in effect choose between a range of different sentences in what has been described as a 'cafeteria' approach (Ashworth 1989). The tradition of judicial independence and the tendency of both magistrates and judges to judge each case on its merits may produce the disparities which have caused so much concern. As Ashworth (1994b: 852) comments: 'unstructured discretion leaves leeway to the personal preferences of the judge, and if the concept of the "rule of law" has any stable meaning, it must exclude such preferences'.

As we have seen, therefore, there have been a variety of attempts to encourage a more consistent approach to sentencing, including the use of statutory criteria, voluntary guidelines and Court of Appeal guideline cases. The CJA 2003 introduced a more coherent approach by identifying sentencing objectives and establishing the Sentencing Guidelines Council, and, in contrast to the CJA 1991, reflected a changing emphasis on the different aims of sentences. The reasons for this shift in emphasis will be explored in more depth in Chapter 12.

Review questions

1 Contrast the six major theories of punishment in terms of the following:
   (a) What do they seek to achieve?

(b) Which are concerned primarily with the impact of the sentence on the offender before the court? Which are concerned with the impact on the public at large?

(c) Which aim to reduce crime in the future?

(d) If the judge or magistrates wish to achieve two objectives with the same sentence, which of the theories are compatible and which are not?

2 Consider the following statements, which are quotations from judges who are describing their approach to sentencing dwelling-house burglars (Davies and Tyrer Research with Crown Court Judges: unpublished). Identify the sentencing objectives that are illustrated in the judges' remarks about sentencing burglars. Which quote is an example of:

■ retribution
■ denunciation
■ deterrent (there are two examples below)
■ incapacitation?

(a) 'I think all these are instances of one thing, which is giving expression to society's reaction to this particular crime . . . whether or not it actually works in a particular way.'

(b) 'While he is inside he can't do it to anybody else.'

(c) 'I believe the primary purpose for this kind of offence . . . is to show that there is a risk of something unpleasant happening to you if you commit this type of offence.'

(d) 'The reason . . . is because everyone needs to know that those who invade the privacy of others in order to steal their property – an all too prevalent offence in our area nowadays – must know that, when they are brought to book, they will be properly punished.'

(e) 'If we were not sending domestic burglars to prison, I would be quite satisfied in my mind that there would be many more . . . burglaries committed . . . you can see it in a totally different context if you look at the fact that it is generally known that if you exceed the speed limit by more than 30 miles an hour you are in danger of being disqualified . . . A fear of the consequences I am certain is a motivating factor in a significant number of peoples' minds.'

3 What are the main sentences available to the court? How can they be related to each of the major aims?

4 List the major constraints and influences which will determine the way the sentencers reach a sentencing decision. Which factors are likely to produce disparity?

5 Describe and evaluate the differing attempts to achieve a more structured approach to sentencing? How is this achieved in England and Wales?

6 In the following three extracts from Court of Appeal decisions on sentencing cases, see if you can identify the aims of sentencing (i.e. an example of a deterrent statement) that are referred to by the court. Identify the statement and indicate which theory it represents.

Extract 1. R v Decino

....

....

....

Extract 2. R v Meggs

....

....

....

Extract 3. R v Knight (Colin)

....

....

....

Extract 1

Kiosk theft justifies jail
Regina v Decino

The offence of theft of money from a telephone kiosk was capable of being so serious that only a custodial sentence could be justified, within the terms of section 1(2)(a) of the Criminal Justice Act 1991.

The Court of Appeal (Lord Justice Beldam, Mr Justice Connell and Mrs Justice Ebsworth) so held on April 21 when allowing an appeal by Nicholas Decino against a sentence of 12 months' imprisonment imposed on January 8, 1993 by Mr Recorder Williams at Cardiff Crown Court, following his conviction on December 8, 1992 at West Berkshire Magistrates' Court of theft of £40.20 from a telephone kiosk.

For that offence he was sentenced to two months, and suspended sentences totalling ten months for burglary and possession of a controlled drug were activated consecutively. The sentences were made concurrent, reducing the total to ten months.

LORD JUSTICE BELDAM says that this was the kind of offence which was capable of depriving members of the public of the use of the public telephone which, to many people, was a lifeline. Of necessity telephone boxes were left unprotected. It was a matter of public policy to deter thefts from such boxes.

There was evidence that the appellant and two other young men provided themselves with the necessary tools and went on a deliberate expedition to rob telephone boxes of their contents.

In their Lordships' view it was, as the recorder has said, an offence capable of being so serious that only a sentence of custody could be justified for it.

(*The Times*, 10 May 1993, © Times Supplements Limited, 1993)

Extract 2

Sentencing in cases of incest
Regina v Meggs

Before Lord Lane, Lord Chief Justice, Mr Justice Kennedy and Mr Justice Hutchinson.
[Judgment February 21]

Cases of incest varied so enormously the one from the other that it was very difficult to derive any assistance from the previous instances which had appeared before the Court of Appeal.

The Lord Chief Justice so stated when giving the judgment of the court on an appeal by Eric William Meggs, aged 50, against prison sentences totalling 10 years passed at the Central Criminal Court by Sir James Miskin, QC, the Recorder of London, on pleas of guilty to specimen counts of incest with two of his daughters, extending, in the case of the elder, for more than 22 years. Sentence of three years on one count, which had been made consecutive, was ordered to run concurrent with the other sentences, totalling 7½ years.

Mr William Clegg, assigned by the Registrar of Criminal Appeals for the appellant.

THE LORD CHIEF JUSTICE said that, having made the elder girl pregnant twice the appellant caused her to have abortions. For a time they had lived as a married couple which, according to Mr Clegg, was what the neighbours thought they were.

The elder daughter became pregnant by her boy friend but the appellant did not desist from having sexual intercourse with her throughout.

The appellant, throughout interviews with the police, denied that anything improper had occurred.

Such cases varied so enormously from one to the other that it was very difficult to derive any assistance from the previous instances which had appeared before the court.

The court had to mark its disapproval and the disapproval of the community of such behaviour. It had to endeavour to deter other men from behaving in such a way.

It had to punish the appellant for using his two daughters, in particular his elder daughter, simply as a chattel to satisfy his own sexual appetite, regardless of the damage he might do to her welfare and happiness and, perhaps most important of all, her ability to enjoy a happy married life herself.

Mr Clegg submitted that insufficient regard was given to the plea of guilty and that overall the totality was too great despite the horrifying features of the case.

He pointed out that the appellant was disowned by his family, which was not surprising, but the effect was that he received no visits and was serving his sentence isolated to a great extent from his fellow prisoners.

They were all matters to be taken into account and their Lordships had concluded that Mr Clegg was correct in stating that the totality was too high.

There was nothing wrong with the individual sentences but their Lordships were concerned with the overall total and the proper course was to order that the sentence on a count ordered to run consecutively should, instead, run concurrent, so that the sentence was reduced by three years.

(*The Times*, 22 February 1989, © Times Supplements Limited, 1989)

Extract 3

Punishment for perjury
Regina v Knight (Colin)

Before Mr Justice McCowan and Mr Justice Leggatt.
(Judgment delivered 26 January)

Punishment for perjury had to be condign and commensurate with the gravity of the offence to prevent conviction of another for which the perjury was committed. The Court of Appeal so stated in dismissing an appeal by Colin Charles Knight, aged 32, against a three-year prison sentence passed at the Central Criminal Court by Sir James Miskin, QC, Recorder of London on a plea of guilty to perjury in that, being lawfully sworn as a witness on the trial of a man called Tobin at the Central Criminal Court, the appellant knowingly falsely described a man who jumped down from a crane.

Mr C Y Nutt, assigned by the Registrar of Criminal Appeals, for the appellant.

MR JUSTICE LEGGATT said that the crane was driven by Tobin into the back of a security van to gain access to it by a group of professional armed robbers. The jury disagreed at his first trial.

At the second trial the appellant, not called at the first trial, gave perjured evidence in saying that he had been in the area at the time of the robbery and described a man different from Tobin getting down from the crane. In the event Tobin was convicted.

In mitigation of the appellant's offence it was suggested that there had been some inducement and threat by an intermediary.

In passing sentence on the appellant, Sir James Miskin had said that armed robbery, planned with exquisite skill by intelligent, determined men for high profit, was one of the most serious crimes known to the courts and there was a great deal too

much of it. Those who intentionally gave false testimony on behalf of such men did so intending to mislead the jury into returning a verdict contrary to true justice and the evidence.

Not having seen one whiff of what had happened and for reward the appellant had entered the witness box and told a whole string of purposive lies. Account was taken of the plea of guilty and good character and implicit show of steel on the part of the intermediary. However, perjury was difficult enough to detect and much more difficult to prove. When it occurred it demanded instant prison.

Three years was imposed so that the appellant might be seen to be punished and, even more importantly, so that every single person in this age who contemplated events like giving false evidence in any case, let alone a serious one, or was minded to tamper with a jury, might know it would always be met by immediate, condign punishment.

Their Lordships agreed with every word of the judge in sentencing and, in particular, that punishment had to be condign. The purpose of the appellant's perjury was to avoid conviction for a grave offence. The punishment had to be commensurate with the gravity of that offence. The maximum penalty was seven years' imprisonment. The judge having made such allowance as could have been made for the appellant's antecedents and plea of guilty, the sentence was unimpeachable. The appeal was dismissed.

(*The Times*, 4 February 1984, © Times Supplements Limited, 1984)

Further reading

Ashworth, A (1992) *Sentencing and Penal Policy* (2nd edn), Weidenfeld & Nicolson: London

Ashworth, A (2002) 'Sentencing', in Maguire. M, Morgan. R and Reiner, R (eds) *The Oxford Handbook of Criminology* (3rd edn), Oxford University Press: Oxford

Cavadino, P and Dignan, J (2002) *The Penal System: An Introduction* (3rd edn), Sage: London

Walker, N and Padfield, N (1996) *Sentencing: Theory, Law and Practice* (2nd edn), Butterworth: London

Wasik, M (2001) *Emmins on Sentencing* (4th edn), Oxford University Press: Oxford

CHAPTER 12

Punishment philosophies and penal paradigms

Main topics covered

➤ Sentencing trends and reforms in the twentieth century

➤ The era of rehabilitation

➤ Just deserts and the justice model

➤ Prison reductionists: Limiting the use of imprisonment

➤ Shifting penal paradigms

➤ Does prison work?

➤ Sentencing for whom?

INTRODUCTION

We saw in Chapter 11 that policy makers, judges and magistrates have sought to find a balance between the six major theories of sentencing, and the twenty-first century has seen a change in the emphasis given to these goals in the Criminal Justice Act 2003. This chapter will focus on these shifting penal paradigms, that is ways of thinking about the causes and consequences of crime and how we should respond to them. The beginning of the twentieth century witnessed a growth in what was seen as a modern or progressive approach which believed that punishment could be replaced with treatment and welfare stratagems to cure criminals through a rehabilitative approach. This was to give way to the back-to-justice approach of the late 1960s as disenchantment with the rehabilitative model set in.

This chapter will start by looking at the history of penal reforms in terms of innovations in the form of new sentences and institutions and the abolition of certain other types of sanctions. It will then consider the ways of thinking about punishment, the penal paradigms, that influenced sentencing reforms and penal practice in the twentieth and into the twenty-first century. First, we will trace the influence of rehabilitative penal objectives, and, secondly, the justice approach based on 'just deserts' ideas of punishment and fairness. The impact of imprisonment on offenders will be considered and we will discuss whether imprisonment works and whether it can deter. Finally, we will examine the question that arises at the sentencing stage, namely who is sentencing for?

12.1 SENTENCING TRENDS AND REFORMS IN THE TWENTIETH CENTURY

By the beginning of the twentieth century the prison was the dominant penal sanction. Transportation had been formally abolished in 1867 and the number of offences that warranted the death penalty had been reduced to four (arson in Her Majesty's Dockyards, treason, piracy and murder) and was primarily used for murder. The Royal Commission on Capital Punishment (1949–53) recorded that for the decade 1900 to 1909, 257 men and 27 women were sentenced to hang; 103 of the men and 22 of the women were reprieved. In contrast, in one year alone (in 1900), there were 149,397 offenders of both sexes and of all ages given a custodial sentence by the courts. By 1910 the number had risen to 179,397, whereas the number of adult and younger offenders, both male and female, given a custodial sentence in 2002 was 111,600.

The term 'custody' covers a variety of sentences given different names over the century, which includes for adults:

> imprisonment, life sentence, corrective training (1949/67), preventive detention (1908/67), extended sentences (1967/91) and the partially suspended sentence (1982/92);

and for younger offenders:

> borstal training (1908/83), those children sentenced under s. 53(1) and s. 53(2) of the Children and Young Offenders Act 1933 for murder and grave offences (1933 onwards), approved school order (1933/70), detention centre order (1953/88), youth custody order (1983/8), detention in a young offender institution (1988 onwards), secure training order (1998 onwards), and detention and training order (1998 onwards).

Over the twentieth century the absolute and relative use of custody by the courts for sentencing has declined:

> In 1894, the total number of convicted criminals sent to prison in that year was 156,466, which represented 526 persons per 100,000 of population ... In 1994, the number given an immediate custodial sentence was 60,800 ... representing 118 persons per 100,000 of population.
>
> (Davies *et al.* 1996: 75)

By 2003 the prison rate had risen to 141 prisoners per 100,000 members of the population (Walmsley 2003: 5). Even though there has been an increase in use of custodial sentences in the last decade of the twentieth century, the trend across the century has been to rely less on custody and to make greater use of fines and community sentences. The decline in the use of custody began during the 1914/18 war. By 1920 the number sent to custody had fallen to 35,439. After the 1939/45 war the numbers sentenced to custody began to rise again and they rose from a total number sentenced to custody of 33,875 in 1950 to a high of 83,300 in 1985. The trend from 1986 to 1993 was downwards, with 58,400 sentenced to custody in 1993. Since then numbers in prison have been going steadily upwards again, with an average daily population of 61,100 in 1997 (*Home Office Statistical Bulletin*, 5/98: 1) and with 73,741 in custody on 30 September 2003 (*Occupation of Prisons*, Home Office, 11 November 2003).

The use of physical or corporal punishments was reformed and then stopped during the twentieth century. In 1908 a person under the age of 16 could no longer be executed. This was raised to 18 by the Criminal Justice Act 1948 and this reform led to one of the prolonged controversies about the death penalty when Derek Bentley was hanged in 1953 and his more culpable 16-year-old accomplice escaped the death penalty. The Criminal Justice Act 1948 also abolished hard labour, and abolished corporal punishment as a sentence of the court, although it was still allowed as a punishment within penal establishments until the Criminal Justice Act 1967. The Murder (Abolition of the Death Penalty) Act 1965 abolished capital punishment for murder and the last execution for murder took place in 1964. The Criminal Damage Act 1971 abolished the death penalty for arson in Her Majesty's Dockyards. The death penalty existed for the offence of high treason and piracy with violence until the Crime and Disorder Act 1998, although the last person executed for treason was William Joyce, in 1946, who made pro-German wireless broadcasts during the 1939/45 war.

The sentence most often given by the courts is the fine. Its use grew throughout the first half of the twentieth century so that by the 1970s it was used for half of all indictable offenders sentenced by the courts. Although its use has declined (see Figure 12.1) with indictable offenders since 1978, it is still the most frequently used sentence and was given in 86 per cent of summary non-motoring offences in 2002 in the magistrates' courts, and was given to 23 per cent of all offenders sentenced for indictable offences.

The use of community sentences has grown over the century as new types of sanctions have become available. These, with the date of introduction, include the following:

- probation (1887 and 1907)
- attendance centre orders (1948)
- community service order (1972)
- curfew orders for younger offenders (1982)
- combination orders (1991)
- curfew orders for adults (1991)
- reparation orders (2000)
- action plan orders (2000)
- drug treatment and testing orders (2000)
- referral orders (2002).

In 2002, of those sentenced for indictable offences, 33 per cent received community penalties and these were used more frequently than custody, which was used for 26 per cent of those sentenced for indictable offences (see Figure 12.1).

Figure 12.1 Sentencing patterns 1975/2002

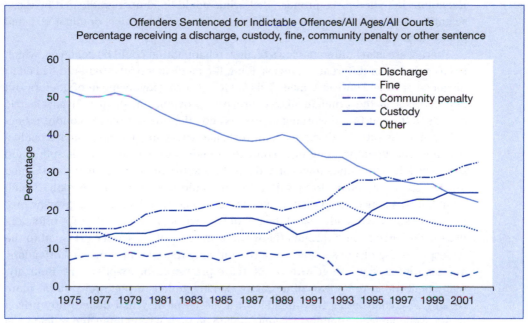

Source: Compiled from *Criminal Statistics England and Wales*, 1975 to 2002.

In the last quarter of the century there were more efforts through sentencing to include measures that benefited victims, such as compensation orders and schemes involving reparation to victims and the community. The shift away from offender-instrumental theories was also evident as new orders were introduced to prevent offenders benefiting from their crime, as with forfeiture orders (from 1983) and confiscation orders, introduced under the Drug Trafficking Act 1986.

Trends in sentencing those convicted of indictable offences from 1975 to 2002 are shown in Figure 12.1.

12.2 THE ERA OF REHABILITATION

During the twentieth century, penal policy throughout Europe and the United States of America was strongly influenced by the theory of rehabilitation. This moved away from earlier emphases on retribution and deterrence which were less concerned with the causes of crime and its treatment than with the justification for and distribution of punishment. Crime was seen as an immoral act that was in need of punishment, which was justified primarily on deterrent or retributive grounds. To rehabilitationists, however, crime, like any other social problem, could be studied scientifically to establish its causes. In what came to be described as a medical model, crime was likened to an illness which could be diagnosed and treated, and, through work with individual criminals and social reform, eventually cured. Thus from the start of the twentieth century experts from the world of medicine, the growing professions of psychiatry and social work, educational specialists and social reformers became increasingly involved in the courts and penal system. Rehabilitation offered the promise that crime could be almost eradicated by these scientific and professional approaches – an orthodoxy which dominated penal policy until the 1960s.

There were many different views on how rehabilitation could be achieved, which led to a variety of different strategies. First, the medical model stressed the need to diagnose, treat and cure criminals. This led to a growing involvement of doctors and psychiatrists in the criminal justice process, providing medical and psychiatric reports to the courts and working in prisons and other institutions. Secondly, others believed in the value of discipline and work, and advocated methods such as industrial and vocational training to encourage offenders to develop self-discipline and good work habits. Unlike medical and psychiatric treatment these measures aimed not to reform offenders from within but to equip them with better skills which would, it was hoped, keep them from committing crimes. Thirdly, the growing profession of social work advocated the use of case work and counselling for offenders both inside prisons and through the work of the probation service. This led to the widespread use of pre-sentence reports outlining the circumstances of offenders, and also influenced the growth of aftercare provision for ex-prisoners. Fourthly, many believed in the power of moral awakening, either through religion or, more recently, by confronting the offender with the harm they had done. Early prison regimes encouraged offenders to contemplate on their wrongdoing and religion has always played a role in prisons. Fifthly, others welcomed rehabilitationist strategies as a more humane way to treat prisoners, which ameliorated the degrading and brutalising aspects of prison life. Thus penal reformers, who had for long sought to improve the conditions of prisoners and who felt that prison could make people worse, supported rehabilitative measures enthusiastically. Lastly, rehabilitation was linked to the ideas of social engineers who identified social deprivation as the root of all social problems and put their faith in growing affluence and the welfare state.

In England and Wales, the rehabilitative paradigm was officially recognised in 1895 in the report of the Home Office Departmental Committee on Prisons chaired by Herbert Gladstone (Home Office 1895). The committee found that 'the moral condition in which a large number of prisoners leave the prison, and the serious number of re-committals have led us to think that there is ample cause for a searching inquiry into the main features of prison life'. It went on to state, 'we start from the principle that prison treatment should have as its primary and concurrent objects deterrence and reformation', and, in what became one of the most influential statements about the aims of prison, continued that:

> ... prison discipline and treatment should be more effectually designed to maintain, stimulate or awaken the higher susceptibilities of prisoners, to develop their moral instincts, to train them in orderly and industrial habits, and whenever possible to turn them out of prison better men and women, both physically and morally, than when they came in.
>
> (Home Office 1895: 8)

The first decade of the twentieth century saw the development of many rehabilitative policies such as the introduction of probation in 1907, of Borstal in 1908, special provision for child offenders in 1913 and new arrangements for the mentally deficient offender in 1914. Welfare officers, psychiatrists and psychologists were recruited into the prison service and in 1919 the prison warder was replaced by the prison officer, a title which marked a changing role. The annual reports of prison commissioners revealed a new mood in which prisons were increasingly seen not negatively, as institutions for incarcerating the bad, but positively, as institutions which could act as agencies of human change.

Although our focus here is on penal philosophy, the growth of rehabilitative policies, especially in prisons, was strongly influenced by individuals. One particularly influential individual was Alexander Paterson, who was involved in social work with the Oxford Medical Mission in Bermondsey where he also worked as an elementary school teacher. Although never chairman of the Prison Commission he was its most dominant figure and his liberal reform values were evident in penal documents from 1921 until his death in 1947. This was a period in which the approach embodied in the Gladstone Report began to crystallise into the dominant penological paradigm. Thus Lionel Fox commented that 'it was in 1921 that gusts of fresh air began to blow through the pages of the reports of the prison commissioners' (Fox 1952). The 1930s were characterised as an age of optimism in penal reform (Hood 1974).

This spirit of optimism is illustrated in extracts from Paterson's evidence to the 1931 Persistent Offenders Committee. This committee also provides a good example of how changing views about the role of prisons legitimated the participation of medical experts. Of the 68 people who gave evidence to the committee, 13 were drawn from the medical world, working within the system as medical superintendents in prisons or in psychiatric hospitals. The growing influence of the medical model and the treatment approach is confirmed in Paterson's evidence. Thus:

> The English Courts today, facing a young offender under 21 in the dock, are not concerned like their predecessors to weigh out a dose of punishment appropriate to the proved offence, but exercised rather to diagnose his condition and to prescribe the right form of training or treatment for the condition. This more thoughtful, sensible and expensive way of dealing with the young offender has inevitably resulted in a marked fall in the number of professional recidivists.
>
> (Evidence to Persistent Offenders Committee 1931: vol 3: 669)

The significance to rehabilitation of other measures was also noted. Thus Paterson comments:

> There has ensued in the last 25 years a whole series of changes in law and practice. The Children's Courts have been established to discover and check the potential tendency of the child offender; the probation system has emerged as a common-sense alternative to the imprisonment of the first offender of any age; the reformatories and industrial schools are no longer convict prisons for turbulent children, but take their place among other educational agencies, as special schools for the backward and the forward; the adolescent offender is sent in increasing proportion for training in a Borstal Institution rather than confinement in a prison.
>
> (Evidence to Persistent Offenders Committee 1931: vol 3: 669)

Paterson was well aware of some of the problems and what have come to be called the 'pains' of imprisonment and the full impact on the individual offender and their families of a period of imprisonment.

> Imprisonment is to be avoided whenever possible. It is often but a clumsy piece of social surgery, tearing a man away from the social fabric of home and work and club and union that has woven round himself, causing distress to others and rendering his replacement in social and industrial life a matter of grave difficulty.
>
> (Evidence to Persistent Offenders Committee 1931: vol 3: 675)

He wished to abolish prisons, and replace them with other institutions which were primarily concerned with reform – thus he also wrote:

> I propose to abolish all prisons.
>
> I propose to replace the prison commission with a Board of Welfare, whose members shall under a director administer:
> (a) Probation and Aftercare
> (b) Reformatory and Industrial Schools
> (c) Borstal Institutions
> (d) Examination Clinics
> (e) Training Centres
> (f) Places of detention
> There shall be no more places called prisons.
>
> (Evidence to Persistent Offenders Committee 1931: vol 3: 675)

While Paterson's ambition of the abolition of prisons was not achieved, his thinking, and the goal of rehabilitation, was paramount in the penal approach. However, the result of rehabilitative policies may have had a surprising outcome: an increase in prison sentence lengths. As we saw in Chapter 11, one implication of rehabilitative theory is that sentence lengths should be flexible and responsive to the needs of the offender. From this came the argument that sentences should be indeterminate along with the idea that offenders needed to be sent to prison for a sufficient time for treatment and training to take effect. Thus Paterson said, 'if we are concerned to train him, a few weeks in prison will be an idle pretence ...' (Paterson 1927). This was a view clearly held by those running the prison system in the inter-war years. Thus the Report of the Commissioners of Prisons for 1925/6 stated:

> ... the short sentence remains an outstanding defect in our penal system and difficulty in prison administration. Repetition on this point is not amiss.
>
> The highest administrative and judicial authorities have taken the same view, and have drawn attention to the uselessness of the short sentence. The International Penitentiary Congress in August 1925 passed a resolution to the same effect. There is not doubt but that the prospect of prison has a strong deterrent effect on those who have never yet passed its gates; nor that, once the disgrace of imprisonment has been incurred, much of that effect has been lost. It can also be readily understood that an impediment to the development of a sound system of prison training is the

presence of a number of men who only come in for a few days, and cannot therefore be taught any work other than the simplest. The difficulty, of course, is to find proper alternatives. The most hopeful prospect lies in the development of the probation system. A point may be reached where many offenders can be so well supervised in the open that, if they fail, a period of custodial training of substantial length will be justified.

(Paterson 1927: xiii)

This extract makes it clear that the prison commissioners did not seek longer sentences for all prisoners. Indeed they advocated non-custodial alternatives for less serious offenders. However, if offenders were to go to prison, the logic was clearly that short sentences would not allow sufficient time to treat and train them to lead a good and useful life. The Prison Rules, first introduced in 1949, took the view that the task of the prison service was to 'encourage and assist the inmate to lead a good and useful life'. In their Annual Report for 1949, the commissioners repeated the need for longer sentences in the context of discussing the new Criminal Justice Act 1948. Thus they argue, 'the purpose of the Act was not to provide some new form of training but to give the courts power to pass sentences long enough to enable the methods of training already developed in training prisons to be effectively applied'. This can be contrasted vividly, as we shall later see, with theories based on punishment and deterrence where the 'short sharp shock' or the 'clang of the prison gates' is urged as the most effective part of imprisonment. The effect of this policy is shown in Table 12.1, which shows prison terms from 1913 to 1975 in absolute and percentage figures.

Table 12.1 shows that sentence lengths increased between 1913 and 1975. This is partly explained by the increasing use of non-custodial sentences from 1913 which meant that fewer petty criminals were sent to prison for short periods of time – thus increasing the average sentence length. The figures also include offenders of all ages, and are therefore affected by the growing use of Borstal and detention centres for those under 21, and by statutory restrictions on sending younger offenders to prison. A major factor in the increase, however, is the influence of the rehabilitative

Table 12.1 (a) Length of prison sentence imposed 1913/75

	1913	*1938*	*1948*	*1958*	*1968*	*1975*
Up to 2 weeks	80,961	8,820	3,366	3,030	2,932	3,161
Over 2 weeks up to 5 weeks	30,359	7,475	5,595	4,922	3,765	5,069
Over 5 weeks up to 3 months	16,862	7,043	8,925	8,398	6,930	10,126
Over 3 months up to 6 months	5,070	3,947	6,447	6,710	7,801	7,483
Over 6 months up to 12 months	2,873	1,881	4,775	4,843	5,858	7,418
Over 12 months up to 18 months	1,033	694	2,361	2,085	3,179	4,546
Over 18 months up to 3 years	774	581	2,478	2,906	4,059	6,197
Over 3 years up to 5 years	231	158	617	733	1,086	1,749
Over 5 years	120	47	123	348	364	532
Life	13	14	30	40	95	153

Table 12.1 (b) Length of prison sentence expressed as percentages

	1913	1938	1948	1958	1968	1975
Up to 2 weeks	58.6	28.7	10.0	8.9	8.1	6.0
Over 2 weeks up to 5 weeks	21.9	24.4	16.7	14.5	10.5	10.9
Over 5 weeks up to 3 months	12.2	23.0	24.7	24.7	19.2	21.8
Over 3 months up to 6 months	3.7	12.9	18.3	19.7	21.6	16.1
Over 6 months up to 12 months	2.1	6.1	14.3	14.2	16.2	16.0
Over 12 months up to 18 months	0.7	2.3	7.1	6.3	8.8	9.8
Over 18 months up to 3 years	0.5	1.9	7.4	8.5	11.3	13.3
Over 3 years up to 5 years	0.2	0.5	1.0	2.1	3.0	3.8
Over 5 years	0.1	0.2	0.4	1.0	1.0	1.2
Life	–	–	0.1	0.1	0.3	0.3

The data includes periods imposed in cases of fine default but excluding sentences of corrective training or preventive detention. The data also includes male and female offenders.

Source: Prison and the Prisoner 1977: 157–8.

arguments outlined above. By 1975, over 28 per cent of offenders sentenced to custody received terms of imprisonment of over 12 months, compared with less than 1.5 per cent in 1913. Thus policies based on rehabilitation appear to have contributed towards the demand for longer prison sentences. This same debate is being re-run in the first decade of the twenty-first century as penal reformers claim that short prison sentences do not allow an opportunity for prisoners to take part in programmes to address the offenders' behaviour.

The 1979 May Report on the prison service also noted the link between sentences and rehabilitation and commented:

> However, confidence in the treatment model as it is usually called has now been waning throughout the Western world for some years. The drive behind the original borstal ideas has fallen away and there is now no belief that longer sentences may be justified because they make actual reformative treatment more possible.
>
> (Home Office 1979: 63)

This last quote indicates that, certainly by 1979, the influence of rehabilitation had waned: the reasons for this will be discussed below.

Rehabilitation reassessed

Rehabilitation fell out of favour largely because its promise was not achieved – it became a faith dashed on the rocks of the unprecedented rise in recorded crime in the post-war years. As this coincided with the growing post-war affluence of the 1950s, it also challenged reformers' claims that crime would be reduced with the growth of social welfare. Thus a 1959 White Paper, *Penal Practice in a Changing Society* (Home Office 1959), lamented:

It is a disquieting feature of our society that in the years since the end of the war, rising standards in material prosperity, education and social welfare have brought no decrease in the high rate of crime reached during the war: on the contrary, crime has increased and is still increasing.

There were several main sources of the declining influence of rehabilitation. The medical model, whose influence has been illustrated above, began to come under considerable criticism. By the 1960s it was apparent that it could justify a range of treatments which seemed far from humane. Many feared the development, for example, of the use of surgery and drug treatment which could readily be used to produce docile inmates. When medical intervention took these more dramatic forms many of the liberal reformers, who supported rehabilitation as a more humane approach, came to realise that punishment might be a better alternative. In addition, the increase in sentence lengths mentioned above, along with the use of indeterminate sentences, made rehabilitative treatments appear harsher than those which would be justified by retributive approaches. Hence, the support from liberal and civil rights groups in the 1970s for the back-to-justice movement, to be discussed below.

A further problem with rehabilitation was its link, seen most clearly in the medical model, with a view that criminality resulted from the pathologies of individual offenders. Yet despite a large volume of research attempting to discover how the characteristics of individual offenders could be related to their criminality, the pathological causes of crime proved hard to identify and apply in individual cases. As seen in Chapter 2, there were also many other approaches to explaining crime, and many offenders possess no clearly identifiable pathology. In addition, from a labelling perspective, excessive intervention risked increasing crime, and adherents advocated the use of minimal intervention (Schur 1973). Thus the promise to diagnose and therefore to devise suitable treatments for offenders was never fulfilled.

One of the greatest problems with the rehabilitative strategies was that they failed to live up to the claim that they would reduce recidivism. The lesson that prisons were not likely to reform offenders was slow to be learned. The results of research seeking to establish the impact of rehabilitative measures led to the gloomy conclusion that 'nothing works' (Lipton *et al.* 1975). During the 1960s the coalition of interests that made up the rehabilitative lobby in Europe and North America began to fall apart. The debate about 'what works' to reduce recidivism continues and the 1997 New Labour Government showed an interest in identifying effective offender programmes. This focus on effectiveness measured in offender-instrumental terms was reflected in the title of the Halliday report (2001), *Making Punishments Work.*

By the 1980s prison service policy documents had abandoned the ambitious mission statements of previous penal epochs, and referred to the much more basic functions of prison. Thus in 1988, a statement by the prison service contained the message that 'Her Majesty's Prison Service serves the public by keeping in custody those committed by the courts'. They had not abandoned, but diluted, the rehabilitative aspirations of the prison and strengthened the concern with humane conditions. 'Our duty is to look after them (inmates) with humanity and to help them lead law-abiding and useful lives in custody and after release' (Prison Service 1988).

By the 1980s the view was established that if rehabilitation was to be achieved then imprisonment was not a suitable location: 'it made bad people worse', to summarise the prevailing orthodoxy. While not claiming that prisons should give up their attempts to rehabilitate inmates, the argument prevailed that if rehabilitation was the primary aspiration of the court at the time of sentence then it would be better to leave the offender in the community. Thus community sentences and the probation service became the main focus of rehabilitative ambitions.

By 2003 this view had been amended to incorporate the idea that to be effective with recidivists there needed to be greater integration between the supervision and programmes in prisons and on release into the community and this logic led to the idea of establishing the National Offender Management Service (NOMS) in 2004 whereby probation and prisons would become an integrated service.

By 2000 the search for effective rehabilitation programmes was back on the agenda of government initiatives for those involved with youth justice and the correctional services. However, these schemes (now and throughout the twentieth century) were not without criticism. First, from a retributive sentencing perspective, there is criticism on the grounds that sentences which stress the primacy of changing offenders' behaviour are likely to be insufficiently punitive. This conflict is seen in the way that community sentences have been presented. When, for example, community service was introduced during the 1960s discussions referred to 'treatment in the community'. In the 1990s, however, the predominant phraseology was 'punishment in the community': for example, the Green Paper issued by the Home Office in 1995 was entitled *Strengthening Punishment in the Community*.

Thus by 1990 the rationale for community penalties had moved on from an alternative to custody approach towards an intermediate sanction rationale in which success will be measured in terms of just deserts and denunciatory goals. In 2003 the pendulum has swung somewhat in the other direction with the search for more effective sentences as measured in terms of recidivism.

Many of the new types of sentences introduced from the 1960s onwards, such as the community service order, were presented as alternatives to custody. That is they were to be regarded as equivalent to custody, and imposed only in circumstances where a prison sentence would have been considered. This implies that the sentences can be substituted for prison and are equivalent; and indeed the Court of Appeal established that 190 hours of community service were equivalent to 9–12 months of imprisonment (*R v Lawrence* 1982). When the community service order was originally introduced, courts were enjoined to indicate whether the order was a direct alternative to custody or not, and to record that fact in the court register (Home Office 1986: 43).

The problem with this kind of approach is that many sentencers and the public simply do not see community penalties as in any way equivalent to prison. Thus there was a tendency for the new, so-called alternatives to prison to be used instead as alternatives to probation. In addition, the mixed rationales underlying the community service order made it difficult to approach in terms of the tariff – how, for example, did such sentences match the seriousness of the offence? If, however, the use of imprisonment was to be reduced while at the same time maintaining a notion of tough sentences, new approaches to community sentences were necessary.

Such new approaches were influenced by the justice model. The logic of just deserts and proportionality implied that penalties should be differentiated according to the severity of the crime and the culpability of the offender. In practice, prison terms are measured in terms of the degree of restriction on the offender's liberty. Community sentences could also, it was argued, be justified in this way. It was suggested that community penalties could be made tougher. This could be done by increasing sentencing options and introducing tougher penalties between probation and prison, thus producing a continuum or gradation of penalties which would reflect sentencers' needs for sanctions proportionate to the seriousness of the offence.

The Criminal Justice Act 1991 made community sentences part of a framework of sentences based on a just deserts approach. These sentences, as revised by the Act, provided for a range of community penalties, with some being more demanding than others. They were no longer merely alternatives to prison but intermediate sentences, a sentence in punitive terms somewhere between prison and probation, and became sentences in their own right with specific aims.

Despite the new role for community penalties as intermediate sanctions, research suggests that some magistrates perceived community penalties as insufficiently demanding to provide the structured steps in a hierarchy of punitiveness between probation and prison. This is illustrated by the following comments from magistrates about the implementation of community service orders:

> To me it's not structured enough. They come and go as they please.
>
> I wouldn't say it was terribly demanding necessarily, only the discipline of having to be there and doing it . . . I wouldn't think they'd break out in a sweat.
>
> I think they tend to lose credibility with me when we have breach hearings and you hear how often the administrator has really bent over backwards to accept their excuse.
>
> The underlying view I think of probation officers would not be to divert people from crime but to divert people from prison.
>
> (Davies *et al.* 1996: 94–5)

These comments reflect in part the ambiguity about the role of community sentences and also the continued debate about the position of the penal objective of rehabilitation: given a secondary role within a sentencing framework established by just deserts and denunciation in the Criminal Justice Act 1991, the Criminal Justice Act 2003 has restored its role to a primary objective of sentencing.

12.3 JUST DESERTS AND THE JUSTICE MODEL

The declining faith in rehabilitation along with the continuing rise in recorded crime led to a reappraisal of sentencing aims in the late 1960s and 1970s. Extremely influential in this process was what came to be known as a back-to-justice policy which affected legislation throughout the 1980s, and most particularly the Criminal Justice Act 1991. There was no one single and comprehensive formulation of the justice model, but it developed out of a number of publications by American academics such as K C Davies (1969), D Fogel (1975), M Frankel (1973) and Andrew von Hirsch (1976). In the United States of America, where the justice model developed and influenced policy more directly, it was influential in shaping reforms of the juvenile courts and the introduction of determinate sentencing laws in California in 1976. These reforms were strongly influenced by the problems of rehabilitative sentencing policies. The long and seemingly harsh sentences associated with rehabilitation, the uncertainty produced by indeterminate sentences and the individualisation of sentences were seen to conflict with the rights of offenders to receive predictable and proportionate sentences. Thus the justice model argues that sentencing should be fair and not aim to achieve anything other than punishing offenders in proportion to the harm they have done. It developed directly out of a critique of rehabilitation and, as Messinger and Johnson (1978) comment, 'it represented ... an outright rejection of previous sentencing policy and seems to be based on the opposite assumptions in every respect'.

The justice model is often linked to and is not logically incompatible with retributive theories; however, it emphasises fairness while retribution is often popularly distorted to support demands for vengeance or harsher sentences. Thus while the justice model stresses punishment as an end in itself it was not called 'back-to-punishment', and von Hirsch (1976) described it as 'vengeance with fairness'. This approach is incompatible with rehabilitation as a primary goal of punishment. It can, however, be included as a secondary aspect of sentencing provided it does not distort the length or type of sentence in terms of the principles of just deserts. There is no clearly articulated theory of just deserts; however, there are four main sets of assumptions and principles that can be identified. These include assumptions about human behaviour, the objective of punishment, the distribution of punishment, and the extension of due process into the prisons.

Assumptions about human behaviour

To advocates of the justice model, individuals are responsible for their own behaviour. Criminal behaviour therefore, like any other, is thus a result of conscious decisions made by responsible, autonomous, self-determined individuals. Thus the rehabilitationist notion that criminality results from some individual pathology or is attributable to the offender's social, economic or personal circumstances was rejected. While it was accepted that these factors could affect behaviour they should not neglect what is seen as the moral imperative of regarding human action as primarily attributable to individual choice. Thus offenders have made a free choice to commit crime, and should therefore be punished. Where they have not been able, for example, because of age or mental disability, to make a free choice, they are not fully responsible for their actions and need not be punished.

The objective of punishment

Punishment is seen as an end in itself and a just and condign reward for morally wrong behaviour. It does not have to be justified by social protection or on the grounds that it is likely to reduce the future likelihood of crime. It should therefore be based simply on the notion of just deserts: culpable criminals should be punished in amounts proportional to or commensurate with the seriousness of the harm done.

This raises important questions. By whom, and how, is culpability to be assessed? What constitutes the proportionate level of punishment for each offence and who should determine this? Thus there can be moral and political objections to this approach. In unequal or unjust societies, just deserts may be determined by those in power and may be far from just to those at the receiving end. In addition, in pluralist societies, cultural differentiation makes shared agreement as to what is right or wrong difficult to assess. Decisions as to how serious a crime is and what its 'just' punishment should be may open up a wider debate on moral, social and political issues. It might not be easy, for example, to distinguish between different offences in terms of seriousness. How can the respective seriousness of rape, burglary or tax fraud be assessed? As we have seen, the public may have very different views over what should be criminalised, and how to rank crime in terms of seriousness. Disagreements are inevitable when citizens are asked to consider the harmful consequences of crime; and the merits of different modes of punishment. However, even if agreement cannot be reached as to what is 'just', it does keep the debate about punishment associated with issues of morality and justice. This point is made by C S Lewis:

> The humanitarian theory removes from punishment the concept of Desert. But the concept of Desert is the only connecting link between punishment and justice. It is only as deserved or undeserved that a sentence can be just or unjust ... we may very properly ask whether it is likely to deter others and to reform the criminal. But neither of these two last questions is a question of justice.
>
> (Lewis 1953)

Von Hirsch, discussing the twin objectives of deterrence and deserts makes it clear that the deserts principle is more important for decisions about the distribution of punishment. Thus he argues:

> ... we think that the commensurate deserts principle should have priority over other objectives in decisions about how to punish. The disposition of convicted offenders should be commensurate with the seriousness of their offences, even if greater or less severity would promote other goals.
>
> (von Hirsch 1976)

The distribution of punishment

Once culpability is established the main determinant of the type or amount of punishment will be the seriousness of the offence. A secondary consideration once this has been established is the degree of responsibility. Thus both mitigating and aggravating circumstances in relation to both the offence and the offender form part of the consideration of the sentence to be given.

Proponents of the justice model aimed to reduce individualised sentencing strategies, which, as we have seen, underlie sentencing disparities, and to eradicate indeterminacy. Thus they wished to see fixed and determinate sentencing with an established tariff for each offence, and uniformity of sentences for offenders committing the same offence in similar circumstances. Hence the move towards more constraints on judicial discretion at the sentencing stage throughout much of the United States of America and the United Kingdom.

Legalism: the extension of due process

Indeterminate prison sentences created a situation whereby the length of a prison sentence depended on discretionary decisions made within the prison. This led to many problems, which, especially in the United States of America, were associated not only with increasing sentence lengths and thus an increase in the prison population, but also with unrest within prisons. Prisoners could not predict how long their sentences were to last nor could they always predict what they had to do to ensure an early release. This could also lead to a situation where release dates and parole decisions could be used as a means of control within the prison system. It also led to apparent injustices as offenders sent to prison for similar offences could in effect serve very different lengths of sentence. This not surprisingly led to much discontent and feelings of inequity. Thus a major argument of the justice model was to extend the principles of due process into the prison system. The clearest impact on prison regimes was achieved by David Fogel, who, as Commissioner for Prisons in Minnesota from 1971 to 1973, attempted to apply the principles of the justice model to prisons. He advocated reforms which would involve more due process; greater openness in decision making and accountability according to the demands of natural justice. His reforms emphasised prisoners' rights and a belief that in the world of the prison community there should be an atmosphere of justice and fairness. This view was later echoed in the Woolf Report 1991 (Home Office 1991a) into prison disturbances in 1990, which will be discussed in Chapter 13.

In the United Kingdom the justice approach made its mark in a more diffuse way than in the United States of America. By the end of the 1970s aspects of prison policy were being scrutinised by the courts and greater attention was paid to prisoners' rights. The indeterminate sentence of Borstal training was replaced by the determinate sentence of youth custody in 1982. Also, as we have seen in Chapter 11, increasing guidance was given to courts to reduce sentence disparity. The 1990 White Paper and the subsequent legislative reforms in the Criminal Justice Act 1991 gave the clearest message that just deserts should be the primary principle for sentencing decisions in England and Wales.

The post-1997 approach to sentencing objectives has eroded the dominance of the justice approach with its emphasis on the seriousness of the offence, and we now have a penal paradigm that gives greater emphasis to the offender-instrumental goals that seek to reduce crime.

12.4 PRISON REDUCTIONISTS: LIMITING THE USE OF IMPRISONMENT

Despite the good intentions of penal reformers, prisons had not achieved the goals claimed by their protagonists in the 1920/50 era in that they were not likely to rehabilitate offenders. Prisons are primarily justified by notions of retribution and denunciation, the uncertain impact of deterrence and a claim to incapacitate. The existence of violence, gangs and drug use within prisons means that even the claim to incapacitate is only partially true.

In addition, prisons are costly institutions and there have been recurrent concerns over the overcrowding of existing prisons and conditions within them. Many prisons in the United Kingdom were built in Victorian times and have few modern facilities. Concerns about overcrowding, on the part of the Prison Officers' Association, were evident in Britain as early as the 1940s and the Prison Commissioners' Annual Reports repeated the warning from 1955 until their demise in 1964. The degrading conditions within prisons also caused considerable concern and were described as an 'affront to civilised society' by the Director General of Prisons in the Annual Report of the Prison Department in 1980.

Out of these concerns grew what came to be known as the 'prison reductionist' movement. Some focused on degrading conditions and overcrowding, while others focused on the adverse effects of prisons and claimed that sentencers were sending too many people to prison. By the 1970s liberal and welfare-oriented groups who had supported rehabilitation came to argue for a reduction in the use of prison. Their message was underlined by media stories of overcrowded cells, antiquated conditions and incidents of unrest in prisons.

Of course, one solution to problems of overcrowding and degrading conditions would be to build more prisons. Moreover, the argument that sentencers send 'too many people' to prison is a difficult one to evaluate given the different aims underlying a prison sentence. Nonetheless, the argument of the reductionists, who shared a common view that the size of the prison population should be reduced, became an influential one. A key part of this argument was that, as prisons could no longer be seen to rehabilitate and indeed could have an adverse effect on prisoners, their use should be curtailed.

This influence was evident in the parliamentary debate on the 1967 Criminal Justice Bill. Thus Roy Jenkins, then Home Secretary, echoed the reductionist position in his speech on the Bill in which he stated that 'the main range of the penal provision of the bill revolves round the single theme, that of keeping out of prison those who need not be there . . . the overstrain upon prison resources, both of buildings and men, is at present appalling'.

From the 1960s official documents started to move away from the grander claims made during the heyday of rehabilitation and towards an acceptance that prisons were not appropriate places to reform individual inmates. It began to be argued that prisons had an adverse effect on inmates, making them reliant on institutional life, and could further deepen their commitment to crime as they mixed freely with other criminals: the prison as the university of crime. In addition, ex-prisoners might face considerable stigma, making it more difficult for them to gain housing or employment. Thus a more limited rehabilitative rationale emerged in arguments that, if rehabilitation was sought by sentencers, it was not likely be achieved in prison. This was made most apparent in the arguments in the Green Paper *Punishment, Custody and the Community* (Home Office 1988a) and the subsequent White Paper of 1990 (Home Office 1990a).

During the late 1980s and early 1990s the reductionist message was paramount. The arguments of those who wished to see prisons reduced on the grounds that they were ineffective and inhumane were echoed by more pragmatic reductionists concerned with the costs, efficacy and the strains caused by the numbers in the system. Thus from the 1980s onwards, as we have seen, successive legislation and policy initiatives began to encourage more consistency in sentencing and imposed limitations on the use of imprisonment, such as the introduction of statutory criteria on the use of prison in the Criminal Justice Acts 1982, 1988 and 1991.

In 1990, explicit recognition was given in a White Paper to the idea that imprisonment has a limited role to play in penal policy. The report is discussed in Chapter 13. Changing prison regimes alone, however, could not alleviate the problems of the prison system and the White Paper argued that prison overcrowding could not be solved in isolation from sentencing policy. Hence the search for sanctions which could be used instead of prison, not necessarily to act as an alternative sentence, but to be placed on the tariff below prison. These sentences should, it was argued, be less severe than imprisonment, but be demanding enough to encourage sentencers to use them for the less serious offences that had previously attracted a prison term.

During Michael Howard's period at the Home Office the prison reductionist view was challenged by the claim that prisons work. This, of course, depended on what prisons were expected to deliver and we discuss this debate in a later section of this chapter.

By 1997 the Labour Party were back in Government and there was to be a shift in policy whereby the rhetoric accepted the argument that prisons were overused and simultaneously the prison population continued to increase to record levels. Custody, in the words of *Justice for All*, has an important role in punishing offenders and protecting the public, but it is expensive and should be limited to 'dangerous, serious and seriously persistent offenders and those who have consistently breached community sentences'.

Reductionism took on a new lease of life when Lord Woolf was appointed Lord Chief Justice in 2000. His report on prison riots in the 1980s had established his liberal credentials and his subsequent actions were based on a view that less use should be made of imprisonment. The controversial decision of the Court of Appeal case on not sending burglars to prison was mainly inspired by the views of Lord Woolf, despite this view being out of touch with his fellow judges, the public at large and the recommendations of the Sentencing Advisory Panel on domestic burglary. In the *McInerney and Keating* Court of Appeal Guideline case (December 2002), he rejected the stepped tariff approach of the Criminal Justice Act 1991, claiming that short prison sentences were ineffective (as selectively measured by recidivism rates) and argued the sentence for burglars should 'ensure the sentence is (a) an effective punishment and (b) one which offers action on the part of the Probation Service to tackle the offender's criminal behaviour and (c) when appropriate, will tackle the offender's underlying problems such as drug addiction'. The emphasis on rehabilitation and changing behaviour had not been so pronounced since the optimistic decade of the 1930s with the belief in science and the medical metaphor of 'cure' and the optimism about the ability to change offenders' conduct.

Another aspect of the prison reductionist case, used by Lord Justice Woolf, is based on the apparent over-punitiveness of the English courts when contrasted to other jurisdictions around the world. Libya was quoted at one stage but more regularly we are referred to what is happening amongst our European Union partners. The crude prison rate of prisoners per population shows England and Wales with more prisoners per head of population than the rest of Europe; but the question is whether the comparison of prison rates should be based on population or related to the amount of crime. Comparing populations with different age profiles and crime rates would not be meaningful whereas comparisons with the amount of crime in general or, more importantly, with the amount of serious crime are more useful in determining whether the judges are more punitive in one jurisdiction than another.

Table 12.2 compares the number of prisoners to the number of recorded crimes across various jurisdictions: the European Union has 17.7 and the figure for England and Wales was 12.7. Measured in this way the British courts do not appear to be as punitive.

The shifts and complexities of the penal paradigm are explored in the next section.

Table 12.2 **The rate of imprisonment in the European Union in 2000**

Country	Prison population	Prisoners per 100,000 pop.	Estimated country population (millions)	Recorded crimes	Prisoners per 1,000 recorded crimes	Crimes per 100,000 pop.
EU Average		**87**			**17.7**	**5,902**
England and Wales	65,666	124	52,939,000	5,170,843	12.7	9,762
Northern Ireland	1,011	60	1,697,800	119,912	8.4	7,095
Scotland	5,868	115	5,114,600	423,172	13.9	8,297
Austria	6,861	84	8,127,024	560,306	12.2	6,909
Belgium	8,524	83	10,239,085	848,648	10.0	8,279
Denmark	3,240	61	5,330,020	504,231	6.4	9,443
Finland	2,887	56	5,181,115	385,797	7.5	7,448
France	48,835	80	58,746,500	3,771,849	12.9	6,405
Germany	79,507	97	82,142,684	6,264,723	12.7	7,620
Greece	8,038	76	10,521,669	369,137	21.8	3,502
Ireland (Eire)	2,887	76	3,790,000	73,276	39.4	1,933
Italy	54,579	94	57,679,895	2,205,782	24.7	3,819
Luxembourg	400	92	435,700	22,816	17.5	5,185
Netherlands	13,847	87	15,940,815	1,173,688	11.8	7,368
Portugal	12,728	124	9,997,590	363,294	35.0	3,558
Spain	45,309	114	39,852,651	923,269	49.1	2,339
Sweden	5,678	64	8,882,800	1,214,968	4.7	1,370

Home Office Statistical Bulletin 5/02, July 2002
EU averages unweighted; OECD Health Data

Source: Civitas website: civitas.org.uk

12.5 SHIFTING PENAL PARADIGMS

By the 1980s, therefore, many factors suggested that there was a need for a review of penal policy. It had been largely recognised that the individualised sentencing associated with rehabilitation had produced disparities and what were seen by proponents of a justice model as injustices. It had become associated with longer and indeterminate sentences, far out of proportion to the crime committed. The belief in the positive rehabilitative effects of custody may have produced a rise in the prison population. However, there were strong arguments in favour of substantially reducing the use of imprisonment, on the grounds of the relative ineffectiveness of prison in terms of rehabilitation, and also on the grounds of its cost-effectiveness. At the same time, however, public concern over rising crime rates, particularly in offences of violence, suggested that reducing the use of imprisonment could be seen as paying insufficient regard to the protection of the public. Community sentences lacked credibility. These issues were reflected in a series of discussion documents and government papers (notably the 1988 Green Paper, *Punishment, Custody and the Community*, and the 1990 White Paper, *Crime, Justice and Protecting the Public*) preceding the Criminal Justice Act 1991, which promised to be one of the most thorough overhauls of sentencing policy. We have already outlined many of the changes brought about by this legislation, some to be quickly overturned in the Criminal Justice Act 1993. This section will place these changes in the context of the shifting penal paradigms outlined in this chapter.

The difficulties of the deterrent approach to sentencing was developed in the White Paper:

> Deterrence is a principle with much immediate appeal. Most law abiding citizens understand the reasons why some behaviour is made a criminal offence, and would be deterred by the shame of a criminal conviction or the possibility of a severe penalty. There are doubtless some criminals who carefully calculate the possible gains and risks. But much crime is committed on impulse, given the opportunity presented by an open window or unlocked door, and it is committed by offenders who live from moment to moment; their crimes are as impulsive as the rest of their feckless, sad or pathetic lives. It is unrealistic to construct sentencing arrangements on the assumption that most offenders will weigh up the possibilities in advance and base their conduct on rational calculation. Often they do not.
>
> (Home Office 1990a: 6)

According to Ashworth, 'The origins of the new law were in the government's white paper of 1990, which stated that desert should be the primary aim of sentencing, that rehabilitation should not be an aim of sentencing but should be striven for within proportionate sentences, and that deterrence is rarely a proper or profitable aim for a sentencer' (von Hirsch and Ashworth 1993: 285–6). The White Paper rejected deterrent sentencing and, while it saw a role for rehabilitation, rejected any notion that rehabilitation should be a primary goal. Denunciation was also seen as significant: thus the 1990 White Paper stated that 'the first objective for all sentences is denunciation of and retribution for the crime' (Home Office 1990a: 6). The emphasis on just deserts meant that the seriousness of the offence was to be the primary criteria for determining the sentence, and it was also envisaged that it should limit the severity of a sentence. This can be seen in the following extract:

> ... the severity of the sentence in an individual case should reflect primarily the seriousness of the offence which has been committed. Whilst factors such as preventing crime or the rehabilitation of the offender remain important functions of the criminal justice process as a whole, they should not lead to a heavier penalty in an individual case than that which is justified by the seriousness of the offence or the need to protect the public from the offender.
>
> (Home Office 1991b: 1)

This extract also shows that, while just deserts is a major principle, the protection of the public is also important; thus the Criminal Justice Act 1991 contained an important incapacitative element. What is often known as bifurcation or a twin-track approach was introduced on the principle that for most offenders the sentence was to be based on the seriousness of the offence, except in circumstances where, as, for example, with sexual and violent offenders, incapacitation was seen to be necessary. This was described largely in terms of distinguishing property offences from those involving violence. While the courts were to be encouraged to use non-custodial sentences for property offenders where possible, prison terms, and terms longer than the offence itself merited, could be used for violent offenders.

One controversial provision of the Criminal Justice Act 1991 (CJA 1991) provided that previous convictions should not be looked at when assessing seriousness (s. 29), the only exception being where earlier offences were taken as aggravating features of the current offence. The offender was to be sentenced on the basis of the current offence and not previous convictions. Another controversial section, referred to as the 'two offence rule', meant that regardless of the number of offences only one offence (the most serious) and only one other would be considered to determine the sentence in typical cases. This was, as had been intended, given a very narrow interpretation by the courts. Both provisions were heavily criticised as limiting the powers available to courts when sentencing the persistent offender whose offences taken individually were not counted as 'so serious'. The Criminal Justice Act 1993 altered this position by repealing these two sections, allowing judges to consider previous offences and the number of offences when sentencing.

A second implication of the approach was that any restriction on liberty should be commensurate with the seriousness of the offence. This applied to both custodial and community sentences. As we have seen, the 1990 White Paper made it clear that imprisonment should not be used for rehabilitative or deterrent motives but might be justified in particular cases on retributive, denunciatory and incapacitative grounds. This is the significance of the statutory criteria to restrict the use of imprisonment, particularly aimed at property offenders. Just deserts was also used to determine lengths of custodial sentences.

In addition, the element of indeterminacy implied by parole was also changed with the introduction of provisions to clarify release dates from prisons with the reform of the system of parole and remission, discussed in Chapter 13.

The CJA 1991 also changed the role, function and organisation of community sentences. Indeed the 1990 White Paper devoted four out of nine chapters to exploring the role of community penalties. To make changes that were acceptable to the public meant that they had to be tied into the just deserts approach, and had to be credible punishments in their own right. Thus the 1990 White Paper referred to a continuum of penalties involving an increasing degree of restriction on the offender's liberty, with custody at one end and probation at the other and with a range of intermediate punishments in the community. This new approach was based on the assumption that the punishment was to be the degree of restriction on the offender's liberty.

Thus it was argued that imprisonment should be retained as the means of punishment for the most serious offences, and fines and discharges for the least serious offences. The Green Paper clarified this point: 'Liberty under the law is highly valued by all of us. The deprivation of liberty is the most severe penalty available to the courts' (Home Office 1988a: 8). Apart from financial penalties, most court disposals place restrictions on offenders' freedom of action. The degree of restriction on offenders' freedom of action thus provides the link between community based forms of punishments and imprisonment. Custody is at one end of the continuum of restrictions on offenders' freedom of action:

> The effect of custodial sentences is to restrict offenders' freedom of action by removing them from their homes, by determining where they will live during the sentence, by limiting their social relationships and by deciding how and where they will spend the 24 hours in each day.
>
> (Home Office 1988a: 3.3)

Thus the CJA 1991 was a logical development in the context of the shifting penal paradigms explored above. In addition, it stated, more clearly than before, the main principles to be used by sentencers, and thus hoped to encourage consistency. Consequently an editorial in the *Criminal Law Review* on the introduction of the Act commented that 'it can be claimed that the 1991 Act differs from its predecessors in one significant respect: its sentencing provisions have some fairly coherent themes' (Ashworth 1992b: 229). Ashworth comments, 'it introduced a primary rationale for English sentencing (desert) and clarified the extent to which other "aims" such as public protection, rehabilitation and deterrence should play a part' (Ashworth 1994b: 853).

The aims and principles of the CJA 1991 were welcomed by many although the details of its implementation – for instance, the system of unit fines – led to opposition in some quarters. Of course, not everyone accepted a sentencing policy based primarily on a just deserts approach which fitted sentences to the seriousness of the offence. One of the problems was that the Act gave little guidance on how this seriousness is to be assessed. There is an assumption, for example, that violent and sexual offences are more serious than property ones, but in practice the delineation of seriousness is far more complex, and perhaps leaves space for individualisation in terms of judging offence seriousness.

Some argued that just deserts policies can lead to an increase in the tariff. This is not inevitable, however – just deserts models have led to more severe sentencing approaches in California (Davies 1989), but not in Scandinavian countries (Ashworth 1997b; Davies *et al.* 1996; Hudson 1993). Much depends on exactly how maximum sentences are conceived and how actual sentencing lengths are determined in practice.

The shift in the penal paradigm was apparent with the changes initiated by the New Labour Government from 1997. It became evident that a number of trends were simultaneously at work and the logic of the sentencing framework of the CJA 1991 was to change away from a primary focus on deserts and denunciation. One important new emphasis was a belief that rehabilitation rates could be improved. Under New Labour the offender-instrumental goals were to be given a heightened and interrelated role, so that more programmes should be in place to help rehabilitate offenders both in and out of prisons, to assist greater monitoring of those left in the community; and the prisons were to be used for punishment, deterrence, incapacitation of recidivists and the attempted rehabilitation of prisoners. The currently fashionable view by 2001 was that there was little penal value in the short prison sentence, which would do little to reduce recidivism – reminiscent of the views of the Prison Commissioners in the 1920s and 1930s. Furthermore, prisons were overused. However, at the same time the use of custody by judges and magistrates was increasing.

These views were found in the Halliday report (2001) entitled *Making Punishments Work*. The message from the foreword to the White Paper *Justice for All* (July 2002) that preceded the Criminal Justice Act 2003 was on the need to be tough and effective.

The White Paper commented, under the heading of 'What is not working', 'Half of all prisoners discharged in 1997 were reconvicted within 2 years' (2002: 24). What was missing was the fact that an equal proportion of offenders given community sentences are reconvicted after 2 years; so, although they claimed to be evidence-based, they had in effect accepted the prison reduction lobby's views (at least about the problems of prisons) even if the judges were still sending more criminals to prison – although the judicial leadership under Lord Chief Justice Woolf did what it could to change this.

The beginning of the twenty-first century saw another departure from the logic that prevailed in 1990 and the CJA 1991. In the Criminal Justice Act 2003 the aims of sentencing have been set out in the statute and 'deterrence' is included but 'denunciation' excluded (see Chapter 11).

The Government is ambiguous about prison. In its 2002 White Paper, *Justice For All*, it says that it wants to send the 'strongest possible message' to criminals that the system will be effective in 'detecting, convicting and properly punishing them'. The role of prison is to be limited to the more 'dangerous, serious and seriously persistent offenders and those who have consistently breached community sentences'.

12.6 DOES PRISON WORK?

Penal reform groups, prison reductionists and policy makers in the 1990 White Paper claimed that a deterrence approach to sentencing is an unrealistic policy because it assumes that criminals make calculations about the likelihood of being detected, arrested and punished and mostly they do not, as most crime is opportunistic or carried out by people who do not make estimates of the likely consequences of their actions. Further, as very few of offences result in a sentence (see Chapter 2) it is assumed that not many people are affected by sentences. In addition, reconviction rates show that the majority of imprisoned offenders will be reconvicted of a new offence in the 2-year period following their release from prison. Thus prisons, it would seem, neither deter nor rehabilitate the majority of offenders who are sent there. These points add up to a view that prisons do not work and that the deterrent theory of imprisonment is invalid. The 1990 White Paper claimed that, 'It was unrealistic to construct sentencing arrangements on the assumption that most offenders will weigh up the possibilities in advance and base their conduct on rational calculation' (Home Office 1990a: 6).

For other critics of imprisonment the question is not whether prison works but whether there are more effective ways of using resources. If the reconviction rates of those sent to prison and those given community sentences are similar, they would argue that it is better to use the cheaper option. Other critics of the use of imprisonment recognise its value for locking up only potentially dangerous offenders.

However, the problem with these different criticisms of prison – that it does not work, or it works but is too costly, or that it should be reserved for dangerous offenders only – is that they focus exclusively on offender-instrumental considerations as if sentencing is only about the consequences on the future behaviour of those already convicted of crimes. These critics ignore the impact on other participants in, or audiences for, the sentence: the public and the victims. The public will include potential offenders who may well be influenced by the general deterrent effect of the sentence and do make estimates as to whether the potential risks of offending are outweighed by the possible gains; and also includes the law-abiding who wish to be reassured that offending does not pay and that the rules of the community are being respected, and that when they are not, a person pays for this in the hard coinage of punishment. Thus a concern with general deterrence, retribution and denunciation means that prisons may well play an effective part in maintaining a stable and law-abiding society.

It can be argued that prisons do not need to be justified in terms of whether they rehabilitate or deter the offenders sent to them, but in terms of the impact on those who do not go to prison. Prisons, it is argued, can work for the following sentencing reasons: first, on retributivist grounds, because they are regarded by the bulk of the public as suitable institutions for punishing people who have done wrong and have been convicted of a sufficiently serious crime such that the offence cannot be ignored and is considered worthy of a serious punishment such as incarceration; secondly, on denunciatory grounds, because they underline society's commitment to defining rules about the appropriateness of certain types of behaviour and censuring others as unacceptable; thirdly, on grounds of incapacitation, in that certain dangerous and sometimes persistent offenders need to be locked up to protect the public. There is a fourth justification based on a general deterrence view that prisons deter crimes from happening because of the fear of punishment. As we have already seen, there is a strongly held view among policy makers that crime is often opportunistic and not based on premeditated calculations of potential gains and losses. However, not all crimes are spontaneous and it is likely that the calculations about the chances of being discovered and punished may well deter some people who contemplate crime. Testing this idea is difficult because it requires a measure of why people do or do not act in a criminal manner.

Let us look at some data about the possible impact of imprisonment, which are part of the debate as to whether prisons work. There are three ways that prisons are considered to be effective: recidivism rates, incapacitation and deterrence.

The reconviction rate for adult prisoners subsequently convicted for offences within a 2-year period since they were discharged was 58 per cent (Spicer and Glickman 2004: 6). Thus over half of adult prisoners reoffend. This is an underestimate as the data excludes those sentenced to fines and discharges. Accurate reconviction rates for community penalties are also difficult to obtain but they also suggest that over half of adults given a community sentence will reoffend. The rate for all types of community sentences was 51 per cent with considerable variation in the rate – 60 per cent of offenders given a CRO reoffending in contrast to 38 per cent of those given a CPO.

Let us look at some data on the idea of incapacitation. The Halliday report, *Making Punishments Work* (2001), quoted a self-report survey of offenders admitted to prison in 2000, which revealed that the average offender admitted to committing 140 offences in the year before they were caught, and offenders who had a drug problem admitted on average to committing 257 offences per year. Thus, on average, for each 1,000 offenders imprisoned for a 12-month period the incapacitation effect would be to reduce offending by 140,000.

The case for the general deterrent effect of custody is difficult to measure with certainty. But one international comparative study, by Langan and Farrington (1998), contrasted six crimes (murder, rape, robbery, assault, burglary and motor vehicle theft) in the United States of America with England and Wales between 1981 and 1996. They contrasted the amount of crime based on crime surveys, with a combined index that brought together the chances of being caught and convicted and the sentence. They were thus able to assess what happened to crime over a 16-year period and assess the likelihood of an average offender being convicted and sent to prison.

Langan and Farrington (1998) found that in England and Wales in the early 1990s, criminals faced a lower risk of conviction and punishment compared with the United States of America. Between 1981 and 1995 an offender's risk of being caught, convicted and imprisoned increased in the United States for all six crimes but fell for all crimes in England and Wales except for murder. For burglary there were 5.5 imprisoned burglars for every 1,000 alleged burglars in the United States, increasing to 8.4 in 1994. In England and Wales there were 7.8 in 1981 but this dropped to 2.2 by 1995.

This decline in England and Wales was due to an increase in the use of cautions and unrecorded warnings; greater procedural safeguards for the accused; the growth in discontinuance of cases by the Crown Prosecution Service; the policy exhortations to judges and magistrates to make less use of prison; and the downgrading of the crime of theft of a motor vehicle in 1988 in England and Wales to a less serious offence category.

Another theorist who has taken up the issue of the deterrence role of imprisonment is Charles Murray, who challenges the liberal orthodoxy of the prison reductionists in *Does Prison Work?* Murray states the case for the theory of general deterrence and the impact of imprisonment, concluding that policy directions have been taken since the 1950s that have helped to promote rather than inhibit the growth of crime. Murray argues that, 'incarcerating people will not, by itself, solve the crime problem ... But if the question is "How can we deter people from committing crimes?" then ... prison is by far the most effective answer short of the death penalty' (Murray 1997: 20).

He shows that the chances of a convicted criminal going to prison has fallen dramatically in the period from 1954 to 1994. The prison reductionist claim about the overuse of custody is unconvincing when one contrasts, as Murray does, the steady but slow rise in prison population figures (doubled in 40 years) with the far more dramatic growth in crime over the period. Murray concludes over the period, 'The risk of going to jail if you commit a crime was cut by 80 per cent' (1997: 1). By contrasting the number of recorded crimes for a particular offence against the numbers given custody in the form of prison or borstal, he concludes:

> The reduction varied from crime to crime. In 1954, the number of people sentenced to prison or borstal for felonious wounding represented one out of five such felonious woundings; in 1994, one out of eight – a drop of 45 per cent. For rape, the number of people sentenced to custody went down from one out of three to fewer than one out of twelve – down 77 per cent. For burglary, from one out of ten to one out of a hundred – down 87 per cent. For robbery, from one out of three to one out of twenty – down 86 per cent.
>
> (Murray 1997: 1)

The evidential basis of his views relates to statistics on offenders sentenced for indictable offences and total crimes recorded taken from *Criminal Statistics England and Wales*. We saw in Chapter 2 that these official statistics can be misleading, but Murray argues that the upward trends in recorded crime from the 1950s represents a real growth in crime. This interpretation is confirmed by data from the British Crime Survey from 1982 onwards. Other evidence for the thesis is given in Figure 12.2, which shows the number of recorded crimes from 1950 to 1996 and the numbers of offenders given a custodial sentence of any form (see the list at the beginning of this chapter for a description of types of custodial sentence) in all courts for men and women of all ages. Figure 12.2 shows a huge growth in recorded crime over the 50-year period but a far less dramatic rise in the use of custody, which provides a small proportion of all those sentenced over the same period, as can be seen in Figure 12.3.

Murray argues that the reduced risk of imprisonment was part of a deliberate policy to switch away from a reliance on custody and towards diversion. This approach is illustrated by the policies as regards younger offenders. 'For more than three decades, English criminal justice policy has taken successive steps to make the criminal justice system less punitive towards youngsters. The motives were noble, but the effect has been that young offenders can be confident that not much is going to happen to them for any offence short of a major felony' (Murray 1997: 25).

Murray also argues that something can be done about crime and that 'the public is not upset about the crime problem only because the crime rate has gone up. Much of the public's anger and anxiety arises from two other aspects of the crime problem: a breakdown in lawfulness and a breakdown in public civility' (Murray 1997: 23).

Figure 12.2 **Crime and custody 1950/2003: total recorded crime and total sentenced to custody for all crimes/ages/male and female**

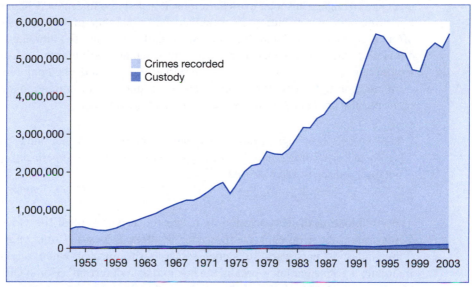

Source: Compiled from *Criminal Statistics England and Wales*, 1950 to 2003.

Figure 12.3 **Sentencing trends and custody 1950/2003 in England and Wales**

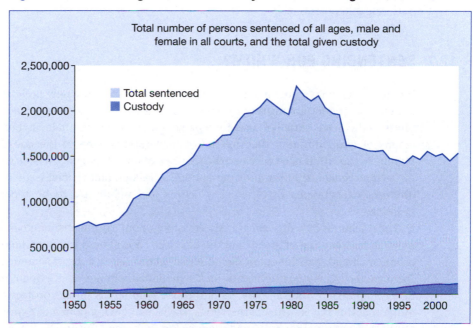

Source: Compiled from *Criminal Statistics England and Wales*, 1950 to 2003.

Prison is one part of a strategy to reduce crime and restore public confidence, built on a deterrence and just deserts approach. Murray believes that public confidence is likely to be undermined in a system of criminal justice if lawlessness is tolerated such that crime is ignored or criminals go unpunished. To help restore public confidence he argues that we need to discard 'most of the system's sympathy for the offender' (Murray 1997: 26). The criminal justice system is not primarily designed to engage in social work solutions. It is first and foremost designed around the principles of retribution to establish the culpability of the accused for the offence. In an adversarial system this puts the offender into the limelight. But after conviction there is no logical reason why offender-instrumental considerations should have priority over the interests of either the victim or the community.

In addition to the deterrence and retributive functions of imprisonment, Murray identifies the denunciatory functions of sentencing. He says:

> The court ... is a stage in the never-ending morality play. It is a public forum in which the peaceful members of the community assert their superiority over the outlaws. It dispenses just deserts.
>
> (Murray 1997: 24)

The combination of denunciation and deterrence was central the Government's White Paper about tackling youth crime, *No More Excuses* (Home Office 1997a). 'Punishment is necessary to signal society's disapproval when any person – including a young person – breaks the law and as a deterrent' (Home Office 1997a: 18). In the final section of this chapter we will be looking in more detail at a penal paradigm which, by the end of the twentieth century, had incorporated a concern for public confidence as well as about the impact of sentencing on the law breakers, both real and potential.

12.7 SENTENCING FOR WHOM?

We have seen above how penal policy has changed, and how new policies and the philosophies underpinning them are based on criticisms of the policies they replace. Shifts in the penal paradigm usually represent a change in the balance between the claims of many different theories and considerations. One of the questions that highlights the differences between the theories of punishment is, 'Who is sentencing for – the offender, the victim or the public?' A related and crucial issue is how the different expectations of offenders, victims and public are to be reconciled in practice.

The dilemmas of sentencing policy are often popularly encapsulated as seeking a balance between the offender and the offence. Thus should the punishment fit the crime or should punishment fit the offender? Many discussions of sentencing policy focus on the individual offender or on the individual offence as is evident in the just deserts approach. But denouncers and those who stress public protection would argue that this focus neglects the wider role of sentencing policy in expressing the public's disapproval of crime and recognising their need for protection. Others see the victim as a forgotten player in the drama of crime and punishment (see Chapter 3).

It is not surprising that a criminal justice system based on adversarial principles should produce a sentencing policy that is geared towards the individual offence, offender and the circumstances of the case. The criminal justice system is after all primarily concerned with implementing the rules which determine criminal liability and it deals with individual cases and individual offenders. Thus as Judge Rhys Davies comments, 'Judges ... must look at the person before them, and all the circumstances, and do what they know to be right conscientiously. That's their duty' (*The Times*, 28 June 1994: 11). To sentencers, therefore, what is fair in the individual case is likely to take priority over abstract principles of justice. This is compounded by the case law tradition of English law in which, as we have seen, there are no penal codes stating general principles but a tendency to judge each case on its merits.

The individualisation of sentencing has also, of course, been justified by the offender-instrumental approach which argues that sentences should aim to prevent further criminality. Also, in the adversarial system, defendants have the opportunity as required by due process to present factors in mitigation. All of this encourages a focus on the circumstances of the convicted criminal.

This individualisation, however, neglects a key person in many offences – the victim. While there is a focus on the harm done, the victim would appear to be little involved in sentencing other than as the potential recipient of a compensation order. As we have seen, some argue that there should be a victim impact statement and others have gone so far as to argue that victims' opinions should be sought. This might seem fair in some respects but is often rejected also on the grounds of fairness and justice. It is, for example, regarded as a key part of criminal law that punishment is undertaken by the state on behalf of the general public (see, for example, Ashworth 1997b). An offence, unlike a civil dispute, is not a private matter; it is a public one. Therefore, the victim should have no role in sentencing, other than when compensation or reparation is considered. In addition, such victim involvement might further compound disparities when different sentences are given to similar offenders on the basis of victim participation. This would add yet further individualised circumstances, this time based on the opinion of the victim, and could produce highly unpredictable sentencing decisions, further undermining any notion of fairness.

In terms of considering fairness, therefore, current discussions focus on fairness to individual offenders and fairness in terms of the sentence being proportionate to the crime. In recent years the balance has shifted with more weight being given to the seriousness of the offence and less to the needs and risks of individual offenders. However, the justice approach does restrict the severity of sentencing and encourage consistency, thus increasing justice to offenders. A major advantage of including in the aims of sentencing the retributivist concern with just desert is that it sets, in principle, limits on that system as to who, how and when it can act against an individual and thus provides the justification for civil rights within the criminal justice system.

However, as we have seen, fairness to individual offenders is not easy to achieve. How much, for example, should their individual circumstances be a factor in sentencing? And how might this lead to other kinds of inequities in sentencing? This can be seen when, as in Chapter 8, we look at the sentences given to those from different socio-economic backgrounds. Thus offenders' domestic, financial, and social circumstances may mean that they are judged favourably or adversely by the court. They may affect how they can present themselves, whether or not they can pay a fine, and the kind of mitigating factors they may put forward. In addition, sentences may have an unequal impact on these different groups.

Some of the above points indicate that sentencing policy cannot hope to include what some would see as the root causes of crime if these lie in social inequalities and the individual circumstances. This brings us back to the limitations of current offender-instrumental approaches to make much of an impact on the volume of crime. To what extent, therefore, can the public be protected or reassured through sentencing policy?

In answer to this it could be argued that tougher policing and tougher sentencing policies are only likely to have a marginal effect on crime prevention if we consider only the impact on offenders before the court. This is because, as we have seen, only a minority of cases reach the courts in comparison with the totality of crime. Less than 100,000 cases reached the Crown Court annually in recent years, and the number is falling, whereas the British Crime Survey suggests that 12 million crimes are committed each year. Even if the police force caught twice as many criminals, the courts could only be dealing with less than 1 per cent of known crimes. Of these cases only a small minority result in a conviction, and of these the overwhelming majority are offences that do not result in a prison sentence. Thus the offender-instrumental approach can at best have only a marginal impact on the amount of crime that the community is subject to. Furthermore, as we have seen, the promise of rehabilitation that crime could be cured and the arguments of deterrent theorists are open to question.

Thus the criminal justice process appears to have an intrinsically limited role to play in reducing or preventing crime. What implication does this have for sentencing policy, particularly in respect of its credibility with the public? The furore caused by unpopular sentencing decisions and the unit fines introduced by the CJA 1991 illustrates, however, that the public do perceive sentencing policy as important. To the denunciation model, as we have seen, punishment is not only a matter for offenders and victims but also involves the community's expectations about standards of behaviour and appropriate punishment. The criminal endangers their civil liberties by threatening their property, physical well-being and shared values.

The CJA 1991 also recognised the denunciatory role of punishment. Thus the 1990 White Paper stated that, 'Punishment can effectively denounce criminal behaviour and exact retribution for it. The sentence of the court expresses public repugnance of criminal behaviour and determines the punishment for it' (Home Office 1990a: 5). The CJA 1991 therefore could be seen as advocating what has been described as a denunciatory-retributivist perspective which by focusing on the morality of the act looks at the consequences of punishment for society as a whole rather than on the convicted criminal (Davies 1993).

Sentencing, after all, is a judgment about an appropriate sentence for a wrong done and is in effect morality in action. The judge condemns the offender in the name of the community and so re-enforces standards of morality. Thus a denunciatory-retributivist approach to sentencing recognises the moral censuring role of sentencing; and that in a democracy the tariff of sentencing should reflect and articulate the moral concerns of the community as well as ensuring fairness to the individual offender before the courts.

Denunciation could add a more positive dimension to a sentencing policy which in many ways has accepted the rather gloomy prognostication that 'nothing works'. One strength of rehabilitative and deterrent arguments was that they appeared to do something positive; they focused on the future rather than on the past. Just deserts focuses on the harm done in the past and therefore could be seen as negative – punishment, however fair, for its own sake. Denunciation, on the other hand, stresses the key role of punishment in focusing public attention onto issues of morality and right and wrong. This in turn draws attention to the social function of punishment. Thus David Garland (1990) comments:

> In designing penal policy we are not simply deciding how to deal with a group of people on the margins of society – whether to deter, reform, or incapacitate them and if so how. Nor are we simply deploying power or economic resources for penological ends. We are also and at the same time defining ourselves and our society in ways which may be quite central to our cultural and political identity. An important part of a society's penal rhetoric is taken up with the suggestion of a social vision.

Thus the importance of punishment for community and society should be recognised. The values embodied in the criminal law demonstrate a society's moral views of right and wrong; and those who breach the laws are doing more than just the physical and financial damage they do to the individual victim, they are challenging the values of society, and threaten the individual's definition of normality. Therefore, the purpose of punishment for the denouncer is not directed at the criminal act or the criminal actor, but at the values which define the rules embodied in the criminal law. The audience is neither the criminal nor victim but the public at large.

Thus the link between punishment and the public involves more than protecting individual citizens from individual criminals, though it is one essential role of the criminal justice system. Crime does more than threaten the individual; it is a threat to the community itself. 'The real significance of crime', wrote Joseph Conrad, 'is in its being a breach of faith with the community of mankind.'

CONCLUSION

This chapter has looked at how sentencing policy must be placed within the context of changing views about the causes of crime and the role of the penal system, especially prison. Thus the rehabilitative model was based on the idea that the problems which caused crime could be established and therefore alleviated. A sentence of imprisonment could be likened to a period of hospital treatment, an approach which had great appeal to reformers who also saw it as more humane. After decades of influence, however, the key ideas of rehabilitation were challenged. Rehabilitative policies were criticised as inhumane and inefficient. To some indeed they represented another way in which the powerful in society could enforce their values on others. Where, for example, did rehabilitation stop and enforced conformity, 'thought reform' or brainwashing begin? Did offenders who were effectively sentenced to be helped not have rights? Were these sentences fair?

The justice model aimed to provide an answer to the many problems of rehabilitation and other offender-instrumental policies. Punishment should not aim to do good, but to do as little harm as possible. Harsher sentences on the grounds of rehabilitation or deterrence could be limited by an approach which stressed linking the sentence to the harm done by culpable offenders. Yet, as we have seen, the application of the justice model raises questions about what is meant by justice and fairness in relation to sentencing.

A key feature of sentencing policy has also been an acceptance of the prison reductionist's aim, whether for idealistic or practical reasons, to reduce the use of imprisonment. This involved stressing the punitive nature of community sentences so as to make them credible to the police and sentencers. Whether or not this will be successful either in terms of reducing the use of imprisonment or making community penalties acceptable as a punishment, remains to be seen.

Changes in penal policy reflect the efforts of policy makers to find a balance between the various aims of sentencing as well as the aims of the criminal justice process as a whole. There is a constant tension between the need for due process, which extends beyond conviction to the sentencing process and the penal system, and the often conflicting claims of public protection. While the CJA 1991 defined the primary aim of sentencing as just deserts it also, with the twin-track approach, allowed for incapacitation through larger sentences for some violent and sexual offences. Incapacitation may conflict with the interests of due process, particularly where an assessment needs to be made of the circumstances in which a particular offender is assessed as dangerous enough that a sentence out of proportion to just deserts is justified.

The revival of rehabilitation and deterrence as part of a wider offender-instrumental penal strategy in the Criminal Justice Act 2003 may require a re-evaluation of existing sentencing practices and penal sanctions. How, for example, might this affect prisons? How will the new emphasis on punishment in the community affect the operation of community sentences previously seen as rehabilitative and offender focused? Some of these issues will be taken up in the next two chapters. Chapter 13 will look at prisons and Chapter 14 will explore developments in community sentencing.

Review questions

1 Explain why the principles of individualisation and indeterminacy followed from a rehabilitative approach to sentencing.

2 What is meant by the term 'disparity'? Explain how it is affected by individualistic strategies of sentencing.

3 What are the main elements of a justice approach to sentencing?

4 Explain the difference between a rationale for community penalties that aims to achieve an 'alternative to custody' and a rationale that seeks an intermediate sanction.

5 What information would you need to be able to assess the question of whether

prison works from a sentencing point of view? Consider the question, first, from the point of view of the likely impact of imprisonment on those offenders given a custodial sentence and, secondly, from the perspective of the general public.

Further reading

Cavadino, P and Dignan, J (2002) *The Penal System: An Introduction* (3rd edn), Sage: London

Davies, M (1993) *Punishing Criminals: Developing Community-based Intermediate Sanctions*, Greenwood: Connecticut

Duff, A and Garland, D (1994) *A Reader on Punishment*, Oxford University Press: Oxford

von Hirsch, A and Ashworth, A (eds) (1993) *Principled Sentencing*, Edinburgh University Press: Edinburgh

Prisons

INTRODUCTION

Despite efforts of the prison reductionists to declare prisons as vestiges of a past era, prisons in the early twenty-first century are thriving in all parts of the world. They must therefore be useful for some purposes but there appears to be no consensus in England and Wales on what is the primary purpose of imprisonment.

In October 1993 in a speech to the Conservative Party Conference, the Home Secretary, Michael Howard, stated that:

> Let us be clear. Prison works. It ensures that we are protected from murderers, muggers and rapists – and it makes many who are tempted to commit crime think twice.

The considerable public debate which followed demonstrated conflicting views about the role, aims and functions of prison along with continuing concerns about aspects of prison regimes, conditions and security. In general terms prisons have credibility with the public as an institution for punishment – the punishment being loss of liberty. This serves a retributive and denunciatory purpose. Prisons are also seen as a potential deterrent for the general public and they incapacitate dangerous and persistent offenders for the period of time they are incarcerated. Whether prison could rehabilitate inmates or deter them from committing further offences is far less obvious in the light of statistics on recidivism. Indeed some argue that it may increase the likelihood that offenders will continue their life of crime – not only have prisons been characterised as schools of crime but they remove offenders from the stabilising effect of their families and the likelihood of obtaining gainful employment. Yet others feel that the prison experience is insufficiently punitive and makes little difference to those with a criminal lifestyle.

In less than a decade the New Labour agenda on crime control has shifted to focus on offender management, a return to the belief that the primary objective was on controlling the criminal rather than the deserved punishment in response to the seriousness of a crime. The current debate is not polarised into a simple punishment versus reform of the criminal, but the new post-1997 agenda has restored a fresh commitment to the corrections penal paradigm with its aim to reduce recidivism by offender change. Phil Wheatley, Director General of the Prison Service, refers to this objective and to the new joined-up agency concerned with offender management:

> From June 2004, the Prison Service is operating within the new National Offender Management Service framework, which in itself brings fresh challenges for the Service. We cannot be complacent, but I believe that these results show that we are well equipped to operate efficiently and competitively within the new arrangements to help drive down re-offending.
>
> (Annual Report and Accounts 2003/4)

This objective for prisons derives from the recommendation in the Halliday report of 2001 to find more effective punishments defined in offender-instrumental terms, and the Home Office aim 'to deliver effective custodial and community sentences to reduce re-offending and protect the public'. The newly restored corrections discourse is seen in the White Paper *Justice for All* (2002), reflecting the New Labour penal paradigm and the prison reductionist logic that sees prisons as 'not working' to reduce recidivism, blames prisons for the break up of families and the acquiring of criminal skills, and sees the record numbers in prison as undesirable (with female numbers doubling between 1993 and 2002). Chapter 12 commented on some aspects of the prison reductionist case that underpins New Labour's strategy on prisons and we will look at other claims in this chapter on prisons.

The challenges facing the correctional services require an enhanced focus on rehabilitative work with offenders but with the edge that greater surveillance and tougher penalties are promised for those who do not comply. Clearly reflecting a shift away from the offence-focused system of the Criminal Justice Act 1991 (CJA 1991) to a focus on controlling offenders, the Criminal Justice Act 2003 (CJA 2003) introduces two new types of custodial sentences. The first is custody plus, with a greater emphasis on supervision following release from prison for short-term prisoners. Under the CJA 1991 there was no supervision following release for prisoners sentenced to less than 12 months. Secondly, intermittent custody is introduced in an attempt to reduce the negative outcomes that can accompany even short periods of full-time custody, such as loss of employment, loss of accommodation, and family disintegration. The logic of NOMS was to achieve a greater coordination between the prison and probation to achieve through-care and enhanced and coordinated supervision of offenders released back into the community.

To those who run prisons, the day-to-day problems of security (ensuring that prisoners do not escape) and control (attempting to prevent riots and violence) may well take precedence over more abstract goals of rehabilitation or deterrence.

This chapter will explore many of these issues. It starts by examining the origins of the penitentiary, and how the use and aims of prison have developed over the last century. The current organisation of the prison system in England and Wales will be outlined, and the numbers and characteristics of the prison population will be considered, followed by examination of the experience of imprisonment, the aims of prisons, and an exploration of the issues involved in assessing whether or not prison can be said to work (see also Chapter 12). Finally, there will be consideration of the question of how to balance the primary purpose of imprisonment (restriction of liberty) consistently with other objectives so as to provide 'humane containment' whilst seeking to help inmates become future law-abiding citizens.

13.1 ORIGINS OF THE PENITENTIARY

The prison as we know it today is a relatively recent social experiment which began 200 years ago. Before that time people were not usually given a sentence of imprisonment. The prisons, dungeons and gaols were owned by a variety of municipal and private bodies, and were used to hold debtors or people who had been arrested and were awaiting trial at the quarter sessions (quarterly sittings of the court). They also held those awaiting the implementation of a sentence. For serious offenders, transportation or execution was the main punishment. For lesser offenders, prison was used to encourage a person to pay a fine and short periods of confinement were prescribed for offenders too poor to pay a fine.

John Howard, in his survey of prisons in the 1770s, estimated a prison population of 4,084. His census of 1776 calculated that the prison population was made up of debtors (59.7 per cent), felons awaiting trial, execution and transportation, along with a few serving a prison sentence (24.3 per cent), and petty offenders (15.9 per cent). Howard was appointed to the post of High Sheriff for Bedfordshire in 1773. One of his duties, usually neglected by other sheriffs, was to report on the prisons in his county. The conditions he encountered so shocked him that he undertook a more widespread review of prison conditions that was printed in 1777, entitled *The State of the Prisons*.

Punishment in the eighteenth century for those convicted of misdemeanours consisted of the stocks, corporal punishment or fines. For serious offenders the sanction was the death penalty, or a substitute. During the eighteenth century, the number of capital offences rose from 50 to 225, and the death penalty became the prescribed punishment for most offences classified as felonies. Juries, however, were often reluctant to convict a person knowing that the person would be executed. 'Pious perjury', according to William Blackstone, became more popular after 1750. By re-evaluating the value of goods stolen to less than a shilling, juries convicted offenders for petty larceny rather than the capital offence of grand larceny. Despite the growth in the number of capital offences, the number of executions declined over the century and transportation became the typical sentence by the end of the eighteenth century. As Table 13.1 shows, in the five years from 1765 to 1769, 70 per cent of criminals sentenced at the Old Bailey were transported.

Table 13.1 **Distribution of punishments, Old Bailey 1760/94**

Year	Per cent death sentence	Per cent transported/hulks	Per cent whip/brand/fine	Per cent imprisoned
1760/64	12.7	74.1	12.3	1.2
1765/69	15.8	70.2	13.4	0.8
1770/74	17.0	66.5	14.2	2.3
1775/79	20.7	33.4	17.6	28.6
1780/84	25.8	24.1	15.5	34.6
1785/89	18.5	50.1	13.2	13.3
1790/94	15.9	43.9	11.7	28.3

Source: Ignatieff, M (1975: 81).

The Transportation Act 1717, providing for transportation to the American colonies as a punishment, was introduced with the purpose of deterring criminals and supplying the colonies with much-needed labour. It became common practice to commute a death penalty to transportation. Although transportation did not stop immediately with the American Revolution of 1776, prisoners began to be housed in hulks which were permanently moored ships. A House of Commons Committee review of transportation in 1779 recommended the continued use of hulks and that two new penitentiaries be built. The idea of the penitentiary was therefore seen at this time as a way forward, even though alternative locations were also being examined to permit the continuation of transportation.

Transportation came under scrutiny because some felt it was not a sufficient deterrent. Indeed, despite the health hazards of the journey it was said that some committed crime in order to be transported. A Transportation Act was passed in 1784 at a time when there was nowhere to send convicts although the Beauchamp Committee of 1785 reported favourably on the practice and cited its potential for reform, its cheapness and the advantages to the colonies of a convict workforce. Alternatives considered included Algiers, Tristan de Cunha and sending convicts down the coal-mines, but Australia was preferred.

Transportation to Australia reached its peak in the 1830s and 1840s with between 4,000 and 5,000 convicts being sent each year. There were also periods in the early nineteenth century when 70 per cent of convicted felons were imprisoned in hulks. The use of hulks and transportation declined after the prison building programme of the 1840s. By 1853 the idea of penal servitude as a substitute for transportation was introduced for those sentenced to under 14 years. In 1857 the last prison hulk went out of service and transportation formally ended in 1867.

Ideological and practical considerations changed the conditions within, and the function of, prison. Among the new penal ideas that emerged at the end of the eighteenth century the penitentiary style of prison was advocated as a place that could change criminals' behaviour by making them penitent. Places of detention were to be transformed from gaols for holding criminals into penitentiaries for transforming them into law-abiding citizens. This new ideology was influenced by a combination of ideas about religious salvation, humanitarian concern with the conditions of prisons and control concerns about the growing urban population. The penal ideology of the era was also shaped by the theories of rehabilitation which were discussed in Chapter 12. These involved isolating the offender from the bad influences of the community in 'total institutions' (Goffman 1961) which cut off the inmate from the environmental sources that were considered by some to be the cause of crime (Rothman 1980). This penal ideology also focused on the importance of surveillance and styles of discipline which could transform prisoners into self-disciplined workers (Bentham 1791; Foucault 1977).

These new ideas were prevalent across the emerging industrial societies of Europe and the United States of America. They were embodied in reforms influenced by Quaker thinkers in Pennsylvania and prison reformers such as John Howard and Elizabeth Fry in England (Rothman 1980). They also represented a shift in views about how to control problem groups in the community (Scull 1977). By the end of the eighteenth century not only prisoners, but orphans, mentally ill, sick and unemployed persons were being assigned to new style institutions such as prisons, orphanages, asylums, hospitals and workhouses. The grand Georgian and late Victorian style of institutions were invented at this time as the solution to deal with 'problem' categories of the population.

The Penitentiary Act 1779 provided the first indication of the new role for prisons as institutions to reform and deter criminals. The influence of John Howard, Sir William Blackstone and William Eden was apparent in the new direction to penal policy. This positive role for prisons was re-echoed in the report of the May Committee on prisons as late as 1979, and in the statements of the Chief Inspector of Prisons in the 1990s, Judge Stephen Tumin. Many ideas on prisons and their roles were utopian – such as Jeremy Bentham's panopticon, a model discussed below (see Figure 13.1). However, these ideas offered a way forward for a penal system which faced three main practical problems.

First, there was concern about growing numbers of migrants coming to the cities in search of work. The old style welfare system, based on parish relief, was no longer viable as the new factory system needed a more mobile labour force. It was no use having large pools of unemployed workers in isolated rural areas away from the new sources of work; hence, the problem of how to care and control those who were moving to rapidly expanding urban areas. This encouraged the search for innovative solutions and the invention of new institutions to cope with those deemed to be either a threat or inadequate – thus the workhouse, asylum and orphanage as well as the penitentiary.

Secondly, there was the practical problem after 1776 that transportation to the colony of Virginia was no longer available as a result of the American Revolution. Thirdly, there was growing disquiet among reformers and thinkers such as Blackstone, Romilly and Beccaria about the large numbers of capital offences. The ideas of Cesare Beccaria about the use of the death penalty influenced debates in the House of Commons. He attacked the widespread use of capital punishment arguing that the death penalty brutalised rather than deterred the population. His views were espoused by William Eden in the reform debates in Britain. Eden's book, *Principles of Penal Law*, was published in 1771. Sir Samuel Romilly took the lead in the parliamentary campaign to reduce the number of capital offences. He realised that to relinquish one mode of punishment the public and Parliament would need to be reassured that a satisfactory alternative was available. Thus some promoters of

Figure 13.1 The Panopticon

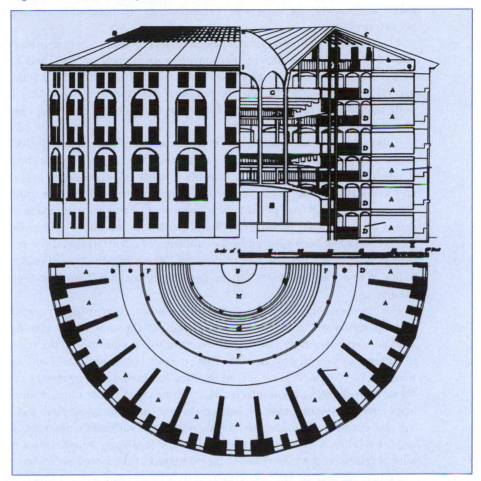

Source: Bowering (1843) *The Works of Jeremy Bentham*, Volume IV, 172–3 cf: 201. Reproduced by permission of The British Library.

the penitentiary argued that it was a more humane alternative to the death penalty, not that it was more efficient, as Bentham and Howard were to argue.

It took 50 years for prisons to become the main mode of punishment used by the criminal courts in Britain. The views of Howard and Bentham influenced prison policy for the next two centuries. Prison became not merely a substitute for the death penalty and transportation but a positive institution in which regimes, if sufficiently constructive, could rehabilitate those sent to them. Regimes were also to be sufficiently austere to deter future lawbreakers. The principle of 'less eligibility' implied that prison conditions were not to be more favourable than those found in the homes of the honest poor lest it encouraged crime.

The most celebrated of the novel ideas for bringing about constructive rehabilitation of convicts was the panopticon design proposed by Jeremy Bentham. The panopticon style prison involved a central viewing tower with rings of cells on each floor facing inwards to be visible to the observation tower. Observation and inspection were the keys to Bentham's approach to a more humane and effective mode of punishment. The panopticon would permit surveillance to allow prison officials to make assessments of prisoners' rehabilitation by constantly monitoring their behaviour.

The coliseum style and circular design of the panopticon was to prove difficult to build and was also inefficient. Pentonville was opened in 1842, and became the model for most Victorian prisons. It had stacked galleries on landings along a central straight corridor. Each corridor met at a central location in a fan-shaped floor plan with a central control and observation point permitting uninterrupted observation of each wing.

This systematic approach to prison design and administration reflected a growing interest in penal reform, which was wider than that of mere philanthropy. As the nineteenth century progressed a growing number of professional experts such as architects and doctors began to take an interest in penal affairs. The intervention of central government into penal policy meant that resources were made available to those who appeared to offer a solution to the problems of crime. Government involvement had been spurred by the problems of where to ship those sentenced to transportation. Having resorted to housing increasing numbers of prisoners in the hulks, it was then necessary for the government to find them work such as river dredging.

For the next 200 years, the government became increasingly concerned in the administration of prisons. The second half of the nineteenth century saw the gradual transfer of responsibility for monitoring conditions and the administration of prisons to central government. This process began with the Gaol Act 1823, in which Peel's administration set out the first comprehensive statement of principles about the running of local prisons. The Act imposed health requirements; required inspection by visiting justices; banned the consumption of alcohol and demanded the classification of inmates and the segregation of different categories. There were to be five classes of inmates, with male separated from female prisoners; and an annual report on the prison had to be submitted to the Home Secretary.

In 1877 all prisons were nationalised in a Prison Act which brought all prisons under central government control. The government established the Prison Commission to run prisons and the first of a number of influential chairmen of the commissioners was appointed, Sir Edmund Du Cane. Some commissioners led the debate on penal reform and were strong advocates of a modern penology based on better prison conditions and strategies to achieve the rehabilitation of inmates. They represented the age of optimism, documented in Chapter 12, about the positive aspects of penal institutions as places of reform. This commitment to the belief that through positive regimes inmates could be encouraged to lead good and useful lives was given official recognition in the Gladstone Committee of 1895 and became one of the leading principles of the prison service when incorporated into the Prison Rules in 1949. This states that the purpose of imprisonment was 'to encourage and assist the inmate to lead a good and useful life'.

During the 1930s the treadmill and arrows on convict uniforms were abolished. During this period also experiments with open prisons for adults were started at Wakefield Prison in 1936, when selected inmates from the prison slept in non-secure accommodation at New Hall Camp. In 1963 the Prison Commission was abolished and prisons were run by the prison service, a branch of the Home Office. The aim was to allow penal policy to be more fully integrated into a more general approach to crime control. This view was to be echoed in the rationale for integration of the prison and probation service.

Events in the 1990s within prisons caused a review of all aspects of prison regimes and staffing. In 1990 prisoners rioted at Strangeways, a local prison in Manchester. It took 25 days for the prison authorities to gain control of the prison. The damage to the prison was valued at £30 million. Rioting spread to other institutions and an independent public inquiry was established under the chairmanship of Lord Justice Woolf to look at the causes of these riots and to make recommendations. The report *Prison Disturbances, April 1990* was published in 1991 (see Home Office 1991a). The first half of the report, written by Lord Justice Woolf, examined the causes of the riots. The second half of this extensive 600-page report was written by Lord Justice Woolf and Judge Stephen Tumin, Her Majesty's Inspector of Prisons. It provided an overview of prison conditions, made 204 specific proposals aimed to reduce future conflicts between inmates and the prison authorities and listed the following 12 key recommendations:

- Closer cooperation between the different parts of the criminal justice system. For this purpose a national forum and local committees should be established.

- More visible leadership of the prison service by a Director General who is and is seen to be the operational head and in day-to-day charge of the service. To achieve this, there should be a published 'compact' or 'contract' given by ministers to the Director General of the prison service, who should be responsible for the performance of that 'contract' and publicly answerable for the day-to-day operations of the prison service.

- Increased delegation of responsibility to governors of establishments.

- An enhanced role for prison officers.

- A 'compact' or 'contract' for each prisoner setting out the prisoner's expectations and responsibilities in the prison in which he or she is held.

- A national system of accredited standards, with which, in time, each prison establishment would be required to comply.

- A new prison rule that no establishment should hold more prisoners than is provided for in its certified normal level of accommodation, with provisions for Parliament to be informed if exceptionally there is to be a material departure from that rule.

- A public commitment from ministers setting a timetable to provide access to sanitation for all inmates at the earliest practical date, not later than February 1996.

- Better prospects for prisoners to maintain their links with families and the community through more visits and home leaves and through being located in community prisons as near to their homes as possible.

- A division of prison establishments into small and more manageable and secure units.

- A separate statement of purpose, separate conditions and generally a lower security categorisation for remand prisoners.

■ Improved standards of justice within prisons involving the giving of reasons to a prisoner for any decision which materially and adversely affects him; a grievance procedure and disciplinary proceedings which ensure that the governor deals with most matters under his present powers; relieving Boards of Visitors of their adjudicatory role; and providing for final access to an independent Complaints Adjudicator.

(Home Office 1991a: para. 15.5)

In response, Kenneth Baker, the then Home Secretary had already begun to introduce some of the proposals to improve conditions within prisons. An increase in visits, letters and access to telephones was implemented together with the start of a programme of works to meet the Woolf deadline of February 1996 for ending the practice of slopping out. The planning and building of new prisons also continued in order to reduce the overcrowding described in the Woolf Report. By early 1994 the prison service could claim that there were no cases of three inmates having to share a prison cell designed for one. Sentencing planning for inmates was introduced on 1 October 1992 for inmates serving 4 years and over and for Category A inmates. For inmates serving between 12 months and less than 4 years the scheme started on 1 November 1993. The CJA 1993 removed the disciplinary powers of the Board of Visitors in line with the recommendations of the Woolf Report; and National and Area Criminal Justice Consultative Councils were established. However, there has been less development with regard to community prisons and a national system of accredited standards.

A second significant incident led to further reviews and reports that considered prison regimes. On 9 September 1994, six prisoners escaped from the high-security prison at Whitemoor. An inquiry was conducted by Sir John Woodcock into that escape and, following the publication of his findings in December 1994, the Home Secretary announced a review of 'physical security and security procedure in the prison service in England and Wales'. This was to be conducted by Sir John Learmont. In the month in which the inquiry team started, Frederick West committed suicide in Winston Green Prison on 1 January 1995 and on 3 January three prisoners escaped from Parkhurst Prison on the Isle of Wight. Whitemoor and Parkhurst were dispersal prisons with regimes designed to prevent the escapes of inmates regarded as a danger to the public. The inquiry found that one of the Parkhurst prisoners was a sheet-metal worker who was given access to workshops where he made the key used in the escape. The inquiry focused primarily on security in dispersal prisons.

The Learmont report (Learmont 1995), *Review of Prison Service Security in England and Wales and the Escape from Parkhurst Prison on Tuesday 3rd January 1995*, made 127 recommendations regarding security in dispersal prisons, including the following:

■ a daily audit of tools and materials used in workshops;

■ visitors to be subject to rub-down searches and x-ray checks and efforts made to prevent smuggling;

■ 360-degree CCTV surveillance in visiting rooms;

■ end family visits in dispersal prisons;

- the volume of inmates' possessions should be limited to that which would fit into two transit boxes;

- the statement of purpose of the prison service should be revised to make custody the primary purpose;

- key performance indicators should be reviewed to show progress towards preventing escapes rather than just measuring the number of escapes, and the degree of success at dealing with the drug problem in prison;

- the concept of drugs-free wings and of drug testing should be implemented where appropriate;

- early release should be a privilege earned through good behaviour;

- all prisoners should be offered meaningful work and wages;

- television in the cells should be an aspect of the privileges schemes and earned through good behaviour.

Whilst the outcomes of these two major reports centred on detailed management within prisons, other recent reviews have focused on the ethos and organisation of the service as a whole. The current organisation, management and monitoring of the prison service are discussed in the next section.

13.2 PRISONS IN ENGLAND AND WALES

In recent years the institutional divide between prison and probation and the consequences of this for offender management has been challenged with the proposed National Offender Management Service. In 2004, staff working in the prison service numbered 48,000. The prison service has the responsibility of operating the prison system in England and Wales, including the prisons operated by private companies. The Prison Act 1877 had created a state monopoly and brought under the control of the Prison Commissioners all those prisons that had previously been in local and private control. On 1 April 1993 the prison service became an executive agency of the Home Office. Agency status gives some degree of independence from Home Office control of daily operations and responsibility for budget and expenditure. The first director of the prison service under these new arrangements was Derek Lewis, who was dismissed in October 1995 and succeeded by Richard Tilt and subsequently by Phil Wheatley.

In 2004 there were 128 prison service establishments in England and Wales, plus 10 contracted out (privately run) prisons. With contracted out prisons the prison service lost the monopoly on operating prisons it was granted in 1877.

The range of prisons reflects the variety of tasks they are used for. Some need to be near criminal courts in urban areas to house those remanded in custody while awaiting trial or sentence. Others deal with specialist populations such as young offenders or females. In 2004 there were 15 female prisons. Others hold inmates for relatively short periods while others need to offer a regime for those prisoners who might spend the rest of their life inside a prison. Some can pay less attention to security because they house prisoners who have shown they can be trusted, while others must contain inmates convicted of serious violent offences who would be a danger to the public if they were to escape, and remain a danger to those inside prison while they are there. The prison service classifies prisons as local, training and dispersal prisons, young offender institutions, remand centres, juvenile institutions and women's prisons. Closed prisons have most security and surveillance to prevent escapes, whereas open prisons have more relaxed security. Open prisons include Ford near Worthing and Leyhill near Bristol. They have little, if any, perimeter security and house Category D prisoners posing a minimal risk to the public. Ford is renowned for the celebrities and white-collar criminals who have spent time there and include George Best who served 3 months for a drink-driving offence, Jeffrey Archer, Lord Brockett (the insurance fraudster) and the Guinness trio of Gerald Ronson, Ernest Saunders and Anthony Parnes.

Local prisons are used to hold those remanded in custody awaiting trial or sentence. After conviction and sentence to a period of incarceration the observation, classification and allocation unit in the local prison carries out an initial assessment and classification. This determines which prison the prisoner will be sent to, depending on security categorisation, the length of sentence and the training, medical and other needs of the inmate.

Those sentenced to a short period in prison will probably stay in the local prison. This is usually near to where they live and so helps facilitate family visits. The local prisons tend to be the older prisons built in the Victorian era and found in urban built-up areas. A new local prison, Belmarsh in East London, was opened in 1991, but this is unusual as most expenditure on prison building went on new training prisons. These are convenient for proximity to the courts and to the prisoners' families but are often the most overcrowded with the oldest facilities. All 37 local prisons are closed establishments.

Remand wings and centres are used in addition to local prisons for holding remand prisoners either in separate remand centres or in parts of local prisons with adult remand wings. Remand centres were created specifically for young offenders in response to growing concerns about mixing young remand prisoners with adults and, in particular, about the level of suicides and self-inflicted harm amongst remand prisoners under 21.

Dispersal prisons are high security prisons which have regimes designed to ensure no escapes as they hold prisoners with the maximum security classification. All sentenced prisoners on arrival in a prison are given a security rating. This ranges from Category A, for those whose escape would constitute a serious risk to the public, to Category D, for those who can be sent to open prisons.

The escape of the Soviet spy, George Blake, from Wormwood Scrubs prison in 1965 led to an inquiry by the Mountbatten Committee (Home Office 1966). Their report in December 1965 recommended that all high-risk inmates be held in one maximum security prison. This recommendation was not approved and, after a further proposal from a committee chaired by Leon Radzinowicz which reported in 1968 (Home Office 1968) it was decided that high security prisoners should be dispersed among a number of prisons with maximum security facilities; hence the term 'dispersal prisons' of which there were nine in 2004 holding on average a daily population of 2,668 prisoners. Three of these have special security units for those Category A inmates most likely to try to escape.

The need for security classifications was another of the recommendations of the

Mountbatten Report. Initial classification is based on the crime committed and the reports made by the assessment unit in the local prison. These categories are reassessed at regular intervals and most inmates are reclassified downwards during their prison term. Category A is for prisoners whose escape from custody would be highly dangerous to the public or to the security of the state. Category B is used to classify inmates who do not constitute such a serious risk. Category C is applied to prisoners who cannot be trusted in open prisons but are deemed unlikely to make an effort to escape, and category D is for prisoners who can be trusted to serve their time in open prisons where the security aspect of the regime is minimal.

Training prisons hold long-term inmates. There are 71 training prisons and they can be open or closed. They provide training facilities, vocational courses and the opportunity to work in the prison industries. At Coldingley Prison, a closed prison, inmates can work making motorway signs or in the large industrial laundry that has a contract with hospitals in the region. Grendon Underwood, opened in 1963, offers a specialist regime based on the therapeutic community concept pioneered by Maxwell Henderson in psychiatric hospitals.

Young offender institutions (YOIs) hold young adult offenders aged between 18 and 20 years of age and juvenile offenders aged 15–17. Juveniles may be kept in custody for remand orders and as a consequence of being given a detention and training order (DTO), which replaced previous custodial sentences for juveniles in 2000. The DTO varies between 4 months and 2 years with half of the period spent in custody and the other half under supervision by a youth offending team. Juveniles sentenced to custody under a DTO may not be sent to a YOI as there is also the option of being sent to a secure training centre (STC) or a local authority secure children's home (LASCH).

Places for incarcerating younger offenders have changed over the years since the Victorian era when the first efforts to separate younger inmates from adults were made with the introduction of reformatories and industrial schools. Borstals were introduced in 1901 and made fully available after the Prevention of Crime Act 1908. Detention centres were introduced in the Criminal Justice Act 1948. Chapter 8 described the changes since 1982 to the name of institutions holding younger offenders. The names may have changed more rapidly than the nature of the regimes that the changes were supposed to signify.

In April 1998 Medway Secure Training Centre was opened near Rochester, Kent. It is the first of a new type of custodial institution for 12–14-year-olds who have committed serious offences. The offenders, called trainees, spend between 3 months to a year in a regime designed to rehabilitate and punish. Trainees are required to attend educational course and programmes to address offending behaviour. It is run by a private firm, Rebound ECD, which is owned by Group 4. This type of secure accommodation for younger offenders is not a prison service institution and comes under the supervision of the Youth Justice Board established by the Crime and Disorder Act 1998.

Female establishments in 2003/4 held an average total population of 4,050. There are 15 female institutions with two more planned to open at Bronzefield in 2004 and Peterborough in 2005. In 2004 there were seven local prisons for females at Brockhill, Eastwood Park, Edmunds Hill, Holloway, Low Newton, New Hall and Styal; six closed training prisons at Buckley Hall, Bullwood Hall, Cookham Wood,

Downview, Foston Hall and Send; and two open prisons at Askham Grange and East Sutton Park. Holloway in London is the largest, with a daily average of 539 inmates (*Prison Service Annual Report and Accounts 2003/4*).

Special hospitals are used for offenders who need treatment for mental disorders under conditions of special security because of their violent or criminal behaviour. These offenders can be sent to one of three special hospitals: Broadmoor, Rampton or Ashworth. These have maximum security facilities similar to a dispersal prison. Special hospitals are run by the Department of Health. All the other types of prisons mentioned above are the responsibility of the prison service.

The prison service is not now the only agency allowed to run prisons. The Criminal Justice Act 1988 allowed for private companies to take over the operation of remand prisons, a sector of the prison establishment where the worst conditions were usually found. Since then companies such as Group 4 have been involved in operating prisons. The prison service has overall responsibility for the 'contracted out' prisons run by the private sector. All contracted out prisons have a prison service controller of governor grade to monitor the delivery of the contract with the prison service, and to undertake adjudications for prisoners charged with offences against disciplinary rules.

Contracted out prisons: The first to open was The Wolds private remand centre near Hull. Now there are 10, including Blakenhurst near Redditch, and Doncaster which opened in June 1994. The government's aim to break down the prison service monopoly in this area was not only influenced by its ideological belief in the virtues of competition. Two other factors played a part: first, a desire to inject new ideas into the running of remand prison regimes; and, secondly, after a series of industrial disputes, a determination to undermine the powerful trade union, the Prison Officers' Association, representing prison officers.

The influence of the Prison Officers' Association has been apparent in a number of industrial disputes over the years. The Labour Government of James Callaghan established an inquiry chaired by Mr Justice May after a long period of deteriorating industrial relations in prisons in England and Wales. It examined the prison population, objectives and regimes, the organisation of the system, resources, the roles of prison officers and governors, pay and allowances, industrial relations and working conditions. The resulting Home Office report was published in 1979 (*The Report of the Committee of Inquiry into the UK Prison Service*, Cmnd 7673). It concluded that 'Central administration ought to have shown itself more responsive to growing feelings of dissatisfaction with the organization and management and service as a whole, especially in the field of personnel management.' With reference to the importance of having clear and agreed aims for prisons – discussed later in this chapter – it commented:

> A great deal of the evidence we received maintained that at the present time these objectives (of imprisonment) were unclear or confused or both, and that this had brought about or contributed not only to a lack of incisive and purposeful leadership but also to indecision, frustration and the consequent lowering of morale throughout the prison service.
>
> (Home Office 1979: 1961)

The May Report found that over one-quarter of junior prison officers were working more than 60 hours' overtime a week, boosting a modest basic salary into reasonably high average earnings. In response to these staffing costs, a new higher basic wage for a 39-hour working week was introduced for prison officers in exchange for abandoning some of the expensive shift work practices.

Fresh Start, as the initiative was called, was introduced in 1987 in an attempt to overcome these staffing costs. The Prison Officers' Association agreed to the scheme because of the rise in basic pay, pension benefits, and officers were allowed to, and were given financial inducements to, buy their own living quarters. This created a longer-term problem for the prison service as it reduced geographical mobility due to the lack of affordable accommodation in some regions.

Industrial disputes were not overcome by the Fresh Start programme and the government sought other ways of curtailing the influence of the Prison Officers' Association. The introduction of 'contracting out' of prison service work to private companies should be seen in this context. The Criminal Justice and Public Order Act 1994 curtailed the right of prison officers and governor grade staff to go on strike.

Employee costs are the major contributor to the cost of imprisonment. In 2003/4 the average cost per prisoner was calculated at £25,718 per inmate per year. These costs ranged from a high end of £46,502 for male dispersal prisons, to £19,016 for male open prisons.

However, this does not mean that sending one less person to prison would save this amount as most of these costs are relatively fixed. Three-quarters of prison service expenditure is attributable to staffing costs. In 2003/4 the prison service employed 48,800 employees. This represents a ratio of under two inmates per officer and compares with a ratio of three to one in 1980. This is a very generous ratio of officers to prisoners compared with prison services around the world.

The prison service is open to inspection by the *Inspectorate of Prisons*, established by statute in 1982 after a recommendation in the 1979 May Report. Members of the inspectorate can make unannounced visits as well as having a number of scheduled visits to certain prisons each year. After a visit a report is made highlighting the strengths and weaknesses of the establishments visited. Some reports have been very damning about conditions in prison establishments and the treatment of prisoners.

Independent Monitoring Boards have taken over the role of the Board of Visitors and perform a vital 'watchdog' role on behalf of Ministers and the general public in providing a lay and independent oversight of prisons. In total there are 1,800 lay members of these boards. Each Board is independent of the prison it monitors and reports each year to the Home Secretary. Board members can visit the prison at any time in order to talk to the staff, inmates or detainees, hear their concerns and check on the conditions they are living and working in. In the past Boards have achieved significant changes through the work of their members.

Until 1992 the Board of Visitors adjudicated on matters of discipline where an inmate might be liable to lose remission for disciplinary offences. As a result of the CJA 1991 prison governors have the right to order up to 14 'added days' for disciplinary offences. The Board of Visitors at Wandsworth prison in the 1980s was among the first to publish a public report, describing the insanitary conditions associated with slopping out and the health hazards of a cockroach infestation near the kitchen area.

In April 1994, the Board of Visitors at Whitemoor prison in March, Cambridgeshire, published a report about the conditions and regime in the prison, which held 514 inmates, 20 per cent of whom were classified as Category A. These included Dennis Nilsen and IRA terrorists. Another 20 per cent were life sentence prisoners. It was in this prison that Leslie Bailey, a paedophile convicted of serious sexual offences against children, was found strangled in his cell in October 1993. The report describes the prison as dirty and the Board of Visitors condemned the illegal brewing of 'hooch' by inmates. The main concern expressed by the Board in its report was that management had lost control of the situation and it quotes a governor who was of the opinion that the prisoners and not the staff were virtually in control of the prison – an allegation that was to be prescient in the light of the subsequent escape attempt in September 1994 by five convicted IRA prisoners in which one prison officer was shot and wounded. All the prisoners were recaptured within hours of the escape. In the same month, quantities of the explosive Semtex were found at Whitemoor. These incidents raised many questions about why no action had been taken and led to demands for the resignation of the Home Secretary, as did the escape in January 1995 of three Category A offenders from another dispersal prison, Parkhurst, on the Isle of Wight.

13.3 PRISON POPULATION

It was shown in Chapter 12 that concerns over prison overcrowding, conditions and the size of the prison population led to policies to reduce the numbers sent to prison. At the same time a prison-building programme started in 1982 designed to improve facilities and reduce cell sharing. The routine of 'slopping out' caused by the lack of toilet facilities in the cells of the Victorian prisons led to the daily morning practice of prisoners forming a queue to the washrooms to dispose of the contents of their chamber pots. The prison service accepted the February 1996 deadline set by Lord Woolf for an end to slopping out. In fact most prisons completed their programme of modernisation to end this practice by 1994.

The daily population in prison varies depending on the time of year. It usually drops in December and rises to a high point in March. The average daily prison population in England and Wales in July 2004 was 74,923. The prison population rose to 50,000 by 1988 and then fell to the 1993 level, since when it has steadily risen. The prison service estimate of the prison population in 2009 will be about 92,000 (*Prison Population Brief* November 2003: 21).

To measure the degree of overcrowding, the prison population is compared with the Certified Normal Accommodation (CNA). In September 2003 the prison population was 111 per cent of its official capacity. Local prisons were most overcrowded with 137 inmates for every 100 places. Some institutions were under capacity, with open young offender institutions at only 64 per cent of capacity (*Occupation of Prisons*, September 2003: 1). The annual averages of the population in custody over the period from 1988 to 2003 are given in Table 13.2.

Table 13.2 Population in custody: annual daily average per year 1988/2003

Year	Under sentence	Remand	Total
1988	38,300	11,400	**50,000**
1989	37,900	10,500	**48,600**
1990	35,500	9,900	**45,600**
1991	35,400	10,100	**45,900**
1992	35,400	10,100	**45,800**
1993	33,300	10,700	**44,600**
1994	35,800	12,400	**48,800**
1995	39,100	11,400	**51,000**
1996	43,000	11,600	**55,300**
1997	48,412	12,131	**60,543**
1998	52,149	12,568	**64,717**
1999	51,691	12,520	**64,211**
2000	52,684	11,274	**63,958**
2001	54,050	11,237	**65,287**
2002	57,306	12,750	**70,056**
2003	59,872	13,034	**74,055**

Note: Excludes non-criminal prisoners.

Source: *Prison Statistics England and Wales 2002*: 29; and *Prison Population Brief* Nov. 2003: 23.

International comparisons

It is often claimed in the press and in broadcasts that the courts in England and Wales make more use of custody than other countries. Comparisons with other western European Union countries is given in the last chapter in Table 12.2, and Table 13.3 shows some comparisons with other prison populations in other advanced industrial countries, some with adversarial legal systems similar to that in England and Wales.

Both figures show average daily populations plus the rate per size of population. In Table 12.2 the number of prisoners per crimes recorded is also shown. There are difficulties in ensuring the data is directly comparable; however, the main question is to ask 'what comparisons make most sense?' Should we compare the prison population against the total size of the population or the amount of crime? Populations vary and we would not expect a country with a larger proportion of infants or elderly citizens to have the same crime problem as others. The problem with comparisons based on the population is that it takes no account of the amount of crime committed, which is, after all, the main reason why people go to prison. The demographic comparative data does not take into account the differences in usage of imprisonment or the risk of imprisonment because of the age of criminal responsibility. Thus it is suggested that a better comparison would be to compare prison populations against crime problems. However, even if this were to be done, we should still ask whether there is any utility in such a comparison because crime definitions and sentencing policies can vary, reflecting different cultures and the different political significance of certain crimes. The cultural significance of types of crime, and modes and the scale of punishment is unlikely to be the same in all countries around the globe.

Table 13.3 International comparison of some prison populations outside Europe 2000/2

Country	2000	2001	2002	Rate per 100,000 population in 2002
England and Wales	65,666	67,056	71,324	137
Australia	21,714	22,458	22,492	116
Canada	31,608	31,547		101
Japan	58,747	63,415	67,354	53
New Zealand	5,720	5,887	5,738	144
South Africa	166,334	174,893	184,142	431
Russia	923,600	979,285	873,000	602
USA	1,935,919			702

Source: *Prison Statistics England and Wales 2002*: 40

Categories of prisoner

Not all inmates held in Her Majesty's Prisons are of the same status. As seen in Chapter 9, some defendants are remanded in custody and held in prison. These unconvicted prisoners have rights distinguishing them from other inmates such as daily access to visitors. There are also those who have been convicted but have not yet been sentenced. In Table 13.2 these two groups are identified as remand prisoners and constitute approximately one-fifth of the average prison population. Young offenders in the prison system are referred to as juveniles if aged 15–17 and young adults if aged 18–20.

Fine defaulters in prison

Although there are many ways in which a fine can be enforced by the courts, as outlined in Chapter 11, the ultimate sanction for non-payment of fines or compensation orders is imprisonment, as indeed it is for non-compliance with community sentences. Fine defaulters are not, however, automatically sent to prison as Mark Romer, a Metropolitan Stipendiary Magistrate explained in a letter to the *Independent*:

> Fine defaulters are not imprisoned because they cannot pay their fines but because, often after many attempts to get them to pay, they will not. Magistrates are forbidden by law to imprison fine defaulters unless either they refuse to pay or, having had the means to pay and other methods of enforcing payment (e.g. by a bailiff's warrant) having failed, they do not pay.
>
> (*Independent*, 5 March 1995: 24)

The average daily population of fine defaulters in prison is 37 and the total number sent to prison for non-payment of fines in 2002 was 1,192 (*Prison Statistics 2002*: 13). The average time served by fine defaulters in 2003 was one week.

The drop in recent years is in part because of a Queen's Bench Judgment on 28

November 1995 (*R v Oldham Justices and Another, ex parte Cawley*) that the courts must consider all other methods of enforcing the fine before committing a fine defaulter to prison. The Magistrates' Association and the Justices' Clerks' Society produced guidelines that required the magistrates to take each enforcement measure in turn to consider whether each measure is appropriate or not. Good practice guidance notes were issued to the courts in July 1996 regarding the enforcement of financial penalties. Under the Criminal Procedure and Invest-igations Act 1996 the method of initiating an attachment of earnings order, in the case of fine default, was changed to allow Justices' Clerks to take proceedings without reference to the magistrates.

Life sentence inmates

In contrast to those who enter prison for a week or two the offender given a life sen-tence has a very different situation to face. Life sentence prisoners spend some time after sentence at a life sentence unit to undergo counselling and preparation for their future life in prison or on licence. They have no entitlement to automatic release but are eligible to apply for *release on licence*. This is discretionary and if released the person is on licence for the rest of his or her life and may be recalled to prison at any time.

For those aged under 21 the following terms refer to the equivalent of a life sentence:

- *Custody for Life* for those aged 18–20 convicted of murder or another life sentence offence
- *Detained during Her Majesty's Pleasure* under s. 90 of the Powers of Criminal Courts (Sentencing) Act 2000
- *Detention for life* under s. 91 of the Powers of Criminal Courts (Sentencing) Act 2000.

In 2003 there were 5,475 inmates in prison with a life sentence including 151 young offenders and 170 women. Most life sentences were for murder (70 per cent) although there were also some offenders given a life sentence for rape, manslaughter and arson (*Prison Population Brief* November 2003: 11). In 2002, 150 lifers were released on licence for the first time and the average time served prior to first release was 13.7 years.

Release on licence for those sentenced to a mandatory life sentence required the authority of the Home Secretary following a recommendation of the Parole Board. The Murder (Abolition of the Death Penalty) Act 1965 allowed the trial judge to specify a minimum period that must be served. The Criminal Justice Act 1967 made it a statutory requirement that the Home Secretary must consult with the trial judge and the Lord Chief Justice whenever a life sentence prisoner is due for release.

The statutory framework concerning the recall of lifers is set out in the CJA 1991, s. 39. When a licence is revoked the person must be told the reason and of his or her right to make representations to the Parole Board. The Parole Board must consider the likely risk to other people when considering the release of a person on licence and the extent to which he or she has complied in the past or is likely in the future to comply with the conditions of a licence. Life licensees can be recalled to prison at any time if they commit an offence or otherwise fail to comply with their conditions of licence.

The time served before release on licence varies depending on the nature of the crime and the perceived risk to the community of releasing a life sentence inmate. Some inmates may never be released. Such is likely to be the situation of Ian Brady, the Moors murderer, convicted with Myra Hindley in 1966 at Chester Assizes for the murder of Lesley Anne Downey, aged 10, and Edward Evans, aged 17. Hindley, who died in prison in 2002, confessed to her role in the murder of three other children.

The responsibility for determining the time to be served under a life sentence and whether this should be a political or judicial decision has occasioned much criticism and the matter came before the European Court of Human Rights in *Dennis Stafford v United Kingdom* (2002) and the House of Lords in *R v Secretary of State for the Home Department, ex parte Anderson and Taylor* (2002). As a result of these cases, legislation allowing the Home Secretary to set the minimum period to be served under a life sentence was declared incompatible with the Human Rights Act 1998 and the CJA 2003 introduced new provisions with effect from December 2003. These provide guidelines for the courts in assessing the tariff for mandatory life sentences and an extensive list of aggravating and mitigating factors which must be taken into account. Whole life tariffs are suggested for multiple and some child murders as well as for murder committed for political or religious causes. Other guideline tariffs are set at 30 years (e.g. for the murder of a police or prison officer, or a murder committed for gain) and at 15 years where none of the aggravating features listed are present. Different considerations are proposed for those under the age of 18.

Female prisoners

The numbers of female prisoners have increased in the last decade. Table 13.4 shows the percentage of female inmates as a proportion of all prisoners over the last one hundred and two years – the table gives data on 5-year intervals from 1900 to 2000 and shows that, despite the recent rapid growth in female imprisonment in absolute terms, current proportions are not as high as in the first half of the twentieth century.

Other data showing the numbers of female prisoners per 100,000 of the whole population over a hundred years indicates a decline from a high of 20 female prisoners per 100,000 of population in 1902. The proportion of female prisoners stabilises from 1929 to 1996 between 3 and 7 per cent, and then rises to 16 by 2002 (*Prison Statistics England and Wales 2002*: 5). From this data the trend from 1996 shows an increasing proportion of women being sent to prison.

The White Paper *Justice For All* under the heading 'What is not Working' states, 'The number of female prisoners more than doubled between 1993 and 2001' (2002: 85). While it identifies a trend towards a higher proportion of women prisoners, any claim that this constitutes evidence that the system is not working is unusual because female offenders are sent to prison by judges and magistrates in response to their crimes. Is there a 'correct' percentage of female prisoners and, if so, what is it?

Table 13.4 Female prisoners as a percentage of the prison population in England and Wales 1900/2002

Year	Male	Female	Total	Females as a proportion (%)
1900	14,459	2,976	17,435	17.1
1905	18,398	3,127	21,525	14.5
1910	18,323	2,581	20,904	12.3
1915	9,244	2,067	11,311	18.3
1920	9,573	1,427	11,000	13.0
1925	9,635	874	10,509	8.3
1930	10,561	785	11,346	6.9
1935	10,587	719	11,306	6.4
1940	8,443	934	9,377	10.0
1945	13,180	1,528	14,708	10.4
1950	19,367	1,107	20,474	5.4
1955	20,156	978	21,134	4.6
1960	26,198	901	27,099	3.3
1965	29,580	841	30,421	2.6
1970	38,040	988	39,028	2.5
1975	38,601	1,219	39,820	3.1
1980	40,748	1,516	42,264	3.6
1985	44,701	1,532	46,233	3.3
1990	43,378	1,597	44,975	3.6
1995	48,983	1,979	50,962	3.9
2000	61,252	3,350	64,602	5.2
2001	62,560	3,740	66,301	5.6
2002	66,479	4,299	70,778	6.1

Source: *Prison Statistics England and Wales 2002*: 16.

Minority ethnic prison population

In February 2003, in the prison population 17,762 were non-white. This higher than expected proportion of minority ethnic prisoners is partly explained because 5,875 males and 748 females were foreign nationals. This has the effect of inflating the ratio of non-white prisoners in the prison population. The prison service therefore also gives data on British nationals, of whom 83 per cent were white, 12 per cent were black, 3 per cent were South Asian (India, Pakistan and Bangladesh) and 2 per cent were Chinese or other ethnic group. This contrasts with the population at risk amongst the general population of British nationals aged 15–64, in which 95 per cent were white, 1 per cent black, 3 per cent South Asian and 1 per cent other (*Prison Population Brief*, November 2003: 18).

Time served

The time served in prison is not usually the amount of time imposed by the judge or magistrate for three reasons: first, time is deducted for pre-sentence periods in custody awaiting trial or sentence while on remand; secondly, because prisoners (except for those serving 4 years and over) are entitled to remission or 'automatic release'; and, thirdly, because of parole and Home Detention Curfew.

The Prison Act 1898 allowed the use of remission of part of the sentence for the good conduct of inmates. The maximum remission, for those given penal sentences, was one-quarter for men and one-third for women. In the 1940s, this was changed to one-third for all inmates. Parole was introduced in 1967 and allowed inmates to apply for early release in addition to remission. This was a discretionary element and, unlike remission, was not automatic. Prior to the changes brought about by the CJA 1991, parole release time was in addition to the one-third deduction from sentence length for remission. Thus with remission (one-third) and parole eligibility starting at the one-third stage of the sentence, before the changes brought about by the CJA 1991, an inmate might be released soon after the one-third stage of their sentence.

Sentence calculations changed with the abolition of the terms 'remission' and 'parole' by the CJA 1991. All inmates were to serve one-half of their sentence, with full allowance for time held on remand in custody. For breaches of prison rules an inmate may serve up to 14 'added days'. Three sets of rules govern release as a consequence of the CJA 1991:

■ *Those serving a sentence of under 12 months* are automatically released at the 50 per cent stage as before. This is referred to as 'automatic unconditional release' (AUR). With the implementation of the CJA 2003 prisoners sentenced to under 12 months are supervised in the community following their release.

■ *Those sentenced from 1 to 4 years* serve 50 per cent of the time but on release will be supervised in the community until the three-quarters period of time. So a person sentenced to 2 years will be released after 1 year, allowing for time spent on remand in custody, and supervised for a further 6 months. This is known as 'automatic conditional release' (ACR).

■ *Those sentenced to 4 years and over* must serve half their sentence, with an allowance for time spent in custody while on remand. But they must still apply after the 50 per cent stage of sentence for release. This is a discretionary decision. They might not be successful, in which case they will serve up to the two-thirds stage of sentence time. Whether they are released at the earliest opportunity (50 per cent stage) or serve all their time to the two-thirds stage, the released prisoner will be supervised in the community after release until the three-quarters stage.

Thus a prisoner sentenced to 10 years who had spent 6 months awaiting trial and sentence would, from the time of sentence, be able to apply for release after a further 4 years 6 months. If successful the prisoner would be supervised on release in the community for a further 2 years and 6 months, i.e. to the three-quarters stage. If unsuccessful in a bid for early release the prisoner would be released finally at the two-thirds stage, i.e. at 6 years 8 months minus the 6 months served on remand. The prisoner would then be supervised in the community for a further 1 year and 4 months, i.e. a total period either in prison or under supervision in the community of 7 years 6 months for a sentence of 10 years.

Under the CJA 2003, the new types of custody discussed in Chapter 11 mean that there will be changes to the early release provisions. The opportunity was taken to clarify and simplify some of the above provisions. For short sentences (up to 12 months) part of the sentence is in custody and part is served on licence as specified by the sentencing court (see Chapter 11). For all longer sentences, other than extended sentences, offenders can be released on licence after half the sentence is served. Those given an extended sentence for sexual or violent offences will not be eligible for automatic release without the Parole Board's approval.

Home detention curfew

The home detention curfew (HDC) scheme was introduced throughout England and Wales in January 1999. It refers to an additional form of early release for those sentenced from 1 to 4 years when they are within 135 days of release (after serving half their sentence). The HDC, originally for 2 months, was extended to 3 months in 2002 and by the CJA2003 to 135 days.

The scheme uses electronic tagging to monitor the released prisoner for periods of curfew. The prisoner released under this scheme would be given specific conditions as to the number of days of electronic surveillance, with a minimum of 14 days. The curfew applies for a minimum of 9 hours and a maximum of 12 hours a day. In 2002, of 55,370 prisoners eligible to apply for the HDC scheme, 20,525 (37 per cent) were released early and 1,478 were recalled to prison because of new charges (16 per cent), breach of release conditions (54 per cent) and change of circumstances (26 per cent).

The Home Secretary, David Blunkett, has claimed that HDC and electronic monitoring has helped to cut reconviction rates. In a press release (21 March 2002) about the benefits of home detention curfew he said: 'Reconviction rates are dramatically lower for those who have been released under HDC than those who have served the final weeks of their sentence in prison. It is an important part of our crime reduction package and our drive to cut reconviction rates.' However, it is likely that those selected by the prisons for early release are by definition those less likely to re-offend so the conclusion that HDC reduces re-offending is not established.

Parole

Parole was introduced in the Criminal Justice Act 1967. It allowed a prisoner to be released early, for in addition to the one-third off for remission, after 1967 they could apply for parole at the one-third point of their sentence. Those released on parole were supervised by the probation service. Before 1967 they would have been released at the two-thirds stage. Introduced as part of a prison reductionist strategy, the parole system provided for an indeterminate element in a sentence between the one-third and two-thirds stage. The decision about suitability for release was made by a Local Review Committee who dealt with short-term prisoners and made recommendations for other prisoners, including life sentence prisoners eligible for release on licence, which went to the Parole Board for consideration and finally to the Home Secretary who could veto a recommendation. The Parole Board was composed of criminologists, judges, probation officers, psychiatrists and independent members. All were part time.

The system was changed by the CJA 1991, which allowed for automatic release at the 50 per cent stage of sentence for all prisoners serving under 4 years. The Local Review Committee was abolished. The Parole Board was left to consider all cases of prisoners sentenced to 4 years and over. It makes the decision in the case of prisoners serving 4 to 7 years and sends recommendations in the case of those sentenced to over 7 years to the Home Secretary. There are now full-time officials in addition to the part-time members. Following recommendations in a review of parole by the Carlisle Committee in 1988, the CJA 1991 introduced a more complex criteria system to be used by the Parole Boards when reviewing cases. For prisoners servicing sentences of up to 15 years the Parole Board makes the final decision. For longer sentence prisoners it makes recommendations to the Home Secretary.

Offenders released under the conditions of parole are supervised in the community by a probation officer up to the three-quarters point of those with a determinate sentence. In 2002/3 the Parole Board received 6,010 requests for release from determinate prisoners, of which 53 per cent were considered eligible for parole by the board.

Under the CJA 2003 the Parole Board will be involved in fewer, more serious offences: those for which extended sentences have been imposed, those involving life cases and cases involving recall to prison for breach of licence. The length of time served is one calculation that the sentenced inmate will be keen to work out soon after reception. However, other considerations will affect the nature of the prison experience that the inmate will face during his or her prison term. Having explained the quantity of time that an inmate will have to serve, what factors influence the quality of time served?

13.4 IMPACT OF IMPRISONMENT ON INMATES

For 200 years, since the introduction of the penitentiary, the impact of prison life on the inmate has been debated. As we saw in Chapter 12, some believed that prison life could provide a positive and constructive experience that would rehabilitate, while others argued that the consequence of imprisonment is to lock an offender further into a life of crime. The 1990 White Paper, *Crime, Justice and Protecting the Public* (Home Office 1990a), made it clear that the effect of imprisonment is unlikely to be beneficial in rehabilitative terms. It is important to bear in mind, however, that individual inmates vary in character and that generalisations about the impact of prison regimes will not hold for every inmate. Empirical studies of how inmates experience and adapt to prison help to shed light on the consequences of being incarcerated, and explain why they have not matched the good intentions of those who saw prison as a means of resocialising inmates.

Toleration of life in prison varies from inmate to inmate. Some will feel their conviction or sentence was unjust, others will accept it, and others will be grateful that the sentence length was no longer. Each prisoner will bring a range of pre-existing impressions and knowledge of prisons.

The National Prison Survey 1991 showed most (57 per cent) sentenced inmates had been in prison before (Walmsley *et al.* 1993). The survey of 4,000 inmates was conducted in January and February 1991 and covered the background characteristics of inmates and asked questions about the regimes and the conditions of imprisonment from the inmates' perspective. Asked about how they got on with staff, 9 per cent said they had been treated badly but most (41 per cent) said the prison staff treated them well. Personal safety questions showed that while most (71 per cent) agreed with the statement that 'most prison officers treat prisoners fairly here', one-quarter also expressed agreement with the statement that 'some prison officers assault prisoners here'. They expressed concern about their personal safety – 18 per cent replied that they did not feel safe from being injured or bullied by other prisoners and 9 per cent reported that they had been assaulted by another inmate in the last 6 months.

These physical aspects of the regime such as food, overcrowding, the time locked up in a cell, access to bath and toilet facilities, and staff attitudes are vital to the trouble-free running of a prison, as was shown in the section of this chapter which considered the findings of the Woolf Report on the riots in 1990.

Regimes, sentence planning and privileges

A framework of privileges and incentives was introduced into prisons in 1995. Intended by the then Home Secretary, Michael Howard, to ensure greater discipline, the scheme allows for a greater number of visits, more disposable cash and community visits for those who comply with the regimes. There are three levels based on the facilities provided:

- *Basic*: the minimum level of facilities to which the prisoner is entitled by law regardless of performance and behaviour of the prisoner.
- *Standard*: set above the legal minimum requirements.
- *Enhanced*: at this level prisoners become eligible for additional privileges.

The aims of the scheme were to ensure that privileges for prisoners are earned through good behaviour and are removable if prisoners fail to maintain acceptable standards of responsible behaviour. The scheme encourages hard work and rewards participation in constructive activity by prisoners. The scheme also enhances the role of sentence planning. Finally, the scheme has a control function in that it seeks to create a more disciplined, better controlled and safer environment for prisoners and staff.

The earnable privileges include:

- access to private cash above a set minimum
- extra visits
- eligibility to take part in enhanced earning schemes
- community visits for Category D inmates
- permission to wear one's own clothing
- time out of cell in association.

Sentence planning was introduced in 1992 following the recommendations of the Woolf Report, to encourage inmates to identify a way of progressing throughout their time in prison so that they might acquire skills and attempt to address their offending behaviour. Following discussion between staff and the inmate, targets are set which aim to reduce future re-offending by agreement to undertake training programmes and activities such as drug counselling or the sex offender treatment programme. At the start of the sentence, information is put together about the inmate's community and family ties, prior training and educational attainments. Information is collected about substance abuse, criminal history and self-harm history. During the period of incarceration comments are kept on file about how the prisoner cooperated with the wing or unit's routines, and how he or she related to other inmates and staff. This information is open to inmates to read and challenge if they regard it as inaccurate.

Inmate adaptation to prison life

How do people cope with being deprived of their liberty? Prisoners do not have the same degree of freedom to decide their daily routines, eating habits, social contacts and sleeping arrangements. Studies of how inmates adapt to prison life illustrate its impact on the inmate and how this is likely to affect their potential for successful rehabilitation. These sociological and psychological studies of prison life give clues about the causes of prison disturbances and riots that we discussed earlier in this chapter (Cohen and Taylor 1972; Fitzgerald 1977; King and Elliott 1977).

How people cope with prison depends on a number of factors. First, if they have had prior experience of prison, they will have some understanding of the routines of prison life. For the novice, initial acquaintance with prison life might be overwhelming and intimidating. Erving Goffman uses the term 'mortification', to describe the induction process in which supports for the person's individuality such as personal name, clothing and hair style are replaced by a prison number, uniform and hygiene requirements (Goffman 1968). This can be lessened and some prison administrators have introduced regimes to normalise some aspects of prison life by, for example, less insistence on uniforms and less restrictions on what might be allowed in a cell, although this might conflict with the needs of containment and security as was suggested in the case of the IRA prisoner escape from Whitemoor Prison.

Prisoner adaptation, whether the inmate is an 'old hand' or a novice, will depend on individual circumstances. Most important is the length of sentence. The nature of the crime committed also influences the prison experience. Thieves, fraudsters and robbers are often regarded with relative degrees of respect and contempt by other inmates, but they will not suffer the fear felt by those convicted of sexual crimes, especially those where the victim was a child. To avoid attacks from other inmates, the 'nonces', as they are called in prison argot, often request to be housed in vulnerable prisoner units and segregated for their own protection under Prison Rule 43, which states:

Another factor influencing prisoners' adaptation is relationships in the outside

> Where it appears desirable for the maintenance of good order or discipline or in his own interest, that a prisoner should not associate with other prisoners, either generally, or for particular purposes, the governor may arrange for the prisoner's removal from association.

world. One of the realities of prison life is that inmates are cut off from ordinary routine interactions with the outside world. Goffman calls prisons, along with other institutions such as monasteries, mental hospitals and boarding schools, 'total institutions'. They are 'total' in that all aspects of life such as sleeping, eating, working and leisure are conducted within the one organisation (Goffman 1968). This means that the array of contacts and opportunities are severely confined and the impact of the outside world is limited. However, this does not mean that there is no outside contact and weekly visits, access to telephones for prisoners and outside visits in pre-release schemes have all been extended in recent years. Of course, the main leisure activities such as watching television, listening to the radio and reading newspapers and magazines mean that inmates in prison can keep up with events that interest them. Regimes will vary between prisons and some, such as open prisons, allow inmates 2 days a month out of the prison for 'town visits'.

The loss of daily contact with the home or workplace is no hardship for some inmates. Others suffer mental anguish when they think about their outside lives, homes and families. The shame of imprisonment on the family and themselves will have an impact on some of those sentenced to imprisonment. Some argue that these factors are of particular significance to women prisoners, especially where they have children (Eaton 1993), and on family life in general.

Justice for All claimed that prison can 'break up families, impede resettlement and place children at risk of an inter-generational cycle of crime' (2002: 85), with over 40 per cent of sentenced prisoners claiming to have lost contact with their families since entering prison. Other research from the Social Exclusion Unit (SEU) states, 'Research shows that prisoners are six times less likely to reoffend if contact with their families is maintained' (Social Exclusion Unit 2002: 106). David Green comments on this:

> There are two main problems with this statement. First, it is not true that simply reinstating family contacts will reduce offending. The SEU reported in 2002 that 43% of prisoners had other family members who had been convicted (compared with 16% of the general population) and 35% had a family member who had been in prison. In such cases the family may be a bad influence ... while it is true that people with strong family ties are less likely to be criminals, it does not follow that *all* people with strong family ties are law abiding ...
>
> Second, it is not true that prison always causes the breakdown of family contacts. Many criminals had few, if any, close family ties before admission to prison. The SEU report shows that 47% of male prisoners had run away from home as a child, and 27% had been in care (compared with 2% of the general population). Some 81% were unmarried prior to imprisonment, nearly 5% were sleeping rough before admission, and 32% were not living in permanent accommodation prior to their imprisonment. Moreover, when their family disowns them or a wife leaves them, it is often because they disapprove of the prisoner's self-chosen conduct.
>
> (Green 2004)

A further factor shaping the way in which inmates adapt to prison life is their attitude towards their offence and sentence. While some accept their guilt and feel ashamed, others feel no remorse. This might be because they are professional thieves who have made a career out of criminal activity and regard imprisonment as an occupational hazard. Individual inmates will vary in their response to conviction. Those incorrectly convicted are entitled to feel outrage and anger. Others are outraged because of the type of person they are. Some are resigned to their fate and 'do their time'. Others will be influenced by the type of company they come into contact with in the prison. Although there is no one factor that determines how a prisoner responds, a number of research studies have indicated patterns of adaptation (Cohen and Taylor 1972).

Some theories accounting for offender adaptation have stressed the importance of institutional traditions and opportunities, particularly focusing on the impact of inmate subcultures and the deprivations associated with a 'closed' institution. Theorists in this tradition include Donald Clemmer, Gresham Sykes and Erving Goffman. Other theorists have focused on the 'importation' model, where the prisoners' adaptations will depend on their pre-institutional careers and lifestyles (Schrag 1944). Schrag's work showed how the social role adopted in prison depended on the inmate's previous lifestyle before imprisonment.

John Irwin's study, *The Felon* (1970), found three types of response among inmates in California prisons: 'jailing', 'doing time' and 'gleaning'. These responses tended to reflect the prisoner's personal history, although Irwin makes the caveat that inmates did not always fit into only one response model and that the three main response patterns did not cover every inmate. Thus 'jailing' was characteristic of 'state raised youth' who had prior institutional contacts from an early age and knew how to exploit the opportunities in a total institution to achieve maximum benefits and status through the rackets and gangs. Prison was not too burdensome for them as they usually had little status outside the institution other than in gang life, which continued in prison. The professional and more mature thieves who were career criminals adopted a different response. Their predominant aim was to get through their sentence as quietly and as quickly as possible. Therefore they were not interested in the rehabilitative programmes of the institution except where it meant an easier life inside or the chance to get out of prison more quickly. Nor were these inmates interested in campaigning or confrontation with the authorities, as were the 'jailing' inmates. The third pattern of adaptation described by Irwin was 'gleaning'. These inmates engaged in the opportunities offered by education, counselling, therapy and work programmes to increase their opportunities of being granted parole and of changing their lifestyles.

In a later study, *Prisons in Turmoil* (1980), Irwin points out that the models of inmate subcultures were easier to identify in the traditional style of penitentiary with more rigid and authoritarian regimes. Clemmer's study in 1940 found a very distinctive and conformist prisoner culture, with an inmate code, defined and enforced primarily through the inmates (Clemmer 1958). Since that time the nature of the prison experience has become more diversified, as new types of inmate and values have been brought into prison. The commitment to rehabilitative strategies in the 1950s brought about more liberal regimes with less emphasis on the convict culture found in many prisons before 1950. The new mix of inmates also undermined the single inmate culture. In the United States of America in the 1960s, as with the British prisons during the period of the 1914/18 war, political prisoners objecting to the war generated a more articulate and politically sophisticated inmate. In the

United States of America the black power movement created another form of politically orientated inmate. Younger inmates convicted of drug and gang-related crimes were not so easily impressed by either the formal or informal cultures of prison life and had their own support and reference groups as gang and drug activities meant that prison contacts became an extension of street life.

More recent theorists and studies have stressed the greater diversity of inmate culture as less strict regimes and more diverse pre-institutional lifestyles have become more apparent in prison in the 1990s and into the twenty-first century.

13.5 AIMS AND PERFORMANCE OF THE PRISON SERVICE

Does prison work, as Michael Howard asserted in the quote at the beginning of this chapter? To answer this it is necessary to ask what the goals of imprisonment are. In clarifying these goals we must distinguish between the function of imprisonment within the criminal justice system (i.e. to carry out the sentence of the court) and the specific goals of prisons as institutions.

Thus prisons work in one sense if they deprive offenders of their liberty for the period of time specified by the court. Hence the main purpose of imprisonment is in terms of sentencing goals. When assessed in terms of whether prisons fulfil this function they are successful if general deterrence, denunciation and just deserts goals are achieved; and at the minimum they fulfil an incapacitative function of keeping away from the community offenders who would, and will, when released, continue criminal activities.

However, the prison service has its own institutionally specific goals reflecting the penal paradigms explored in Chapter 12. In 1979 the report of the May Committee referred to the loss of faith in the treatment objective in prison and recommended the rewriting of Prison Rule 1 and adopting the idea of custody which is both 'secure and yet positive'. 'Positive custody' was defined in four ways. It should:

- create an environment which can assist them (the inmates) to respond and contribute to society as positively as possible;
- preserve and promote their self-respect;
- minimise, to the degree of security necessary in each particular case, the harmful effects of their removal from normal life;
- prepare them for and assist them on discharge.

(Home Office 1979: 67)

In the 1990s the prison service set out the following goals of imprisonment in its mission statement:

> Her Majesty's Prison Service serves the public by keeping in custody those committed by the courts. Our duty is to look after them with humanity and help them lead law-abiding and useful lives in custody and after release.

In terms of the institutional goals the prison service has set itself, prisons can be assessed as to their effectiveness by monitoring their success at achieving the objectives set. Key performance indicators (KPIs) were introduced for this purpose. In 2004 the objectives and KPIs were as follows.

Prison service objectives and KPI targets

The blend of containment, concern with conditions and capacity, rehabilitative aspirations and non-prison-specific objectives associated with the organisational culture are evident in this statement of objectives set out in the Prison Service's Corporate and Business Plan 2003/4:

- maintain security and prevent escapes
- ensure safe and decent conditions for prisoners
- improve prisoners' prospects on release
- provide capacity
- increase diversity and equality
- improve performance
- introduce organisational development and change.

These objectives are turned into targets through key performance indicators (KPIs). The *Prison Service Annual Report 2004* indicates that, over the past year, the prison service met KPIs in the following areas:

- There were 15 escapes from prisons and prison escorts compared with 17 in the previous financial year and no Category A escapes since 1995.
- There was only one escape from escort per 39,377 prisoners, compared with the target of one escape from escort per 20,000 prisoners.
- The average staff sickness rate was 13.3 days against a target of 13.5 days.
- The rate for timely delivery of prisoners to court (a new KPI) was 82% against a target of 81%.
- In the resettlement sphere, 32,592 prisoners had a job, education or training outcome within a month of release, 12% more than the target of 29,044.
- 5.5% of staff were from a minority ethnic group, exactly meeting the target of 5.5%.
- Education targets were significantly exceeded in most areas:
  - Prisoners achieved 103,583 Work Skills awards compared to the target of 52,672
  - Prisoners achieved 43,731 Basic Skills awards compared to the target of 34,482
  - Within this, the KPI for delivery of Basic Skills Level 2 qualifications was narrowly missed, with 13,338 completions against a target of 13,648
- 9,169 offending behaviour programmes were completed. Within this, the target of 1,168 sex offender treatment programme completions was not achieved, but the actual figure of 1,046 is the highest ever figure for completions.

The prison service failed, however, to meet the following key performance targets:

- The rate of positive mandatory drug tests was 12.3% against the target of 10%.
- The rate of self-inflicted deaths was 135.9 per 100,000 prisoners against a target of 112.8. This represents a small improvement on the rate for 2002/3.
- The provision of purposeful activity was an average 23.2 hours per week against a target of 24 hours, although this also represents an improvement on the previous year's performance.
- The average rate of doubling, or the number of prisoners held two to a cell designed for one, was 21.7% against a target of 18%.
- The rate of serious assaults was 1.54% against a target of 1.20%.

(Prison Service Annual Report 2004)

In general debates about the role and success of prisons the details of KPIs are subsumed under more general issues as to whether those sent by the courts are retained until the proper release date and whether this represents adequate punishment for the crime, and the possibility of rehabilitation within the prison.

Rehabilitation and offender management

The re-emphasis on rehabilitation in 2004 was further emphasised in the plans to integrate the prison and the probation services into the National Offender Management Service. The objective is to ensure that offenders are managed throughout the whole of their sentences, whether in custody or in the community and the delivery of integrated offender management. This will require new arrangements for case management based on a common system operating in custodial and community settings.

A number of pilot projects are already running. Resettlement strategies work with offenders on critical issues such as offending behaviour, learning and skills and employment, through the whole sentence. The developing arrangements for offender management will link closely with a range of public and private partners.

Another project that concentrates on integrating prisoners into the community is the 'Restorative Prison' which applies the principles of restorative justice in the prison. The North East Restorative Community Partnership project started in 2000 and is based on the idea of the community prison referred to in the Woolf report. The community prison is based on the principles of restorative justice: prisoners work with victims, prisoners work for the benefit of the community, and an approach to resolving conflicts in prison that avoids formal and adversarial process and uses mediation procedures. The claim is that this will result in a better atmosphere in prison, with prisoners feeling better about themselves; prison is boring, so this gives them something to do; and work done in public parks is giving something back to the community.

The project to link prisoners with the community and to instil civic values is also evident in the campaign to give prisoners the vote, with the aim of making them more responsible citizens (see the question at the end of this chapter and the arguments produced by the Prison Reform Trust in 2004).

This restored optimism in the rehabilitative role of imprisonment is in contrast with the pessimism of the previous decades. The 1990 White Paper concluded they were counter-productive in this regard. The Report states:

> It was once believed that prison, properly used, could encourage a high proportion of offenders to start an honest life on their release. Nobody now regards imprisonment, in itself, as an effective means of reform for most prisoners ... however much prison staff try to inject a positive purpose into the regime, as they do, prison is a society which requires virtually no sense of personal responsibility from prisoners. Normal social or working habits do not fit. The opportunity to learn from other prisoners is pervasive. For most offenders, imprisonment has to be justified in terms of public protection, denunciation and retribution. Otherwise it can be an expensive way of making bad people worse.
>
> (Home Office 1990a: 6)

The Green Paper *Punishment, Custody and the Community* cited the many unintended consequences of imprisonment which made them counter-productive in rehabilitative terms. Paragraph 1.1:

> ... they are not required to face up to what they have done and to the effects on their victim.

Paragraph 1.1 commented further:

> ... if they are removed in prison from the responsibilities, problems and temptations of everyday life, they are less likely to acquire the self-discipline and self-reliance which will prevent re-offending in the future.

Paragraph 1.6:

> Imprisonment is likely to add to the difficulties which offenders find in living a normal and law-abiding life. Overcrowded local prisons are emphatically not schools of citizenship.

Paragraph 2.15:

> [With regard to young offenders] Even a short period of custody is quite likely to confirm them as criminals, particularly if they acquire new criminal skills from more sophisticated offenders. They see themselves labelled as criminals and behave accordingly.
>
> (Home Office 1988a)

The mood a decade on was that more could be done to reduce the recidivism rates of prisoners. One aspect of this strategy was to challenge the efficacy of the short prison sentence on rehabilitative grounds. *Justice for All* noted that prisoners given short sentences were reconvicted at a higher rate than those who served longer sentences. David Green (2004) comments on this argument that it 'implies that a prisoner's subsequent conduct is determined by his short time in jail. Consider someone aged 20 who has been a regular offender and only just been caught. How likely is it that 3 months in jail will become the main cause of his later conduct? It is more likely that the attitudes acquired in the previous 20 years continue to exert a powerful influence.'

The University of Maryland's review of What Works evidence concluded that there was no evidence that prison increased the likelihood of increasing recidivism. 'The evidence seems to point to an overall picture of criminals, particularly property criminals, generally "returning to work" after their time in prison' (Murray 2003: 9).

Part of the new emphasis has been based on a faith in cognitive skills programmes with prisoners to make them more aware of what they were doing when they committed a crime. Two evaluations have been published by the Home Office about the impact of cognitive skill programmes with prisoners. In July 2003, *Findings* 206 (Falshaw *et al.* 2003), acknowledged, 'This evaluation found no differences in the two-year reconviction rates for prisoners who had participated in a cognitive skills programme between 1996–1998 and a matched comparison group. This contrasts with the reduction in reconviction shown in the previous evaluation of cognitive skills programmes for prisoners, delivered between 1992 and 1996'.

The test of the success of working with prisoners is primarily measured through reconviction rates as an indicator of recidivism. Chapter 12 showed that the average re-offending rate following imprisonment is the same as that for community sentences. The 2-year recidivism rates measure the proportion of offenders reconvicted for a further offence in a 2-year period from release. These figures show that imprisonment is likely to be related to future re-offending. However, they also show that non-custodial sanctions are not much better at reducing the likelihood of re-offending.

Perhaps sentencing an offender, whether to prison or in the community, has little to do with the influences on offending behaviour. If it is difficult to establish the proposition that prisons work to reduce the criminality of offenders following their release, the value of imprisonment should be assessed in terms of its functions other than those concerning its effect on individual offenders (see Chapter 12).

So the answer to the question of whether prisons work is that it depends on what we expect of them. The failure to meet the original high expectations of those pioneering the penitentiary as an institution to change offenders into law-abiding citizens is apparent. But prisons meet other demands, particularly as the most credible way to achieve retribution, denunciation, general deterrence and incapacitation.

Finally, no doubt the 'success rate' of imprisonment, in terms of any of its aims could be improved if more money is spent on the prison system. What would be the cost of ensuring no escapes? Would the taxpayer wish to pay this cost? For those who think prisons have failed in all or most respects, the onus is on them to say what they would put in its place as the major institution symbolising punishment.

CONCLUSION

This chapter has shown that prisons have been expected to perform many functions. The rehabilitative paradigm discussed in Chapter 12 influenced the design, organisation and regimes of prisons from their inception to around the 1960s. Thus prisons were seen not as degrading and punitive institutions but as institutions where inmates should be encouraged and assisted to lead a good and useful life through a regime of treatment and training. These ideals, however, were not achieved, and some of the reasons why prisons may not be able to achieve rehabilitation have been noted. They are, after all, institutions in which inmates are deprived of their liberty, which may have an adverse effect on their sense of individuality and purpose. Some prisoners are wedded to a life of crime; others, particularly those on long sentences, may simply wish to forget the outside world and see no hope for the future. Prisons indeed may have a damaging rather than a positive effect.

Intermittent custody, introduced in the Criminal Justice Act 2003, attempts to reduce the negative outcomes that can accompany even short periods of full-time custody, such as loss of employment, loss of accommodation, and family disintegration.

The demise and resuscitation of rehabilitative goals, however, has a profound effect on the institutions making up the prison system. One attraction of rehabilitative goals to penal reformers was that it held out the promise of treating prisoners with humanity. With its demise, these conditions also declined, many training programmes ceased and prisoners were locked up for longer periods in their cells. These conditions arguably contributed to the disturbances in the early 1990s.

It is important to distinguish between the aims of sentencers in sending offenders to prison and the aims of the prison system itself. Thus while sentencers and policy makers talk of incapacitation and the deprivation of liberty, these do not provide constructive goals for the institutions who must carry out these aims. Reducing the goal of prison to that of simply keeping offenders from escaping until they are due to be released ('warehousing') might further distance staff from inmates and undermine programmes aimed at reforming them.

Prisons must deal with those whom the courts send to them and attempt to prevent them escaping and creating disturbances. Yet the interests of security and control may run counter to positive regimes and humane conditions in a cost-conscious climate. The debate over the balance between security, control, costs and changing offender behaviour in prison is likely to continue into the next millennium.

Review questions

1 What are the different security categories of prisons run by the prison service in England and Wales?

2 Calculate the actual amount of time served by an inmate if he or she is sentenced to: (a) 8 months; and (b) 2 years. What rules apply to the prisoner sentenced to over 4 years?

3 What are the different aims of imprisonment? What kind of evidence should be examined to explore whether or not these aims are being achieved?

4 What arguments are involved in considering whether more prisons should be built or greater efforts should be made to reduce the prison population?

5 Using the information in Table 12.2, showing the comparative use of imprisonment in western European countries, consider:

(a) where England and Wales is ranked among the countries and jurisdictions listed, in terms of the numbers of prisoners in 2002;

(b) where England and Wales is ranked among the countries listed, in terms of the numbers of prisoners per 100,000 of the population in 2002;

(c) where England and Wales is ranked among the countries listed as a proportion of the number of crimes recorded in 2002.

(d) which of the comparisons (the total numbers in prison, the numbers compared with the population as a whole, or the numbers compared with the amount of recorded crime) do you regard as most useful for assessing claims about the overuse of custody in England and Wales.

6 Would giving prisoners a vote in elections re-integrate them into the community as responsible citizens or has their offending behaviour caused them to forfeit their rights? Search the Prison Reform Trust website using the search term 'vote' for information on the Trust's views.

Further reading

Cavadino, M and Dignan, J (2002) *The Penal System: An Introduction* (3rd edn), Sage: London

Harding, C, Hines, B, Ireland, R and Rawlings, P (1985) *Imprisonment in England and Wales* Croom Helm: London

Morgan, R (2002) 'Imprisonment', in Maguire, M, Morgan, R and Reiner, R (eds) *The Oxford Handbook of Criminology* (3rd edn), Clarendon Press: Oxford

CHAPTER 14

Probation service and community penalties

Main topics covered

➤ The development of community sentences

➤ The probation service

➤ 'What Works' and why, and recent initiatives in community sentences

➤ The effectiveness of community sentences

INTRODUCTION

In this chapter we will discuss the work of the probation service and look in more detail at community sentences.

The development of community sentences reflects the search in England and Wales for non-prison punishments. The desire for such punishments has been justified by arguments based on cost-effectiveness, on a just deserts philosophy and on the basis of the need for reform and rehabilitation rather than punishment of offenders.

The role and function of community penalties have changed considerably since their inception in the late nineteenth century, changing particularly rapidly in the last decade. First seen as largely rehabilitative, probation orders (and later community service orders) were a key part of attempts to divert offenders from custody. At times some community orders were specifically described as 'alternatives to prison' and at other times as 'punishment in the community' and as an intermediate punishment: between prison and probation (see Chapter 12).

Affected severely by the pessimism of the 'nothing works' era, a new optimism has surrounded recent emphases on 'What Works' in community sentences, and on implementing programmes aimed at reducing the likelihood of an offender re-offending, signalling a return to rehabilitative methods on the grounds that they can best have an impact on recidivism. This has been accompanied by rapid changes in the structure and organisation of one of the main agencies involved in community sentences, the probation service, and the setting of ambitious targets to reduce recidivism rates by 5 per cent.

This chapter will start by outlining the development of community sentences, illustrating many of these changes and highlighting their fluctuating objectives. It will then describe the role of the main agencies responsible for community sentences and supervision: the probation service. Thereafter, the text will explore current thinking about how community sentences can be delivered effectively. Finally, some of the ways in which the effectiveness of community sentences can be evaluated will be considered.

Before this it is important to define what is meant by community sentences – which in theory can encompass all sentences of the court where the offender is left in the community and not sent to prison. The terminology, however, conventionally excludes financial penalties and discharges: where no further intervention takes place. Community sentences or penalties are usually defined as 'court ordered punishments ... structurally located between custody, on the one hand, and financial or nominal penalties (fines, compensation and discharge) on the other' (Bottoms *et al.* 2001: 1). They can be distinguished from fines and discharges as in these sentences no further intervention is made. In community sentences, however, some contact takes place whether by way of attendance in a programme of counselling or treatment as in a community rehabilitation order (the renamed probation order), a programme of unpaid work in the community as in a community punishment order (the renamed community service order), or active surveillance as in electronic monitoring and the curfew order.

14.1 THE DEVELOPMENT OF COMMUNITY SENTENCES

The idea that offenders can be dealt with in the community has a long history. In the late nineteenth century many juvenile offenders were 'saved' from prison by police court missionaries who agreed to be responsible for them – the forerunners of the probation service. The historical development of probation was linked to reforms brought about by the Summary Jurisdiction Act 1879, which introduced conditional discharge for younger and first-time offenders. The court could add the requirement of supervision. Volunteers and friends offered to supervise, and from this developed the role whereby people, sometimes police officers, supervised and acted as mentors to offenders. The Probation of First Time Offenders Act 1887 specified the term 'probation' and outlined its role. The Probation of Offenders Act 1907 provided that the courts could appoint and pay probation officers and defined their duties, which were seen as being to 'advise, assist and befriend offenders'. The Criminal Justice Act 1925 formalised the role and required each petty sessional division to employ at least one probation officer.

After this the work of the probation service expanded considerably. Probation officers became responsible not only for work in the criminal courts but also for civil work involving divorce. They provided social enquiry reports to the court giving information about offenders' circumstances and attitude to offences and gave the court advice about what sentence would be appropriate. They also began to work with ex-prisoners, reflected in the use of the term probation and after-care service. Their role was strongly linked to the rehabilitative philosophies outlined in Chapter 12, and the service became professionalised. Most probation officers were trained as social workers and for much of the mid-twentieth century probation officers worked according to a treatment model and practised what was described as social casework (Raynor and Vanstone 2002).

Some features of probation in this era were of considerable importance both to the rehabilitative philosophy and to the role of probation within the penal system. Probation was not in itself a sentence but a release according to conditions – a period quite literally of probation. Offenders who breached the conditions of supervision, and who re-offended, could in theory be taken back to court and sentenced for the original offence, although this was in practice relatively rare. Offenders had to agree to be placed on probation, as it was felt that rehabilitation and supervision had to be voluntarily accepted rather than seen as a punishment which was imposed – thus setting the tone of the relationship between caseworker and offender.

The legitimacy of probation was challenged during the disillusionment with rehabilitation which followed and the 'nothing works' pessimism outlined in Chapter 12. In addition, there was little demonstrable evidence of the effectiveness of probation in making any real impact into offenders' lives – once on probation, some argued, nothing much else happened. Offenders saw probation officers at intervals, sometimes as little as once a month. While there were some experiments with more intensive supervision such as IMPACT programmes, again these were not fully evaluated for their effect on offenders, with whether or not the offender had completed a period of supervision normally being taken to be the benchmark of success.

Probation did, however, constitute an alternative to custody and growing concerns over rates of imprisonment led many to see the primary role of community sentences as being to reduce the prison population. These arguments influenced the introduction of new measures during the 1960s and 1970s. Parole and the suspended sentence were introduced in 1967 and the Criminal Justice Act 1972 introduced community service orders (CSOs), made available nationally in 1975. Community Service Orders proved popular because they combined so many sentencing aims. They could be seen as a form of retributive punishment by depriving offenders of their free time – as a 'fine on time' which in itself could also be construed as a deterrent. The element of unpaid work, often with voluntary organisations, could be seen as a form of reparation, and it was also assumed that working with community organisations could contribute to rehabilitation. They proved popular, and by 1988 they accounted for 8 per cent of all sentences for indictable offenders. This may have been due to their 'Jack of all Trades' image, although in practice their role has been affected by 'philosophical confusion' (Gelsthorpe and Rex 2004: 230). While the legislation itself made no specific reference to their use for those who would otherwise have been sent to prison, they were expected to be used primarily as an alternative to prison (Cavadino and Dignan 1997), although research suggested that they were used rather as an alternative to probation and placed lower down the tariff than originally intended.

During the 1970s and 1980s new elements were added to community sentences. In 1973 provisions were made that offenders on probation could be required to attend day training centres. The Criminal Justice Act 1982 provided that courts could require full-time attendance at day centres for a maximum of 60 days. Day centres were viewed with concern by many probation officers who saw their use as increasing their control function (May 1994). Other policies during the 1970s involved targeting selected offenders for intensive probation supervision and during the 1980s some schemes involved tracking offenders. There were, however, considerable local variations in provision and, despite the addition of new strategies, community sentences could be seen as a 'soft option' to those calling for tougher punishment.

Throughout the 1980s Home Office policy sought to reduce local variations and to increase the punitive elements of sentences. There was an attempt to exert greater control over community sentences, the strong welfare orientation within the probation service being seen as an impediment (May 1994). In 1984 a Statement of National Objectives for Probation (SNOP) was issued which stated that the priorities of the probation service were to provide alternatives to custody and prepare social inquiry reports for the court. A major theme was that offenders with a high risk of imprisonment were to be targeted, signalling a shift away from the traditional role of the service as dealing with less serious offenders who would benefit from treatment, help or support (May 1994). In 1988 an Action Plan called on every local probation area to develop its own strategy for targeting more intensive supervision on young adult offenders.

Changes were also made to community service orders. In 1989 a set of national standards for community service was introduced which encouraged the adoption of more exacting procedures for dealing with lateness, non-compliance and unsatisfactory behaviour (*National Standards for the Supervision of Offenders in the Community*). A strong preference for manual labour was indicated, laying emphasis on tasks such as cleaning up graffiti. Following the Criminal Justice Act 1991 (CJA 1991) and the influence of 'just deserts' policies, the emphasis was laid on the amount of restriction of liberty being commensurate with the offence. This criterion was in addition to the criterion for the imposition of a community sentence itself: that the offence or offences were 'serious enough' for the imposition of a community penalty. Thus the choice of specific penalty had also to reflect seriousness and just deserts. This created a notional ranking of the punitiveness of the sentences involved, and their variability in terms of lengths and intensity. To further increase this range and in response to criticisms, the combination order was introduced to enable the combination of the punishment aspects of community service with the rehabilitative aspects of probation in the CJA 1991. A probation order could be combined with additional specified requirements, under which the court could order that the offender undergo particular programmes, or treatment.

Initially it was a prerequisite of most community sentences that the offender give his consent to the order. Failure to consent was a ground for imposing a custodial penalty. This provision was thus criticised on two grounds: first, that it was conceptually bizarre to ask an offender to consent to the sentence, and secondly, that asking for consent with the threat of prison in the event of a refusal was nonsensical. The requirement for consent was removed in most cases, therefore, by the Crime (Sentences) Act 1997.

Although the reparative and reintegrative effects of orders were stressed in the CJA 1991 its practical effect was, argue Gelsthorpe and Rex (2004), to intensify the distinction between probation as rehabilitation and community service as punishment.

Probation, too, was increasingly affected by the punitive turn in policy during the 1990s. Following considerable controversy surrounding the perceived laxness of community sentences typified in press reports of offenders being sent to holiday camps as part of their order, the Home Secretary, addressing the annual conference of the Central Probation Council in May of 1994, commented that 'probation services are working with offenders but for the community and not the other way round'. The courts and the public, he went on to say, must have confidence in community sentences as punishment, and, while he was in favour of programmes making demands on offenders, they should not be given 'privileged access to opportunities which law-abiding members of the community cannot afford'. While community sentences had for many years been described as 'treatment in the community', the new emphasis on just deserts and punishment were associated with a new terminology – 'punishment in the community' – as used, for example, in the title of a Green Paper issued by the Home Office in 1995, *Strengthening Punishment in the Community*. Less emphasis was thus placed on *diversion* from custody, but rather a community sentence was considered as a rigorous and punitive sentence in its own right that was less severe than custody; hence, an intermediate sentence in the tariff. The turn in policy was signalled by the then Home Secretary Michael Howard's claim that 'prison works' and a consequent lessening of the desire to use community sentences as merely diversions from custody.

The desire to gain judicial and public acceptance of community punishments was accompanied by a range of measures aimed at 'toughening up' the delivery of community sentences. In August 1994 the Government announced new national standards which included a ban on safari and domestic holidays and requirements that work on community sentences should be demanding and usually physical in nature.

Before the imposition of a community penalty courts had usually been required to obtain a social enquiry report from the probation service. In the CJA 1991 these were renamed pre-sentence reports which in part refocused their purpose as an aid to the sentencer. This heralded a different approach to the preparation of the pre-sentence report and underlined the role of probation officers as officers of the court, responsible for helping the court assess the risk of re-offending. Criticisms that probation officers had often made unrealistic suggestions as to the appropriate sentence were answered by making probation officers assess offending seriousness in the same way that a court might.

This reflected the range of changes which arguably altered the role of the probation officer and the nature of probation supervision. From 1991 onwards, probation orders had become a sentence in their own right with a place in the tariff, rather than an order *instead* of a sentence. In the mid 1990s the requirement that probation officers be qualified social workers was abolished, which many see as a change that symbolised the changing function of probation – from a social work service providing welfare and rehabilitation to offenders to a law enforcement, 'correctional' agency (Raynor and Vanstone 2002; Robinson and McNeill 2004). As mentioned above, in 1997 the requirement that offenders consent to an order was withdrawn, making it more like an imposed punishment than a voluntary contract. There was also a successive tightening up of requirements for law enforcement should offenders breach the requirements of their order. Hitherto probation officers had had considerable discretion whether to take the offender back to court for breaching their order, but this discretion was successively removed. To many this further signalled a move towards law enforcement, raising the spectre of armed probation officers (as in the United States of America) who have rights to pursue and arrest those who do not comply (Raynor and Vanstone 2002). Discussions of electronic monitoring of community orders further underlined this trend. In 2004 the transition became complete with the probation and the prison services jointly considered as correctional services and managed together under the National Offender Management Service.

Nonetheless, attention to rehabilitation was still prominent, and the legitimacy of probation could be strengthened by evidence that it could make a difference to reducing offending through effectively intervening in offenders' lives to encourage them to stop offending. This in turn could be justified by appeals to public protection as offenders were turned away, if the intervention was successful, from committing crimes in the future. Attention turned to looking at what works in relation to offending behaviour, an agenda which has become prominent in the early twenty-first century, and which will be discussed below. While this received some criticism (Mair 2004), it has provided a considerable source of optimism for some and has arguably provided a new *raison d'être* for the probation service. While less immediately applicable to community service, with its more punitive emphasis, many argue that the 'what works' literature can also affect the effectiveness of community service (Gelsthorpe and Rex 2004). This will be discussed below.

In short, therefore, the probation service has seen many changes, having been profoundly affected by the pessimism following the 'nothing works' era and moving away from its roots in social work and dealing with the welfare of offenders to being more concerned with law enforcement, public protection and correctionalism. This contrasts with the position in Scotland where, unlike in England and Wales, the probation service was abolished in the late 1960s and the provision of what is called 'criminal justice social work' became part of generic social work services. While this approach has had its problems, the provision of community sentences in Scotland has continued to be more affected by anti-custodialism, social inclusion and stressing the value of welfare and social-work based interventions. Moreover, it did not have to face the recasting of its work as 'punishment in the community', although it currently faces a major review with suggestions for a single offender management agency (McIvor 2004; Robinson and McNeill 2004).

14.2 THE PROBATION SERVICE

In 2001 the implementation of the Criminal Justice and Courts Services Act 2000 meant that the probation service in England and Wales became a national service: divided into 42 local services matching police force boundaries for the first time. In organisational terms this completed the move to co-terminous boundaries for the main criminal justice agencies: police, CPS and probation.

In 2002 there were 17,300 staff: 8,000 were probation officers. Below is a summary of their workload in 2002 indicating the range of tasks undertaken by the probation service.

■ *Writing reports for courts*: 253,000 pre-sentence reports (PSR). Youth Offending Teams (YOTS) now produce reports for the youth courts. Courts can now ask the probation service to make a rapid assessment, without the need for an adjournment of the case to another day, of the suitability of a single specified community sentence. This provision was introduced so that probation views could be canvassed where a certain community sentence was uncontentious, without the cost and time involved in the preparation of a full PSR.

■ *Supervision of court orders*: 127,000 offenders started community sentences in 2002. Figure 14.1 shows the growth and relative change in the imposition of CPOs, CROs and CPROs from 1992 to 2002. Drug treatment and testing orders introduced nationally in 2000 were also commenced in 5,800 cases in 2002. Approximately 1,300 money payment supervision orders, where the probation service assists offenders to manage fines and other payments due to the court, were dealt with in 2002.

The growth in the use of court ordered community sentences has been considerable and is illustrated by the fact that, in 1992, of all offenders sentenced for indictable crimes in the Crown Court and magistrates' courts, 23 per cent were given a community sentence. By 2002 this had risen to 33 per cent. Obviously this type of sentence has become more fashionable and, despite the publicity given to the rise in the prison population, the rise in the use of community sentences has been more dramatic.

■ *Pre and post-release supervision*: 31,400 offenders aged 21 or over who had been sentenced to 12 months or more in prison began statutory post-prison supervision. Added to this number of people being supervised in relation to prison sentences were 12,400 young offenders and 7,200 who underwent voluntary supervision. Thus at the end of 2002 138,400 offenders were under probation supervision in the community either under a community sentence or after release from prison.

■ *Contacting victims*: since 2000, the probation service has a statutory duty to

Figure 14.1 **Persons starting court order supervision by the probation service: England and Wales**

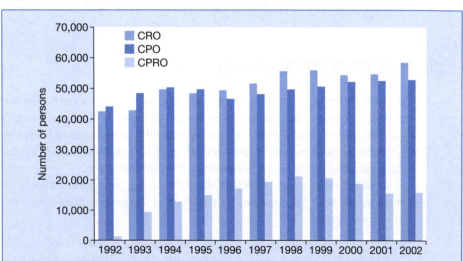

Source: Probation Statistics 2002 (Home Office 2004)

consult and inform victims in relation to the release arrangements of certain offenders. Between April 2002 and March 2003 the probation service informed 16,000 victims.

- *Hostels for bail and probation requirements*: the service run hostels which cater for those on probation or bail with a condition of residence in a hostel and those on licence after release from prison.

- *Advice and training*: providing support for offenders in need in areas such as housing, basic skills, and employment.

Once on a community order, offenders face a variety of experiences. These may include a programme of meetings with their supervising officer or attendance at counselling or therapy sessions for alcohol and drug abuse or anger management. Some will require help finding accommodation and work, others with welfare and social security applications. Others may participate in a variety of projects: for example, motor projects which provide offenders who have been involved in car crime with an opportunity to drive and work with cars legitimately. Other offenders are sent on programmes involving physical exercise to improve their ability to use leisure time constructively and cooperate within teams and groups.

The range of programmes can vary across the country and will reflect demand and resources. For example, in the Thames Valley Probation area (covering Buckinghamshire, Berkshire and Oxfordshire) in 2003 the following programmes were available as an aspect of a community sentence:

- *Aggression replacement training*: aimed at persistent offenders with a pattern of violent or aggressive behaviour other than domestic violence or sex offenders. The programme consisted of 5 sessions on risk assessment, 18 weekly group work sessions developing anger control and social and reasoning skills, and 5 post-programme individual evaluation and relapse prevention sessions.

- *Anti-violence group work programme*: aimed at male domestic violence offenders involving weekly sessions of 2 hours for 24 weeks and 'home work' assignments. Under this programme partners of such offenders were offered information about the offender's progress and advice.

- *Drink-impaired Drivers' Programme*: aimed at drivers with up to 4 previous convictions for driving with excess alcohol and involves 4 sessions on risk assessments and 14 weekly group work sessions concentrating on social and decision-making skills and information about the effects of alcohol on driving capability. The course is followed by 6 individual evaluation and relapse prevention sessions.

- *One to one*: aimed at persistent offenders on post-release licence after custody or a CRO or CPRO, with personality or social skills problems that would make group work less effective. The programme is not suitable for those whose social functioning problems stem from mental disorder or drug abuse or those with learning difficulties. The programme is composed of 21 sessions and can be undertaken by those who must reside in a probation hostel.

- *Think First*: aimed at persistent offenders other than sex offenders, domestic violence offenders and drink drivers, who do not think through the consequences of their actions (hence the name).

Table 14.1 Persons supervised by the probation service by type of supervision

England and Wales 31 December										Number of persons	
Type of supervision	1992	1993	1994	1995	1996	1997	1998	1999	2000	2001	2002
Criminal supervision											
Court orders											
CRO	49,747	49,243	54,313	53,666	54,148	56,660	60,977	60,329	57,482	56,678	61,593
C&YP 1969	2,228	2,281	2,348	2,545	2,670	2,567	2,369	1,911	322	48	201
Suspended	2,657	1,061	490	514	642	807	811	767	708	574	583
MPSO	7,388	6,679	6,465	5,838	7,937	7,486	7,112	6,879	6,959	6,787	2,411
CPO[1,2]	31,586	35,592	36,947	34,657	32,463	33,632	37,321	34,388	37,694	37,290	34,491
CPO[3]	–	–	–	–	–	–	168	256	267	272	16
CPO[4]	–	–	–	–	–	–	564	637	706	672	4
CPO (breach)	17	352	843	1,112	1,506	1,587	1,697	2,125	2,359	2,034	2,470
CPRO	1,385	8,739	14,165	16,756	19,675	21,767	25,090	22,069	21,719	21,053	18,245
DTTO	–	–	–	–	–	–	–	76	304	2,863	3,887
All court orders	88,543	96,563	107,257	107,333	110,274	115,622	126,876	120,945	119,904	120,174	116,859
All pre and post-release supervision	50,325	51,631	54,293	56,102	62,934	71,730	80,622	87,017	89,183	91,871	78,188
All criminal supervision	136,612	145,039	158,313	160,764	170,332	184,271	203,497	204,000	204,647	207,423	192,856
Family court supervision	388	442	456	405	520	356	246	144	232	3	9
All supervision	137,000	145,481	158,769	161,169	170,852	184,627	203,743	204,144	204,879	207,426	192,864

(1) Community punishment order (CPO). Previously known as community service order (CSO).
(2) Excludes community punishment orders which have run for more than 2 years.
(3) CPO for persistent petty offending.
(4) CPO for fine default.

Source: Probation Statistics 2002 (Home Office 2004)

- *Sex offender group work*: aimed at male sex offenders who are over 21, other than those who have mental health problems. This programme involves a psychometric assessment to determine the relevant blocks to be undertaken. The available blocks are:
  - Foundation: full time 9am–5pm attendance for 2 weeks
  - Victim empathy: attendance twice weekly for 4 weeks
  - Lifeskills: attendance twice weekly for 10 weeks
  - Relapse prevention: attendance weekly for 24 weeks.

Clearly there is a range of tasks undertaken by probation officers in their work to supervise offenders and to help reduce offending. The caseload would include writing court reports, supervising offenders as individual cases and contacting victims. In 2002 the average supervisory caseload was 21 per officer, and with an average court order caseload of 12.5. The average number of reports completed per main grade probation officer was 76.2. Such analysis and measurement of caseload reflects concerns that have existed over understaffing and consequent delays in providing services to the courts and to develop more intensive programmes of supervision for the highest risk offenders. The effectiveness of community sentences has been a key concern in their delivery and development and is considered in the next section.

The latest development in community sentencing is the introduction of the single generic community order by the CJA 2003 (discussed in Chapter 11) which provides for the individually tailored approach to sentencing, allowing the courts to impose a range of requirements to meet the specific needs, threats and risks of the offender in order to prevent re-offending and the just deserts of the particular offence.

It is also important to consider the conflicting objectives of community sentences. The increasing emphasis on cost-effectiveness monitoring and the deprivation of liberty may have an impact on how offenders respond to some schemes. For example, pressures of cost-effectiveness may lead to offenders being placed on a scheme that happens to be available in a locality that might not always be appropriate to a particular offender's needs. Thus resource constraints and competing objectives make probation work difficult to carry out and difficult to evaluate.

Along with other criminal justice agencies, in keeping with the trend to managerialism, the National Probation Service is subject to targets and inspection. HM Inspectorate of Probation reports to ministers in relation to probation service achievements. In addition the Prisons and Probation Ombudsman investigates complaints from those subject to probation supervision, as discussed in Chapter 4.

Efforts to define finding a key role for probation by the beginning of the twenty-first century led to the search for tougher multi-purposed community penalties – to meet punishment and rehabilitative goals – that are credible with the public and sentencers, will contribute to reducing the prison population, and will achieve the crime reduction targets set by the Government. In the White Paper *Justice for All* the search was on for a third way, for 'tough community sentences' that are a 'credible alternative to custody', with multiple conditions like tagging, reparation and drug treatment and testing. As noted in Chapter 1, a new model of criminal justice

was launched which focused on offenders and sought to punish, control and rehabilitate through more demanding and multi-purpose community sentences.

14.3 'WHAT WORKS' AND WHY, AND RECENT INITIATIVES IN COMMUNITY SENTENCES

It was seen above that probation practice has now become dominated by what has
been described as a 'What Works' agenda – often taken to be a response to research
which, while not entirely negative, seemed to suggest that 'nothing works'. Much of
the What Works research originated in Canada. What worked in terms of changing
offender behaviour had not been so prominent in the 1980s/early 1990s when efforts
were being made to identify a punishment role of community sentences. It re-emerged
with the emphasis on evidence-based policy of the new Labour Government and, in
particular, in June 1998 with a circular entitled *The Effective Practice Initiative:
National Implementation Plan for the Supervision of Offenders* (Mair 2004: 1). Early
work revealed that there was considerable variation in programmes, with little clear
evidence of success, and a Pathfinder project was set up which contained several cognitive behavioural programmes which were to be closely evaluated. The accreditation
of programmes increased and a Joint Prison/Probation Accreditation Panel was
formed in 1999 which favours cognitive behavioural approaches.

The What Works programmes vary in focus. Some emphasise the importance of
cognitive behavioural therapy, which focuses on addressing the 'risk factors' associated with offending which include habits of thinking ('cognition'), and patterns of
behaviour which are identified with deficiencies in skills – such as, for example,
'social skills'. Cognitive skills courses encourage offenders to change attitudes. The
'change' element includes teaching educational skills, both general and vocational,
and providing 'offending behaviour programmes' inspired by cognitive-behavioural
therapy. They are based on the belief that criminals carry out crimes because of mis-
perceptions, so that they think that no one gets hurt, e.g. victims of property crimes
are assumed to be insured, or they perceive innocent actions as confrontational, for
example, by aggressive responses such as 'what are you looking at?'.

In the 1990s much effort went into finding out what works. Meta-analyses of a
number of studies pointed to shared findings about what interventions were likely
to be successful and research on programmes with offenders considered to be at a
'high risk' of re-offending found that interventions of various kinds could make a difference to offenders' propensity to re-offend.

Iain Murray (2003: 15–16) develops the framework of Andrews, Bonta and Hoge
(1990) to identify effective recidivism-reducing strategies:

- *Risk*: programmes must differentiate between the risk of re-offending of individual offenders.

- *Needs*: programmes must address the specific crimogenic (e.g. drug use) and non-
  crimogenic needs (e.g. low self-esteem) of the offender.

- *Responsivity*: the offender's willingness to participate and join in the programme
  is crucial.

- *Professional discretion*: staff must be allowed to vary activities in response to the individual offender they are dealing with.

- *Programme integrity*: there must be a well-resourced and properly implemented programme.

In the United Kingdom another meta-analysis claimed that some forms of intervention could produce reductions in offending, it was claimed, of between 10 and 20 per cent. Raynor and Vanstone (2002: 88) provide a useful summary of elements that are included in the most effective programmes, being those which:

- target high-risk offenders who are otherwise considered likely to re-offend (they are less successful with low-risk offenders who gain little benefit or are harmed);

- focus on 'criminogenic need' – the circumstances or characteristics of offenders held to have contributed to their offending;

- follow a tight structure which makes clear demands and follows a logical sequence;

- use a directive working approach so that those involved are clear about what they are meant to be doing;

- use cognitive behavioural approaches to provide opportunities to learn new thinking and behaviour;

- are located in the community, although they can also be used in prison;

- have programme integrity, with clear procedures;

- are implemented by appropriately trained staff;

- are adequately resourced;

- are evaluated, preferably by external researchers.

The optimism about community sanctions in England and Wales since 2001 has been built around a faith in the multi-dimensional features of Intensive Supervision and Surveillance Programmes (ISSP) for offenders aged 10–17. The related programme, Intensive Control and Change Programme (ICCP) scheme, introduced in 2003 is for 18–20-year-olds.

The target group for these programmes, being the most serious and prolific young offenders, was thought to be responsible for a quarter of all youth crime. The programmes are available for convicted young offenders and also aim to prevent persistent young offenders on bail from committing more crimes while awaiting trial. They subject the offender to intensive surveillance and monitoring for up to 24 hours a day, 7 days a week, if necessary. Electronic tagging and telephone voice verification can be used in addition to police and probation surveillance. The minimum requirement is for two surveillance checks per day. In addition, for rehabilitative purposes, offenders are subject to a structured programme of activities for 25 hours a week for the first 3 months, after which the supervision continues at a reduced intensity (a minimum of 5 hours per week) for a further 3 months.

The evidence regarding the effectiveness of these programmes is open to dispute, with the Youth Justice Board claiming success for these programmes but the large study in the United States of America (University of Maryland) not finding systematic evidence to support a view that they were successful. In England and

Wales there has been one evaluation of a pilot scheme in Rotherham conducted in 2000/01. This showed that 27 young offenders on the Rotherham Intensive Supervision, Support and Advocacy Programme (RISSAP) had been convicted of 160 offences in the 9 months before the scheme, but during the programme they committed only 47 offences. The programme group was 35 strong and the control group only 18. Seven out of 18 members of the control group did not offend (39 per cent) compared with 16 out of 35 members of the programme group (46 per cent). These numbers are far too small to reach any conclusion as one person switching from the offending to non-offending category would change the outcome.

There are also varied conclusions about the evaluation of the impact of electronic monitoring as a surveillance device to control criminal conduct for those on community sentences. Work in Canada is used to support the claim about the effectiveness of rehabilitative programmes that are reinforced via electronic monitoring (Bonta *et al.* 1999).

David Green summarises the Bonta *et al.* study:

> The main finding of the study, *Electronic Monitoring in Canada*, was that recidivism rates of offenders did not change significantly as a result of electronic monitoring. The study considered three methods of punishment and control: Electronic Monitoring, probation and prison. The crude scores initially suggest a benefit from Electronic Monitoring. Reconviction rates were 26.7% for Electronic Monitoring participants, 33.3% for probationers and 37.9% for offenders who had been imprisoned (Bonta, pp. 46–7). However, the three groups were not equal. They had all been assessed on a 'risk-needs' scale previously found to be a reliable indicator of future offending. The report concluded that the 'lower recidivism rates found with Electronic Monitoring participants could be explained by the differences in risk-needs levels'. Consequently, the reduced re-offending was not the result of the type of sanction. The researchers concluded that adding Electronic Monitoring to the supervision of offenders had 'little effect on recidivism' (Bonta pp. 47–8). Moreover, they found no lasting post-programme effect on criminal behaviour (Bonta, p. 54).
>
> The only benefit of EM was the one mentioned by the Youth Justice Board, namely that offenders subject to EM who attended the educational programme were more likely to complete it than the probationers (87.5% for those on Electronic Monitoring and 52.9% for those on probation). However, the probation sample was small (17 people) and the researchers thought that the additional requirements of EM, including 'the threat of a return to prison for non-cooperation' might explain the difference (Bonta et al., p. 16).
>
> (David Green 2003)

The largest meta-analysis of over 500 evaluation studies of What Works in terms of reducing recidivism was produced by the University of Maryland in 1997 for the US Congress, *Preventing Crime: What Works, What Doesn't and What's Promising*. While the original thesis of Martinson that 'nothing works' in 1974 had been modified, the subsequent evaluation trials had not come up with much that supports the level of optimism as was to be found in the 1997/2003 period in the United Kingdom. The study found some programmes that were promising but had not been fully evaluated. The conclusion seems to be that any specific programme is unlikely to deliver a large reduction in recidivism because of the complexities that affect the life opportunities and choices of offenders. Responding to the risk factors of individual offenders might offer a more realistic chance of reducing recidivism.

In England and Wales the evidence about what works in terms of community sentences is still unclear; while in Government, prison reductionist pressure groups and some academic circles in the United Kingdom there have also been signs of a growing confidence that community service can contribute to reducing recidivism (Gelsthorpe and Rex 2004; McIvor 2004). Some studies have found lower reconviction rates than would be expected for those sentenced to community service and there is some evidence that some features of it do have reintegrative and rehabilitative potential. Particularly important can be the acquisition of skills and the experience of work for some offenders, which can give rise to feelings of confidence and self esteem. In addition, some placements with community-based agencies can make offenders aware of other people and their ability to deal with them.

However, there is also scepticism about the evidence supporting What Works programmes and in the way in which 'what works' research has been interpreted and implemented in practice – often focusing on a more narrow concept of cognitive skills rather than on the wider social and economic needs of offenders (Mair 2004).

Some have questioned the strength of the 'evidence' base on which claims about effectiveness are made – many are based on local initiatives and on inconsistent findings about the effectiveness of programmes on different groups of offenders and there have been concerns that the growth in accredited programmes has preceded the collection of evidence. Indeed, even supporters of the initiatives accept that the evidence base in Britain is still small (Raynor and Vanstone 2002), and one critic comments that the 'foundations of What Works in England and Wales cannot be said to be neat, evidence based, carefully considered and well planned' (Mair 2004: 21). In addition there have been problems in implementation, some of which are attributable to a shortage of qualified staff across the National Probation Service along with a lack of administrative support and difficulties in ensuring adequate evaluation.

To some critics the emphasis on cognitive behavioural approaches implies a return to the medical model of deviance with its assumptions that offenders are somehow 'different' and 'deficient' and that they are to be treated as 'others' – which can become exclusive rather than inclusive (Mair 2004). This in turn may be related to the way in which What Works research has been implemented in England and Wales – in terms which stress individual responsibility and cognitive skills rather than taking a more 'holistic' view of the broader personal and social problems which offenders face. For offenders faced with pressures of unemployment and homelessness, it could be argued, programmes to encourage them to learn social skills may not provide sufficient motivation to cease offending and indeed the pressures of their circumstances may impede attendance at programmes. In Scotland – where there is more emphasis on social inclusion and a welfare approach – what works can potentially include a broader approach focusing on the wider factors which affect desistance, which may include personal problems, feelings of confidence, employment, education and feelings of achievement, suggesting the importance of a more personalised approach (Robinson and McNeill 2004; McIvor 2004).

14.4 THE EFFECTIVENESS OF COMMUNITY SENTENCES

There have been many pressures for community sentences to establish their effectiveness. Yet we have also seen that, given the different functions accorded to community sentences, it may be difficult to assess what is meant by effectiveness. Is their effectiveness to be judged in terms of how well they provide an alternative to prison? Or in terms of how many offenders are diverted from further crime? Alternatively, given the high costs of imprisonment and pressures for cost-effectiveness should we subject community sentences to a cost–benefit analysis? Finally, irrespective of any of these measures, should we look at the extent to which offenders are helped by these schemes, whether or not they re-offend?

In relation to the first question – their effectiveness as alternatives to prison – evidence is mixed. To start with, in what sense are community sentences an alternative to prison (i.e. an equally valid option)? In just deserts terms this was not considered credible. The cost and effectiveness of comparing imprisonment and community sentences were discussed in Chapters 12 and 13. The prison population has continued to rise despite the introduction of measures which in part were aimed at reducing it; and it appeared that the so-called alternatives to prison acted instead as alternatives to existing non-custodial sentences. This may even have resulted in more people being sent to prison – if, for example, an offender failed to comply with an order or committed further offences, they could be sent to prison, thus moving more rapidly up the tariff than they might otherwise have done. Another possible reason was that the courts, viewing community sentences as too soft, were not prepared to use them for offenders that they would otherwise have sent to prison.

This may continue to be the case – rates of the use of both Community Punishment and Community Rehabilitation Orders for summary offences have risen to the extent that almost half of community penalties are now made for summary offences, rather than for those convicted of more serious offences (Mair 2004). In addition, there has been a decrease in those receiving orders who have experience of custody and an increase in the use of orders for first-time offenders – suggesting that community penalties are increasingly being used for less serious offenders who might otherwise have been given a fine, as the proportionate use of fines has also decreased. Thus less serious offenders are being given more punishment (Mair 2004), community sentences have slipped down the tariff and appear to be having little impact on the use of custody (Gelsthorpe and Rex 2004).

Effectiveness can be measured by looking at the number of offenders who complete their sentence rather than being returned to court for breaching orders. The enthusiasm of the judges and magistrates for the new Drug Treatment and Testing Order (DTTO) might not be supported by the initial evidence with regard to completion rates. The first evaluation by the National Audit Office (2004: 26) *The Drug Treatment and Testing Order: Early Lessons* finds that the majority of drug offenders do not complete their community sentence and 28 per cent do. This figure includes those with orders that expired while offenders were waiting formal revocation by the courts.

The non-completion of a community sentence may result in a breach and a return to court. In 2002, 32 per cent of offenders on community punishment orders, 25 per cent of those on community rehabilitation orders and 50 per cent of those on community punishment and rehabilitation orders were the subject of breach proceed-ings (*Criminal Statistics England and Wales* 2002: 125). While these figures might be regarded as a success by those familiar with the problems of dealing with offenders, from another perspective they represent a failure of offenders to com-plete the sentence given by the court; a sentence usually proposed in the pre-sentence report by the probation service.

A second measure is their effectiveness in preventing re-offending. This is usually expressed in terms of the number of follow-up convictions in a two-year period since the offender started a community sentence, or in the case of prisons, com-pleted their prison sentence. These figures are normally based on formal con-victions, which makes them less than reliable if we recognise that only a few of all crimes that are committed result in a conviction (see Chapter 2).

Reconviction rates may be useful for comparing success with certain types of offenders, or certain types of offence. The two-year reconviction rate for all offenders commencing community penalties in 1999 was 56 per cent, and the com-parative rates for the years 1987 to 1999 are shown in Figure 14.2. They vary in terms of type of different community sentences which overall has remained stable at 56 per cent over the last five years; community punishment was lower at 48 per cent (i.e. more successful at reducing re-offending) and community rehabilitation orders (probation orders) were less effective at 61 per cent.

The problem of interpreting these figures is not simple as the measurement of reconviction rates does not take account of the original risk of re-offending. Risk of re-offending may be affected by age, sex, previous history of offending, type of offence, as well as by the sentence imposed. For offences committed in 1999, the two-year reconviction rate varied between under 30 per cent for those whose orig-inal conviction was for sex offences, to 80 per cent for offenders whose original conviction was for theft from a vehicle. Additionally, the criminal justice system can

Figure 14.2 **Two-year reconviction rates by type of community penalty order since 1987**

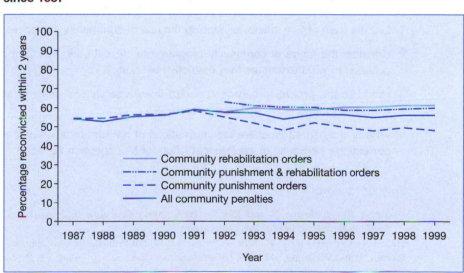

Source: Probation Statistics 2002 (HMSO 2004)

itself affect the statistics as some of the 'reconvictions' are for offences dealt with after the original one but committed before (pseudo-reconvictions) (see Lloyd *et al.* 1994).

It can be seen that the reconviction rates are broadly similar and do not fluctuate over time very greatly. Looking at the data in more detail shows that, for community sentences, the reconviction rate will vary by gender, age, type of offence, but is not so influenced by length of sentence given.

CONCLUSION

This chapter has shown that community sentences and the probation service have undergone considerable changes since their inception in the early twentieth century. In particular with community sentences in the last 20 years we have seen a re-interpretation of their role: between seeing them as primarily a rehabilitative measure, a diversionary measure or as part of the higher tariff sentences of the criminal justice process, concerned more with public protection and punishment. There has also been the reawakening of an interest in rehabilitation, seen in the increasing attention paid to what works and the use of cognitive therapy, and a recognition of the personal, social and economic circumstances of offenders which might impede efforts to make them less likely to re-engage with crime. An important issue with community sentences has always been their credibility and legitimacy, with many seeing them as a 'soft option'; in part, the increasing emphasis on What Works and an evidence base can be taken as an attempt to address this issue. The recent development of a multi-purpose and intensive intervention with high-risk offenders justifies our inclusion of the new model of criminal justice we introduced in Chapter 1.

Review questions

1 List the main arguments for enhancing the use of community sentences.

2 Consider the range of community programmes described in this chapter: in what way and to what extent are they restrictive of liberty?

3 How has the probation service changed from a service to befriend and support offenders to a service to manage offenders?

4 What's in a name? What are the implications of having probation as part of (a) the correctional services; (b) the National Offender Management Service?

Further reading

Bottoms, A, Gelsthorpe, L and Rex, S (eds) (2001) *Community Penalties: Change and Challenges*, Willan Publishing: Cullompton

Mair, G (ed.) (2004) *What Matters in Probation*, Willan Publishing: Cullompton

Raynor, P and Vanstone, M (2002) *Understanding Community Penalties: Probation, policy and social change*, Open University Press: Buckingham

CHAPTER 15

Conclusion

The beginning of a new century provides an opportunity to take stock of the developments over the past one and to speculate about the trends that provide clues to the future. In 1900 it is unlikely that we would have found a commentator who would have predicted the extent of changes in the field of criminal justice. Some changes were unforeseeable: the impact of information technology and its ability to process a mass of information which can be sent almost instantly around the world; the development of the computer and its contribution to the phenomenon called globalisation. World news and international travel are aspects of life in wealthy western society which are taken for granted at the beginning of the twenty-first century. Whilst enhanced travel and career opportunities are thus provided, so are opportunities for international crime, be it international terrorism or trafficking in illegal drugs, weapons or people, or the opportunities provided by the use of computers for new methods to facilitate fraud, theft and pornography.

What conclusions can be made concerning the frenetic pace of reform in the United Kingdom since 1997, which has left no agency or aspect of criminal justice untouched, in the name of effectiveness, evidence-based reforms and modernisation? Partly this is a response to the heightened public anxiety about crime. No rationalisation in terms of moral panics can fully explain the level of public concern and fear of crime. By 2000 it appeared that some aspects of middle-range crime – burglaries for instance – were responding to focused targeting. However, this did not allay public anxiety as everyday street level incivilities and yobbishness meant people felt threatened when using public transport or visiting town centres once the bars, pubs and vicinity were taken over by alcohol and drug-fuelled rowdy youths. Then came the new nightmare of the twenty-first century as, around the world, people witnessed the unthinkable as passenger aircraft were flown into the twin towers of the World Trade Center in New York City on 11 September 2001. The fear of terrorist actions in busy urban areas provided the new paranoia, which turned, in a short period of time, to reality for those killed by terrorist bombs in Madrid, Istanbul and Bali.

At the same time other fundamental changes were taking place in matters previously taken for granted and vital in dealing with crime. Membership of the European Union was changing the nature of sovereignty and the role of the nation state. New rules, regulations and institutions were forthcoming. New crimes were being defined in Brussels and Strasbourg and new cross-European arrangements were introduced. If the United Kingdom remains within the European Union this will provide the major source of change to the criminal justice system in the foreseeable future.

Even so, at the start of the twenty-first century we are aware that in England and Wales there is a system that has slowly evolved over a thousand years, built on the key principles of the rule of law. Societies that go through periods of lawlessness, such as, in recent times, Kosova and Serbia, quickly learn the consequences of living in fear of other people and the unpredictability of everyday life when there is no rule of law.

In England and Wales crime policy became part of the political debates partly in response to rising crime and partly as a result of the reform era of the 1960s and 1970s. Social change in this period was to shift the cultural roots and social arrangements of people undertaking everyday activities in the home, the community and at work. The 1970s seemed to be a different country from the drearily austere and conformist post-1939/45 war Britain of the 1950s. Change and consequent uncertainty was apparent in the debates about the causes of crime and the role of criminal justice agencies. In the 1990s human rights reforms and data protection legislation was to cause further uncertainty; with tragic consequences in the case of the latter when the Humberside police did not keep effective records about allegations of sexual offences by Ian Huntley, who went on to murder Holly Wells and Jessica Chapman in Soham in 2003.

Few of the traditional institutions have remained untouched as laws provided new rights, and intervened into spheres previously regarded as private, such as the home. The pre-1950s political consensus on crime was to become polarised as reformers imposed changes that were not shared by the majority. The abolition of capital punishment was one such example.

Change and uncertainty was rife in many aspects of everyday life and crime policy was no exception. Therefore it was no surprise when in July 2004 a new 5-year plan was announced by the government for more action against anti-social behaviour, with more police community support officers and community wardens on the beat, a better deal for victims and tougher and focused action against the prolific offenders who seem immune to the interventions of the current system.

In an ambitious attempt to do something about the persistent offender the New Labour Government shifted the focus from the CJA 1991, with its just deserts approach to achieving a standardised and proportionate response to the crime committed, and adopted an 'offender-management' model with its many layered interventions which seek to be part rehabilitative, part surveillance and also part punishment. Thus the offender and not the crime has become the new emphasis of the criminal justice system by 2004.

This textbook has considered aspects of the criminal justice system in terms not only of the work and effect of the agencies involved, but also the policy and political contexts in which they operate and the often conflicting pressures and objectives that influence their operation. By using various models of considering the criminal justice system the text has highlighted how processes can be analysed to put them into a wider context. It has identified how change in one area can impact on another: the crucial inter-relatedness of the system underpins the New Labour Government's avowed quest for 'joined-up criminal justice'. These matters have been examined largely by following a process chronology: the sources and definitions of crime, government and administrative interventions and crime prevention, the commission and investigation of crime; the courts and trial process; and the penal system.

The first sections of this text examined the changing nature of what is considered a crime and differing approaches to key players: note was taken of the increased focus on victims of crime and on desires to include them in the criminal process as well as to make amends for the crimes committed against them.

Varying political approaches to the 'crime problem' and the initiatives under New Labour to curtail crime by an offender-management approach have been considered, including, in this context, the impact of the desire for cost-effective, measurable outcomes and monitoring of achievements by targets and KPIs. A combination of cost-effectiveness and political considerations also has affected the widespread privatisation of many aspects of criminal justice.

The increasing focus on cost-effectiveness may conflict with other influences on penal policy. Governments face a dilemma in pursuing strategies, often seen as politically desirable, which stress being tough on crime while at the same time taking account of economic considerations. Tougher and more punitive policies may involve higher costs of prosecution and an increasing use of imprisonment. This has led to a tendency towards bifurcation, whereby tougher policies are reserved for more serious offences and offenders, while others are diverted from the system at various stages. Some may be diverted before prosecution by the use of cautions and victim–offender mediation schemes and diverted from prison by the greater use of community sentences. This can, of course, conflict with notions of just deserts and denunciation and with the interests of victims who see their offenders going unpunished.

Many of the strategies to make the system more effective have been accompanied or based on new technologies both for the management of systems and the control of the offenders within it. More offenders can be kept out of prison if they are monitored by what is popularly known as electronic 'tagging' and many town and city centres and other public spaces are subject to surveillance by closed circuit television.

There has also been an enormous growth of what is often described as 'private' policing. Local authorities increasingly employ security companies and many have their own municipal security – as in, for example, parks – and some have extended this to council property, housing estates and public places. There has also been a growth of auxiliary police and community wardens, and a general wish to include the community in policing and crime prevention.

The processes and changes in court procedure and particularly the criminal trial have also been considered, with examination of the tensions between due process and bureaucratic efficiency models. Diversionary strategies referred to above can increase efficiency in the court process but can lead to public disquiet on the grounds that offenders may be perceived as being 'let off too lightly', and denunciationists might argue that offenders should be publicly tried. In addition, diversionary policies raise issues of justice and due process in that decisions about these offenders are being made in private and may thus be less accountable. This divergence may also disadvantage those who choose to contest their guilt and are seen as taking up officials' time unnecessarily and who may receive a harsher disposition as a result. It also raises questions of the degree to which some minor offences may in effect be decriminalised, as happened in the downgrading of cannabis from a class B to a class C drug, thus carrying lower penalties and symbolically allowing the police to treat possession of the drug more lightly.

The final stage considered, the penal system, has also undergone much institutional review and examination with a reconfiguration of its role and objectives.

The 'what works' debate had dominated the agenda about prisons. The prison reductionist arguments about the high cost of prison and the recognition that prisons have only a limited rehabilitative potential raise important questions for the prison system. Should a steady increase in the prison population be accepted, or should steps be taken to reduce numbers in prison? If they are increasingly to be used for more serious, hard-core offenders, for largely incapacitative purposes, how should regimes be organised and what should they aim for? If there are few goals other than security and control, popularly expressed as 'keeping them in and keeping them quiet', do they become, as Cohen (1985) argues, effectively 'human warehouses' which may lead to more unrest? In 2004 the Home Secretary announced a cap on the prison population of 80,000. As this text shows, such an aim is not simple to accomplish without significant changes elsewhere in the system.

Since the election of the New Labour Government in 1997, legislative reforms have proceeded apace (see Chronology). The most all-encompassing is the Criminal Justice Act 2003. This Act, building on the reports by Auld and Halliday, though not implementing all their suggestions, is one of the most far-reaching pieces of criminal justice legislation in modern times. Its impact relates to bail, police conduct, the composition of the jury, the conduct of criminal trials, rules of evidence, sentencing, appeals, prison and probation.

These sweeping reforms, in addition to the plethora of initiatives introduced since 1997, are indicative of the all-encompassing approach of New Labour to modernisation and the pursuit of change.

It is clear, therefore, that in the twenty-first century the criminal justice system faces considerable change and continuing dilemmas. The different models of criminal justice outlined in Chapter 1 continue to influence thinking and remain significant, although the limitations of the system in reducing or preventing crime are more widely recognised. It is, more than ever, clear that criminal justice policy and agencies must be seen in a wider social, cultural, economic, national and international context.

Glossary of criminal justice terms

Absolute discharge A sentence of the court in which no further action is taken.

Accused The person suspected and accused of committing a crime.

Acquittal Finding of not guilty.

Actual bodily harm (ABH) An offence of violence where assault results in any physical or mental injury. More serious than common assault but less serious than grievous bodily harm (GBH).

Actus reus A Latin phrase referring to the acts (the guilty act) constituting a criminal offence. It refers to the part of a definition of a criminal offence that relates to the activity or consequence. For example the actus reus of murder is 'causing the death of a living person'.

Adversarial justice The system of justice based in criminal cases on the assumption that the prosecution must prove the guilt of the person accused of committing a crime by presenting admissible evidence that demonstrates the guilt of an offender beyond reasonable doubt. It is open to the defence to challenge this evidence.

Arrest An action whereby a suspect is lawfully detained, usually by the police, but in certain circumstances by any individual. (The latter is sometimes called a 'citizen's arrest'.)

Attorney General The Government Minister answerable for prosecution policy and the CPS in Parliament.

Automatism A criminal defence on the basis that the actions of the defendant took place without the defendant being aware of them, as in sleep-walking but not drunkenness.

Bail Release of a suspect or defendant before the conclusion of a case, to return at a specified time to the police station or court, where failure to do so can result in punishment.

Barrister A professional lawyer who acts as an advocate in the courtroom who can only be instructed by a solicitor.

Borstal A type of custodial institution which, from 1908 to 1982, sought to re-habilitate young offenders aged from 16 to 21.

Brief Instructions to a barrister from a solicitor regarding an appearance in court; and also used as a slang term to refer to a defence barrister.

British Crime Survey (BCS) A Home Office crime victimisation survey covering England and Wales carried out usually every two years since 1982.

Burglary   The criminal offence of illegally entering premises and committing or intending to commit acts such as theft, rape, serious assaults and criminal damage. Referred to in Scotland as housebreaking.

Capital punishment   The death penalty as a sentence.

Category A   One of four security classifications that relate to the security risk of an inmate.

Caution   (1) A formally worded statement made at the time of arrest by the police warning the suspect that whatever he or she says or does not say may be referred to as evidence in court. The caution also advises suspects that failure to reveal information may harm their court defence in certain circumstances

(2) An official caution in lieu of conviction and sentence is a means by which offenders who admit their guilt may be given an official warning by the police and are not sent to court for trial. It is a means of diversion. Cautions given to younger offenders are called reprimands and warnings. Conditional cautions were introduced by the CJA 2003 and can lead to prosecution if the conditions are breached.

Certified mentally ill   A person certified as not criminally liable because of the state of his or her mental health.

Clear-up rate   The detection rate expressed as a ratio of crimes cleared up as a percentage of those recorded by the police. A crime is cleared up if a person has been charged, cautioned or summonsed, or if an offender asks for crimes to be taken into consideration, or if a prisoner admits to a crime, or no further action is taken because the criminal is below the age of criminal liability.

Closed circuit television (CCTV)   A photographic system used as a means of security and surveillance.

Co-defendant   A person charged in the same case as another.

Committal   A stage in pre-trial proceedings whereby arrangements are made to transfer a case from the magistrates' court to the Crown Court for trial or sentence.

Common law   Law developed by court decisions, case law, and not embodied in statute.

Community Punishment Order (CPO)   Sentence of the court providing for an offender to do unpaid work for the community for between 40 and 240 hours over the course of one year. Formerly named Community Service Order. Replaced under CJA 2003 by an unpaid work requirement for 40 to 300 hours

Community Punishment and Rehabilitation Order (CPRO)   Sentence of the court combining CPO and CRO in specified ways. Formerly named Combination Order

Community Rehabilitation Order (CRO)   Sentence of the court providing for rehabilitation by way of supervision by the probation service. Formerly named Probation Order. Lasts between 6 months and 3 years. Replaced under CJA 2003 by a supervision requirement for up to 3 years

Community sentence   A community sentence can be made up of a range of different orders, which under the Criminal Justice Act 2003 includes a variety of requirements (such as unpaid work, activity or treatment requirements). Prior to the introduction of these orders, community sentences included Community Punishment Orders, Community Rehabilitation Orders, Community Punishment and Rehabilitation Orders, Curfew Orders and Atttendance Centre Orders).

Compensation Order   A monetary payment ordered by the court to be paid by the offender to the victim.

Condign   Merited or deserved as in a sentence.

Conditional discharge   A sentence of the court that results in no further action for the current offence, but which allows the court to sentence in some other way if another offence is committed within the time specified.

Conviction   Formal ascription of guilt in a criminal court.

Coroner's court   A tribunal to investigate sudden or violent deaths presided over by a coroner.

Counsel   Synonymous with barrister.

Court of Appeal   The court to which appeals from the Crown Court against conviction or sentence generally go.

Crime control model   An objective, or model, of criminal justice which stresses the aim of reducing crime.

Crimes without victims   Crimes that do not have an obvious or direct victim so they are less likely to be reported to the police, for example, prostitution, gambling, drug taking.

Criminal Injuries Compensation Authority (CICA)   A non departmental public body that administers a system of financial compensation in the form of payments for those injured as a result of criminal activities.

Criminal liability   Legal responsibility for an offence.

Criminal statistics   Officially published statistics of crimes recorded by the police.

Crown Court   The higher criminal court that replaced the Assize and Quarter Sessions in 1972 where trials on indictment take place before a judge and jury.

Crown Prosecution Service (CPS)   The agency that, since 1986, has been responsible for prosecuting most criminal offences.

Culpability   Responsibility of an offender for a crime. Blameworthiness.

Curfew   a) A sentence that requires the person to remain in a specified place such as his or her home at specified times.

b) A condition of bail to the same effect.

Custody   A sentence of imprisonment, or, for those aged 21 and under, detention in a young offenders' institution.

Custody plus   Sentence introduced by CJA 2003 for short term custodial sentences where a term of custody is followed by release under supervision.

Defendant   The person in the trial who has been accused of committing an offence.

Denunciation   An objective of sentencing and punishment where the aim is to reinforce community values by indicating that certain behaviour is regarded as reprehensible and will not be tolerated.

Detention and Training Order   Custodial sentence for young offenders.

Deterrence   An objective of sentencing and punishment the purpose of which is to reduce the likelihood of a crime being committed in the future by the threat or anticipation of a penalty.

District judges (magistrates' courts)   Legally qualified and paid magistrate, appointed from solicitors and barristers of at least 7 years' standing. Formerly called stipendiary magistrate.

Director of Public Prosecutions (DPP)   The appointed head of the CPS answerable to the Attorney General.

Dispersal Prison   Type of prison designed for high risk, Category A prisoners.

Disposal   Another term for a sentence of the court.

Diversion   Using strategies such as cautioning to keep offenders out of the criminal justice system.

DNA   Deoxyribonucleic acid, a component of all living matter present in blood, hair, bones, fingers, nails and bodily fluids which is used for identification purposes in criminal investigations and at a trial.

Doli incapax   The Latin term used to describe children who are deemed in law incapable of committing an offence because they are regarded as being too immature to appreciate the wrongfulness of their actions.

Double jeopardy   At risk of being punished twice for the same matter.

Due process   The term used to describe the legally required procedure so as to ensure that a criminal investigation and the trial is conducted in a fair manner and is regarded as protecting the civil liberties of the defendant.

Duress   A defence referring to serious threats made to a person who commits a crime as a result. It does not apply to murder or treason.

Evidential Sufficiency   One of the two criteria the CPS must apply in reviewing all cases before they may proceed to trial to ensure that sufficient and appropriate evidence has been collected by the police.

Green Paper   A preliminary discussion paper issued by a government department inviting comment on proposed changes to the law.

Grievous bodily harm (GBH)   Really serious harm such as broken ribs.

Hidden figure of crime   Sometimes referred to as the dark figure; the number of crimes that go unrecorded.

Home Affairs Committee (HAC)   A select committee of the House of Commons that monitors criminal justice issues.

Home Office   The government department responsible for law and order policies and the overall responsibility for the police, probation and prison services.

Homicide   Offences involving the unlawful killing of a person, for example, murder, manslaughter, infanticide.

Hooliganism   Rowdy and disorderly behaviour, usually in a group, that is regarded as threatening by others.

Incapacitation   Sentencing or punishment strategy that makes it impossible for the criminal to re-offend by imposing physical restraints on him or her such as imprisonment.

Incorrigible   An offender who refuses to change his or her criminal behaviour; unmanageable; unreformable.

Independent Police Complaints Commission   Body established from April 2004 to deal with complaints about the police.

Indeterminate sentence   A sentence that is not fixed in length, such as a life sentence.

Indictable   A criminal offence that may be tried in the Crown Court. Indictable offences are thus those that can only be tried in the Crown Court and triable either way offences.

Indictment   The formal document that contains the charges against a defendant for Crown Court trial.

Inmate   A person kept in prison or in a mental hospital.

Intermittent custody   Court sentence introduced under CJA 2003 allowing a custodial sentence to be served over longer periods of time, not on consecutive days.

Joyriding   A popular term for the criminal offence of aggravated vehicle taking.

Jurisdiction   The geographical and legal extent of the powers of an agency or court.

Jury   The twelve adults who are selected to decide, in Crown Court trial, whether from the evidence they have heard the accused is guilty or not. A jury is also used in the Coroner's Court.

Jury vetting   Examining the jury list before trial to exclude jurors with extreme political views: only possible in terrorist and national security trials.

Just deserts   Sentencing approach in which the sentence should be appropriate for the offence.

Justice model   Punishment model based on just deserts.

Labelling   The process of stereotyping social categories such as delinquents.

Lay magistracy   Justices of the Peace other than district judges.

Litigation   Using the courts to pursue a legal remedy.

Lord Chancellor's Department or Department of Constitutional Affairs   The government department responsible for the courts and the appointment of magistrates and judges.

Magistrates   The men and women appointed to decide matters in the magistrates' courts: District Judges (magistrates' courts) and lay magistrates.

Magistrates' court   The lower of the two criminal courts that try criminal cases.

Mandatory   Something that must happen as set down by legislation, for example, mandatory sentences: the court has no choice.

Manslaughter A criminal offence of causing death without the intention necessary to be guilty of murder, or where murder is reduced to manslaughter because of provocation or diminished responsibility.

Mens rea A Latin term meaning guilty mind, used to cover the various levels of the mental element (eg intention or recklessness) in the definition of an offence. For example, in the case of murder the *mens rea* is the intention to kill or to cause grievous bodily harm.

Metropolitan Police The police force for London and the surrounding area.

Miscarriage of justice A term commonly used to describe a case where a defendant, after serving a term of imprisonment, is later found to be not guilty. The term is rarely used in respect of mistaken acquittals.

Mitigation Factors that reduce an offender's culpability for a crime without being a defence and thus are used in decisions about sentences.

Mode of trial The way a defendant is tried, i.e. summarily or on indictment, hence the mode of trial decision/procedure is concerned with this choice in triable-either-way cases.

Moral panic An alarmed reaction to a social problem. The media is blamed for over-reacting to a type of crime and making it appear more serious or prevalent than it is.

Mugging A commonly used word to refer to a street robbery.

Murder Causing the death of another human being intending to cause his or her death or intending to cause grievous bodily harm.

Nolo contendere The defendant does not dispute the facts of the case for which he or she is accused.

Notifiable offences These are offences recorded by the police and broadly refers to most indictable (including triable either way) offences, although a few summary offences are included such as unauthorised taking of a motor vehicle. Not as extensive as the List of Standard Offences.

Organised crime Refers to the serious crimes of organised gangs and criminal syndicates.

PACE Police and Criminal Evidence Act 1984.

Paradigm A way of thinking about a subject of study or professional practice.

Parole Board Body responsible for decisions about the release of prisoners.

Penitentiary A prison. In earlier use in the USA it was a prison committed to rehabilitative aims.

Plea The answer of the accused to the question of whether he or she is guilty or not to the crime of which he or she has been accused.

Plea bargaining Process of a defendant pleading guilty to certain lesser charges when more serious charges are dropped or an indication of a likely sentence is given.

Plea before venue Name given to magistrates' court procedure where plea to a triable either way offence is taken before a decision is made as to whether the case is tried in the magistrates' court or Crown Court.

Plea in mitigation   Argument on behalf of an offender after conviction with an aim of reducing the sentence.

Police Complaints Commission   see Independent Police Complaints Commission.

Positivism   Application of scientific methods to the study of crime.

Pre-sentence report (PSR)   A report, prepared by the Probation Service in the case of those over 16 and the social services for those under 16, describing the background and circumstances of the offender with a view to providing information that might be useful in the sentencing decision. It replaced the social enquiry report (SER) in 1992.

Presumption of innocence   The principle that governs the conduct of a trial, and puts the entire burden of proving guilt onto the prosecution. The accused is not required to give any explanation or defence. The outcome of the trial does not lead to the conclusion that the accused is innocent but that he or she has not been proved to be guilty.

Presumptive sentences   Sentencing guidelines that are not mandatory but give a strong suggestion as to the sentence appropriate for different types of offences and offender histories.

Prison: Certified Normal Accommodation (CNA)   The designed capacity of a prison.

Prison: open   A prison with minimum security arrangements, in contrast to a closed prison.

Prison: receptions   The annual total of people sent for whatever reasons into the prison system.

Prisoners' Aid Society   Founded by Lord Shaftesbury in 1854 to help released prisoners to find work and provide welfare support for their families.

Proactive policing   The police initiating enquiries without relying on citizen complaints.

Probation: breach   Failing to comply with the terms of a probation order.

Probation Order   see Community Rehabilitation Order.

Professional crime   Crimes committed by a career criminal.

Public interest criterion   The second criterion that the CPS must apply in determining whether a case should be started or continued.

Queen's Counsel (QC)   A senior barrister appointed on the recommendation of the Lord Chancellor.

Rape   Having sexual intercourse with a man or a woman without his or her consent.

Reactive policing   The police responding to citizens' reports of crime in contrast to preventative or proactive policing.

Recidivist   A persistent repeat offender.

Recorder   A part-time judge who presides in the Crown Court; also certain judges with specific administrative responsibilities or traditional duties such as the Recorder of London.

Reformatory   A custodial training institution for younger offenders (1854/1933).

Rehabilitation   Sentencing objective concerned with the reform of the offender.

Remand centre   Place of detention for those remanded in custody before a criminal case is completed.

Remand in custody   Detention of a suspect/defendant in custody pending the next stage in his or her case.

Remand on bail   Release of defendant pending the next stage in his or her case under compulsion to return to court or police station.

Reparation   Making amends for a wrong done; repairing the damage.

Requisition   Document accompanying written charge requiring suspect to appear in magistrates' court.

Restitution   Compensation for the victim of a crime.

Restorative justice   An approach that seeks reparation for the victim from the offender.

Retribution   A purpose of sentencing and punishment to exact vengeance for wrongdoing. Just deserts.

Right of Audience   The right to speak in court.

Robbery   An offence that involves the theft of property through the use or threat of violence.

Rule 43   The Prison Rule that allows a prisoner to be held in isolated accommodation for his or her own protection, or because they are disruptive.

Self-report study   A survey which asks the respondents about how many offences they have committed.

Silk   Synonymous with Queen's Counsel.

Solicitor   A lawyer who can be approached directly by the public with rights of audience mainly in the magistrates' court.

Standard list offences   A list of offences for which the name of the offender and details of each sentence have been collected by the Home Office. Covers all indictable only, triable either way and some summary offences such as assault on a police constable, and criminal damage under £5,000. Data from this is used for the Offender Index and for reconviction studies. More comprehensive than the List of Notifiable Offences.

Statutory law   The law set out in Acts of Parliament.

Statutory sentence   A sentence provided for by Act of Parliament.

Stipendiary magistrate   see district judge.

Strict liability offence   A crime not requiring any intention or mental element.

Summary offence   A category of criminal offences (one of three). Offences that are tried in the magistrates' court only.

Summary trial   Trial in the magistrates' court.

Summons   A written notice to appear in court on a specified date to answer a criminal charge.

Taken into consideration (TIC)   Offences taken into consideration, i.e. not specifically charged but which the court takes account of when sentencing.

Theft   Dishonest appropriation of property belonging to another with the intention of permanently depriving that other of it (stealing).

Total institutions   A sociological term for an institution such as a prison in which the entire round of life is conducted within the one place with the same people, isolated from the rest of society.

Triable either way (TEW)   A category of criminal offence (one of three). These offences may be tried either in the magistrates' court or the Crown Court.

Trial   Contesting liability in any court.

Vandalism   The offence of criminal damage.

Victimology   The study of victims of crime.

Victim Support   Voluntary organisation concerned with giving advice and support to victims of crime.

Victim survey   A survey, such as the BCS, which asks people about their experiences as a victim.

Warrant   An order of the court; for example, an arrest warrant which gives power to the police to arrest someone.

White collar crime   A term referring to crimes relating to business or professional activities.

White Paper   A report published prior to legislation indicating the policy direction of reforms from a government department such as the Home Office.

Younger offender   Defined as child (offender aged 10–14); juvenile or youth (offender aged 14–17) and young adult (offender aged 18–21).

Young Offender Institution   A custodial institution for those aged between 15 and 21.

Youth Court   The name since 1992 of the part of the magistrates' court that deals with younger offenders aged under 18. Previously known as the Juvenile Court.

Youth Justice Board   Body responsible for oversight of juvenile and youth justice policy.

Zero tolerance   A crime prevention strategy of not tolerating or ignoring breaches of the law no matter how trivial.

Appendix 1
Practical Exercises

Exercise 1: Crime data exercise

You should consider how crime is defined. Look at various sources of information about crime, particularly at the media and official sources. Why are some kinds of crime seen as more serious than others? To understand the creation and interpretation of official data about crime, you will need to examine the processes underlying the reporting of crime – by the public, victims and the police. The reliability of official criminal statistics will depend upon these factors.

Interpreting crime statistics

Consult extracts from the criminal statistics and answer the following questions, illustrating your answers with figures taken from statistics. Specify your source of information. Give the title of the publication you consulted and indicate which year the data covers:

Title: ....

Year: ....

(a) By how much has the total volume of crime known to the police increased in recent years?

....

....

....

(b) What percentage of all crimes reported to the police do the following constitute?

murder ....

rape ....

robbery ....

theft ....

fraud   ....

car theft   ....

Consider which crimes are likely to be proportionately over-represented and why?

....

....

Which crimes are likely to be under-represented and why?

....

....

(c) Give examples of the variations in the rate at which different kinds of crimes are 'cleared up' by the police.

....

....

What does it mean to say that a crime is 'cleared up'?

....

....

Why are some offences more likely to be 'cleared up' than others?

....

....

(d) Which groups in the population are most 'at risk' from 'personal crime'?

....

....

Should we be more afraid of strangers, acquaintances or family? Why?

....

....

(e) What percentage of known offenders are male?

....

....

Taking into account the process of 'creating' statistics – how accurate do you think the ratio of male to female known offenders is?

....

....

Exercise 2: Victim survey

You should use the following 'Crime Victim Questionnaire' and interview eight people (four male, four female). Note their age. Try to include a range of people.
   Consider the following:

1 Which offences are respondents most/least likely to be the victims of? Are there any significant age/gender differences?

2 Which offences are more likely to be reported?

3 What reasons do victims give for not reporting crimes?

Crime victim questionnaire

In the last two years, how many times have you been the victim of the following crimes?	*If so, was this reported to the police?*	*If not reported, why not?*
Theft:		
of a motor car	....	....	....
from a motor car	....	....	....
of a bicycle	....	....	....
at work	....	....	....
from your person	....	....	....
Burglary	....	....	....
Assault:		
with injury	....	....	....
no injury	....	....	....

Robbery:

in street ....

in bank/post office ....

Insulted/bothered:

by strangers ....

Any other?

describe briefly ....

Exercise 3: Magistrates' court observation report

We recommend you observe a morning session of a magistrates' court, which will normally start at 10 am and go on until lunchtime. If you are unable to attend during the week it may be possible to find inner urban courts that sit on Saturday and there is at least one evening court in the London area.

1 Name: ....

Location of magistrates' court: ....

Date of visit: ....

Time of arrival: ....

Time of departure: ....

2 Before you go give some impression of what you expect to see in a magistrates' court.

....

....

3 How many courtrooms were there? ....

How many cases were scheduled to be heard in each?

....

....

4 After 10 minutes, from your time of arrival at the magistrates' court, describe your initial impressions.

....

....

5 Can you identify the following (*please tick*):

Bench ☐
Clerk's desk ☐
Advocates' seats ☐
Dock ☐
Witness box ☐
Press box ☐
Usher's seat ☐
Public seating ☐
Seating for defendants on bail or summons ☐

6 Personnel in the courtroom.

How many magistrates were there? ....

Name the other functionaries.

....

....

Who else was in the court?

....

....

7 Defendants

How many defendants appeared while you were in the court?

8 What sort of cases did you observe (*please tick*)?

a remand ☐
a decision as to mode of trial ☐
an adjournment ☐
a decision to grant bail ☐
a remand in custody ☐
a community order being made ☐
a disqualification from driving being ordered ☐
a guilty plea being entered ☐
a trial ☐
a fine being imposed ☐

9 How would you describe the types of defendants you saw?

....

....

10 Were there some defendants who seemed unable to understand the proceedings?

....

....

11 Outcomes

How many cases were disposed of, from plea to sentence? ....

How many defendants were remanded in custody? ....

How many defendants were given bail with conditions? ....

How many defendants were given bail without conditions? ....

How many defendants were sent for trial to the Crown Court? ....

How many cases were adjourned to a future date? ....

If they were adjourned, give the reasons why.

....

....

12 What were your impressions of the performance of the Crown Prosecutor?

....

....

13 What was your impression of the magistrates?

....

....

14 What was your impression of the defence lawyer?

....

....

15 Using keywords, describe your general impression of the magistrates' court.

....

....

16 What time did the court commence business? ....

17 Was the conduct of the court efficient in your view? If not explain why not.

....

....

18 Are there any other comments you wish to make about your observations?

....

....

Appendix 2
List of websites

Part A: Introduction to criminal justice

Information for citizens

This website 'CJ online' gives an official overview of the criminal justice system in England and Wales. Its Citizens' Arena gives basic information for victims, witnesses, defendants and jurors:

www.cjsonline.org/home.html

Information for citizens and police announcements:

www.criminal-justice-system.gov.uk/home.html

Government

Home Office main site with many points of relevance:

www.homeoffice.gov.uk

Department of Constitutional Affairs (DCA) took over the duties of the Lord Chancellor's Office in 2003 and is responsible for legal appointments and constitutional matters:

www.dca.gov.uk

Government documents:

www.open.gov.uk

See, for a comprehensive index of UK public sector information on the Internet:

www.open.gov.co.uk

Audit Commission is an independent body charged with scrutinising the government's use of public money; posts its reports on policing, crime and punishment and youth justice on the web:

www.audit-commission.gov.uk

Criminal Justice Information Technology (CJIT) website:

www.cjit.gov.uk/home.html

Lawmaking and reform

HMSO website with full texts of Acts published since 1988:

www.legislation.hmso.gov.uk/acts.htm

Parliamentary website with information on bills and details of recent Acts of Parliament:

www.publications.parliament.uk

Law Commission is an independent body mandated by Parliament to recommend law reform and website includes consultation papers:

www.lawcom.gov.uk

Crime prevention

Home Office sets out the government's Crime Reduction Strategy:

www.crimereduction.gov.uk

Home Office site with information on community safety initiatives:

www.homeoffice.gov.uk/crime/communitysafety/index.html

Victims

Victim Support:

www.victimsupport.org

Home Office site for victims:

www.homeoffice.gov.uk/justice/victims/index.html

Home Office site with Victims Charter:

www.homeoffice.gov.uk/justice/victims/charter/index.html

Home Office information on the release of prisoners and Information for victims:

www.homeoffice.gov.uk/justice/victims/release/index.html

Criminal Injuries Compensation Authority (CICA). Information about compensation for victims of violent crimes:

www.cica.gov.uk

Crime data and reports on crime

Data and research reports on subjects including: courts, crime, drugs, firearms, prisons, probation, terrorism:

www.homeoffice.gov.uk

National Statistics online site lists specific Scottish and Welsh findings from the British Crime Survey and current statistics on crime in Northern Ireland:

www.statistics.gov.uk

Research by Home Office RDS on aspects of crime:

www.homeoffice.gov.uk/rds/onlinepubs1.html

Youth justice

Youth Justice Board England and Wales:

www.youth-justice-board.gov.uk

Home Office website on sentences and order available for young people:

www.homeoffice.gov.uk/justice/sentencing/youthjustice/index.html

For information about the Scottish Children's Hearings system:

www.childrens-hearings.co.uk/youthjustice.asp

International

European Union Justice and Home Affairs website:

europa.eu.int/pol/justice/index_en.htm

Criminal Justice weblinks europe:
  www.leeds.ac.uk/law/ccjs/ukweb-3.htm

US Bureau of Justice Statistics:
  www.ojp.usdoj.gov/bjs

US Bureau of Justice online source book statistics:
  cscmosaic.albany.edu/sourcebook

National Criminal Justice Reference Service (USA NCJRS):
  www.ncjrs.org

United Nations Crime and Justice Information Network:
  www.uncjin.org

UN Office on Drugs and Crime:
  www.unodc.org/unodc/crime_cicp_sitemap.html

Australian Institute of Criminology:
  www.aic.gov.au

Other: Think Tanks, and other sources
Civitas Institute for the Study of Civil Society:
  www.civitas.org.uk

Mental Health Foundation:
  www.mentalhealth.org.uk

Zito Trust – a mental health charity concerned about the mentally ill and the implications for community safety:
  www.zitotrust.co.uk

Part B: Law enforcement

Policing
On-line resources listed for policing:
  www.acpo.police.uk/links/index.html

Official police site:
  www.police.uk

Police discussion official site:
  www.policereform.gov.uk

Police Federation:
  www.polfed.org

Association of Chief Police Officers in England and Wales (ACPO):
  www.acpo.police.uk

Metropolitan Police (London):
  www.met.police.uk

White Papers on policing:
  www.policereform.gov.uk
  www.policereform.gov.uk/whitepaper/index.html

National Criminal Intelligence Service (NCIS):
www.ncis.co.uk

Interpol – an international law enforcement agency:
www.interpol.int

Independent Police Complaints Commission:
www.ipcc.gov.uk

Forensic Science Service:
www.fss.org.uk

Crimestoppers Trust:
www.crimestoppers-uk.org

Prosecution

Crown Prosecution Service (CPS):
www.cps.gov.uk

Serious Fraud Office (SFO):
www.sfo.gov.uk

Part C: Criminal courts

Courts and the legal system

The Court Service:
www.courtservice.gov.uk

Criminal Cases Review Commission:
www.ccrc.gov.uk

Legal Service Commission Information on legal aid and the Criminal Defence Service:
www.legalservices.gov.uk

Home Office site with information on sentencing:
www.homeoffice.gov.uk/justice/sentencing/index.html

Law Society of England and Wales:
www.lawsociety.org.uk

Witness support:
www.victimsupport.org.uk

Magistrates' Association:
www.magistrates-association.co.uk

Judicial Studies Board – provides training for the judiciary:
www.jsboard.co.uk

Old Bailey historical records of trials and criminal proceedings 1674–1834:
www.Oldbaileyonline.org

Part D: The penal system

Prisons
Prison Service:
   www.hmprisonservice.gov.uk

HM Inspector of Prisons England and Wales:
   www.homeoffice.gov.uk/justice/prisons/inspprisons/index.html

Howard League for Penal Reform:
   www.howardleague.org

National Association for the Care and Resettlement of Offenders (NACRO):
   www.nacro.org.uk

Penal Reform Trust:
   www.prisonreformtrust.org.uk

Prisons and probation ombudsman:
   www.ppo.gov.uk

King's College London's International Centre for Prison Studies:
   www.prisonstudies.org

International Corrections and Prisons Association:
   www.icpa.ca

Scottish Prison Service:
   www.sps.gov.uk

Security Industry Authority – licensing of private security firms:
   www.the-sia.org.uk

Probation
Probation Service:
   www.probation.gov.uk
   www.cjsonline.gov.uk/working/homeoffice/probation.html

Probation statistics:
   www.homeoffice.gov.uk/rds/pdfs2/probation2002.pdf

National Offender Management Service (NOMS):
   www.probation.homeoffice.gov.uk

Sentencing
Sentencing Guidelines Council and Sentencing Advisory Panel:
   www.sentencing-guidelines.co.uk

Bibliography

Aitchison A and Hodgkinson J (2003) 'Patterns of Crime', in Simmons J and Dodd T (eds) *Crime in England and Wales 2002/3*, London: Home Office National Statistics.

Alderson J (1978) *Communal Policing*, Exeter: Devon and Cornwall Constabulary.

Allen C (2004) *A Practical Guide to Evidence* (3rd edn), London: Cavendish.

Amir M (1971) *Patterns of Forcible Rape*, Chicago: University of Chicago Press.

Anderson S, Kinsey R, Loader I and Smith C (1994) *Cautionary Tales: Young People, Crime and Policing in Edinburgh*, Aldershot: Avebury.

Andrews D, Bonta J and Hodge R (1990) 'Classification for Effective Rehabilitation', *Criminal Justice and Behaviour*, **17**: 19–52.

Ashworth A (1989) 'Criminal Justice and Deserved Sentences', *Criminal Law Review*: 340–55.

Ashworth A (1992b) *Sentencing and Penal Policy* (2nd edn), London: Weidenfeld & Nicolson.

Ashworth A (1994a) *The Criminal Process*. Oxford: Clarendon Press.

Ashworth A (1994b) 'Sentencing', in Maguire M, Morgan R and Reiner R (eds) *The Oxford Handbook of Criminology*, Oxford: Clarendon Press.

Ashworth A (1997b) 'Sentencing', in Maguire M, Morgan R and Reiner R (eds) *The Oxford Handbook of Criminology* (2nd edn), Oxford: Clarendon Press.

Ashworth A (1998) *The Criminal Process* (2nd edn), Oxford: Clarendon Press.

Ashworth A (2000) 'Victims' Rights, Defendants' Rights and Criminal Procedure', in Crawford A and Goodey J (eds) *Integrating a Victim Perspective within Criminal Justice*, Aldershot: Ashgate/Dartmouth.

Ashworth A (2002) 'Sentencing', in Maguire M, Morgan R and Reiner R (eds) *The Oxford Handbook of Criminology* (3rd edn), Oxford: Clarendon Press.

Ashworth A (2003) *The Criminal Process* (3rd edn), Oxford.

Audit Commission (2004) *Youth Justice 2004: a Review of the Reformed Youth Justice System*, London: Audit Commission.

Auld Report (2001) *Review into the Workings of the Criminal Courts in England and Wales*, London: Home Office

Ayres Murray and Fiti (2003) Arrests for Notifiable Offences and the Operation of Certain Police Powers under PACE, *Home Office Statistical Bulletin*, 17/03.

Baldwin J and McConville M (1979) *Jury Trials*, Oxford: Clarendon Press.

Barclay G (ed) (1995) *Digest 3: Information on the Criminal Justice System in England and Wales*, London: HMSO.

Bennett T (1990) *Evaluating Neighbourhood Watch*, Aldershot: Gower.

Bennett T (1994a) 'Recent Developments in Community Policing', in Stephens M and Becker S (eds) *Police force, Police Service: Care and Control in Britain*, London: Macmillan.

Bennett T (1994b) 'Community Policing', *Criminal Justice Matters*, No 17, Autumn 1994: 6–7.

Bennett T and Lupton R (1992) 'A National Activity Survey of Police Work', *Howard Journal of Criminal Justice*, **31** (3): 200–23.

Bentham J (1791) *Panopticon: or the Inspection House*, London: Payer.

Blumberg A (1967) *Criminal Justice*, Chicago: Quadrangle Books.

Bonta J, Wallace-Capretta S and Rooney J (1999) *Electronic Monitoring in Canada*, Ottawa: Solicitor General Canada.

Bottoms A, Gelsthorpe L and Rex S (eds) (2001) *Community Penalties: Change and Challenges*, Cullompton: Willan Publishing.

Bowling B and Foster J (2002) 'Policing and the Police', in Maguire M, Morgan R and Reiner R (eds) *The Oxford Handbook of Criminology* (3rd edn), Oxford: Clarendon Press.

Bowling B and Phillips C (2003) 'Policing Ethnic Minority Communities' in Newburn T (ed) *Handbook of Policing*, Cullompton: Willan Publishing.

Brand S and Price R (2000) 'The Economic and Social Costs of Crime', Home Office Research Study 217, Economics and Resource Analysis, Research, Development and Statistics Directorate, London: Home Office.

Bratton W (1997) 'Crime is Down in New York City: Blame the Police' in Dennis N (ed) *Zero Tolerance: Policing a Free Society*, London: IEA.

Brown D (1997) *PACE Ten Years On: A Review of the Research*, Home Office Research Study No 155, London: Home Office.

Cain M (1973) *Society and the Policeman's Role*, London: Routledge & Kegan Paul.

Cashmore E (2001) 'The experiences of ethnic minority police officers in Britain: under-recruitment and racial profiling in a performance culture', *Ethnic and Racial Studies*, **24** (4): 642–59.

Cavadino P and Dignan J (1997) *The Penal System: An Introduction* (2nd edn), London: Sage.

Cavadino P and Dignan J (2002) *The Penal System: An Introduction* (3rd edn), London: Sage.

Chibnall S (1997) *Law and Order News*, London: Tavistock.

Clarke (1980) 'Situational Crime Prevention: Theory and Practice', *British Journal of Criminology*, **20**: 136–47.

Clarke R and Hough M (1984) Crime and Police Effectiveness, *Home Office Research Study* 79, London: HMSO.

Clemmer D (1958) *The Prison Community*, New York: Holt, Rinehart & Winston.

Cloward R and Ohlin L (1960) *Delinquency and Opportunity: A Theory of Delinquent Gangs*, New York: Free Press.

Cohen S (1980) *Folk Devils and Moral Panics*, Oxford: Martin Robertson.

Cohen S (1985) *Visions of Social Control*, Cambridge: Polity Press.

Cohen S and Taylor L (1972) *Psychological Survival*, Harmondsworth: Penguin.

Coleman C and Moynihan J (1996) *Understanding Crime Data: Haunted by the Dark Figure*, Buckingham: Open University Press.

Coleman C and Norris C (2000) *Introducing Criminology*, Cullompton: Willan Publishing.

Collison M (1996) 'In Search of the High Life: Drugs, Crime, Masculinities and Consumption', *British Journal of Criminology*, **36** (3): 428–44.

Condon P (1994) Address to meeting of British Society of Criminologists, London, January 1994.

Crawford A (1998) *Crime Prevention and Community Safety: Politics, Policies and Practices*, London: Longman.

Crawford A and Goodey J (eds) (2000) *Integrating a Victim Perspective within Criminal Justice: International Debates*, Aldershot: Ashgate.

Croall H (2001) *Understanding White Collar Crime*, Buckingham: Open University Press.

Croall H (2003) 'Combating Financial Crime: Regulatory versus Crime Control Approaches', *Journal of Financial Crime*, **11**: 144–55.

Crown Prosecution Service (annually) *Annual Report*, London: HMSO.

Davies K (1969) *Discretionary Justice: A Preliminary Inquiry*, Baton Rouge: Louisiana State University Press.

Davies M (1989) 'An Alternative View: Square Deal Punishment in the Community: It is Cheaper But Who Will Buy It?', in Rees H and Hall Williams E (eds) *Punishment, Custody and the Community: Reflections and Comments on the Green Paper*, Suntory Toyota International Centre for Economics and Related Disciplines.

Davies M (1993) *Punishing Criminals: Developing Community-based Intermediate Sanctions*, Connecticut: Greenwood.

Davies M (1997) 'Sentencing Trends and Public Confidence', in Murray C, Davies M, Rutherford A and Young J (eds) *Does Prison Work*, London: IEA and *Sunday Times*.

Davies M, Takala J-P and Tyrer J (1996) *Penological Esperanto and Sentencing Parochialism*, Aldershot: Dartmouth.

Davies P (2003) 'Crime Victims and Public Policy', in Davies P, Francis P and Jupp V (eds) *Victimisation: Theory, Research and Policy*, Basingstoke: Palgrave/Macmillan.

Davies P, Francis P and Jupp V (eds) (2003) *Victimisation: Theory, Research and Policy*, Basingstoke: Palgrave/Macmillan.

Department of Constitutional Affairs (2003) *Judicial Appointments Annual Report 2002/3*, London: DCA.

Dicey A (1959) *Introduction to the Study of the Law of the Constitution*, London: Macmillan.

Dignan J and Wynne A (1997) 'A Microcosm of the Local Community', *British Journal of Criminology*, **37** (2): 184.

Ditton J and Duffy J (1983) 'Bias in the Newspaper Reporting of Crime News', *British Journal of Criminology*, **23**: 129.

Ditton J and Short E (1999) 'Yes, it works – no, it doesn't: compare the effects of open-street CCTV in two adjacent town centres', *Crime Prevention Studies*, 10, pp 201–23.

Duff A and Garland D (1994) *A Reader on Punishment*, Oxford: Oxford University Press.

Durkheim E (1970) *Suicide*, London: Routledge & Kegan Paul.

Eaton M (1986) *Justice for Women?*, Milton Keynes: Open University Press.

Eaton M (1993) *Women after Prison*, Milton Keynes: Open University Press.

Eden W (1777) *Principles of Penal Law*, London: B White & T Cadell.

Ekblom P 'Situational Crime Prevention', in McLaughlin E and Muncie J (2001) *The Sage Dictionary of Criminology*, London: Sage.

Ernst and Young (2000) 'Reducing Delay in the Criminal Justice System: Evaluation of the Indictable Only Initiative', London: Home Office.

Evans R and Wilkinson C (1990) 'Variations in Police Cautioning Policy and Practice in England and Wales', *Howard Journal of Criminal Justice*, **29** (3): 155–76.

Eysenck H J (1977) *Crime and Personality*, London: Routledge & Kegan Paul.

Felson M (2002) *Crime and Everyday Life* (3rd edn), London: Pine Forge.

Fielding N, Kemp C and Norris C (1989) 'Constraints on the Practice of Community Policing', in Morgan R and Smith D (eds) *Coming to Terms with Policing*, London: Routledge.

Fitzgerald M (1977) *Prisoners in Revolt*, Harmondsworth: Penguin.

Fitzgerald M and Hale C (1996) *Ethnic Minorities: Victimisation and Racial Harassment: Findings from the 1988 and 1992 British Crime Surveys*, Home Office Research Study No 154, London: Home Office.

Fletcher G and Allan J (2003) 'Perceptions of and Concerns about Crime in England and Wales', in Simmons J and Dodd T (eds) *Crime in England and Wales 2002/3*, London: Home Office National Statistics.

Flood-Page C and Mackie A (1998) *Sentencing practice: an examination of decisions in magistrates' courts and the Crown Court in the mid-1990's*, Home Office Research Study No. 180, London: Home Office.

Flood-Page C, Campbell S, Harrington V and Miller J (2000) *Youth Crime: Findings from the 1998/99 Youth Lifestyles Survey*, Home Office Research Study 209, London: Home Office Research, Development and Statistics Directorate Crime and Criminal Justice Unit.

Fogel D (1975) *We are the Living Proof: The Justice Model for Corrections*, Cincinatti: W H Anderson.

Foster J (1989) 'Two Stations: An Ethnographic Study of Policing in the Inner City', in Downes D (ed.) *Crime and the City*, London: Macmillan.

Foster J (2003) 'Police cultures', in Newburn T (ed.) *Handbook of Policing*, Cullompton: Willan Publishing.

Foucault M (1977) *Discipline and Punish*, Harmondsworth: Penguin.

Fox L (1952) *The English Prison and Borstal System*, London: Routledge & Kegan Paul.

Frankel M (1973) *Criminal Sentences: Law Without Order: The American Friends Service Committee 1971 Struggle for Justice*, New York: Hill & Wang.

Garland D (1990) *Punishment and Modern Society*, Oxford: Oxford University Press.

Gelsthorpe L and Morris A (1994) 'Juvenile Justice 1945–1992', in Maguire M, Morgan R and Reiner R (eds) *The Oxford Handbook of Criminology*, Oxford: Clarendon Press.

Gelsthorpe L and Rex S (2004) 'Community Service as reintegration: exploring the potential' in Mair G (ed.) *What Matters in Probation*, Cullompton: Willan Publishing.

Gill M and Mawby R (1990) *Volunteers in the Criminal Justice System: A Comparative Study of Probation, Police and Victim Support*, Milton Keynes: Open University Press.

Goffman E (1961) *Asylums: Essays on the Social Situation of Mental Patients and Other Inmates*, Golden City, New York: Doubleday.

Goffman E (1968) *Stigma: Notes on the Management of Spoiled Identities*, Harmondsworth: Penguin.

Graham J and Bennett T (1995) *Crime Prevention Strategies in Europe and North America*, Helsinki: Heuni.

Graham J and Bowling B (1995) *Young People and Crime*, Home Office Research Study No 145, London: Home Office.

Green D (ed.) (2000) *Institutional Racism and the Police: Fact or Fiction?*, London: Civitas.

Green, D (2004) 'Crime Reduction: Are Government policies likely to achieve its declared aims?', www.civitas.org.uk.

Gross H (1979) *A Theory of Criminal Justice*, New York: Oxford University Press.

Hagell A and Newburn T (1994) *Persistent Young Offenders*, London: Policy Studies Institute.

Halliday Report (2001) Making Punishments Work: Review of the Sentencing Framework for England and Wales, London: Home Office.

Hannibal M and Mountford L (2002) *The Law of Criminal and Civil Evidence*, Harlow: Pearson.

Harding C, Hines B, Ireland R and Rawlings P (1985) *Imprisonment in England and Wales*, Beckenham: Croom Helm.

Harman H and Griffith J (1979) *Justice Deserted: The Subversion of the Jury*, London: NCCL.

Hart H L A (1968) *Punishment and Responsibility*, Oxford: Clarendon Press.

Hartless J, Ditton J, Nair G and Phillips S (1995) 'More sinned against than sinning: A Study of Young Teenagers' Experience of Crime', *British Journal of Criminology*, **35** (1): 114.

Hawkins K (1984) *Environment and Enforcement: Regulation and the Social Definition of Pollution*, Oxford Socio-Legal Studies: Clarendon Press.

Heal K and Laycock G (1986) *Situational Crime Prevention: From Theory to Practice*, London: Home Office.

Hedderman C and Moxon D (1992) *Magistrates' Court or Crown Court? Mode of Trial and Sentencing Decisions*, London: Home Office.

Heidensohn F (1992) *Women in Control? The Role of Women in Law Enforcement*, Oxford: Oxford University Press.

Hentig H von (1948) *The Criminal and his Victim*, New Haven: Yale University Press.

Hirsch A von (1976) *Doing justice – The Choice of Punishment*, York: Hill & Wang.

Hirsch A von (1986) *Past or Future Crimes*, Manchester University Press.

Hirsch A von and Ashworth A (eds) (1993) *Principled Sentencing*, Edinburgh: Edinburgh University Press.

Hobbs D (1991) 'A Piece of Business: the Moral Economy of Detective Work in the East of London', *British Journal of Sociology*, **42** (4).

Holdaway S (1983) *Inside the British Police*, Oxford: Basil Blackwell.

Holdaway S (1997) 'Some Recent Approaches to the Study of Race in Criminological Research', *British Journal of Criminology*, **37** (3): 383–400.

Holdaway S and Barron A (1997) *Resigners? The Experience of Black and Asian Police Officers*, London: Macmillan.

Home Office (1895) *Report from the Departmental Committee on Prisons* (chaired by Herbert Gladstone), London: Home Office.

Home Office (1959) *Penal Practice in a Changing Society*, London: Home Office.

Home Office (1966) *Report of the Inquiry into Prison Escapes and Security* (chaired by Earl Mountbatten), London: HMSO.

Home Office (1968) *Report on the Regime for Long-term Prisoners in Maximum Security* (chaired by Sir Leon Radzinowicz), London: HMSO.

Home Office (1977) *Prison and the Prisoner*, London: HMSO.

Home Office (1979) *The Report of the Committee of Inquiry into the UK Prison Service* (chaired by Mr Justice May), Cmnd (for 1956 to Nov 1986) 7673, London: HMSO.

Home Office (1984) *Criminal Justice: A Working Paper*, London: Home Office.

Home Office (1986) *The Sentence of the Court*, London: HMSO.

Home Office (1988a) *Punishment, Custody and the Community*, Cm 424, London: HMSO.

Home Office (1990a) *Crime, Justice and Protecting the Public*, London: Home Office.

Home Office (1991a) *Prison Disturbances, April 1990,* Report of an inquiry presented to the Home Office by Lord Justice H Woolf and Judge Stephen Tumin, Cm 1456, London: HMSO.

Home Office (1991b) *A General Guide to the Criminal Justice Act 1991,* London: HMSO.

Home Office (1991c) *Custody, Care and Justice: The Way Ahead for the Prison Service in England and Wales,* Cm 1647, London: HMSO.

Home Office (1994) *Home Office Research Findings,* No 14, London: HMSO.

Home Office (1996) Victims Charter, London: Home Office.

Home Office (1997a) *No More Excuses – A New Approach to Tackling Youth Crime in England and Wales,* Cm 3809, London: Home Office.

Home Office (1997b) *Getting to Grips with Crime – A New Framework for Local Action,* London: HMSO.

Home Office (1997c) *Review of Delay in the Criminal Justice System* (chaired by M Narey), London: HMSO.

Home Office (1998) *Statistical Bulletin* 7/98, London: Home Office.

Home Office (2000) Victim Respect: ensuring the victim matters, London: Home Office.

Home Office (annually) *Prison Statistics England and Wales 2000.*

Home Office (annually) *Judicial Statistics ...*

Home Office (annually) *Justice for All.*

Home Office (annually) *Prison Statistics England and Wales 2002.*

Home Office (annually) *Probation Statistics ...*

Home Office (2002) *Race and the Criminal Justice System,* London: Home Office.

Home Office (2002) *Mobile Phone Theft,* Home Office Research Study 235, London: Home Office.

Home Office (2004) Occupation of Prisons, Remand Centres, Young Offenders Institutions and Police Cells England and Wales (monthly), London: Home Office.

Home Office (2003) *Prison Population Brief,* London: Home Office.

Home Office (2003) *Respect and Responsibility – taking a stand against anti-social behaviour,* London: Home Office.

Home Office (2003) *Statistics on Women and the Criminal Justice System 2003,* London: Home Office.

Home Office (2004) *One Step Ahead: A 21st Century Strategy to Defeat Organised Criminals,* London: Home Office.

Home Office (annually) *Criminal Statistics England and Wales,* London: Home Office.

Hood R (1965) *Borstal Re-assessed,* London: Heinemann.

Hood R (ed.) (1974) *Crime, Criminology and Public Policy,* London: Heinemann.

Hope T (1997) 'Inequality and the future of community crime prevention', in Lab S P (ed) *Crime Prevention at a Crossroads,* American Academy of Criminal Justice Sciences Monograph Series, Cincinnati, OH: Anderson Publishing.

Howard J (1777) *The State of Prisons*

Hudson B (1993) *Penal Policy and Social Justice,* London: Macmillan.

Hughes G (2002) 'Crime and Disorder Partnerships: The Future of Community Safety?' in Hughes G, McLaughlin E and Muncie J (eds) *Crime Prevention and Community Safety: New Directions,* London: Sage.

Ignatieff M (1975) *A Just Measure of Pain: The Penitentiary in the Industrial Revolution 1750–1850,* London: Macmillan.

Irwin J (1970) *The Felon,* Englewood Cliffs: Prentice Hall.

Irwin J (1980) *Prisons in Turmoil,* Toronto: Little, Brown & Co.

Jefferson T (1990) *The Case Against Paramilitary Policing*, Milton Keynes: Open University Press.

Jones T and Newburn T (1994a) *How Big is the Private Security Industry?*, London: Policy Studies Institute.

Joutsen M (1990) *The Criminal Justice System of Finland: A General Introduction*, Helsinki: Ministry of Justice.

Jowell R, Curtis J, Lindsay B, Ahrendt D with Pork A (eds) (1994) *British Social Attitudes, 11th Report*, Aldershot: Dartmouth Publishing Co.

King M (1981) *The Framework of Criminal Justice*, London: Croom Helm.

King R and Elliott K (1977) *Albany: The Birth of a Prison, the End of an Era*, London: Routledge & Kegan Paul.

Langan P and Farrington D (1998) Crime and Justice in the United States and in England and Wales 1981–96, Washington: US Department of Justice.

Lea J and Young J (1992) *What is to be Done about Law and Order?* (2nd edn), London: Pluto Press.

Learmont J (1995) *Review of Prison Service Security in England and Wales and the Escape from Parkhurst Prison on Tuesday 3rd January 1995*, Cm 3020, London: HMSO.

Legal Services Commission, *Annual Report 2002/3*, London: HMSO.

Leishman F, Loveday B and Savage S (eds) (1998) *Core Issues in Policing* (2nd edn), London: Longman.

Leng R, McConville M and Sanders A (1992) 'Researching the Discretions to Charge and to Prosecute', in Downes D (ed.) *Unravelling Criminal Justice*, London: Macmillan.

Levi M (1987) *Regulating Fraud: White Collar Crime and the Criminal Process*, London: Tavistock.

Levi M (1989) 'Suite Justice: Sentencing for Fraud', *Criminal Law Review*: 420–34.

Levi M (2002) 'The Organisation of Serious Crimes', in Maguire M, Morgan R and Reiner R (eds) *The Oxford Handbook of Criminology* (3rd edn), Oxford: Clarendon Press.

Lewis C S (1953) 'On Punishment', *Res Judicatae*, **6**, 1952–4.

Lipton D, Martinson R and Wilks J (1975) *Effectiveness of Correctional Treatment*, Springfield, Mass.: Praeger.

Lombroso Cesare (1897) *L'Uomo Delinquente* (5th edn), Torino: Bocca.

Loveday B (1992) 'Right Agendas: Law and Order in England and Wales', *International Journal of the Sociology of Law*, **20**: 297–319.

MacPherson W (1999) *The Stephen Lawrence Inquiry: Report of an Inquiry by Sir William MacPherson*, London: Home Office.

Maguire M (2002) 'Criminal Statistics: the "Data Explosion" and its Implications', in Maguire M, Morgan R and Reiner R (eds) *The Oxford Handbook of Criminology*, (3rd edn), Oxford: Clarendon Press.

Maguire M, Morgan R and Reiner R (eds) (1997) *The Oxford Handbook of Criminology*, (2nd edn), Oxford: Clarendon Press.

Maguire M and Pointing J (eds) (1988) *Victims of Crime: A New Deal?*, Milton Keynes: Open University Press.

Mair G (ed.) (2004) *What Matters in Probation*, Willan Publishing: Cullompton.

Mathews R, Hancock L and Briggs D (2004) 'Jurors' perception, understanding, confidence and satisfaction in the jury system: a study in six courts', Home Office Research Findings 227.

Mawby R C and Wright A (2003) 'The Police Organisation', in Newburn T (ed.) *Handbook of Policing*, Cullompton: Willan Publishing.

May T (1994) 'Probation and Community Sanctions', in Maguire M, Morgan R and Reiner R (eds) *The Oxford Handbook of Criminology*, Oxford: Clarendon Press.

Mayhew P, Clarke R, Sturman A and Hough J (eds) (1976) *Crime as Opportunity*, Home Office Research Study No 34, London: HMSO.

Mayhew P, Elliot D and Dowds L (1989) *The 1988 British Crime Survey*, London: HMSO.

McCabe S (1988) in Findlay M and Duff P (eds) *The Jury Under Attack*, London: Butterworth.

McConville M and Wilson G (2002) *The Handbook of the Criminal Justice Process*, Oxford: Oxford University Press.

McNeill and Batchelor S (2004) 'Persistent Offending by Young People: Developing Practice', *Issues in Community and Criminal Justice*, Monograph 3.

McIvor G (2004) 'Getting Personal: developments in policy and practice in Scotland' in Mair G (ed.) *What Matters in Probation*, Cullompton: Willan Publishing.

Merton R K (1938) 'Social Structure and Anomie', *American Sociological Review*, **3**: 672–82.

Messinger S and Johnson P (1978) 'California's Determinate Sentencing Statute History and Issues', in *Determinate Sentencing: Reform or Regression*, National Institute of Law Enforcement and Criminal Justice, Washington, DC: Government Printing Office.

Mirrlees-Black C, Mayhew P and Percy A (1996) 'The 1996 British Crime Survey: England and Wales', *Home office Statistical Bulletin*, Issue 19/96, London: HMSO.

Morgan J and Zedner L (1992) *Child Victims: Crime, Impact, and Criminal Justice*, Oxford: Clarendon Press.

Morgan R (1989) 'Policing by Consent: Legitimating the Doctrine', in Morgan and Smith (eds) *Coming to Terms with Policing: Perspectives on Policy*, London: Routledge.

Morgan R (1997) 'Imprisonment', in Maguire M, Morgan R and Reiner R (eds) *The Oxford Handbook of Criminology* (2nd edn), Oxford: Clarendon Press.

Morgan R and Jones T (1992) 'Bail or Jail?', in Stockdale E and Casales S (eds) *Criminal Justice Under Stress*, London: Blackstone.

Morgan R and Newburn T (1997) *The Future of Policing*, Oxford: Clarendon Press.

Morgan R and Russell N (2002) 'Survey on Public View on Residential Burglary', in Sentencing Report to the Court of Appeal (2002) *Domestic Burglary*, London: Sentencing Advisory Panel.

Morris A and Giller H (1987) *Understanding Juvenile Justice*, London: Croom Helm.

Moss B (2004) 'Coming Soon to a Court Near You', *Counsel*, June 2004: 22.

Muncie J (1999) *Youth and Crime: A Critical Introduction*, London: Sage.

Muncie J (2003) 'Youth, Risk and Victimisation', in Davies P, Francis P and Jupp V (eds) *Victimisation: Theory, Research and Policy*, Basingstoke: Palgrave Macmillan.

Muncie J, McLaughlin E and Langan M (eds) (1999) *Criminological Perspectives*, London: Sage.

Murphy P (1992) *A Practical Approach to Evidence*, London: Blackstone Press.

Murray C (1997) *Does Prison Work?*, London: IEA and Sunday Times.

Murray I (2003) 'Making Rehabilitation Work', www.civitas.org.uk.

Newburn (2002) 'Young People, Crime and Youth Justice', in Maguire M, Morgan R and Reiner R (eds) *The Oxford Handbook of Criminology*, (3rd edn), Oxford: Clarendon Press.

Newburn T (2003a) *Crime and Criminal Justice Policy*, (2nd edn), London: Longman.

Newburn T (ed) (2003b) *Handbook of Policing*, Cullompton: Willan Publishing.

Newman O (1972) *Defensible Space: Crime Prevention Through Urban Design*, New York: Collier-Macmillan.

Nicholas S and Wood M (2003) 'Property Crime', in Simmons J and Dodd T (eds) *Crime in England and Wales 2002/3*, London: Home Office National Statistics.

Norris C and Armstrong G (1997) *The Unforgiving Eye: CCTV Surveillance in Public Space*, Centre for Criminology and Criminal Justice: University of Hull.

Norris C and Armstrong G (1999) *The Maximum Surveillance Society: The Rise of CCTV*, Oxford: Berg.

Packer H (1968) *The Limits of the Criminal Sanction*, Stanford, CA: Stanford University Press.

Pain R (2003) 'Old Age and Victimisation', in Davies P, Francis P and Jupp V (eds) *Victimisation: Theory, Research and Policy*, Basingstoke: Palgrave/Macmillan.

Painter K (1998) *Lighting and Crime – The Edmonton Project*, Enfield: Middlesex Polytechnic.

Painter K and Farrington D (1998) 'Marital Violence in Great Britain and its Relationship to Marital and Non Marital Rape', *International Review of Victimology*, **5**: 257–76.

Parker H, Sumner M and Jarvis G (1989) *Unmasking the Magistrates*, Milton Keynes: Open University Press.

Paterson A (1927) *Report of the Prison Commission*, London: HMSO.

Pease K (2002) 'Crime Reduction', in Maguire M, Morgan, R and Reiner R (eds) *The Oxford Handbook of Criminology* (3rd edn), Oxford: Clarendon Press.

Peay J (2002) 'Mentally Disordered Offenders', in Maguire M, Morgan R and Reiner R (eds) *The Oxford Handbook of Criminology* (3rd edn), Oxford: Clarendon Press.

Phillips C (2002) 'From Voluntary to Statutory Status: reflecting on the experience of three partnerships established under the Crime and Disorder Act 1998', in Hughes G, McLaughlin E and Muncie J (eds) *Crime Prevention and Community Safety: New Directions*, London: Sage.

Phillips C and Bowling B (2002) 'Racism, Ethnicity, Crime and Criminal Justice', in Maguire M, Morgan R and Reiner R (eds) *The Oxford Handbook of Criminology* (3rd edn), Oxford: Clarendon Press.

Porter M (1997) *Tackling Cross Border Crime*, Home Office Research Report, London: Home Office.

Povey D and Allan J (2003) 'Violent Crime', in Simmons J and Dodd T (eds) *Crime in England and Wales 2002/3*, London: Home Office National Statistics.

Prison Commissioners (1925) *Annual Report*, London: HMSO.

Prison Service (1988) *Briefing*, November, London: HMSO.

Prison Service (annually) *Annual Report and Accounts 2000*.

Raynor P and Vanstone M (2002) *Understanding Community Penalties: Probation, policy and social change*, Buckingham: Open University Press.

Reeves H and Mulley K (2000) 'The New Status of Victims in the UK: Opportunities and Threats', in Crawford A and Goodey J (eds) *Integrating a Victim Perspective within Criminal Justice*, Aldershot: Ashgate Dartmouth.

Reiner R (2000) *The Politics of the Police*, London: Harvester Wheatsheaf.

Robertson G, Pearson R and Gibb R (1995) *The Mentally Disordered Offender and the Police*, Home Office Research Findings, No 21.

Robinson G and McNeill F (2004) 'Purposes matter: examining the "ends" of Probation', in Mair G (ed.) *What Matters in Probation*, Cullompton: Willan Publishing.

Rothman D (1980) *Conscience and Convenience: The Asylum and its Alternatives in Progressive America*, Boston, Mass.: Little, Brown.

Runciman, Lord (1993) *The Report of the Royal Commission on Criminal Justice* (chaired by Lord Runciman), London: HMSO.

Ryan M (2003) *Penal Policy and Political Culture in England and Wales: Four essays on policy and process*, Winchester: Waterside Press.

Sanders (2002) 'Prosecution Systems', in McConville M and Wilson G (eds) *The Handbook of the Criminal Justice Process*, Oxford: Oxford University Press.

Sanders A and Young R (1994) *Criminal Justice*, London: Butterworth.

Sanderson J (1992) *Criminology Textbook*, London: HLT.

Schlesinger P and Tumber H (1994) *Reporting Crime: The Media Politics of Criminal Justice*, Oxford: Clarendon Press.

Schrag C (1944) 'Social Types of a Prison Community. Quoted in Ditchfield J (1990)', *Control in Prisons: A Review of the Literature*, London: HMSO.

Schur E (1969) *Our Criminal Society*, Englewood Cliffs: Prentice Hall.

Schur E (1973) *Radical Non-Intervention. Rethinking the Delinquency Problem*, Englewood Cliffs: Prentice Hall.

Scottish Executive (2003) 'Criminal Proceedings in Scottish Courts, 2001', Scottish Executive Statistical Bulletin Cr/2002/9.

Scull A (1977) *Decarceration: Community Treatment and the Deviant – A Radical View*, Englewood Cliffs: Prentice Hall.

Shapland J, Willmore J and Duff P (1985) *Victims and the Criminal Justice System*, Aldershot: Gower.

Shawcross (Lord) (1951) House of Commons Debate, Vol 483, 29 January 1951.

Simmons, J and Dodd T (eds) (2003) *Crime in England and Wales 2002/3*, London: Home Office National Statistics.

Skolnick J (1966) *Justice Without Trial*, New York: Wiley.

Smith D J (1997) 'Race, Crime and Criminal Justice', in Maguire M, Morgan R and Reiner R (eds) *The Oxford Handbook of Criminology* (2nd edn), Oxford: Clarendon Press.

Smith D J and Gray J (1985) *Police and People in London: the PSI Report*, Aldershot: Gower.

Social Exclusion Unit (2002) *Reducing Re-offending by Ex-prisoners*, London: Office of Deputy Prime Minister

Soothill K (1993) 'Sex Crime in the News Revisited', Unpublished paper presented to the British Criminology Conference, Cardiff, July 1993.

Soothill K and Walby S (1991) *Sex Crime in the News*, London: Routledge.

Spencer S and Stern B (2002) *Reluctant Witness*, London: NCCL.

Sprack J (2004) *Emmins on Criminal Procedure* (10th edn), London: Blackstone Press.

Taylor, Lord Chief Justice (1993) *17th Leggatt Lecture – What do we want from our Judges?* University of Surrey.

Thomas D A (1979) *Principles of Sentencing*, London: Heinemann.

Tilley N (1993) 'Crime Prevention and the Safer Cities Story', *Howard Journal of Criminal Justice*, **32** (1): 40–57.

Tilley N (2002) 'Crime Prevention in Britain, 1975–2010: breaking out, breaking in and breaking down', in Hughes G, McLaughlin E and Muncie J (eds) *Crime Prevention and Community Safety: New Directions*, London: Sage.

Tilley N (2003) 'Community Policing, problem-oriented policing and intelligence-led policing' in Newburn T (ed.) *Handbook of Policing*, Cullompton: Willan Publishing.

Tonry M (1987) *Sentencing Reform Impacts*, Washington, DC: US Department of Justice.

Utting D, Bright J and Henricson C (1993) *Crime and the Family: Improving Child Rearing and Preventing Delinquency*, Occasional Paper 16, Family Policy Studies Centre.

Van Dijk JJM and de Waard J (1991) 'A Two-dimensional Typology of Crime Prevention Projects: with a bibliography', *Criminal Justice Abstracts*, **23**, pp 485 – 503.

Vennard J (1985) 'The Outcome of Contested Trials', in Moxon D (ed.) *Managing Criminal Justice*. London: HMSO.

Victim Support (1995) *The Rights of the victims of crime*, London: Victim Support.

Victim Support (2003) *Insult to Injury: How the criminal injuries compensation system is failing victims of crime*, London: Victim Support.

Walker M (1987) 'Interpreting Race and Crime Statistics', *Journal of the Royal Statistical Society A*, **150**, Part 1: 39–56.

Walker N and Padfield N (1996) *Sentencing: Theory, Law and Practice* (2nd edn), London: Butterworth.

Walklate S (1989) *Victimology: The Victim and the Criminal Justice Process*, London: Unwin Hyman.

Walmsley R (2003) *World Prison Population: List* (5th edn), Home Office Findings, London: HMSO.

Walmsley R, Howard L and White S (1993) *The National Prison Survey 1991: Main Findings*, Home Office Research Study No 128, London: HMSO.

Wasik M (1993) *The Magistrate*, October.

Wasik M (2001) *Emmins on Sentencing*, (4th edn), Oxford: Oxford University Press.

Wasik M and Taylor R (1994) *Criminal Justice Act, 1991*, London: Blackstone.

Watson L (1996) *Victims of Violent Crime Recorded by the Police, England and Wales, 1990–1994*, Home Office Statistical Findings, Issue 1/96, London: HMSO.

Webb B and Laycock G (1992) *Tackling Car Crime: The Nature and Extent of the Problem*, Home Office Crime Prevention Paper No 32.

Wells C (1988) 'The Decline and Rise of English Murder: Corporate Crime and Individual Responsibility', *Criminal Law Review*: 789–801.

West D J and Farrington D (1973) *Who Becomes Delinquent?*, London: Heinemann.

West D J and Farrington D (1977) *the Delinquent Way of Life*, London: Heinemann.

Whitelaw W (1989) *The Whitelaw Memoirs*, London: Arum Press.

Wilson J Q and Kelling G (1982) 'Broken Windows', *Atlantic Monthly*, March: 29–38.

Windlesham Lord (1993/2001) *Responses to Crime* (4 vols), Oxford: Clarendon Press.

Wright A (2002) *Policing: An introduction to the concepts and practice*, Cullompton: Willan Publishing.

Wright R (2000) 'Financial Markets at Risk: The Threats to Stability and Integrity of the Financial Order and the Good Governance of the Financial Services Industry', speech delivered to the 18th International Cambridge Symposium on Economic Crime, 11 September 2000.

Zander M (2003) *The Police and Criminal Evidence Act 1984*, (4th edn), London: Sweet & Maxwell.

Zedner L (2002) 'Victims', in Maguire M, Morgan R and Reiner R (eds) *The Oxford Handbook of Criminology* (3rd edn), Oxford: Clarendon Press.

Zito Trust (1997) *Community Care Homicides*, London: Zito Trust.

Index